SAMS
Teach Yourself

Mac OS® X
Tiger™

Robyn Ness
John Ray

All in One

SAMS   800 East 96th Street, Indianapolis, Indiana, 46240 USA

Sams Teach Yourself Mac OS· X Tiger™ All in One

Copyright © 2005 by Sams Publishing

International Standard Book Number: 0-672-32705-8

Library of Congress Catalog Card Number: 2004093744

Printed in the United States of America

First Printing: June 2005

08   07   06   05   4   3   2   1

Trademarks

All terms mentioned in this book that are known to be trademarks or service marks have been appropriately capitalized. Sams Publishing cannot attest to the accuracy of this information. Use of a term in this book should not be regarded as affecting the validity of any trademark or service mark.

Warning and Disclaimer

Every effort has been made to make this book as complete and as accurate as possible, but no warranty or fitness is implied. The information provided is on an "as is" basis. The author and the publisher shall have neither liability nor responsibility to any person or entity with respect to any loss or damages arising from the information contained in this book.

Bulk Sales

Sams Publishing offers excellent discounts on this book when ordered in quantity for bulk purchases or special sales. For more information, please contact

U.S. Corporate and Government Sales
1-800-382-3419
corpsales@pearsontechgroup.com

For sales outside of the U.S., please contact

International Sales
international@pearsoned.com

Acquisitions Editor
Betsy Brown

Development Editor
Jonathan A. Steever

Managing Editor
Charlotte Clapp

Project Editor
Matthew Purcell

Copy Editor
Margo Catts

Indexer
Eric Schroeder

Proofreader
Suzanne Thomas

Technical Editor
John Traenkenschuh

Publishing Coordinator
Vanessa Evans

Designer
Gary Adair

Page Layout
Stacey Richwine-DeRome

Contents at a Glance

Table of Contents

Contents

Contents

About the Authors

John Ray is an award-winning developer and security consultant with more than 17 years of programming and administration experience. He has worked on projects for the FCC, the National Regulatory Research Institute, The Ohio State University, Xerox, and the State of Florida. He has written or contributed to more than 10 books currently in print, including *Mac OS X Unleashed, Special Edition Using TCP/IP, Sams Teach Yourself Dreamweaver MX Application Development in 21 Days*, and *Maximum Mac OS X Security*. He bought his first Macintosh in 1984 and remains a strong proponent for the computer and operating system that revolutionized the industry.

Robyn Ness holds a master's degree in psychology with a specialization in judgment and decision making from The Ohio State University. She currently works as a web developer, focusing on issues of usability and content design. In her spare time she tests the bounds of iPhoto by taking a ridiculous number of digital photographs, the best of which can be seen at www.floraphotographs.com.

Dedication

For family, friends, and TiVo.

Acknowledgements

We would like to acknowledge the dedicated people at Sams Publishing who worked to make this book possible. Specifically, Betsy Brown, Jon Steever, Matt Purcell, and Margo Catts were instrumental in bringing you *Sams Teach Yourself Mac OS X Tiger All in One*. We offer a sincere thank you as well to John Traenkenschuh for his thorough technical review. Through the tireless effort of this team, we're able to bring you, our readers, this helpful guide to Mac OS X Tiger.

We Want to Hear from You!

As the reader of this book, *you* are our most important critic and commentator. We value your opinion and want to know what we're doing right, what we could do better, in what areas you'd like to see us publish, and any other words of wisdom you're willing to pass our way.

You can email or write me directly to let me know what you did or didn't like about this book—as well as what we can do to make our books stronger.

Please note that I cannot help you with technical problems related to the topic of this book, and that due to the high volume of mail I receive, I might not be able to reply to every message.

When you write, please be sure to include this book's title and author as well as your name and phone or email address. I will carefully review your comments and share them with the author and editors who worked on the book.

Email: consumer@samspublishing.com

Mail: Mark Taber
            Associate Publisher
            Sams Publishing
            800 East 96th Street
            Indianapolis, IN 46240 USA

Reader Services

For more information about this book or another Sams Publishing title, visit our website, at www.samspublishing.com. Type the ISBN (excluding hyphens) or the title of a book in the Search field to find the page you're looking for.

Introduction

Our goal in creating this book is to give you the most information possible about Mac OS X 10.4 (also known as Tiger) in as friendly and straightforward a manner as possible. Although we've included tips that even seasoned Mac users can benefit from, this book is especially written for the following:

▶ People who have recently switched to the Mac who want to learn the basics of the operating system, as well as some of the best Mac programs available.

▶ Long-time Mac users who want to learn the new Mac OS X operating system, as well as work more productively with common OS X applications.

▶ People who are already familiar with some aspects of Mac OS X but want a helpful reference for those parts they haven't yet mastered.

How This Book Is Organized

The chapters of this book are categorized into six sections:

Part I, "Mac OS X Basics," explores fundamental elements of the operating system, including the Finder, the Dock, and System Preferences. It also explains the basics of how to work with windows, files, and applications.

Part II, "Common Applications and Hardware," introduces several applications that come with OS X (and some that you need to purchase separately), as well as how to work with displays, printers, and USB and FireWire devices.

Part III, "Internet Applications," covers how to connect to the Internet and several applications from Apple that use a network connection, including the Safari Web browser, the email program Mail, and the instant messaging client iChat AV.

Part IV, "Apple's iLife Applications," explores Apple's digital media applications—iTunes, iPhoto, GarageBand, iMovie HD, and iDVD.

Part V, "System Administration and Maintenance," explains several topics—such as setting up your Mac for multiple users, securing your system, recovering from crashes, and backing up your data—that can make your system run more smoothly or, at least, help in times of trouble.

Part VI, "Advanced Topics," introduces some aspects of Mac OS X that the average user may not be aware of, including using the Unix command line, running AppleScript, and working with various system utilities.

2

An Invitation from the Authors

If you have questions or comments about Mac OS X or this book, please feel free to email us.

Thanks for reading!

Robyn Ness (robynness@mac.com)
John Ray (johnray@mac.com)

PART I

Mac OS X Basics

CHAPTER 1

Introducing Mac OS X

This chapter begins with a quick look at the initial setup of Mac OS X and at the components that give Mac OS X its power. It then examines basic desktop controls, System Preferences, and some of the applications included with 10.4, which are examined in depth in later chapters.

Setting Up Mac OS X

The first time Mac OS X starts, it runs Setup Assistant, which helps you set up the basic features of the operating system. During the setup procedure, your network settings are configured and your registration details are sent back to Apple.

Creating Your Account

Mac OS X requires you to create an account for one user during the setup process. You can add other user accounts later, but the original account is an administrator account, which is used to control access to the system and to prevent unauthorized changes from being made to your software.

Mac OS X is a multiuser operating system that allows you to create multiple user accounts. This allows each user to have his or her own files and system preferences and requires each user to access the system with a username and password. Passwords provide a measure of security. On the other hand, if you're the only user and don't want to log in each time, you can set up your system to start without a login. Chapter 31, "Sharing Your Computer with Other Users," discusses the options further.

Did you Know?

The account setup fields are explained here:

▶ Name—Enter your full name.

▶ Short Name—The short name is the name of your account. It should be composed of eight or fewer lowercase letters or numbers. Spaces and punctuation aren't allowed.

Give some thought to what you choose as the short name for your account because it will be used as an identifier in a lot of system files and is very, very difficult to change later. Changing the short name of an account requires you to edit files that most users don't even know exist!

▶ Password—The Password field is used to enter a secret word or string of characters that Mac OS X uses to verify that you are who you say you are.

▶ Verify—The Verify field requires you to type the same string you entered in the Password field. This step ensures that the password you typed is actually what you intended.

▶ Password Hint—Type a phrase or question that reminds you of your password. If you attempt to log in to your system three times without success, the hint is displayed.

After you fill in this user information, click Continue to proceed.

Additional Settings

After you create a user account, you can set up your Internet connection. If you already have Internet access, but don't have all the information required to connect to your network or dial in to your ISP, skip this step for now. Specifics about Internet access are covered in Chapter 13, "Connecting to the Internet."

The next step is to specify the time zone for your computer. After you choose the appropriate zone and set the date and time, click Continue.

Congratulations! You've reached the last step of the configuration process. When prompted, click the Done button, and Mac OS X takes you to the desktop, as shown in Figure 1.1.

If you are switching from one computer running any version of OS X to one running Tiger, you can use the Migration Assistant utility (located inside the Applications folder under the Utilities folder) to transfer the contents of your old computer to your new one. After you connect the two computers with a FireWire cable, the Migration Assistant asks whether you want to move your applications, your user accounts, or both. It may also prompt you if it notices additional settings that require your consideration.

FIGURE 1.1
The Mac OS X desktop—your gateway to productivity and entertainment.

Now let's take a brief look at what goes inside Mac OS X.

A Peek Under the Hood

The technology that gives OS X all its power and stability is a Unix-based system called Darwin. If Mac OS X were a building, Darwin would be the rock-solid foundation on which the other elements stand. Unix (pronounced YOU-nix) is an operating system developed at Bell Labs during the 1970s. Unix was created to be a development platform for computer programmers. However, it has traditionally been run in the form of text commands typed at a command line, which can be a bit intimidating for casual computer users. Mac OS X preserves the power of Unix while adding the usability of a Mac interface.

Although this might seem complex, the good news is that Mac OS X shields all these technical details from your view—unless you choose to know more. Although software developers can delve into the Unix side of OS X, the rest of us need do nothing more than sit back and reap the benefits. (Those who want to learn more about using Unix from the command line can look forward to Chapter 37, "Using Basic Unix Commands.")

Applications Included with Mac OS X

As you've already learned, Mac OS X was built to allow the continued functioning of many applications written to operate under Mac OS 9. However, in the time since Mac OS X was unveiled, many fun and helpful programs have become available for use with Mac OS X.

Here are just a few of the applications that come bundled with Mac OS X:

▶ iTunes—Helps you store and play music files and burn custom CDs, as well as listen to Internet radio stations and purchase music files via the iTunes Music Store. Figure 1.2 shows iTunes' Visualizer, which displays colors and patterns in time with the music. You learn more about iTunes in Chapter 21, "Using iTunes."

FIGURE 1.2
Here's a glimpse of iTunes.

▶ Safari—This Web browser comes bundled with Mac OS X. In Chapter 14, "Using Safari," you find out about accessing the Web.

▶ Mail—Sends and receives email, including text and image attachments. Chapter 17, "Using Mail," explores email and related settings.

If your favorite applications weren't mentioned, remember that many other applications are included with Mac OS X and still more are available for purchase or download. Additional software that you might want to add is discussed in Chapter 9, "Installing Additional Software."

Now it's time to explore the desktop!

The Mac OS X Desktop

One of the best features of the Macintosh operating system has always been its interface filled with pictorial icons and easy-to-access menus. The Mac OS X desktop, shown in Figure 1.3, continues that tradition.

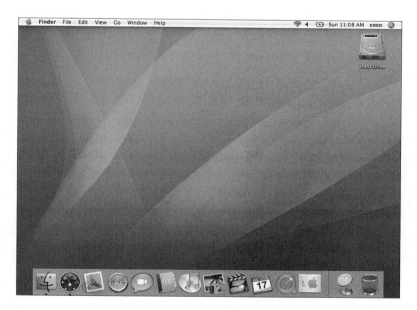

FIGURE 1.3
The Mac OS X desktop.

As you may already know, the Mac desktop is part of the Finder, which manages your computer's tasks and organizes your files. The desktop is a neat and orderly place with a row of menus across the top (called the menu bar), a row of icons along one edge (called the Dock), and plenty of wide open space to hold all the application windows you'll soon be working with.

Let's take a look at several elements of the Mac OS X environment and their basic use. The exploration is continued in greater depth with discussion of the Finder in Chapter 2, "Using the Finder," and the Dock in Chapter 3, "Exploring the Dock."

The Apple Menu

The Apple menu provides access to system controls. You open the Apple menu by clicking the Apple icon in the menu bar. It remains accessible, and its options are unchanged regardless of which program is in use. Figure 1.4 shows this menu.

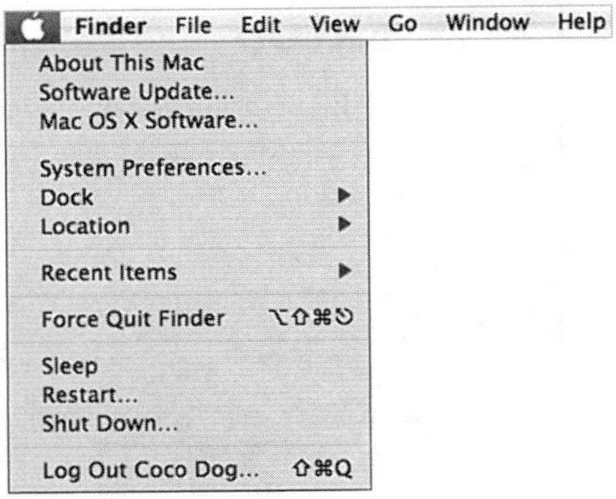

FIGURE 1.4
System-wide
preferences and
information are
located under
the Apple menu.

| Finder | File | Edit | View | Go | Window | Help |

About This Mac
Software Update...
Mac OS X Software...

System Preferences...
Dock   ▶
Location   ▶

Recent Items   ▶

Force Quit Finder   ⌥⇧⌘⏻

Sleep
Restart...
Shut Down...

Log Out Coco Dog...   ⇧⌘Q

These options are available in the Apple menu:

▶ About This Mac—Displays information about the computer, such as the current version of the operating system, the amount of available memory, and the type of processor that the system is using.

▶ Software Update—Launches the Software Update feature, where updates to currently installed Apple software are listed as they become available for your download. Chapter 34, "Maintaining Your System," talks more about Software Update.

▶ Mac OS X Software—Launches the user's preferred Web browser and loads the URL http://www.apple.com/downloads/macosx/. At that Web page, you can download third-party applications from Apple's list of available Mac OS X software.

▶ System Preferences—Launches the application used to change preferences and settings for almost all aspects of the Mac OS X—from the appearance of your desktop to network connection settings. Relevant System Preferences are discussed as we cover different topics, and any that are left out are covered in Chapter 5, "Setting System Preferences and Universal Access Options."

▶ Dock—One of the most visible features of the Mac OS X interface. The Apple menu provides quick access to common Dock preferences, such as the option to hide or show the Dock. Chapter 3 discusses Dock preferences further.

▶ Location—Enables you to quickly adjust the Mac OS X network settings for your current location.

▶ Recent Items—Displays the most recently launched applications, documents, and servers so you can quickly return to them.

▶ Force Quit—Opens a list of open applications and enables you to select which to quit. You can also access this list by pressing Command-Option-Esc. You'll learn more about Force Quit in Chapter 35, "Recovering from Crashes and Other Problems."

Traditional Mac users know that Command-Option-Esc is an example of a *key command,* which is a kind of shortcut activated by holding down a set of keys. For those new to the Mac, the Command key shows outlines of an apple and a clover-leaf.

By the Way

▶ Sleep—Places your computer in a sleep state that requires very little power and yet can be restarted in a matter of seconds without the need for a full reboot.

Although the Sleep option is convenient for momentarily powering down and allowing a quick start, PowerBook/iBook users might want to prevent battery drain by shutting down their computers completely instead of putting them to sleep for long periods.

Did you Know?

▶ Restart—Quits all applications, prompts the user to save open files, and gracefully reboots the computer.

▶ Shut Down—Quits all applications, prompts the user to save open files, and shuts down the computer.

▶ Log Out—Quits all applications, prompts the user to save open files, and then returns to the Mac OS X login screen.

The Application Menu

Immediately to the right of the Apple menu is the application menu, which provides functions specific to the application currently in use. When an application launches in Mac OS X, a menu based on its own name appears to the right of the Apple icon. For example, if you start an application named TextEdit, the TextEdit application menu is the first menu item after the Apple icon.

The application menu contains items that act on the entire application rather than on its files. Figure 1.5 displays the application menu for Mail—an application included with Mac OS X.

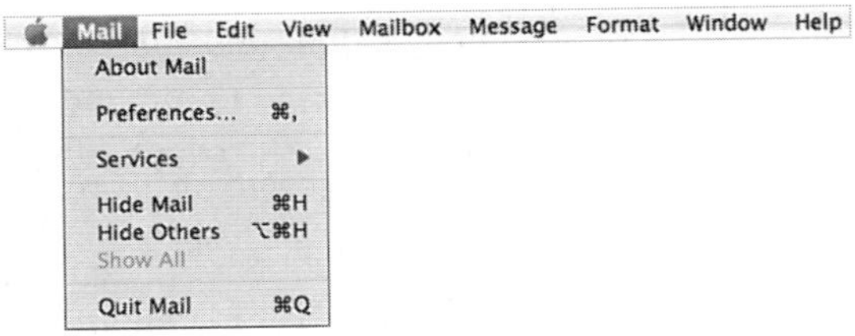

FIGURE 1.5
Application
menus contain
functions that
act on an entire
application.

Seven default items make up an application menu:

▶ About—Reveals information about the running program, such as its version number.

▶ Preferences—Each application menu provides a standardized location for application preferences.

▶ Services—An interesting feature of Mac OS X, services help an application use other system features or applications. (Note, however, that the application has to have been specially written to use services, so they aren't always available.) For example, if you want to have a portion of an email message read aloud by your computer, you could select the text in your Mail window and then choose Start Speaking Text from the Speech submenu under Services.

▶ Hide—Hides all windows of the active application.

▶ Hide Others—Hides the windows of all applications other than the front-most application. This effectively clears the screen except for the program you're currently using.

▶ Show All—Shows all hidden applications.

▶ Quit—Quits the current application. Command-Q is the universal Quit shortcut.

The remaining menus vary widely by application, so we'll cover them for specific applications in later chapters as needed.

Windows

One of the most obvious places in which you interact with the Mac OS X interface is through onscreen windows, as illustrated in Figure 1.6. Let's take a brief look at the controls for a Mail window.

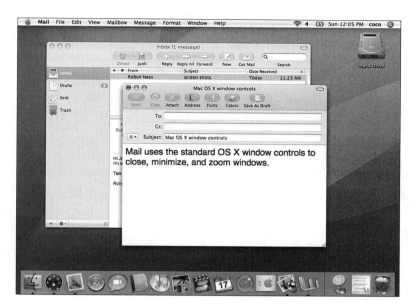

FIGURE 1.6
Mac OS X win-
dows have sev-
eral common
features.

Close/Minimize/Zoom

In the upper-left corner of each window are the Close (red X), Minimize (yellow –),
and Zoom (green +) buttons. Differentiated only by color and position, the corresponding symbol appears in each button when the mouse cursor nears them.

> The Close, Minimize, and Zoom buttons in the currently active window have color,
> whereas those in windows that don't have the system's focus don't have color.

Clicking the Close button closes the open window. The Mac OS X Minimize button
shrinks the window into an icon view and places it in the Dock. This icon is a
miniature of the original window—down to the items it contains. In some cases,
Dock icons even update their appearance when the parent application generates
new output. Clicking the icon in the Dock restores the window to its original position and size on the screen.

> There is a preference option that makes double-clicking the title bar of a window
> have the same effect as clicking the Minimize button. This option can be found in
> the Appearance section of the System Preferences, which can be opened from the
> Apple menu.

Did you Know?

The Zoom button (usually) opens the window to the size necessary to display the available information. Most Windows PC users expect the maximized window to fill the entire screen. However, if there are only three icons to be shown, Mac OS X doesn't waste space by filling up your window with blank area.

> Holding down Option while clicking the Minimize or Close button results in all the windows in the current application being minimized or closed.

Toolbar Button

In the upper-right corner of some windows (including Finder and Mail windows) is an elongated button, called the Toolbar button, that can be used to quickly show or hide special toolbars in the top of some windows. Figure 1.7 shows the result of hiding the toolbar in the Mail application.

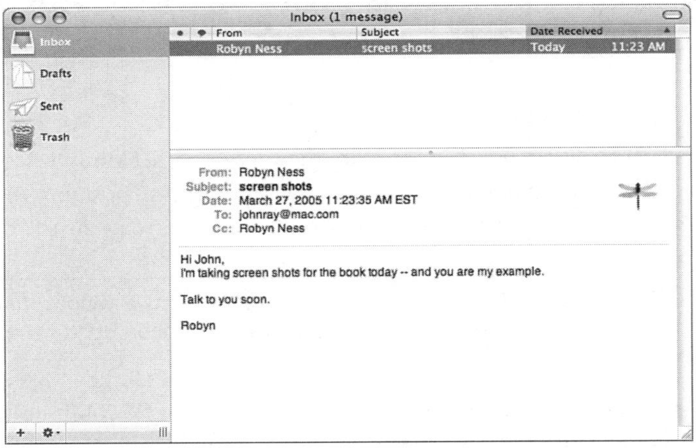

FIGURE 1.7
With the task toolbar hidden, the window occupies less screen space.

Apple advocates the use of toolbars in applications to increase usability and efficiency. However, because individual programmers must write their programs to support the toolbar button, you shouldn't expect all applications with toolbars to have the Toolbar button.

Window Moving and Resizing

Another characteristic of some Mac OS X windows is the borderless content area. As shown in Figure 1.8, the display in most Mac OS X application windows (except those with a metal appearance) stretches to the edge of the content window. In contrast, some operating systems such as Mac OS 9 and Windows offer window borders for dragging.

FIGURE 1.8
The content in a window goes right to the edge.

To drag a window in OS X, you must grab it by its title bar. For windows with a metal appearance, you can grab them by any "metal" area.

To resize a window, click and drag the size control in the lower-right corner of each window. Many applications in Mac OS X (such as email messages in Mail) take advantage of live resizing; that is, as you resize the window, its contents adjust in real time.

Window Usage Tips

It is possible to resize a window to the point where it becomes so large that you can't reach the size control—or to choose a lower screen resolution so all your windows are in that condition. If you can't reach the size control, how do you make the window smaller? Click the green Zoom button, which makes a window only as large as it needs to be to show its contents or makes the window fit within the viewable screen area.

Chapter 4, "Working with Folders, Files, and Applications", talks about a feature called Exposé, which enables you to temporarily view the full windows of everything open on your desktop all at once. The settings for this feature are accessed in the System Preferences, discussed later in this chapter.

There are a few other neat tricks you can use when working with Mac OS X windows. If you hold down the Command key, you can drag inactive windows located behind other windows. If fact, holding down Command enables you to click buttons and move scrollbars in many background applications.

Another fun trick is holding down the Option key while clicking on an inactive application's window. This hides the front-most application and brings the clicked application to the front.

Finally, instead of switching to another window to close, minimize, or maximize it, you can position your cursor over the appropriate window controls to highlight them—enabling you to get rid of obtrusive windows without leaving your current workspace.

Sheet Windows and Window Drawers

Two other unique interface elements in Mac OS X are *sheet windows* and *window drawers*. Sheets are used in place of traditional dialog boxes. Normally, when a computer wants to get your attention, it displays a dialog box containing a question such as, "Do you want to save this document?" If you have 10 open documents on your system, how do you know which one needs to be saved?

Sheet windows connect directly to the title bar of an open window. As shown in Figure 1.9, these messages appear inside the window with which they're associated.

Sheet windows are used just like regular dialog boxes, except that they're attached to a document. Unlike many dialog boxes, which keep you from interacting with the rest of the system until you interact with them, sheet windows limit access to only the window in which they appear.

A window drawer is used to store commonly used items, such as settings or additional content, that might need to be accessed while a program is running. Figure 1.10 shows the Preview application's window drawer containing a series of open images.

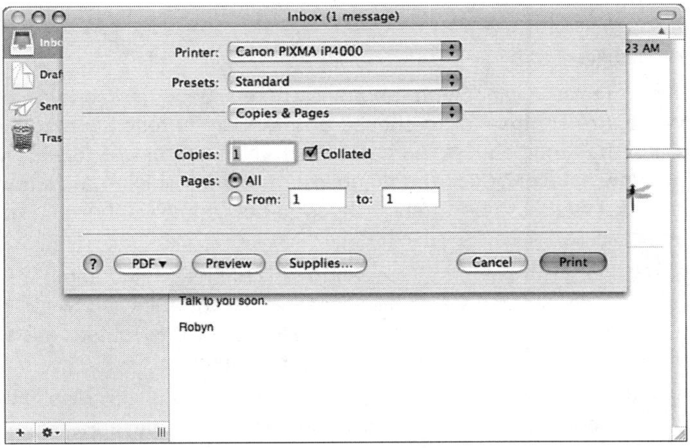

FIGURE 1.9
The sheet window appears to drop from an open window's title bar.

FIGURE 1.10
Window drawers hold options that are needed often while a program is in use.

To use active drawers in applications that contain them, you typically click a button in the toolbar. After a drawer is open, you can often drag its edge to change the drawer's size.

Interface Elements

Other functions of the interface are activated by *graphical interface elements*. Figure 1.11 shows samples of many of the Mac OS X interface elements.

FIGURE 1.11
These are (most of) the Mac OS X interface elements.

OS X interface elements include the following:

▶ Pushbuttons—These are rendered as translucent white or aqua ovals or as square-ish buttons with appropriate label text. They're typically used to activate a choice or to respond to a question posed by the operating system or application. The default choice, which is activated by a press of the Return key, pulses for easy visual confirmation.

▶ Check boxes/radio buttons—Check boxes are used for choices involving multiple attributes (AND), whereas radio buttons are used for choices between attributes (OR).

▶ List views—Clicking a category, such as the Date Modified heading shown in Figure 1.11, sorts items by that selection. Clicking the category again reverses the direction of the sort (ascending to descending or vice versa). To resize category headings, click the edge of the heading and drag in the direction you want to shrink or expand the column.

▶ Pop-up menus—Single-clicking a menu drops down the menu until you make a selection. The menu can stay down indefinitely. With Mac OS X's multitasking system, other applications can continue to work in the background while the menu is down.

▶ Disclosure triangles—Click the triangle to reveal additional information about an object.

▶ Disclosure pushbuttons—Like disclosure triangles, these pushbuttons are used to reveal all possible options (a full, complex view) or to reduce a window to a simplified representation. They are used in the File Save sheets.

▶ Scrollbars—Scrollbars visually represent the amount of data in the current document by changing the size of the scrollbar slider in relation to the data to display. The larger the slider, the less data there is to scroll through. The smaller the slider, the more information there is to display.

▶ Button bar—Button bars, made up of several buttons, enable you to move between separate settings within a single window when you can choose only one available option at a time. When long lists are broken up in this way, windows with many options are less overwhelming, but you might have to click between sections to find the settings you're looking for.

System Preferences

Mac OS X enables you to control many aspects of your system, from desktop appearance to user access. Conveniently, you can tailor these settings to your own needs from one centralized place, System Preferences, as shown in Figure 1.12.

To access System Preferences, choose System Preferences from the Apple menu, or simply click the Dock icon that resembles a light switch (it should be located in the row of icons at the bottom of your screen). As you can see in Figure 1.12, the items in System Preferences are organized by function. You'll learn more about System Preferences in Chapter 5 and throughout this book as different topics are discussed.

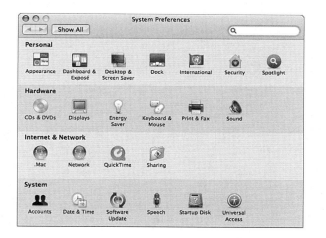

FIGURE 1.12
Many system settings are accessible through System Preferences.

Menu Extras

Mac OS X offers a feature that gives users quick access to common system settings: menu extras. They appear as icons at the upper right of the menu bar. Figure 1.13 shows a number of menu extras.

FIGURE 1.13
Menu extras provide quick access to system settings.

Each extra is added to the menu bar through individual System Preferences panes that correspond to an item's function. You can activate or deactivate an extra by clicking Show <option> in the Menu Bar check box for the corresponding option. For example, under Displays in the Hardware group, you can turn on the Displays Menu Extra.

A few of the menu extras available under Mac OS X include

▶ Date & Time—Displays the date and time graphically as a miniature clock or in the standard text format.

▶ Displays—Adjusts the display's resolution and color depth from the menu bar.

▶ Volume—Changes the sound volume.

▶ Battery—For PowerBook and iBook users, this option tracks battery usage and recharge time.

▶ AirPort—Monitors AirPort signal strength and quickly adjusts network settings. (The AirPort is a device that enables computers to be connected to the Internet without wires. It's discussed further in Chapter 13, "Connecting to the Internet.")

Clicking a menu extra opens a pop-up menu that displays additional information and settings. Items such as Battery and Date & Time can be modified to show textual information rather than a simple icon status representation.

You can alter the order of menu extras by holding down the Command key and dragging an icon to a different position.

Summary

A lot of care went into making Mac OS X the versatile, powerful, and attractive system that's available today. In this chapter, you learned about the structure of Mac OS X, as well as some basic features to help you find your way around the Mac OS X desktop. The focus was on elements such as the Apple and application menus and window controls. This chapter also briefly discussed some of the applications bundled with Mac OS X and the System Preferences, which are covered in more detail in later chapters. In Chapter 2, you explore the Mac OS X file system and some useful shortcuts to your favorite applications.

CHAPTER 2

Using the Finder

You're now ready to take a closer look at Mac OS X and its operation as we focus on the Finder. The Finder is the application that Mac OS X uses to launch and manipulate files and applications. Unlike other tools and utilities that you activate, the Finder starts immediately after you log in to the system and is always active. In addition to helping you locate your files, the Finder handles all common tasks, such as creating, deleting, moving, and copying files and folders, which we'll talk about in Chapter 4, "Working with Folders, Files, and Applications."

You can interact with the Finder in several different ways. There's a menu bar for the Finder, but there's also the Finder window, which has several different modes and view options. Using the Finder window is perhaps the easiest way to understand and move through the Mac OS X file system, so let's look at it first.

The Finder Window

To help people manage their files, the Finder includes a specialized window, which is accessed by clicking the Finder icon in the Dock or by double-clicking the icon for the Mac OS X hard drive on the desktop. (The Dock is the row of icons along one edge of your screen; it is discussed in detail in Chapter 3, "Exploring the Dock.")

Mac OS X has two modes of operation in the Finder window. In the first of the two window modes, shown in Figure 2.1, a sidebar appears along the left, and a toolbar appears at the top. Content area takes up the rest of the window. In this mode, which we'll call the toolbar mode, double-clicking a folder displays its contents in the content area of the current window, replacing what was there before.

The second mode, a toolbar-less version of the Finder window, can be entered by clicking the Hide/Show toolbar button in the upper-right corner of the Finder window. In this mode, shown in Figure 2.2, double-clicking folders opens additional windows to display their contents while leaving the original window as it was.

FIGURE 2.1
The toolbar version of the Finder window enables you to move forward and back through the contents of your hard drive—and even your local network.

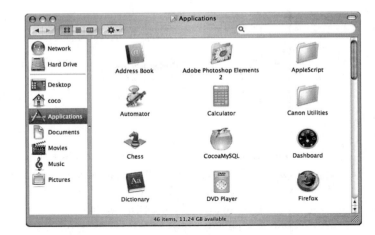

FIGURE 2.2
The toolbar-less version of the Finder window shows only the contents of a selected folder or drive.

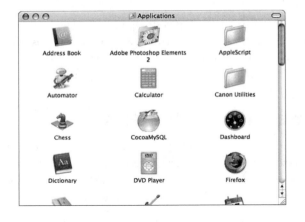

By the Way

At the top of the toolbar-less version of the Finder window is the status bar, which shows the number of items in a folder and the amount of space available on the drive. You can toggle the status bar on and off by using the Show/Hide Status Bar command in the Finder's View menu.

The Finder Window Toolbar

The toolbar version of the Finder window provides several useful controls for viewing and navigating your files.

In the upper-left corner of the toolbar is the Back arrow—click it to return to the previous folder. Using this technique, you can dig many levels deep into the file system and then quickly back out by using this button. The Forward arrow enables you to follow the same path back to inner levels.

By default, there are several other elements in the toolbar, as shown previously in Figure 2.1. From left to right, you see the View selector, the Action pop-up menu, and the Search text field. Using the Finder to find files is discussed further in the section "Performing File and Content Searches—Spotlight to the Rescue" later in this chapter.

You can customize your Finder toolbar by adding other predefined Mac OS X shortcuts or by removing the default items in this way:

1. Choose View, Customize Toolbar from the menu.

2. From the sheet window containing all the available shortcuts (shown in Figure 2.3), locate the items you want to add.

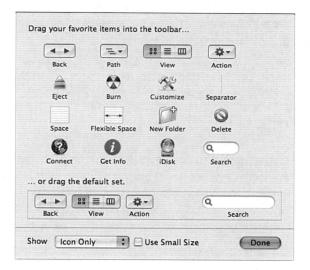

FIGURE 2.3
Finder shortcuts give you single-click access to special features.

3. Add a shortcut by dragging it from the window to wherever you want it to appear on the toolbar.

By the Way

When you modify your toolbar, it's modified for all Finder windows in your workspace, not just the currently open folder. However, the changes that you make to your toolbar don't affect other user accounts on the same computer.

While the Customize Toolbar sheet window is visible, you can also rearrange or remove any toolbar shortcuts. To rearrange, simply drag a shortcut to a new location—the others will move aside. To remove, drag the shortcut icon outside the toolbar area. It disappears with a whoosh and a puff of smoke.

Now that you've seen the Finder window, it's time to explore the Finder's file system.

The File System

If you double-click the icon for your Mac OS X drive, you see a collection of permanent folders, as shown previously in Figure 2.1. These folders contain preinstalled applications, utilities, and configuration files for your system, known collectively as *system folders*. You should not modify these system-level directories or move them from their default locations. However, you can create folders and files *within* these locations.

The following list describes the folders at this level, which serve as the starting point for accessing most of your system's functions:

▶ Applications—Contains all the preinstalled Mac OS X applications, such as iTunes, Mail, Safari, and many others. Within the Applications folder is the Utilities folder, which contains the tools necessary to set up your printers, calibrate your display, and perform other important tasks.

You can move, rename, or delete the system folders if you want (though you may have to type a password to authorize the changes), but such changes should be made only with great caution because the performance of some applications could be disrupted.

▶ Library—Although it doesn't have a strict definition, Library mostly stores system-wide application preferences, application libraries, and information that should be available to anyone using the computer. Some of the folders in Library are used by applications to store data such as preferences, whereas others hold printer drivers or other system additions made by the user.

▶ System—Next on the list is the Mac OS X System folder. By default, the System folder contains only a folder called Library—a more specific version of the other Library folder. Within System's Library folder are the components that make up the core of the Mac OS X experience. These files and folders shouldn't be changed unless you're aware that any modifications you make could cause your computer not to start up or otherwise operate as expected.

▶ Users—As mentioned in Chapter 1, "Introducing Mac OS X," Mac OS X is a true multiuser operating system in which each user has a private account and password to access the operating system. The Users folder contains the home directories of all the users on the machine. ("Home" directories are covered next.)

Let's take a closer look at the Users directory, where folders are created for use by each individual user on your system. Figure 2.4 shows the Users folder in List view for a system with three users: robyn, jray, and coco. There is also a Shared folder to hold files that all users can access easily.

FIGURE 2.4
All users have their own home folders, but they cannot access most of the contents of each other's home folder.

Your home folder can be considered your workplace. It's yours alone because most of the files and folders stored there are protected from other users. Even though you can see the folders for every user, you can access only the Public and Sites folders in another user's home folder. (Chapter 31, "Sharing Your Computer with Other Users," further discusses setting up additional user accounts.)

The Home Directory

Your home directory, as shown in Figure 2.5, is the start of your personal area on Mac OS X. There, you can save your own files, and no one can alter or read them from another account on the computer.

FIGURE 2.5
The default folders in a user's home directory.

Your home directory is named with the short name you chose when you created your Mac OS X user account. Several default folders are created inside your home directory. Those folders and their purposes are as follows:

▶ Desktop—Contains all the files, folders, and applications that you've saved to your desktop.

▶ Documents, Movies, Music, and Pictures—These four folders are generic store-all locations for files of these kinds. You don't have to use these folders; they're merely recommended storage locations to help you organize your files. (Applications such as iPhoto, iTunes, and iMovie store their files in the appropriate folders by default.)

▶ Library—Serves the same purpose as the top-level Library folder and the Library folder in the System folder, except what is stored here is available for your use only. Within the subfolders in this folder, you can store fonts, screensavers, and many other extensions to the operating system—especially those you don't want to share with other users of the computer.

▶ Public—Provides a way for you to share files with other users on your computer without granting total access. Also, if you plan to share your files over a network, you can do so by placing them in the Public folder and activating file sharing in the Sharing System Preferences panel. This is discussed further in Chapter 31.

▶ Sites—If you want to run a personal website, it must be stored in the Sites folder. To share your site with the outside world, you also have to enable Personal Web Sharing, which is discussed in Chapter 31 and Chapter 32, "Sharing Files and Running Network Services."

Although folders for different file types exist by default, you can do nearly anything you want with your home folder. However, some folders in your home directory should be treated with caution: the Desktop, Library, Movies, Music, and Photos folders. They are critical to system operation and specific applications (such as iMovie, iTunes, and iPhoto) and must not be renamed or removed. (Also, you shouldn't remove any of the items in the Library folder unless you put them there to start with.)

The Sidebar

Now that you've seen the file structure, let's take a look at the default items in the sidebar along the left side of the toolbar version of the Finder window, as shown previously in Figure 2.5.

Although you can choose to display your computer's hard drive on the desktop, it is also visible in the top portion of the sidebar. Any additional FireWire or USB drives (and other types of removable media, including CDs) currently recognized by the system also appear.

In the bottom portion of the sidebar are icons for the home directory of the current user, the applications folder, and several folders within the current user's home directory.

Clicking any drive or folder in the sidebar fills the content space of the Finder window with a view of the files it contains.

Customizing the Sidebar

Just as you can customize the toolbar, you also can add your own shortcuts to favorite folders, files, and applications by adding them to the sidebar.

> If you want to change the width of the content area or the sidebar, you can click and drag the narrow strip separating the two areas. Double-clicking the strip toggles the sidebar open and closed.

By the Way

When folders and applications are added to the sidebar, a single click on the icon opens or launches the selected item. You can also drag documents onto an application icon or folder icon in the toolbar, either to open the file by using the application or to move the file into a folder.

To add something to the sidebar, locate the item's icon and drag it to the list. A blue insert bar appears, as shown in Figure 2.6, to show you where the file will be added. If you drag an item onto an existing folder or storage device (including your hard drive) in the sidebar, that folder is then outlined in blue, as shown in Figure 2.7, to let you know the item you are dragging will be placed inside it.

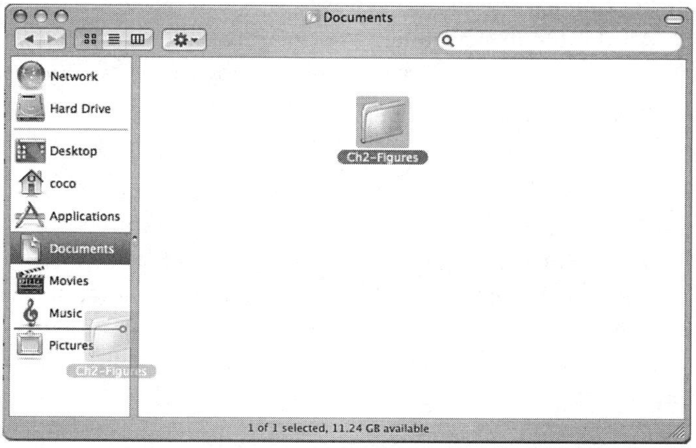

FIGURE 2.6
Add an item to the sidebar.

FIGURE 2.7
Place a file
inside an item
in the sidebar.

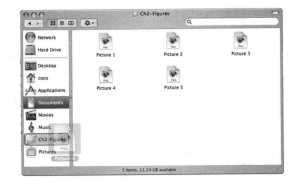

Finder Window View Options

In addition to the options to switch between the toolbar and toolbar-less versions of the Finder window, there are other display options from the Finder window. Three View buttons in the toolbar enable you control the way information is displayed in the Finder window.

Icon View

The first time you log in, the Finder is in toolbar mode and in Icon view. If you've already been using the Finder and are no longer in Icon view, you can quickly switch to Icon view by choosing As Icons from the menu or by clicking the first of the View buttons in the toolbar. (Refer to Figure 2.5 to see the Finder window in Icon view.) In Icon view mode, you navigate through the folders on your drive by double-clicking them.

List View

The next view to explore is the Finder's List view. You can switch to List view by clicking the middle button in the Finder's View selector or, if the toolbar isn't present, by choosing View, As List from the Finder's menu. Demonstrated in Figure 2.8, the List view is a straightforward means of displaying all available information about a file or folder.

The columns in the List view represent the attributes for each file. Clicking a column highlights it and sorts the file listing based on that column's values. For example, if you want to locate the most recently created files in a folder, you can view the folder contents in List view and click the Date Modified header. By default, the column values are listed in descending order. Clicking a column header again reverses the sorting order. An arrow pointing up or down at the right of each column indicates the current sort order.

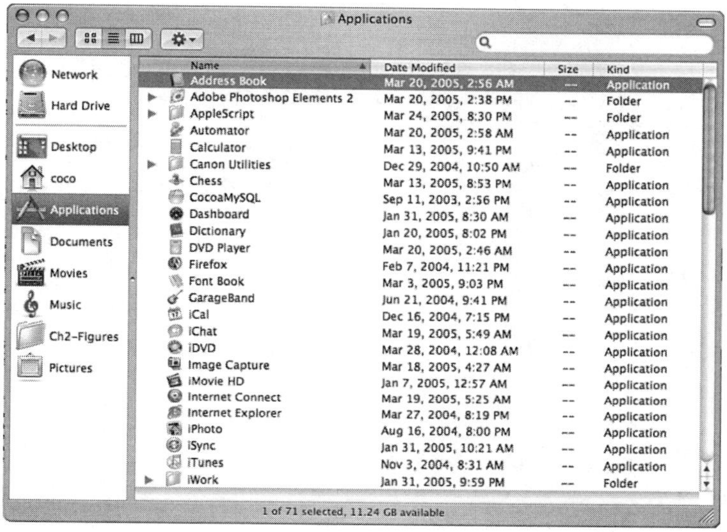

FIGURE 2.8
List view packs
a lot of informa-
tion into a small
space.

You can change the width of the columns by placing the mouse cursor at the edge
of the column and click-dragging to the left or right. You can reposition the columns
by clicking and dragging them into the order you want. However, the first column,
Name, cannot be repositioned.

When a folder appears in the file listing, a small disclosure triangle precedes its
name. Clicking the triangle reveals the file hierarchy within that folder. As with Icon
view, double-clicking a folder in this view either opens a new window (if you're in
toolbar-less mode) or refreshes the contents of the existing window with the contents
of the selected folder. (Double-clicking applications or files opens them in any view.)

Column View

Unlike other views, which can either overwhelm you with information or require
multiple windows if you want to move easily from point to point, the Column view
is designed with one thing in mind: ease of navigation.

The concept is simple: Click an item in the first column of the content area, and its
contents are shown in the next column. Click a folder in this new column, and its
contents are shown in the next column, and so on. Figure 2.9 shows a multicolumn
display that reaches down two levels.

FIGURE 2.9
Using the Column
view, you can
easily navigate
through the fold-
ers on your hard
drive.

> If you use the horizontal scrollbar to move back along a path, the folders you've
> chosen remain highlighted in the columns. You can, at any time, choose a differ-
> ent folder from any of the columns. This refreshes the column to the right of your
> choice. There's no need to start from the beginning every time you want to change
> your location.

One big bonus of using Column view is the capability it gives you to instantly see
the contents of a file without opening it. If you choose a file or application, a preview or description of the selected item appears in the column to the right. For an
example, take a look at the far right column in Figure 2.9, where a representation of
an image file is displayed. When you choose an application or a file that cannot be
previewed, only information about the file is displayed, such as the creation/modifi-
cation dates, size, and version.

Show View Options

For each of the three Finder window views, there are additional settings that you can
customize by choosing View, Show View Options from the menu. For Icon and List
views, you can also choose whether your changes apply to the current window only
or to all Finder windows.

For Icon view, you can scale icons from the smallest to largest size by dragging the
Icon Size slider from the left to the right. You can choose how the icon is labeled,
including the font size and label placement. You can set how the icons are arranged
and what color the window background is.

List view enables you to choose small or larger icons, text size, and which columns of information to display with the filenames. You can also choose to show relative dates, such as "Today" and "Yesterday," or to calculate the sizes of all files. (Be warned, however, that calculating files sizes does consume some system resources.)

Column view gives you options for text size and whether to show icons or the pre-view column. There are no global settings for this view.

Now that you understand how to navigate within the Finder window and alter your view options, let's move on to exploring the desktop. (We'll save discussion of the Action pop-up menu that appears in the Finder window toolbar until Chapter 4.)

The Desktop

The desktop is, for all intents and purposes, a global Finder window that sits behind all the other windows on the system. The primary difference between the desktop and the other window modes discussed so far is that the desktop is always in Icon view mode.

As with other Finder windows, the desktop layout is controlled by the View Options in the View menu. Use the Icon Size slider, text, and arrangement settings exactly as you would adjust any other window in Icon view mode.

You can change the background image of your desktop in the Desktop & Screen Saver pane of System Preferences. There you'll find many background images from which to choose, and you can even add images of your own!

Did you Know?

The Desktop and Exposé

In addition to being a window-like object that displays icons, the desktop is also your workspace. As you open Finder and application windows, they cover the desktop; as you open more and more windows, they cover each other. To help you find buried windows, or even just focus your attention, Apple has introduced a feature called Exposé, which rearranges and resizes the windows currently open so that you can see them all at one time, as demonstrated in Figure 2.10. From this view of open windows and applications, you can then choose the one on which you want to work.

You set up Exposé from the System Preferences pane shown in Figure 2.11. There you can choose what activates the various states of Exposé. Those states are

▶ All Windows—Displays all open windows, as shown previously in Figure 2.10. You can then move your mouse cursor over the window you want to bring to the front and select it. The other windows on the desktop reappear in their original locations behind it.

FIGURE 2.10
Exposé can display all open windows while dimming the desktop.

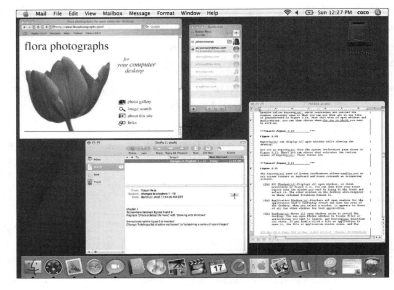

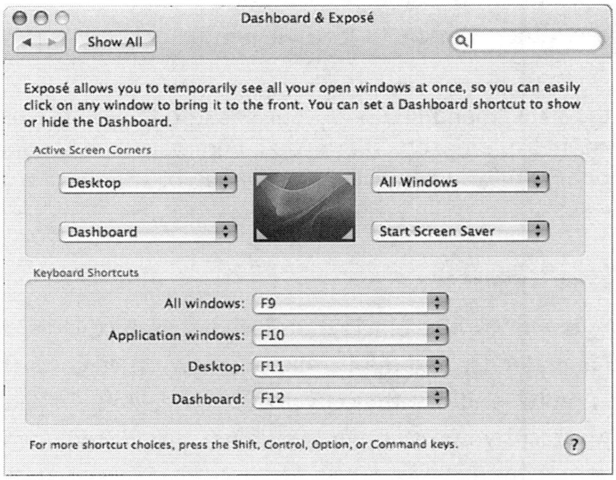

FIGURE 2.11
The Exposé pane of System Preferences enables you to set screen corners or keyboard and mouse commands as triggering actions.

▶ Application Windows—Displays all open windows for the application that's currently active and dims the rest of the desktop. When you select a window, it appears in front of all the other windows for that application.

▶ Desktop—Moves all open windows aside to reveal the desktop. You can open Finder windows to locate files or applications you want to launch, and Exposé maintains its state. If you double-click a file or application to open it, the file or application window opens, and the other windows on the desktop reappear in their original locations behind it.

▶ Dashboard —Reveals dashboard. See section "Dashboard" immediately following.

If you would prefer using keyboard commands to activate Exposé, you can set those options instead. (Or even set both screen corners and keyboard options.)

Dashboard

Apple introduced something new to the Desktop in Mac OS X 10.4—Dashboard, a virtual workspace for all the little applications that make life easier (see Figure 2.12).

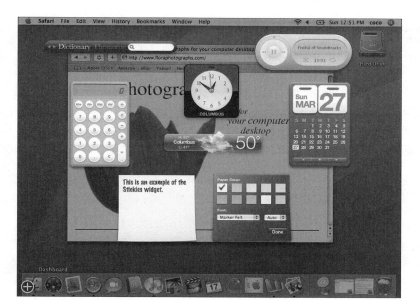

FIGURE 2.12
Dashboard widgets of all sorts.

Called "widgets," these applications include a calendar, calculator, and interfaces to applications such as iTunes and Address Book. Widgets can also provide up-to-the-minute information on a wide range of topics, from your local weather to the stock market, by connecting to the Internet. (If the idea of widgets to handle all those functions you need in a day appeals to you, you'll be happy to know that Apple has been encouraging software developers to write widgets of their own.)

Dashboard starts up automatically when you login into OS X, but remains hidden until you call for it. By default, you can access Dashboard by clicking the Dashboard icon in the Dock, or by pressing the function key F12. (You can change that function key under the Exposé pane of the System Preferences, shown in Figure 2.11.)

One interesting thing about Dashboard is that it acts like a single application, where the many different widgets are files within it. To choose which widgets appear when you start Dashboard, click the "X" at the lower left of your screen to open the Widget Bar along the bottom of you screen. Then click on a widget in the Widget Bar to open it on your Desktop. You can open multiple instances of a single widget by clicking multiple times.

To change the settings of each individual widget, you simply "flip" its window and see what can be changed. As you mouse-over each widget, its Info button, labeled with an *i*, appears. Click the button to flip the window. When you're finished changing settings, click the Done button and the widget flips again. (In Figure 2.12, two instances of the Stickies widget are shown at the bottom of the screen. The one on the left shows the location of the Info button, while the one on the right shows the settings that appear when you click the Info button.)

To exit Dashboard and return to your regular desktop, click outside the widget windows or use the same function key you used to bring up Dashboard.

The Finder Preference Options

The Finder Preferences can be used to adjust settings that control how you interact with your desktop and icons. Open these settings by choosing Preferences from the Finder application menu. Figure 2.13 shows the options available in the General pane of the Finder Preferences.

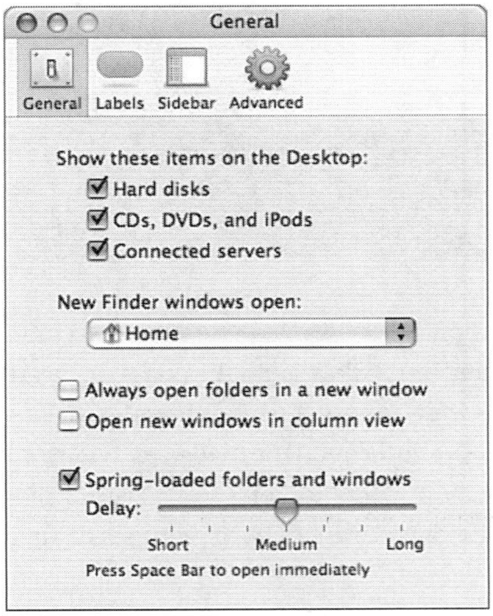

FIGURE 2.13
The Finder's general preferences control what's visible on the desktop and how new Finder windows behave.

By the Way

You can change the appearance of Finder windows and system-wide elements from the Appearance pane of the System Preferences. There, you can choose the color of highlighted items and the interface elements (as discussed in Chapter 1, "Introducing Mac OS X").

Among the General preference settings are whether to display icons for the hard drive, removable media, or connected servers on the desktop and the default content displayed by new Finder windows. *Spring-loading* is the desktop behavior that occurs when you drag a file or folder on top of another folder and it springs open to let the dragged item move inside and then closes again to return the desktop to its previous state.

The Labels settings relate to a feature discussed in Chapter 4, so we'll discuss this pane further in the "Adding Color Labels" section of that chapter.

The Sidebar section allows you to choose which items appear in the sidebar of the Finder window while it is in toolbar mode. Check and uncheck the boxes in front of the options, which include computer, hard disks, network, removable media, desktop, and applications.

The Advanced section pertains to a variety of Finder features and functions. You can set whether to show file extensions. Traditionally, Mac users have paid little attention to whether a filename ends in .doc or .txt, but Windows users are used to seeing these extensions. (That's because the Windows operating system uses these extensions when determining which application can open a given file; Macs, on the other hand, used to rely on hidden information stored in the file itself to make that determination.) Checking this option reveals file extensions.

The option to show hidden files will show files used by your system that you normally don't know are there. There's also an option to display a warning that appears when you empty the Trash to give you a second chance to reconsider.

Close the Finder Preferences pane when you're satisfied with your settings.

Performing File and Content Searches—Spotlight to the Rescue

In addition to organizing your files, the Finder enables you to search for applications and folders by name and documents by filename or by content—as well as by a plethora of other criteria associated with these items (including file types, dates created, and even hidden "metadata" stored with an item).

An easy way to search for an item with a keyword or phrase is by clicking the Spotlight icon at the far right of the menu bar. A text field appears, where you can type your search term. Results begin to appear below the text field even as you continue to type, as shown in Figure 2.14.

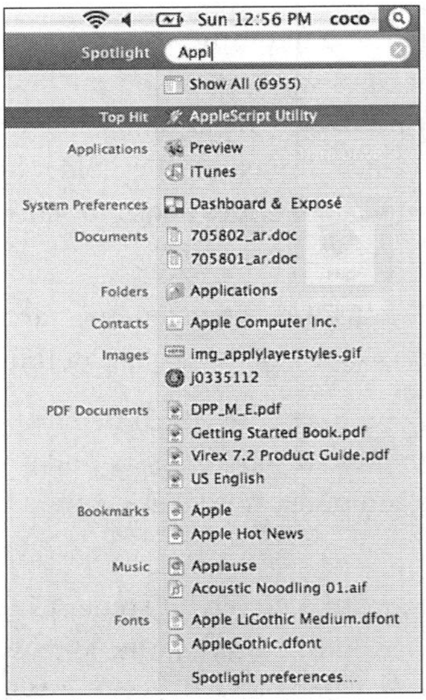

FIGURE 2.14
Searching by keyword is fast and easy with Spotlight.

If you select a search result, the item will open. If you click Show All from the top of the list, a separate window for the results opens (see Figure 2.15). The results are grouped by type—use the categories on the right side to choose what to group by, how to order the items, and any timeframe or specific locations to constrain what is shown.

By the Way

Apple's Spotlight technology is new in Mac OS X 10.4, and its speed and depth of coverage are already widely praised. Although searches of file content in previous versions of Mac OS X required that the directory containing the file be indexed or cataloged, that is no longer the case. Spotlight is continuously cataloging the content on your system so it's ready at a second's notice.

The Spotlight icon isn't the only way to tap into the powers of Spotlight. To be a bit more selective about what you are searching, you can also search using the search field in the Finder window or by opening a New Search window.

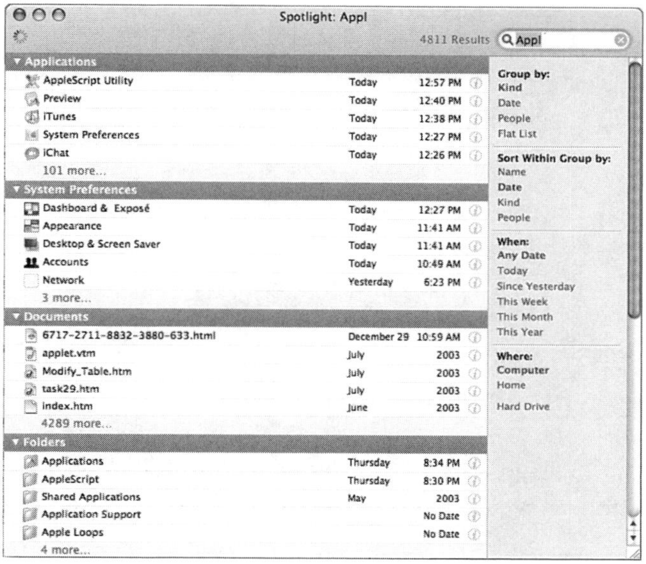

FIGURE 2.15
Sort your results for easy scanning.

To search from a Finder window, double-click your hard drive icon on the desktop, the Finder icon in the Dock, or the folder containing the file you want to find. Then type your search term in the Search box in the toolbar. To search, begin typing a word in the text field. The content area of the window immediately begins showing results. You can add further search attributes by clicking the + button at the upper right. (Available attributes are covered in just a moment.)

> Remember, if the toolbar isn't visible in a Finder window, you can show it by clicking the oblong button at the upper right of the window's title bar. If the search box isn't visible, you might have to enlarge your window by dragging the resize control in the bottom-right corner.

Did you Know?

To open a fresh New Search window (where you can set search attributes immediately), choose File, Find from the menu (or use the key-command Command-F). Figure 2.16 shows the New Search.

To set search attributes, click the popup menu and choose what you're interested in. (Use the + button to add more types of search criteria.) Enter your search term into the appropriate field(s).

FIGURE 2.16
Use the New
Search window
to locate files
by kind, name,
content, or
other criteria.

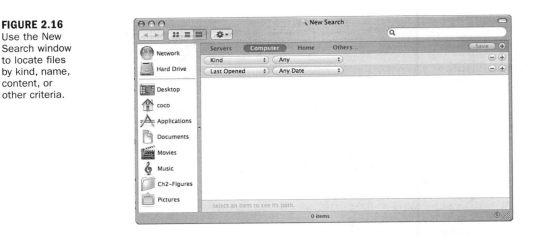

Although Name, Contents, Size, Last Modified, and Created are obvious, some of these search attributes require a bit of explanation.

▶ *Kind* refers to whether the item sought is an application, folder, document, audio file, image, movie, or an alias (or shortcut) to a real file.

By the Way

Although the "normal" list of search criteria is impressive, you can have even more control of your search by choosing Other from the popup menu. A separate window of search attributes appears for your perusal. (By the way, those attributes include some very specialized settings, such as information stored by iPhoto about the camera settings used to take a specific digital photograph and characteristics stored by iTunes about music files.)

▶ *Keywords* refers to metadata (or "data about data") in files that isn't displayed in the document itself, but is attached to the file to describe the content. (If you want to find a word that actually appears in one of your documents, be sure to use the Contents attribute!)

▶ *Color Label* refers to a color-coding system you can apply to your files to help you organize and prioritize them. (Labels are discussed further in Chapter 4.)

After setting your criteria, click the Search button to start the search.

In a few moments, the search results are displayed by document type, as shown in Figure 2.17. After an item is highlighted, the path required to reach it on your hard drive is shown at the bottom of the window. Double-clicking any portion of the path opens the file, folder, or application.

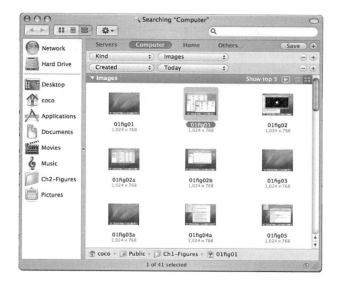

FIGURE 2.17
Scroll through the results to choose the file you were looking for.

The search results are interactive, so you can launch located programs, applications, and files by double-clicking their icons in the results window. Also, dragging a file or folder to the desktop or a Finder window moves that object to a new location. This is a quick way to clean up when you accidentally save a file to the wrong folder.

Now that you have a good understanding of search attributes, let's take a look at a related feature—Smart Folders.

Smart Folders

You may be wondering what makes a Smart Folder smarter than a regular folder. The answer, as hinted at earlier, is search criteria.

Smart Folders are really just saved search attributes. In fact, if you choose File, New Smart Folder from the menu, you get a window that looks exactly like a search window with search attributes at the top. After you set your search attributes, click the Save button at the upper right. You then need to choose what to save the Smart Folder as and where you want to save it. (You can also check or uncheck the option to have the Smart Folder appear in the sidebar of your Finder windows.)

Smart Folders display a gear-like icon to show that their content is dynamic. As documents that match the search attributes you set are created on your system, they too appear in the Smart Folder. Likewise, if you set date-sensitive search criteria, such as Last Modified or Last Opened, files disappear from the Smart Folder when they haven't been modified or opened within the time specified in your search.

The Finder Menu Bar

You've learned about the Finder window, but there's also a Finder menu bar, which provides access to a range of features. Some of those features are standard and shouldn't require much description. The standard features include options in the Edit menu to Undo/Redo, Copy, Paste, and Select All, and an option in the Window menu to access all open Finder windows.

Some menu bar options offer other ways to perform actions that have already been discussed. For example, several of the View options duplicate settings in the Finder window toolbar. Some of the unique options are covered in the following sections.

The File Menu

The options in the File menu mostly have to do with creating, opening, duplicating, and getting information about an item. Chapter 4 talks about these.

The Find function and Smart Folders, discussed earlier, are also accessed from the File menu.

However, there is are two unexpected and useful features in the Finder File menu—New Burn Folder and Burn Disc.

Burn Disc

Mac OS X makes writing a CD similar to moving files to any other storage device.

> This section focuses on burning a CD by moving items to the CD icon that appears when a blank CD is in the drive. In a moment, we talk about "burn folders," which enable you to assemble the contents of a CD before inserting a blank CD.

To make the process as simple as possible, Mac OS X stores applications, files, and folders that you want to write to CD in a special folder until you tell the system to burn the CD. Files are transferred to the CD only after the burn starts.

> To choose File, Burn Disc from the menu, the active Finder window must be the CD's window. If the CD is not the active window, the menu item is disabled.

These are the steps to write your own data CD using the Finder:

1. Insert a blank CD into the CD writer. The Mac OS X Finder prompts you to prepare the CD, as shown in Figure 2.18. (This doesn't actually write anything to the CD yet, but it tells the computer what your intentions are for the disc.)

FIGURE 2.18
When you insert a blank CD, your computer asks what you intend to use it for.

If you want to insert a CD in the drive but don't want to prepare it (for use in another CD-burning application), click Ignore rather than OK in the window that appears when you first insert a CD.

Did you Know?

2. Choose the Open Finder option from the Action pop-up menu. (Chapter 21, "Using iTunes," talks about burning CDs from iTunes.)

3. Enter a name for the CD you're writing. The disc appears with this name on the desktop.

4. Click OK to start using the CD on your system. An icon representing the CD appears on your desktop. At this point, you can interact with it as you would any other folder or storage device under Mac OS X. You can copy files to it, delete files, and so on.

5. When you create the CD layout you like, you can start the burn process by choosing File, Burn Disc from the menu (or by clicking the Burn toolbar shortcut if you've added it). In addition, dragging the CD to the Trash also prompts burning to begin. This process takes a few minutes and is tracked by the Finder much as it does with a normal Copy operation.

If you decide against writing the CD, you can choose File, Eject from the menu and then click the Eject button in the CD burning window to remove the media and erase the CD layout you created.

New Burn Folder

The previous section described how to add content to a CD if you've got a blank CD in your drive. But what if you want to prepare contents for a CD ahead of time, or to arrange content for several CDs simultaneously? The answer is Burn Folders.

A burn folder, shown in Figure 2.19, serves as a container for other items, just like a regular folder. However, rather than hold the actual items, a burn folder holds only references (or aliases) to them. (This makes sense because you don't want to move the items from their original locations just to burn them to a CD.)

Did you
Know?

Because you are creating references to content and not copying it to the burn folder, whatever you add updates as the original changes. For instance, if you want to write a CD containing your household budget files, you can add them to a burn folder and still continue to update them until you are ready to create the CD. Likewise, if you add a folder to a burn folder, anything you add to the folder appears on the CD.

FIGURE 2.19
Burn folders are marked with the yellow-and-black disc burning icon.

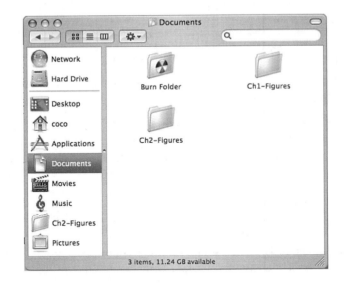

To create a burn folder, choose File, New Burn Folder from the menu. Then begin dragging items to it as you would any other folder. As shown in Figure 2.20, the icons for the items appear in the folder with small arrows next to them to show they aren't the originals, while the originals stay where they were.

When you want to burn a disc containing the contents of a burn folder, insert a CD, select the burn folder, and choose File, Burn Disc from the menu. Alternately, you can open a finder window by double-clicking the burn folder and clicking the burn button at the top, as shown in Figure. 2.20.

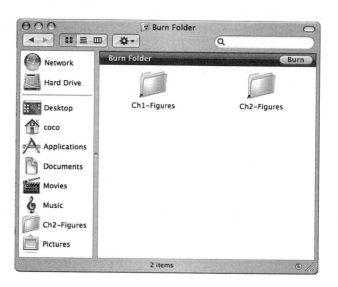

FIGURE 2.20
Add content to your burn folder as you would any other folder.

The Go Menu

If you want to navigate quickly to commonly used folders or drives, you can use the folder shortcuts in the Go menu. This menu enables you to jump to one of several predefined locations. These options are the same ones that can be set in the Finder window's sidebar.

The Go menu also enables you to type the name of a directory you want to browse. Choose Go, Go to Folder from the menu to open the Go to Folder dialog box (Shift-Command-G). Here, you can tell the Finder where you want to be, based on the pathname you enter. Figure 2.21 shows the Go to Folder dialog box.

FIGURE 2.21
The Go to Folder dialog box lets you enter your desti-nation by hand.

You can type any folder pathname in the Go to the Folder field. Folder names are separated by the / character (think of a pathname as being similar to a Web URL). For example, if you want to open the Documents folder in your home directory, you would type the following:

```
/Users/[your Home directory name]/Documents
```

As you type, OS X tries to anticipate which folder or item you have started to type.

Also in the Go menu is the option Connect to Server for connecting to remote computers, which are discussed in Chapter 32, "Sharing Files and Running Network Services."

Summary

The Mac OS X Finder is a powerful tool for managing your files and folders. It offers a high degree of customization to help you work efficiently. In addition to the expected file search capabilities, the Finder also provides some special functions, including CD burning, that make it more than just a filing system.

CHAPTER 3

Exploring the Dock

Along one edge of your screen (the bottom, left, or right) is a colorful row of icons known as the Dock. The Dock, shown in its default state in Figure 3.1, acts as a taskbar to show open applications and minimized or reduced versions of a document window. It also offers quick access to favorite applications, shows feedback from open applications, and provides a resting place for the Trash.

FIGURE 3.1
The Dock is useful for organizing your desktop.

Here's a fast overview of the Dock's arrangement:

▶ Left (or Top) portion—At left (or top) are icons for applications. The ones you've opened have a triangle under or next to them.

▶ Right (or Bottom) portion—At right (or bottom) are document icons representing the documents you've reduced or minimized.

Remember: To minimize a document, you can click the yellow (center) button at the top left of each window. You can also minimize by double-clicking the window's title bar if you've checked that option under the Appearance settings of the System Preferences.

▶ Trash—At the extreme right (or bottom) is the Trash, the place to drag files that you want to throw away.

You can also drag URLs into the right (or bottom) side of the Dock. A single click launches your default Web browser and opens it to the saved address.

▶ Separator bar—The separator bar splits the Dock into the application and file/folder areas.

To make the icons in the Dock larger or smaller, click the separator bar and then move the mouse up to increase the size or down to reduce it if positioned horizontally, or move it left and right if your Dock is positioned vertically.

Applications and the Dock

The left (or top) portion of the Dock contains all docked and currently running applications.

To launch an application whose icon is in the Dock, just click its icon once, and your computer takes it from there. When you launch an application that isn't in the Dock, its icon then appears in the Dock.

As the application launches, you'll see the icon bounce. When opened, a small triangle appears with its icon to show that it is running—as you can see with the first icon on the left in Figure 3.1. When you quit or close the application, the triangle disappears. (For applications that haven't been set to remain in the Dock, the icon also disappears from the Dock.)

To switch between active applications, just click the icon in the Dock that you want to become the active application. You can also switch between open applications by holding down Command-Tab. This moves you through active applications in the Dock in the order in which they appear. When you reach the item you want to bring to the front, release the keys to select it.

Dropping is a shortcut for opening document files in a specific application. To drop a file, you can drag and drop a document icon on top of the icon of the application in which you want it to open. In Mac OS X, you can use the application's Dock icon instead of having to locate the original application file on your hard drive.

Also, to force a docked application to accept a dropped document that it doesn't recognize, hold down Command-Option when holding the document over the application icon. The application icon is immediately highlighted, enabling you to perform your drag-and-drop action. (Keep in mind, however, that many applications can work with files in only certain formats—forcing an application to open something it doesn't have the capacity to read won't get you very far!)

By the Way

Adding and Removing Docked Applications

You can add applications to the left side (or top) of the Dock to create a quick launching point, no matter where the software is located on your hard drive. Dragging an application icon to the Dock adds it to that location in the Dock.

When the Dock expands to the full width of the screen, it automatically decreases the scale of its icons to fit along the edge of your screen. As you open more applications or add more icons to it, each icon appears smaller.

By the Way

To make an open application a permanent member of the Dock, simply do the following:

1. Locate the application's icon if it appears in the Dock. (If it's not in the Dock, the application isn't open!)

2. Click and hold on the icon to pop up a menu, as shown in Figure 3.2.

3. Choose the option Keep in Dock. (If the application already has a place in the Dock, you won't be given this option.)

After you've placed an application on the Dock, you can launch it by single-clicking the icon.

Moving an icon to the Dock doesn't change the location of the original file or folder. The Dock icon is merely an alias to the real file. Unfortunately, if the original files for a docked application have been moved since it was added to the Dock, the Dock can no longer launch that application.

By the Way

To remove an application's icon from the Dock, make sure that the application isn't running and drag it out of the Dock. It disappears in a puff of smoke (try it and see).

FIGURE 3.2
Click and hold on an application's icon in the dock.

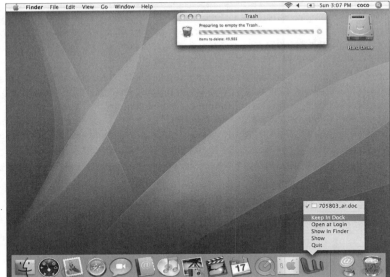

Getting Information from the Dock

In addition to providing easy access to commonly used applications, the Dock also gives you feedback about the functioning of applications through their icons.

The icon of an application that's opening bounces in the Dock (unless configured not to) and continues bouncing until the software is ready. Also, if an open application needs to get your attention, its icon bounces intermittently until you interact with it.

The Dock also signals which applications are running by displaying a small triangle, or arrow, with their application icons. This is a good way to see which applications are open, even if you've hidden them or closed all their windows.

In addition to telling you which applications are open, Dock icons can also give you a convenient way to close applications. Simply click and hold the icon of an open application and choose Quit from the menu that appears.

Dock icons also offer quick access to documents open in an application. For example, when you have multiple Finder windows open, you can view a list of those windows by clicking and holding on the Finder icon in the Dock. From the list, as shown in Figure 3.3, you can easily choose the one you want.

Did you Know?

Some applications, such as System Preferences and Sherlock, take "Dock menu-ing" even further. If they are open, you can choose from among all their sections, whether those sections are open or not, by click-holding on their icons in the Dock.

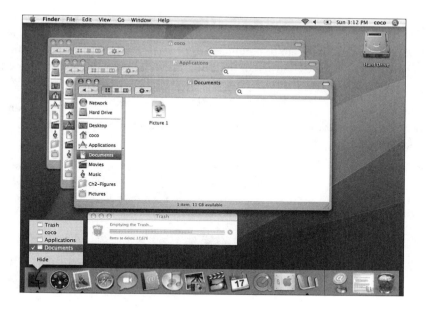

FIGURE 3.3
Click and hold on the Dock icon of an open application for a list of open windows.

Some applications even have customized Dock's icons to display information about events occurring in the application itself. For example, the Mail program displays the number of unread email messages in a red seal that appears in the icon in the Dock, as shown in Figure 3.4. (Mail is covered in detail in Chapter 17, "Using Mail.")

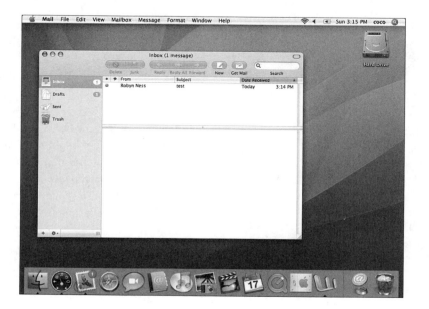

FIGURE 3.4
View the Number of Unread Messages on Your Mail Icon in the Dock.

Docked Windows, Files, and Folders

Now, let's talk about the right, or bottom, portion of the Dock. You can drag commonly used documents to this area of the Dock, and a link to them is stored for easy access, as shown in Figure 3.5.

You can also drag commonly used folders to this portion of the Dock. Click-holding (or right-clicking) a docked folder displays a list of its contents and the contents of the subfolders in that folder, as shown in Figure 3.6.

Minimized application windows are also placed in this portion of the Dock. They are labeled with the icon for their associated application for easy identification, as shown in Figure 3.7.

FIGURE 3.5
Add an important document to the Dock.

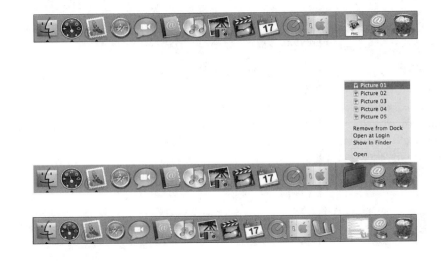

FIGURE 3.6
View the contents of docked folders with ease!

FIGURE 3.7
Temporarily store your work-in-progress in the Dock.

In addition to reducing desktop clutter, these window miniatures can serve another useful purpose. Depending on the application, minimized windows might continue to update as their associated applications attempt to display new information. QuickTime Player and DVD Player, for example, continue to play movies.

Trash Can

Another important resident of the Dock is the Trash (see Figure 3.8). The Trash is where you drag files, folders, or applications when you want to delete them from your computer. Figure 3.8 shows the Trash when empty. Figure 3.9 shows the Trash filled with one or more files.

The Trash is also used for ejecting disks, CDs, or DVDs. (It is also used to unmount external hard drives that you may attach to your computer for extra storage.) To allay user
fears that this might hurt the contents of the item being ejected, Mac OS X changes the
Trash icon into the Eject symbol when you drag a disk icon to it, as shown in Figure 3.10.

> You don't have to use the Trash when ejecting disks. An Eject icon appears in the
> sidebar of the Finder window next to any discs or drives to which it can be
> applied. Ctrl-clicking a mounted volume opens a contextual menu with an Eject
> option. Alternatively, you can highlight the disk to remove and choose File, Eject
> (Command-E) from the Finder's menu. (Some models of the Macintosh's keyboard
> also include an Eject key bearing the same eject symbol shown in Figure 3.10.)

By the Way

Deleting Files

To get rid of unwanted files, simply follow these steps:

1. Click and drag a program's icon onto the trash can icon, which is highlighted
   as soon as the icon is brought atop it. See Figure 3.11 for the effect.

2. Choose Empty Trash from the Finder's application menu, which opens the
   request for confirmation, as shown in Figure 3.12.

> When you click and hold the Trash icon, you see an Empty Trash command, which
> is a fast way to delete its contents. But be forewarned: There is no second
> chance, no warning. When you choose this command, there's no opportunity to
> change your mind.

Did you Know?

When you click OK, the file is deleted.

Finder File Edit View Go Window Help
Sun 3:34 PM coco
Hard Drive
PNG
Picture 1
Trash

FIGURE 3.11
When you release the mouse, the file is placed inside the Trash can.

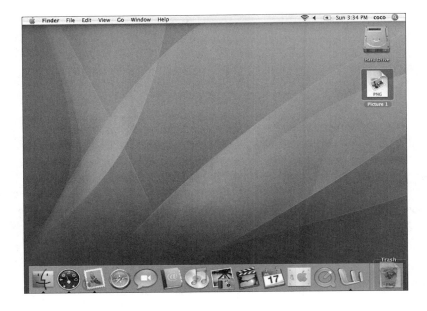

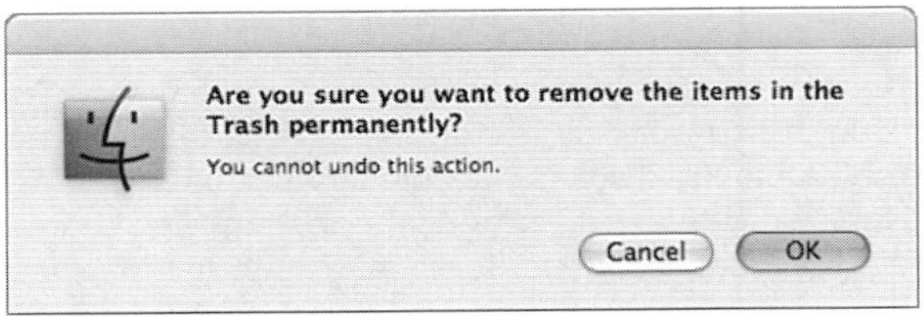
Are you sure you want to remove the items in the Trash permanently?
You cannot undo this action.
Cancel
OK

FIGURE 3.12
Do you really want to delete the files in the Trash?

Did you Know?

The Trash works like a folder. If you're not sure what's inside, just double-click it to open a window displaying its contents. If you decide to keep something after all, click and drag that icon out of the Trash window onto the desktop.

Secure Empty Trash

The files you delete using the normal Empty Trash command are no longer available for use. However, special software exists for the purpose of recovering deleted files. If you want to ensure that your deleted files can't be recovered, choose File, Secure Empty Trash from the menu.

Secure Empty Trash works by deleting a file and then filling the space it occupied on a drive with meaningless data to obscure any traces of the file that may still be readable.

Customizing the Dock

After you've used the Dock for a while, you'll probably want to customize it to better suit your needs.

If you have a small monitor, you might want to resize the Dock icons to cover less area. The easiest and fastest way to resize them is to click and hold on the separator bar that divides the Dock areas. As you click and hold on the separator bar, drag up and down or left and right (if your Dock is placed vertically). The Dock dynamically resizes as you move your mouse. Let go of the mouse button when the Dock reaches the size you want.

> After playing with different Dock sizes, you might notice that some sizes look better than others. That's because Mac OS X icons come in several native icon sizes, and points between those sizes are scaled images. To choose only native icon sizes, hold down the Option key while using the separator bar to resize.

By the Way

Dock Preference Options

For more fine-tuning of the Dock, open the Dock pane of the System Preferences. This pane, shown in Figure 3.13, includes settings for adjusting the Dock's size and icon magnification and for making it disappear when not in use.

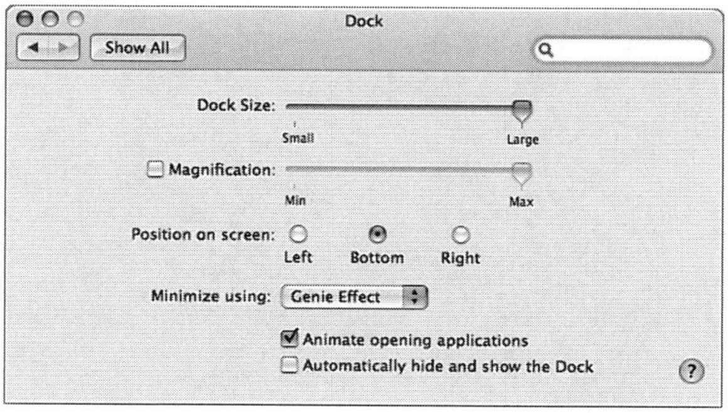

FIGURE 3.13
Configure your Dock to the size you want, or make it disappear when not in use.

> Even if you choose the option to hide the Dock, it's not really gone; it reappears for your use when you bring your mouse cursor to the Dock's edge of your screen.

By the Way

You can also shut off the animation effects that occur when document windows are minimized and stored in the Dock.

When you've made your selections, choose Quit (Command-Q) from the System Preferences application menu, or click the Close button at the top of the window.

Summary

The Dock is an important part of the OS X interface. In this chapter you learned how to use it to launch applications as well as receive feedback about them as they run. You also learned how to store files, folders, and document windows in the Dock—and to use the Trash to delete files, folders, and applications you no longer need.

CHAPTER 4

Working with Folders, Files, and Applications

In the first three chapters, you learned how to work with the desktop and windows and how to navigate the file system. Along the way, you encountered folders, files, and applications. In this chapter, we'll take a closer look at using them productively. Let's begin with a brief explanation of each.

Folders, Files, and Applications

Folders, files, and applications appear as icons on the desktop and in the Finder window, as shown in Figure 4.1.

FIGURE 4.1
A variety of folder, file, and application icons.

The folders on your computer are like folders in an office—they hold collections of (hopefully) related items, including other folders. (Most folders look alike, but some are customized with an icon.) To create a new folder, choose File, New Folder from the Finder menu or use the keyboard shortcut Command-Shift-N. A new folder appears on the Desktop or inside an existing folder, depending which item was selected when you created the folder. The default name of new folders is "untitled folder"—that text is selected immediately after a folder is created so you can type a more descriptive name. To look inside an existing folder, double-click its icon and a Finder window opens to reveal the contents.

Files, on the other hand, contain information of some kind. File icons reflect their type or the application that will be used to open them. (In Figure 4.1, for instance, the bottom item in the column of icons on the right is a PDF that would be opened by the Preview application, whose icon is displayed upper right in the open Finder window.) If you double-click a file icon, the application that made (or one that recognizes) the file is launched, and the file opens in a window on your screen.

To move a folder or file, click its icon and drag to a new location. You can even drag files into folders if you feel like getting organized.

As you may have gathered from the discussion in the previous chapters, applications are computer programs designed for various purposes. Double-clicking an application's icon (in a window or the Dock) launches the application so that you can use it.

Creating Aliases

Aliases are shortcuts that point to a folder, file, or even an application. They let you have access to things you need from anywhere you need them—without making redundant copies or moving the original from its current location.

Figure 4.1 shows an alias icon. The little arrow at the lower left indicates that this is not the actual folder or file, but a pointer to it (hence the arrow). Double-click the alias icon for a folder, and you'll see the contents of the original folder.

To create an alias for an original, press Command-L when you select an icon. You can also select a folder, file, or application icon and choose File, Make Alias from the menu, or hold down Command-Option while dragging an icon, to accomplish the same thing.

Watch Out!

> If you move the alias of a file to the trash, the original is not deleted, just the alias. If you really want to delete the original, too, you need to drag both icons to the trash. If you trash the original and not the alias, the latter becomes nonfunctional, although the Finder usually gives you the chance to pick another file for it to point to when it's double-clicked.

Renaming, Copying, and Deleting

To rename a file or folder in the Finder, click once to select the file, pause, and click a second time on the file's name. The filename becomes editable in a few seconds, as shown in Figure 4.2. (If you tend to accidentally open items when clicking to rename them, you can also rename them in the Name & Extension section of the Info window, discussed later in the section "Getting Info.")

You should avoid using colons (:) in file and folder names because your system uses them to indicate separation between folders in the path to an item. Also, avoided using a period (.) as the first character of a filename because Mac OS X reserves this use of the period to denote invisible system files.

By the Way

Be cautious about which items you rename. It's best not to rename applications because other applications or system processes may not be able to locate them. Also, do not rename folders or files that are accessed by specific applications. For instance, do not rename the Movies, Music, and Pictures folders in your home directory, which are accessed by iMovie, iTunes, and iPhoto, respectively.

Watch Out!

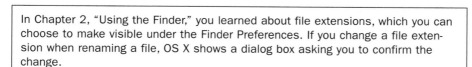

FIGURE 4.2
Clicking the name of a selected icon's label makes it editable.

In Chapter 2, "Using the Finder," you learned about file extensions, which you can choose to make visible under the Finder Preferences. If you change a file extension when renaming a file, OS X shows a dialog box asking you to confirm the change.

By the Way

Copying

Copying a file or folder creates an exact duplicate of an original. (Note that this is different from creating an alias to a file, which is just a pointer and not a separate object.) The new file contents and creation/modification dates are identical to those of the original. There are a number of ways to create a copy in Mac OS X:

▶ Drag a file to a different disk or drive—Dragging a file to a disk or drive other than the one on which it is currently stored creates a copy with the same name as the original.

▶ Drag a file while holding down the Option key—If you hold down the Option key while dragging a file icon to a folder on the same disk as the one on which it is currently located, a duplicate of that file is created in the new location. The copy has the same name as the original—unless you drag the icon within its current folder, in which case the word *copy* is appended to the name. (As you drag the file icon, a + appears next to your cursor.)

▶ Choose Duplicate from the Finder menu or contextual menu—If you want to create an exact duplicate of a file within the same folder, highlight the file to copy and then choose Duplicate from the Finder's File menu (Command-D), or Ctrl-click the icon and choose Duplicate from the pop-up contextual menu. A new file is created with the word *copy* appended to the name.

As the file is copied, the Finder displays an alert box in which you can see the progress of the copy operation. If multiple copies are being made at the same time, the statuses of the operations are shown stacked on one another in the Copy alert box.

If you attempt to copy over existing files of the same name, the Finder asks whether you want to replace the files. Also, if you attempt to replace existing files that you don't have permission to access, the copy operation fails.

Deleting

Your Mac enables you to delete folders, files, and applications.

As with copying a file, there are a number of ways to delete one:

▶ Drag to Trash—Dragging an icon from a Finder window into the Dock's Trash is one of the most obvious and easy ways to get rid of a file.

▶ Finder toolbar—A Delete shortcut can be added to the Finder's toolbar (refer to the section "The Finder Window Toolbar," in Chapter 2 for details). Any items selected can be quickly moved to the Trash if you click the Delete shortcut. Delete is *not* one of the default toolbar icons.

As you learned in Chapter 3, "Exploring the Dock," moving an item on your desktop to the Trash does not delete it permanently. Instead, it places the item inside the trash folder. To completely remove a file from your system, choose Empty Trash from the Finder's application menu or press Command-Delete.

If you want to rescue a file you've accidentally moved to the Trash, you can click the Trash icon and drag the file's icon out of the window.

> In Mac OS X, you can delete applications by moving them to the Trash. However, some applications create additional files, such as application preferences, that you may also need to delete. (Such files are often in the Library folders, either in your home directory or at the system level.)

By the Way

The Finder Window Action Menu

In Chapter 2's discussion of the Finder window, we postponed discussing the Action pop-up menu in the toolbar. It's time to return to it now to see how it can be used to make working with folders, files, and applications more convenient.

The items in the Action menu are context dependent, which means they differ depending on whether a folder, file, or application is selected. The Action menu for files, shown in Figure 4.3, contains the most options, so we start by listing those options.

FIGURE 4.3
This is the Action menu when a file is selected.

▶ New Folder—Creates a new, empty folder at the same level as the selected file.

▶ New Burn Folder—Creates a new folder of a special kind at the same level as the selected file. When you place an item or a folder in a burnable folder, only an alias to the item is added. That way, you can continue to work with the original file or continue adding items to a regular folder, but be ready to burn a CD of your work at a second's notice. (See Chapter 2 for more information about using burnable folders.)

▶ Open—Opens the selected item.

▶ Open With—Enables you to choose which application installed on the system will be used when the selected file is opened. A list of recommended applications is presented, along with the option Other, which allows you to select any application on your hard drive or connected to it. When you select an application, the file is opened in it.

▶ Print—Enables you to print a file without having to open it.

▶ Get Info—Opens the Info window for the selected item. (The Info window is covered in greater detail later in the chapter.)

The Get Info option appears in the Action menu when you select your hard drive. If you select a removable drive, such as an external hard drive, Get Info and Eject appear in the Action menu.

▶ Move to Trash—Provides another way to place an item in the Trash for deletion from your system.

▶ Duplicate—Provides another way to copy an item. When Duplicate is used, the copy appears in the same place as the original with the word *copy* appended to its name.

▶ Make Alias—Provides another way to make an alias of an item.

▶ Create Archive—Creates a compressed, or "zipped," version of an item that takes up less space than the original.

▶ Copy/Paste—Provides yet another way to copy an item. When Copy is used, the file is copied but not pasted. You can then navigate to the location where you want the copy, and choose Paste from the Action pop-up menu. (The Paste option is visible only after an item has been copied.)

▶ Color Label—Enables you to color-code the selected file for easy identification. Also, if you recall from Chapter 2, you can perform file searches for items marked with a specific color. (Using Color Labels is covered in just a moment.)

The options available for a folder are similar to those for a file, except that the options Open With and Print are not given.

For applications, the list of available options includes New Folder, New Burn Folder, Open, Get Info, Move to Trash, Duplicate, Make Alias, Create Archive, Copy/Paste, and Color Label. There is also the option Show Package Contents, which opens a second Finder window to display the supporting files associated with the selected application.

Applications on your drive are often really folders of items that work together. When you choose Show Package Contents, you can see elements "inside" the application that are normally hidden from view. Although it's interesting to see how things work, you shouldn't rename or remove any of the items needed by a program unless you are prepared to deal with the consequences.

Watch Out!

Adding Color Labels

Previously, you learned that one of the items in the Action pop-up menu is Color Label, which can be used to color-code your files and folders. You can choose from seven colors. In addition to helping you visually locate important documents, the colors can be used as search criteria in the Find window.

You can change the names of the color labels from simply their colors to more meaningful terms, such as *work* or *book project*, in the Labels section of the Finder preferences. You can access the Finder preferences under the Finder application menu.

By the Way

To apply color labels to a selected file or folder, do the following:

1. Locate the item you want to label in the Finder window and select it.

2. Click the Action pop-up menu to open it and reveal the Color Label options, as shown previously in Figure 4.3.

3. Click one of the seven colors to apply it to the selected file or folder.

The color appears as a background behind the file or folder's label, as shown in Figure 4.4.

To remove a color label, select the item, open the Action pop-up menu, and choose the "x" under the Color Label option.

Now it's time to take a close look at the Info window that can be launched from the Action pop-up menu.

FIGURE 4.4
Eye-catching
color labels can
make finding
important docu-
ments easy.

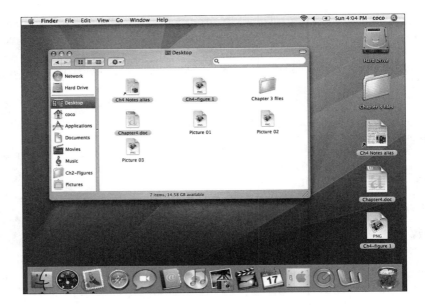

Getting Info

The Info window displays detailed information, such as graphical previews and user permissions, about your folders, files, and applications. You can display the Info window by selecting the file you want to examine in the Finder, and then choosing Get Info from the Action pop-up menu in the Finder toolbar. Alternatively, you can select an item and choose File, Get Info (Command-I) from the menu.

Like the options in the Action pop-up menu, the Info window is context-dependent, with slightly different options depending on what it's giving information about. Let's examine the information available in the Info window.

General

As shown in Figure 4.5, the General section supplies basic facts about the selected resource, including the kind, size, and date of creation.

If the item you're viewing is an alias file (remember, an *alias* is a shortcut to the place where the real file is stored), the General section shows the location of the original file along with a Select New Original button that enables you to pick a new file to which the alias should be attached.

In the General section of the Info window is a check box labeled Locked, and for files, one labeled Stationary Pad. If an item is locked, a small lock appears in its icon that shows you won't be able to move or delete it. If you try, your system displays a message that it can't comply because the item is locked. You also won't be able to rename an item.

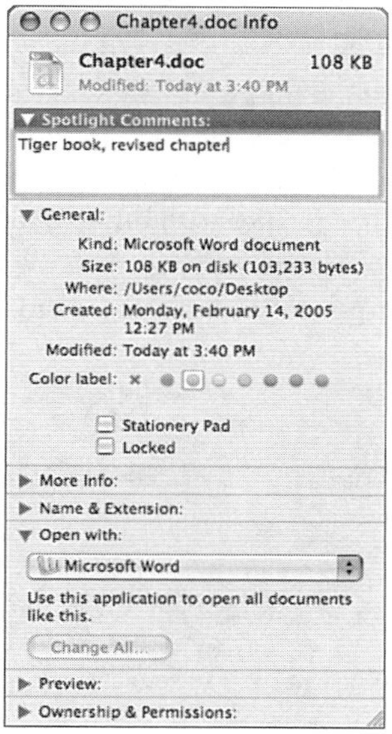

FIGURE 4.5
General informa-
tion includes
basic size, loca-
tion, and type
information
about a file.

Stationary Pad is an option only for files—and only if they aren't already locked. Checking this box makes a file into something of a template. If you double-click a file set as stationary pad, it doesn't open, but an exact copy of it is made in the same place so that you can make changes to the copy while the original remains untouched.

Although an identifying icon appears for locked items, there is no indication that a file is a template—except that a duplicate file automatically appears whenever you try to open the file. It's a good idea to title stationary pad files to indicate their purpose so that you'll know which files are affected this way.

Watch
Out!

More Info

The More Info section offers just that—additional information about an item. For nearly all items, this section shows the date and time last opened. If the item is an application, the information includes copyright information and version number. For image files, details such as the resolution of the file and its color space are displayed. (If you don't know what color space is, don't worry. We'll talk about it more in Chapter 11, "Working with Displays and Peripheral Devices.")

Name & Extension

Under Name & Extension, you view the name of the selected item and choose whether to show its file extension. As you've learned, a filename can contain an extension—a period followed by several letters at the end of a name that indicates what kind of file it is. Common examples of file extensions are .doc for Microsoft Word documents and .html for Web pages. The Name & Extension section, shown in Figure 4.6, enables you to choose whether to view the filename with or without its extension. If you plan to exchange files with other systems (Windows), you should verify that your files include the extensions because Windows systems use file extensions to determine in which applications to open them.

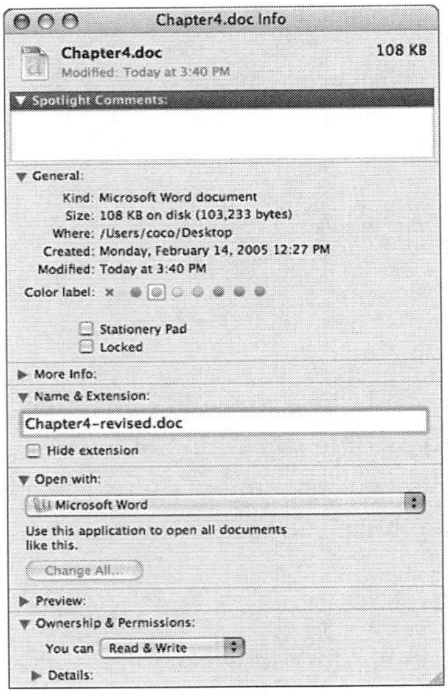

FIGURE 4.6
Change a file's name and choose whether to hide or show its file extension.

For folders and applications, the Name & Extension section simply shows the name of the item.

Open With

If you select a file icon (not an application or a folder), you can access the Open With section in the Info window, which is similar to the Open With item in the Action menu discussed previously. If you download a file from a non–Mac OS X system, your computer might not realize what it needs to do to open the file. The Open With section lets you pick an application to open the file.

If there are multiple files you want to have open with a different application than is currently configured for them, you can select them all by holding down the Command key as you click the files' icons. Then you can open the Info window and change the Open With settings for all of them at once.

To use this feature, click the disclosure triangle next to Open With. The default application name is shown as the current choice in a pop-up menu containing alternative application choices. Use the pop-up menu to display options and make a selection. If the application you want to use isn't shown, choose Other, and then use the standard Mac OS X Open dialog box to browse to the application you want to use.

If you have a group of files that you want to open with a given application, you can select the entire group and follow the same procedure, or use the Change All button at the bottom of the window to update all files on your system simultaneously.

Preview

If you select a QuickTime-recognized document, Preview enables you to quickly examine the contents of a wide variety of media files, including MP3s, CD audio tracks (AIFFs), JPEGs, GIFs, TIFFs, PDFs, and many more (see Figure 4.7).

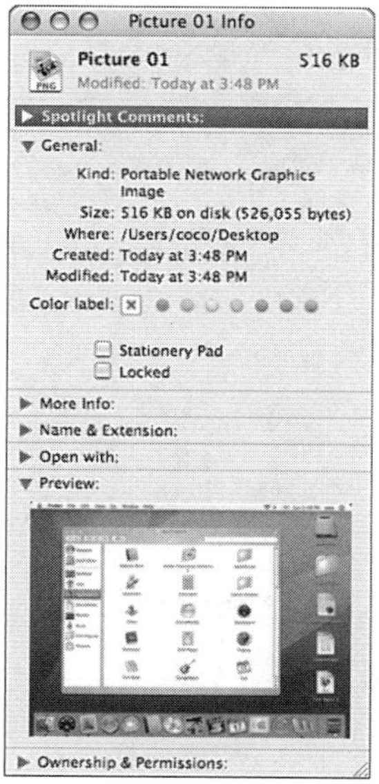

FIGURE 4.7
View an image file with the Preview feature.

If you're previewing a video or audio track, the QuickTime Player control appears and enables you to play the file's contents.

If you select a folder or an application, the Preview section displays its icon.

Languages

For an application, the Info window includes a section called Languages that enables you to see which languages the application supports. If the language you've set in the International section of the System Preferences isn't supported, the first supported language listed in the Info window is used to display menus. You can uncheck or remove supported languages to ensure they aren't used. (See Chapter 5, "Setting System Preferences and Universal Access Options," for more details about the International preferences.)

Ownership & Permissions

Mac OS X is a multiuser system, and by default all the files and folders on your system identify themselves with the user who created them. That means only the owner, or someone with special administrative powers, can move or modify them. Applications have different permissions depending whether they are shared or stored in a personal account. The Ownership & Permissions section, shown in Figure 4.8, enables you to change who owns a file, what other groups of users can access it, and what actions can be performed on it. You learn more about working with multiple user accounts and administrative access in Chapter 31, "Sharing Your Computer with Other Users."

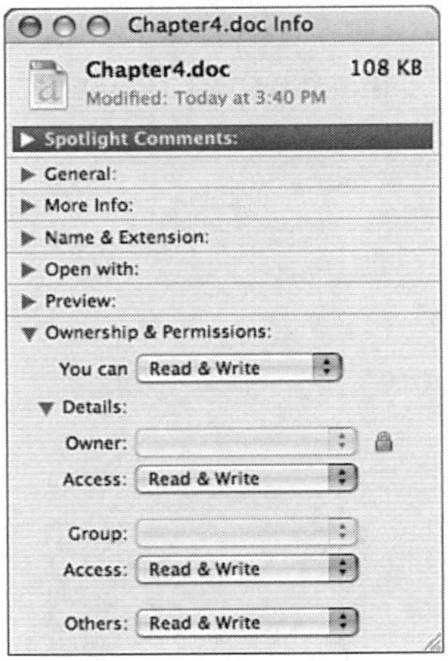

FIGURE 4.8
Determine, or alter, who has access to an item on your system.

```
                  ● ○ ○   Chapter4.doc Info
                  ┌─────┐  Chapter4.doc         108 KB
                  │     │  Modified: Today at 3:40 PM
                  ▶ Spotlight Comments:
                  ▶ General:
                  ▶ More Info:
                  ▶ Name & Extension:
                  ▶ Open with:
                  ▶ Preview:
                  ▼ Ownership & Permissions:
                    You can  [ Read & Write    ▼ ]
                    ▼ Details:
                      Owner:   [            ▼ ]  🔒
                      Access:  [ Read & Write ▼ ]

                      Group:   [            ▼ ]
                      Access:  [ Read & Write ▼ ]

                      Others:  [ Read & Write ▼ ]
```

Did you Know?

You can select a group of items and change the ownership and permissions for them all at once. Hold down the Command key as you click to select multiple items; then open the Info window and change the settings.

Spotlight Comments

The Spotlight Comments section enables you to create notes attached to specific files, folders, and applications. The content of notes doesn't appear in the actual file, but it can searched by Spotlight when you set Keyword attributes in a search. (Refer to Chapter 2, "Using the Finder," for more information about searching your files with Spotlight.)

Additional Tips for Using Applications

Later chapters explore specific applications ranging in complexity from Calculator to iMovie. For now, however, let's talk about some fairly common practices for working with applications.

Using Open and Save Dialog Boxes

Although you can launch an application by double-clicking a file created by it, sometimes you are already in an application and want to open additional files. To open existing files in an open application, choose File, Open from the menu. This launches the Open dialog box, as shown in Figure 4.9.

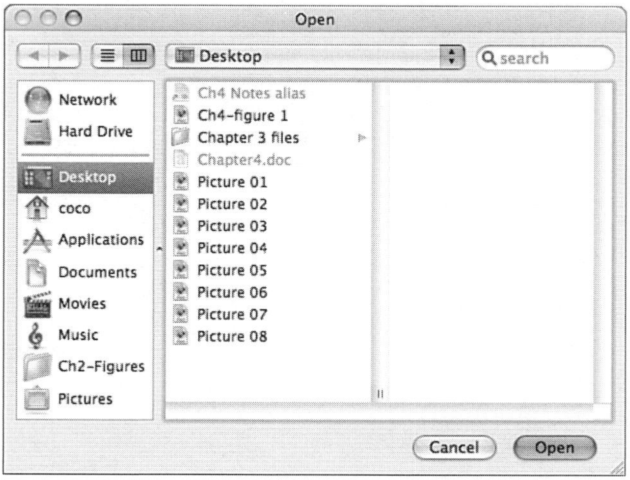

FIGURE 4.9
In the Open dialog box, the shortcut list and content area should look familiar.

The Open dialog box is a modified Finder window where the toolbar has been replaced with a pop-up menu to help you quickly navigate to a different level of the file system. There's also a pair of buttons, Cancel and Open, at the bottom of the window so that you can cancel the dialog box or open a selected file.

By the Way

> In addition to Open and Save, other common dialog boxes and helpers are the Page Setup and Print windows and the Font panel, which are discussed in Chapter 12, "Printing, Faxing, and Working with Fonts."

You can use the shortcut list and content area to move through the file system to locate a specific file. Applications can't be opened in another application. You can, however, click folders to open them. The Open button at the bottom of the Open dialog box is grayed out until you select a file.

Did you Know?

> You can select more than one document to open in the current application by holding down the Command key on your keyboard. If you want to select a long list of files all in a row, you can hold down the Shift key and select the first and last file in the list—all the files in between are then also selected.

When you are using an application, you are likely to create new documents that you want to save. To save a document, choose File, Save or File, Save As from the menu. This opens a Save sheet window attached to the current document, as shown in Figure 4.10.

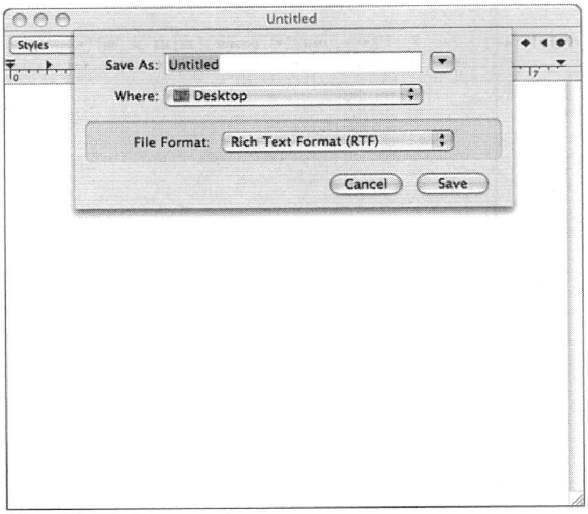

FIGURE 4.10
The "short" version of the Save sheet window.

By the Way

> The first time you save a new document, Save and Save As cause the same outcome. Later, however, there is a difference. Save saves changes to the file you've already created. Save As allows you to rename your document and save—which is especially useful if you want to keep the original intact for comparison later or if you want to save a copy to a new location.

If you want to save your document in its current location, as indicated by the Where pop-up menu, you can simply enter a title and click the Save button. (Use the Cancel button if you've changed your mind about saving.)

If you want to save the document to another location (or if aren't sure where the Where pop-up is putting your document), click the disclosure triangle button to the right of the Save field. An expanded version of the Save sheet window appears, as shown in Figure 4.11.

FIGURE 4.11
Navigate to the location where you want to save your file.

The expanded Save sheet window is like the Open dialog box, with a few additional options. You can use it to move to any folder on your hard drive, or even to connected storage devices. The New Folder button enables you to create and name a new folder into which to save your document. You also have the option to show or hide the file extension, as discussed previously.

When you've chosen the location and given your file a name, click the Save button to store your file.

Running Classic Applications

Using the Classic environment is a way for you to operate some older Mac software while still using the Mac OS X operating system. If you use Classic, almost any application that was functional in Mac OS 9 can run inside Mac OS X.

You must have at least 128MB of memory to use Classic. Also, a 400MHz G3 (or faster) computer is recommended. Why? Classic is a process running under Mac OS X. When it's in use, your computer is really supporting two operating systems simultaneously. As you can imagine, this is resource intensive.

Launching Classic

The Classic environment needs to be launched only once during a Mac OS X login session, and it can be launched manually or automatically. After it's running, Classic remains active (but mostly unnoticeable) until you log out or manually force it to shut down.

How can you find out whether a piece of software on your hard drive is indeed a Classic application? You can always ask the Finder. Simply select the icon for the program in question and choose File, Get Info (or press Command-I) from the Finder's menu. If Classic Application is listed in the General section next to Kind, the software requires Classic to operate.

There are two ways to launch the Classic environment: through the Classic pane in System Preferences or by double-clicking a Classic application.

First, let's start Classic from the System Preferences pane. Here's what to do:

1. Locate the System Preferences icon in the Dock and double-click it (the icon looks like a wall-mounted light switch), or choose System Preferences from the Apple menu.

2. In System Preferences, click the Classic icon to open its Preferences pane, shown in Figure 4.12.

3. Click the Start/Stop view of the Classic Preferences pane. Here you see several options, including a Stop or Start button for manually turning Classic off or on, Restart for when you want to reboot Classic, and Force Quit for when the Classic system is unresponsive after a crash.

4. Click the Start button to launch Classic. Mac OS 9 takes a few minutes to boot and then you're ready to run your older applications.

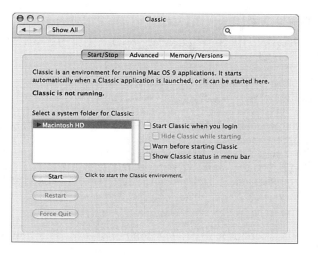

FIGURE 4.12
The Classic pane enables you to start/stop, restart, or force-quit the Classic environment.

By the Way

The first time you start Classic, your system requests permission to make some changes that allow Classic to operate.

Let's try the second way to launch Classic:

1. Locate an older, non–Mac OS X application and double-click it.

Yes, there's only one step. If Classic isn't already running, it boots automatically before the application you've chosen is launched. It may take a little while for both Classic and the application you've launched to open and be ready for use. Remember that after it's started, Classic remains in the background until you log out of Mac OS X or manually stop Classic. Even when you log out of all Classic applications, Classic itself is still running.

By the Way

The Classic System Preferences pane shows the status of the Classic environment—that is, whether or not it's running. Because Classic does not appear as an active task in the Dock, this is one way to check its status.

Although it's true that in most cases Classic runs until you log out or manually stop the process, it's still (like Mac OS 9 was) susceptible to crashes. If Classic crashes, so do any applications running within it. You must restart Classic to continue working.

Using Classic Applications

The first time you open a Classic application, you'll notice that several interesting things happen.

> Be careful not to alter settings in a Mac OS 9 control panel! When running Classic, the Mac OS X menu bar is replaced by the Mac OS 9 menu bar with a rainbow apple at the upper left in place of the solid-color one you usually see. Using the Mac OS 9 Apple menu, you can access all the earlier system's control panels and associated functionality. Settings in control panels such as Appearance and Sound are harmless enough, but it's possible to accidentally disrupt your network connections by working with the TCP/IP and AppleTalk control panels. It's best to avoid the Mac OS 9 control panels altogether.

Visually, Classic applications look different from applications that run under OS X. These older applications appear just as they would under Mac OS 8 and 9. The appearance of Mac OS X interface elements does not carry over to their windows or buttons, but the Mac OS X Dock and Process Manager do recognize Classic applications, as shown in Figure 4.13.

FIGURE 4.13
A mixture of OS X and OS 9 interface elements appears.

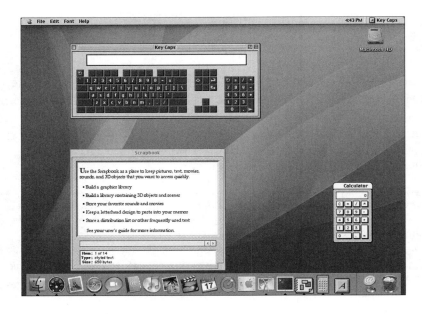

After it starts, Classic is easy to use without extra detail about how it interacts with Mac OS X. You simply operate programs as you normally would. However, there are a few exceptions that might be confusing for you:

▶ Copy and paste/drag and drop—Two of the most common means of moving data in the Mac OS suffer when working between native and Classic applications. It can take several seconds before data copied from one environment is available for pasting into another. Dragging and dropping text and images between native and Classic applications fails altogether.

▶ Open and Save dialog boxes—Mac OS X applications are aware of the special folders and files used by the system and take care to hide them. The same cannot be said for Classic applications. The Open and Save dialog boxes clearly show the invisible items. Although normal, these invisible files could be alarming to users not accustomed to seeing them.

Note that when using the Classic environment, applications still need to access all hardware through Mac OS X, so software trying to access hardware directly fails for devices not compatible with Mac OS X.

By the Way

Summary

This chapter covered many of the basics of interacting with folders, files, and applications. It examined options in the Finder window's Action menu and the Get Info window. You also learned how to rename, copy, delete, and create aliases for files, folders, and applications. Finally, it discussed some more special techniques for working with applications, including running older Mac applications in Classic mode.

CHAPTER 5

Setting System Preferences and Universal Access Options

System preferences are settings that control aspects beyond a single application and that might even affect the entire system. Some of Mac OS X's system preferences have already been covered within specific topics. However, some settings don't apply elsewhere. This chapter fills in the remaining gaps in system configuration and lets you know where to find the system preferences discussed in other chapters. It gives special attention to the accessibility features available in System Preferences.

As you've seen in previous chapters, System Preferences items are categorized into four groups, as shown in Figure 5.1. They are Personal, Hardware, Internet & Network, and System.

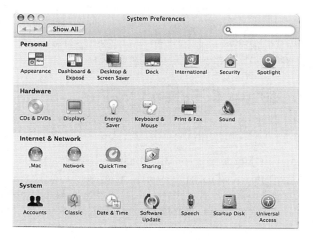

FIGURE 5.1
The System Preferences panes are loosely categorized.

Within those sections, each button may have many features (accessible after it's been clicked) and contain buttons or pop-up menus that organize its features into smaller units. This could mean that you have to click through several options before you locate the setting you want to change. Use the button labels and explore pop-up menus to help guide you. Also, if you want to view all the system preferences again after selecting a specific one, click Show All at the upper left in the System Preferences window.

Personal System Preferences

The options in the Personal section of System Preferences affect your personal desktop. Each user can decide individual settings without interfering with the settings of others.

Appearance

The Appearance pane enables you to choose between Blue and Graphite for a general color scheme for menus, buttons, and windows on your desktop. You can also pick the highlight color for selected items. Other settings are the placement of arrows in the scrollbars, whether clicking the scrollbar jumps to the next page or the corresponding location in the window, the number of listings for recent applications and documents, and activation of font smoothing for optimal font appearance on different screens.

Dashboard & Exposé

Dashboard is a collection of small applications, such as a calculator and sticky notes, that appear on the desktop. Exposé is a feature that temporarily shifts the windows on your desktop so that you can view the desktop or see all open windows. You can set Active Screen Corners or keyboard and mouse combinations to trigger different modes of Exposé and to activate Dashboard. Exposé and Dashboard are covered in Chapter 2, "Using the Finder."

Desktop & Screen Saver

The Desktop Preference pane, shown in Figure 5.2, enables you to choose the background on which all the items on your desktop will be displayed.

You can choose from among the images in the Apple Images, Nature, or Abstract folders provided by Apple, or use your own images stored in your Pictures folder or iPhoto Library or elsewhere on your system. You can also choose a solid color. To set a new background, simply select a category from the left column and click a thumbnail image that appears at the right.

If you like variety, select an item, check the Change Picture box, and set a frequency for the change. Your desktop background phases between all the images in that folder. You can also check the Random Order box if you want.

Under Screen Saver preferences, you can choose among several preinstalled screensavers. The preview window, shown in Figure 5.3, enables you to view your selection before applying it.

FIGURE 5.2
Choose a desktop background to brighten your day—or to minimize distraction.

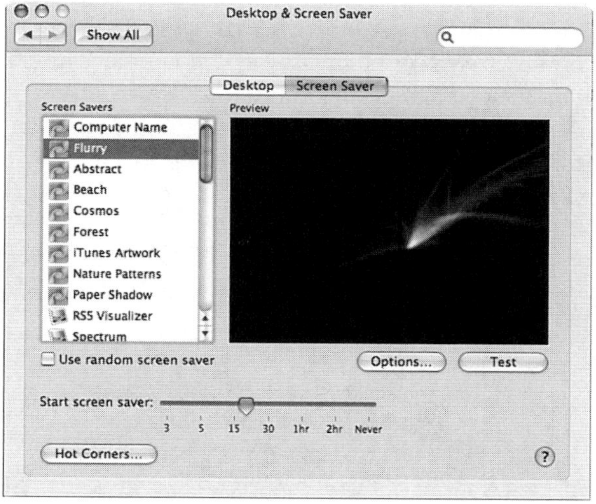

FIGURE 5.3
Choose a screensaver and how it activates.

You can also choose how the screensaver activates by setting the time until activation. The Hot Corners button enables you to pick corners of the screen that activate or prevent activation of the screensaver when your mouse enters a given corner.

Dock

The settings under Dock enable users to customize the appearance of the Dock by resizing it or positioning it on the left, bottom, or right edge of the screen. Other options include graphic effects that occur when documents are minimized into the

Dock or when applications are launched. The Dock is discussed in greater detail in Chapter 3, "Exploring the Dock."

International

The International settings control the language displayed, as well as date, time, and number formatting conventions. You can also choose keyboard layouts to support different languages from the Input Menu section.

Security

Under Security preferences, shown in Figure 5.4, you can choose to activate a feature called FileVault to encrypt your entire Home folder to ensure that no one will be able to read your files. This feature operates in the background, so you can use your files a usual. However, if someone steals your computer or connects to your computer remotely and doesn't know your password, your files will be undecipherable without a great deal of effort. To turn on this feature, click the Turn On FileVault button. Note that you need spare room on your hard drive for the encryption to take place. You can also set a master password that can be used to unlock any files in any FileVault account on your computer.

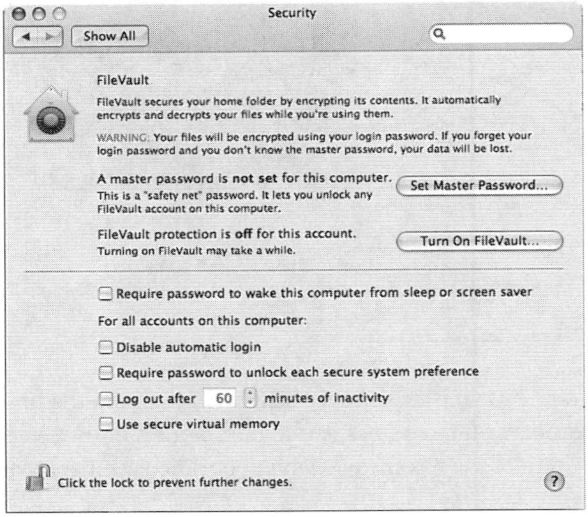

FIGURE 5.4
Security features range from encrypting your entire account to requiring a password to wake your computer from sleep.

Encryption, when done right, isn't easy to crack. If you forget both your account password and the Master password, which was set when you first set up your account, your files will remain securely encrypted even from you! For this reason, FileVault is a serious security option, not a toy—use it wisely.

In the lower portion of the Security pane, you can set whether a password is required to wake your computer from sleep or from screensaver, to log in to user accounts, or to unlock secure system preferences. Secure system preferences, such as the Security pane shown in Figure 5.4, are marked by a lock icon in the lower left of the pane. If the lock is "locked," you must type the username and password of an "administrator" to make changes to the preferences. An administrator is a user with special privileges—the account you created the first time your computer ran OS X is automatically an administrator. Other accounts can be set up to be administrators as well, which is discussed in Chapter 31, "Sharing Your Computer with Other Users."

If you can't remember your login name, you can find it in the Accounts pane as your "short name," which is discussed later in this chapter. If you can't remember your password, you can reset it by using your OS X installation disk as described in Chapter 35, "Recovering from Crashes and Other Problems."

By the Way

You can also choose to have the computer log out any user after a specific period of inactivity to prevent passersby from using an unattended workstation.

The final option, Use Secure Virtual Memory, encrypts virtual memory to ensure that no one can read information from it—this protects confidential files by ensuring that traces of them stored in virtual memory can't be recovered easily.

Spotlight

As you learned in Chapter 2, "Using the Finder," Spotlight is a search technology that doesn't require you to index the content on your computer—that's because Spotlight is continuously cataloging. The Search Results pane of the Spotlight preferences enable you to choose which categories of results will be displayed and in what order. You can also set keyboard shortcuts for activating the Spotlight menu and the Spotlight window.

The Privacy pane enables you to exclude folders from the Spotlight search.

Hardware System Preferences

Hardware preferences, such as those for display, keyboard, and mouse, are found in the Hardware section of System Preferences.

For those with compatible graphics tablets, the Ink preferences also appear in this section, as discussed in Chapter 8, "Working with Address Book, Keychain Access, iSync, and Ink."

By the Way

Bluetooth

If you have a Bluetooth-enabled computer, the Bluetooth preference pane is the first item in the Hardware section of the System Preferences. Bluetooth is a popular wireless technology that allows you to form a wireless *PAN–Personal Area Network*. Through this wireless network, you can synchronize PDAs, connect to the Internet through your cell phone, print to printers, use Apple's wireless keyboard and mouse, and so on.

Although Bluetooth *is* an accepted standard, a limited number of devices currently use it, and not all Macintosh systems are Bluetooth enabled. If you're interested in Bluetooth, you can purchase a Bluetooth USB dongle that will Bluetooth-enable your Mac.

The Settings pane enables you to make changes to your first Bluetooth device—your Macintosh. Options include turning Bluetooth on or off, making your computer "visible" (or discoverable) to other Bluetooth devices, and showing Bluetooth status in the menu bar.

Use the Devices pane to add, delete, disconnect, and otherwise alter the devices to which your computer connects over the Bluetooth network. In the upper-left corner of the pane is a list of Bluetooth devices paired with your computer. Below the list is a detailed display showing information about the selected device.

To add a new device, click the Set Up New Device button in the Device pane. The Bluetooth Setup Assistant walks you through the steps of adding a new device. During setup, you may need to enter the passkey from your device's documentation to verify that you have permission to create a connection, or a pairing, between the device and your computer.

Did you Know?

Paired Apple Bluetooth keyboards and mice add new settings to the Keyboard & Mouse preferences, including showing their battery level.

The Sharing pane enables you to which services are active on your Bluetooth-enabled computer. Click a service in the list, and then use the Start or Stop buttons or On check box beside its name to enable or disable it. In addition to simply starting and stopping a service, you can also force incoming connections to generate and validate a passkey. To ensure that only authorized devices connect, click the Key check box beside each service name, or highlight the service and then check the box for Require Pairing for Security.

CDs & DVDs

The CDs & DVDs preferences enable you to tell your computer what to do when CDs and DVDs are inserted in your drive. The default configuration, shown in Figure 5.5, launches the appropriate application included with Mac OS X when you insert a music CD, picture CD, or video DVD. When you insert blank media, the Finder prompts you to choose an application to suit your purpose.

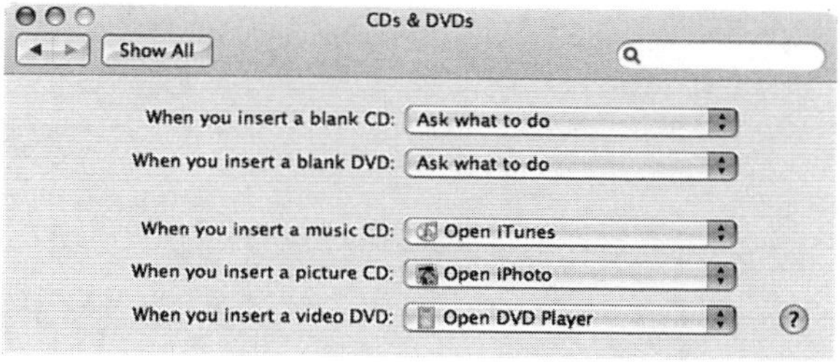

FIGURE 5.5
Choose which application is activated when you insert a CD or DVD.

Displays

The Display pane of the Displays preferences enables you to set your screen resolution, brightness, and the number of colors displayed. You can also choose to show Displays in the menu bar as a menu extra for convenient access to resolution settings. In the Color pane, you can choose a display profile, which is a specific color balance setting, or recalibrate your display. Both the Displays and Color panes are examined further in Chapter 11, "Working with Displays and Peripheral Devices."

Energy Saver

The Energy Saver preferences, shown in Figure 5.6, enable you to set Sleep and Wake options for your machine. Laptop users also have the option to show the battery status in the menu bar. Notice that separate settings exist for the display and the hard disk.

After you've set Sleep options, use the Options pane of the Energy Saver pane to set Wake options.

Click the Schedule button to set your computer to start up and shut down at a given time on weekdays, weekends, every day, or a specific day.

When performing functions that require lengthy periods of keyboard inactivity, such as CD burning or digital video rendering, it's best to set the Sleep option to Never to avoid disruption to the process that can result in skips in the output.

Watch Out!

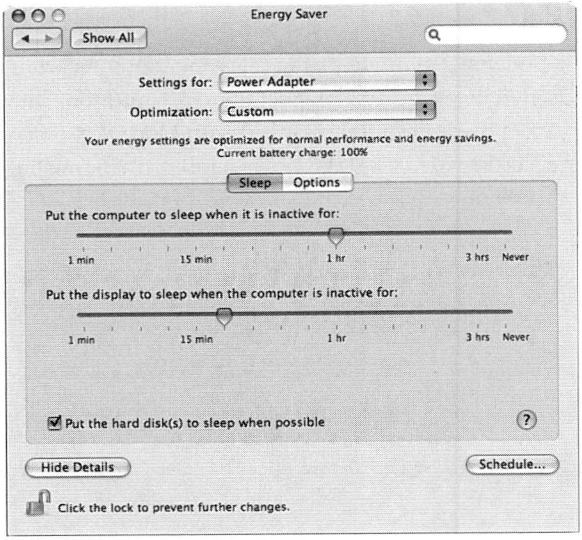

FIGURE 5.6
Energy Saver
lets your system
conserve power
in response to
monitor and
hard drive inac-
tivity.

Keyboard & Mouse

In the Keyboard pane, you can set the repeat rate of the keyboard and the delay before keys start to repeat when you hold them down.

Just as the Keyboard pane enables you to control keyboard sensitivity, the Mouse pane enables you to control tracking and double-click speeds. You might need to test the options a bit to find the most comfortable settings for your system.

By the Way

> For laptop users, who don't have a mouse on their system, the Mouse pane appears under the label Trackpad.

Laptop users also see a Trackpad pane with settings similar to the Mouse pane. The Trackpad settings also include Trackpad Gestures options to enable you to select and drag items without pressing the trackpad button. The Ignore Trackpad While Typing option disables the trackpad temporarily while the keyboard is being used, and the Ignore Trackpad When Mouse Is Present disables the trackpad when a mouse is plugged in.

If you have a Bluetooth keyboard or mouse, the Bluetooth pane enables you to set them up to work with your computer and also show the battery levels of these devices after they've been set up.

The Keyboard Shortcuts pane, shown in Figure 5.7, can be used to customize keyboard shortcut settings that enable users to control menus, windows, and other interface elements from the keyboard.

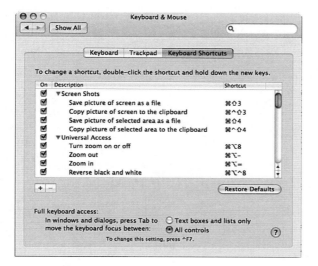

FIGURE 5.7
Use keyboard controls in addition to your mouse to change system focus and navigation.

Print & Fax

The Printing pane gives you access to an application called Printer Setup Utility where you can set up printers. You can also choose the selected printer that will appear in the Print dialog box and a default paper size.

Under Faxing, you can check the box to receive faxes on your computer and enter the phone number of the phone line connected to your computer. You can also choose how received faxes will be handled.

In the Sharing pane, you can choose whether to share your printer with other computers over the network and whether to allow others on your network to send faxes through your computer.

Printing and Faxing are discussed further in Chapter 12, "Printing, Faxing, and Working with Fonts."

Sound

The Sound preferences contain Sound Effects options (see Figure 5.8) and volume controls for alerts and the main system, as well as the option to choose your sound output and input devices. You can also change the overall volume levels from the keyboard sound controls. In addition, you can use the Show Volume in Menu Bar check box to add a volume control menu extra to your menu bar.

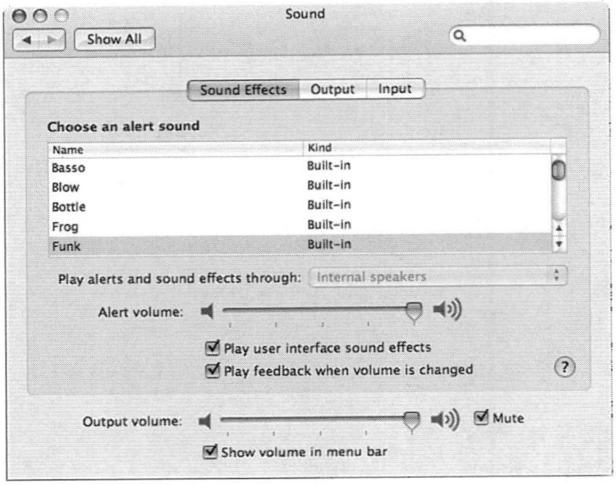

FIGURE 5.8
The Sound pref-
erences pane
enables you to
pick error alerts
and select from
which audio out-
put they
emanate.

If you have multiple sound input and output devices (such as an iSub speaker) connected to your computer, you can choose between them in the Output and Input
panes. For output devices, set the balance between left and right speakers. For Input
devices, set the Input volume.

Internet & Network System Preferences

The next grouping of preferences, Internet & Network, determines how your
machine talks to other computers on the network and works with your Internet services, such as email and Web.

.Mac

Pronounced "dot Mac," the .Mac preferences allow you to set up a for-pay account
with Apple that includes an email account and Internet-accessible storage space
referred to as iDisk. We discuss the .Mac services and these preferences in detail in
Chapter 16, "Exploring .Mac Membership."

Network

The Network preferences are used to set up your computer's Internet connection.
These settings are explained in Chapter 13, "Connecting to the Internet."

QuickTime

QuickTime, which is often used as a browser plug-in, requires information about your Internet connection. We cover the QuickTime preferences in Chapter 7, "Using QuickTime and DVD Player."

Sharing

Sharing refers to giving other users access to resources and files on your system. Chapter 31, "Sharing Your Computer with Other Users," Chapter 32, "Sharing Files and Running Network Services," and Chapter 33, "Securing Your Computer," explain various aspects of the Sharing preferences.

System Preferences

The System section of System Preferences controls settings relating to your overall system rather than to a single user or to a specific application.

Accounts

The Accounts preferences enable you to create additional user accounts so that others can have their own place to store files and keep their own desktop preferences without interfering with yours. You can also edit a user's information. We discuss options for setting up additional user accounts in Chapter 31.

> In an earlier note, you learned that you have to use a system installation disk to reset your password. That's because although you can change your password from the Accounts pane, you have to enter your password to authorize that change!

By the Way

The Login Items pane of the Accounts preferences, shown in Figure 5.9, enables you to choose applications or files to open automatically whenever your account is active. To add an item, simply click the "+" button and navigate to it in the window that appears. To temporarily disable an item, uncheck the box in front of it. To remove an item from the list, select it from the list and click the "–" button.

> Be careful not to start too many applications at startup, or you may have to wait a long time for your system to be ready for use!

Watch
Out!

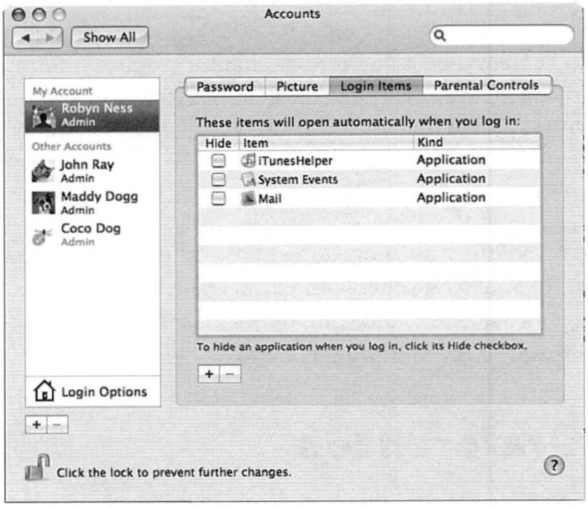

FIGURE 5.9
You can choose
to have Mail
automatically
start up when-
ever you log in.

FIGURE 5.9
You can choose
to have Mail
automatically
start up when-
ever you log in.

Classic

Chapter 4, "Working with Folders, Files, and Applications," talked about running
Classic applications, which were written for Mac OS 9. The Classic preferences
enable you to start Classic for use with those applications and to restart or force-quit
Classic if it misbehaves. The Advanced pane of the Classic preferences enables you
to fine-tune some aspects of Classic if you are a frequent user, whereas the
Memory/Versions pane displays applications running in Classic and the memory
used by them.

Date & Time

Not surprisingly, you set the system date and time in the Date & Time pane of the
Date & Time preferences. If your computer remains connected to the Internet, you
can choose Set Date & Time automatically and select a network time server to control your system clock. You can set your time zone in the Time Zone pane.

In the Clock pane you can choose whether to show the date and time in the menu
bar or as a window on your desktop, as shown in Figure 5.10. You also can choose
what form it should take—digital like a stop watch or analog like a pocket watch.
Finally, you can have your computer announce the time on the hour, on the half
hour, or on the quarter hour, and choose a voice.

FIGURE 5.10
Put a clock on
your desktop—
and even give it
a second hand.

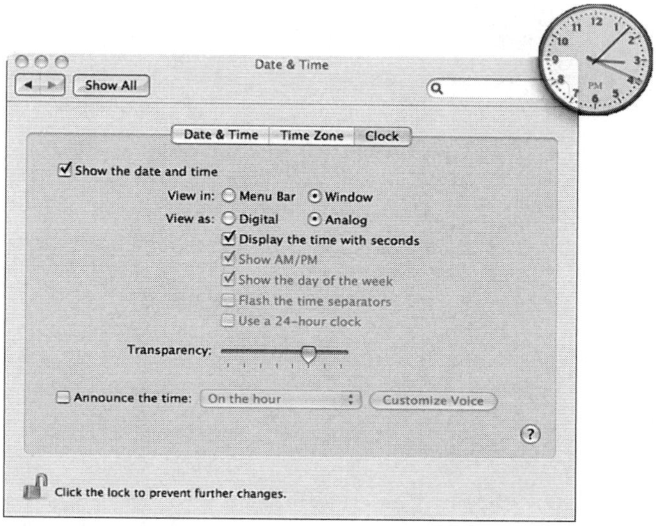

Software Update

As software updates become available, use the settings in the Software Update preferences to install them. You can also view what updates have been installed. This is discussed further in Chapter 34, "Maintaining Your System."

Speech

The Speech preferences control two separate, but related, elements: speech recognition
and text-to-speech conversion.

In the Speech Recognition pane, shown in Figure 5.11, the primary option is to turn the
Speakable Items feature on or off. As the name suggests, Speakable Items is a group of
commands; when you speak one of these commands, your computer reacts to it. Click the
Commands button to open a panel of helpful speech-recognition tips. You can also choose
which microphone to use or to calibrate your microphone to improve performance.

The Listening section of the Speech Recognition pane enables you to choose how you
interact with the computer when speaking commands to it. The first option is whether
you must press the Listening key before voicing your command or whether you can
address the computer without using the Listening key.

If you choose not to interact with the keyboard before your commands, you can assign
a keyword so that the computer knows when you're issuing commands, or you can
hope that your computer recognizes the commands without warning by setting the
Keyword Is pop-up menu to Optional Before Commands.

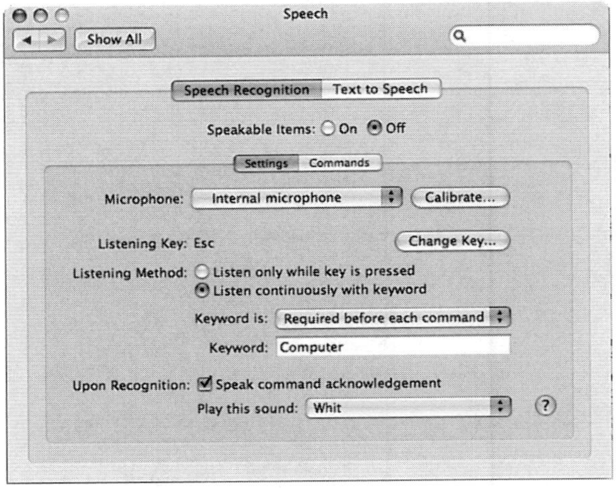

FIGURE 5.11
Use Apple's speech recognition application to perform elementary system functions.

> Keep in mind that using a keyword to prompt your computer that a command will be spoken means that it is always listening unless you manually toggle listening with the chosen key. No, this statement isn't meant to stir up paranoia. But it does mean that your computer has to determine which sounds are directed toward it and which ones are environmental or incidental. Depending on the circumstances, this might be difficult, and your computer would be unable to obey—or may take action when you didn't intend it to. To avoid undue frustration, it's preferable to use Speakable Items with the Listening Key option enabled.

Watch Out!

The final option enables you to choose a feedback sound to inform you when your commands have been recognized.

In the Commands section of the Speech Recognition pane, you can choose which system features will be accessible by spoken commands.

When you turn on speech recognition, the circular Speech Feedback window appears on your screen, as shown in Figure 5.12. This unusual window shows the level of sound detected by the microphone by filling in the lines in the lower portion of the window. The Speech pane of System Preferences and the Speech Commands window are accessible when you click the arrow at the bottom of the window. The Speech Commands window shows the commands that you may speak to the computer. It also displays a log of all recognized commands and the system response enacted.

The Text to Speech pane of the Speech preferences lets you set the voice and rate of speech used by applications that speak. For example, the Finder may use this feature to read alerts that haven't generated a response after a reasonable amount of time has passed. To test each voice, select it from the System Voice pop-up window and click the Play button.

FIGURE 5.12
The Speech Feedback window shows how much sound is being picked up by your microphone, and the Speech Commands window shows a record of the functions carried out.

Startup Disk

Some computers have multiple operating systems available on them, which are installed on different sections of the hard drive or attached via external drives. In the Startup Disk preferences pane, you can choose which system to use when you next start up your computer.

If multiple operating systems are available to your computer, such as when you have an operating system installed on an external drive, you can choose which to use by holding down the option key as you turn on your computer. As the computer starts up, a special screen appears where you can select the bootable drive you want to run.

Now, let's look at the accessibility features built into Mac OS X under the Universal Access preferences.

Universal Access

The Universal Access preferences enable you to interact with your computer in alternative ways to provide greater accessibility for those with disabilities. The Seeing and Hearing panes contain special settings for users with vision or hearing loss. If you have difficulty using the keyboard and the mouse, Universal Access also enables you to customize their sensitivity.

Seeing

The options under the Seeing pane, shown in Figure 5.13, turn on VoiceOver, which is a utility that provides a spoken interface, and affect the size or contrast of the elements onscreen.

FIGURE 5.13
The Seeing settings control zoom and contrast options.

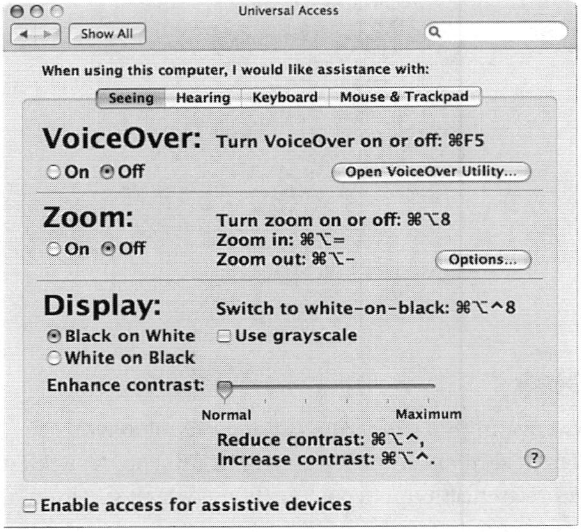

Zoom activates a feature that enlarges the area of the display near the mouse cursor. Using key commands, you can zoom in (Command-Option-=) several levels to examine text or detail in any application, and then zoom back out (Command-Option---). To toggle zoom on or off, use the key command Command-Option-8. In Zoom Options, features such as degree of magnification can be configured.

The settings under Display enable you to adjust the contrast of items on the screen. White on Black (Command-Option-Control-8) reverses the dark and light areas of the display to show white detail on a dark background; Black on White is the normal mode. Check the Use Grayscale box to change the display from color to grayscale, which shows only white, black, and shades of gray. A slider control enables you to vary the contrast between light and dark areas on your screen from a normal level to a maximum. (Key commands Command-Option-Control-, and Command-Option-Control-. decrease and increase contrast, respectively.)

VoiceOver

The VoiceOver utility enables you to use your keyboard and mouse to move around the screen as VoiceOver reads onscreen text and describes buttons and controls under the VoiceOver cursor.

You can activate VoiceOver in the VoiceOver section of the Seeing pane. Though you can activate VoiceOver from the System Preferences, to customize its settings you must launch VoiceOver, shown in Figure 5.14. In these preferences, you can set the amount of detail spoken, set navigation options, choose different voices, set visual display options, and add custom pronunciations for items that are phonetically difficult.

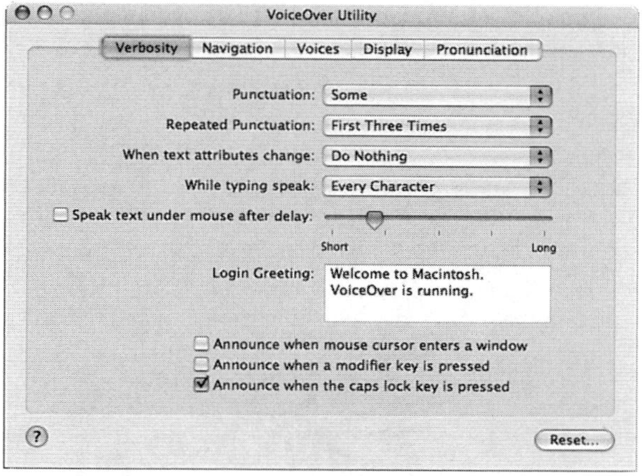

FIGURE 5.14
Configure the
VoiceOver utility.

You can open the Universal Access pane in the System Preferences, or open it from the Utilities folder inside the Applications folder.

Did you
Know?

To navigate your screen using VoiceOver, you primarily use preset keyboard commands in place of the mouse to control the computer. You can view the commands by choosing Help, VoiceOver Commands from the menu. These commands are divided into the categories General, Orientation, Navigation, Text, and Interaction. As you issue commands, press the Control and Option keys together to signal that you are directing commands to VoiceOver, and not to any active application that may also accept keyboard commands.

Hearing

The Hearing pane enables you to have your computer notify you of alert sounds by flashing the screen. You can also open the Sounds preferences pane to adjust volume.

Keyboard

The Keyboard pane is shown in Figure 5.15. The top portion of the preferences relate to Sticky Keys, an option that enables you to press one key at a time when typing key combinations, such as Command-C. After Sticky Keys is enabled, you can choose to turn the feature on or off by pressing the Shift key five times in succession. You can also choose to receive feedback by having the system beep when each modifier key is pressed or having it display pressed keys on screen.

By the Way

When Sticky Keys is enabled, you can cancel a keystroke by pressing the same key again. For example, if you pressed the Shift key by mistake, pressing that key again removes it from the key sequence.

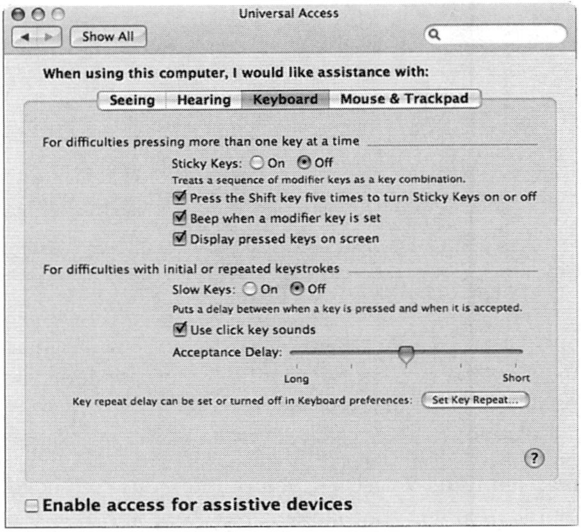

FIGURE 5.15
Change keyboard and mouse sensitivity in Universal Access.

The bottom portion of the window pertains to how much delay the system gives between key presses. You can also use the Key Repeat button to open the Keyboard pane settings to minimize accidental multiple key presses.

By the Way

The settings in the Keyboard and Mouse & Trackpad panes of the Universal Access preferences are not the same as the settings available under the Keyboard & Mouse preferences. The Universal Access options offer extra features to help users who have difficulty with precise motions, while those under Keyboard & Mouse are used to configure more basic hardware settings.

Mouse & Trackpad

Under the Mouse & Trackpad pane, set control options for mouse functions. For those who would rather use the numeric keypad than the mouse to direct the cursor, you can turn on Mouse Keys. Similar to Sticky Keys, you can turn Mouse Keys on or off by pressing the Option key (instead of Sticky Keys' Shift key) five times. The Mouse & Trackpad pane also contains settings to control the speed and delay of mouse cursor movement. The final setting changes the size of the mouse cursor to make it easier to see.

Summary

This chapter gave a synopsis of System Preferences options that aren't discussed elsewhere in this book. These preferences adjust settings for system functions ranging from the individual user's desktop settings to overall hardware configurations. They also include features that make Mac OS X accessible to a wide range of users with different physical abilities. To help you realize the range of their effect, Mac OS X has arranged them into four groups based on their spheres of influence. Also, preference panes with a larger number of settings have been broken into multiple panes or sections available via pop-up menus.

PART II

Common Applications and Hardware

CHAPTER 6

Using Calculator, Grapher, Preview, and TextEdit

Mac OS X includes a number of utilities and applications that enable you to start working as soon as your Mac is up and running. This software includes two not-so-basic calculators, a PDF and image file viewer called Preview, and a basic text editing program called TextEdit. Because they require no installation or additional setup, we recommend giving each of these applications a try as a way to familiarize yourself with the Mac OS X desktop.

> You may recall that there is also a very basic calculator widget included in Dashboard, as discussed in Chapter 2, "Using the Finder."

By the Way

Calculator

The Calculator application, shown in Figure 6.1, is located in the Applications folder. You can toggle between basic, scientific (which supports trigonometry functions and exponents), and programmer view, which converts numbers between hexadecimal, octal, and decimal, and performs other calculations useful in computer programming, under the View menu.

> There's an even more basic calculator included with Dashboard, an application that includes an assortment of little applications. (Incidentally, the long-time Mac staple Stickies, which enables you to post virtual stickie notes on your desktop, has also been reincarnated as a part of Dashboard.) Refer to Chapter 2 for more information about Dashboard.

By the Way

You can operate the Calculator by clicking the buttons in the window or by using your numeric keypad. The number keys on your keypad map directly to their Calculator counterparts, and the Return key is equivalent to clicking the equal button.

FIGURE 6.1
The Calculator in basic view supports common arithmetic functions.

Under the View menu is the option to switch the calculator to RPN, or Reverse Polish Notation. In this mode, the Equal button is replaced by an Enter key. When in RPN mode, you type each number you want to calculate with, followed by the Enter key, and then enter the operation (addition, subtraction, log, and so on) you want to apply to them.

If you want to view a record of your calculations, choose View, Show Paper Tape. This opens a separate window to display inputs, as shown in Figure 6.2. You can print the tape by choosing File, Print Tape (or even save it by choosing File, Save Tape As) from the menu.

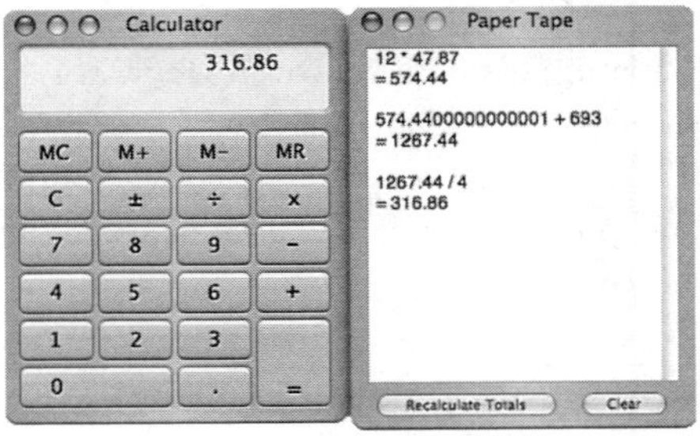

FIGURE 6.2
Keep records of your calculations by saving or printing the Paper Tape.

Another useful, if unexpected, feature is the Calculator's Conversion function. It enables you to easily perform conversions of currency, temperature, weight, and a variety of other measurement units. Simply enter a value in the Calculator and then choose the desired conversion type from the Convert menu.

Currency exchange rates fluctuate over time—be sure to check the time they were last updated, and update as needed, in the Convert menu before making your calculations.

In the sheet that appears from the top of the Calculator, choose the units to convert from and those to convert to and click OK. Figure 6.3 depicts a currency conversion.

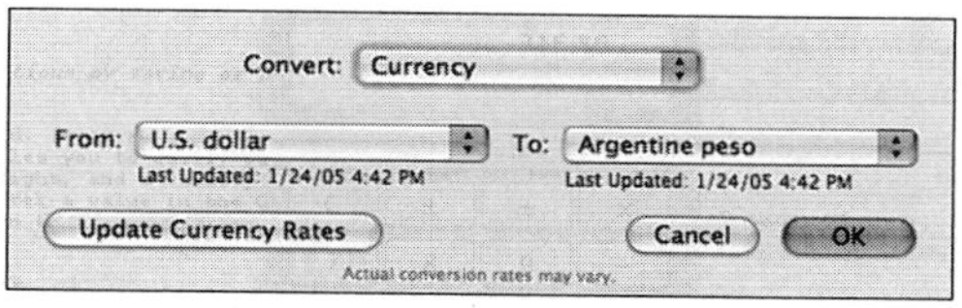

FIGURE 6.3
You can update currency rates when choosing monetary units in the currency conversion sheet.

Grapher

In addition to Calculator, Mac OS X also comes with the Grapher, a graphing calculator application. Grapher is located in the Applications folder inside the Utilities folder. An example of Grapher in action is shown in Figure 6.4.

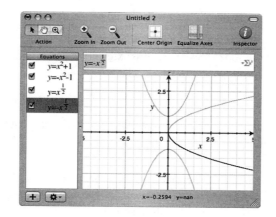

FIGURE 6.4
Use Grapher to display a series of equations in two or three dimensions.

To use Grapher, you need to choose a coordinate system for your graph from the window shown in Figure 6.5.

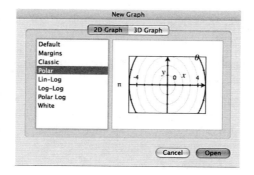

FIGURE 6.5
Choose a classic grid pattern or a polar or log option. (Refer to Figure 6.4 for the default option.)

After choosing the type of graph, enter your equations in the text box above the graphing space, as shown in Figure 6.4. To insert additional equations in the same graph, click the + button below the Definitions pane and type another equation in the text box above the graph.

> Under the Object menu, options to add arrows and text enable you to label your graph. (The equations in Figure 6.4 were added this way.)

When you are finished with a graph, you can save your file in the usual way. Your data is stored as a Grapher document with the file extension `.gcx`.

In the Grapher application preferences, located under the Grapher menu, you can choose a default font size for equations, number format notation style, and set thresholds for calculation accuracy.

Preview

For viewing PDF files and images of all sorts, Mac OS X comes with the Preview application, which can be found in the Applications folder.

> Preview can be used to view images in JPG, GIF, TIF, PSD (Photoshop Document), PICT, PNG, BMP, and SGI formats. Preview can also open PostScript (PS) and Encapsulated PostScript (EPS) files as PDFs.

Preview can be launched in a number of ways. First, you can double-click the application icon. Doing so starts Preview, but doesn't open any windows. You must then choose File, Open from the menu to select a file to view.

> Another common application for viewing PDF documents is Adobe Acrobat.

Second, you can open Preview by dragging the image or PDF files onto the Preview icon in the Finder or Dock.

Third, Preview is integrated into the Mac OS X printing system, so clicking Preview in any Print sheet window starts it.

> If you want to view a series of images in one Preview window, select them all and drag the set on top of the Preview icon in the Applications folder or in the Dock.

When you open an image or PDF document in Preview, it shows up in a window with a toolbar across the top, as shown in Figure 6.6. The following options are located in the toolbar when viewing text-based PDF files:

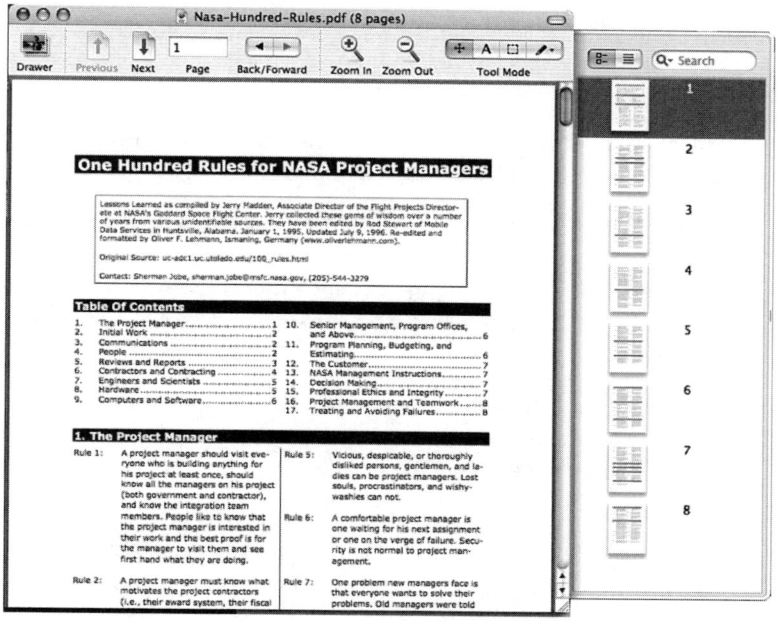

FIGURE 6.6
The Preview window includes a toolbar where you can easily alter the viewing style of your files or move between pages.

▶ Drawer—Opens and closes a drawer, shown in Figure 6.6, which displays either a list of page headings or a series of thumbnail images representing the pages or files open in the current Preview window. Clicking a page heading or thumbnail image shows that page in the main viewing area. (For text documents, you can choose whether the drawer contains text or thumbnails by using the View buttons at the top of the drawer.)

▶ Previous and Next—If you're viewing a multipage file, you can move through the pages sequentially by using the Previous and Next arrows.

▶ Page—When you're viewing a multipage PDF file, Page Number enables you to enter a page number to jump directly to that page.

▶ Back/Forward—If you've viewed several pages in a multipage file out of sequence, you can page back and forth in the order you visited by using the Back/Forward arrows.

- ▶ Zoom In and Zoom Out—These two options enable you to view a larger or smaller version of the selected image or PDF. If the image is larger than the Preview window, scrollbars appear.

- ▶ Tool Mode—This set of buttons, which varies depending on whether you are viewing a text or image file, contains the following tools:

    - ▶ Scroll Tool—Enables you to scroll within a selected page by clicking and dragging in the main viewing area. To move between pages, you still need to use the Page Up/Page Down controls or select another page in the drawer. (The mouse cursor appears as a hand icon while you are in this mode.)

    - ▶ Text Tool—Enables you to select text in a PDF. When selected, you can copy and paste the text to another document by using standard commands under the Edit menu. (Note, this tool is available only in text-based documents.)

    - ▶ Select Tool—Enables you to select a portion of a page, which you can then copy by using the Edit, Copy command from the menu. When copied, you can create a new PDF document containing only the selected area by choosing File, New from Clipboard from the menu. Unlike the Text Tool, you can select either text or images with the Select Tool, but the result when copied is an image-based PDF format, not editable or searchable text.

    - ▶ Annotate Tool—Enables you to type notes on a highlighted background ("Text Annotate") or to circle in red ("Oval Annotate"). To use, simply choose the kind of annotation you want to make and drag your mouse cursor to create your annotation. (You can also reposition your notes or circles by selecting them and dragging, and delete by selecting and pressing the Delete key on your keyboard.)

For image files, the toolbar contains the options to Rotate Left and Rotate Right, to view Actual Size and Zoom To Fit to match window size, and to Zoom In to see details and Zoom Out to view more of image within the window.

You can search text-based PDFs by using the search box at the top of the drawer. Just start typing your search term, and pages containing the string you've typed appear in the drawer for your convenience.

By the Way

Just as you can for Finder windows, you can hide the Preview toolbar by using the toolbar button at the upper right of the window's title bar. Note, however, that you can't simply scroll to reach another page of the PDF unless you activate Continuous Scrolling from the View menu.

In addition to viewing files, you can use Preview to convert a file to one of several common file types and export it to a new location. To do this, choose File, Save As from the menu and enter a filename. Then choose a location in which to save and a file format. The Quartz Filter button reveals additional settings for color depth, so you can save in black and white or even sepia tone.

By the Way

Bookmarking PDFs

In addition to annotating PDF files, you can also use Preview to bookmark pages so you can easily return to a specific spot. To add a bookmark to a page currently open in Preview, choose Bookmarks, Add Bookmarks from the menu, which opens the window shown in Figure 6.7.

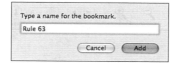

FIGURE 6.7
Create your bookmark by giving it an easily-recognized name.

In that window, type a name for the bookmark and click Add. Now, the next time you want to return to that page (even if you don't have that PDF open in Preview) you can choose that bookmark from the bottom of the Bookmarks menu, as shown in Figure 6.8.

FIGURE 6.8
Return to a bookmark you created earlier.

Preview saves each bookmark as a reference to a given page for a given file. This information is separate from the actual PDF file, which means your bookmarks don't appear if you send the PDF to someone else. Also, your Preview bookmarks aren't available from another computer.

Watch Out!

Preview Preference Options

As you learned in Chapter 1, "Introducing Mac OS X," one of the standard items in an application menu is Preferences, which enable you to customize some aspects of how an application responds. For applications with many preference settings, the Preferences window may have a row of buttons along the top, as shown in Figure 6.9, so you can choose those settings on which you want to focus.

The General pane enables you to use the standard system Colors window to choose a thumbnail size and a background color for the window, as shown in Figure 6.10.

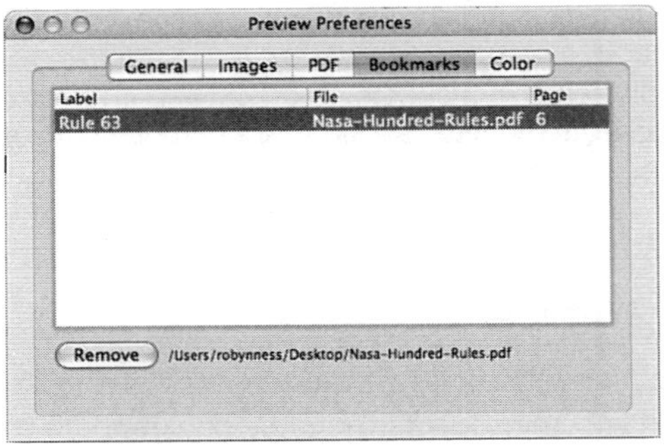

FIGURE 6.9
The Bookmarks pane of the Preview Preferences.

FIGURE 6.10
The Colors window is a standard part of OS X.

In the Images and PDF preference panes, you can choose the default size at which images and PDF documents are opened—fit to screen or some other size. You can also choose some aspects of how images or text are rendered on screen.

The Bookmarks pane, shown in Figure 6.9, enables you to edit and delete bookmarks you've created in Preview. (This pane also opens if you choose Bookmarks, Edit Bookmarks from the menu.) To edit a bookmark, double-click its label and type a new one. To delete, select a bookmark so its row is highlighted in blue and click the Remove button.

The Color pane gives options for how you want documents' colors displayed while using Preview. (Color management and color spaces can be a complex topic, but we'll discuss the basics in Chapter 11, "Working with Displays and Peripheral Devices.")

TextEdit

Mac OS X comes with the text editor TextEdit in the Applications folder. TextEdit can save files in plain text or the RTF format and uses many built-in Mac OS X features to give you advanced control over text and fonts. Its Rich Text Format (RTF) files can be opened in popular word processing programs, such as Microsoft Word, and display all formatting attributes, such as bolding, italic, and special fonts. Even better for some, the current version of TextEdit can open, edit, and save Word documents, which allows documents to be traded back and forth between Word and TextEdit users. TextEdit can also be used as a simple Hypertext Markup Language (HTML) editor for writing web pages.

About Unicode

TextEdit also handles Unicode editing. Unicode is a character-encoding format that uses 16 bits (as opposed to the traditional 8) for storing each character. This allows more than 65,000 characters to be represented, which is necessary for some languages such as Japanese and Greek. Eventually, Unicode is expected to entirely replace ASCII encoding (which can represent a total of only 255 characters).

When you start it, TextEdit opens a new Untitled.rtf document for you to begin working, as shown in Figure 6.11.

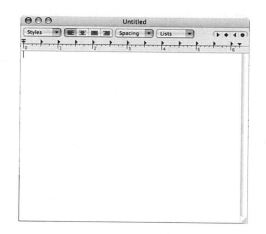

FIGURE 6.11
The basic TextEdit workspace.

If you want to open an existing document, choose File, Open (Command-O) from the menu. However, be sure the file is of a supported document type, such as plain text, HTML, Microsoft Word documents, or RTF. Figure 6.12 demonstrates TextEdit's rich text editing capabilities.

FIGURE 6.12
TextEdit can edit styled text documents stored in RTF.

You will find the options to change the size or font style of text using TextEdit under the Font item of the Format menu. Choose Show Fonts to launch the OS X Font window, where you can choose between any of the fonts installed on your system. (We'll talk more about fonts in Chapter 12, "Printing, Faxing, and Working with Fonts.")

To change the text color, choose Format, Font, Show Colors from the menu. This launches the Colors window shown previously in Figure 6.10.

If you change your mind about all the fonts and color modifications you've made and just want to stick with simple, unadorned text, choose Format, Make Plain Text from the menu. Figure 6.13 shows the plain text version of the document displayed in Figure 6.12. (Also notice that the ruler at the top of the document window has disappeared; to bring it back, choose Format, Make Rich Text from the menu.)

Untitled.txt
This is NOT styled text.

FIGURE 6.13
This document
is *not* a rich text
document!

> The ruler is available only for Rich Text Documents. Using the ruler, you can visually adjust tabs and other layout features of the active document. You can also use it to easily and visually change formatting and placement of text.

By the Way

For the most part, you should be able to open TextEdit and start creating and editing text documents. However, you can use a number of preferences and features to customize its appearance and functionality.

Preferences

The TextEdit Preferences window controls the default application preferences. Many of these options can be chosen from the menu bar and stored on a per-document basis as well as for the entire application.

The New Document pane of the Preferences, shown in Figure 6.14, is broken out into several sections. The first section includes an option for Rich Text or Plain Text. It enables you to select the Wrap to Page check box so that lines fit the page width. You can also choose the default width (in characters) and height (in lines) of new windows.

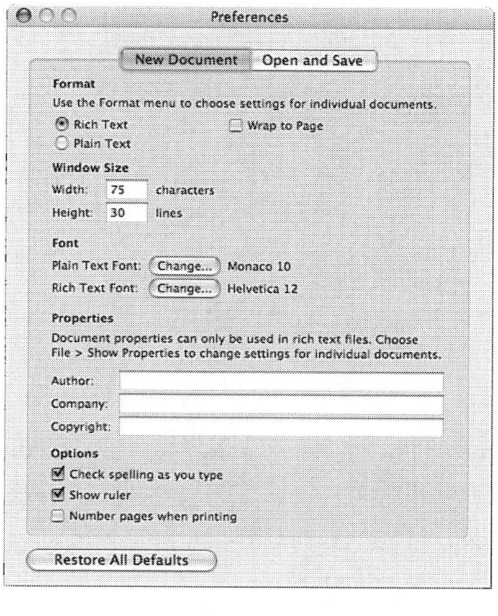

Preferences

New Document | Open and Save

Format
Use the Format menu to choose settings for individual documents.
⦿ Rich Text   ☐ Wrap to Page
○ Plain Text

Window Size
Width: 75   characters
Height: 30   lines

Font
Plain Text Font: (Change...) Monaco 10
Rich Text Font: (Change...) Helvetica 12

Properties
Document properties can only be used in rich text files. Choose File > Show Properties to change settings for individual documents.
Author:
Company:
Copyright:

Options
☑ Check spelling as you type
☑ Show ruler
☐ Number pages when printing

(Restore All Defaults)

FIGURE 6.14
The New
Document pref-
erences control
a range of fea-
tures related to
freshly created
documents.

Use the Set buttons in the Default Fonts section to choose new default fonts for rich text and plain text documents. The default fonts are Helvetica 12 and Monaco 10, respectively.

Under the Properties settings, you can enter information about your document that is saved with the document, but won't be visible in the text of the document. (This kind of information is called "metadata"—data about data.) You can provide information about the document's author, company, and the copyright status.

The Options section includes some basic features typically including in a word processing program. To have TextEdit automatically check your spelling as you type, select the Check Spelling as You Type check box in the Editing section. Misspelled words are underlined in red. Ctrl-click the misspelled word to open a contextual menu that enables you to choose from a list of corrections, ignore the word, or add it (the Learn option) to the Mac OS X dictionary. You can also choose to show the ruler in the TextEdit window and to show the number of pages when printing.

The Open and Save pane of the TextEdit preferences is shown in Figure 6.15.

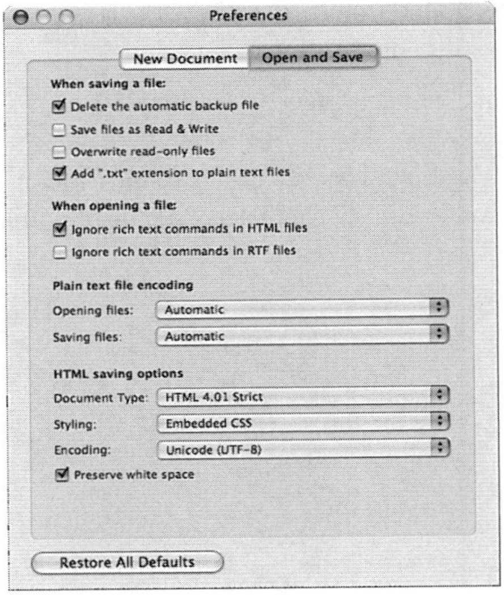

FIGURE 6.15
The Open and
Save prefer-
ences.

Under the heading When Saving a File, your options include

▶ Delete the Automatic Backup File—Removes the TextEdit backup file after a document is successfully saved.

▶ Save Files Read & Write—Saves read-only files with write permissions turned on; that is, they can be edited later.

▶ Overwrite Read-only Files—Overwrites files, even if their permissions are set to read-only.

▶ Append `.txt` Extension to Plain Text Files—Adds a `.txt` extension to the end of plain text files for cross-platform compatibility and ease of recognition.

Under the heading When Opening a File, you can control how different kinds of files appear. To disable rich text commands in HTML and RTF files, click the corresponding check box in the Rich Text Processing section. Ignoring the style information opens the document as a plain text file, showing all the control codes and tags used to embed the original styles. This is required for editing HTML tags within a Web page.

The options for Plain Text File Encoding require a bit of explanation. By default, TextEdit attempts to read style information in whatever file it opens. Allowing automatic detection enables TextEdit to open files created on other operating systems, such as Windows, and transparently translate end-of-line characters. When opening or saving a document, TextEdit gives you the opportunity to override automatic detection of the appropriate file encoding type to use. To choose an alternative encoding, such as Unicode, use the pop-up menus in the Default Plain Text Encoding section.

The HTML Saving Options apply to the way TextEdit writes HTML, the markup language used to create Web pages. You can choose a document type, a style for Cascading Style Sheets, and an encoding format for characters. There is also an option to preserve whitespace to make it easier to indent HTML.

To save your settings, close the TextEdit Preferences panel. To revert to the original configuration, click the Restore All Defaults button.

Menus

As you learned earlier, the TextEdit menus provide control over fonts. They also control other document-specific information. Most of the application preferences can be overridden on a per-document basis from the main menus.

You can open, save, and print documents by using the File menu.

The Edit menu contains the basic copy and paste functions, along with the find, replace, and spell-checking features.

The Format menu enables you to control your font settings, colors, and text alignment. In addition, you can toggle wrapping modes, rich text and plain text, and hyphenation.

The Window menu enables you to choose among open TextEdit windows or bring all to the front.

Summary

Mac OS X includes a wealth of applications and utilities, ranging from the simple (but not so simple!) Calculator to a versatile PDF viewer. The experience of using one application applies to others you will encounter. This is especially true for TextEdit, which uses the Mac OS X system-level color-picker, spell-checking, and font controls.

CHAPTER 7

Using QuickTime and DVD Player

In the previous chapter, you learned to use several practical applications that come with Mac OS X. In this chapter, you get a chance to try out some more entertainment-oriented applications—QuickTime and DVD Player.

QuickTime

You learned in Chapter 1, "Introducing Mac OS X," that QuickTime is one of Mac OS X's built-in imaging components. By using its technology, system applications can support reading or writing many different image formats.

You might also know that QuickTime is a popular media player used to enjoy media, both from within a Web browser and as an application on your desktop. The first half of this chapter looks at using QuickTime 6.

QuickTime supports most common digital media formats, including those for movies, MP3 files, WAV files, images, and interactive applications. QuickTime 6 also supports MPEG-4, the global standard for multimedia, which is designed to deliver high-quality video using smaller file sizes.

You can learn more about the supported formats by visiting Apple's QuickTime specification page at www.apple.com/quicktime/whyqt/.

Did you Know?

Watching QuickTime movies play in your Web browser window is one of the most common uses for QuickTime, so let's take a look at the controls of the QuickTime browser plug-in. Figure 7.1 shows a QuickTime movie playing in the Safari Web browser.

If you're a movie fan, you'll love Apple's movie trailers Web page, located at www.apple.com/trailers/.

 By the Way

FIGURE 7.1
Many users
experience
QuickTime
through their
Web browsers.

The movie controls are located across the bottom of the video. There's a volume control at the far left, with a Play/Pause button immediately to its right. The progress bar takes up the middle. At the right are buttons to Rewind or Fast-forward, and a downward pointing arrow to get information and change settings.

If you've used a VCR or other media player, you've certainly seen these before. However, you might want to know a few shortcuts. For example, clicking the speaker icon on the far left can instantly mute the volume. You can also control the volume level using the up-arrow and down-arrow keys on the keyboard.

Did you Know?

> To increase the volume beyond its normal limit, hold down the Shift key while dragging the volume control.

Playback controls also can be activated from the keyboard, so you don't have to mouse around on your screen. To toggle between playing and pausing, press the Spacebar. To rewind or fast-forward, use the left-arrow and right-arrow keys, respectively.

If the movie being played is streaming from a remote server, some of these controls might not be available. For example, on-demand streaming video can't be fast-forwarded or rewound, but static files can be.

The QuickTime Player

In addition to the QuickTime plug-in, there's also the QuickTime Player. The QuickTime Player application provides another means of viewing movies and other QuickTime-compatible media, including digital images and music files, directly from your desktop.

> Minimizing a QuickTime Player movie while it is playing adds a live icon to the Dock. The movie (with sound) continues to play in the minimized Dock icon. Even if you don't have a use for this feature, give it a try—it's extremely cool!

Did you Know?

To use QuickTime Player, open it from its default home in the Dock or from the Applications folder. The default QuickTime window is shown Figure 7.2.

FIGURE 7.2
The default QuickTime Player window shows previews and samples.

If you click the video (or immediately below it on the space labeled Click Here for More Information), QuickTime launches your default Web browser and brings up a page listing the related content. Selecting a listed item does one of two things: It either launches a new Apple QuickTime window in your desktop to play the item, or opens a new Web browsing window where you can view the QuickTime element using the QuickTime plug-in.

When QuickTime starts to load a streaming video clip, it goes through four steps before displaying the video:

1. Connecting—Makes a connection to the streaming server.

2. Requesting data—Waits for acknowledgement from the remote server.

3. Getting info—Retrieves information about the QuickTime movie.

4. Buffering—QuickTime buffers several seconds of video to eliminate stuttering from the playback.

If the player stalls during any of the four steps that precede the video display, there might be a problem with the remote server or your transport settings (how your computer talks on the Internet). Try another streaming source, and if it still fails, use the QuickTime System Preferences pane to change your settings. (QuickTime preferences are discussed in the "QuickTime Preferences" section later in this chapter.)

Did you Know?

If you have a streaming server URL, you can choose File, Open URL in New Player (Command-U) from the menu to open the stream directly.

Using QuickTime Player to Play Other Media

You can use QuickTime Player to play information from other sources besides those from the Web. For example, you can open and play CD audio tracks and MP3s by selecting File, Open Movie command from the menu. Even though there aren't any visuals, these media types are referred to as *movies* in QuickTime's vocabulary.

You can open local movie files by choosing File, Open Movie in New Player from the menu (Command-O) or by dragging a movie file onto the QuickTime icon in the Dock or Applications folder.

QuickTime Preferences

In the QuickTime application menu, there are two different choices for preferences: Preferences, which relate to the QuickTime Player, and QuickTime Preferences, which relate to system-level QuickTime preferences including management of the QuickTime browser plug-in.

Figure 7.3 shows the Player Preferences dialog box.

Use the following options in the Player Preferences dialog box to control how the application handles multiple movies and playback:

▶ Open Movies in New Players—By default, QuickTime Player reuses existing windows when opening new movies. To open new movies in new windows, select this check box.

▶ Automatically Play Movies When Opened—Does what it says! When checked, QuickTime Player starts playing a movie immediately after it's opened.

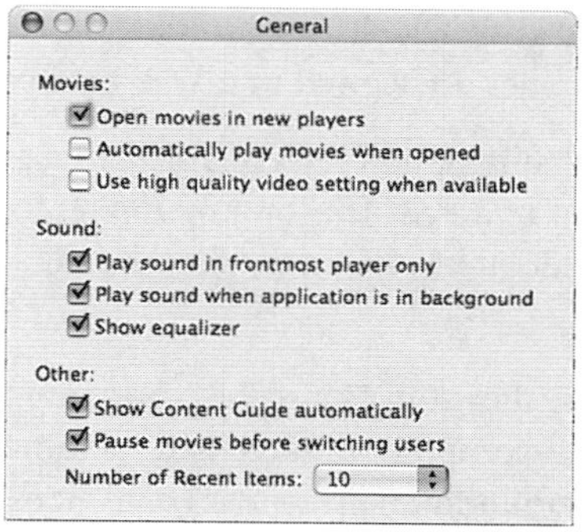

FIGURE 7.3
Choose how QuickTime Player reacts to opening and playing movies.

▶ Use High-Quality Video Setting when Available—When checked, QuickTime Player uses more of your computer's processing power to produce a better-quality picture.

▶ Play Sound in Frontmost Player Only—By default, sound is played only in the active player window. To hear sound from all playing movies simultaneously, uncheck this option.

▶ Play Sound When Application Is in Background—If this option is checked, sound continues to play even when QuickTime Player isn't the active application.

▶ Show Equalizer—Displays the sound levels to the right of the progress bar.

▶ Show Content Guide Automatically—Automatically fetches and displays a current entertainment blurb when QuickTime Player is started. (Click just above the status bar to bring up Apple's QuickTime "What's On" page, which displays recent items with links to QuickTime previews.)

▶ Pause Movies Before Switching Movies—Pauses active movies, switching from one user account to another using Fast User Switching. (Setting up and working with additional user accounts is covered in Chapter 31, "Sharing Your Computer with Other Users.")

▶ Number of Recent Items—Controls the number of files that will be listed under the menu item File, Open Recent.

Close the window to save the application preferences.

The QuickTime System Preferences are located in the Internet & Network section of System Preferences. These preferences enable you to change QuickTime's settings for better quality playback and to make other modifications. This section discusses some of the more useful settings.

Browser settings control how the QuickTime browser plug-in operates. (Remember, plug-ins are used when movies are viewed in a Web browser.)

The Play Movies Automatically option directs QuickTime to start playing a movie after enough of it has been buffered. This option applies to movies that aren't streamed. Select the Save Movies in Disk Cache option to temporarily store a clip to speed up repeated viewings.

The Streaming preferences, shown in Figure 7.4, configure the type of network access QuickTime can expect your computer to have and the amount of delay to allow for streaming media. This information helps QuickTime choose the appropriate type of media to display, depending on how fast it can be received. Check the box for Enable Instant On if you want to play streaming media without a delay, or use the slider to set the amount of delay. (Delaying the play of streaming media can be a very good thing—the delay acts as a buffer to prevent choppy playback if the data stream is uneven or temporarily interrupted.)

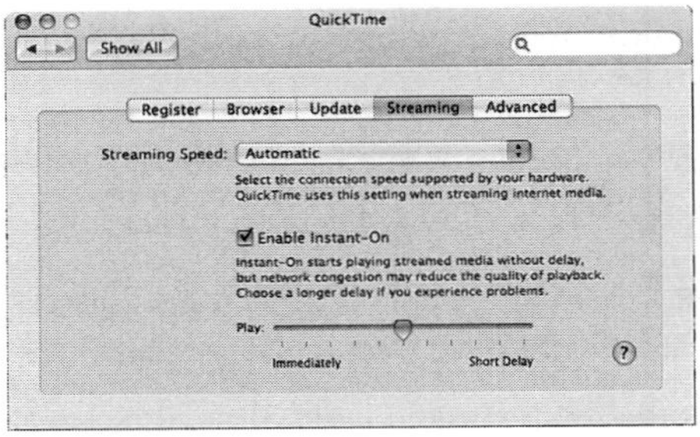

FIGURE 7.4
Choose your connection speed and an acceptable amount of delay for streaming media.

Under the Advanced preferences, shown in Figure 7.5, are several interesting settings.

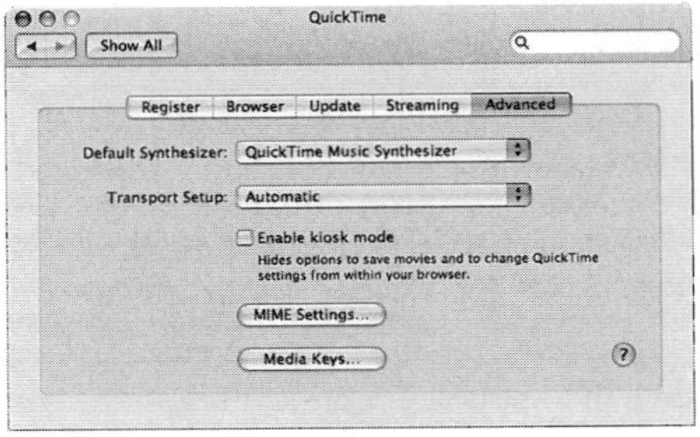

FIGURE 7.5
Advanced preferences include customizing QuickTime's MIME settings.

▶ Transport Setup—Enables you to choose the protocol used for streaming. By default, QuickTime attempts to choose the best transport based on your network type. (It's best not to change these settings unless you're having difficulty viewing media, and if you do make changes, write down the original settings so you can restore them if needed.)

▶ Enable Kiosk Mode—Makes it possible for movies to run continuously, unattended, for demonstrations and presentations.

▶ MIME Settings—Opens a list of all the MIME types that QuickTime can handle and everything it's currently configured to display so you can check and uncheck them. (MIME stands for Multipurpose Internet Mail Extension and defines a set of document types, such as text, HTML, and so on.)

▶ Media Keys—Enables you to enter authentication keys for secured media that requires a key to be played.

> In relation to computers and the secure exchange of data, keys are issued to give the holder permission to decrypt a file for viewing. The use of keys for sending and receiving secure email messages is discussed in Chapter 17, "Using Mail."

By the Way

DVD Player

Included with Mac OS X is DVD Player, an application for displaying DVD content on computers equipped with internal DVD drives. To start DVD Player, simply insert a video DVD into your system, or double-click the application icon in the Applications folder.

By default, Mac OS X launches DVD Player automatically when it detects a DVD in the drive. At startup, the DVD begins to play, and a playback controller appears onscreen. Figure 7.6 shows the playback controller.

> Unless you've changed your DVD Player preferences, DVDs automatically play full-screen when a DVD is inserted. If you want to view the DVD in a window so you can do other things on your computer as you watch, you can switch to one of three windows sizes. To view the DVD in a small window, use the keyboard shortcut Command-1. To view it in a normal-size window, use Command-2. To view it in a window of maximum size, use Command-3. To return to fullscreen, use the keyboard shortcut Command-0. (These options are also available under the Video menu.)
>
> If you view a DVD inside a window instead of fullscreen, you can minimize the DVD Player window—the picture plays in the Dock and the sound continues to be audible.

By the Way

Use the controller window as you would a standard DVD remote. Basic playback buttons (Play, Stop, Rewind, and Fast-forward) are provided, along with a selection control and a volume slider directly under the primary playback controls. Also available are buttons to access the menu, display the title of the current scene, and eject the DVD.

Did you Know?

Typically, viewers navigate through DVD menus with arrow keys on their DVD controllers. Because your DVD Player is run on your computer, you have additional options. To navigate onscreen selections without the use of a controller, you can simply point and click at a DVD menu item to select it. To move quickly through chapters in a DVD with the keyboard, use the left and right arrow keys.

Six additional advanced controls are accessible if you click the far right edge of the controller window. In Figure 7.7, the controller window is shown with the window tray extended. This opens a window drawer containing two columns of buttons that control playback or special features of DVDs. Those controls, from top to bottom, left to right, are Slow, Step, Return, Subtitle, Audio, and Angle buttons.

If you prefer a vertically oriented player control, as shown in Figure 7.7, choose Control, Use Vertical Control (Option-Command-C) from the menu. You can switch back to the horizontal layout at any time by choosing Controls, Use Horizontal Control (Option-Command-C) from the same menu. To hide or show the Controller regardless of its orientation, use the key command Command-Shift-C.

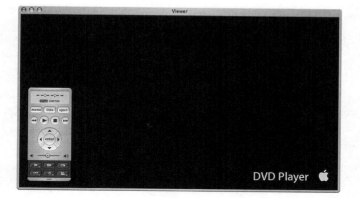

FIGURE 7.7
Same controls, different arrangement.

Using the DVD Player Menu

Although the onscreen controller can be used for almost everything, some helpful features can be accessed in the DVD Player menus. (If a DVD is playing in full-screen view, move your mouse to the top of the screen to reveal the menu bar.)

Under the Video menu, you can choose the size of the window playing your movie— half size, normal size, maximum size, or full screen.

The following options are available under the Controls menu:

> Many of the options under the Control menu, such as Play/Pause, Fast-forward/ Rewind, and Volume, as well as some options in the other menus, can also be performed with keyboard commands. Those commands, in the following list, also appear in the menu so you can easily look up the ones you'll need most often.

Did you Know?

- ▶ Play/Pause—(Spacebar) Play or pause the video.

- ▶ Stop—(Shift-Command) Stop the current video from playing.

- ▶ Scan Forward—(Shift-Command-right arrow) Speed through the video playback.

- ▶ Scan Backwards—(Shift-Command-left arrow) Move backward through the video playback.

- ▶ Scan Rate—Set the rate at which you fast-forward—2×, 4×, 8×, 16×, or 32×.

- ▶ Volume Up—(Command-up arrow) Increase the volume.

- ▶ Volume Down—(Command-down arrow) Decrease the volume.

- ▶ Mute—(Option-Command-down arrow) Mute the sound.

- ▶ Closed Captioning—(Option-Command-T) Display captioning on DVDs for which it is available. (It can be set to appear either over the video as it plays or in a separate window under the Closed Captioning item of the Controls menu.)

▶ Timer—Set time for beginning and ending play.

▶ New Bookmark—(Control-=) Create a bookmark at a specific moment in a DVD. (To go to a bookmark, choose Go, Bookmarks from the menu bar and select the one you want from the submenu.)

▶ New Video Clip—(Control—) Mark a video clip for easy viewing later. (To use, set start and stop points and then name your clip. To view, choose Go, Video Clips from the menu bar and select the clip you want to view from the submenu.)

When creating bookmarks or marking video clips, DVD Player is merely storing references to specific moments in the DVD. No changes are made to the DVD itself and no video footage is actually copied to your computer.

▶ Use Horizontal/Vertical Controller—Toggle between Horizontal or Vertical orientation.

▶ Close/Open Control Drawer—Toggle between open and closed control drawer.

▶ Eject DVD— (Command-E) Eject the current DVD.

Did you Know?

During fast-forwarding or rewinding, the view is displayed at an accelerated rate. Use the Scan Rate option under the Controls menu to set the speed to two, four, or eight times faster than normal.

In addition to the Bookmarks and Video Clips items mentioned above, here are some other useful items available under the Go menu:

▶ DVD Menu—(Command-`) Stop playback and load the menu for the active DVD.

▶ Previous Chapter—(Right arrow) Skip to the previous chapter on the DVD.

▶ Next Chapter—(left arrow) Skip to the next chapter on the DVD.

The Window menu gives you access to various windows for settings, information, and video display. You can open or close the View window and hide or show the onscreen controller. Here are some other extremely useful options you can access under the Window menu:

▶ Navigate—Enables you to move around in a DVD by chapters or time and to change options for audio, subtitles, volume, bookmarks, and video clips—all without blocking much of your viewing area, as shown in Figure 7.8.

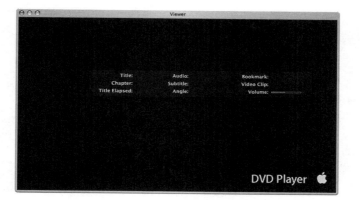

▶ Bookmarks and Video Clips—Enables you to view, add, or delete bookmarks and video clips for the current DVD.

▶ Video Zoom, Video Color, and Audio Equalizer—Customize the play of your DVD by altering zoom (how it fills the screen), color (brightness, contrast, and so on), and sound quality (as shown in Figure 7.9).

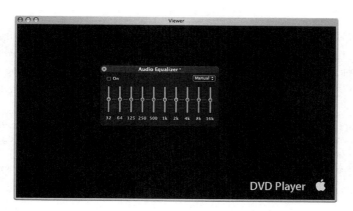

DVD Player Preferences

The preferences for DVD Player are split into five sections. The Player pane, shown in Figure 7.10, enables you to set how DVD Player reacts on system startup and insertion of a DVD. You can also choose the viewer size, whether to enable closed captioning when muted, and whether to mute audio when connecting to an audio or video chat in iChat, an application discussed in Chapter 18, "Using iChat AV."

The Disc Setup pane contains settings for default language and the option to enable DVD@ccess, which allows DVD Player to recognize and react to embedded hot spots that link to Internet Web sites. You can also change audio output settings.

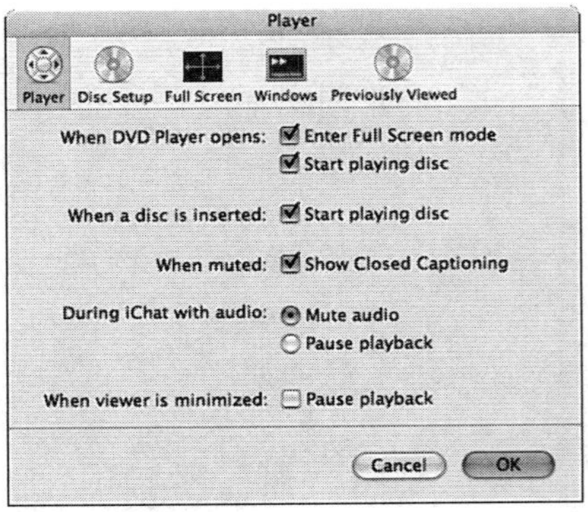

FIGURE 7.10
Change how
DVD Player is
activated and
the size of the
viewing window.

The Full Screen pane enables you to set an inactivity interval after which the Controller will be hidden. Options are also available for dimming other windows while DVD Player is active, remaining in full screen when DVD Player is inactive, and disabling the menu bar (kiosk mode) so that viewers can't exit the program.

By the Way

> If you disable the menu bar, you need to exit the DVD Player by ejecting the DVD.

The Windows pane controls whether the controller fades away or just disappears when it is hidden, and turns on and off status information that appears while a movie is playing. You can also choose the color and transparency of these messages, as well as the color and transparency of closed captioning.

By the Way

> Transparent text and gradual fade of the controller when it is hidden are features enabled through the use of Quartz Extreme, which enables some graphics cards to take some of the graphics-processing load off Mac OS X.

Under the Previously Viewed pane of the DVD Player preferences, you can choose whether a previously-viewed DVD will begin play from the beginning, the last position played, or a default bookmark—or whether the application should ask you each time. You can also decide whether the disc settings override any manual settings made in the Video Zoom, Video Color, or Audio Equalizer windows.

Summary

In the first half of this chapter, you learned to use QuickTime, both as a plug-in for your Web browser that can be used to view movies online and as a standalone player that runs on your desktop. The last half looked at DVD Player, which enables you to view DVDs on your desktop.

CHAPTER 8

Working with Address Book, Keychain Access, iSync, and Ink

Chapter 6, "Using Calculator, Grapher, Preview, and TextEdit," and Chapter 7, "Using QuickTime and DVD Player," explored several basic applications that come with OS X. This chapter continues in that vein. However, the applications discussed here can be considered "helper" applications because they typically work with other applications rather than run on their own. Address Book and Keychain Access store information that other programs can access. iSync synchronizes information between your computer and other devices—for example, it can be used to synchronize your calendar between your iPod and your computer. Finally, Ink enables you to interact with your computer and applications by writing rather than typing; note, however, that it does require additional hardware to accomplish this.

Address Book

The Mac OS X Address Book is more than a simple contact manager. It is a system-wide database that stores all your contact information and is accessible from other applications that use contact information, such as the email application Mail. Address Book data is also available in the Safari web browser, the search utility Sherlock, the scheduling program iCal, your system's Fax function, and the instant messaging program iChat!

> Address Book is also available as a part of Dashboard. See Chapter 2, "Using the Finder," for more about Dashboard.

By the Way

Using Address Book

The main Address Book window, shown in Figure 8.1, has two view modes—Card and Column view and Card Only view. To toggle between them, use the View buttons at the upper left. You will do most of your work with Address Book in Card and Column view. The Card Only view displays only a single contact at a time.

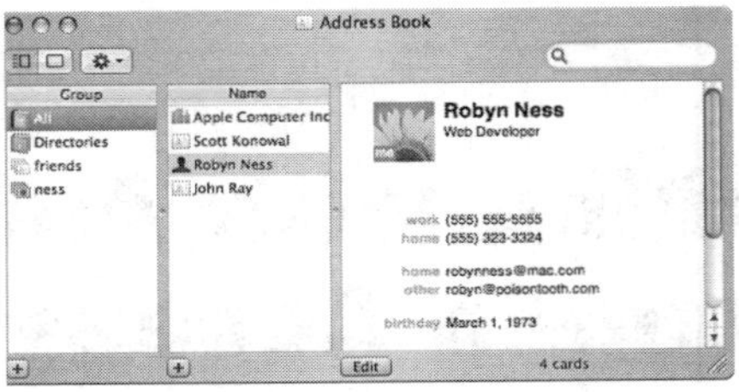

FIGURE 8.1
The Address Book, shown here in Card and Column view, keeps track of your contact information with a simple uncluttered interface.

The Card and Column view displays a three-column view of the Address Book with these columns:

▶ Group—A list of all the groups of contacts on your system. There are three pre-defined groups: All, which shows the contents of all your groups, Directories (LDAP Servers), and Last Import, which contains the last card/cards you imported via LDAP or from an external source.

▶ Name/Directory—The contacts (or available directory servers) within the selected group.

▶ Card—A "business" card view of the currently selected contact.

At the bottom of the Group and Name columns are + buttons that add new Groups and Contacts to the system. Under the Card column is an Edit button that switches the current contact information to Edit mode.

You can browse through your contacts much as you use the Finder's column view. Choose a group, choose a contact within the group, and then view the information in the Card column. The search field at the top of the Address Book window searches the currently selected group for a string of your choice.

Working with Cards

Because Address Book maintains contact information, the base "unit" of information is a single person or organization stored in a card. Each card can store multiple addresses, phone numbers, and pieces of contact information for an individual, making it unnecessary to maintain multiple cards for a single person.

Add/Edit Cards

To add a card, select the group that should contain the contact and then click the + button below the Name column. This opens a blank card in the Card column where you can type the information you want to save.

There are fields for first and last name, an array of phone numbers (work, home, mobile, fax, and so on), email address, names of friends/relatives, AIM screen name, and mailing address, as well as a space at the bottom for notes. You can tab between fields or click into the ones you want to insert. You can add as much or as little information as you want, but an email address is required if you plan to use the card with Mail, and an AIM screen name is required for use with iChat.

You may not need to type all you contacts' information in order to add them to Address Book—if they use vCards, or "Virtual Cards," which are sent as attachments in email messages. If you have contacts who include vCards with their email messages, you can drag the vCard attachments from the Mail application into Address Book. It will automatically be read. (By the way, vCards are a standard format that works across different operating systems and applications.)

If the label to the left of the field doesn't match the information you want to add, you can adjust it by clicking the up/down arrows icon. This opens a pop-up menu with several common labels as well as an option to customize. In some cases, such as adding a phone number, you may want (or need) to add multiple values. When you're editing a field that supports multiple entries, + and – buttons appear to the left of the field. Clicking + adds a new field of the same type; clicking – removes the field. To add completely new fields, choose Card, Add Field; then select from any of the available fields.

The default template for creating new cards can be changed in the Address Book application preferences, or by choosing Card, Add Field, Edit Template.

In the upper-left corner of the card column is a picture well. If you want to add a custom picture, you can paste it into the well. Alternatively, double-click the picture well or choose Card, Choose Custom Image from the menu to open a window where you can drag an image file and zoom/crop the image. (You can even take a video snapshot if you have a web camera, such as Apple's iSight camera.) To clear a custom image, choose Card, Clear Custom Image from the menu.

When you're finished adding information, click the Edit button again, and the unfilled fields disappear.

To edit a card you've already created, select the individual's name from the Name column and click the Edit button below the card column, or choose Edit, Edit Card (Command-L) from the menu.

To delete a card, select it and press the Delete key on your keyboard. You are asked to confirm the action before it is carried out. You can also remove a card by choosing Edit, Delete Card from the menu, but you are not prompted to confirm before the card disappears.

Special Card Settings and Functions

When editing a card, a few special properties and functions can be applied. The first—Card, Make This My Card—sets the current card so that it represents *you*, the owner of the active system account. Your Address Book card is represented with a "head" icon in Address Book listings, unlike other cards.

A second property, set by choosing Card, This Is a Company, or by clicking the Company check box when editing a card, swaps the company name and contact name information in the card display and alters the card icon in the listing to resemble a small building.

If you are displeased with the first/last name ordering in a card, choose Card, Swap First/Last Name, and they are reversed in the card view. To reset to the default ordering, choose Card, Reset First/Last Name to Default.

A final option, Card, Merge Cards (Command-|) is useful if you've accidentally created multiple cards for the same person. You can merge information in two or more cards by selecting them in the Name column and then choosing the Merge Cards option. (To select two cards that aren't adjacent, hold down the Command key as you select them.)

View Cards

When a card is not in edit mode, many of the labels in the card view provide links to useful functions. Clicking the "friend/relation" label displays the option to show that person's contact card, if it exists.

A unique feature Apple provides is the capability to display a web-based map of any street address in your Address Book. Click the label to the right of any address field and choose Map Of from the pop-up menu. Your web browser opens to a map of the location. You can also choose to copy the URL of the map.

By the Way

> You can also copy the address to the Clipboard in address label format by clicking the label to the right of any address field.

If you have the Apple Bluetooth adapter and a Bluetooth-enabled phone, you can pair the devices under the Bluetooth pane of the System Preferences. After they are paired, you can send cards from Address Book to your phone. In addition, BlueTooth-paired phones automatically trigger Address Book to display the card (if available) for incoming calls and enable you to choose to answer the call or send the call to voice mail.

Adding/Editing Groups

You can arrange your cards into your own custom groups, which, in addition to creating organization, can be used to send email to a collection of people.

> If you have many cards to work with but no need for mailing to custom groups, you can enter keywords in the Notes section of the cards and then use the Search function, located at the upper right of the Card and Column view, to see only those cards that contain your chosen keyword.

To create a group, click the + button under the Group column and type a name for it. You can then start adding contacts to the group, either by using the method discussed previously, or by selecting another contact group (such as All) and dragging contacts from the Name column to populate the new group. You can hold down the Command key to select more than one addressee at a time.

> The + button is a common feature in many of Apple's applications, including iPhoto and Safari, and is used to create a new collection. The column arrangement and method of dragging items into a newly created collection also carries over to these applications.

Address Book also lets you create Smart Groups, which are dynamic groups that are updated automatically based on the rules you set. To create a new Smart Group, choose File, New Smart Group from the menu and then set your attributes. For example, you can create a Smart Group selecting all employees of a specific company.

> You can also create a Smart Group by entering a search term in Address Book's search field and then choosing Save Search from the Action menu at the top left of the window.

Distribution Groups

An Address Book group can be used with Mail to send messages to a group of people simultaneously if you drag the group into the Address field in Mail. When used in this manner, the group is considered a *distribution group*. All Address Book groups can be used as distribution groups, but before using them, you may want to choose which email address each contact in the group is to use when the message is sent. To do this, highlight your group in Address Book; then choose Edit, Edit Distribution List. A window similar to that in Figure 8.2 appears.

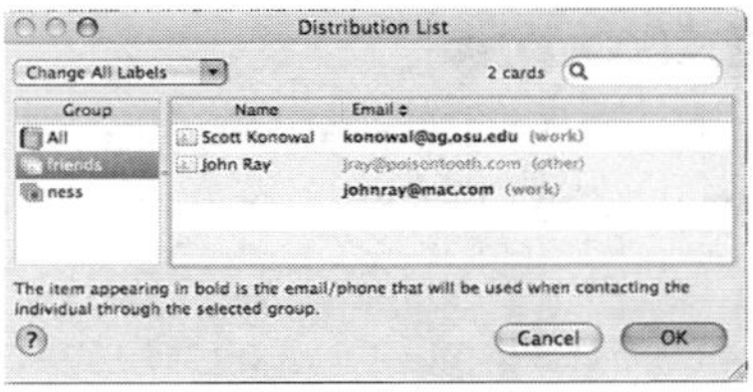

FIGURE 8.2
Choose the address to use if a group is used to send email.

Use the pop-up menu in the upper-right corner of the Distribution List window to switch all contacts in the group to their work, home, or other addresses. To switch on a person-by-person basis, simply click the correct contact address in the list to highlight it.

When all the correct addresses are selected, click OK. You can now use your Address Book group as a mailing distribution list.

Printing Contact Information

Built into Address Book is the capability to easily print mailing labels, envelopes, mailing lists, and a pocket address book.

To print one of these options, first select the group you want to print; then Choose File, Print. Address Book displays the dialog box shown in Figure 8.3.

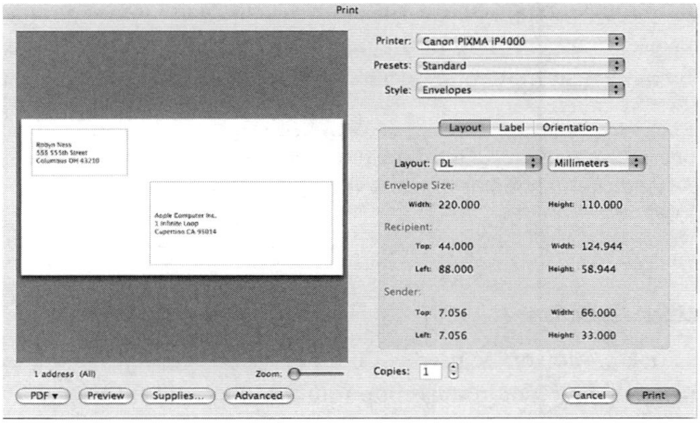

FIGURE 8.3
Print envelopes, lists, and mailing labels with ease.

Use the Style pop-up menu to choose what you want to print. The Mailing labels option provides settings for controlling your paper layout under the Layout pane, including several label standards. The Label pane displays settings for choosing between which Address Book addresses are printed (Home or Work), sorting, font options, and an image that can be printed beside each address.

When printing envelopes, you can choose the type of envelope, the order in which envelopes are printed, and the orientation of the envelopes in the printer. When printing lists, as shown in Figure 8.3, you are given the option of choosing which attributes are printed in the list. When printing a pocket address book, you can choose which attributes to include.

Make your setting choices and view the results in the preview on the left side of the window; then click Print to start printing.

Preferences

The Address Book preferences, accessible from the Address Book menu, are used to choose sorting, display, and vCard preferences and to configure LDAP servers for use with the Address Book directory services.

General

The General pane, shown in Figure 8.4, enables you to choose the Display order for names (first or last name first), how the contacts should be sorted, the Address format, and the display font.

FIGURE 8.4
The Address Book General Preferences.

To automatically send updates that are made to your personal card to a group of people in your Address Book, click the Notify People When My Card Changes check box. When you change any piece of information in your card, a prompt asks whether you want to email the update to your contacts. You can choose the groups to which to send email, and type a brief message to them.

Template

The Template pane provides control over the "default" Address Card format. Using the same controls available when creating a card entry, you can create your own custom template, as shown in Figure 8.5. Use the Add Field pop-up menu to add fields to the template.

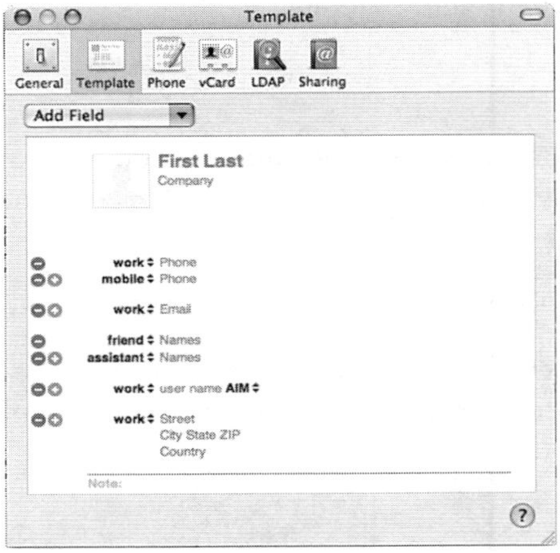

FIGURE 8.5
Define a custom Card template.

Phone

The Phone pane enables you to choose custom phone layouts and activate/deactivate automatic formatting of phone numbers.

Use the Formats menu to choose from one of the predefined formats, or click the disclosure button to display the format editor. To use the format editor, Click + to add a new format and type the number format as you want it to appear, substituting the pound (#) sign for the actual phone number digits.

Use the – button to remove phone number formats, or the Edit button to edit existing formats. The formats can also be dragged in the listing if you want to change their order.

vCard

As you learned above, vCards are used to attach contact information to email in a standardized format. Use the vCard pane to choose the default format of your own vCard "address card."

> To attach your own vCard, you can drag your card from the Address Book into a new message window in most email programs.

By the Way

You can also ensure the privacy of your personal card by enabling the Enable Private "Me" Card option. This keeps everything but your *work* contact data from being exported with your card.

Use the Export Notes in vCards option to include the notes field when exporting cards. Because notes are typically personal information, they are not exported by default.

LDAP

LDAP (Lightweight Directory Access Protocol) defines a means of querying remote directory systems that contain personnel data. The Address Book can use LDAP server connectivity to retrieve contact information from network servers. This pane of the Address Book preferences is used to set up Address Book for LDAP queries. Speak to your network administrator if you want to know more about this option.

Sharing

If you have a .Mac account, the Sharing pane enables you to share your contacts with other .Mac users. To share your Address Book, check the box labeled Share Your Address Book and then click the + button to choose .Mac members in your contact list with whom to share. The contacts you approve for sharing must then choose File, Subscribe to Address Book from the menu and enter your .Mac username.

Keychain Access

Keeping track of passwords for email servers, file servers, websites, and other private information can be difficult. That's why Apple has included a security utility called Keychain Access to make managing your collection of passwords and PIN numbers much easier.

Think of Keychain Access as a database of your most sensitive information, all accessible through your Mac OS X account password. The Keychain Access software automatically stores passwords from Keychain Access-aware applications, such as Mail—which means that you don't have to enter your password every time you check your email.

> Not all applications have been constructed to interact with Keychain Access. In those instances, you can manually add your own passwords or even store credit card information for convenient lookup when you need it.

Automated Access

If you open Keychain Access from the Utilities folder within the system Applications folder, you can see the contents of your default keychain. For an account that has set up email and enabled the Safari web browser to store web logins, the Keychain Access window looks similar to the one shown in Figure 8.6.

The obvious question is, "How did these items get here?" They were added by Mac OS X applications. Typically, when an application wants to store something in Keychain Access, you're given the option of storing it. For example, choosing the Remember Name and Password option in the Safari web browser automatically adds the entered password to the default keychain. Over time, your keychain becomes populated with these items.

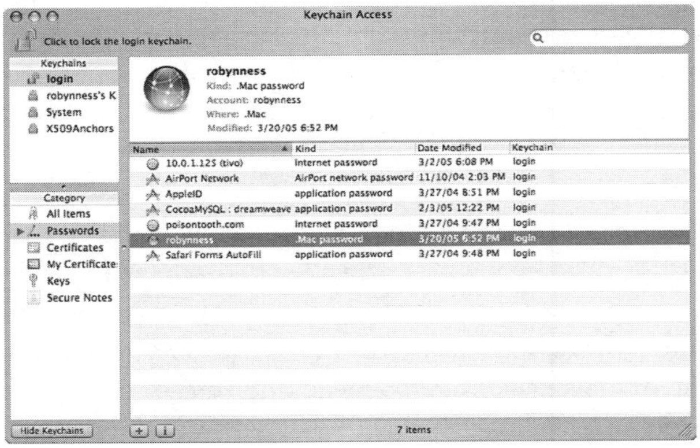

FIGURE 8.6
The Keychain Access window displays a list of accounts with stored passwords.

You can view information in a keychain in the Keychain Access window. You can view each item stored in the keychain by selecting it in the lower pane of the Keychain Access window.

> If Keychain Access is something you want easy access to, you can add a menu extra to your menu bar in the Keychain Access preferences by checking the box for Show Status in Menu Bar. A lock icon, open or locked, appears in the menu bar to show the status of your keychains. Clicking it gives you options to lock or unlock all keychains and to open the Keychain Access utility.

Attributes and Access Control

Double-clicking an item opens another window with more detail and more options, as shown in Figure 8.7. Two sets of information exist for each Keychain Access item: Attributes and Access Control.

FIGURE 8.7
Attributes of an item in the keychain.

The Attributes settings provide basic information about the stored item, as shown in Figure 8.7. You can also add comments about the item by typing them in the Comments field. Check the Show Password box to display your password. To authorize revealing your saved password, you are prompted to type your account password.

> When authorizing Show Password, you're asked for your password to access Keychain Access itself. At that time, you have the option to Allow Once, Always Allow, or Deny Permission. Because Keychain Access isn't listed as having unlimited access to stored items, it asks each time it needs to retrieve the information unless you choose the Always Allow option.

By the Way

The Access Control settings, shown in Figure 8.8, enable the user to choose which applications can use information from Keychain Access. When a Keychain Access–aware application wants to access information from your keychain, it must first make sure that the keychain is unlocked. Your default Mac OS X keychain is automatically unlocked when you're logged in, making its passwords accessible to the applications that stored them.

Click Allow All Applications to Access This Item to allow access to the resource with no user interaction. If you prefer to monitor use of your passwords by programs on your system, click the Confirm Before Allowing Access radio button to be prompted to allow Keychain Access to share each password when needed.

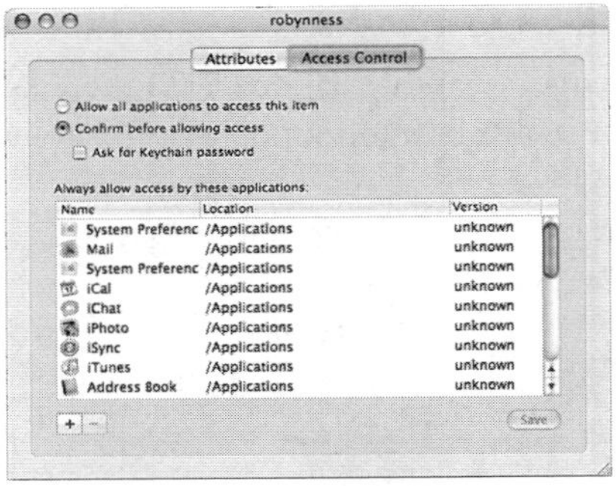

FIGURE 8.8
Access Control enables you to choose which applications can apply your passwords.

> You can manually lock or unlock the entire keychain by clicking the Lock button in the toolbar of the Keychain Access window. After the keychain is locked, you're asked to enter a password—which, for the default keychain, is your account password—whenever an application attempts to access keychain information. Also, the details of keychain items within Keychain Access won't be shown until a password is entered. (However, the names of the items and when they were created are displayed.)

You can further specify how individual applications deal with passwords in the Always Allow Access by These Applications section. Use the + and – buttons to add and remove applications from the list.

Adding New Entries to Keychain Access

You can add new items to Keychain Access by clicking the "+" button at the bottom of the Keychain Access window or by choosing File, New Password Item from the menu. This action opens the window shown in Figure 8.9, in which to enter the data to be stored.

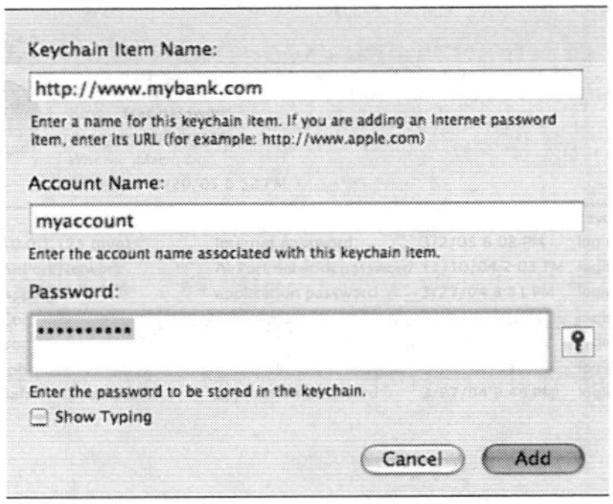

FIGURE 8.9
It's easy to add new items manually to an existing keychain.

To add a new item, follow these steps:

1. In the Name field, enter the name (or for password-protected websites, the URL).

2. In the Account Name field, enter the username associated with the data.

3. In the Password field, enter the account password. By default, the password is hidden as you type. To display the password as it's typed, click the Show Typing check box.

OS X includes a Password Assistant to help you choose strong passwords. Click the key icon to the right of the Password field in Figure 8.9 to access it. (Password Assistant is discussed further in Chapter 31, "Sharing Your Computer with Other Users.")

Did you Know?

---

4. When you've completed these fields, click Add.

To remove any item from Keychain Access (whether it was automatically or manually entered), select its name in the list and then press the Delete key on your keyboard, or choose Edit, Delete Keychain from the menu.

In addition to adding new passwords to your keychain, you can also create Secure Notes. Choose File, New Secure Note Item from the menu. A new window opens in which to type your note. When you've typed the name and content of the note, click the Add button to save. The note is added to the list of items.

To view the contents of a secure note, check the box labeled Show Note and enter your account password for authorization. You can then edit the note and save changes (see Figure 8.10).

FIGURE 8.10
Private information can be stored as a secure note within Keychain Access.

Adding and Managing Keychains

Each user has a default keychain that's unlocked with the system password, but you can have as many keychains as you want. Sensitive information can be placed into a secondary keychain with a different password so that someone with your account password doesn't have access to all your information.

To add a new keychain, do the following:

1. Choose File, New Keychain from the menu.

2. You are prompted for a name and save location for the keychain. (The default save location is the Library folder in your home folder.) When you've set these options, click Create.

3. The New Keychain Password window appears, prompting you to enter and verify the password that unlocks the new keychain. (It's best to choose something different from your account password to prevent people who might gain access to your account from seeing your most sensitive information.)

4. Click OK.

To switch between different keychains, select the one you want from the Keychains list at the top of the sidebar.

iSync

iSync helps you synchronize contact and calendar information between your computer and devices, such as an iSync-compatible Bluetooth or USB mobile phone, a Palm OS device, or an iPod. iSync works by comparing information stored in compatible applications on your computer, such as Address Book, with the address and contact information stored on a device.

By the Way

> A list of devices that work with iSync is online at www.apple.com/isync/devices.html.

Did you Know?

> Apple's .Mac Internet service works with iSync to synchronize information across different computers. This is especially useful for synchronizing your contact information in Address Book, your web bookmarks from the Safari web browser, and schedule to-do items in the iCal application. Chapter 16, "Exploring .Mac Membership," explains .Mac synchronization capabilities further.

Connecting Portable Devices to iSync

To use iSync, you first need to connect a device. When correctly set up, a device appears in the iSync window, as shown in Figure 8.11.

Apple recommends that you sync USB and Bluetooth phones and Palm devices to only one computer to avoid unpredictable results, such as duplicated information. If you need to sync with a different computer, connect it first to the computer originally synced and remove the device by choosing Device, Remove Device from the menu. You can then connect the device to a new computer without unpleasant side effects.

Watch Out!

Connect iPods and USB Phones

To connect an iPod or USB phone, connect the device to the computer using the cable that came with it and then start iSync from the Applications folder. Next choose Device, Add Device from the menu and double-click the device you connected.

Connect Bluetooth Phones

To connect a Bluetooth mobile phone to a Bluetooth-enabled computer, first make sure the phone is set to discoverable mode. Then open the Device settings of the Bluetooth pane of the System Preferences, choose Set Up New Device, and follow the onscreen instructions. After pairing your Bluetooth phone and computer, your phone appears in the iSync window the next time your open it.

Connect Palm Devices

Connecting Palm devices is slightly more complex than connecting other kinds of devices. To begin, be sure you have installed Palm Desktop 4.0 or later and have synced at least once using the HotSync Manager before attempting to connect your Palm device to iSync.

Visit www.palmone.com/us/Macintosh for information on Palm Desktop.

By the Way

Then, open iSync and choose Devices, Enable Palm OS HotSync from the menu. Follow the onscreen instructions. (This step enables you to synchronize information on your Palm device with information on your computer by using Palm Desktop.)

Next, open the HotSync Manager from the Palm folder inside your Applications folder and choose HotSync, Conduit Settings from the menu. In the window that opens, choose iSync Conduit settings and check the box for Enable iSync for This Palm Device. (This step allows iSync to synchronize your information.)

Syncing Information

After you've added a device, you can use iSync to synchronize contact information from Address Book and calendar information from the iCal application with information on your device.

To synchronize with a non-Palm device, click the device icon in the iSync window, choose which information you want to synchronize, and click the Sync Devices button. To synchronize with a Palm OS device, HotSync the device by pushing the button on its cradle and the information is updated.

In the event that iSync locates conflicting information while syncing the information on your computer with the information on a device, it replaces the information in both places with one version but saves the other version in the Conflict Resolver. To view and resolve any conflicts, open the iSync preferences, enable Show Status in Menu Bar, and choose Conflicts from the iSync menu that appears on the right side of the menu bar. The Conflict Resolver window opens, in which you can choose which version of the information to keep.

By the
Way

> You can replace any contact and calendar information on your device with the information on your computer by choosing Devices, Reset All Devices from the menu. If you have your computer configured the way you want it and don't want to sync for fear of messing up your settings, Reset All Devices allows you to override the information stored on your other devices with what is contained on your computer.

To investigate past synchronizations from the current computer, choose Window, Sync Logs from the menu. Click the disclosure triangle to reveal details about each sync listed.

iSync Preferences

Use the iSync application preferences, shown in Figure 8.12, to turn on syncing for your computer. The option for Display Palm Hotsync Warning allows you to enable reminders to click the HotSync button if you had disabled this feature at the time the device was connected. You can also add an iSync status menu to your menu bar. From the iSync status menu, you can synchronize your devices, open iSync, or view any unresolved information conflicts.

Within the preferences, you can also choose the amount of data that has to change for iSync to display a warning message and reset your sync history, which makes your computer act as though it is syncing with a device for the first time.

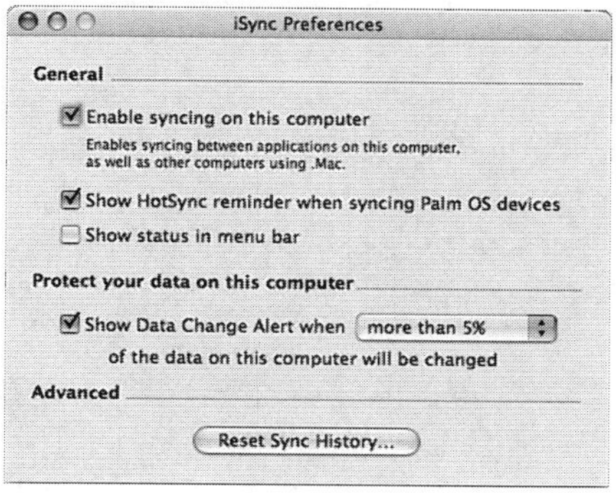

FIGURE 8.12
Use the iSync preferences to add a menu extra to your menu bar.

Ink

Mac OS X includes a handwriting recognition feature called Ink, which enables you to write input to any application including word processing programs, email applications, and even web browsers. Ink requires no special alphabet, although people with messy handwriting might require practice to understand how Ink interprets characters. Figure 8.13 shows Ink being used with Mail, Mac OS X's built-in email program.

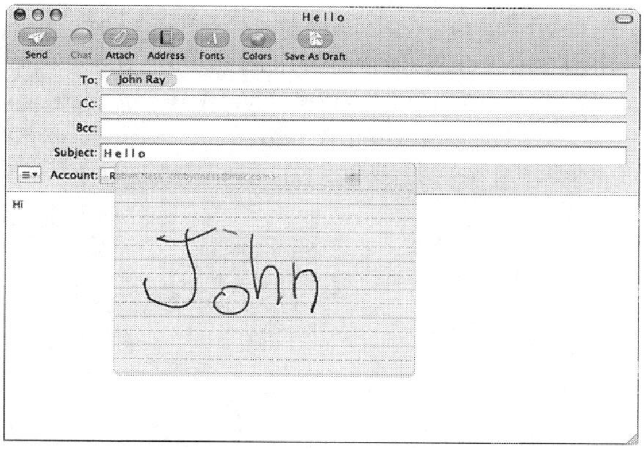

FIGURE 8.13
Ink enables you to set your keyboard and mouse aside.

> To run Ink, you must have a compatible graphics tablet, such as a Wacom graphics model. You must also install the appropriate driver for Mac OS X . (If you need more information about downloads or software installation, read Chapter 9, "Installing Additional Software.")

By the Way

When a graphics tablet is plugged into one of your computer's USB ports, the Ink icon shows up under the Hardware section of System Preferences. The Ink preferences, shown in Figure 8.14, give you options to turn handwriting recognition on or off and to change several settings.

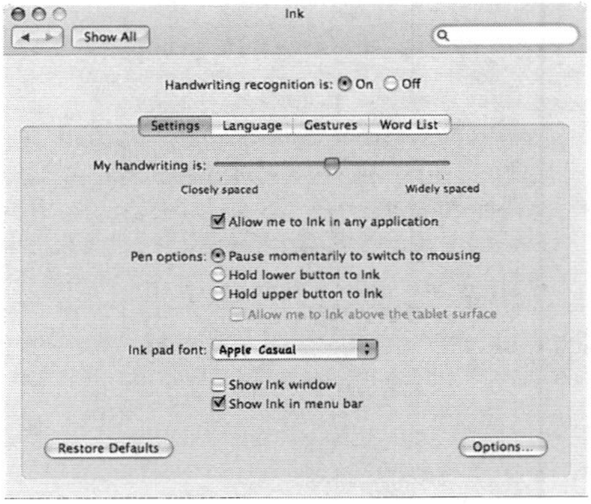

FIGURE 8.14
To activate Ink, you need to go to the Ink preferences in the System Preferences.

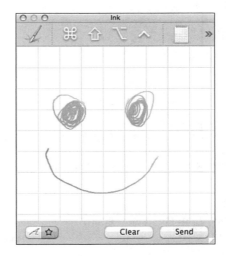

By the Way

If you plan to use Ink regularly, check the Show Ink in Menu Bar check box in the Settings pane of the Ink preferences. This adds a menu item from which you can turn Ink on and off as needed. It also enables you to toggle Write Anywhere on and off, which determines whether you write directly into applications or use the Ink window, which is discussed next, as an intermediary.

The Ink window floats on top of all other application windows. From the toolbar at the top, you can toggle between handwriting recognition mode and pointer mode, select common menu command and keyboard shortcut characters, and open the Ink pad, as shown in Figure 8.15. With the Ink pad open, you can switch between the writing and drawing modes, using the buttons at the lower left.

FIGURE 8.15
Ink pad provides a space for you to write or draw.

The text or drawings you create in Ink pad can be inserted into other documents. Create the content of your choice in the workspace and click the Send button to add it to the active document at the current insertion point. For instance, when you finish composing the text of an email message, you could sign your name in the drawing view of Ink pad and insert your signature at the bottom of your message. Note, however, that you cannot insert pictures into applications that don't support image display.

Although Ink pad enables you to compose your additions before you add them to a document, you can also write directly into a program. To add text directly to an application, touch the stylus to the tablet to open a writing space with guiding lines in which to form characters and begin writing words. An example of this is shown in Figure 8.13. If a writing space doesn't appear, try touching the stylus to the graphics tablet in a different place. Because your stylus can also act as a mouse, some areas of the screen, such as window controls or menus, activate commands rather than opening a writing space.

> If a writing space doesn't appear no matter where you touch the stylus to the tablet, double-check that the option Allow Me to Ink in Any Application is enabled in the Settings pane of the Ink preferences.

Watch Out!

Although Ink doesn't require you to learn special letter forms, you must write linearly—as if you were using paper—instead of writing letters on top of one another as you would on a personal digital assistant (PDA). When you pause, your markings are converted to text at the top of the writing space. To correct a mistake, draw a long horizontal line from right to left and pause to see the last character disappear. If you have larger sections to delete, switch to pointer mode in the Ink window, select the part you want to redo, and switch back to writing mode to try again.

> Some applications that don't use standard Mac OS X text controls behave unpredictably with Ink's text recognition. If you're using an application in which spaces don't appear between words as needed, try writing your content in Ink pad and using Send to insert it in the other application.

By the Way

Ink Preferences

Now that you know a little about what Ink is and how it works, let's take a closer look at the Ink preferences panes. The following adjustments can be made under the Settings pane (shown previously in Figure 8.14):

▶ My Handwriting Style Is—Move the slider to describe your handwriting as closely spaced, widely spaced, or somewhere in between.

▶ Allow Me to Ink in Any Application—Choose whether you can write to all programs or only in the Ink pad.

▶ Pen Options—Choose whether pausing momentarily switches the pen action to mousing or whether the lower or upper button on the pen activates Ink functions.

▶ Ink pad Font—Set a font for display in the Ink pad. For greatest accuracy, Apple recommends keeping the font set to Apple Casual, which contains letter shapes that are the most similar to those recognized by Ink so that you can model your writing after it.

▶ Show Ink Window—Brings up the Ink window when Ink is activated.

▶ Show Ink in Menu Bar—Adds a menu extra to turn Ink on and off.

Clicking the Options button opens a sheet window with additional handwriting recognition options, including the amount of delay before writing is converted to type, how much the stylus must move before a stroke is recorded, and several other options. If you change your mind about configurations you've made in either the Settings pane or the Options sheet, choose Restore Defaults to revert to the originals.

Use the Language pane to choose the language in which you will be writing.

The Gestures pane displays shapes that have special meaning in Ink, such as vertical or horizontal spaces, tab, and delete. Click on an item to see both a demonstration of drawing the shape and a written description of it. You can also activate or deactivate Gesture actions using the check box in front of each item. Apple recommends that you provide extra space in front of a Gesture shape and exaggerate the ending stroke so that the system does not confuse it with a letter.

The Word List pane enables you to add uncommon words that you use frequently. Ink uses a list of common words to help decipher people's input. If you come across a word that Ink doesn't know, click the Add button and type the new word in the text box.

Summary

This chapter explored four "helper" applications—Address Book, Keychain Access, iSync, and Ink—that work with other applications rather than run on their own. Address Book integrates with several applications that use contact information, whereas Keychain Access stores private information (such as passwords) securely. iSync synchronizes information between your computer and portable devices. With the addition of a compatible graphics tablet, Ink can be used as an input device in place of your keyboard and mouse.

CHAPTER 9

Installing Additional Software

Although Mac OS X comes with programs and tools offering a wide range of features, at some point you'll probably want to add software to your system. This chapter talks about how to install additional software in Mac OS X. (Even though software installation is not difficult, Mac OS X supports several different methods of doing so.) It also looks at some software issues for multiuser systems and recommends some interesting applications available for your system.

Software Sources

When it comes to expanding your collection of software, your first question might be "What are my options?" You'll be pleased to hear that a number of good online libraries feature Mac OS X software. (If you need to learn more about how to get online or how use a web browser, those topics are discussed in Chapter 13, "Connecting to the Internet," and 14, "Using Safari.")

The following sites present the latest and greatest Mac OS X programs available for download or on CD-ROM (by purchase):

▶ VersionTracker—www.versiontracker.com/macosx/—Updated continually, VersionTracker's website is often the first to carry new Mac OS X software. As a nearly comprehensive catalog, it also works as a handy reference guide. To find what you need, just type the name or a keyword for a product into the search field.

▶ MacUpdate—www.macupdate.com/index.php?os=macosx—Similar to VersionTracker, MacUpdate lists a broad selection of Mac software.

▶ Mac OS X Apps—www.macosxapps.com/—This site features in-depth discussions about new software and uses.

▶ Apple's Mac OS X Downloads—www.apple.com/downloads/macosx/—Although less expansive than the previous sites, Apple's software compendium is well documented and easily navigated.

Later in this chapter, we recommend several interesting applications mentioned on these sites that you might want to try.

Downloading and Installing Software

Although there's no single installation technique for all software available for the Mac OS X, let's look at two common methods. Obviously, you should read the documentation that comes with your software if you want to be certain of the results, but for those who are anxious to double-click, this section offers a basic description of what to expect.

If you would rather purchase your software from a mail-order or in-store vendor, just make sure to read the product information to ensure compatibility with Mac OS X. The installation process for disc images (explained later in this section) still applies.

Open a web browser, such as Safari (see Chapter 14, "Using Safari"), and go to one of the sites mentioned previously to find trial versions or freeware that you want to try. After you locate something interesting, you're ready to begin:

1. On the software download page, determine which version your system requires and click that link. Remember to choose a version that's made for Mac OS X.

2. As your system begins downloading your selection, a Downloads window, similar to that shown in Figure 9.1, appears on your screen.

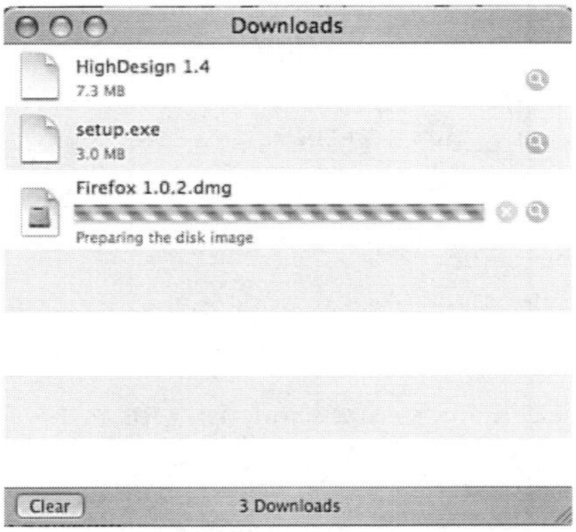

FIGURE 9.1
In Safari and most web browsers, you can monitor an item's status as it downloads.

3. When the download is finished, several icons appear on your desktop, so that it looks similar to Figure 9.2. The icon with the extension .dmg represents a special file that has been encoded as a disk image for easy storage and download. Other common types of download files end with a .gz, .zip, or .sit

extension and contain the files in encoded or compressed form. We'll talk more about this in the "Opening Compressed Files with StuffIt Expander" section later in this chapter.

4. The final installation step may differ, depending on the application you're using. Here are the three major variations:

   If a folder icon appears on your desktop, you must open it to reach the application file. The folder also usually contains a ReadMe file that explains what to do next. This kind of install exists for smaller programs. (If you download new fonts, as discussed in Chapter 12, "Printing, Faxing, and Working with Fonts," they often appear in this way.)

   If a file icon with the extension .pkg or .mpkg appears, double-clicking starts the Apple Installer, which provides a simple step-by-step guide to installation.

   Finally, if a disk image icon appears, as with the Firefox disk icon shown second from the bottom in Figure 9.2, double-clicking it mounts the disk image, which you can then double-click to open a Finder window containing instructions. Disk images have the .dmg file extension.

   For example, when installing the Firefox web browser, opening the disk icon results in the screen shown in Figure 9.3, which contains an application icon for you to drag to the Applications folder on your hard drive.

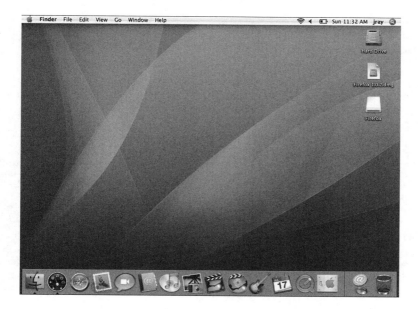

FIGURE 9.2
When you download software, new icons appear on the desktop unless you've set another location.

When you've placed the file or folder where you want it, your application is ready for use. You can drag all the files that appeared on your desktop during download and installation to the Trash.

FIGURE 9.3
To install Firefox, simply drag the application icon to a folder in a Finder window—preferably the Applications folder.

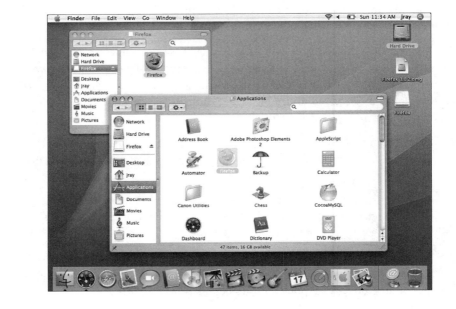

By the Way

You cannot eject a disk image from your computer while running the software contained on that disk.

If you try to drag a disk image to the Trash and receive an error message, it is likely that you didn't copy the contents of the disk image to your hard drive and are instead working off the disk image. To be able to eject the disk image, you need to close the application, and then copy the disk image to the Mac OS X drive.

To uninstall most software, simply locate the application file or folder and drag it to the Trash. Under Mac OS X, you should find most application folders in the system-wide Applications folder.

Watch Out!

Although you can drag most application files or folders to the trash to uninstall them, you may need to delete other files, such as preferences, that they leave behind before reinstalling the same application again. Preference files are stored in the system-wide Library folder in another folder called Preferences.

Opening Compressed Files with StuffIt Expander

Because applications tend to be large files, they come in a compressed form that takes up less space and makes downloading them faster and easier. These compressed files are also referred to as archive files because they're compact and easily stored. Compression can be done in several different ways. Mac OS X can compress and uncompress .zip files, which is a common format used on Windows machines, as well as .tar and .gz files, which are Unix standards. (Recall that you can zip a file or folder by using the Archive option of the Action menu in the Finder window, as discussed in Chapter 4.)

When opening some other types of compressed files, such as .sit (StuffIt) files, you may need the assistance of an application such as StuffIt Expander, whose Progress window appears in Figure 9.4.

FIGURE 9.4
When the download is finished, StuffIt Expander goes to work.

StuffIt Expander uncompresses most common archive types, including some formats that Mac OS X doesn't. You can download StuffIt Expander at www.stuffit.com/mac/expander/.

> StuffIt Expander is freeware, which means you can download and use it without purchasing a license code.

By the Way

After you download a compressed file, StuffIt Expander opens automatically when it's needed and leaves uncompressed folders on the desktop along with the original archive file. You might never need to start it manually, but you can configure a number of settings in its Preferences dialog box to control actions, such as how StuffIt deals with files after extraction.

Software Considerations in a Multiuser System

Mac OS X is a multiuser system. When it comes to installing software, this seemingly small detail really matters. For one thing, not all users might have the same privileges on the system. When you set up user accounts, as will be explained in Chapter 31, "Sharing Your Computer with Other Users," you have the option to prevent others from modifying the system in any way. That includes installing additional software.

> When installing some software, or even updating existing software, you may have to enter the password you created when you set up your account. This is meant to ensure that you, the administrator of your computer, approve of whatever changes are being made.

Also, when you install applications, keep in mind that other users don't necessarily have access to items stored in your home directory. If you install a large application in your home directory, you might be the only person who can use it, which could lead to other users installing copies of this same application on the same machine. To best utilize disk space and resource sharing, major applications should be installed in the system's Applications folder or in a subdirectory of Applications rather than inside your home directory.

One other issue: Be sure to read your software license agreements regarding operation by multiple users. If an application is licensed for only a single user (rather than a single computer), it should not be placed in the Applications folder where other users of your system can have access.

Some Software Suggestions

For the rest of the chapter, we look at some interesting applications available for Mac OS X. These programs have been selected based on their unique features and immediate availability (either in full or demo form) over the Internet.

> Software recommendations are also made in other chapters of this book, as appropriate. For example, several programs to protect your computer from viruses are discussed in Chapter 35, "Recovering from Crashes and Other Problems."

Although we recommend the following software, keep in mind that many other fine programs are available, and that the number grows daily. The following should serve only as a starting point for exploring the possibilities.

Web Browsing Applications

Web browsing is a popular pastime, and you can choose from many different web browsers with different helpful features. The following sections describe a few of them. Some you might have heard of, whereas others are entirely new to the Mac platform.

Firefox

Firefox (www.getfirefox.com) is a popular, open-source browser from the Mozilla Project, a group that has also worked on recent versions of Netscape. Firefox offers pop-up blocking, tabbed browsing so you can open several web pages in one open window (see Figure 9.5), and strong security features. It also renders web pages *amazingly* fast—seriously, you need to see it to believe it.

FIGURE 9.5
Firefox is an amazingly fast web browser.

Open source means that software is developed by a community of programmers and isn't owned by a specific company. Rather, open source software is meant to be distributed freely and improved by anyone who can make improvements.

OmniWeb

OmniWeb, by the Omni Group (www.omnigroup.com/), is an alternative web browser that supports standards-compliant web technologies. Omniweb will update you when the URL of a bookmarked site has changed. It also allows you to search your history files for any word you recall from a web page so that you can find your way back to a site without knowing the name.

Productivity Applications

Here are a few practical applications for your word processing, image editing, and computer programming needs.

Nisus Writer Express

Nisus Writer Express is a word processing program with an interface worthy of Mac OS X. Also, one of its special features is support for noncontiguous selection, so you can copy and paste bits and pieces of information easily. It's available for a free 30-day trial at www.nisus.com/Express/.

OmniGraffle 3

OmniGraffle 3, from the makers of OmniWeb (www.omnigroup.com), is a charting/diagramming program that you can use to draw organizational structures and flow charts. (It may not sound exciting, but it does these things so well!) Without a license, you're limited to the use of 20 objects per document.

Graphic Converter X

If you've been looking for a program that can open and save image files of just about any format, Graphic Converter is for you. It's available as shareware from Lemke Software (lemkesoft.com/en/graphcon.htm).

Desktop "Helpers"

A host of small programs have been written to make working with your desktop more efficient. Here are a couple of the most well-loved.

▶ WindowShade X—If you find yourself double-clicking the title bars of windows expecting the window to collapse to a title bar as it did in OS 9, try WindowShade X from Unsanity (www.unsanity.com).

By the Way

> WindowShade and Graphic Converter are *shareware*, which means that the developer makes software available for your use (at least in a limited trial) but requests a small payment in return. If you try any shareware applications and like them, paying the fee is the right thing to do!

▶ Drop Drawers X—Drop Drawers, available as shareware from Sig Software (www.sigsoftware.com/dropdrawers/), adds "drawers" to the edge of your screen where you can store notes, URLs, or files for easy access. Simply double-click their handles, and the drawers open. Figure 9.6 shows an example.

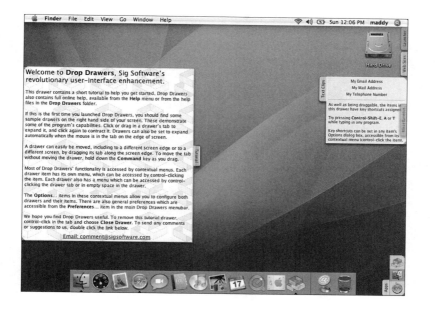

FIGURE 9.6
Add storage to your screen with Drop Drawers.

Games

If you're looking for recreation, try one of these:

▶ Burning Monkey Solitaire (www.freeverse.com/bms2005/), available as shareware, offers several versions of the Solitaire card game, including Klondike, Freecell, and 52 Card Pick-up, delivered in an interface filled with taunting monkeys. A limited demo is available without purchase of a license code.

▶ BabelBloX, available as shareware from illumineX at www.illuminex.com/software/games/babelblox.html, offers several addictive games in one, all involving the arrangement of colorful squares. A limited demo is available without purchases of a license code.

▶ Enigmo, available as shareware from Pangea Software (www.pangeasoft.net/enigmo/), is a challenging puzzle/strategy game with a fun interface and catchy music. See Figure 9.7 for a glimpse. A limited demo is available without purchases of a license code.

FIGURE 9.7
The objective of Enigmo is to direct droplets of water (and sometimes fire) into containers, using only the tools provided.

Screensavers

Mac OS X comes with many attractive screensavers, but many people delight in finding new and interesting ones. Spice up your system by downloading one of these excellent replacements:

▶ Mac OS X Screensavers 3.0 (www.epicware.com/macosxsavers.html) is a collection of popular screensavers that have been transplanted from another platform. Although several years old, this set is still pleasing to the eye.

▶ Hotel Gadget (www.zugakousaku.com/index.cgi?hotel&cover&en&) generates a series of black-and-white rooms where objects randomly appear. Think "MC Esher meets Rene Magritte"! (See Figure 9.8 if that description doesn't help.)

▶ Neko.saver (homepage.mac.com/takashi_hamada/Acti/MacOSX/Neko/index.html) turns one or more animated cats loose on your desktop to play, sleep, and scamper across your screen.

To install a screensaver, place its application file in the system folder Library/Screen Savers or in your own ~/Library/Screen Savers folder, depending on whether you want public or private access. After you've installed a new screensaver, you still must choose it in the Screen Saver section of the Desktop & Screen Saver pane of the System Preferences to activate it.

FIGURE 9.8
The Hotel
Gadget screen-
saver renders
surreal hotel
rooms to puzzle
your family and
friends.

Customizing Desktop Icons

In addition to downloading and installing new and interesting screensavers, you can customize your desktop by downloading and installing new icons for your files, folders, and applications—and even your hard drive icon. One popular source for free, custom icons is the Icon Factory (www.iconfactory.com/), which both develops and holds yearly open contests for new icon sets.

To customize an icon, start by locating a set of icons you like and downloading it. (The Icon Factory offers icons in a couple of different formats—be sure to download icons made for the Macintosh.) When downloaded, the icon set uncompresses with help from StuffIt Expander and is ready for use.

Next, open the folder containing the icon set, select the icon you want, and open the Info window for it by choosing Get Info from the File menu at the top of the Finder window. When the Info window opens, select the icon at the top of the window so that a highlight appears around it (as shown in Figure 9.9); then choose Edit, Copy from the menu.

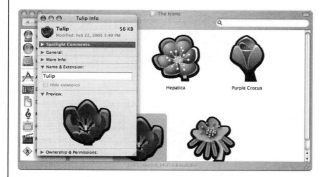

FIGURE 9.9 Select the icon in the General section of the Info window to copy it.

Then open another Finder window and navigate to a point where you can see the folder, file, or application icon you want to customize. Select the item and open the Info window as you did for the custom icon. Select the icon at the top of the Info window, and choose Edit, Paste from the menu.

The custom icon now appears in place of the standard icon both in the Info window and on your desktop.

If you decide you'd rather use the standard icons, simply select the item with the icon you've switched, open the Info window, and select and delete the custom icon. The original icon will appear as if it had never been gone.

If you decide you want to replace all your system icons with one custom icon set, download CandyBar from the Icon Factory web site. This application works with specially packaged icon sets to change all your icons at once.

Summary

This chapter discussed the basics of adding new software—from finding what you need to downloading and installing it. Although we focused on easy-to-obtain, downloadable software, the issues we discussed also apply to software you purchase on CD or DVD. Remember that, in Mac OS X, it matters where you place new applications on your system if you want to share with other users of the computer.

CHAPTER 10

Using iWork—Pages and Keynote

This chapter briefly introduces iWork, a software package from Apple that you may want to purchase for use with Mac OS X. iWork consists of two applications, Pages and Keynote. Pages is a word processing application with built-in templates for documents of all kinds. Keynote is specifically for creating stylish onscreen presentations, including animations and multimedia.

Pages

Pages is a word processor and layout tool for designing polished publications, such as newsletters, reports, and brochures. It's greatest strength is a library of templates, most with an assortment of page styles that you can use to customize your document. An example of a document created with Pages is shown in Figure 10.1.

FIGURE 10.1
A sample catalog created in Pages—notice the distinct, yet coordinating, page styles.

> In addition to Pages, Apple also sells AppleWorks, a versatile application for word processing, spreadsheets, and drawing.

The Pages Toolbar

Along the top of the window in Figure 10.1 is the default Pages toolbar, which offers easy access to many of Pages' most useful features. (We discuss them in order, left-to-right, as they appear in Figure 10.1.)

Did you Know?

> You can choose which tools appear in the toolbar by choosing View, Customize Toolbar from the menu. A window containing icons for many text and object formatting tools appears so that you can drag additional tools to the toolbar. (You can remove any tools you don't use by dragging them out of the toolbar.) It you add more tools than there is room for in the toolbar, check the box labeled Use Small Sizes to shrink the tool icons.

The first two tools apply to the pages in your document and their basic layout.

▶ Pages—Adds a new page to the end of your document. As shown in Figure 10.2, clicking the Pages tool reveals an assortment of page styles for the template you selected when you first created your document.

FIGURE 10.2
An array of page styles perfectly coordinated for each template.

▶ Columns—Sets the number of columns for a text object or page.

You can see how columns are set up, even on blank pages, by choosing View, Show Layout from the menu.

The next set of tools enables you to control the appearance of text.

▶ Style—Displays basic text styles for your chosen template, such as Heading and Body Text.

▶ List—Displays options for creating bulleted and numbered lists.

Choose View, Show Styles Drawer from the menu to open a drawer on the right side of the Pages window to show the styles and list types.

The next two items are used to work with objects (texts, shapes, tables, and charts) and the text that surrounds them.

▶ Objects—Inserts a new text object, shape, table, or chart that you can then position and customize.

▶ Wrap—Displays options for how nearby text will flow around a selected object.

The four tools on the right side of the toolbar offer even greater control over your document than the preceding tools.

Items in the toolbar marked with a downward-pointing arrow open a menu of options; those without arrows open in a separate window.

▶ Inspector—Opens the Inspector window (see Figure 10.3), which has separate sections for different elements of your document, such as pages, text, and objects. (See the next section, "The Pages Inspector," for details.)

▶ Media—Opens the Media Browser (see Figure 10.4), which connects to your iTunes library, iPhoto library, and your Movies folder.

FIGURE 10.3
The Inspector window with the Document pane visible.

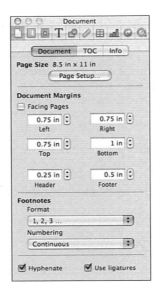

FIGURE 10.4
The Media Browser links directly to your iPhoto library.

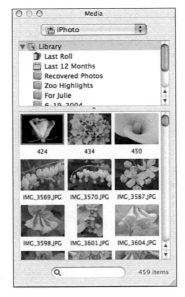

By the Way

It seems odd that you can add audio or movies to your Pages document, but it is true. (Perhaps these features exist in Pages because they exist in Keynote, which has a very similar structure.) If you want these multimedia elements to play for someone on another computer, you need to select Copy Audio and Movies into Document when you save the document.

▶ Colors—Launches the standard Mac OS X Colors window, where you can set colors for selected objects or text.

▶ Fonts—Opens the standard Mac OS X Fonts window, where you can select any font installed on your system. (Refer to Chapter 12, "Printing, Faxing, and Working with Fonts," for details.)

The Pages Inspector

The Inspector window in Pages enables you to perform fine customization of elements in a document. After you've added a page or an object (such as text, a shape, chart, or table), you can select it, open the Inspector window, and choose the option containing the settings you want to customize.

Make sure that you've chosen the proper Inspector option for the selected object, or none of the settings will be active. If all the settings appear grayed out, or faded, you may need to try a different object or different Inspector to make the changes you intend.

Watch Out!

The sections of the Inspector window are

▶ Document Inspector—Controls document-wide attributes. In the Document section, shown in Figure 10.4, set page size and margins. You can also choose a footnote style, whether to hyphenate, and whether to allow use of ligatures if supported by a given font. In the TOC section, choose which text to automatically add to a table of contents by selecting the font style of headings used in your document. In the Info section, label your document with information about its author and content, as well as view statistics about your document, such as word count.

A *ligature* is a feature available in some fonts that combines two or more characters into one for a more custom appearance.

By the Way

▶ Layout Inspector—Under the Layout settings, view details about column settings and column margin. Under the Section settings, choose how pages are numbered and which pages have different headers and footers. (For example, you can decide that left and right pages show different information.)

▶ Wrap Inspector—Offers additional control for how text wraps around objects in documents.

▶ Text Inspector—Controls color and alignment, spacing, and margins, as well as bullets and numbering of text.

▶ Graphic Inspector—Related to the characteristics of the object currently selected. The sections in this pane include Fill, Stroke, Shadow, and Opacity, which is used to change the transparency of an object to allow objects and the background behind it to show through.

▶ Metrics Inspector—Controls the size and placement of objects. The sections in this pane are File Info, Size, Position, Rotate, and Flip. (The Size and Position settings are set in pixels, which is a standard measure for onscreen graphics. Also, the Position is given by x (horizontal) and y (vertical) coordinates relative to the top-left corner of the slide.)

▶ Table Inspector—Changes the characteristics of tables. Use the Rows and Columns sections to set the number and size of each. Further customize table appearance by changing the Cell Border options.

▶ Chart Inspector—Changes the characteristics of a chart, including the chart type and details of data display.

▶ Hyperlink Inspector—Enables you to link text or objects to a website, another page in the current document, or an email address for sending messages.

By the Way

To link to another page in the current document, you first need to add a bookmark. To do this, select the text you want to bookmark and then choose Insert, Bookmark from the menu. Any bookmarks you add then appear in the Hyperlink Inspector when you choose to enable a bookmark or view the Bookmarks section.

▶ QuickTime Inspector—Sets various aspects of an inserted QuickTime movie, including repeat status and volume.

Creating and Customizing a Document in Pages

Integrated templates are one of Pages' strongest features, so we focus attention on them.

When you open Pages or choose File, New from the menu, a dialog window appears so you can select a template, as shown in Figure 10.5. When you make a selection, a single page based on that template opens. In that page, you can change the placeholder text and images to fit your needs.

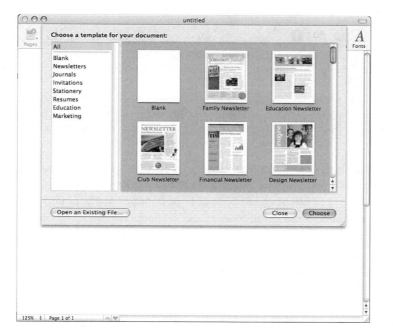

FIGURE 10.5
Select a template for your project.

If you have chosen a document type other than a card, envelope, or invitation, you can insert additional pages with layout that coordinate with the template you have chosen. For example, if you create a newsletter, Pages starts you with only the front page; you choose the interior pages and a back cover to complete the document.

To insert a page, click the Pages icon in the toolbar to open a menu of options for your current template (see Figure 10.2). Select an option and the page is added following the page currently selected.

> There is no simple way to delete or move pages in Pages after they have been added. (The not-so-simple ways are explained below.) To avoid difficulties, outline your project before you begin so you know which pages you need and the order in which you need them to be.

Watch
Out!

Delete or Move a Page

To delete a page, you delete all the objects and text on the page. When it is empty, the page disappears.

Pages are made up of two items: text and images that are arranged on the page itself and objects (such as shapes, graphs, and additional images and text boxes) that are "floating on top" of the page. Items that are on the page itself are aligned according to the page margins and column settings; objects can be positioned anywhere on a page.

To tell the difference between the two, try to select an item. If white squares, technically called *resize handles*, appear at the corners, the item is an object. If text highlights or gray squares appear around an image, the item is on the page itself.

To delete all the objects, select each one and press the Delete key on your keyboard. (You can select more than one object at a time by holding down the Command key as you click on the objects.) Any text that is on the page itself, rather than part of an object, remains. You must also select and delete this text.

Watch Out! Do not use the command Select All from the Edit menu instead of selecting each item on the page—this selects all the objects in your entire document, which you probably don't want to delete.

When the page is entirely blank, it disappears. If it doesn't disappear, choose View, Show Invisibles to locate and remove any hidden characters, such as spaces or tabs, that you may have missed. You may also need to remove an initial paragraph break. To do this, place your cursor at the top of the blank page and press the Delete key on your keyboard.

By the Way If you are nervous about deleting portions of your document, save before you begin the process. If anything goes wrong, you can close without saving and open the original copy.

To move an existing page, you need to copy the objects and text it contains and paste them into a new page. You then delete the original page.

Following are the basic steps for moving the content of a page to a different location in the document:

1. Begin by inserting a new page in the position where you want it. If possible, choose a text page with no other objects from the Pages tool in the toolbar—it will have the basic column layout of your template without any objects.

2. Go to the page you want to move, select an object, and choose Edit, Copy from the menu. Next, return to the new page you created, click to place your cursor, and choose Edit, Paste from the menu. If the pasted object is not exactly where it was on the original page, you may have to select it and move it

into position. Choose View, Show Layout to see the column guides for more precise positioning.

3. Repeat the process to transfer all the objects to the new page. To speed up the process, now is a good time to learn the key command for copying, Command-C, and for pasting, Command-V, so you won't have to open the menu twice for each item.

You can select multiple objects by holding down the Command key as you click them. However, you can't select the text in the actual page along with the objects. Also, if you select and copy more than one object at a time, objects sometimes appear on separate pages when you paste. (This happens most often when one or more of the objects span multiple columns.)

4. When all the objects are in place, select the text from your original page and copy and paste it to the new page. When your new page matches your original, you can return to the original page and delete it as described previously.

Work with Placeholder Images

Nearly all of Pages' templates include spaces for images, which are temporarily filled by placeholder images.

To replace a placeholder image with your own image, drag an image from the Finder or the iPhoto pane of the Media Browser onto the placeholder image.

The image with which you replace a placeholder image is itself a placeholder image, so you can replace it if you change you mind. If you want to make an image permanent, choose Format, Advanced, Define as Image Placeholder. (A check mark in front of that option indicates that an image is currently set as a placeholder.)

If the placeholder is surrounded by text, it doesn't matter what size or shape of image you insert—the text rewraps to fit. To resize an image, select it and drag one of the selection handles that appear at it corners and edges, as shown in Figure 10.6. To delete a placeholder image altogether, select it and press the Delete key on your keyboard.

FIGURE 10.6
Click and drag a
selection handle
to resize an
image.

You can resize an object to an exact size in the Metrics Inspector. You can also return an object to its original size by clicking the Original Size button in the Metrics Inspector.

In some templates, images that are a different size from the original placeholder image require extra formatting to fit the page's layout. For example, if the original placeholder image was square, a standard, uncropped photo doesn't fill exactly the same area. To fit a new photo into the square space, you need to mask part of the image.

An image can be masked only if it is fixed to the page so it doesn't move as text flows across the page. (By the way, you can still resize an image that has been fixed to the page.) To fix an object to the page, open the Inspector window and select the Wrap Inspector (see Figure 10.7). Then select the image you want to mask and click the option Fixed on Page from the Object Placement settings.

FIGURE 10.7
Use the Wrap
Inspector to fix
an image to the
page before
masking it.

When the image is fixed to the page, follow these steps to mask it:

1. Select image and choose Format, Mask from the menu. As shown in Figure 10.8, a dotted border appears around the image with selection hands for resizing.

2. To reposition the mask on the photo, click in the unclouded area and drag it to highlight the area of the photo you want to emphasize.

3. To set the mask, click outside of the image.

If you want to revert to the original form of the image, select it and choose Format, Unmask from the menu.

FIGURE 10.8
Change the
position and
size of the
mask.

Did you Know?

> When a masked image is selected, its borders appear as dotted lines, so you can easily tell if the full image is not visible.

Replace Placeholder Text

To replace placeholder text, either within the page or as part of an object, click to select it and press the Delete key on your keyboard. The layout and text style are retained to format the text you type in its place.

By the Way

> When you delete placeholder text, other objects in the text area may shift positions. For instance, boxes for pull quotes or a newsletter table of contents may move to fill the open area left when the placeholder text was removed. Do not be alarmed. As you type your own text, the other objects move to make room. Also, if you want to manually position one of these objects, select it and drag it to the spot you want it to fill.

If you type more text than will fit in a template, a blank page with the same column layout as the template is added immediately after it to hold the overflow.

Watch Out!

> The new blank page is linked to the page before it because the text from the first page continues on it; Pages does not allow you to insert a page between the two pages. You can, however, add a page after the overflow page and then cut and paste the text from the overflow page into the page template you chose. When the overflow page is empty, Pages removes it.

Style Text

After adding your text, you can leave it in the style Pages applied, choose a paragraph style created by Pages for your template, or change individual words or lines of the text.

To view the paragraph styles designed for your current template, choose View, Show Styles Drawer from the menu to open the Styles drawer shown in Figure 10.9. When you select a text element in your document, the style applied to it highlights in the Styles drawer. To apply a style, select the text you want to change and then click a paragraph style from the list.

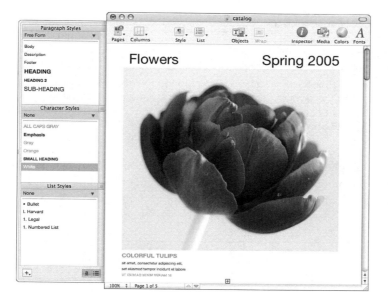

FIGURE 10.9
The Styles drawer makes choosing between styles easier.

Some templates, such as School Report and Term Paper, automatically generate a table of contents by recognizing the heading styles used where sections begin. This features works especially well if you have been consistent in your use of section heading styles, but you can also add defined styles to the list of styles under the TOC pane of the Document Inspector.

Did you Know?

To make changes to a default paragraph style, select text displaying the style you want to modify, select the style from the list, and click the arrow that appears to the right of the selected style. A menu opens in which you can choose the option Create New Paragraph Style from the Selection, and Pages prompts you to name your new style. To make changes to the new style's appearance, use the tools in the Text Inspector or the Font and Text items of the Format menu.

To change the typeface, choose Format, Fonts, Show Fonts from the menu to open the standard Mac OS X Font window. Select a new font family, typeface, and size. You can also apply to selected text bold, italic, underline, and outline, or increase or decrease font size, by choosing Format, Fonts and the appropriate option from the menu.

To change alignment options, choose Format, Text and the desired alignment option from the menu. To create or remove text that is inset from the normal page or column margins, choose Format, Text, Increase/Decrease List Indent Level.

You can apply style from one section to another selection by using the Copy Character Style and Copy Paragraph Style options under the Format menu. These options enable you to select text that appears as you want it, copy its style, and "paste" only the style to another area of text.

If you want to change all instances of a paragraph style easily, select one instance, click the arrow after the style that has been applied to it, and choose Select All Uses Of *(style)* from the menu. You can then apply a change to all selected text in one step.

If the paragraph styles provided don't meet your needs, or if you want to change an isolated word or phrase within a paragraph, you can make other changes to the text of your document. Select the text you want to change, and use the Font and Text items of the Format menu described above.

If you choose not to use the defined paragraph styles, remember that less is more when it comes to applying fonts to achieve professional-looking documents.

Importing and Exporting Documents with Pages

Pages opens Microsoft Word, AppleWorks, and rich-text format documents with ease. Choose File, Open from the menu and select the file you want Pages to open.

If you want to export a Pages document to share with those who don't have access to Pages, choose File, Export from the menu. The window shown in Figure 10.10 appears, in which you can select an export option. Click the Next button to name the exported document and choose a location in which to save it.

The options for exporting are

▶ PDF—Saves a document so its layout is perfectly preserved, but the resulting file is less easily edited than those of the other options.

▶ Word—Converts the document to a format that Microsoft Word can read and edit.

▶ HTML—Exports an HTML version of the document that can be viewed in a web browser, such as Safari. (A folder containing the images is also created.)

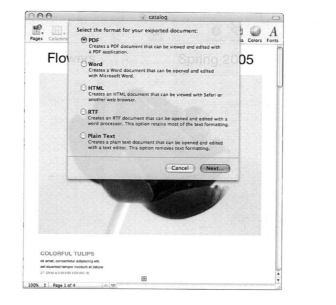

FIGURE 10.10
Exporting a
Pages docu-
ment.

> The way web pages are laid out is much different from the way word processing documents are, and the HTML version of a Pages document may require extra editing to look as you intended. (HTML documents can be edited in the TextEdit application discussed in Chapter 6, "Using Calculator, Grapher, Preview, and TextEdit.") Always test the HTML documents created by Pages in a web browser before assuming they are ready to show to others.

Watch Out!

▶ RTF—Creates a rich-text format document that keeps most of the formatting, but can be opened by a variety of applications, including TextEdit, Word, and AppleWorks.

▶ Plain Text—Exports only the text and keeps no text styling; plain text documents can be opened by all basic text editor applications, such as Microsoft's Notepad.

Pages Preferences

To view the application preferences, choose Pages, Preferences from the menu.

▶ For New Document—Choose whether the Theme Chooser appears each time you create a new document, or settle on a default theme.

▶ Editing—Enable or disable use of smart quotes, display of size and position of elements when moving them, and reduction of images to fit on slides.

▶ Invisibles—Choose a color with which to display invisible attributes, such as section breaks and paragraph marks.

▶ Hyperlinks—Text that matches the pattern of an email or web address is linked automatically.

▶ Ruler Units—Set the units that are used by the rulers provided by Keynote. It also lets you choose to number outward from the center of a ruler and to display ruler units as a percentage.

▶ Alignment Guides—Choose a color with which to display alignment guides used when placing objects. Also, set whether guides mark the center of the selected object(s) and/or the edges.

Keynote

Keynote is a flexible tool for creating elegant presentations involving slide animation, images, audio, text, charts and graphs, and even QuickTime movies, such as those from iMovie. You can also use it to create non-linear slideshows where viewers can choose their own path.

Figure 10.11 shows the Keynote interface in Navigator view, with the current slide and slide organizer visible. Under the View menu, you can choose to view only the slide or to show the outline (all the text you've added to your slideshow) in place of the slide organizer.

FIGURE 10.11
The Keynote interface in Navigator view.

The Keynote Toolbar

The Keynote Toolbar, shown above in Figure 10.11, contains several groupings of tools to help you create presentations. . These tools are covered in the order in which they appear, from left-to-right.

The first grouping of buttons affects the slides in your presentation. Here are the buttons in this group:

- ▶ New—Adds a new slide after the currently selected slide.

- ▶ Delete—Removes the currently selected slide.

- ▶ Play—Plays the slideshow as it currently exists in full-screen mode. (To exit a slideshow and return to Keynote, press the Esc—or Escape key—on your keyboard.)

The next three items relate to slide setup and how you view the content of your presentation.

- ▶ View—Changes the viewing mode between Navigator (shown in Figure 10.11), Outline, and Slide Only. You can also view the slide masters for each slide, which are discussed next, or open a Note pane at the bottom of the Keynote window, in which you can type comments that don't appear inside the presentation.

- ▶ Themes—Opens the Themes window (shown in Figure 10.12), where you can choose a theme to apply to your presentation. (Themes in Keynote are like templates in Pages.)

- ▶ Masters—View a list of "master" slide layouts for the current theme. Masters show the placement and style of all the elements on a slide; you can edit the masters to change your slideshow's appearance to suit your needs.

The next group of buttons enables you to add objects and text to your slide:

- ▶ Text—Creates a text object. The text object appears in the center of the screen with the word "Text" in it; you can drag it where you want and double-click to type your own text.

FIGURE 10.12
Choose a
theme to give
all the slides in
your presenta-
tion a unified
appearance.

▶ Shapes—Creates a shape object. The options are line, line with arrowhead, line with two arrowheads, rectangle, rounded rectangle, oval, triangle, right triangle (which has one 90-degree angle), arrow, double arrow, diamond, and quote bubble. Shapes appear in the center of the screen; you can drag them where you want and customize them by selecting them and dragging one of their selection handles.

Did you Know?

You can resize, reshape, or change the direction a shape faces with the selection handles. To change a shape's direction, click on the selection handle opposite where you want the shape to flip and drag in the direction you want the shape to flip.

▶ Table—Creates a table in which to organize information. Resize tables as you would a shape. Use the Table Inspector to set the number and size of rows and columns; customizing table dimensions is covered in the section on the Inspector window later in this chapter.

▶ Chart—Opens a Chart Data Editor window in which to enter information you want to display in a graph. You can customize a chart by using the Chart Inspector window, which is examined later in the chapter.

The next set of tools is used to position objects:

▶ Group—Used to link two or more objects that you want to treat as one item; this is useful if you've carefully positioned a set of shapes or text boxes and want to move them on the slide.

Did you Know?

> To select more than one object in a slide, hold down the Command key as you click.

▶ Ungroup—Used to separate objects that you've grouped.

▶ Front—Puts the selected object on top of all other objects in a slide while leaving it where it was positioned.

▶ Back—Puts the selected object underneath all other objects in a slide while leaving it where it was positioned.

The group of options at the far right opens additional windows you may need to customize your slides. (These tools may seem familiar because they are very similar to their counterparts in Pages.)

▶ Inspector—Opens the Inspector window, which contains specific tools for various slide elements. (See the upcoming section, "The Keynote Inspector," for more information.)

▶ Media—Opens the Media Browser, where you can choose to insert content from your iTunes library, iPhoto library, or your Movies folder.

▶ Colors—Opens the Mac OS X Colors window, where you can choose colors to apply to objects and text.

▶ Fonts—Opens the Mac OS X Fonts window, as discussed in Chapter 12, "Printing, Faxing, and Working with Fonts."

Now, let's move on to the Inspector window, which contains additional sets of useful tools.

The Keynote Inspector

Keynote's Inspector window is almost identical to the Inspector window for Pages (discussed earlier in the section "The Pages Inspector"). To customize a slide or object, select it and open the appropriate pane of the Inspector to reveal related settings.

The sections of the Inspector window that differ from those in the Inspector window for Pages are

▶ Document Inspector—Enables you to set whether a presentation plays automatically upon opening, whether it loops, and whether if is self-playing or "normal." You can also set the size of the slides to fit the screen on which they play and choose music from your iTunes library to accompany the visuals.

▶ Slide Inspector—Under Transitions, decide which animation effect to use to transition from the current slide to the next one and set duration, direction, what will trigger the transition, and any delay before it starts. Under Appearance, change the slide master for a selected slide or choose whether title or slide body text is visible. The Background settings enable you to make the background a color, gradient, or image fill—or to leave the background empty.

You can change the background image of a selected slide by dragging any image file into the image well in the Background section of the Slide Inspector pane.

▶ Build Inspector—Controls animation effects used to make objects appear (Build In) and disappear (Build Out) from a slide. Settings, as shown in Figure 10.13, include Effect, Order, Direction, and Delivery. Click the Automatic Builds button to open a drawer where you can choose to trigger builds with a click or have them start automatically.

FIGURE 10.13
Animate objects and text in the Build Inspector.

▶ Hyperlink Inspector—Enables you to link text or objects to another slide in the current presentation, another presentation, a website, or an email address for sending messages.

Creating a Presentation in Keynote

When you first launch Keynote or create a new document, you are shown the Theme Chooser dialog, as shown in Figure 10.14.

FIGURE 10.14
Pick a theme to begin designing your presentation.

> In the Keynote preferences, you can choose a theme to automatically use for new presentations and when Keynote is launched. If you make this change, you don't see the Theme Chooser dialog unless you select Choose Theme from the File menu.

Did you Know?

After your theme is in place, you just click the placeholder text to replace it with your own. The theme's font colors and styles are applied automatically, but you can adjust them to your tastes by using the Text Inspector, as described earlier.

Work with Object Placeholders in Keynote

If you've chosen a theme with an object placeholder, you can insert your own image (or even your own movie).

To easily add a photo from your iPhoto library, open the Media Browser by clicking its icon in the toolbar and selecting iPhoto from its pop-up menu. You can then drag any image into the placeholder space. If the image you want to add is not in your iPhoto library, you can open the folder containing it and drag it into the placeholder space. (You can add a movie in QuickTime-compatible format, such as something you've produced with iMovie, in much the same way. See Chapters 24 through 28 for coverage of iMovie.)

> If you insert a movie into the object placeholder, you can change settings for that movie, such as volume and repeat, in the QuickTime Inspector.

You may have to scale your image to fit the space provided by Keynote. To do this, select the image, grab any of the white resize handles that appear, and drag them to reduce the image's size.

Watch Out!

> You can increase a photo's size in a presentation by dragging the resize handles, but if you enlarge a photo too much the image quality declines as the pixels that make up the photo spread out to fill the space.

If you want to add an image to a slide, but only want a portion of the image to show onscreen, you can mask the image. Masking is similar to cropping a photo, except masking hides portions of a photo but doesn't alter the original.

To mask an image you've already added to a slide, follow these steps:

1. Select the image and choose Format, Mask from the menu. An area with clouded edges appears on top of the image so you can change the area of the photo you want to show, as shown in Figure 10.15.

2. Click in the unfaded area of the mask to reposition it on the photo, or click on the faded area to reposition the photo within the mask borders.

3. If you so desire, change the masks' dimensions by dragging the resize handles—if they are not visible, click near the mask border to reveal them. (Be aware, however, that if your mask isn't similar in shape and proportion to the placeholder space you are working with, your image may not fit seamlessly into the slide layout.)

4. When you are satisfied with the portion of the photo that is showing, click outside your slide to set your mask.

After your image is masked, you may need to resize the image to fill the placeholder space in the slide. To remove masking, select the masked image and choose Format, Unmask from the menu.

FIGURE 10.15
Reposition your
photo within the
mask area.

Add and Move Slides in Keynote

To add other slides to your presentation, click the + button at the upper left. A new
slide of the same kind as the one you already have is added.

If you want to change the slide's layout from a title slide layout to something else,
click the Masters tool in the toolbar to reveal the page types available for your chosen theme, as shown in Figure 10.16. With your theme in place, you can then
change the text or photos as discussed previously.

FIGURE 10.16
Choose a slide
style with the
Masters tool.

If you want to rearrange your slides, make sure you are in Navigator view, previously shown in Figure 10.11. In the slide organizer along the left side, select a thumbnail image of one slide and drag it up or down in the list. A blue line appears as you drag to show where the slide would be placed if you released the slide.

To move several slides at the same time, hold down the Command key as you select them.

If you've added a slide, but change your mind about using it, select the unwanted slide so it appears in the slide area and click the – button at the upper left.

Add Effects in Keynote—Slide Transitions and Builds

After you've got at least 2 slides, you can add a transition effect for switching between them. To do this:

1. Open the Slide Inspector, shown in Figure 10.17.

FIGURE 10.17
Set transitions
between slides.

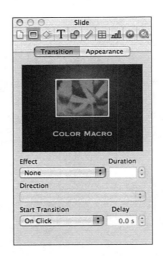

When a transition has been added to a slide, a small triangle appears in the lower-right corner of its thumbnail in the slide organizer.

2. Choose an effect, a duration, whether the transition happens automatically or on click, and a delay. For some effects, you may also be able to set a direction, such as whether the Iris transition makes its path in or out.

Many of the transition effects can be also used to make objects and text appear on a slide with their own timing and style. These are known as Build Effects, and you set them using the Build Inspector, shown previously in Figure 10.13. To apply build effects:

1. Select an object or text and open the Build Inspector.

2. Choose whether you want to add a "build in"—how the object appears—or a "build out"—how the object disappears. (You can add both, just not at the same time!)

3. Next, choose an effect and the order in which it will occur in relation to the other builds for that slide. For some effects, you may have the option to change direction or delivery settings as well.

> If you've selected a text object to which you want to add a build, you see many more Effects than for images and movies. Keynote includes effects that can be applied to individual letters or words that simply don't apply other objects.

By the Way

After you've added a couple of builds, you can fine-tune their order and add automatic timing. To do this, click the Set Automatic Builds button to open a drawer showing all the builds you've added to this slide. Drag a row to reorder the builds, or select one to change the Start Build pop-up menu from On Click to Automatically.

For builds following first one, you will have the option to tie their start with the build that came before—for example, you may see the options Automatically With Build 1 or Automatically After Build 1. (Note that the options shown depend on whether two builds can be performed at the same time.)

Customize Slide Masters in Keynote

Earlier, you learned how to use the Masters tool to choose a slide layout. Although there are a variety of default slide options for each theme, sometimes you may want to customize their layout or visual design for your specific project.

If you want to create your own page layout, follow these basic steps:

1. Click the Inspector tool in the toolbar to open the Inspector window.

2. Select the Slide Inspector and reveal the Appearance settings, as shown in Figure 10.18.

FIGURE 10.18
Create your own
slide layout.

3. Choose a starting point for your new layout from the list of existing page layouts—choose Blank if you want to start with an empty slide.

4. Next, check or uncheck the Title, Body, Object Placeholder, or Slide Number
   option to add or remove them.

5. When you have chosen the elements you want, work in the slide space to
   arrange and resize them.

Watch Out!

Some of the themes include slides with backgrounds specially designed for their
object placeholders. These kinds of placeholders appear with a border or frame
that is built into the slide background. You can't remove them from a slide even
with the Appearance settings in the Slide Inspector. If you can't get the desired
appearance with such slides, try choosing a different slide layout or begin with a
blank page.

If you make changes, but then change your mind, you can choose Format, Reapply
Master to Slide to return to the default layout of the slide type you originally chose.

Did you Know?

In addition to modifying the slide master for a single slide, you can modify an
existing slide master and save it for use later. To do this, click the View tool and
choose Show Slide Master. Choose the master slide you want to change from the
upper portion of the slide organizer on the left and then choose Slide, New Master
Slide from the menu. Give your new master slide a title and use the Appearance
settings of the Slide Inspector, as you learned earlier, to edit the slide.

Playing and Exporting Keynote Presentations

As you are working on your presentation, you will probably want to preview it to ensure that it looks as good full-screen as it does in the workspace.

To play a slideshow, click the Play button at the upper left. If you haven't added transitions, effects, or at least automatic start events, you need to click to progress through the slide show. Your slideshow plays on your screen until it reaches the end. If you want to exit the slideshow before that, press the ESC key on your keyboard.

Use the back arrow key on your keyboard to replay slides without stopping and restarting the slideshow.

If you want to automatically skip over a slide without deleting it, select the slide and choose Slide, Skip Slide from the menu. (If you want to restore a skipped slide, choose Slide, Don't Skip Slide.)

Did you Know?

When presenting your slideshow for an audience, you may want to set additional play options, such as automatically starting the slideshow or changing the screen resolution for better display with a projector. These settings and more can be found in the Document Inspector, shown in Figure 10.19.

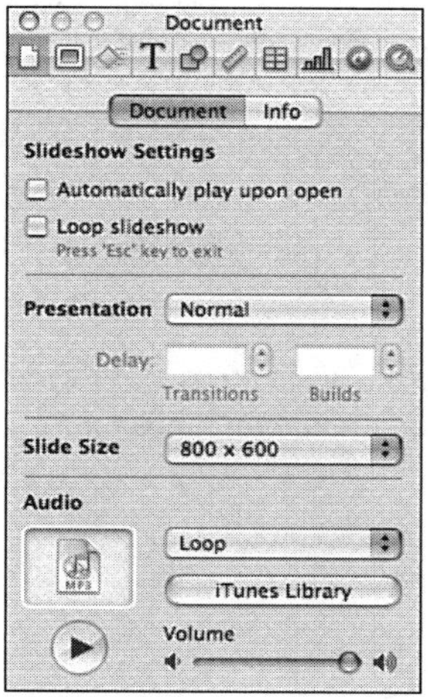

FIGURE 10.19
Set how your slideshow will play in the Document Inspector.

Under Slideshow settings, choose whether to Automatically Play on Open and whether to Loop Slideshow.

In the Presentations settings, choose whether your document will be played as a normal slideshow, a self-playing slideshow (with automatic transitions), or as hyperlinks only (where viewers click onscreen objects to move between slides).

Use Slide Size to set the slide resolution to optimize display—several default sizes matching common screen resolutions are provided, but you can customize the size if you'd prefer.

With the Audio settings, you can choose background music from your iTunes library, set whether it loops, and its volume.

In addition to the document-specific settings in the Document Inspector, there are also settings for slideshows in general that you can set in the Slideshow section of the application preferences. To view them, choose Keynote, Preferences from the menu.

Under the Slideshow section of the preferences, you can elect to scale your presentation to fit the display, to exit automatically after the last slide, and to show the mouse pointer when the mouse moves or only on slides containing links. You can also choose whether to show your slideshow on the primary or a secondary display, though this option may require additional setup in the Display settings of the System Preferences. (See Chapter 11, "Working with Displays and Peripheral Devices," for more information about the Display System Preferences.)

By the Way

> If you're using a PowerBook or another model of Mac that supports dual displays, you can choose to show your presentation on one screen and your own notes on another that only you can see. You can configure the way these notes appear in the Presenter Display settings of the application Preferences.

When your slideshow is complete—including transitions, background music, and any auto-play settings—you can export it for easy distribution and nearly fool-proof display.

To export your slideshow, choose File, Export from the menu. You see the window displayed in Figure 10.20, where you can choose a format.

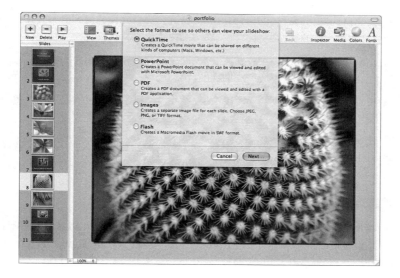

FIGURE 10.20
Pick a format
for export.

Keynote Preferences

It's important to talk about some of the application preferences you haven't already seen before your tour of Keynote is complete. To view the preferences, choose Keynote, Preferences from the menu.

The General section includes the following application-wide settings:

▶ For New Document—Choose whether the Theme Chooser appears each time you create a new document, or choose a default theme.

▶ Editing—Enable or disable use of smart quotes, display of size and position of elements when they are moved, and reduction of images to fit on slides.

▶ Saving—Choose whether to back up the previous version when saving in order to keep the previously-saved version as well as the newest version. Also choose whether to copy images and movies into the document instead of simply linking to them, and whether to copy theme images into the document. (These options are important for people who want to circulate a presentation as a working document to other people with Keynote who may not have exactly the same supporting files available on their computers; however, be aware that making copies of a lot of images and movies can take up a lot of system resources.)

▶ Hyperlinks—Choose whether to show underline on hyperlinks and whether text that looks like an email or web address is linked automatically.

▶ Outline View—Set a font and font size for use with outline view.

The Rulers preferences control the units that are used by the rulers and guides provided by Keynote. It also lets you choose a color for the alignment guides.

The Slideshow and Presenter Display preference were discussed earlier in the section "Playing and Exporting Presentations."

Summary

Apple's iWork is a software package that consists of two applications: Pages and Keynote. Pages is a combination word-processing/page layout application that comes with templates with multiple-page designs for newsletters, reports, and catalogues. Keynote is an easy-to-use presentation builder, with a built-in set of themes. These applications have similar interfaces and features, and both offer ways for sharing their files which other users who may not have access these applications.

CHAPTER 11

Working with Displays and Peripheral Devices

Your Macintosh is a fantastic tool for communicating visually. The first half of the chapter walks you through the process of calibrating your system's display and introduces ColorSync, your Mac's built-in utility for ensuring consistent color reproduction on different output devices. You learn everything you need to know about color calibration with ColorSync and how to work with Mac OS X's display settings.

In the second half of the chapter, you learn about connecting peripheral devices, such as printers, digital cameras, and external hard drives, to your Mac. You also learn a bit about the common connection standards USB and FireWire.

Let's begin by exploring settings for displays.

Configuring Displays

To change settings for your display, be it a cathode ray tube (CRT) monitor or a liquid crystal display (LCD) screen, there's one convenient place to do it: the Displays pane in the Hardware category of your System Preferences. This pane is a bit unusual in that it can change drastically depending on what type of monitor is connected to your system. Users of Apple's CRTs see geometry information for adjusting image tilt, size, and so forth. The exact display depends on the monitor type. Those who have more than one monitor can arrange the monitors' locations on the desktop and choose where the menu bar appears.

Resolution and Colors

To access your Display settings, open the Displays pane of System Preferences and make sure that the Displays button is highlighted at the top of the pane. Here you can see the basic settings for your monitor—color depth, resolution, and refresh rate—as shown in Figure 11.1. Again, what you see might vary slightly depending on the type of monitor you're using.

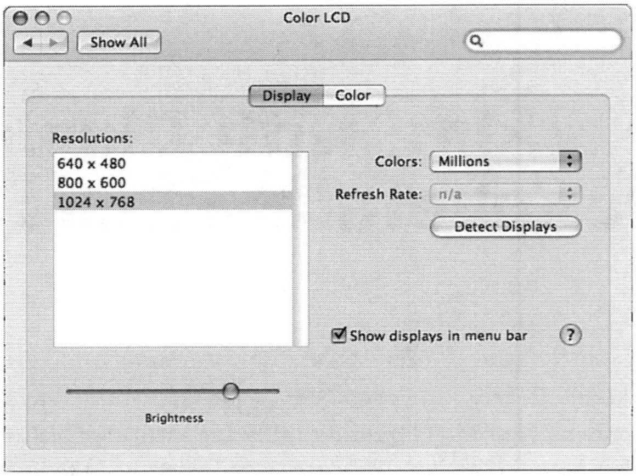

FIGURE 11.1
The Display
section of the
Displays System
Preferences
panel controls
monitor colors
and resolution.

Available resolutions for your display are listed in the left column. Choosing a new resolution immediately updates your machine's display. If you plug a monitor into your computer after it has already booted (such as on a PowerBook or a PowerMac G5 with a dual-monitor video card), you can click Detect Displays to force your Macintosh to recognize the new monitor and start displaying on it.

Displays Menu Extra

If you find yourself switching colors or resolutions often, click the Show Displays in Menu Bar check box. This activates a menu extra, shown in Figure 11.2, that makes it simple to switch between different settings. The menu extra displays recent modes (resolution/refresh/color settings) that you've used—much as the Apple menu shows you recent applications and documents. To change the number of recent modes displayed, use the pop-up menu. The default is three.

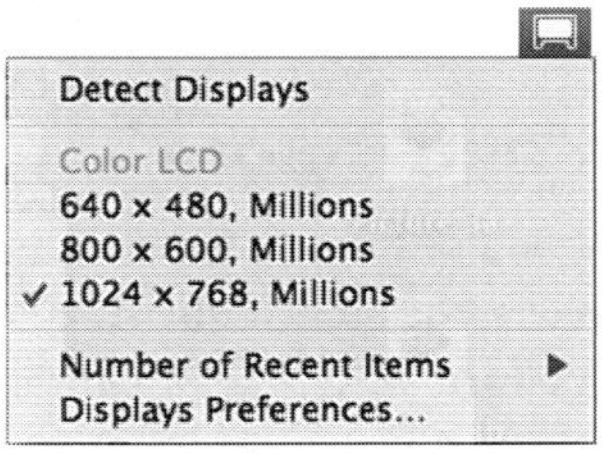

FIGURE 11.2
The Displays
menu extra
provides instant
access to color
and resolution
settings.

Multiple Monitors

If you're lucky enough to have multiple monitors to connect to your system, Mac OS X enables you to use them all simultaneously as a single large display. Note that you still need a video card for each monitor you're connecting or dual display support from a single video card. Users of iBooks and iMacs see a mirroring of their desktop on any added monitors rather than an addition of a new desktop area.

Mac OS X automatically recognizes when multiple monitors are connected to the system and adjusts the Displays Preferences panel accordingly by adding an Arrangement button at the top of the pane. For example, Figure 11.3 shows the settings for a PowerBook G4 with an external VGA monitor connected.

> There's no need to reboot to connect an external display. Just plug it in, click Detect Displays from the System Preferences pane or menu extra, and start mousing!

By the Way

If you click the Arrangement button, you can control how the two monitors interact by dragging the corresponding rectangles. To move a monitor so that its portion of the desktop falls on the left or right of another monitor, just drag it to the left or right in the Arrangement settings section. You can also move the menu bar by clicking its representation in the Arrangement section and dragging it to the monitor on which you want it displayed. The changes you make to the arrangement take effect immediately; no need to reboot!

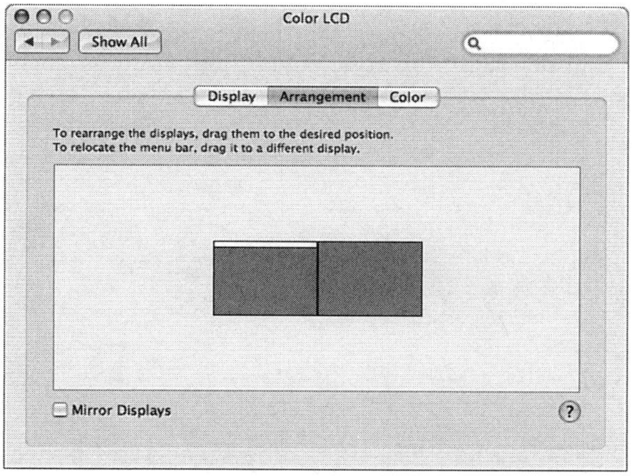

FIGURE 11.3
The Displays System Preferences pane changes to handle multiple monitors.

If you have multiple monitors connected, you'll also notice that each monitor has its own copy of the Displays System Preferences pane displayed in the center of the screen. By using these separate panes, you can change the color and resolution for each display independently. You should also see a small "overlapping rectangle" button (visible in Figure 11.3) displayed in the upper-right corner of the pane. Clicking this button moves the configuration pane from the other monitors directly under the pane with which you are working. This cuts down on the need to mouse back and forth between monitors to make setting changes.

Geometry

If you're using an Apple CRT display or a third-party CRT display that supports geometry settings through software, you might see an additional Geometry button in the Displays Preferences pane. Click this button to fine-tune the image on your display through actions such as rotating or resizing so that it has no obvious distortions. Read the operator manual that came with your monitor for more information. Using these controls actually creates minuscule adjustments to the voltages that produce images on your screen. LCD displays generate their pictures in an entirely different manner and don't require separate geometry settings.

Color

The final button in the Displays System Preferences pane, Color, is where you can create the ColorSync profile for your monitor or choose from one of the preset profiles that come with the system. A ColorSync profile is a collection of parameters that define how your device (in this case, your display) outputs color. Figure 11.4 shows default color settings.

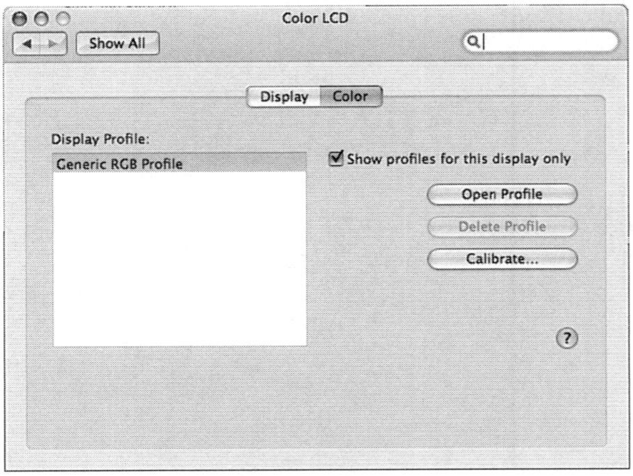

FIGURE 11.4
Use the Color settings to implement your chosen ColorSync display profile or launch the calibration utility to make a new profile.

By default, Mac OS X tries to pick the profile it thinks is best for your system, but that doesn't mean it is necessarily in "sync" with your display. The color quality of both CRTs and flat panels varies over time, so you still might want to run a calibration even if there's already a setting for your display. To start the color calibration process, click the Calibrate button.

Using the Display Calibrator Assistant

The Display Calibrator application is a simple assistant that walks you through the process of creating a profile for the displays connected to your computer.

The steps in the calibration process differ greatly depending on the type of display you're using and whether you're in "expert" mode. Adjustments roughly follow these steps: set up, native gamma, target gamma, target white point, admin, name, and conclusion. For most LCD displays, the calibration process skips several of the steps that aren't applicable.

Follow these steps to calibrate your display:

1. When the Display Calibrator Assistant starts, it provides a brief explanation of what it's about to do and gives you the option of turning on Expert mode, as shown in Figure 11.5. Click the Continue button at the bottom of the window to begin. You can use the Continue and Go Back buttons at any time to move forward and backward between the different steps.

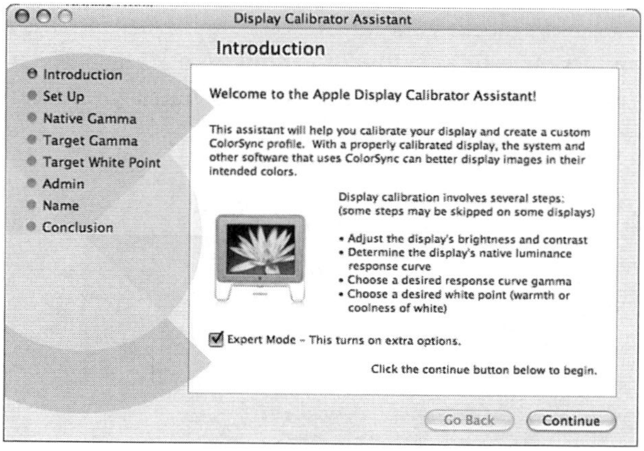

FIGURE 11.5
Turning on Expert mode enables more precise adjustment; sticking with the normal mode limits your options to predefined settings.

2. The first step, Set Up: Display Adjustments, matters for CRT displays only. It helps you adjust the brightness on your display to achieve the right black levels. To begin, turn the contrast control on your display up as high as it

goes. Next, take a close look at the block in the middle right of the window. At first glance, the block might look completely black. In reality, the dark block is composed of two rectangles with an oval superimposed on them.

Using your monitor's brightness control, adjust the image so that the two rectangles blend together and the oval is barely visible. It's best to sit back a little, away from your screen, to gauge the effect.

3. The next step, Determine Your Display's Native Gamma, applies to both LCD and CRT displays, but usually only in Expert mode. Brightness does not increase linearly on computer displays. As the display increases a color's brightness on the screen, the step isn't necessarily the same size each time. To correct this, a gamma value is applied to linearize increases in brightness. In the second step of the calibration process, you adjust the gamma settings for the different colors your computer can display. For more information about Gamma, visit www.bberger.net/rwb/gamma.html.

    On your screen you should see a block containing an Apple Logo. Using the sliders, adjust the logo's brightness and hue so that it matches the background color as closely as possible. It's impossible to get a perfect match, so don't worry if you can still see the apple. It's best just to squint your eyes until you can't make out the text on your screen, and then perform the adjustments.

4. The next step, for both CRT and LCD displays, is Select a Target Gamma. The target gamma for your display is useful for deciding what images on your monitor look like on other displays. PCs and televisions have varying gamma settings that don't match your Macintosh defaults. This makes it difficult to create graphics on your Mac that look right on a PC display. Using the target gamma settings shown in Figure 11.6, you can make your Mac's display look much like that of a standard PC.

FIGURE 11.6
Choose the gamma setting to use on your display.

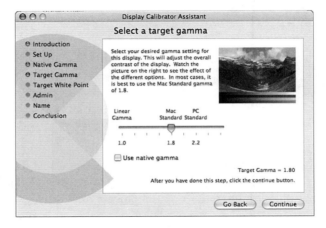

To adjust the gamma setting, select the radio button corresponding to your viewing needs. The picture in the upper-right corner of the window gives you an idea of what your choice does to your display's output. Choosing Use Native Gamma usually results in a very bright and washed-out image. (Those in Expert mode use a slider to set the gamma, which offers more precise control.)

> If you play games on your Mac, you might have noticed that some environments appear too dark in places. To compensate for this, just decrease your display's gamma settings.

Did you Know?

5. The final calibration step for both CRT and LCD displays is Select a Target White Point. As you know, the color white is not a color and is hardly ever truly white. When your computer displays a white image, it probably has tinges of blue, yellow, or even red. This variation is known as the *white point*. Figure 11.7 displays the white point settings.

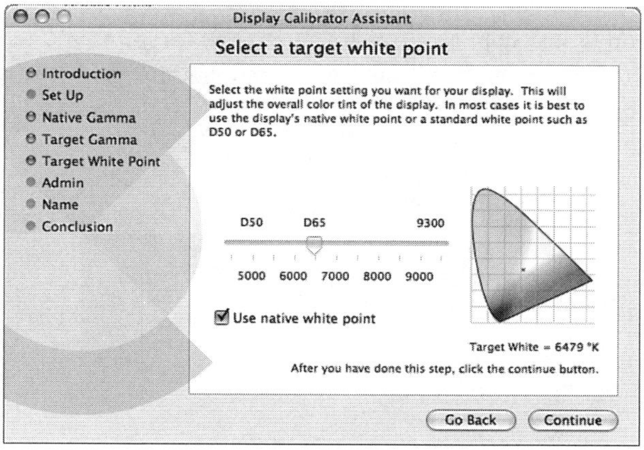

FIGURE 11.7
Choose the target white point setting to use on your display.

To set a white point, choose from the listed options by selecting the appropriate radio button. Once again, those in Expert mode have a slider to set a more precise level. The higher the white point value, the cooler (bluer) the display; the lower it is, the warmer (redder) the display. You might need to uncheck the No White Point Correction (Native) check box before you can make any modifications (in Expert mode).

6. The Admin step, shown in Figure 11.8 and available only in Expert mode, provides a valuable feature for multiuser systems. Instead of allowing only *you* to use the profile you've created, it enables you to save it for use by any user on

the system. On a machine with a few dozen accounts at a graphic arts firm, this saves the headaches of each person needing to calibrate the display separately.

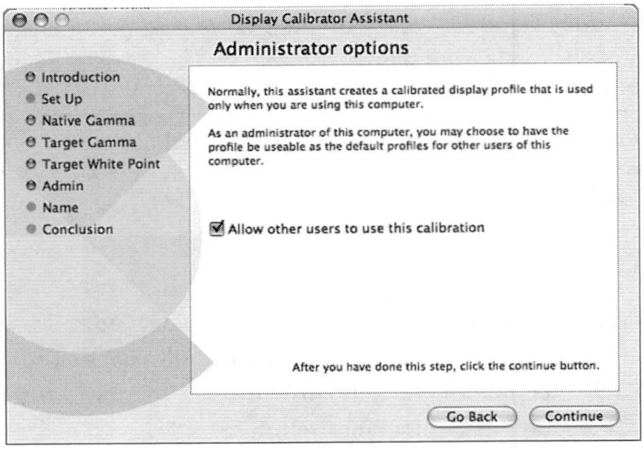

FIGURE 11.8
In Expert mode, you can choose to make the profile available to all users on the system.

7. The second to last step, Name (see Figure 11.9), prompts you to name your profile. Entering a descriptive name for your creation makes it simple to tell them apart.

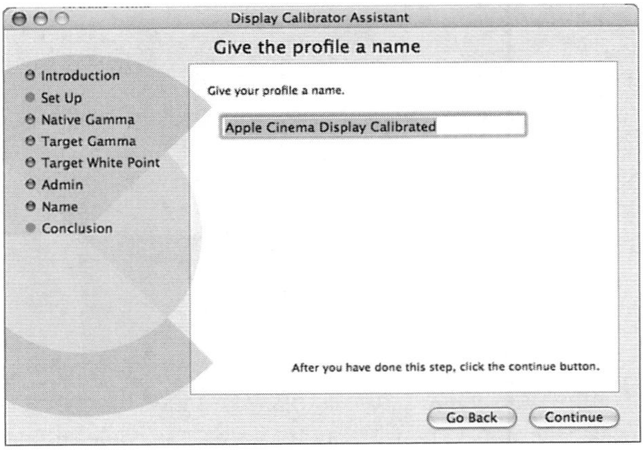

FIGURE 11.9
Enter a name for your calibrated profile.

8. Finally, the Conclusion screen displays a message signaling the successful completion of the calibration process, or, if you're in Expert mode, a summary of the profile you've created, demonstrated in Figure 11.10. Click the Done button to save and exit. The new profile goes into effect immediately. Remember that you can switch between profiles in the Color area of the Displays System Preferences pane.

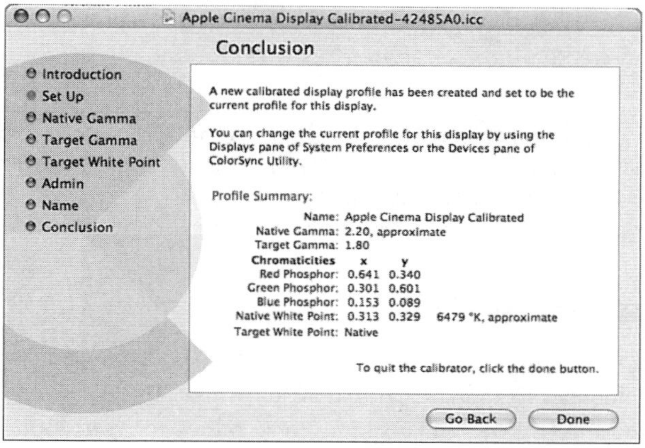

FIGURE 11.10
When finished, the calibration profile is immediately active.

Introduction to ColorSync

As you work with color images and color output devices, you will soon realize that there is no standard color display, printer, or scanner. A *color space* represents the possible output colors for a device by using a hypothetical one- to four-dimensional space. Each dimension in the space represents different intensities of the components that define a color. For example, a common space is RGB (red, green, blue). This three-dimensional color space is defined by the three primary colors of light. (The primary colors of pigment are commonly known to be red, yellow, and blue, but light combines differently.) Many other spaces exist that address other specific needs, such as printed color.

Although every display you buy is undoubtedly an RGB display, the RGB color space it supports varies depending on the quality of the display's components. Different phosphors produce slightly different shades of red, green, and blue. Cheap CRT monitors might have a slight yellow or green tint to them, whereas LCD panels have vibrant hues but may have less consistency in gradations than professional CRT displays.

The same goes for printers and scanners. A scanner that costs more is likely to have a far broader and more consistent color space than its cheaper cousins. If you've ever seen a scan that looks dull and muddy, you're seeing a limitation of the scanner's supported color space.

ColorSync's challenge is to make sure that the colors you intend to print or display are what you end up getting. To do this, ColorSync uses a CMM, or color matching module, to translate between different color spaces. In addition, different devices (including your display) can have ColorSync profiles that describe the range of color they can reproduce. Using Display Calibrator Assistant, as discussed in the previous section, you can create a profile for your system's display.

You'll often find other profiles on the disks that come with your peripheral devices. You can install profiles by dragging them to the /Library/ColorSync/Profiles folder at the system level or in your home directory.

ColorSync Utility

To make it simple to switch between different groups of ColorSync settings, or *workflows*, Apple included a ColorSync Utility (/Applications/Utilities/ColorSync Utility) in Mac OS X. Using this utility, you can set up a workflow for your input devices, display, and output devices.

In addition, ColorSync Utility enables you to set default profiles for each of the ColorSync-supported color spaces (RGB, CMYK, and Gray Tone) and choose a default color-matching technology that maps from one ColorSync profile to another. (Note, however, that some of these features aren't active unless you've installed additional software on your computer.)

To switch between the utility's different functions, click the icons at the top of the window.

Let's work through the different panes in ColorSync Utility, from left to right.

Profile First Aid

The Profile First Aid feature shown in Figure 11.11 verifies that installed color profiles conform to the ICC profile specification. If they do not, it can usually repair them. Click the Verify or Repair button to locate or correct any installed profiles on the system.

Profiles

The next feature is the profile viewer, which you can view by clicking the Profiles icon. In this window, you can navigate through the installed ColorSync profiles on the system and display details for each one by selecting it from the list at the left of the display. Figure 11.12 shows the details for one of the profiles on my system.

Among the details given are the name and location of the profile, its color space, when it was created, and the amount of space it takes up. An interesting graph, called a Lab Plot, also appears to depict the relationship of colors to one another. (The yellow-blue axis runs vertically, and the green-red axis runs horizontally.)

FIGURE 11.11
Verify and repair installed profiles.

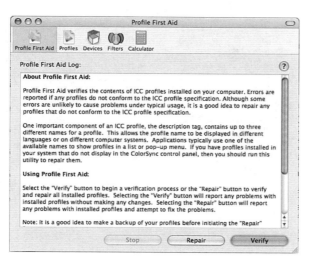

FIGURE 11.12
Easily navigate through all the installed profiles and display their details.

Devices

In the Devices preferences, you can view information about devices and their attached profiles. Each type of device is displayed as a category at the left of the window. Expanding a category shows the supported devices in that classification. For example, the Displays category includes my monitor (an Apple LCD display), as shown in Figure 11.13. If you select a device from the list, the right side of window displays information, including any custom calibration profile you've created for it. Use the Current Profile pop-up menu to choose a new profile, and click the Make Default Display button to set the current device as the default to be used in a given ColorSync category.

FIGURE 11.13
View the available ColorSync devices on your system.

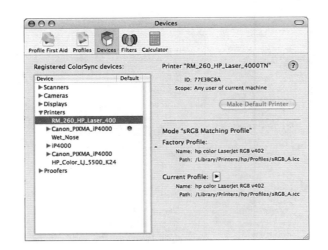

Filters

An interesting part of the ColorSync Utility is Filters. When applied to an image, ColorSync Filters change its appearance. ColorSync filters are applied to an output device (such as your display or printer) and modify anything you're outputting, but they don't change the source file! Figure 11.14 shows the filter setup screen, including a list of default filters.

FIGURE 11.14
Create and manage ColorSync filters.

You can see the details for each of the filters in the default list by clicking the disclosure triangle on the left and then clicking any further disclosure triangles. You cannot change the settings on a default filter, so the options are grayed out.

To make changes to a default filter, click the downward-pointing arrow to its right and choose Duplicate Filter. An editable version of the selected filter appears with the word Copy appended to its name. Click the downward-pointing arrow to the right of the new filter to fine-tune Color Management, Image and PDF handling, and Domains. You can also choose to add comments.

If you want to create a new filter, click the ± button at the bottom of the ColorSync Utility window. You can then click the downward-pointing arrow to the right of the filter to set up your filter.

To remove a filter you've created, select it and a click the – at the lower left.

After you have created filters, you can use them in any ColorSync-aware application that supports filters. For most users, this means the Mac OS X printing system. When printing from any application, you can change the Quartz Filter pop-up menu to choose any of the ColorSync filters (shown in Figure 11.15).

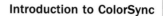

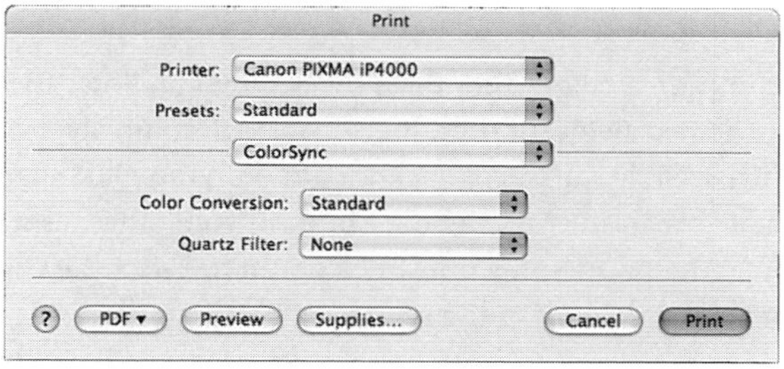

FIGURE 11.15
Apply a filter to temporarily alter a document's tones for printing—Lightness Decrease, which darkens, and Lightness Increase, which lightens, are especially useful.

> If you apply a filter in the print window and then choose the option Save as PDF, the PDF is saved with the filter applied. (Remember, applying filters doesn't change the original file, but in this case you would be saving the Print Preview that has the filter applied—so no rules are broken!)

Did you Know?

Calculator

The Calculator pane, shown in Figure 11.16, enables you to convert color values from one space to another.

Use the pop-up menus on one half of the window to choose the color space of interest and whether to interpret it as perceptual, relative, saturation, or absolute. You can also choose any profiles set for the color space you selected. The sliders and text fields toward the lower part of the window then fill in with details about the color shown in the color sample area—by default, the color is black.

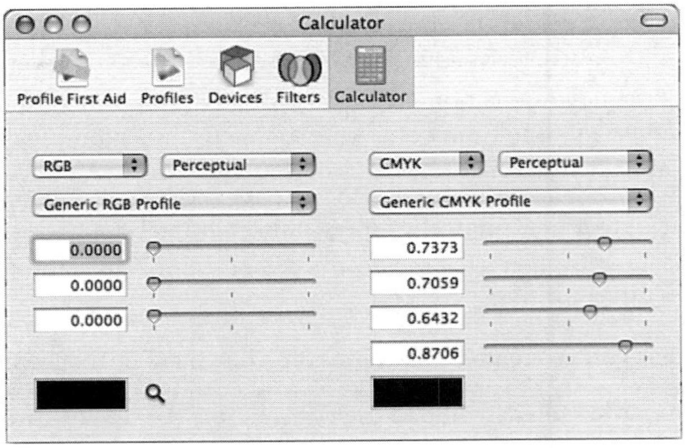

FIGURE 11.16
The Calculator makes side-by-side comparison of the same color in different color spaces easy.

To compare the color to the equivalent color in another color space, choose the setting on the other half of the window. (Note that in Figure 11.15, I'm comparing CMYK and RGB.)

If you want to compare a color other than black, you can enter the numeric values for that color in the text fields, or drag the sliders. Alternatively, if the color you want to examine is visible onscreen, click the magnifying glass icon near the lower left and move your cursor over it. The area around your cursor is magnified so you can choose exactly the point you want. Click again to select the color and read the color values from the right half of the screen.

Did you Know?

> Mac OS X includes another application, DigitalColor Meter, that also helps you pick colors from your screen. It's also located in the Applications/Utilities folder. We discuss its use in Chapter 38, "Exploring the Utilities Folder."

I know that color spaces and calibration sound complicated, and, frankly, they are! But color management is an important part of the Macintosh operating system and part of what makes it widely revered among graphics professionals. Even if you don't fall within that group, it's good to know about ColorSync because it can breathe new life into a display that has a less-than-perfect picture.

Now let's take a look at using peripheral devices that connect to your computer through USB or FireWire ports.

Connecting Peripheral Devices

Although your Mac is a marvelous tool in and of itself, you might want to supplement its capabilities with peripheral hardware, such as printers, scanners, digital cameras, and even additional hard drives. Fortunately, recent Macs come equipped with USB and FireWire ports, which make connecting to such things easy. USB and FireWire are two different standards used to convey data between computers and various devices.

If you have an older peripheral device that connects via SCSI instead of USB or FireWire, you can check with your local Apple computer vendor for a SCSI-to-USB adapter or a SCSI-to-FireWire adapter. Such adapters enable you to use older scanners, hard drives, and other devices on your computer. The only downside is with hard drives; they run more slowly on a USB port. (The SCSI-to-FireWire adapter is better if your computer has FireWire.)

USB Basics

Your computer comes with a type of flexible connection port called USB (short for *Universal Serial Bus*). USB enables you to attach up to 127 separate and distinct items that can expand your computer's capabilities. The USB ports on your computer have a flat, rectangle shape and are marked with the symbol shown in Figure 11.17. USB cables also often display the symbol.

FIGURE 11.17
The USB symbol.

The USB ports on your computer may be either USB 1.1 or USB 2.0—the difference is the speed at which they transfer data. (USB 1.1 provides data transfer at a rate of 12 megabits per second, while USB 2.0 is significantly faster, providing data transfer at a rate of up to 480 megabits per second.) USB devices will work regardless of whether your computer uses USB 1.1 or USB 2.0. However, the type of USB determines the rate of data exchange between your computer and the device.

To find out which type of USB your computer uses, open the Apple System Profiler by choosing About This Mac from the Apple menu and then clicking the More Info button. In Apple System Profiler, select USB from the Hardware section and look to see if any of the USB buses are labeled "USB High-Speed Bus."

By the Way
> USB cables have two types of plugs, so that you can connect the correct end to the correct end. The part that plugs into your computer (or a hub) is small and rectangular. The side that goes into the device itself may be square. Some USB devices support a different style of connection, but it is always obvious which end goes where.

Did you Know?
> If you use a lot of peripheral devices and have filled all your computer's built-in USB or FireWire ports, you can purchase a hub to add more ports.

USB is *hot-pluggable*, which means that you can attach and detach USB-connected items without having to turn off or restart your computer.

Watch Out!
> There are times when you shouldn't unplug the device to stop using it. For example, if you have an external hard drive, Zip drive, or similar product, eject the drive or disk by dragging its icon from the desktop to the trash can before detaching the device from your computer. (As you drag a drive or disk toward the trash, the trash icon changes to show that you're ejecting it—not actually "trashing" it!).

FireWire Basics

Developed by Apple, FireWire is much faster than the other popular standard, USB. For that reason, FireWire is ideal for working with information-rich content, such as audio and video.

By the Way
> The speed of USB 2.0 equals that of FireWire. However, FireWire 800, which works at twice the speed of USB2 and traditional FireWire, has also been introduced. As these improvements cancel each other out, it appears that USB will still be used mainly for lower-performance peripherals, and FireWire will continue to be used for working with large amounts of data, as in digital video. (Also, remember that both USB and FireWire capabilities are a hardware issue—if you don't have a USB2 or FireWire 800-enabled computer, you won't experience their benefits.)

FireWire enables you to hook up all sorts of high-speed devices to your Mac. Most digital camcorders, for example, have FireWire connections, and if you plan to use iMovie, which is explored in Chapters 24 through 28, you need a computer and a camera that are FireWire-equipped.

You can also use your Mac's FireWire capability to hook up FireWire-based hard drives, CD drives, tape backup drives, and scanners. FireWire features a plug-and-play capability similar to USB. You install the software and then plug in the device, and it's recognized, just like that.

Not all FireWire-compatible devices refer to this technology as FireWire. Depending on the manufacturer, it might also be known as IEEE 1394 or i.LINK, but they work just the same.

You can recognize FireWire ports and connector cables by the symbol shown in Figure 11.18.

FIGURE 11.18
The FireWire symbol.

Like USB, FireWire devices are also hot-pluggable.

Connecting FireWire and USB Devices

If you've set up a desktop Macintosh, you already have some experience with peripheral devices—the standard Mac keyboard and mouse are connected via USB. Some devices, however, require an additional step or two to work.

Here's the basic method for setting up a FireWire or USB device (some changes might apply to specific products, and the documentation will explain them):

1. Unpack the device.

2. If a CD comes with your product, it means that special software (a driver) may be needed to make the device work with your computer. To install the device driver, place the installation CD in your computer's drive. (Note, it's important to use the installation CD intended for the Mac—some products come with both Mac and PC discs.)

Mac OS X has built-in support for many of the things you connect via FireWire or USB. But some printers, scanners, and CD or DVD burners may need special software. Before you try to use any of these products, check the documentation or the publisher's website to confirm that the product works with Mac OS X. Or visit VersionTracker.com (www.versiontracker.com) to search for the latest updates.

3. Double-click the Installer icon and follow the instructions to install the new software.

> Under Mac OS X, you might see a prompt where you have to authenticate yourself as the administrator of your computer before a software installation can begin. Because Mac OS X is a multiple-user operating system, it wants to know that you are authorized to make serious changes to the system. To continue, type the password you created when you first set up Mac OS X.

4. After installation, you should be able to connect and use your device right away. However, in some rare cases, you might be asked to restart your computer before continuing.

5. Connect one end of the device's cable to an unused port on your Mac. (Be sure to plug the cable into the right kind of port and to do so gently—don't force things to fit or you may damage your computer.)

> FireWire and USB are totally separate technologies. You cannot hook up a USB device to a FireWire port, or vice versa (the plug layouts don't even match).

6. Connect the other end of the cable to your peripheral device and turn it on. (You should read that manual the comes with the device to learn how to operate it.)

Summary

In this chapter, you learned about display settings and calibration as well as the ColorSync system and the related System Preferences panels and utilities. Even if you don't use your Mac for precise graphic design and composition, you might find that creating custom ColorSync profiles for your system can benefit games, amateur photography, and anything else that involves color display on your screen. You also learned about using USB and FireWire to connect additional devices to your computer.

CHAPTER 12

Printing, Faxing, and Working with Fonts

This chapter looks at font and printer management—two important factors in producing quality output from your system. We talk about setting up printers and basic print settings. We then look at configuring and using Mac OS X's built-in faxing capability. Finally, we discuss adding new fonts and using the Font Book application and system Font panel.

Using the Printer Setup Utility

In Mac OS X, the Printer Setup Utility application maintains and manages everything related to the printer. You can find it in the Utilities folder inside the Applications folder.

When you start the Printer Setup Utility, it opens a window listing all the available printers detected by your system, as shown in Figure 12.1.

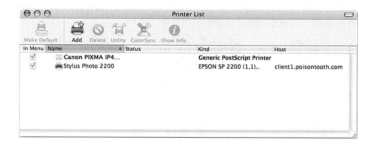

FIGURE 12.1
The Printer Setup Utility shows a list of available printers for you to add.

If a printer is set as the default printer, its name appears in bold type. You can make a different printer the default by selecting its name in the list and then choosing Printers, Make Default (Command-D) from the menu.

Setting Up Printers

To begin, you need to set up your printer and attach it to your computer, as discussed in Chapter 11, "Working with Displays and Peripheral Devices"! With your printer connected, you are ready to set up a printer on your system. To do this, open the Print Setup

Utility and click the Add button at the top of the Printer List window. The Printer Browser window appears, which is similar to the one in Figure 12.2.

There's a pane called Print & Fax in the System Preferences. If you click the + button under the list of printers, the Print Browser window of the Printer Setup Utility launches. (The Print & Fax preferences are covered later in the chapter.)

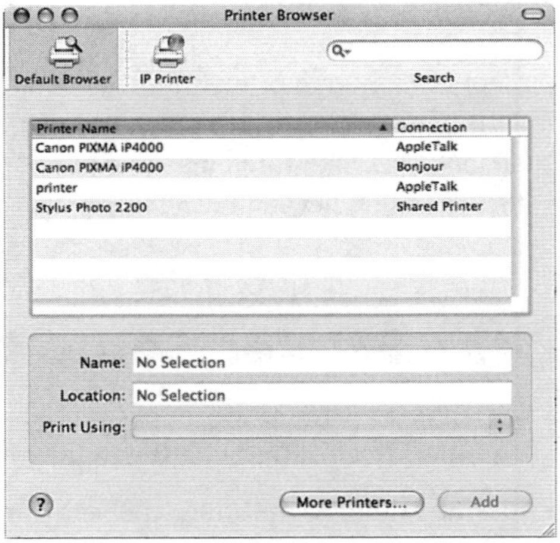

FIGURE 12.2
Use the Printer Browser window to configure any connected printing devices.

At the top of the window are buttons that represent different ways in which you can find and connect to your printer:

▶ Default Browser—Default Browser is the choice to make if you're connecting to a personal or local network printer. (When you set this option, printers in your local AppleTalk Zone appear along with any printers that are Bonjour enabled.)

Bonjour is a technology that allows devices, such as computers and printers, to automatically locate each other on a network. It can also be used by the iChat AV application to allow people on a local network to chat with each other without a lot of setup. (By the way, iChat AV is covered in Chapter 18, "Using iChat AV.")

▶ IP Printer—This option is used for many types of printers that allow access over TCP/IP. If you need to access a printer that isn't on your local network, this is probably the choice you want to make.

Other printer options are available if you click the More Printers button at the bottom of the Printer Browser window. If you want to access a printer located in another AppleTalk zone, choose AppleTalk and choose the zone to see a list of available printers. If you want to access a Bluetooth-enabled printer, select Bluetooth and wait for your computer to automatically detect it. If you are part of a mostly Windows network, select Windows Printer to choose your local network and a printer on it. There are also some manufacturer-specific drivers to choose from.

By the Way

When you choose Default Browser, any printers located by your computer are listed. To finish adding a printer, select it from the list of detected devices. Mac OS X then attempts to automatically detect the type of printer you've chosen and select the appropriate driver. Sometimes, however, you must use the More Printers pop-up menu at the bottom of the window to manually pick a printer type. Finally, click Add to add the selected printer to the Printer Setup Utility listing.

IP printers are configured a bit differently. If you click the IP printers button at the top of the window, you're asked for information on where the printer is located and how to connect.

Talk to the printer's administrator to determine the IP address and queue name for the remote device. Many times you can choose to use the default queue and simply enter an IP address. Because of the nature of IP connections, you must manually choose a printer model. Click Add to finish adding the printer.

For any of the printer connection types, if Mac OS X can't automatically find your printer model, you might need to do some trouble-shooting to correct the problem. First, make sure the printer is powered on. (If the printer is shared via another computer, make sure that the sharing computer is powered on and that printer sharing is enabled in the Services section of the Sharing pane of the System Preferences.) If that doesn't solve the problem, you may need to download additional drivers from the printer manufacturer's website.

By the Way

Managing Your Printer Queue

After you start using your printers, you might occasionally want to cancel a print job that you've created or see what other print jobs are slowing down yours. You can easily do this by accessing the printer's *queue*—a list of the print jobs on which it is currently working. To examine the queue, simply double-click the printer name in the Printer Setup Utility printer listing. Figure 12.3 displays a printer queue.

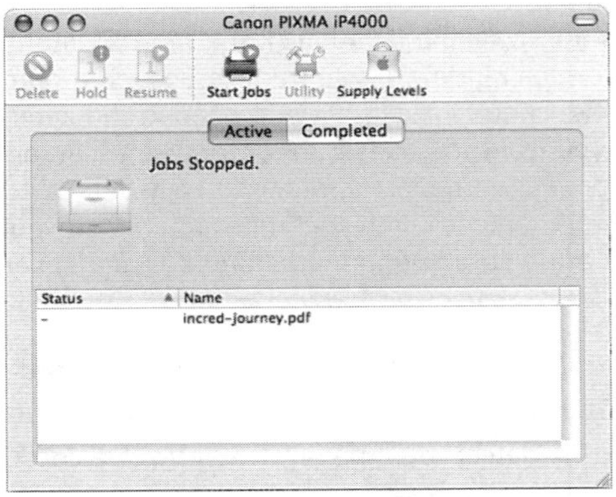

FIGURE 12.3
Double-click a printer's name to display its queue; this queue shows a stopped print job.

When viewing a printer queue, you can drag an individual print job up and down in the listing to adjust its priorities. You can also select a job and use the Delete button to remove it from the print queue entirely.

To completely stop the printer, click the Hold button. This prevents any further jobs from being processed. To resume printing, click the Resume button.

The Page Setup and Print Windows

Before anything shows up in the print queue, it must first be submitted to the printer. In most applications, you can print a document by choosing File, Print from the menu. You can also use two menu commands shared by most applications:

▶ Print (Command-P)—Print the active document and configure settings for your chosen printer.

▶ Page Setup (Shift-Command-P)—Choose how the document is laid out when printing.

Let's start with the standard page setup sheet window, shown in Figure 12.4.

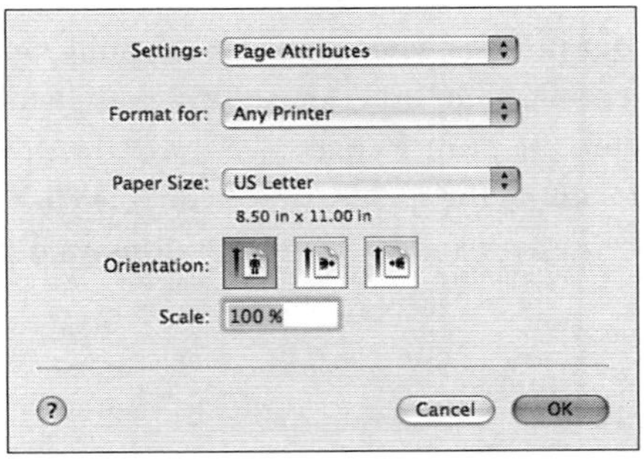

FIGURE 12.4
Choose the basic layout settings for your print job.

In the page setup sheet window, you can use the Settings pop-up menu to choose Page Attributes, Custom Paper Size, or Summary to see a description of how the page will be printed, including margin and size information.

When printing image files (those saved as .jpg, .gif, .tiff, or .png files) from the Preview application, the options for page layout appear in the Print window so you won't have to go through the extra step of opening the page setup before printing.

Did you Know?

The Format For pop-up menu enables you to choose for which printer the page is being laid out. Because different printers support different page sizes and margins, it's important to format a document for the appropriate printer before starting the print process.

Use the Paper Size settings to select from standard paper sizes that your device supports.

Finally, you can use the Orientation buttons to choose from normal, landscape, and reverse landscape layouts, and to set the Scale value to enlarge or shrink the output.

After making your Page Setup settings, it's time to use the Print sheet window shown in Figure 12.5 to finish configuring your printer and start the print job. Choose File, Print from the menu or use the keyboard shortcut Command-P to open the Print window.

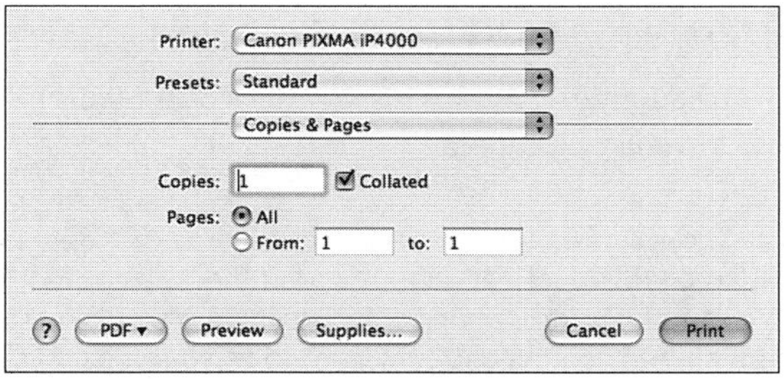

Printer: Canon PIXMA iP4000

Presets: Standard

Copies & Pages

Copies: 1   ☑ Collated

Pages: ● All
       ○ From: 1   to: 1

? | PDF ▾ | Preview | Supplies... | Cancel | Print

FIGURE 12.5
The print settings are used to configure the printer and start the print job.

If you've used a printer before, you probably recognize most of these settings. You can choose a printer and enter your page print range, the number of copies, and so on, and then click Print to start printing the document.

The default information displayed when you open the Print window is the Copies & Pages settings. Using the pop-up menu near the middle of the dialog box, you can select other common setting panes for your printer. (If you don't see a window that looks like Figure 12.5, look for the Advanced button to toggle to a window with more settings.) These are a few that you may see:

For some printers, such as high-quality photo printers, additional options appear under the Printer Features settings to let you choose print quality and paper type. Review the manual that came with your printer to learn about other options that may be available to you.

▶ Layout—Have your printer print multiple document pages per printed page. This setting is useful if you want to print a long document for review. You can choose how to arrange the pages and whether to put borders around them.

▶ Paper Handling—Choose in what order to print the pages, whether to print all pages or odd/even pages, and the paper size to which you are printing.

▶ ColorSync—If you use a color printer, you may be interested in the ColorSync settings, which enable you to apply a filter—such as Black & White or Sepia— to your print job without the need for a graphics program. (See Chapter 11, "Working with Displays and Peripheral Devices," for more discussion of ColorSync filters.)

▶ Cover Page—Choose whether to print a cover page with your document to help you separate print jobs.

▶ Error Handling—You can choose how the system responds to errors that occur during printing. The options are No Special Reporting and Print Detailed Report.

▶ Paper Feed—Many printers have multiple paper trays. The Paper Feed settings enable you to choose which feed is active for a given print job.

▶ Summary—The Summary settings display the status of all the preceding settings in one convenient location.

In some applications, additional options appear in the Copies and Pages drop-down menu. For example, when printing from Mail, OS X's built-in email program, an option called Mail lets you choose how best to fit your message on the printed page—scale to fit, rewrap text, or keep the same apparent font size as you see onscreen.

If you change several settings and want to save them for use from time to time, choose Save As under the Presets pop-up menu. Your custom settings show up under Presets at the top of the Print sheet window for any later work.

A nifty extra of the Mac OS X printing system is the Printer Setup Utility icon. When printing, it displays an animation of pages going through your printer and a count of the remaining pages to print. If there is an error, it displays a red page containing an exclamation mark to get your attention.

By the Way

At the bottom of the Print window are buttons to Preview, Fax, Save as PDF, Cancel, or Print. If you choose to preview your document, it literally opens in the Preview application (discussed in Chapter 6, "Using Calculator, Preview, and TextEdit") to show you what the pages will look like as, well, pages. Save as PDF opens a save window where you can choose a name and location for the PDF file that's created. Cancel exits the Print window, and Print does as it says.

Now, let's discuss faxing from your computer.

Faxing from the Print Window

Essentially, faxing is printing over the phone. With OS X, you can fax a document from the standard Print window (refer to Figure 12.5). Note, however, that you need to be connected to a phone line for it to work—if you dial in over a modem to connect to the Internet, you're all set to send faxes.

We'll talk about receiving faxes through your email account in the "Print and Fax Preference Options" section, later in the chapter.

By the Way

Click the PDF button and choose Fax PDF to bring up the sheet window shown in Figure 12.6.

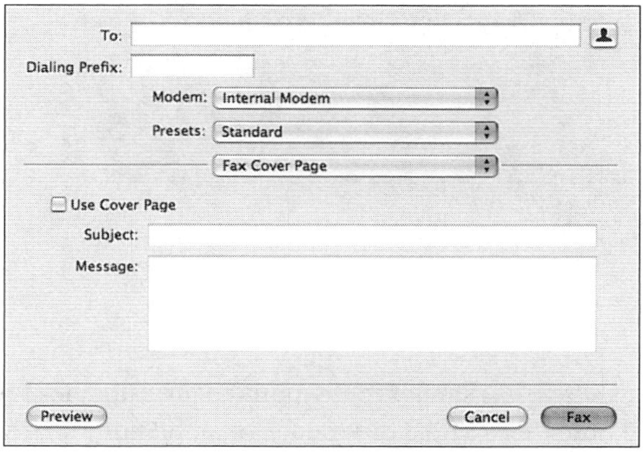

FIGURE 12.6
Prepare to send your fax.

▶ To—Enter the name of the recipient, or click the button on the right to choose a contact from the Address Book. (Note that you can select only contacts for whom fax numbers are listed.)

▶ Dialing Prefix—If you need to dial long distance or enter a prefix to dial outside your organization, enter those digits here.

▶ Modem—Choose the "fax" machine that is to send your document. Modem is the default—and likely only—choice.

▶ Presets—Presets enable you to save a configuration for reuse or choose one you've saved, just as in printing.

The section in the middle of the window also echoes the printing window, with options such as Copies & Pages, Layout, Cover Page, and Error Handling. The Cover Page option lets you choose to include a cover page for which you can type a subject and a message.

> To use the cover page, select it in the pop-up menu; then be sure to click the Cover Page check box that appears.

When you've entered all the appropriate information, click the Fax button. The icon for an application called Internal Modem appears in the Dock. If you double-click it, the window appears to display the fax status, as shown in Figure 12.7.

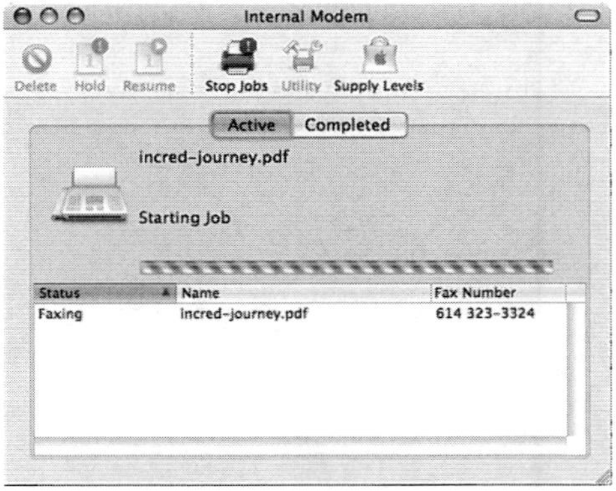

Figure 12.7
Check your fax's status.

The modem status window is similar to the print queue listing for Printer Setup Utility. You can choose Delete, Hold or Resume, or Stop/Start Jobs. (Note, however, that the name applied to the fax job is the document's title, not the name you entered in the Fax sheet window.)

Print and Fax Preference Options

Figure 12.8 shows the Printing pane of the System Preferences, easily accessed through the Apple menu. Any printers you have set up appear at the top of the window along with details, such as kind and activity status. To add or edit a printer, you can click the Printer Setup button or the "+" button to open the Printer Setup Utility, which was discussed earlier.

Click the Print Queue button to view the print queue for the selected printer. You can also choose which printer will appear as the selected printer in the Print sheet window: the last printer used or a specific printer you have set up. You can also choose a default paper size to appear in the Print sheet window.

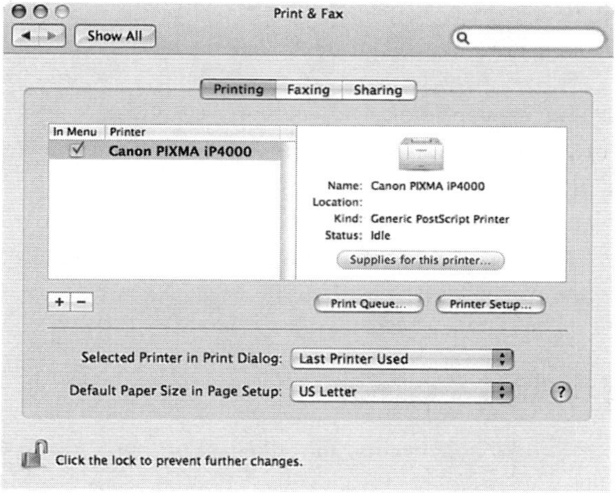

FIGURE 12.8
View information about the printers you've added.

The Faxing pane, shown in Figure 12.9 allows you to set up your computer to receive faxes. (As you learned previously, faxing from your computer is as easy as printing.) After connecting your computer to a phone line, you can check the box for Receive Faxes on This Computer and enter the number for the phone line. You can choose how many rings before incoming faxes are accepted, as well as where to store them and a default printer to print them. If you entered an email address in the system, it appears by default as the address to which faxes are to be emailed.

At the bottom of the pane is the Set Up Fax Modem button, which opens the Modem window shown in Figure 12.9, where you can watch the status of outgoing faxes. You can also choose to show fax status in the menu bar.

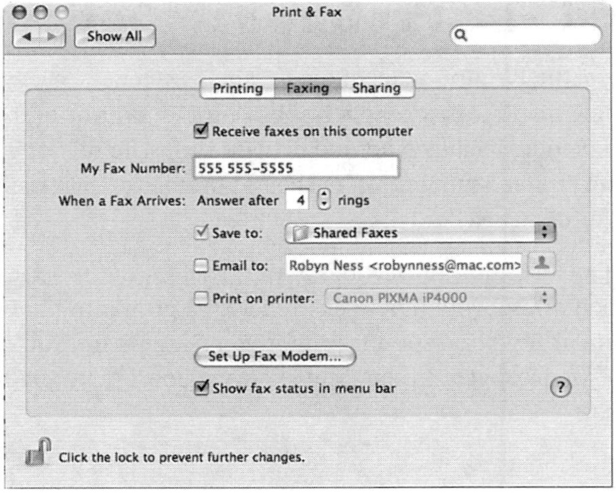

FIGURE 12.9
Turn your computer into your fax machine.

The Sharing pane enables you to give others on your network access to printing or faxing capabilities set up on your systems. The option Share These Printers with Other Computers gives people on your local network access to USB and FireWire printers connected directly to your computer—and you can choose with which printers to share access. At the bottom of the pane is the option for you to allow others to send faxes through your computer.

Working with Fonts

Mac OS X comes with a large collection of fonts and supports many common font formats, including

- `.dfont` suitcases
- `.ttf` TrueType fonts
- `.ttc` TrueType font collections
- `.otf` OpenType fonts
- PostScript Type 1 fonts
- All previous Macintosh font suitcases

In short, if you have a font, chances are that you can install it on Mac OS X and it will work.

Font files are stored in the system `/Library/Fonts` folder or in the `Library/Fonts` folder inside your home directory. If you have a font you want to install, just copy it to one of these locations and it becomes available immediately. You must restart any running applications that need access to the fonts, but you don't need to restart your computer.

Organizing Fonts with Font Book

To add a new font, you can simply place new fonts in the Fonts folder inside either the system or user-level Library folder. However, the Font Book application exists to help you view and manage a large font collection effectively. You can find Font Book in the Applications folder.

The Font Book window, as shown in Figure 12.10, has three columns. The one on the left contains collections, or categories, of fonts. The first item in the list displays all fonts available to the current user. Several categories, such as Classic and Fixed Width, are listed by default. To add your own collections, maybe for a specific project or of a certain look, click the + button below the column. You can also choose to see fonts installed by other users of the computer—if they have installed them in the system Library/Fonts folder, and not a folder in their home directories.

FIGURE 12.10
Font Book helps you categorize (and even hide) your many fonts.

The middle column displays any fonts included in the selected collection. (Expanding the list by clicking the disclosure triangles shows the related fonts.) Clicking the + button at the bottom of the window enables you to navigate to fonts stored on, or connected to, your system in folders other than one of the Library/Font folders.

The Disable button enables you to remove an option temporarily from a collection. For instance, if you feel you're in a rut and want to disallow the use of Courier in all your documents, choose it from the All Fonts list and click Disable. After you confirm that you really do mean it, Courier and its related fonts will be grayed out in the Font Book window, but in the system as a whole, they won't even appear! (To bring Courier back when you realize how much you've missed it, select it in the All Fonts list of Font Book and click the Enable button.)

Some fonts are used by your system and can't be disabled. Those fonts have a small lock icon in front of their status information at the lower right.

The right column shows an A-to-Z and numeric sample of the selected font. Drag the size slider to view the font at different sizes, or leave the Fit at its default.

Watch Out!

Although it's fun to try uncommon fonts, it doesn't work to share them via outgoing email messages. If your recipients haven't installed the font you chose, the message will appear in one of the default fonts on their systems, rather than with the look you wanted.

Using the Mac OS X Font Window

Applications that enable you to choose fonts often use the built-in font picker shown in Figure 12.11. This element of the Macintosh operating system is designed to make fonts easier to find and more accessible among different pieces of software. To see the Font window for yourself, open the TextEdit application found in the Applications folder, and then choose Format, Font, Show Fonts from the menu.

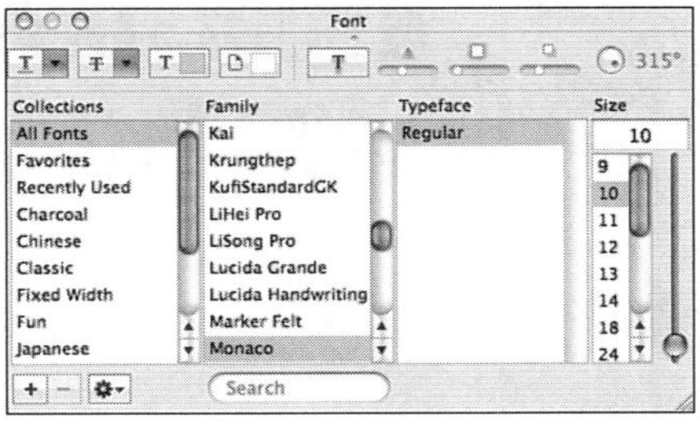

FIGURE 12.11
The Font window is a systemwide object for choosing fonts.

In its default form (as shown in Figure 12.11), the Font window lists four columns: Collections, Family, Typeface, and Size. Use these columns much as you use the Column view of the Finder—working from left to right. Click a collection name (or All Fonts to see everything), and then click the font family, typeface, and, finally, the size.

To view settings before applying them, open the preview space by clicking just under the Font title bar and dragging.

> The Font window is quite a chameleon. In addition to the two views already mentioned, there's a more simplified view as well. If you want to save space, use the window resize control in the lower-right corner of the panel to shrink the Font window to a few simple pop-up menus. (The pop-up menus also appear if you expand the preview space to its full size.)

At the top of the Font window is a line of four buttons that, from left to right, control underlining, strikethrough, font color, and background color. To the right of these buttons is another set of controls for adding a drop shadow to the font and controlling its placement.

Along the bottom of the Font window are several additional controls. The + and – buttons enable you to add and remove collections in the Collections list. The search field enables you to locate a font by name or character string rather than scroll endlessly.

The Action pop-up menu (the little "gear" icon) gives you access to several special features of the font system:

▶ Add to Favorites—Add the current font choice to the Favorites font collection.

▶ Show/Hide Preview—Shows or hides the preview space at the top of the window.

▶ Show/Hide Effects—Shows or hides the font effects toolbar at the top of the Font window.

▶ Color—Pick a color for the font.

▶ Characters—Shows the Character Palette, shown in Figure 12.12, displaying each of the characters for a selected font.

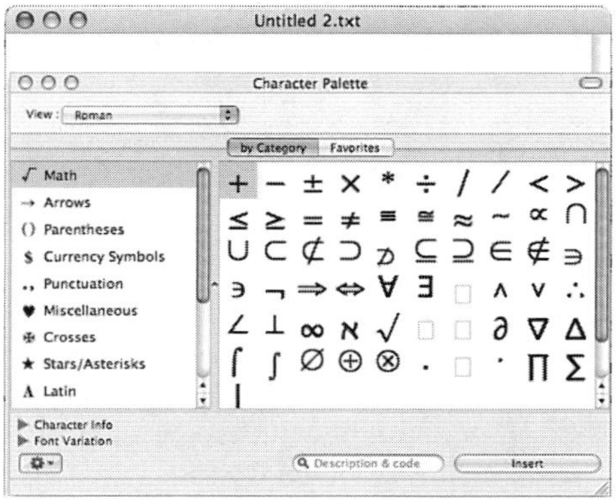

FIGURE 12.12
The Character Palette gives easy access to characters and symbols, including those for math or simply decoration.

> Instant access to the Character Palette from any application can be added in the Input Menu pane of the International panel in the System Preferences. Simply check the box in front of Show Input Menu in Menu Bar, and a menu extra appears. To remove the icon, return to the Input Menu tab and uncheck the box. In some applications, you can access the Character Palette directly from the Edit menu if you choose Special Characters.

▶ Typography—Opens the Typography window, where you can make adjustments to the spacing of letters and lines.

▶ Edit Sizes—Opens a sheet window, where you can customize the font sizes or the range of font sizes available in the Font window. You can also pick whether to use a list of fixed sizes, a slider, or both for choosing font sizes in the default Font window.

▶ Manage Fonts—Launches Font Book, where you can create and edit new collections of fonts.

One final note about fonts: Not all applications use the system Font window. When it's not supported, as with applications such as Microsoft Word, you're likely to see pull-down menus listing every installed font.

Summary

The focus during this chapter has been printing and faxing. In Mac OS X, printers are managed through the Printer Setup utility and often share a common look and feel throughout each of the settings panels. Also, faxing is built right into the standard print window so that you no longer have to print things out to fax them.

The font system is equally easy to use. Font Book and a system-wide Font window make it simple to build font collections and find your way through hundreds of available typefaces.

PART III

Internet Applications

CHAPTER 13

Connecting to the Internet

Mac OS X is easy to configure for dial-in, ethernet, AirPort, cable modem, and DSL service. If you have a connection to the Internet, this chapter helps you set up your Mac to access it. Specifically, you learn what tools exist for setting up your network, where to configure your connections, and how to manage multiple locations.

Creating an Internet Connection

The first step in connecting to any network (including the Internet) is determining what, exactly, is being connected. Mac OS X supports a number of technologies out of the box, such as standard wired (ethernet) networks, wireless AirPort networks, and, of course, broadband and dial-in ISPs. For each different type of network, you may need to collect connection information before continuing. Chances are good that your Internet Service Provider (ISP) can configure your settings automatically through the magic of Dynamic Host Configuration Protocol (DHCP).

If DHCP doesn't fill in the required information, your network administrator or ISP should be able to provide the details of your network access, including

▶ IP address—An Internet Protocol address that's used to uniquely identify your computer on the Internet

▶ Subnet mask—A filter that helps your computer differentiate between which machines are on the local network and which are on the Internet

▶ Router—A device address used to send and receive information to and from the Internet

▶ Domain Name Server (DNS)—A computer that translates the name you see in your web browser, such as www.poisontooth.com, into the corresponding IP address

▶ ISP phone number—A number used when creating a dial-in connection

▶ Account name—A username for your ISP Internet account

▶ Password—A password for your ISP Internet account

▶ Proxy—A computer through which your Macintosh may go to reach websites

By the Way

> Proxy servers are mainly used to boost performance when surfing the Web. Contact your ISP or network administrator for details.

You should be absolutely positive that you have all the necessary information before you continue; otherwise, your computer may not connect because of problems that are difficult to diagnose. You may want to keep a log of the settings you used in case you need to call your ISP's support line for help with connection problems.

Watch Out!

> Under no circumstances should you ever attempt to guess an IP address for your computer. Entering invalid information could potentially disrupt your entire network or cause intermittent (and difficult to diagnose) problems for other users.

With connection information in hand, open System Preferences, and click the Network button in the Internet & Network section. The Network pane is the control center for all your network connections. Figure 13.1 shows that pane's Network Status section.

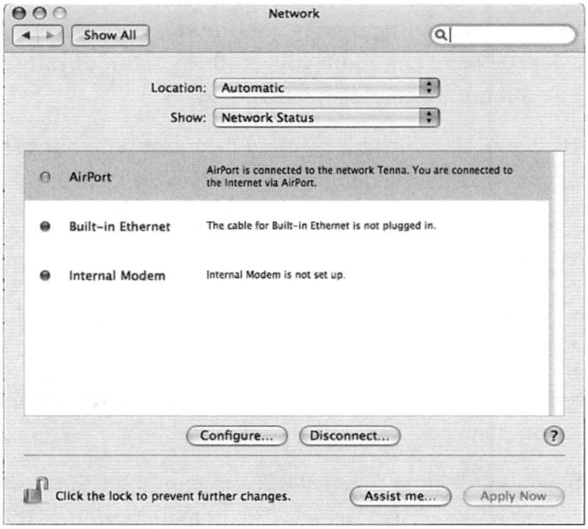

FIGURE 13.1
See the status of potential network connections.

By the Way

> At the bottom of all the sections in the Network Preferences pane is the Assist Me button. Clicking it launches the Network Setup Assistant, which asks you a series of questions to try to help you set up your Internet Connection. Basically, it collects the same information discussed in the rest of this chapter. If you aren't sure which option is for you, the Setup Assistant's questions may help you decide.

Near the top of the panel is the Show pop-up menu. Use this menu to choose between the different types of connections that your computer can use, such as Internal Modem, Built-in Ethernet, and AirPort. Let's look at each one and how it can be set up for your ISP.

If you're a laptop user who needs to use different types of connections (for example, a modem at home and AirPort at work), don't worry. In the section "Setting Network Port Priorities and Locations" later in the chapter, you'll see how several different connection types can get along without any conflicts.

By the Way

Internal Modem

If you use a modem to connect to the Internet, choose the appropriate Modem option in the Show pop-up menu. The lower portion of your screen changes slightly to reflect the type of connection you're configuring. You see four buttons that lead to four individual setting panes:

▶ PPP—The most important pane, shown in Figure 13.2, the PPP settings enable you to set your username, password, and ISP phone number.

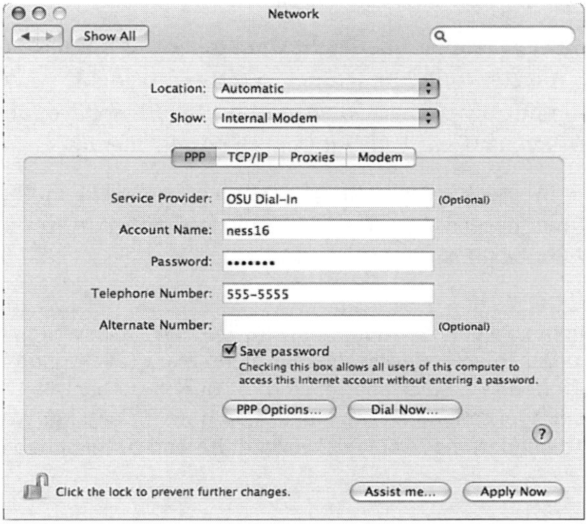

FIGURE 13.2
The PPP options are usually the only things you need to make a connection that uses your internal modem.

▶ TCP/IP—TCP/IP settings are rarely needed for dial-in connections. Unless you know otherwise, I recommend not touching anything found here.

▶ Proxies—If your ISP has provided proxy servers for your use, you need to enter them here. A *proxy* acts on your behalf, retrieving web pages for you and storing commonly-requested web pages in a cache. (Retrieving web pages from the cache is much faster than retrieving them from the computer on which they are officially hosted.)

By the Way

> Your ISP may or may not require use of a proxy server. If use is required, you may need to use a proxy server ID and password, possibly separate from your account username and password. Review your service documentation, and contact your ISP if you have any questions.

▶ Modem—Settings specific to your computer's modem. If you don't like hearing the annoying connection sound, you can shut off the speaker here. Most important, you can activate the option to Show Modem Status in Menu Bar, which provides a menu extra that enables you to easily connect and disconnect from the Internet without opening extra windows.

In the PPP section, enter the username and password you were given for your ISP, along with the ISP's phone number. If you want to keep your password stored with the machine, click the Save Password check box.

There are a number of settings you might want to look at by clicking the PPP Options button. You can configure settings in a sheet to enable you to redial a busy connection, automatically connect when starting TCP/IP applications, and automatically disconnect if you choose Log Out from the Apple menu.

Click Apply Now to save the PPP settings. If you chose the PPP option to connect automatically when needed, you should be able to start Safari (see Chapter 14, "Using Safari") and begin surfing the Web.

By the Way

> If you didn't choose to connect automatically, you can choose Show Modem Status in Menu Bar to activate the modem menu extra (this option is in the Modem section) to add a quick-control icon to your menu bar. Alternatively, the Internet Connect application can start and stop a dial-in setting. We talk more about that in "Using Internet Connect" toward the end of this chapter.

Built-in Ethernet

The next type of connection we look at is the built-in ethernet connection. If you have a DSL/cable modem hookup or are part of a wired 10BASE-T LAN, this is where you'll need to focus your attention. Choose Built-in Ethernet from the Show pop-up menu. Again, several sections enable you to fine-tune related areas.

The sections for the ethernet settings are

▶ TCP/IP—The Ethernet TCP/IP pane, displayed in Figure 13.3, offers configuration options for setting your IP address, either automatically using DHCP or manually.

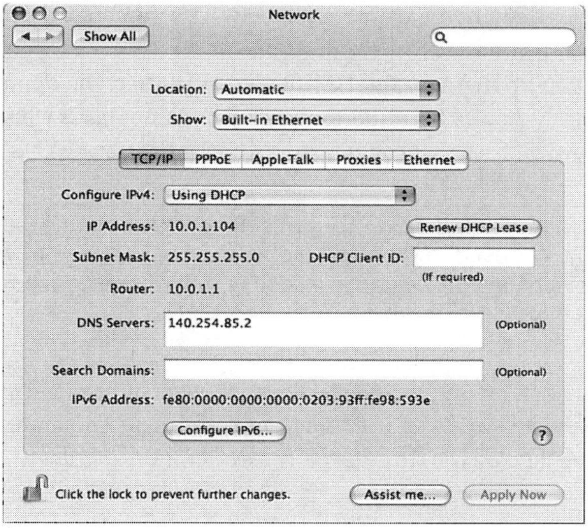

FIGURE 13.3
TCP/IP settings are important for ethernet-based connections.

▶ PPPoE—PPP over ethernet is a common way for DSL-based services to connect. They generally require a username and password as a modem-based PPP connection does, but operate over a much faster ethernet wire.

▶ AppleTalk—The AppleTalk section is used to control whether you become part of a local AppleTalk network. AppleTalk is Apple's traditional file-sharing protocol and is discussed further in Chapter 32, "Sharing Files and Running Network Services."

▶ Proxies—If your ISP has provided proxy servers for your use, you will need to enter them here.

▶ Ethernet—If you need to look up your Ethernet ID (also known as a MAC address or NIC address), this is the place to look. Although IP addresses are identifying numbers assigned by your network that can be used to associate a computer with an action, Ethernet ID numbers are unique identifiers associated with the hardware of your computer. (The Configure pop-up menu can be used to access advanced settings, but do not change them unless you have help from your system administrator.)

As you saw in Figure 13.3, you definitely need to know a few details before you can successfully operate an ethernet connection. Fill in the information that you collected from your network administrator or ISP now. If you're lucky, at least a portion of these settings can be configured automatically by a boot protocol (BOOTP) or Dynamic Host Configuration Protocol (DHCP) server on your network.

BOOTP and DHCP often provide automatic network setup on corporate and cable modem networks. If your network supports one of these services, you can use the Configure IPv4 pop-up menu in the TCP/IP section to select the appropriate protocol for your connection. Again, it's important that you do not *guess* what you need to connect—using invalid settings could disrupt your entire network.

By the Way

> The TCP/IP section of the Built-in Ethernet settings has a button labeled Renew DHCP Lease. This is used to "refresh" the IP address assigned to you by your local network. Sometimes, if your connection is misbehaving, renewing your IP address can correct the problem.

If your ISP requires that you use PPPoE, click the PPPoE button. In this pane, you can supply a username and password for your connection and enter optional identifying data for the ISP. (By the way, PPPoE is used almost exclusively with DSL accounts.)

Near the bottom of the pane is a check box that enables you to view your PPPoE status in the menu bar. Clicking this check box adds a new menu extra that displays activity on your connection and gives you quick control over your settings.

Click the Apply Now button when you're satisfied with your ethernet setup. You should be able to immediately use the network software on your computer, such as Mail and Safari.

AirPort

The next connection method, AirPort, is available only if your computer has an AirPort card and is within range of a wireless base station. AirPort is Apple's wireless networking device that enables you to connect to the Internet without the burden of running network wires or phone lines.

By the Way

> Wireless technologies, regardless of their manufacturers or product names, interoperate well. You can use a non-Airport wireless access point with your Mac, and share your Airport wireless network with PC users.

To configure your AirPort connection, choose AirPort in the Show pop-up menu. AirPort setup, surprisingly, is identical to ethernet. The same TCP/IP, AppleTalk, and Proxies sections apply. There is, however, one additional section that's essential to configure properly: the AirPort section, shown in Figure 13.4.

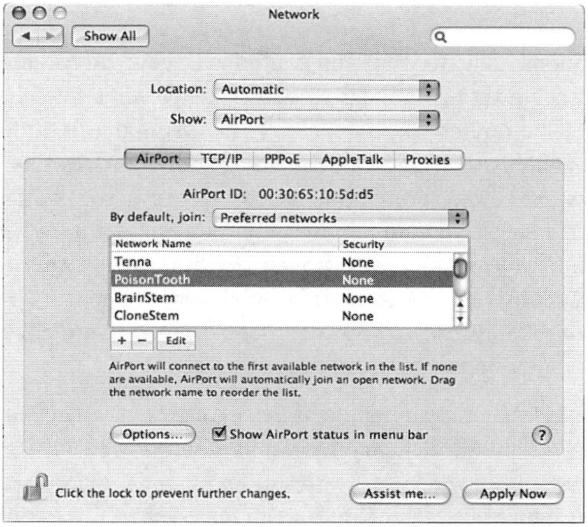

FIGURE 13.4
Choose the AirPort network to which you want to connect, or set criteria so that your system can choose.

In the AirPort section, you can direct your computer to Join Automatic, which is whatever network is available, or Join Preferred Networks.

AirPort networks are identified by a network name. When Join Preferred Networks is selected, you can add an AirPort by manually typing the name into the Network Name text field.

As with the modem and ethernet settings, you can activate yet another menu extra—the AirPort signal strength—by clicking Show AirPort Status in Menu Bar. This menu extra also enables you to instantly switch between the different available wireless networks and even shut down AirPort service if you want.

> Airport wireless connection does use additional power. If you're a PowerBook or iBook user, you may want to turn Airport off to conserve battery power when you're not using Internet applications such as web browsers and email programs.

By the Way

Although the settings discussed so far are typically all you need to connect to an AirPort Network, clicking the Options button reveals some additional features related to AirPort networks.

First, you can decide whether your computer should ask for your permission before connecting to an open AirPort network. AirPort networks, unless password-protected, can be joined by anyone with a wireless-enabled computer, which can be a security hazard to both the network and its users. Having your computer ask before joining an open network can help you know whether you're outside the safety of your own network.

The next two options relate to what you can do with your AirPort-enabled Mac without "administrator" authorization. (In this case, the administrator is the person responsible for the computer—probably you!) The first option is quite straightforward. In the previous paragraph, you learned a bit about AirPort security issues; requiring a password before changing to a new wireless network offers an additional line of defense. The second option requires a bit more explaining: AirPort-enabled Macs are able to broadcast their own wireless signal to create a network with other wireless-enabled computers. Once again, opening your computer up to other computers can pose a security risk, so you can choose to reserve the power to create a computer-to-computer network for the administrator.

The remaining check boxes don't require much explanation—you can choose to allow your computer to automatically add other wireless networks to its list, to have your computer disconnect from wireless networks when no one is logged in, and to enable interference robustness (which can help smooth out a shaky wireless connection).

Click Apply Now to start using your wireless network.

Computers with AirPort cards can create computer-to-computer networks with other AirPort-enabled computers even if no official network is present. To create a computer-to-computer network, open the Network pane of the System preferences and choose Airport from the Show pop-up menu. Check the option to Show AirPort Status in Menu Bar; then click on the AirPort Status menu extra and choose Create Network. In the window that appears, enter a name for your network and click OK. (If you want to be sure that only specific people join your network, click the Show Options button and enter a password that will be required to join your network.) Others in your vicinity will be able to join your network as if it were another AirPort-based network by choosing it from their AirPort Status menu extra.

You may notice there is one more option in the Show menu of the Network pane of the System Preferences: Built-in FireWire. This option enables you to create a network by connecting a series of computers, using their FireWire ports (see Chapter 11, "Working with Displays and Peripheral Devices"). This is probably not a feature you'll need to explore, but the options are very similar to those for Built-in Ethernet.

Setting Network Port Priorities and Locations

That wasn't so bad, was it? Everything that you need to get yourself connected to the Internet is all located in one System Preferences panel. Unfortunately, not all users' network setups are so easy. Many of us use our PowerBooks at home to dial in to the network, and then go to work and connect via ethernet, and, finally, stop by a coffee shop on the way home to relax and browse the Web via AirPort.

In Mac OS X, all your different network connections can be active simultaneously! This means that if it is possible for your computer to find a way to connect to a network, it will! Obviously, you don't want it trying to dial the phone if it has already found a connection, and, true to form, Mac OS X is smart enough to understand that if it *is* connected, it doesn't need to try any of the other connection methods. In fact, you can alter the order in which it tries to connect to the network by choosing Network Port Configurations in the Network Preferences pane's Show pop-up menu. Figure 13.5 shows this configuration pane.

Here you can see four available port configurations, including Internal Modem, Built-in Ethernet, AirPort, and Built-in FireWire. You can drag these different configuration settings up and down in the list to determine the order in which Mac OS X attempts to use them. If you prefer that the computer *doesn't* attempt to connect through one of these configurations, deselect the check box in front of that item.

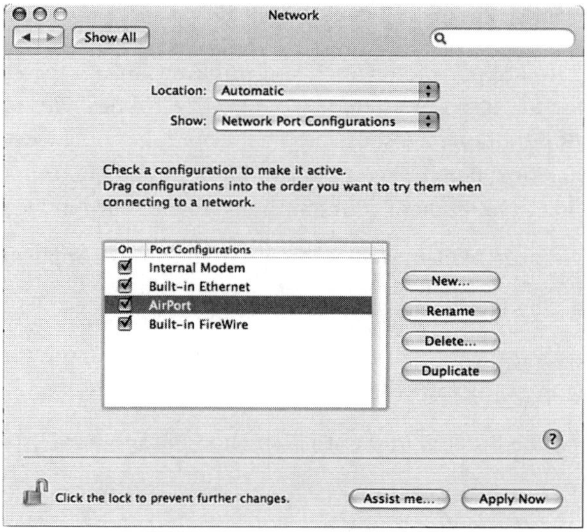

FIGURE 13.5
Adjust which connection settings take precedence over the others.

Using the New, Delete, and Duplicate buttons on the right side of the pane, you can create alternative configurations for each of your built-in connection methods. These new configurations appear in the Show pop-up menu and are set up just as you set up the modem, ethernet, and AirPort connections earlier.

Locations

Mac OS X creates collections of port settings called *locations* that you can easily switch between. So far you've been dealing with a location called Automatic, shown in the Location pop-up menu of the Network Preferences panel.

To create a new location, choose New Location from the Location pop-up menu. After you create a new location, you can edit the port configurations and priorities just as you have under the default Automatic location. To manage the locations that you've set up, choose Edit Locations in the Location pop-up menu.

Switching from one location to another is simply a matter of choosing its name in the Location pop-up menu or the Location submenu under the system-wide Apple menu.

Watch
Out!

Choosing a new location causes the new network settings to take effect immediately and could disrupt any connections currently taking place.

Using Internet Connect

The Internet Connect application, which you can launch from the Applications folder, is the final stop in your tour of Mac OS X network utilities. This is a rather strange application that offers a shortcut to several of the same features found in the Network Preferences panel. It can be used for both modem and AirPort connections to quickly log in to different configurations in your current location.

Figure 13.6 displays the Modem side of the Internet Connect application.

To log in to your ISP via modem, follow these steps:

1. Choose the modem configuration you created earlier in the Configuration pop-up menu at the top of the window.

2. Enter the phone number for your ISP or choose from those listed in the pop-up menu.

3. The login name should already be set as configured in the Network Preferences panel. If you didn't save your password in the panel, you must enter it here.

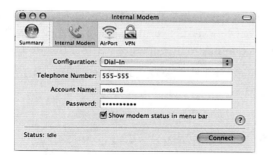

FIGURE 13.6
The Internet
Connect applica-
tion enables
you to easily log
in to your ISP.

4. Click the Show Modem Status in Menu Bar check box to add the modem menu extra to your screen.

5. Click Connect to start using your dial-in connection.

After you've connected to your ISP, the Connect button changes to Disconnect, giving you a quick way to break the modem connection.

AirPort users also stand to benefit from the Internet Connect application. Along with modem configurations, AirPort settings are also shown in the Configuration pop-up menu. Choosing an AirPort-based configuration displays the status of the connection and signal strength, as shown in Figure 13.7.

FIGURE 13.7
Internet
Connect can
also control
your AirPort
settings.

Use the Turn AirPort Off (and subsequent Turn AirPort On) button to disable or enable the AirPort card in your computer. To switch to another wireless network, use the Network pop-up menu.

Finally, to see a readout of the signal strength at all times, check the Show AirPort Status in Menu Bar check box. As you can see, many features of the Internet Connect application are already accessible through the Network Preferences panel. However, Internet Connect has one more setting that we haven't seen before: VPN, which stands for Virtual Private Network. VPN allows remote users to connect to a specially configured network securely and interact as if they were within the local network. Your system administrator will know whether this would apply to you.

Regardless, the Internet Connect application offers a quick means of viewing your connection status and changing common settings.

Summary

In this chapter, you learned how to set up your Mac OS X computer for network access through traditional wired networks, wireless AirPort connections, and, of course, dial-up ISPs. Mac OS X networking has a number of advantages, including the capability to automatically configure itself to whatever type of network is currently available. This feature, combined with a simplified locations manager, makes it easy to adapt your computer to any sort of network environment.

CHAPTER 14

Using Safari

As you saw in Chapter 13, "Connecting to the Internet," it's easy to configure Internet settings in OS X. In this chapter, you learn how easy it is to use Safari, Apple's own web browser, to explore the World Wide Web.

The Safari Interface

Figure 14.1 shows Safari's default configuration. Figure 14.2 shows all available interface options. You can add the toolbar items by choosing Customize Address Bar under the View menu. The status bar along the bottom of the window can also be turned on and off under the View menu. (In Figure 14.2, a feature called "tabs" is also activated; they are discussed later in the section "Using Tabs.")

FIGURE 14.1
Apple's Safari web browser with a typical set of interface options.

FIGURE 14.2
The elements of
the Safari inter-
face.

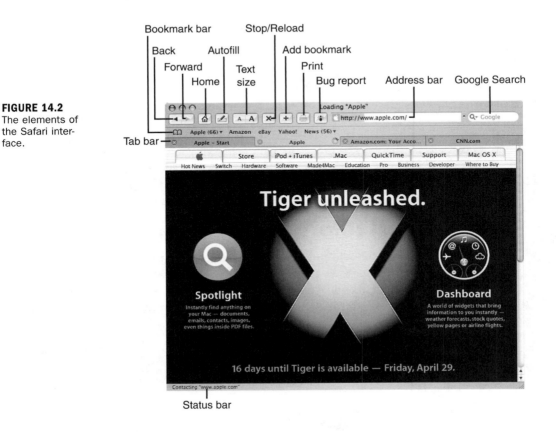

Address Bar

The top row of controls in the Safari window is the Address bar. It contains the basic
tools you need to move between web pages, as well as a few tools to make your use
of the Internet easier.

▶ The Back and Forward buttons work together. You use the Back button to
return to the web page you viewed previously. After you've gone back, you
can use the Forward button to move ahead to where you were. If you haven't
gone back through any pages you've already viewed, the Forward button is
grayed out to show that it is not currently an active option.

▶ The Home button returns you to the page set as your default startup page.
Think of it as a shortcut for connecting to a site you visit frequently.

To change the page that comes up automatically when Safari is launched, choose Preferences from the Safari application menu, and click the General option from the toolbar. (If you don't see a toolbar, click the transparent oval-shaped button at the upper right of the Preferences window.) You can type a new web address in the field labeled Home Page or, if your Safari window is open to the page you want to use, simply click the button marked Set to Current Page.

Also, if you prefer, you can have new windows open with your list of bookmarked pages rather than a default page. Simply change the setting in the New Windows Open With pop-up menu from Home Page to Bookmarks.

By the Way

▶ The Autofill button activates a service that helps you complete online forms, such as registration and login pages, where you have to provide basic personal information. It works by storing information you've previously entered in web page text fields so that it can repeat them on later visits.

▶ The Text Size button enables you to easily increase or decrease the font size in the current page.

▶ The Stop/Reload button changes depending on whether the current page identified in the Address field has been loaded or is loading. If a page has been loaded, you see the Reload button, as shown in Figure 14.1, which enables you to refresh the page. This can be useful if you view a page that is updated frequently throughout the day and you want to make sure that you are viewing the most current version. The Stop button, shown in Figure 14.2, appears as a page is loading to allow you to stop it from loading. In cases where a page takes a long time to load, and you'd rather give up than wait, the Stop button lets you return Safari to an idle state so that you can enter the address for a new page.

▶ Clicking the Add Bookmark button, which looks like a +, adds the current page to your bookmark list so that you can easily visit it again without writing down the address. Bookmarks are discussed later in this chapter in the section "Working with Bookmarks."

▶ The Print button provides a quick way to print the current web page without choosing File, Print from the menu.

▶ For cases when you find pages that simply don't work in Safari, the Report Bugs button was included to enable you to report any problems you experience in viewing pages. When you click that button, a window appears where you can type a description of the problem you're experiencing. (Click the button labeled More Options to classify the type of problem, or to include a picture of the page and/or the source HTML of the page you're having difficulties viewing.)

▶ The Address Field is where you can type web addresses of sites you want to visit. It also shows the addresses of pages you reach through links in other pages or through pages you've bookmarked. In addition to showing addresses, the Safari Address field also shows the status of pages as they are loading. As shown in Figure 14.2, a blue-shaded bar moves from left to right across the Address field as information for displaying the current page is received.

Did you Know?

> If the Status bar stops moving, there may be a problem loading the page. Use the Stop button to tell Safari to stop trying to load the page. You can try to connect again by clicking the Refresh button.

▶ On some sites with specially configured content, the Show RSS button appears at the far right of the Address Field (see Figures 14.1 and 14.2). RSS, which stands for RDF Site Summary or Real Simple Syndication, is another way that websites can distribute their content for easy skimming. For example, to see a summary of all of Apple's recent headlines, you can click the Show RSS button to see a listing of those stories, as shown in Figure 14.3.

FIGURE 14.3
Safari's RSS interface enables you to focus on text-based content.

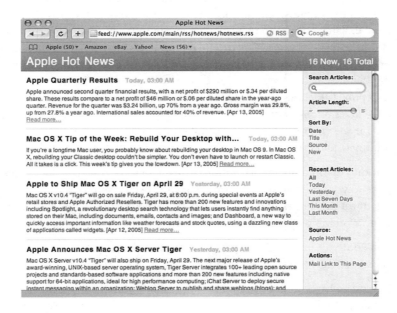

▶ The Google Search field enables you to type a word or phrase of interest and use the powerful Google search engine to locate relevant sites. The results listing appears in your browser window.

Did you
Know?

On the right side of the Safari RSS interface, you can search articles on the current RSS feed, sort by a variety of characteristics, and choose whether to see a brief or long write-up for each item.

These features become even more useful if you create folders of RSS sources in your Bookmarks: You can display all the headlines from the different sources and search or sort them.

By the
Way

Google, located at www.google.com, is a popular search engine with a reputation for strong performance. However, just because a site isn't in Google doesn't mean that it doesn't exist. Search engines work by cataloging sites, not by actually searching all websites at the moment you request the information. Sometimes newer or more obscure sites haven't been cataloged, or a technical glitch results in a site "disappearing" temporarily from the listing.

Bookmarks Bar

Earlier, you were introduced to the Add Bookmark button in the Address bar, which enables you to add the current page to a list of bookmarked pages. The Bookmarks bar holds links to sites you want to keep close at hand.

You can add sites to the Bookmarks bar by clicking the icon in front of the address in the Address field and dragging it into the Bookmarks bar. A sheet window appears where you can enter a name to identify the site, as shown in Figure 14.4. Remove a site by dragging the address outside the Safari window. If you drag addresses within the Bookmarks bar area, you can rearrange them.

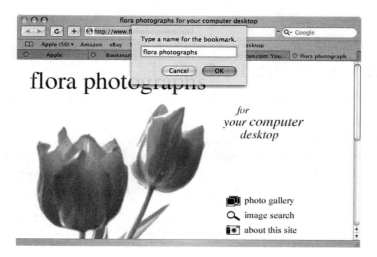

FIGURE 14.4
Keep the page's official title or enter one you'll remember better.

Because only a limited number of items remains visible in the Bookmarks bar, you can also store and organize favorite addresses in an expanded Bookmark view. This is where addresses go when you click the Add Bookmark button. You can open it by clicking the icon that looks like an open book at the far left of the Bookmarks bar. Managing bookmarks is covered later in the chapter in the section "Working with Bookmarks."

Tab Bar

Tabs are an option in Safari that enable you to have several web pages open at one time without all the clutter of extra browser windows. The Tab bar shown previously in Figure 14.2 has three open pages between which you can click. The section "Using Tabs," later in the chapter, talks more about this.

Status Bar

The Status bar, which you can choose to include at the bottom of the Safari window, displays information about a page as it loads. For example, in Figure 14.2, the page has been reloaded, so the Status bar reads Contacting "www.apple.com."

The Status bar also provides information about hyperlinked elements on a page as you move your mouse cursor across them. For example, if you run your mouse across a text link or a linked image, the address to which the link goes appears.

By the Way

Don't underestimate the value of the Status bar. In some cases, seeing the linked address can help you decide whether you want to click. You may decide not to follow links that lead outside the current site, or not to click on links that lead to documents in PDF format.

Web Browsing in Safari

Now that you know what the parts of the Safari interface can do, it's time to do some web browsing.

To visit a website for which you know the address, type the address in the Address field in the Button bar and press Return on your keyboard. You see a blue shaded bar move across the Address field as the page loads, and, if you've chosen to view the Status bar, a countdown of the page elements that are loading.

When a page has loaded, you can click text links, linked images, or buttons to move to other pages, or click in the Address field to type a new address.

Web pages aren't a single object—typically, they are composed of a page file and separate image files. (In some cases, there may be additional supporting files containing page content or formatting information as well.) The countdown in the Status bar as a page loads tells you just how many files it requires!

By the Way

Websites don't always work. If you try to visit a site and receive a `Safari Can't Find The Server` message, as shown in Figure 14.5, the problem is not likely to be Safari. Such a message occurs when there are network problems or technical difficulties for the computer hosting the website, or when a site is no longer available. To make sure the problem was not a momentary glitch, first try reloading the page. If that doesn't work, your next step is to double-check the address you've entered. If the address is correct, you may need to wait before trying the site again, in case there's some kind of temporary server outage.

If the site doesn't return, you can try a Google search on the name of the site to see whether a "cached" version of the content is still available. (By the way, a cached page is the version of the page saved by Google when it cataloged the page's content, and it may not be up to date.)

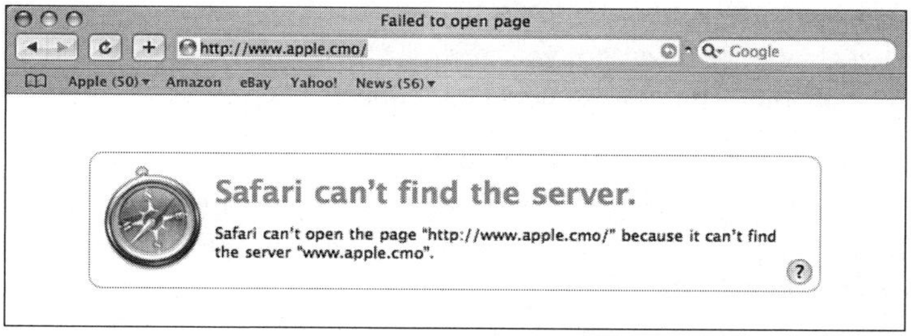

Did you Know?

Safari can't find the server.

Safari can't open the page "http://www.apple.cmo/" because it can't find the server "www.apple.cmo".

FIGURE 14.5
This message lets you know when an address can't be reached. (In this example, the trouble is a misspelling in the intended address.)

If you begin to type in an address you've visited recently, Safari tries to autocomplete it. A drop-down menu of addresses for pages you've visited that match what you've typed so far appears. Also, Safari's best guess of which address you're typing appears, highlighted in blue, in the text field. If the page you want to view is listed in the drop-down menu, use your mouse cursor to select it. If it isn't listed, continue to type the rest of the address in the Address field.

Shopping online has become a popular time (and money) saver in recent years, but it's important to use caution when sending personal information (such as credit card numbers) over the Internet. To make sure that the site accepting your data is configured to transfer data securely, look for a lock icon at the upper right in the Safari window (as in Figure 14.7, later in this chapter). (Note, however, that even a secure site may fall prey to a persistent criminal.)

By the Way

Using Snap-Back

As you use Safari, you may notice an icon displaying a "return" arrow in an orange circle at the far right side of the Address field. That's the Snap-Back button. It appears in any page you navigate to through links within other web pages. If clicked, the Snap-Back button takes you back to the last address you physically typed in the Address field.

You can also manually set a page to be the one to which Snap-Back returns. Simply choose History, Mark Page for Snap-Back from the menu, or use the keyboard short-cut Command-Option-K. This is a convenient way to mark a specific page while you continue following links.

Using Tabs

As you saw previously, Safari's tabs enable you to have several web pages open at one time without the clutter of extra browser windows.

If you want to use tabs, choose Preferences from the Safari menu, open the Tabs pane (shown in Figure 14.6), and check the Enable Tabbed Browsing box. You can also decide whether tabs containing freshly loaded pages will be selected automatically or whether they will wait for you to click them. Finally, you can choose whether to show the Tab bar even when only one tab exists.

After you've enabled tabs, you're ready to try them out. Tabs are easy to use. When you want a new one, choose File, New Tab from the menu (or use the keyboard shortcut Command-T). A row containing tabs appears just below the Address bar. Each tab is labeled with the name of the web page it contains, as shown in Figure 14.7, so you can easily click between them to view different pages. If you want to close a tab, click the close icon on its far-left side.

FIGURE 14.6
The Tabs prefer-ence pane con-tains a few options as well as a list of key-board short-cuts.

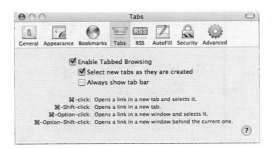

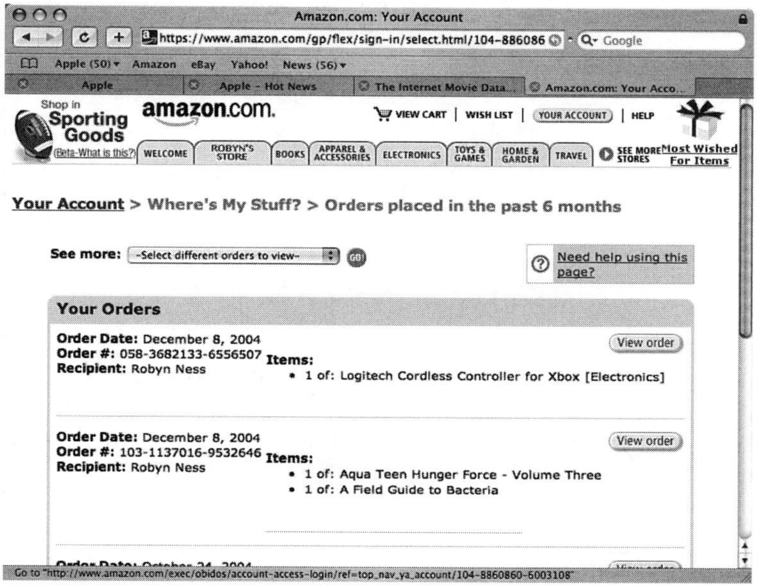

FIGURE 14.7
A row of tabs,
each represent-
ing a web page
ready for view.

If tabbed browsing isn't enabled in the Safari preferences, you don't see the option to open a tab under the File menu.

Watch Out!

If you want to open a linked page in a new tab, hold down the Command key on your keyboard as you click the link.

Did you Know?

Downloading Files

In addition to viewing web pages with Safari, you can also use it to download files linked from web pages.

Downloadable files commonly linked from web pages include PDF files, word-processing or spreadsheet documents, and compressed (or "zipped") files and folders. Compressed files and folders include software applications, such as those discussed in Chapter 9, "Installing Additional Software."

By the Way

When you click a link for certain types of documents, Safari automatically opens a Downloads window, as shown in Figure 14.8. Depending on your preference settings, this window may list other files you've downloaded, as well as show status of the current download.

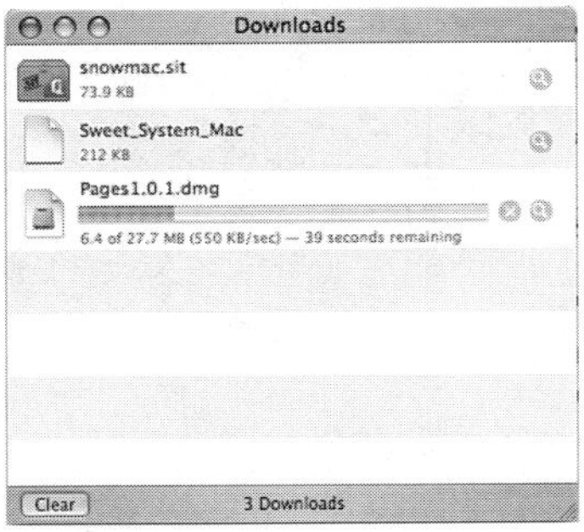

FIGURE 14.8
See the progress of a file as it downloads.

When the download is complete, the file will be on your local computer. By default, Safari stores downloaded files on your desktop, but you can change this option in the General pane of the system preferences, which is discussed in the "Safari Preference Options" section later in this chapter.

Watch Out!

There is a potential for downloaded files to transfer malicious code, such as computer viruses or software that spies on your keystrokes, to your computer. Files from trusted sources are usually safe, but it is smart to exercise caution and to install quality virus-protection software. For information about virus protection, see Chapter 35, "Recovering from Crashes and Other Problems."

Working with Bookmarks

Earlier, you learned to drag a web address from the Address field into the Bookmarks bar to quickly store it for later reference. As useful as that feature is, there's limited space for all the pages you want to keep. However, there is plenty of room in the Bookmarks window, shown in Figure 14.9, which you can open by clicking the Show All Bookmarks button in the Bookmarks bar.

By the Way

In addition to any pages you've bookmarked, Safari also stores all the pages you've visited in the past seven days. You can view them under the History menu or in the History category of the Bookmarks window.

By default, Safari comes with several common websites already stored as bookmarks, but you can add your own simply by clicking the Add Bookmark button in the Address bar when you are viewing a page you want to add. (If the Add Bookmark button is not visible, go to the View menu to select it.) Safari displays a sheet window, shown in Figure 14.10, where you can name your bookmark and select a folder in which to store it.

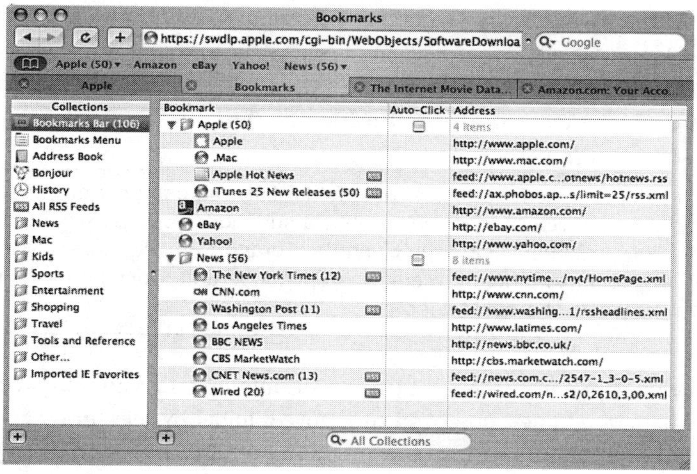

FIGURE 14.9
A special win-
dow to view and
organize lists of
your favorite
websites. (When
opened, it dis-
plays the last
section you
visited.)

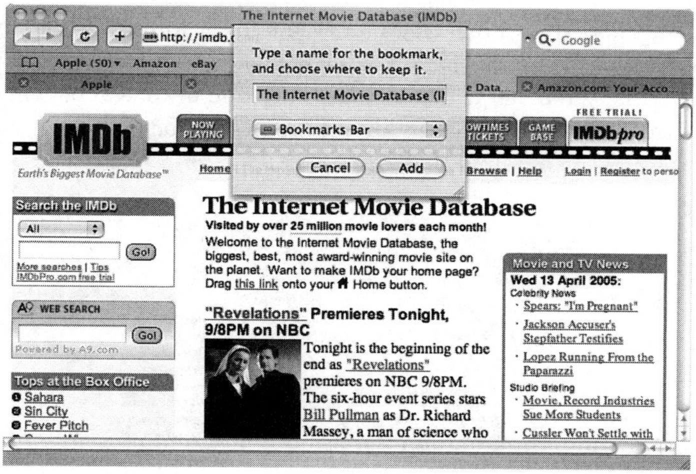

FIGURE 14.10
Name and cate-
gorize the site.

If you had another web browser, such as Internet Explorer, on your computer at the time Safari was installed, Safari may have created a folder of the bookmarks saved for its use.

By the Way

To return to a page you've bookmarked, open the Bookmarks window and choose the folder where you stored it.

If you decide another category would be more appropriate for something you've already bookmarked, you can drag it from one folder into another. If you want to remove a page altogether, select it and press the Delete key on your keyboard. (You can also drag unwanted items to the Trash in the Dock.)

Did you Know?

> If the new category is added to the main folder list, you can drag existing bookmarks into it easily. However, if you created a subfolder, you may have to drag bookmarks into its parent folder first and then drag them into place. Alternatively, you could select bookmarks from elsewhere, choose Edit, Copy from the menu, and paste them into the new folder.

Although Safari's preset category folders are straightforward, you may want to rearrange them or add new ones. You can move a folder by selecting it and dragging it to a new location in the list. An insertion bar appears to show you where it will be placed.

You can create more specialized folders (or even a folder within a folder) by clicking the Create a Bookmarks Folder button at the bottom of the Bookmarks window. Use the button at the bottom left to add a main folder, and the one at bottom center to add a subfolder to the current folder. An untitled folder is added where you can type your new category, as shown in Figure 14.11.

FIGURE 14.11
A new bookmarks subfolder has been named.

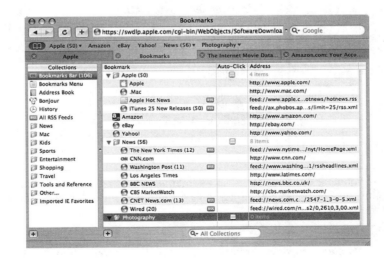

Bookmarks are useful things, but what happens if you use more than one computer? How can you have access to all your bookmarks? Apple has a solution—using iSync (discussed in Chapter 8, "Working with Address Book, Keychain Access, iSync, and Ink") and a .Mac membership, you can synchronize your bookmarks across computers and even view them from nearly any browser over the web. The details are explained in Chapter 16, "Exploring the .Mac Membership."

The Safari Menu Bar

Several features discussed previously in this chapter can be accessed through the Safari menu bar, but additional features are available. Let's review the menu items you've already seen and take a brief look at the others.

Safari Menu

The Safari menu contains many options typically found in an application menu. You can view information about Safari or open the Preferences window, as well as access available services (mentioned during the tour of the menu bar in Chapter 1, "Introducing Mac OS X") and hide or quit the application.

From the Safari menu, you can also report bugs to Apple or easily activate and deactivate the option to block pop-up windows. If you want to prevent Safari from storing information about your browsing activities (such as what pages you view, what files you download, what Google searches you do, and what you entered into online forms), you can turn on Private Browsing. To remove your browser settings altogether, choose Reset Safari from the Safari menu to erase your browsing history, cached files, list of downloads, Google search entries, any cookies set on your computer, and all the data saved for used by the Autofill feature. Choose Empty Cache to delete the web pages and images saved by Safari.

Sometimes, after websites have been updated, web browsers continue to show them (or parts of them) as they used to appear because of images stored in the cache. If this happens, try choosing Empty Cache from the Safari menu and then revisit the site.

File Menu

The File menu contains the basic options for opening and closing new windows or tabs. As in most other applications, the Page Setup and Print features are also located here. The Open Location option places the mouse cursor in the Address field, ready for you to enter a web address. Open File enables you to navigate to web page or image files on your computer that you want to view in Safari. You can also export your current bookmarks into a file so you can transfer them to a different computer, or import such a file.

Edit Menu

The Edit menu contains the standard Copy, Cut, and Paste commands, as well as Select All and Delete.

Undo and Redo options are also found under the Edit menu. They pertain not to moving between pages—you have Forward and Back buttons for that—but rather to changes you make to your bookmarks. Find can be used to quickly locate a word or phrase of interest on a page. For example, in a long list of names and addresses, you can choose Find to go immediately to the entry for the person you want to contact.

Autofill Form, like the Autofill button mentioned earlier, helps you fill in online information.

The Spelling option doesn't check the spelling in websites so that you can recognize when they are poorly proofread. Rather, it enables you to check any text you enter in a text field on a page. For example, if you type a search term in the Search field on the Google web page or in the Google field in the Safari Address bar, you can check its spelling before running a search. You can choose the Check Spelling as You Type option to see a wavy red line under any term your system doesn't recognize.

View Menu

You learned earlier that you can choose which interface options appear in the Safari window in the View menu. You can also control the more advanced options for text encoding and view source. You may know that web pages are written in HTML. Choosing View Source from the View menu allows you to see the HTML that the browser is using to display a given web page.

The Text Encoding option lets you tell Safari in which format to display character sets used in web pages. There is a default setting in the Appearance pane of the Safari preferences, but you can make temporary changes by using this Text Encoding menu option.

History Menu

The History menu contains duplicates of the basic controls for moving through pages: the Back, Forward, and Home items work the same as the buttons typically found in the Address bar. Also in the History menu are the settings to mark a page for Snap Back and to snap back to the currently marked page. Finally, the History menu displays a list of addresses for pages visited in the past week and the option to clear the history.

Bookmarks Menu

The Bookmarks menu provides an alternative way to view and add bookmarks in Safari. (See the "Working with Bookmarks" section earlier in this chapter.)

Window Menu

The Window menu contains options related to viewing Safari windows—including the download manager—and tabs. It also includes the standard "minimize" and "zoom" window controls for covering or uncovering your desktop.

Help Menu

The Help menu gives you access to Apple-created instructions for using Safari and to the acknowledgements and user license agreement for the software. It also enables you to view which plug-ins recognized by Safari are installed on your system. Figure 14.12 shows an example.

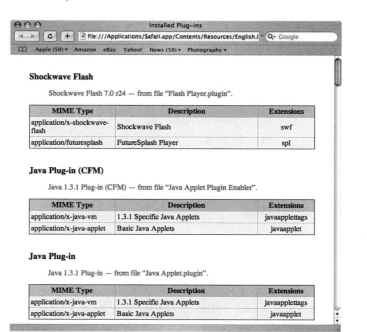

FIGURE 14.12
See what plug-ins are available on your computer for Safari to use.

Plug-ins are supplemental programs that enable you to view content from web pages created in a format other than plain HTML. Examples include the QuickTime and Flash Players, which play movie-like elements in your browser window.

Safari Preference Options

You've seen how to change your default home page in the General section of the Safari preferences, as well as how to change settings for tabs. This section reviews the preferences already covered and looks at any that were left out.

General Preferences

Options under General preferences, shown in Figure 14.13, include many common settings related to how a Safari window is launched and how pages and files are accessed.

FIGURE 14.13
Choose your default web browser and default home page in the General preferences pane.

The first option is a choice of your default web browser, or the web browser that launches automatically whenever you click a link received in email or through another program. The drop-down menu lists any application recognized as a web browser by your system.

You also have the option of choosing whether new windows that open come up with a specific home page that you've chosen, as an empty page, with any page currently open, or in Bookmarks mode. (Setting a default home page was covered in a note in the "Address Bar" section earlier in this chapter.)

The next three options pertain to downloading files. You have the option to save downloaded files to the Desktop or to choose another location from the standard OS X file browser. You can also decide how items are to be removed from your Download list: manually, when Safari quits, or upon successful download. (Note that removing items from the list doesn't affect files that have been downloaded.) If you like to keep a record of what you've downloaded, set it to Manually; if you prefer a clean slate, choose one of the other options.

The third download-related preference is the Open "Safe" Files After Downloading check box. Safe files, by Safari's definition, are files unlikely to cause harm to your system, including media files, such as images and sounds, PDF or text files, and disk images. If this option is checked, any "safe" files automatically become active when they are downloaded; otherwise, you need to double-click downloaded files to launch or uncompress them.

The final setting relates back to how Safari reacts to links you open from other applications. You can decide whether to open links in a new window or in the current window.

Appearance

The Appearance pane, shown in Figure 14.14, contains the web page display settings over which the viewer can have some input. You can choose any font on the system to be used on web pages where another font is not specifically specified. You can also choose a *fixed-width font,* a font in which all letters take up the same area in a line of text, to be used when the specified font needs to align in a specific way.

FIGURE 14.14
Choose fonts and character encoding preferences.

You can also decide whether to load images in a web page, in case you'd rather not wait for them to download. Finally, you can set default character encoding, which tells your browser how to interpret characters in a web page. For example, if you regularly read Japanese websites, you need your character encoding and the web page to use the same setting to see the correct characters.

Bookmarks

Choose whether to include web pages listed in your Address Book or available on your local network (through Rendezvous) in the Bookmarks bar or Bookmarks menu.

You can also choose to synchronize your bookmarks across computers using .Mac, as discussed earlier.

Tabs

As mentioned earlier, the Tabs pane, shown previously in Figure 14.6, allows you to control preferences related to tabbed browsing. You can enable tabbed browsing and choose whether the tab bar will be visible even when only one window is open. You can also set whether to open tabs as they are created, or allow them to open in the background and wait until you choose to open them.

RSS

The RSS preferences, shown in Figure 14.15, let you choose your default RSS reader (why not Safari?). It also lets you choose whether or not to automatically update the data from RSS feeds and how often. (You can also choose a color to highlight new articles for easy scanning.) Finally, set a time for removing old RSS articles or click the Remove Now button to clear the list.

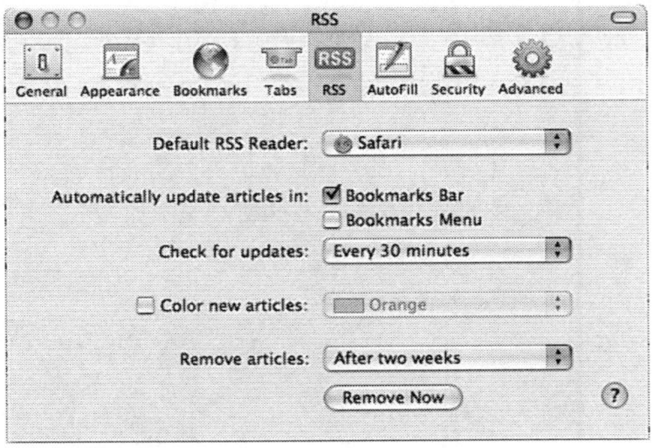

FIGURE 14.15
Change your
RSS settings.

Autofill

In the Autofill pane you can choose whether to allow Autofill access to information stored in your card in the Address Book, based on sites and passwords you've entered for it to use, or based on data from other forms you've filled in. After each option is an Edit button. Clicking the Edit button allows you to view or remove any information stored for use by Autofill.

Security

The Security pane, shown in Figure 14.16, contains settings for how Safari should respond to different elements it encounters as you visit web pages. The first group of options are common elements of web pages employed mostly for benevolent uses, but that can be abused.

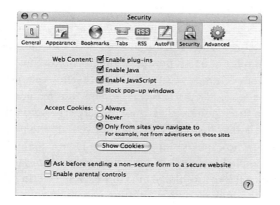

FIGURE 14.16
Security options include how your browser interacts with websites.

As you learned earlier, plug-ins are supplemental programs that enable you to view content from web pages created in a format other than plain HTML. If you don't want to allow this content, you can choose to disable plug-ins. Keep in mind, however, that the elements created for use with plug-ins are not readable.

Java is a computer programming language for creating interactive applications that run either inside or outside a web browser. You may choose to disable Java to prevent such applications from running on your computer.

JavaScript is a simple scripting language often used to make regular web pages show some interaction. For example, JavaScript is often used to make images change when you move your mouse cursor over them. If you find motion onscreen distracting, you can disable JavaScript. However, be aware that some pages are more difficult to understand and may even have content that is visible only to people who have JavaScript enabled for their browsers.

Another common use of JavaScript is to open new browser windows on your screen—sometimes whether you want them or not. Pop-up ads are often used for web advertising, but Safari gives you the option to block these additional windows. Although this can be a good way to eliminate annoying ads, keep in mind that some sites open additional windows containing important content in the hopes of getting people's attention. Those who block pop-up windows may miss real content.

> You can easily activate or deactivate pop-up window blocking from the Safari
> application menu.

Another tool often used by web developers is *cookies*. Cookies are small pieces of
data stored on your local computer by the computer that hosts a website. This is
done so that the site can identify you as a unique visitor.

Mostly, cookies are used so that a website can provide better service. For instance, if
you purchase books at Amazon.com and then return to the site, you are welcomed
by name and shown a list of books that may interest you because the site identifies
your account with your computer. Use of cookies also enables a person to move
freely between pages in some types of secure systems that require user login. Cookies
often are required in these situations because the server hosting the website needs to
know on every page within the secure section that you are the person who logged
in, and not someone who's simply skipped over the login page without authorization. In the first example, the cookie would be stored for a long time—perhaps a
year or more—so that the site would be able to welcome you. In secure sections,
cookies may last only until you quit out of the Safari application.

Although many sites use cookies for benevolent visitor tracking, there is the potential for cookies to be used to track people's habits on the web even outside the site
that issues the cookie. Many people find this an invasion of privacy. For this reason,
Safari gives you the option to always accept cookies, never accept cookies, or to
accept cookies only from sites to which you purposely navigate. You can also click
the Show Cookies button to view any cookies currently stored on your computer and
to delete any you want to remove.

The last option on the Security pane is a check box to ask before sending a nonse-
cure form to a secure server. Activating this feature alerts you when you may be
sending sensitive data over the web through a web connection not designed to
ensure privacy.

Advanced

The Advanced pane, shown in Figure 14.17, includes settings most people don't
need to change.

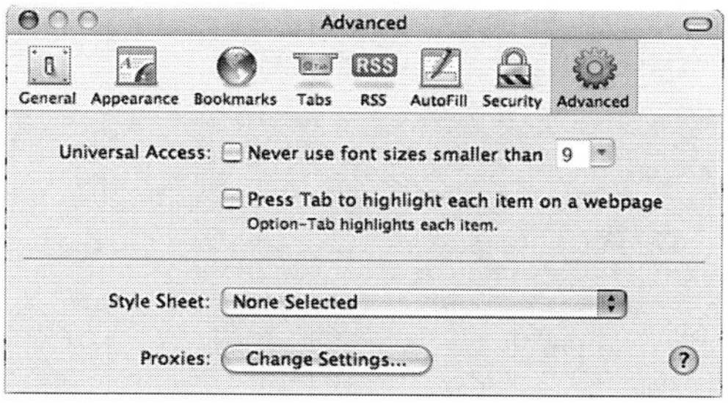

FIGURE 14.17
The default settings of the Advanced options should probably be left intact.

Under Universal Access settings are two options that make web browsing easier. You can set a minimum font size, or enable the option to tab through links on a web page rather than use your mouse.

The next option allows you to set your own style sheet, which is a specially formatted description of how text on a page should be displayed. For example, with a carefully written style sheet, you could have text in web pages that is coded as a heading appear in extremely large type, or even change its color, or reset the background of a page to another color to increase or reduce contrast. (Although this feature can be useful, writing style sheets is outside the scope of this book.)

Changing settings for proxies is another topic outside the scope of this book. Proxy servers are computers that serve as intermediaries between a user's computer, such as yours, and the computer that serves a web page. The proxy server may be used to manage the flow of data over a network that is due to requests from many users. If your computer is part of a local network with a network administrator, you may want to ask about any proxy servers and settings that may be recommended.

Summary

You became acquainted with the Safari web browser in this chapter, as well as some basics of web browsing. You learned how to view web pages and download files. You also learned how to create and organize bookmarks to favorite web pages. Finally, you learned what preference options you can use to customize Safari to suit you.

CHAPTER 15

Using Sherlock for Internet Searches

As its name implies, the Sherlock application is something of a detective, tracking down information on the Internet from the clues you provide. With specialized search categories, including yellow pages and a dictionary, Sherlock will quickly become your one-stop reference tool.

Sherlock is basically a collection of Internet search functions, each packaged in its own "channel." The default channels are listed in the Channels menu of the Channels pane, as shown in Figure 15.1. They're also listed in the toolbar at the top of the window.

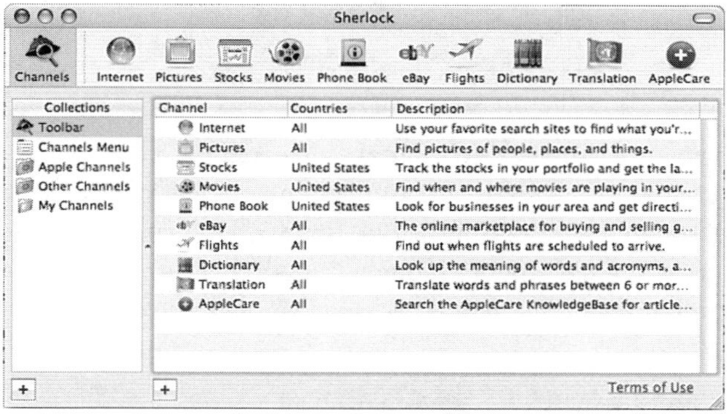

FIGURE 15.1
The Channels area of Sherlock displays the available search functions and brief descriptions of each.

> Long-time Mac users might be confused by the more recent incarnation of Sherlock, which doesn't include the option to search the local machine's files. That feature is now available directly from the Finder, either in the Search option in the toolbar of the Finder window or in a separate Find window opened by selecting Find from the Finder's File menu (or by using the keyboard shortcut Command-F). Refer to Chapter 2, "Using the Finder," for further information.

By the Way

Each channel provides a specific kind of information, gathered from another source and displayed within the Sherlock interface. Notice that at the bottom of the Channels pane is a Terms of Use link, which opens a sheet explaining that Apple doesn't produce most of the content displayed in Sherlock.

Let's take a look at each default channel's use and special features.

The Internet Channel

The Internet channel compiles search results from popular Internet search sites, such as Ask Jeeves and Lycos. As shown in Figure 15.2, each search result lists the title and address of a web page, a relevance ranking, and the search site or sites that provided the entry.

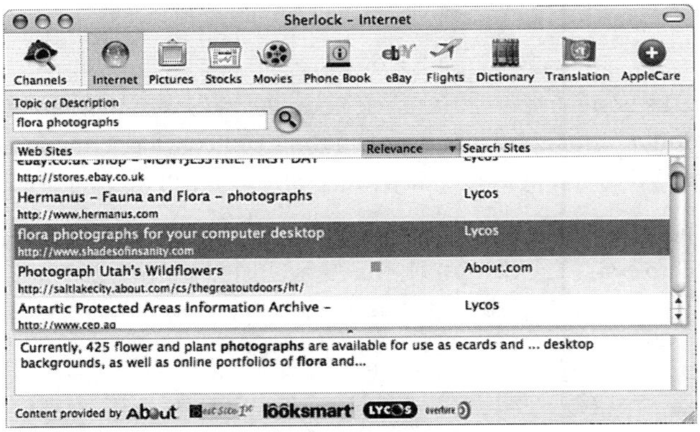

FIGURE 15.2
Searching the Internet from a variety of search engines is simplified by Sherlock.

To perform an Internet search, simply type your search terms into the text entry field at the top of the Internet channel pane and click the green Search button or press Return. When the results listing appears, you can select an entry with a single click to see a site description, if one is available. Double-clicking launches your default web browser and opens the page you requested.

The Pictures Channel

In a manner similar to searches using the Internet channel, the Pictures channel queries photo databases for digital images based on your search terms. Thumbnail images of the results are displayed in the results pane, as shown in Figure 15.3. Double-click a thumbnail image in the results to open a web page displaying the full-sized picture.

Watch Out!

The photos displayed in the Pictures channel searches might not be free for commercial use. Read the terms of service from the originating site if you have any questions about what's allowed.

FIGURE 15.3
Results appear
as thumbnail
images—
double-click
one to see
the original.

The Stocks Channel

The Stocks channel, shown in Figure 15.4, provides details about the market performance of publicly traded companies. The information shown includes the stock price at last trade, price change, price range over the course of the day, and the volume of shares traded. You can also view charts of a company's performance over the past year or week or for the current day.

FIGURE 15.4
Enter a company's name or
market symbol
to see information about it,
including recent
news stories.

To find information about a company, enter its name or market symbol. Market symbols are unique identifiers, but many companies have similar names or several separate divisions. If you enter a name, you might see a sheet asking you to choose the company in which you're interested, as shown Figure 15.5. Select the correct name or symbol and click the Add button or press Return.

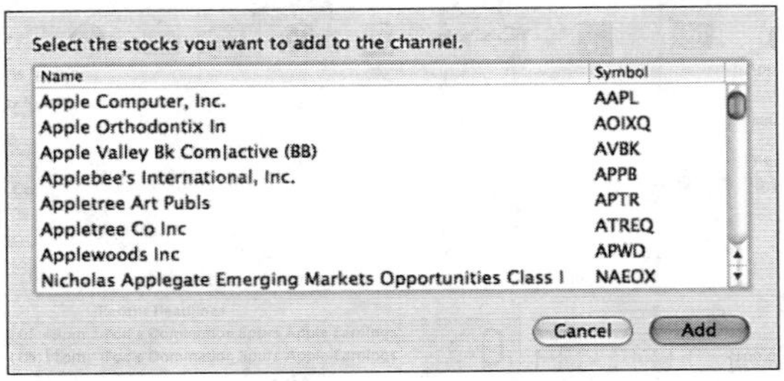

FIGURE 15.5
If you enter a string of letters that appears in more than one company name, a sheet window appears where you can choose the company in which you're interested.

Select the stocks you want to add to the channel.

Name	Symbol
Apple Computer, Inc.	AAPL
Apple Orthodontix In	AOIXQ
Apple Valley Bk Com|active (BB)	AVBK
Applebee's International, Inc.	APPB
Appletree Art Publs	APTR
Appletree Co Inc	ATREQ
Applewoods Inc	APWD
Nicholas Applegate Emerging Markets Opportunities Class I	NAEOX

Cancel   Add

Watch Out!

Market symbols and companies with similar names can make it difficult to ask for the listing you really want. If you don't enter the exact market symbol, some guesswork might be involved for Sherlock to return any results. Always check to make sure that the displayed information is for the company you thought you requested!

As you view information for different companies, they are added to the list in the middle of the Stocks pane so that you can easily return to them. If you want to remove a listing, simply select it and press the Delete key on your keyboard.

In addition to providing stock quotes, Sherlock also displays recent news articles pertaining to the selected company. To read a story, select its headline from the left of the chart, and the bottom pane displays the full text.

The Movies Channel

Sherlock's Movies channel, shown in Figure 15.6, pulls together all the information you need to choose a movie and a theater in which to view it.

To use the Movies channel, you need to enter either your city and state or your ZIP Code in the Find Near box. (If you start typing letters, the Find Near box tries to auto-complete with a city that matches the letters you've typed so far.) Then you can choose to search either Movies or Theaters in your area. The Showtime pop-up menu enables you to choose the date of interest to you.

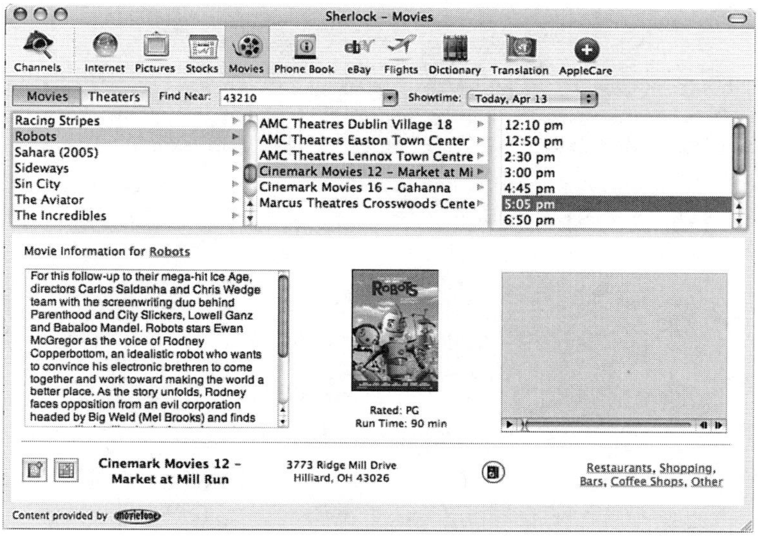

FIGURE 15.6
The Movies channel displays a QuickTime preview of the selected movie, as well as theater addresses.

Choose the movie and theater listings at the top of the panel that are of interest to you, and the bottom of the window fills with theater and movie information. In addition to a text summary of the movie, you can watch a preview in QuickTime format for the selected option.

> To play the QuickTime preview, you might be prompted to set your network connection information in QuickTime Preferences if you haven't already done so. Refer to the section on QuickTime in Chapter 7, "Using QuickTime and DVD Player," for more details.

By the Way

The Phone Book Channel

The Phone Book channel has two modes: a person search and a business search.

The person search mode, shown in Figure 15.7, enables you to find a phone number and address by entering a person's name and a general location. To perform a person search, click the information button at the upper left (the one with an "i" in a white circle). Enter a last name, a first name, and either the city and state or the ZIP Code of the area to search. Then click the green Search button. In the middle pane, choose from among the list of potential matches to see detailed information, including a map.

FIGURE 15.7
Locate a person
by name and
location.

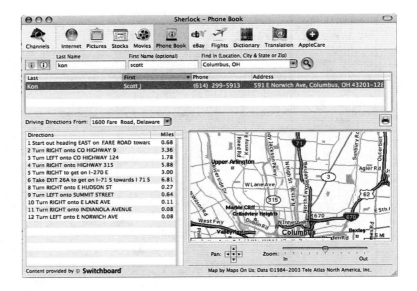

Use the business search, shown in Figure 15.8, to obtain the phone number and
address for a business and to view a map to its location. Simply click the information button on the right (the one with an *i* in a yellow circle), enter the business
name and either the city and state or the ZIP Code of the area to search, and click
the green Search button. In the middle pane, choose from among the list of potential matches to see detailed information.

FIGURE 15.8
Obtain contact
information and
personalized
driving direc-
tions to busi-
nesses.

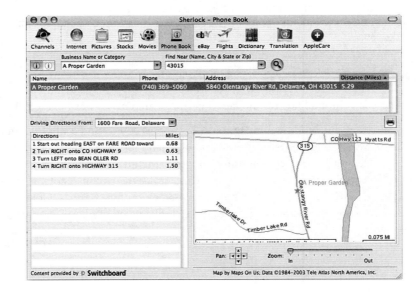

To receive driving directions to addresses turned up in either the person or business search, enter an address in the Driving Directions From text field. The Directions pane fills with step-by-step instructions.

You can then select the location you added in the Driving Directions From pop-up menu.

The eBay Channel

From the eBay channel, you can search active eBay auctions and track those of interest to you. To search, enter keywords in the Item Title text entry field and set your other parameters, such as product category, region, and price range; then click the Search button. When you choose a result from the search, its details fill the bottom panes of the screen, as shown in Figure 15.9.

To track an item, highlight it in the results listing and click the Track Auction button at lower right. Changing to Track mode (using the button just below the search field) reveals a list of only those items you're tracking. To remove an item, select it and press Delete on your keyboard.

FIGURE 15.9
If you enjoy online auctions, the eBay channel will delight you.

The Flights Channel

For information on current flights, go to the Flights channel. Here you can view flight status by route or by airline and flight number. Select a specific flight for details about the aircraft and flight. For some entries, you can also view a chart depicting the plane's position en route, as shown in the lower-right corner of Figure 15.10.

FIGURE 15.10
View the status of specific flights, including a chart of the flight path.

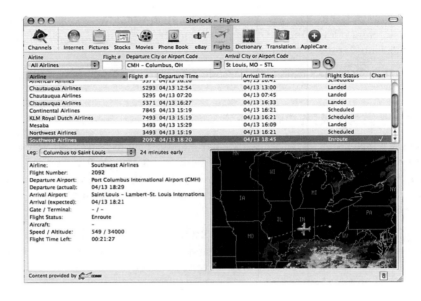

You can click the small switchlike button at the bottom right of the Flights pane to set preferences for the Flights channel. As shown in Figure 15.11, you can choose airlines and airports by continent.

FIGURE 15.11
Choose a continent to select all airlines flying in a region, or check boxes for all continents whose airports you want to include in your search.

The Dictionary Channel

As you might expect, you look up word definitions in the Dictionary channel (shown in Figure 15.12). For some words, you also see a list—in the lower half of the pane—of phrases that contain that word or relate to it.

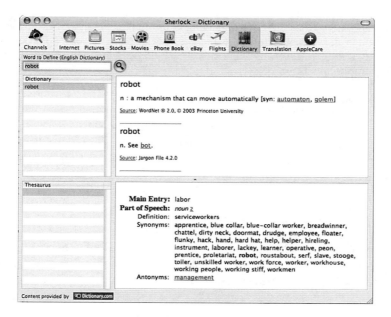

FIGURE 15.12
Expand your vocabulary with help from the Dictionary channel.

The Translation Channel

The Translation channel, shown in Figure 15.13, performs rough translations between different languages. English speakers can translate into Simplified and Traditional Chinese, Dutch, French, German, Greek, Italian, Japanese, Korean, Portuguese, Russian, and Spanish, and then back to English.

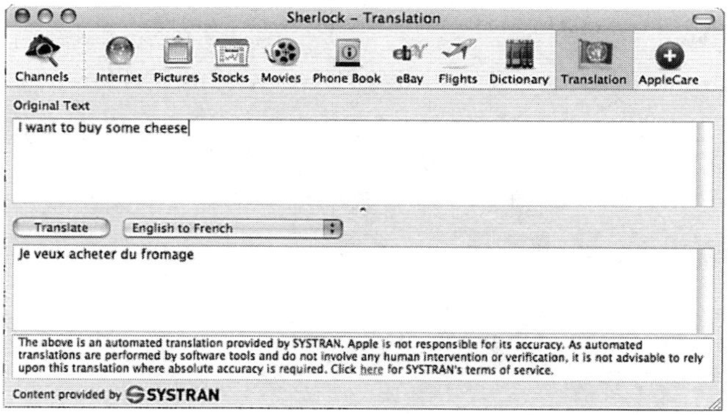

FIGURE 15.13
To translate text, type the original text into the top text field, choose an option for translating the original language into another language, and click the Translate button.

If there is a large block of text in a document or email message that you want to translate but don't want to retype, you can select the text, choose Edit, Copy from the menu, and then switch to Sherlock's Translation channel and choose Edit, Paste from the menu.

When using this service, keep in mind that computer-generated translations do not match the output of a skilled human translator. Don't use the Sherlock's translations for serious issues, such as business correspondence. Many expressions don't translate literally between languages, and you run the risk of sending gibberish instead of conveying the message you intended.

The AppleCare Channel

If you have a specific technical question about Apple software or hardware that OS X's Help Viewer can't resolve, use the AppleCare channel, shown in Figure 15.14, to search the AppleCare Knowledge Base for reports about Apple products and issues.

FIGURE 15.14
A quick search of the AppleCare Knowledge Base can answer many of your questions about Apple products.

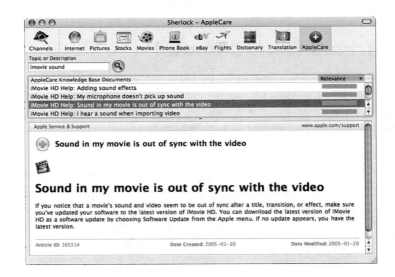

Now that we have explored the default channels, let's take a quick look at some channels written outside Apple.

Third-Party Channels

In addition to the channels you've see so far in this chapter, which were created by Apple, there are many channels written by others to enable you to view information on topics ranging from news to astrology and from weather to sports calendars.

To access this information, click the Channels button at the upper left of the Sherlock toolbar to open the Channels pane. Next, choose Other Channels from the list along the left side of the window. As shown in Figure 15.15, a plethora of channels appears in the right column, along with the countries to which they apply and a brief description.

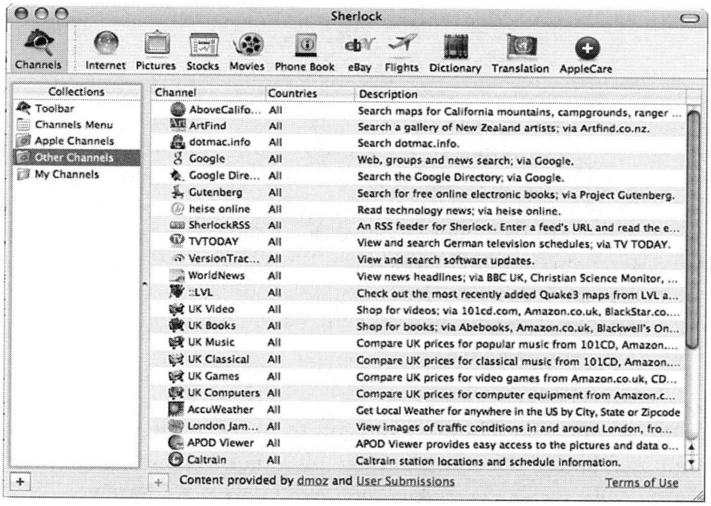

FIGURE 15.15
The list of channels created outside Apple.

To open one of these channels, double-click its listing. Each channel has its own interface to support the information it displays; you have to follow the cues in the channel's interface to figure out what information will be provided and how to perform a search.

The quality of third-party channels varies greatly. Some are helpful; others merely frustrate.

Before this tour of Sherlock is complete, it's important examine the features accessible in Sherlock's preferences.

The Sherlock Preferences

The Sherlock Preferences, as shown in Figure 15.16, are minimal. You have the option to allow Sherlock to accept cookies always or never as it searches the Internet on your behalf. *Cookies* are small files sent to your computer from some websites that provide specific types of services, such as personalized user accounts and online shopping.

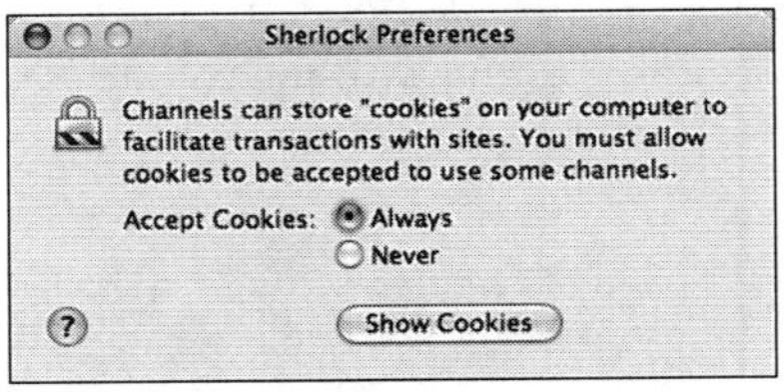

FIGURE 15.16
Choose to accept or decline cookies, or show a list of any cookies currently stored on your computer.

Sites use cookies to keep track of you as you interact with the site. (This is because the computer running the website doesn't have another way to recognize that you're the same person who looked at the preceding page.) Even though cookies are mostly harmless, some people don't like the idea of having others track their movements on the Internet, even if the information is most likely never seen by human eyes. That's why Sherlock gives you the choice of whether to accept cookies. (Note, however, that some sites require use of cookies for you to interact with them successfully.)

By the Way

If you click the Show Cookies button, you can see a list of the cookies accumulated on your computer, both by Sherlock and by any other web browsing applications you use. If you want to remove cookies, you can select them individually and click the Remove button or choose to delete all stored cookies with a click of the Remove All button. When finished with the list of cookies, click Done. Remember, however, that removing cookies can interfere with your ability to access some websites; if you delete the cookie that gives you access to an online account you may need to re-register to use the site.

Summary

In this chapter, you learned how to use Sherlock, your system's built-in Internet search tool. You saw the wide range of specialized search channels available from Apple, including movie listings and stock quotes, as well as a source for channels written by third parties.

CHAPTER 16

Exploring .Mac Membership

.Mac (pronounced "dot Mac") is a for-pay, Internet-based service available from Apple. It includes a range of services built around storage space on Apple's .Mac server and is integrated with the OS X operating system and several of Apple's applications in key ways. This chapter takes a look at those services.

Defining .Mac

The easiest way to define .Mac is to enumerate the services it offers:

▶ .Mac Email—Apple-hosted email services, including a user-friendly web interface, are included as part of the subscription. An account holder receives 125MB quota of mail storage. Additional accounts can be added to a .Mac account for a small fee.

Apple lists iChat as one of the .Mac features. iChat, however, is available for free to any Mac OS X user. A .Mac account name can serve as your buddy name; however, even if you just sign up for a demo account, you get to keep the account name indefinitely and can use it with iChat as you like. (See Chapter 18, "Using iChat AV," for more information about iChat.)

By the Way

▶ Network storage (iDisk)—The .Mac iDisk offers 125MB of network-accessible storage. Using your iDisk, you can access your files from other machines or even share them with friends.

▶ Synchronization services—.Mac, in conjunction with iSync (discussed in Chapter 8, "Working with Address Book, Keychain Access, iSync, and Ink"), provides a means for all your Macs to share the same bookmarks for the Safari web browser, Address Book information, and calendars through the iCal application.

▶ Exclusive software—Apple offers two pieces of .Mac "member's only" software: Virex (virus protection) and Apple's own Backup (personal document backups). These pieces of software make .Mac an especially good value if you need the functionality they offer. If you were, for example, planning to buy a virus protection package for $50 already, that's half the cost of a .Mac subscription. (See Chapter 34, "Maintaining Your System," for more about backups and Chapter 35, "Recovering from Crashes and Other Problems," for more about Virex.)

▶ Communication-oriented web services—The .Mac HomePage feature provides page templates and site management controls that make it easy to create custom websites—either by using files from your iDisk or by exporting them from within iPhoto. Users can also send iCards created with their own or professionally photographed images.

▶ Training—Basic Macintosh tutorials and training materials are available online for common family/consumer activities such as using iTunes, creating web pages, and so on. These features serve as nice introductions for beginners.

▶ Software Discounts—Special software discounts are offered through .Mac for select packages.

Because describing how to use a website (www.mac.com) is not the purpose of this book (and the information contained on the site is variable in nature), we won't attempt to document the features that you access through your web browser. Instead, we look at how .Mac's features are used in the Mac OS X desktop and then take a brief walk-through of the web services so that you can make the decision of whether you want to join .Mac.

Setting Up .Mac Service

To set up your .Mac services, open the System Preferences application and open the .Mac pane under the Internet & Network section. Your screen should resemble Figure 16.1.

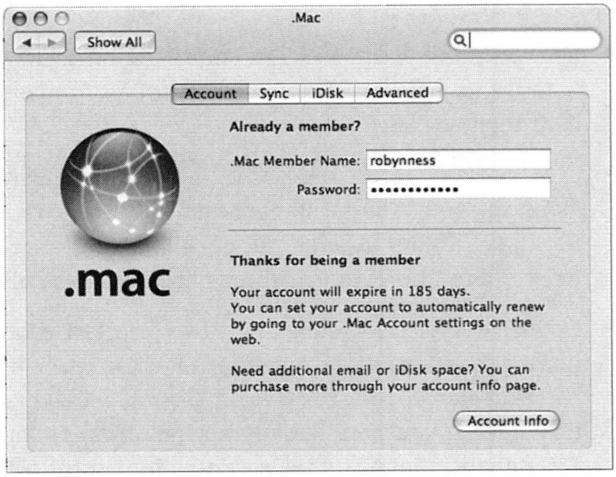

FIGURE 16.1
Configure or create .Mac services in the .Mac preference pane.

Your choices are limited: Either enter an existing .Mac member name and password, or click the Learn More button to create a new account. If signing up for the first time, your web browser launches, and you are taken to the .Mac sign-up page. Keep in mind that you don't need to commit to a full account immediately. You can apply for a 60-day free trial and try many of the members-only features (except for the exclusive software and access to .Mac Support discussions) before you buy.

If you already have a .Mac account, enter your account information in the appropriate fields and then either close the preference window or click the iDisk button at the top of the window to view the status of your iDisk. (This is a quick way to verify that the account information is entered correctly and everything is working as it should.)

Using the iDisk

The Apple iDisk is storage space to which your system automatically "knows" how to connect without additional information. iDisk is the cornerstone of the .Mac service and is what makes most of the other services possible. For example, without a central storage place to keep iSync information, there would be no means of synchronizing multiple computers on different networks.

iDisk requires a network connection and is barely usable on dial-in lines. Cable and DSL should be considered the minimum tolerable network requirement for making a connection.

Watch Out!

iDisk enables you to keep a copy of its contents on your local machine so that you can use it when not connected to the Internet; the next time you are connected, the folders are synchronized automatically. This means that you always have an up-to-date offline copy of the files in case your Internet connection goes down.

iDisk appears like any other connected disk or drive, whether you work with the contents online or use the local copy. The synchronization occurs unobtrusively. As you make changes to the files, they are noted and automatically uploaded to the .Mac server in the background. You can also choose to synchronize files manually if you want.

iDisk Storage Space and Settings

You can customize how your iDisk works and view a quick status of how much space is available by clicking the iDisk button within the .Mac system preferences pane. The pane is shown in Figure 16.2.

FIGURE 16.2
Configure your
iDisk and view
the space avail-
able.

At the top of the pane is the amount of storage currently in use and the total available. You can buy additional iDisk storage space by clicking the Buy More button.
Additional iDisk space is sold, like .Mac, on a subscription basis.

You can also choose whether a local copy of your iDisk is created that can be synchronized with your actual iDisk space. To do this, click the Start/Stop button under
iDisk Syncing. If you don't enable iDisk Syncing, your iDisk is accessible only over
the Internet, and you cannot work with the contents without an active network connection.

Did you Know?

You can force synchronization at any time by clicking the chasing arrow (circular
arrows) icon to the right of the iDisk icon in the sidebar of the Finder window. If
you've chosen to have your Mac automatically synchronize the iDisk, you can tell
when synchronization is in progress by watching the chasing arrow—it spins while
synchronizing.

After you enable iDisk syncing, you can use the radio buttons to select whether it
happens automatically or manually. If you have a slower Internet connection or
don't plan to access your iDisk files often, you might want to set it to Manually.

By the Way

If you disable synchronization between your iDisk and the local copy, Mac OS X
creates a disk image file of the local copy on your desktop. This ensures that you
don't lose any data that hasn't been transferred to your iDisk, but also prevents
you from making changes to your local copy that can no longer be saved to your
iDisk. You can mount that disk image to get at the contents or throw it away if you
want.

Also in the iDisk pane are controls for determining how your public folder is accessed. The iDisk public folder is a special directory on the iDisk that can be read by other Mac OS X users without your .Mac login information. You can use the Public folder as a place to exchange files.

To keep things under your control, Apple provides the option of choosing whether other users (that is, not you) have read-only or read-write access to your folder, and whether the folder should be password-protected. If you choose to password-protect the folder, you are prompted to set a new password—*do not* use your .Mac password. This is a password that you give out to your friends so that they can connect to your Public folder.

Click out of the iDisk pane to activate your iDisk settings.

Do *not* store copyrighted/pirated material in your public folder.

If you enable read/write access to your Public folder, be aware that you've turned over a portion of your iDisk storage space to the public. If your public folder is filled, it counts against your 125MB iDisk total.

Accessing and Synchronizing Your iDisk

After entering the membership information needed to connect to your iDisk, you can immediately start using the service. To access your iDisk, open a Finder window and click the iDisk icon in the sidebar, or chooe Go, iDisk, My iDisk from the menu (Shift-Command-I). After a few seconds, thes iDisk icon (a blue orb) appears on your desktop.

Open the iDisk as you would any other disk. If you click the iDisk icon in the Finder sidebar, the Finder window refreshes to show its contents. If you mounted it from the Go menu, you can double-click the iDisk icon on the desktop to open the window shown in Figure 16.3.

An iDisk contains nine folders, some of which are similar to the folders in a Mac OS X user account (as discussed in Chapter 2, "Using the Finder"):

▶ Backup—A folder used by the .Mac Backup application to back up your files. This folder is read-only, so you can view the files it contains but can't add new ones; only Backup can add and remove items from this folder.

▶ Documents—Your personal storage space for "stuff." No one has access to these files but you.

FIGURE 16.3
The folders in
your iDisk are
stored on the
.Mac server.

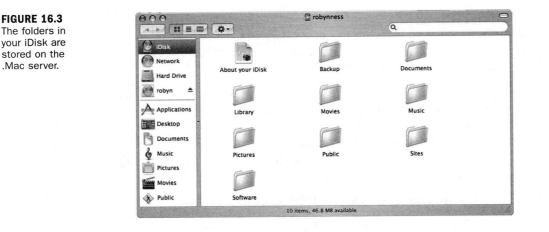

▶ Library—Data storage for applications such as iSync. Again, these files are maintained automatically and probably shouldn't be touched.

▶ Movies—A place to store your movie files. Movies placed in this location are available for use within the .Mac HomePage website builder utilitys.

▶ Music—A place for you to store your music files. With the advent of the Apple Music Store, it's reason to guess that Apple will be adding the capability to download song purchases to this folder in the future.

▶ Pictures—Like Music and Movies, Pictures provides a content-specific place for you to drop your image files. Images placed in the Pictures folder are available within HomePage and the Apple's iCard builder.

▶ Public—Your online folder that can be opened to the public. Files stored here can be accessed (if you choose) by friends or anyone in the world.

▶ Sites—The files for your Apple-hosted mac.com website are stored in the Sites folder. Files placed here are accessible via the URL homepage.mac.com/ *<mac.com username>/<filename>*.

▶ Software—Apple's collection of freeware and demo Mac OS X software and music. If you need a quick software fix, you can find it here.

Work with iDisk as you would your hard drive or a network share, but be aware that copying files to or from the iDisk takes time. If you are configured to maintain a local copy of the iDisk, transfers seem nearly instantaneous, but the actual transfer occurring in the background may take minutes or hours, depending on the quality of your connection and the amount of data to be transferred. If you are working with large files via your iDisk, it may be to your benefit to work off a local copy because your work will be saved and retrieve locally quickly, all the while transferring to you remote iDisk.

Accessing Other Users' iDisks

To access the iDisks of other users, simply choose iDisk, Other User's iDisk from the Finder's Go menu. You are prompted for the user's membership sname and password, as shown in Figure 16.4.

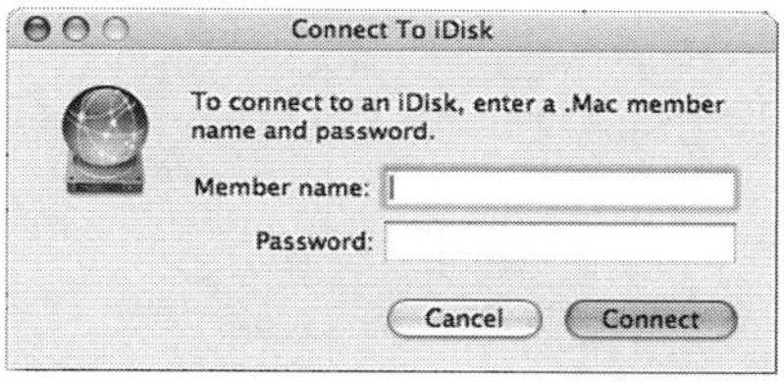

FIGURE 16.4
Mount another
user's iDisk.

To mount a user's Public folder, choose iDisk, Other User's Public Folder from the Go menu. In this case, you are prompted for the member name, but you do not need to supply a password unless one has been set by the owner of the remote iDisk account.

As in previous versions of Mac OS X, you can mount the iDisk volume with Connect To Server by supplying the URL idisk.mac.com/<*mac.com username*>.

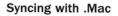

Did you Know?

Syncing with .Mac

Probably the most compelling web service for advanced users is the access to traditionally "desktop" information while on the go. iSync (discussed in Chapter 8) used with .Mac keeps everything "connected" so that what you see on your desktop is available on other computers overs the network, and vice versa. Figure 16.5, for example, shows the Bookmark browser.

Likewise, .Mac email and address book entries are also accessed through a web interface—and carry the feel of a native Mac OS X application along with them. Figure 16.6 shows the .Mac web-based email.

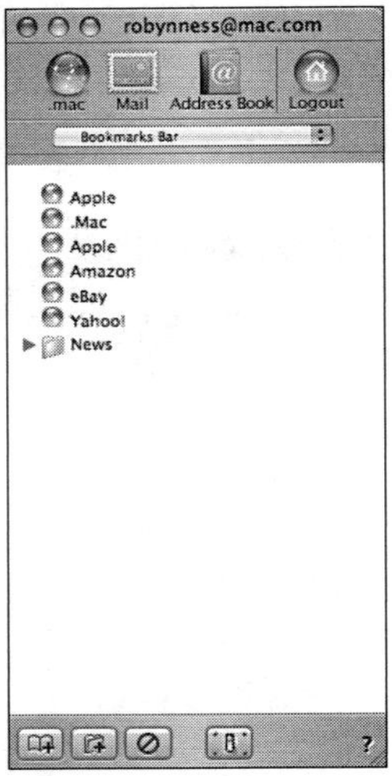

FIGURE 16.5
The Bookmark browser enables you to access and update bookmarks from anywhere.

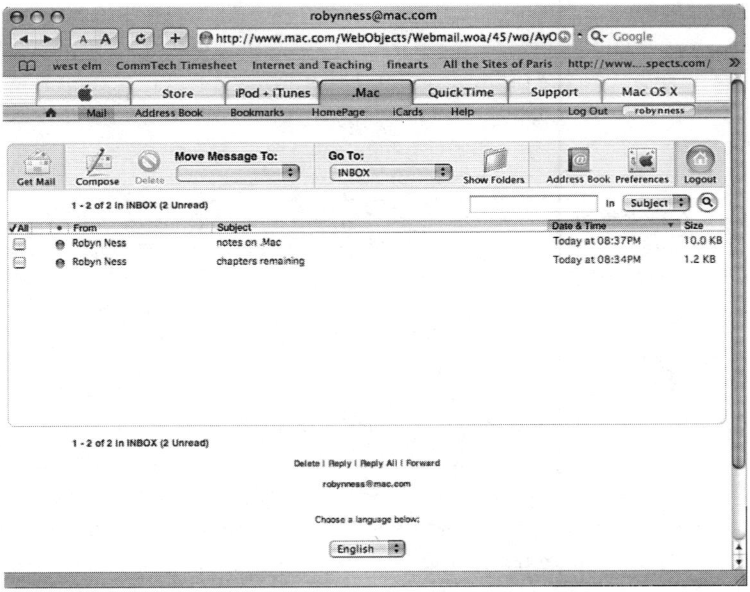

FIGURE 16.6
It's like your Mac OS X email application—in a web browser.

> **By the Way**
>
> Under the Account settings of the Preferences in the .Mac Mail interface, you can choose to forward you .Mac mail to another account. You can also set your .Mac mail account to check other email accounts—this is a convenient way to check POP email accounts when you are away from your regular computer without making the messages inaccessible from your regular computer later. (Refer to Chapter 17, "Using Mail," for more information about POP mail accounts.)

Setting Up Syncing

To enable .Mac to sync with various applications and settings on your computer, open the System Preferences, choose the .Mac option, and click the Sync button. You can choose which items to syncronize from the listed options, including Bookmarks, Calendars, Contact, and Mail Accounts, as shown in Figure 16.7. You can also choose when syncing occurs—every hour, every day, every week, manually, or automatically.

FIGURE 16.7
Enable which applications and functions are synchronized with other computers in the Sync pane.

You can synchronize several different computers swith a single .Mac account. The Advanced pane of the .Mac preferences, shown in Figure 16.8, allows you to see which computers are set up to synchronize data with your .Mac account. Your computer is automatically added to the list if you opt to synchronize with .Mac under the Sync settings, but in the Advanced pane you can unregister computers with which you no longer wish .Mac to sync.

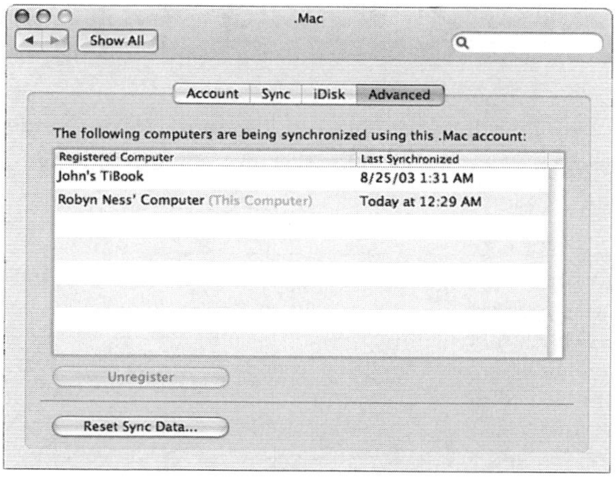

FIGURE 16.8
View a list of computers that are synchronized with the current one in the Advanced pane.

.Mac Web Services

The final .Mac features to cover in this chapter are communication-related web services. Accessed with a web browser through www.mac.com, these services include easy-to-create web pages and iCards.

Websites

The HomePage website builder, shown in Figure 16.9, allows anyone to create web pages without any knowledge of HTML. Simply copy images and movies to your iDisk (in the appropriate folders, of course), choose a HomePage template, and then add your own content.

FIGURE 16.9
Use the HomePage builder to create instant websites.

Apple provides templates for photo albums, resumes, iMovies, and more. If you're an advanced user, you can always add your own content directly to the iDisk Sites folder and create any site you want.

By the Way

You can create simple photo album pages from within iPhoto. Find out more in Chapter 22, "Using iPhoto."

iCards

The Apple iCards are a collection of elegant photographs to which you can add a message to and then forward to your friends, demonstrated in Figure 16.10. Images that you've placed in your iDisk Pictures folder also are available for your use.

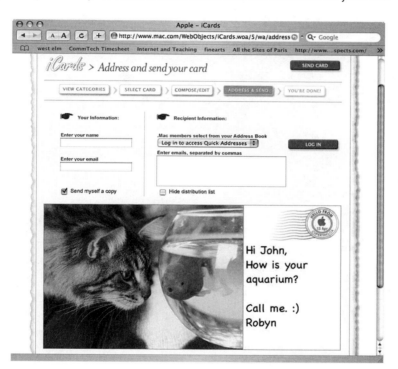

FIGURE 16.10
Create your own iCards to send to friends.

In addition to sharing photos through your .Mac web page or a custom iCard, you can create a .Mac screensaver that enables users to view albums created in iPhoto. Refer to Chapter 22 for details.

Did you Know?

Summary

Apple's .Mac is a subscriber-based service that includes Internet-accessible storage space, email services, and access to members-only software deals. .Mac also enables synchronization of desktop applications on different computers. As an easy-to-use method for storing and synchronizing data, you may find .Mac worth the $99.95 price.

CHAPTER 17

Using Mail

The Mail application is the email application that comes with OS X. Mail provides a powerful search mechanism, junk-mail filter, and message thread display that can make managing hordes of email messages painless.

If you've used other common email programs, you'll be completely comfortable in Mail. A toolbar at the top of the window gives access to commonly used functions for creating, responding to, and searching messages. (We go into detail a bit later, but Figure 17.1 gives a sneak peek at the main window of a loyal Mail user.)

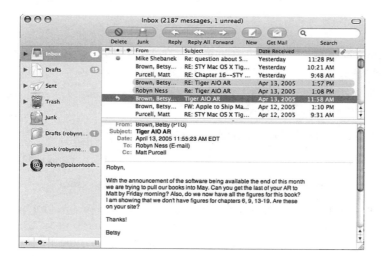

FIGURE 17.1
Mail provides a pleasant (and organized!) interface for working with email.

Setting Up Mail

During the Mac OS X setup procedure (assuming that you've installed from scratch or purchased a new machine with OS X), the installer prompts for a default email account. Although this creates a single account for a single person, additional users and multiple accounts can created within Mail itself. For many people, the first task is setting up a new account—this provides a perfect place to start.

To create a new Mail account, choose File, Add Account from the menu. The setup window to configure a new email account, as shown in Figure 17.2, appears to walk you through the process of setting up an account.

FIGURE 17.2
Provide the necessary setup information when prompted by the assistant.

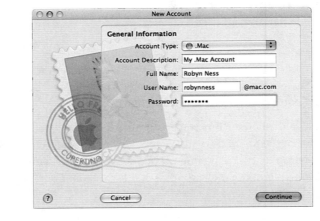

Eight pieces of information, at most, are required to create an email account (.Mac users are required to enter just their name, password, and an Account description):

▶ Account Description—A name that you want to use to refer to your account (Home email, for example).

▶ Full Name—That thing that people call you by.

▶ Email Address—Your email address (for example, jray@mymailmachine.com).

▶ Incoming Mail Server—The server that stores your email.

▶ Account Type—Almost all ISPs support the POP3 protocol for accessing email, but IMAP offers more features. Apple's .Mac servers and MS Exchange servers use IMAP, but are configured as their own account type. Read further for more information on both POP3 and IMAP and the differences between them.

▶ User Name—The username used to access an email account. This is the text that comes before the @ in your email address (that is, jray is the username for jray@mymailmachine.com).

▶ Password—The password required to retrieve mail for your email account. Leaving this field blank causes Mail to prompt the user to enter the password when needed.

▶ Outgoing Mail Server (SMTP)—The server required to send messages and any username/password required to send mail.

If you are unsure of any of these fields, contact your ISP or network administrator. Follow through each step of the setup assistant, clicking Continue to move to the next screen. After each entry, Mail attempts to verify the information you've added and notifies you if there are any problems.

Upon reaching the end of the setup, you are prompted to create another account, or click "Done" to begin using Mail. If it is the first time you've run Mail, you are also given the option of importing mail from another application.

POP3 Versus IMAP

If your email provider supports both the POP3 and IMAP protocols, you're in luck! The POP3 protocol, although extremely popular, is not practical for people with multiple computers. I access the same email account from a number of different computers—one at work, one at home, and another while on the road. Keeping all these machines in sync is virtually impossible with POP3.

POP3 (Post Office Protocol v.3) works much as it sounds: Email is "popped" from a remote server. Incoming messages are stored on the remote server, which in turn waits for a connection from a POP3 client. The client connects only long enough to download all the messages and save them to the local hard drive. Unfortunately, after a message transfers from the server, it's gone. If you go to another computer to check your mail, it won't be there.

IMAP takes a different approach. Instead of relying on the client for message storage, IMAP servers keep everything on the server. Messages and mail folders remain on the server unless explicitly deleted by the client. When new messages arrive, the IMAP client application downloads either the message body or header from the server, but the server contents remain the same. If multiple computers are configured to access the same email account, the email appears identical between the machines—the same folders, messages, and message flags are maintained. In addition, the IMAP protocol supports shared folders between different user accounts and server-based content searches.

If your ISP does not support IMAP, you can sign up for a .Mac account. Apple's POP and IMAP service provides everything you need, along with exclusive Mac OS X downloads and online services.

Importing Mailboxes

After entering your basic account information, Mail immediately starts downloading any available messages for that account and, at the same time, prompts you to import mailboxes from another email program such as Entourage or Eudora. This provides a convenient way to migrate to Mail without having to launch your old mail application to read past messages. Click Yes if you want to pull your old messages into Mail from a supported email application. You are then prompted for the mail application from which you will be importing, as shown in Figure 17.3.

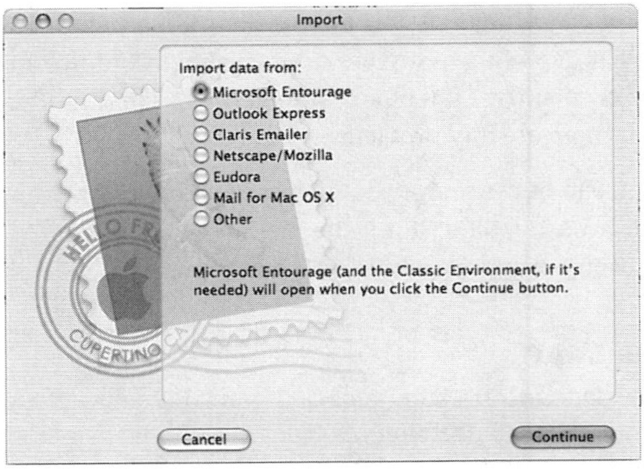

FIGURE 17.3
Choose the mail
application from
which you want
to import.

By the Way

You can import mail you've received in other email programs on your computer at any time (not just during the initial setup) by choosing File, Import Mailboxes from the menu.

Next you are prompted for *what* you want to import—which mailboxes or contacts you want to bring into Mail. Mail can't necessarily import *everything* from everywhere. If you don't see your contacts listed, importing them isn't supported—it isn't an error in mail, just a shortcoming.

After choosing the items to import, click Continue. Mail displays a progress bar as it copies the information. When finished, you are notified that the data is now available in Mail.

Adding and Modifying Accounts and Settings

Mail supports multiple email accounts for a single user. After setting up the initial account, you can add other email accounts through the Accounts pane of the Mail preferences, shown in Figure 17.4. Choose Preferences from the application menu; then click the Accounts icon.

To add a new account to the list, click the + button—this is the same as choosing File, New Account. To remove an account, select it and click –.

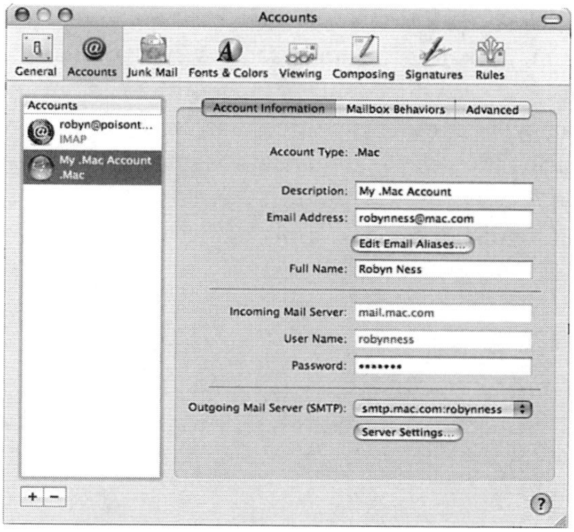

FIGURE 17.4
Multiple email accounts can be added through the Accounts pane of the Mail preferences.

To edit existing accounts, select them in the account list, and then use the three buttons—Account Information, Mailbox Behaviors, and Advanced—to alter and further configure the account information. Let's take a look at these three views:

▶ Account Information—The Account Information options, displayed in Figure 17.4, contain all the settings that you initially collected and entered when adding an email account (see "Adding Accounts" earlier for more information). You can edit these if your server name changes or your account information is otherwise altered. Click the Server Settings button to reveal advanced options related to sending email, as shown in Figure 17.5.

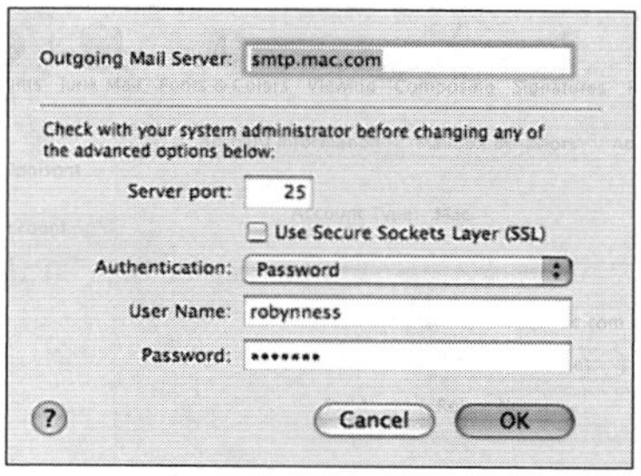

FIGURE 17.5
Check with your system administrator about any special settings needed in order to send mail.

If you have multiple email return addresses and you want to be able to choose which address shows up in the From field on the final message, enter multiple addresses separated by commas in the Email Address field. This adds a pop-up menu to the message composition window where you can choose from the listed addresses.

Did you Know?

▶ Mailbox Behaviors—The Mailbox Behaviors view controls what Mail does with Draft, Sent, Junk, and Trash messages. When configuring an IMAP, Exchange, or .Mac account, as shown in Figure 17.6, you can choose whether these "special" types of mailboxes are stored on the server, and when mail should be deleted from these server-based Mailboxes. POP accounts are not given the option of storing special messages on the server. Instead, POP users only can choose when messages in any of the special mailboxes are erased or moved.

FIGURE 17.6
Special
Mailboxes store
Drafts, Junk,
and other types
of messages.

▶ Advanced—The Advanced settings fine-tune how Mail interacts with your email server. Depending on the account type that you've chosen, the available options change. Figure 17.7 displays the Advanced tab for IMAP (or Mac.com) accounts. Choices available on the Advanced tab when using IMAP (or .Mac) include the following:

   ▶ Enable This Account—Includes the account in the available account listing. If not enabled, it is ignored.

   ▶ Include When Automatically Checking for New Mail—If selected, the account is polled for new messages at the interval set on the Preferences Account pane. If not, the account is polled only when the user manually checks his mail.

   ▶ Compact Mailboxes Automatically—Cleans up the local mailbox files when exiting Mail. The benefit of using this is slight, and it can slow down the system when dealing with large mailbox files.

FIGURE 17.7
Each type of
email account
has different
available
options.

▶ Account Directory—The local directory where the Mail application stores
your messages.

▶ Keep Copies of Messages for Offline Viewing—After a message is
received on the server, the IMAP client has the option of immediately
caching the text of the message on the local machine (cache all messages locally), caching read messages (cache messages when read), or
never caching messages on the local drive (don't cache any messages). If
you want to be able to read your mail while offline, you probably want
the default setting of synchronizing all messages and their attachments.

▶ Automatically Synchronize Changed Mailboxes—When Mail notices a
change in a mailbox and this option is selected, it automatically downloads the changes instead of waiting for the mailbox to be opened or
manually synchronized.

▶ IMAP Path Prefix—The IMAP prefix required to access your mailbox.
This field is normally left blank unless a value is specified by your mail
server administrator.

▶ Port—The default IMAP port is 143. If your server uses a different access
port, enter it here.

▶ Use SSL—Enable SSL encryption (IMAPS) of the email traffic. This setting
must be supported by the server to be used.

▶ Authentication—Choose how you will authenticate with the remote server. Most ISPs use a plain password; special server configurations may require more secure authentications options. Check with your ISP or system administrator if you have questions.

By the
~~Way~~

> If possible, use SSL encryption for POP and IMAP traffic instead of the defaults, which transmit passwords in cleartext, making them highly interceptable. Check with your system administrator or ISP to see if it's supported.

If you are using a POP account, you can control how messages are retrieved and when they are deleted from your account, among other things:

▶ Enable This Account—Include the account in the available account listing. If not enabled, it is ignored.

▶ Include This Account When Checking for New Mail—If selected, the account is polled for new messages at the interval set on the Mail Preferences Account pane. If not, the account is polled only when the user manually checks his mail.

▶ Remove Copy from Server After Retrieving a Message—Choose the length of time (if any) messages should remain on the server after downloading. By leaving the messages on the server, you can create an IMAP-like environment where multiple computers can download the same messages. This is a "poor-man's" IMAP and does not support multiple server-based folders, shared folders, and so on. Click Remove Now to remove downloaded messages manually.

▶ Prompt Me to Skip Messages over <#> KB—Automatically skips messages over a set number of kilobytes. This setting is useful for keeping attachments from being downloaded.

▶ Account Directory—The local directory where the Mail application stores your messages.

▶ Port—The default POP port is 110. If your server uses a different access port, enter it here.

▶ Use SSL—Enable SSL encryption (POPS) of the email traffic. This must be supported by the server to be used.

▶ Authentication—Choose how you will authenticate with the remote server. Most ISPs use a plain password; special server configurations may require more secure authentications options. Check with your ISP or system administrator if you have questions.

Configure and Manage SMTP Servers

Near the bottom of the Account Information pane are options for setting your SMTP servers. Use the Outgoing Mail Server pop-up menu to add a new SMTP server, or just choose an existing server. The Server Settings button edits the currently selected SMTP server.

> Many people who have added and removed accounts end up with a very large list of SMTP servers unless they manually remove servers associated with inactive accounts. To manage the servers, choose Edit Server List from the pop-up menu. This displays a list of *all* SMTP servers and shows which accounts are using which servers. Use the + and – buttons to add and remove servers from this list.

By the Way

When adding or editing an SMTP server, you are prompted for the server name, port (if different from 25), and security information. If you are accessing an SSL-protected mail server (IMAPS, POPS), click the Use Secure Sockets Layer (SSL) check box. In addition, if your server uses authenticated SMTP, choose the authentication method and provide a username and password. Check with your system administrator or ISP if you have questions about SMTP settings.

Reading and Managing Email

If you've used an email program such as Eudora or Outlook Express, you'll be completely comfortable with Mail's interface, shown in Figure 17.8.

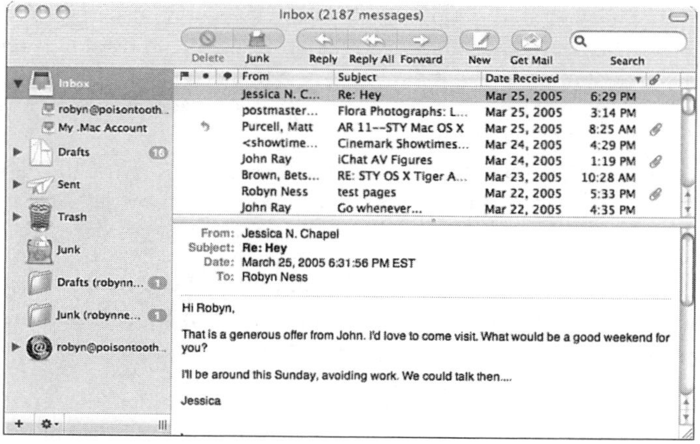

FIGURE 17.8
Tiger's new Mail has a streamlined interface and under-the-hood improvements.

On the left are mailboxes and accounts; messages and message content appear on the right. The toolbar at the top of the window holds commonly used functions for creating, responding to, and searching for messages.

Checking Mail

When you set up an account in Mail, it is automatically configured to go online and check for new messages every five minutes. To manually check your account for messages, click the Get Mail button in the toolbar. You can also use the menus—choose Mailbox, Get *All* New Mail to get all new messages from all accounts. Or, to retrieve email from a specific account, choose Mailbox, Get New Mail, <*account-name*> from the menu.

Did you Know?

> You can set up how frequently Mail checks for new messages within the General pane of the application preferences.
>
> When new messages are received, Mail automatically plays Apple's "New Mail Sound." You can also customize this sound and enable/disable sounds for other email events (such as deleting messages) within the General application preferences.

If Mail finds new messages for your account, they are downloaded to the main "Inbox" folder in the mailbox list. Click the "Inbox" folder to display the messages you've received.

By the Way

> If you have multiple accounts, you'll notice that the Inbox can be expanded by clicking a disclosure arrow to the left of its name. Expanding the main Inbox shows all the individual Inboxes for each of your accounts. To display a summary of all the messages in either the main Inbox or a specific account Inbox, click to highlight it. The upper-right pane of the screen (the Message list) refreshes with the contents of the selected mailbox.
>
> This same concept applies to other special Mailboxes such as Trash, Drafts, and so on. You'll learn more about Mailbox management later in the chapter.

The Message list columns display the default columns' read/unread status, iChat status, subject, and day/time sent. Additional columns can be accessed under the View, Columns submenu. To sort columns, you click their headings.

New messages appear with a small "dot" in front of their names (the read/unread status field). If this isn't obvious enough for you, change the Viewing preferences to force unread messages to be displayed in bold within the listing.

Mail integrates with iChat such that any email message from a contact who is also on your IM buddy list displays that person's IM status in a column within Mail. To launch an iChat AV session with an online buddy, highlight the message you received in your message list; then choose Message, Reply with iChat (Command-Option-I). This feature also can be added as a toolbar customization.

By the Way

Sorting by the message number is the best way to keep track of new messages as they come in. If a sender includes incorrect time or time zone information when sending a message, it is sorted incorrectly if you use Date and Time as the sort field.

Unfortunately, Mail uses different numbers to number different accounts, so this works best on a single account, or when viewing one account at a time.

Did you Know?

To enlarge the viewing area for the message list, you can either drag the divider bar at the bottom of the message list, or simply double-click it. This instantly drops the bar to the bottom of the Mail window, filling the window with *just* the message list. Double-clicking the bar again returns it to the original position.

When an Internet connection isn't available, you may still find yourself wanting to read your mail. This isn't a problem if an account is using POP3 (all messages are stored on your local machine), but IMAP and .Mac store messages on a mail server. To synchronize IMAP/.Mac messages for offline reading, highlight a mailbox in the account you want to sync and then choose Synchronize from the Mailbox action button. You can also choose Mailbox, Synchronize from the menu and select a specific account, or Mailbox, Synchronize All Accounts to synchronize all your active email accounts.

To set mailbox synchronization to happen automatically whenever mailboxes are changed (new mail comes in, is deleted, and so on), select the Automatically Synchronize Changed Mailboxes option in the Advanced area of the Accounts application preferences.

By the Way

Reading and Deleting Messages

To read a message, highlight it in the list; the lower-right portion of the window refreshes with the message content. Mail is capable of using the Safari rendering engine to display plain-text and styled/HTML messages.

To delete a message, select it in the Message list and click the Delete button in the toolbar, press the Delete key, or choose Message, Delete from the menu. You can select multiple messages at once by holding down Shift (for a range) or Command (for non-contiguous blocks of messages) while you click.

Did you Know?

By default, Mail hides some information from you—specifically, the headers that are attached to the message. Message headers can reveal the network addresses that handled a piece of email before it reached you, along with other interesting information such as the mail client that transmitted the message. To view headers, choose View, Message, Long Headers from the menu.

For full control over the default headers shown, use the Show Header Detail option within the Viewing pane of the Mail preferences. You can also customize the Mail toolbar (View, Customize Toolbar) to include a Show Headers button that shows/hides mail headers.

Deleted messages are not immediately removed from the system; they are transferred to a Trash mailbox. What happens from there (deleting after a week, for example) can be configured from the Mailbox Behaviors pane of the Accounts application preferences. Alternatively, one can use the Mailbox, Erase Deleted Messages menu options to erase deleted mail from all accounts or just a specific account. To view the contents of your Trash mailbox, just select it as you would the Inbox—the message list refreshes to show the contents.

By the Way

You can mark the message as unread (to remind you to read it again, or perhaps so that another email program detects it as "unread") by choosing the appropriate option from the Message, Mark submenu. You can also add a button for this feature to the toolbar (View, Customize Toolbar).

Messages Attachments

If the message contains an attachment in a format that Mac OS X can display (such as an image or PDF), it renders the attachment directly in the message.

Watch Out!

Exercise caution when you open attachments, especially from people you don't know. Email attachments are a common way to spread computer viruses, and while few viruses affect the Mac, it's better to be safe than sorry. (See Chapter 35, "Recovering from Crashes and Other Problems," for information about virus protection.)

By the Way

Messages that include image attachments include a Save button with a submenu option that enables you to import image attachments directly into iPhoto.

Also, a Slideshow button located beside the Save button plays a slideshow of the image attachments in the message. Moving your mouse during the slideshow displays a control bar for moving back, pausing, moving forward, displaying a thumbnail sheet, expanding the images to fill the screen, or closing the slideshow.

If attachments cannot be directly displayed, they appear as icons in the body of the message. To open an attached file, double-click the file directly in your email message. To save it, drag it to a Finder window or the Desktop.

> If you have a message with many attachments, it may be easier to work with them by using the expandable list directly following the message headers. When expanded, you can drag the attachment icons to your desktop, or click the Save button to reveal a submenu where you can save one or all of the attachments to a given location.

Mail saves downloaded attachments in the folder ~/Library/Mail Downloads, and removes attachments automatically from the default download folder when the original message is deleted. You can use the General application preferences to remove attachments from the download folder each time Mail quits, or never—meaning that you'll have to clean up after yourself.

Messages Threads

To make message reading easier, Mail provides threaded browsing of your message list, as shown in Figure 17.9. A *thread* is a "conversation" you've had with someone over the span of several messages scattered throughout your other messages. To enable threads, choose View, Organize by Thread from the menu.

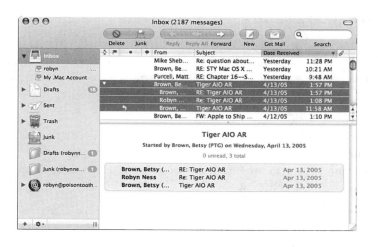

FIGURE 17.9
Organize your messages into threads.

Threads are identified by a blue highlight and the presence of an arrow in front of the initial message subject that started the thread and a number in the status field showing how many unread messages are in the thread, if any. Highlighting the first message subject line displays information about the thread in the message content pane, such as who started the thread, when, how many messages it contains, which contain attachments, and how many of them are unread. Clicking a line within the content pane list jumps you immediately to the chosen message.

> Mail bases threads on a message's subject. If you have multiple messages with the same subject that *aren't* a thread, they are still displayed as a thread.

To browse the thread within the message list, click the arrow at the front of the thread subject line. The message thread expands to show all the available emails within the thread and immediately jumps you to the first unread message. To collapse the thread, click in the first column (down and up opposing arrows) of any message within the thread or on the arrow in front of the initial thread subject line. The thread immediately collapses back to a single line.

The View menu's Expand/Collapse All Threads options can be used to quickly open and close all threads in your mailbox.

> To change the color used to highlight related messages (whether viewing as threads or not) use the Highlight Related Messages Using Color option in the Viewing application preferences.

Searching Messages

To search your messages, use the Search field in the toolbar. Simply start typing and search results begin to appear. If you want to limit your search to a specific header field, click the appropriate heading directly under the toolbar. Figure 17.10 displays a sample search using the Entire Message option, which targets any content from any message.

You may notice that a Save button appears to the right of the criteria for constraining the search. This button saves the search results to a Smart Mailbox, which is similar to a Smart Folder in the Finder. You learn about this in more detail in the section "Managing Email with Mailboxes."

To reset the search results, click the "X" button at the end of the search field.

Coping with Junk Mail

Mail includes a built-in feature to help you manage the ever-increasing sea of junk mail (aka, spam) that threatens to overtake your mailbox. When Mail thinks it has found a piece of spam, it highlights the item in brown in the message listing and displays a "spam" warning when you view the message, as shown in Figure 17.11.

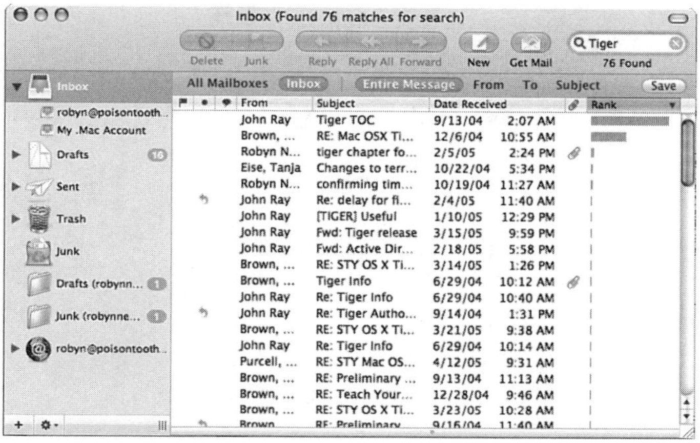

FIGURE 17.10
Search results
fill the message
area.

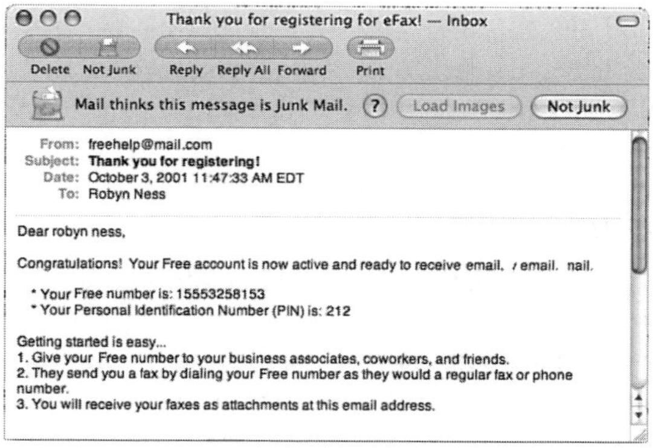

FIGURE 17.11
Mail provides
built-in spam
sensing rules.

Click the Not Junk button in the warning to tell Mail that it incorrectly labeled the message as spam. You can also use the Junk/Not Junk toolbar buttons to flag (or unflag) the currently selected messages(s) in the message listing as spam. The more you "train" Mail, the better it gets at identifying good and bad email.

The Junk Mail application preferences, shown in Figure 17.12, are used to fine-tune how junk mail is handled.

To help keep Mail from getting false positives, it is configured by default to *not* mark something as spam if the sender is in your address book, is a recent recipient of an email you sent, or has addressed you using your full name. If you'd prefer not to perform these checks, they can be disabled in the Junk Mail application preferences.

FIGURE 17.12
Help Mail deter-
mine what is or
isn't spam and
what it should
do with it.

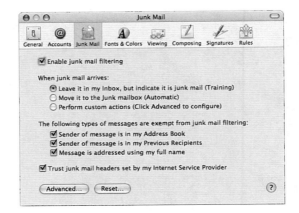

When Mail has gotten to the point where it is consistently identifying spam, you can use the Junk Mail preferences to automatically move messages to a special Junk mailbox rather than leave them in your inbox. If you want to reset the junk mail system to its defaults, click the Reset button. Mail will "forget" everything it has learned about what is/isn't spam on your system.

Block Dynamic Image Links

Spammers are nasty. They use special tricks such as identifying whether your email account is active by sending HTML messages with dynamic image links to your address. If your email reader loads the images, the spammer immediately knows that the email account is active and capable of viewing HTML mail—even if you never click a link in the message! Mail understands this and provides the option of disabling the display of inline images.

Under the Viewing preferences, you can enable or disable the option to Display Remote Images in HTML Messages. When images are disabled, Mail adds a Load Images button at the top of the message content area. Only after the button is clicked are images loaded—preventing the spammers from getting any feedback from your computer.

Bounce Messages

Another method of defeating spam is to bounce mail back to them to create the appearance that your account doesn't exist. This can result in having your address removed from their lists. (Unfortunately, many spammers use fake reply-to address-es, which simply bounce your own bounce back to you.)

To bounce a message, highlight the email in your message list and then choose Message, Bounce (Shift-Command-B). Alternatively, you can add a Bounce button to the Mail toolbar for fast access.

Managing Email with Mailboxes

As you receive messages, they are stored in your Inbox. If you're a casual emailer, that doesn't pose a problem—but if you rely on email for managing your life, you'll almost certainly need to start categorizing and filing messages. To do this, you can create any number of mailboxes (think "folders") that are stored locally or, in the case of IMAP and .Mac servers, on the remote mail server itself.

Mail displays all the active accounts and the mailboxes inside those accounts in the pane on the left side of the window. Because accounts hold mailboxes and mailboxes themselves can hold more mailboxes, this pane is managed very much like a list view in the Finder. You can use the disclosure arrows to collapse and expand the hierarchy of mailboxes. The number of unread messages is displayed in parentheses to the right of each mailbox.

You can expand the mailbox pane by using the handle in the lower right corner of the pane. Double-clicking the handle or the separator bar alternates between collapsing the Mailbox pane to fit the mailbox names perfectly and fitting only the mailbox icons. To hide the mailboxes entirely, choose View, Hide Mailboxes from the menu. You can also customize the toolbar (View, Customize Toolbar) to include a shortcut for hiding/showing the mailbox pane.

> The default icons in the Mailbox pane are *huge*. If you have a bunch of mailboxes created, choose View, Use Small Mailbox Icons to fit more in the window.

By the Way

File Messages

To file one or more message into a mailbox, click and drag it from the message list to the mailbox you want to use. Alternatively, you can use the Move To or Copy To options from the Message menu. Control-clicking a message in the listing opens a contextual menu from which you can choose to move the message. (From the contextual menu, you can also access most of the options available in the Message menu.)

Certain mailboxes, such as In, Out, Drafts, and Trash, are "special" in that they contain all of a specific type of mailbox for each account and are filled automatically:

- ▶ In—Contains all the Inboxes for all your accounts. You can either expand the master Inbox to pick a specific account's Inbox, or use the top-level Inbox to show all incoming messages in all your accounts, be they POP3, IMAP, or .Mac accounts.

- ▶ Out—Messages that are *going* to be sent but have not yet left your system.

▶ Sent—Messages that have already been sent from your computer.

▶ Trash—Like the Inbox, the Trash is a collection of messages—in this case, all messages that have been marked for deletion but are not yet deleted.

▶ Drafts—Messages that you are working on but have not yet sent.

The Mail icon displays the total number of unread messages in *all* the Inbox folders. Unfortunately, there is currently no way to change the mailboxes it monitors for the unread count.

Create New Mailboxes

To create new mailboxes, choose Mailbox, New from the menu, or click the + button at the bottom of the Mail window drawer. You are prompted for where the Mailbox will be created, and what it should be called, as demonstrated in Figure 17.13.

FIGURE 17.13
Choose where to create the new mailbox and what it should be called.

If you're using a POP account, your only option for Location is On My Mac. This creates a mailbox at the top level of the Mailbox listing that is stored directly on your computer. IMAP/.Mac users can choose an email account from the Location pop-up menu. This stores the mailbox on the remote server. To create a mailbox inside another mailbox, type the full path of the mailbox you want to create. For example, if you already have a mailbox called Work and you want to make the mailbox Monkey inside it, type **Work/Monkey** in the Name field.

Mailboxes can also be rearranged by dragging them from one location to another. You can place mailboxes inside other mailboxes or even copy a mailbox from one IMAP/.Mac account to another.

To delete or rename a mailbox, highlight it in the mailbox list, and then use Rename or Delete from the Mailbox menu.

> As a shortcut for creating mailboxes within mailboxes, highlight the mailbox inside of which you want to create another mailbox, and then click + or choose the Mailbox, New Mailbox from the menu.
>
> Also, notice that, like the Finder, the mailbox pane has an action button. This button can be used to access many of the same functions as those you can find under the Mailbox menu bar.

Assign Special Mailboxes for Sent, Trash, Draft, and Junk Email

Mail automatically creates mailboxes for storing Sent Items, Trash, Drafts, and Junk Mail. Unfortunately, if you use email on other platforms or your mail ends up with multiple mailboxes serving the same purpose ("Sent Messages" and "Sent Items," for example), you may need to do a bit of clean up. To force Mail to use a specific mailbox for Sent, Trash, Draft, or Junk Mail, highlight the mailbox you want to use, then from the menu bar choose Mailbox, Use This Mailbox For, followed by the purpose of the mailbox.

Rebuild Corrupt Mailboxes

There may be times that Mail gets "out of sync" with your IMAP/.Mac mail server. The symptoms are usually missing messages or messages with the wrong content.

From my experience, this happens most often when you access the mail server from another client and rename/move mailboxes. To rebuild the contents of any mailbox, choose Mailbox, Rebuild from the menu. Mail redownloads the contents of the mailbox and (you hope) corrects the problem.

Create Smart Mailboxes

"Smart" things are everywhere in Mac OS X: Smart Playlists in iTunes, Smart Folders in the finder, and now Smart Mailboxes in Mail. Similar to the other Smart elements, a Smart Mailbox is essentially a saved search that is attached to a virtual mailbox. When you open the folder, the search is performed and you see only the messages matching the search. A Smart Mailbox, for example, might be set to search for messages from a specific person and display only those messages. This eliminates the need to manually file the messages or to write rules that move the messages around—unless you want to!

Smart Mailboxes search all your accounts and account mailboxes. They appear as purplish "geared" folders at the top level of your mailbox listing, as shown in Figure 17.14. Clicking the folder displays the messages that it "contains"—just like any other folder.

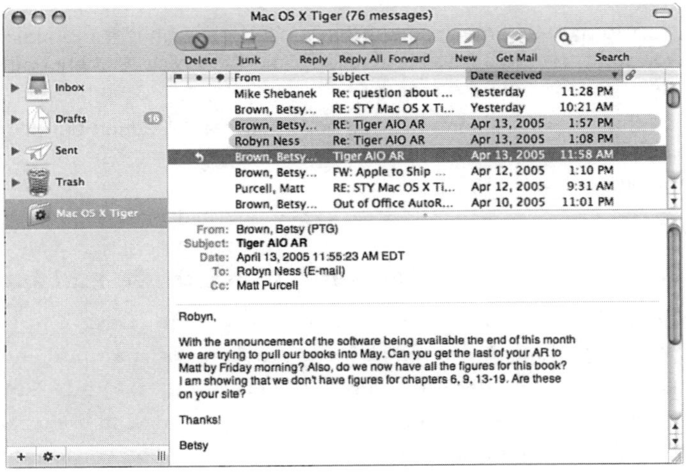

FIGURE 17.14
Smart Mailboxes appear at the top level of your mailbox hierarchy and aren't attached to a specific account.

To create a new Smart Mailbox, choose Mailbox, New Smart Mailbox from the menu. The Smart Mailbox creation screen appears, as shown in Figure 17.15.

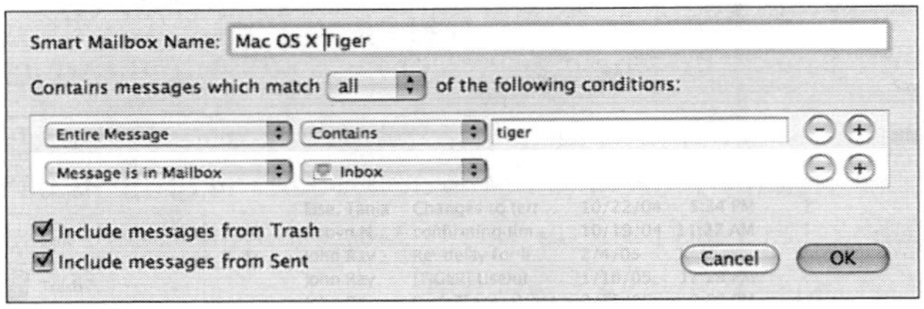

FIGURE 17.15
Set search attributes to create a new smart mailbox.

First, name the mailbox and decide whether you want *any* or *all* of the search conditions to apply. Next, add each of the conditions that you want to be met for a message to appear in the mailbox. Use the + and – buttons to add or remove conditions as needed.

Did you Know?

If you have a message selected when you create a new Smart Mailbox, Mail automatically creates a condition necessary to match the sender of that message. You need to manually click the + button to fill in additional conditions.

If you want the Smart Mailbox to also include messages that are in the Trash or your Sent mailbox, use the two check boxes at the bottom of the dialog box. When finished, click OK. Your mailbox is added to the Mailbox pane and should be ready for use.

Like normal mailboxes, you can delete Smart Mailboxes by using Mailbox, Delete, or rename them by double-clicking their names in the Mailbox list or using the menu item Mailbox, Rename. If you decide you want to change the Smart Mailbox search criteria, editing is just a matter of selecting it in the Mailbox list and choosing Mailbox, Edit Smart Mailbox from the menu.

Smart Mailboxes aren't like normal mailboxes in that you can't drag them around to place them inside another mailbox. As a result, you may end up with dozens of smart mailboxes cluttering up your Mailbox list. To help organize these virtual objects, Apple provides "Smart Mailbox folders," which can be used to file and organize all your Smart Mailboxes. To create a Smart Mailbox Folder, choose Mailboxes, New Smart Mailbox Folder from the menu. When prompted, type the name for the folder and click OK. A new folder that looks just like a Smart Mailbox is added to your Mailbox list. After a Smart Mailbox Folder is created, you can drag your Smart Mailboxes in and out of the folder (or other Smart Mailbox Folders) and organize them as you see fit. You may *not*, however, use the folder for any other purpose or drag it into an email account.

Composing and Sending Messages

To write a new email, click the New button in the toolbar or choose File, New Message (Command-N) from the menu. If you'd prefer to reply to an existing message, select that message in the mail list, and then click the Reply button or choose Message, Reply (Command-R). To address the outgoing message to everyone who received the original message and not just the original sender, choose the "Reply All" from either the toolbar or menu.

By the Way

In addition to replying to existing messages, you can also forward or redirect them. The difference between forwarding and redirecting is that a forward is the equivalent of copying and pasting the original message and basic headers into a new email and sending it from your account. A redirected message, on the other hand, appears to come from the original sender. A forward is most appropriate if you want to include your own comments, whereas a redirect is better suited for passing an original message without any modifications to another recipient.

To forward or redirect a message, select it in the message list, and then choose Redirect or Forward from the message menu. You can also add forward/redirect buttons to the toolbar by choosing View, Customize Toolbar from the menu.

Regardless of how you go about starting your message, the composition window appears, as shown in Figure 17.16.

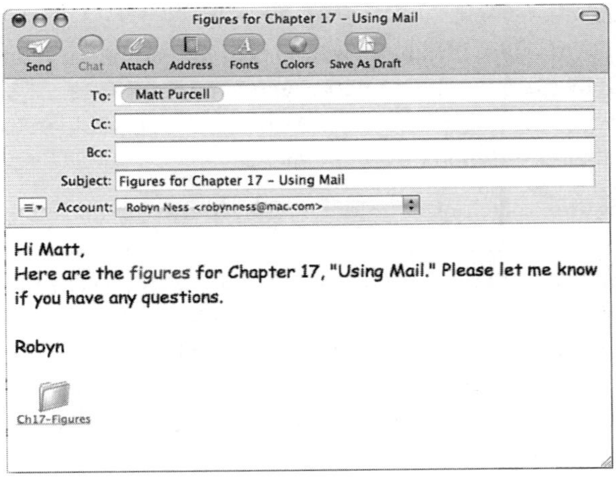

FIGURE 17.16
Mail supports
styled mes-
sages and drag-
and-drop attach-
ments.

Did you Know?

When replying to a message, it is common to quote another message. If text from the original message is selected when you choose to reply, it is included in the new message as a quote from the original message. If nothing is selected, the entire message is quoted.

By default, the quoted material is indented and the font changes color. (If you quote a quote, it is indented twice.) This differentiation between text added in different messages is called the *quote level*, and it can build up over the course of a conversation. Sometimes, the quote level of a message isn't what you want—something you want to be indented *isn't*, whereas something you don't want indented is. To adjust the levels of quoting, select the text to change and use the menu selections Format, Quote Level, Increase or Decrease. You can also control the quoting of text and whether the quote level is automatically increased when replying within the Composing application preferences.

Addressing Your Messages

Four fields are initially provided for addressing the message. Use the To line for single or multiple addresses that serve as the primary recipients of the message. A comma should separate multiple addresses. The Cc: line adds additional recipients who are not part of the main list. The primary recipients can see these addresses. Next is a Bcc field. A Bcc (Blind Carbon Copy) works like a normal carbon copy but does not allow the recipients to view each other's email address or name. Finally, the Subject line is used to set the email's subject or title.

To enter an address in a field, simply start typing the contact's name or email address. As you're typing into any of the available fields, Mail attempts to recognize the address either from your Address Book or from other addresses you've used recently to autocomplete the address as you type. If it gets the correct address, press Tab or click outside the area where you are typing and the address is entered as an object—Mail treats every email address it recognizes as an object. If multiple email addresses are associated with a name (home and work addresses, for example), click on the address object and use the pop-up menu to choose from the different addresses available for that person, as shown in Figure 17.17.

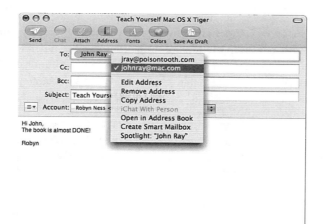

FIGURE 17.17
Choose which address you want to use for a given person.

From the same pop-up menu, you can also choose Edit Address to enter and edit the address manually, Remove Address to delete the address object from the field, iChat with Person (to start an iChat session if available), Open in Address Book to open the Address Book application and display the appropriate record, and Add to Address Book to add the address to the Address Book application. Finally, you can choose to create a new Smart Folder that displays only messages with the highlighted address.

Adding Content and Attachments

To create the message itself, type the text into the window's content area. The toolbar can be used to attach files or pick fonts and colors. These options are also available from the Message and Format menus.

> If you use special fonts or font colors in a message, it must be sent in a Rich Text format. Be aware that to receive rich text email, the remote user must have an email program capable of displaying styled text and have the right fonts installed. To create a message that anyone can receive, compose the content in Plain Text mode. Plain text messages cannot convey any text-styling information. You can toggle between Plain and Rich text messages with the Format menu. If moving from Rich to Plain, any style information you've added is lost.
>
> If you are replying to a message, you can have Mail automatically set your reply format in the format of the original message. Choose Use the Same Message Format as the Original Message again in the Composing application preferences.

To add attachments, drag images and files (and even folders!) directly into the message, click the Attach button in the toolbar. Depending on the type of file, it is added to the message as an icon (application, archive, and so on) or displayed within the body (JPG, PDF, and so on). When sending to Windows recipients, you may also want to choose Edit, Attachments, Always Send Windows Friendly Attachments.

When you're finished, click Send in the toolbar, or choose Message, Send (Shift-Command-D) from the menu. If you want to save the message and work on it later, choose File, Save as Draft (Command-S). This saves the message to your Drafts mailbox, where you can open it and resume work at a later date.

> If you are sending large files as attachments, you can reduce the space they take up by compressing them. This reduces the amount of space the files take up in your recipient's mailbox and speeds up message downloads. To compress a file in Mac OS X, select the file in a Finder window or on your Desktop and choose File, Create Archive from the menu. You can add the .zip file that is created to your message as you would any other file.

> To help guard against sending sensitive email outside your company, Mail can be configured so that email addresses of messages to recipients in domains outside a given "safe" domain are highlighted in red as they are entered. To activate this feature, open the Composing pane of the application preferences; then choose Mark Addresses Not in This Domain and fill in the appropriate domain in the accompanying field.

Spell Checking Messages

By default, Mail automatically spell-checks your messages as you type them. Words that it has identified as being incorrect are highlighted and underlined in red. To correct an error, Control-click the word and a list of potential corrections is displayed; choose the corrected term and the original word is replaced in the message. You can also choose to ignore the word (and any other instances of it in the message) or learn it for future use.

> Even if a word isn't spelled wrong, you can still Control-click it and choose to look it up in the OS X dictionary, Google, or even Spotlight.

Did you Know?

You can also choose to have Mail perform spell checking after you click Send rather than as you type. This can be less intrusive than the "underline" method and ensures that you catch everything before the email goes out. To activate this feature, use the Check Spelling pop-up menu in the Composing application preferences to choose When I Click Send.

Managing and Adding Signatures

Everyone needs an email signature—something to identify authors as individuals or at least tell others how to contact them. The Mail application handles multiple different signatures for multiple accounts with ease. Signatures are configured through the Signatures application preferences, demonstrated in Figure 17.18.

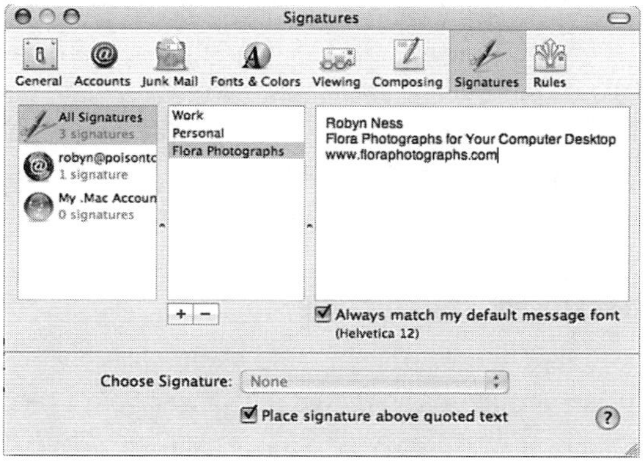

FIGURE 17.18
Create multiple signatures within the Mail application.

The Signature management interface is divided into three columns. The first displays all your email accounts (including a generic All option). The second column shows a list of signatures for the selected account. Finally, the third column displays the actual editable signature.

To add a signature, choose the account to which you want it to be attached (or All, for all the accounts), click the + button in the middle column, name the new signature, and enter the signature in the column on the far right. To remove a signature, select it in the center column and click the – button.

The signature entry area is a full "rich text" field. As you type, you can use the same Format menu options to style the signature text. To help make things consistent, click the Always Match My Default Message Font check box to change the signature to match whatever you set for your default font in the Fonts and Colors application preferences.

After typing your signatures, you can choose which is displayed by default (if any) for each email account. Pick the email account in the left column, and then use the Choose Signature pop-up menu to pick a specific signature.

A final setting is the capability to place the signature above quoted text. This is useful if you typically reply to messages and quote the original text directly after your reply. Rather than pasting your signature at the very bottom of the message, it appears above the original (quoted) text.

If you've chosen a default signature, it is inserted automatically whenever you compose a message. If, however, you didn't set a default, you can insert a signature by using the signature pop-up menu in the lower-right corner of the message composition window.

Using Advanced Features of Mail

So far in this chapter you've learned how to set up your account, receive and send messages, and work with mailboxes. Those basics probably represent the bulk of your Mail needs. However, there are several additional features of Mail that you may find useful: setting parental controls, synchronizing Mail with .Mac, and applying rules to messages to automate how Mail treats them.

Applying Parental Controls

If you're a parent, you may not want your child being able to email (and receive email from) every other person on the planet. Much like Safari can restrict the URLs a user can visit, Mail can restrict the email addresses a user can send messages to or receive them from. To active this feature, open the Accounts pane of the System Preferences, select the user you wish to restrict, and then click the Parental Controls button. Click the Mail check box; then click Configure. A dialog, shown in Figure 17.19, prompts you for the appropriate restrictions. Use the +/- buttons to add and remove addresses from the list.

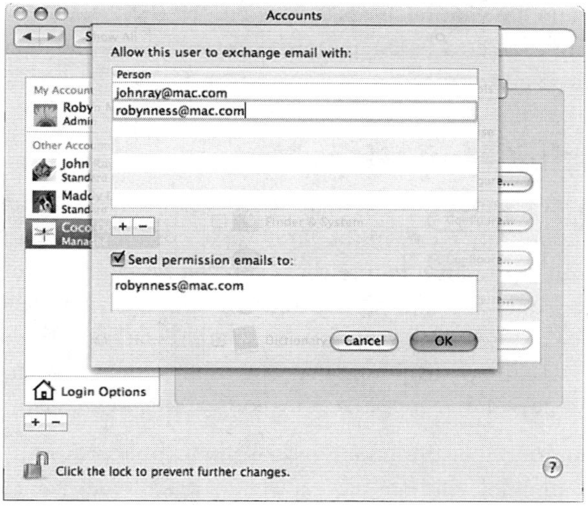

FIGURE 17.19
Enter the allowed email addresses and the person who will oversee the account.

If you want to give the user the flexibility to request approval for additional addresses, check the Send Permission Emails To check box and enter a valid email address. When the permissions feature is activated, the user is prompted to ask for permission upon any attempt to email an unlisted address. The permission request message is sent to the address provided during setup with an Always Allow button at the top, as shown in Figure 17.20.

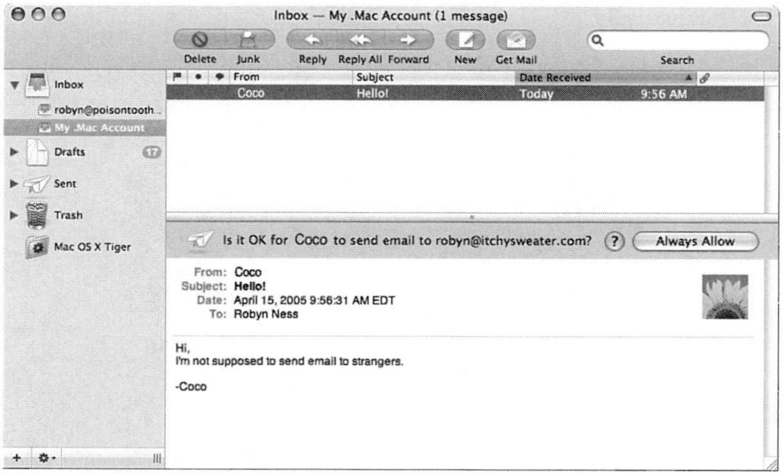

FIGURE 17.20
A restricted user can ask for permission to send email.

Click the button and the email address is added to the restricted user's allowed list. You can, at any time, go back to the permission email and click No Longer Allow to restrict the address again.

Synchronizing Mail with .Mac

If you have multiple computers in different locations, it helps to be able to access the same information from each. To this end, Apple has included basic .Mac syncing features to Mail. With a few mouse clicks you can synchronize your mail rules, signatures, Smart Mailboxes, and Accounts across multiple computers. That is, of course, if you have a .Mac account. Assuming you do, you can activate these features within the General application preferences or directly in the .Mac system preference pane, as discussed in Chapter 16, "Exploring .Mac Membership."

There is no configuration for this option aside from turning it on. After it is activated, iSync keeps your email configuration current across all registered .Mac machines.

Applying Rules to Messages

Rules (filters) can perform actions on incoming messages, such as highlighting them in the message listing, moving them to mailboxes, or playing special sounds. Much as the built-in junk mail detector highlights spam messages in brown, you can write your own rules to do similar things.

Rules are managed through the Rules pane of the application preferences, shown in Figure 17.21.

FIGURE 17.21
Rules can auto-mate the process of going through your messages.

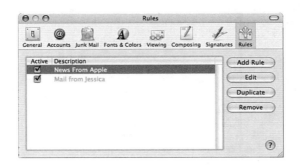

Each rule in the list is evaluated once per incoming message (unless the Active box is unchecked). In fact, multiple rules can act on a single message. To change the order in which the rules are applied, drag rule entries in the list to put them in the order you want.

By the Way

Apple includes a default rule for dealing with Apple mailings. If you aren't subscribed to any Apple lists (or if you are and don't want them to be highlighted), you can delete or uncheck this rule.

There are four options for manipulating the rule list: Add Rule, Edit, Duplicate, and Remove. The function of each option is self-explanatory.

Creating a New Rule

Rule creation is simple. Each rule consists of *conditions* that look at portions of the incoming message and determine what *actions* to perform.

To create a new rule, click the Add Rule button to display the rule creation dialog, as shown in Figure 17.22. First enter a description to identify the rule in the listing. Next, decide whether the rule you're creating requires *all* of a series of conditions to be met or *any* of the conditions to be matched. Use the If pop-up menu to choose Any or All condition matching.

Next, compose the conditions. The Rule starts with a single condition; you can add conditions by clicking the + button at the end of the condition line. Conditions can be deleted with the – button. The conditions are extremely flexible and enable you to match search attributes against your Address Book entries and the message content itself.

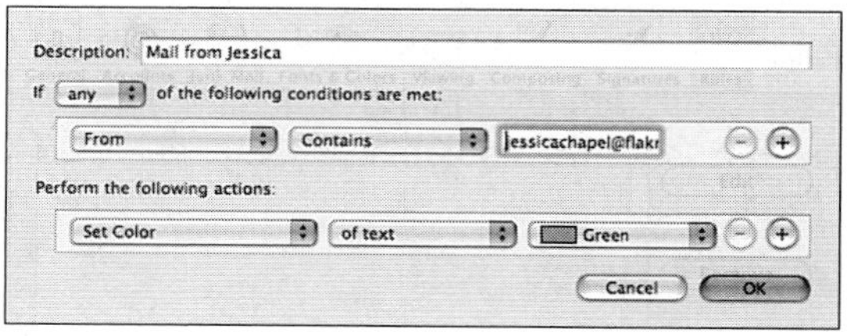

FIGURE 17.22
Mail's rules
are simple to
create.

Finally, choose the actions. Use the + and – buttons to add and delete as many actions as you want.

▶ Move Message—Move the message to another mailbox.

▶ Copy Message—Copy the message to another mailbox, leaving a copy in the default mailbox.

▶ Set the Color—Set the highlight color for the message.

▶ Play Sound—Play a system (or custom) beep sound.

▶ Bounce Icon in Dock—Bounce the Mail icon in the Dock.

▶ Forward/Redirect/Reply To—Send the message to another email address. Click the Message button to enter text that will be included with the message being sent.

▶ Delete the Message—Delete the message. Useful for automatically getting rid of common spam messages.

▶ Mark as Read—Mark the message as read.

▶ Mark as Flagged—Flag the message, which marks message with a flag icon.

▶ Run AppleScript—Run an AppleScript for advanced processing.

▶ Stop Evaluating Rules—Stop processing any further rules in the filter.

Click OK to set and activate the rule; new messages are automatically evaluated and acted on as appropriate.

To manually apply new rules to existing messages, simply select the Messages, Apply Rules (Option+Command+L) from the menu.

Mail Utilities and Diagnostic Tools

To help you get the most out of Mail and figure out what in the world it is doing as the little cursor spins, Apple has included several tools within Mail that help in monitoring, diagnosing, and using the application. These aren't settings or features you'd need to access every day, but they can be helpful.

Viewing Account Info

It isn't uncommon to have an email account with a quota but have no idea of how much space you're using. Mail provides an Account Info display that quickly provides a summary of your account settings, size, and quota. To access the Account Info window, select an account within the Mailboxes pane and choose Command-I or "Get Info" from the Mailbox action menu. The Account Info window appears, as demonstrated in Figure 17.23.

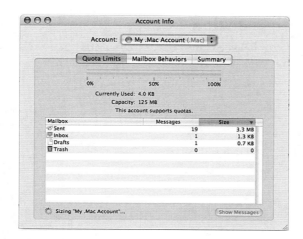

FIGURE 17.23
The Account Info window can be used to get a summary of your account usage and setup.

Use the Account pop-up menu at the top of the window to switch between any of your accounts. Below that you can move between three different information summaries:

▶ Quota Limits—Visible for IMAP/.Mac accounts, this shows the size of your account, the total capacity, and the sizes of each mailbox. To view a mailbox's contents, select it in the list and click the Show Messages button; Mail opens a new viewer with that Mailbox.

▶ Messages on Server—Available for POP users only, this displays the messages that are stored on the POP server, removed from your local account, or those that have been downloaded to your computer. Selecting a message in this list also provides the option of removing it from the server without downloading it into your mailbox—useful for extremely large attachments on a dial-in connection.

▶ Mailbox Behaviors—Displays the settings for the Drafts, Sent, Junk, and Trash Mailboxes. This view is identical to the Mailbox Behaviors within the account settings and can be used to quickly change how your account interacts with these default mailboxes.

▶ Summary—Shows a simple uneditable summary of your account information.

Viewing Mail Activity

The Activity Viewer shows tasks Mail is completing, along with a description of the action that is currently taking place. If Mail appears to be frozen, choose Window, Activity Viewer from the menu. To cancel or stop an action, click the Stop button.

Using the Connection Doctor

The Connection Doctor helps you locate settings that may be wrong in your email accounts. To use the Connection Doctor, choose Window, Connection Doctor from the menu. The window shown in Figure 17.24 is displayed.

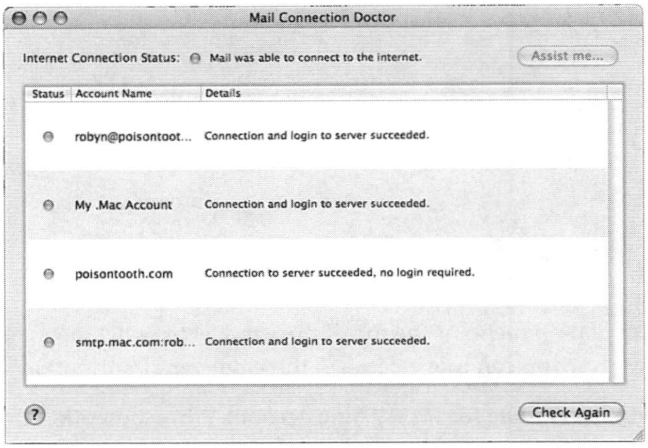

FIGURE 17.24
The connection doctor helps identify problems with your email account settings.

At the top of the window is your Internet status. If there is no Internet, there's no mail. If the status shows anything other than green, click the Assist Me button to launch the Network system preference panel and identify the issue.

The Connection Doctor displays a line for each email account and SMTP server configured. If connecting to the server is successful, a message to that effect is displayed next to the account/server name. If an error has occurred, the connection doctor provides a summary of the problem and an educated guess of what might be causing it.

To fix an error, double-click the error line in the Connection Doctor window and Mail displays the setting that it has determined is causing the problem. After making the necessary changes, click Check Again in the Connection Doctor window to verify that the problem is solved.

Summary

This chapter took an in-depth look at OS X's built-in email Application, Mail. You learned how to set up your email account, as well as how to transfer messages from your existing mail program. You also learned how to read and send mail. Finally, you learned how to use some of Mail's advanced features, such as parental controls and rules, as well as some tools to help you diagnose email problems.

CHAPTER 18

Using iChat AV

iChat AV enables you to hold text-based conversations with friends and family in real time—or, with the proper equipment, to have audio or videoconferences.

To make full use of iChat, you need an AOL Instant Messenger (AIM) account, a .Mac username, or a Jabber server account. You can sign up for a free AIM account at www.aim.com or a free .Mac username at www.mac.com, which comes with a 60-day trial of .Mac. (After the .Mac trial expires, the username is still usable for iChat.) Jabber is used to set up private instant messaging servers within corporate or secure environments. For more information on Jabber, visit www.jabber.org/.

As mentioned in Chapter 12, "Printing, Faxing, and Working with Fonts," Bonjour is a technology that allows devices to automatically locate each other on a network. If other users on your local network use iChat AV, you don't need an AIM or .Mac account to chat with them. Bonjour has been incorporated into iChat so that it can automatically generate a buddy list of users within your local network. This list appears in a Bonjour window separate from AIM or .Mac contacts you specifically add to iChat.

Did you Know?

Setting Up iChat AV

The first time you start iChat AV, you are prompted for either your AIM or .Mac iChat username, as shown in Figure 18.1. To register for a free .Mac username, click the Get an iChat Account button.

Next, iChat prompts you to set up Jabber Instant Messaging. Unless your company or organization has a Jabber Server, skip this configuration and click Continue. If you *do* have a Jabber server, check the Use Jabber Instant Messaging box and supply an account name and password. Click Continue to carry on setting up iChat AV.

Next, you are prompted for whether you want to use Bonjour messaging. If you have a relatively small local network, turning on Bonjour probably isn't an issue. If you're part of a large network with hundreds of iChat users, however, your Bonjour buddy list may be overwhelming and not worth activating. Click Continue to move on.

FIGURE 18.1
Enter your
account infor-
mation.

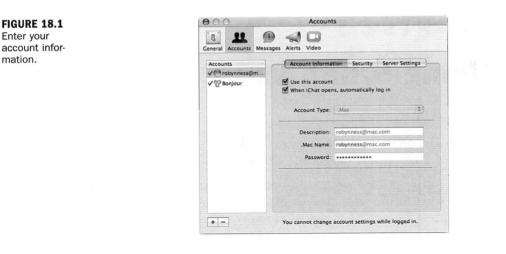

If you turn on firewall protection in the Sharing pane of System Preferences, you might be unable to receive messages from other Bonjour users. To use Bonjour, check the box in the Firewall section of the Sharing pane to allow iChat Bonjour.

Finally, iChat provides a preview of your audio and video input. Make sure that if you have a camera and a microphone attached that the inputs are visible before continuing. Your setup is now complete. Click the Done button to begin using iChat AV.

Adding or Editing Accounts

To modify accounts after iChat AV has completed the initial setup process, choose iChat, Preferences from the menu. Click the Accounts icon to open the Account manager, as shown in Figure 18.2.

iChat accounts settings are laid out with accounts on the left side of the window and account settings on the right. To edit an existing account, choose it in the list—the settings appear to the right.

Although you can have only one of each account type active at a time, you can create as many AIM, .Mac, or Jabber accounts you'd like and switch between them at will. The accounts that are currently active are marked by check marks. To add an account, click the + button. An account creation window appears, as shown in Figure 18.3.

Use the Account Type pop-up menu to choose between AIM, .Mac, or Jabber, and then supply your account information and a description of the account in the provided fields. If you want the account to become the default active account, select the Use This Account check box. Click Add to save the account information.

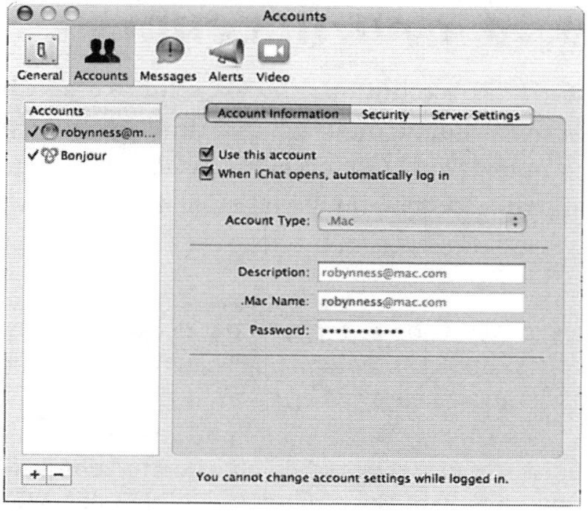

FIGURE 18.2
You can manage
many different
IM accounts
within iChat.

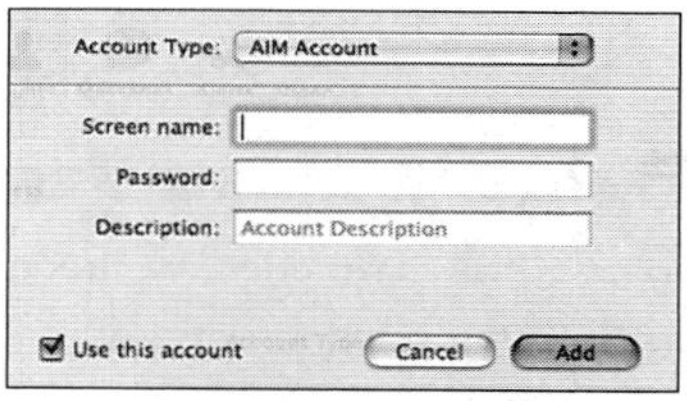

FIGURE 18.3
Enter the infor-
mation for your
new account.

Advanced Account and Server Settings

After an account is added, selecting it in the account list displays its associated properties in the pane on right side of the window. You can use the buttons at the top of the pane at the right to switch to up to three settings views:

▶ Account Information—Basic settings for the account, username, password, and so on. These settings also determine whether an account is currently active (Use This Account) or whether it is logged in to automatically when iChat starts (When iChat Opens, Automatically Log In.)

▶ Security—Determines who can (or can't) see that you are online. The iChat security options are discussed later in this chapter.

▶ Server Settings—The server settings can be used to configure proxy connections for your IM servers or set non-standard ports for communication. With Jabber servers, these settings also control SSL encryption of the chat session.

When you are finished adding and configuring all your accounts and account settings, close the application preferences. You can now begin using iChat AV.

Logging In to Your Accounts

Unless you've configured the Account Information settings otherwise, iChat AV automatically logs in to your default accounts when it starts up and logs out when you quit. To manually log in to or out of an account, use the Log In and Log Out selections under the iChat application menu. If you have multiple AIM, .Mac, or Jabber accounts, you can switch between them by choosing Switch To from the iChat menu.

Did you Know?

> A few system events can be used to trigger iChat or shut it down. If you have an iSight camera, iChat can be set to automatically launch when the camera iris is opened, which turns on the camera.
>
> Similarly, the Fast User switching feature automatically logs you out when you switch to another user account; this can be changed to keep you online but show you are away. Use the Video and General panes of the iChat AV preferences to make these adjustments, respectively.

Showing iChat Status in Menu Bar

Although starting and stopping iChat is an effective means of logging in and out of your accounts, it also means that you have to remember to do it. To make logging in and out of iChat easier (and automatic), you can activate the iChat status menu by opening the General application preferences pane, as shown in Figure 18.4.

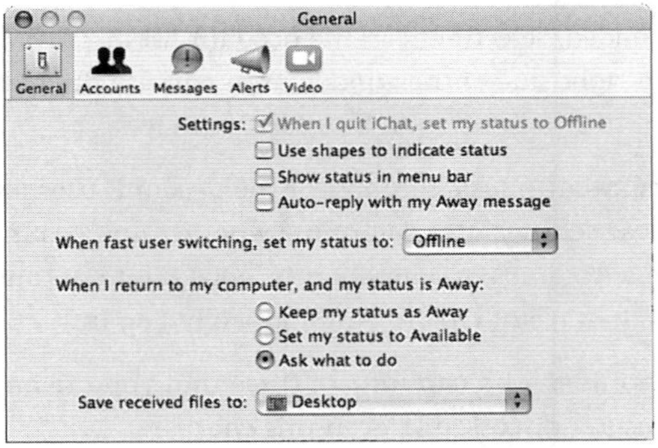

FIGURE 18.4
Add an iChat status menu to your menu bar in the General preferences.

Click the Show Status in Menu Bar check box to display a "speech bubble" icon on the right side of your menu bar. After the iChat status menu is active, you do not have to have iChat AV open to set your online status, or to initiate a chat session. Simply activate the menu and choose Available to log in or Offline to log out. The last status setting you've chosen is applied automatically when you log in to your Mac OS X user account.

Configuring Your Online Information

Other users can see a number of pieces of information when you're online—such as your account status, an AIM profile, and a picture you've chosen to represent yourself. You can control these settings so you can be certain that your buddies are seeing what you expect them to.

Setting Your Account Status

When you are logged in to iChat AV, other members can see whether you are available for a chat. By default, your status, as well as the status of your buddies, is indicated by green (available), red (away), and orange (idle) dots next to each name (including yours) in the Buddy List window and iChat AV Status menu. You can set your account to use two default status states: Available and Away—accessed from either the iChat Status menu or the drop-down menu under your name at the top of the Buddy List window. However, if your computer has been idle for several minutes, iChat automatically switches to an idle state to show that you haven't been using your computer.

If you have trouble differentiating between the colors or just want a change of pace, you can change the availability indicators to shapes in the General pane within the iChat AV application preferences.

Even though you can set your account to only two real states manually, you can apply your own custom labels to these states. To create custom labels, use the two Custom selections found under the availability menu in the Buddy List, which you access by clicking directly below your iChat name in the Buddy List heading.

A custom state called Current iTunes Track shows you as available and displays the current iTunes track you are listening to.

By the Way

For even greater control, choose Edit Status Window to open the window shown in Figure 18.5.

Click the + button under the appropriate column to add messages to your Available or Away pool. Use the – button to delete existing messages. If you want iChat to remember the messages you've typed between sessions, be sure the Remember Custom Messages check box is selected.

FIGURE 18.5
Edit the
Available and
Away messages
for your
account.

By default, if you receive a message while you're away, iChat does nothing. To configure iChat to automatically respond with your custom Away message, select Auto-reply with My Away Message in the General preferences.

You can also use the General preferences to automatically have iChat change your Away status back to Available when you start using your computer after being away.

Changing Your AV Capability Status

In addition to the availability status, iChat also sends your AV capability status to your buddies. This information tells the remote systems whether you are capable of accepting video and/or audio chats. While *there are times when* you want to use these features, sometimes you may want to temporarily disable them.

To disable/enable your Microphone and Camera devices, uncheck the Microphone Enabled or Camera Enabled menu items under the Audio or Video menus. Your AV capabilities update immediately in your friends' buddy lists.

Updating Your Profile

Your AIM profile is nothing more than a few paragraphs of text that say whatever you want. You can use the profile as a means of communicating with your friends or leaving a note larger than just a custom Away or Available message. In addition, the profile is visible even if you aren't online.

To change your profile, choose Buddies, Change My Profile from the menu. The profile window shown in Figure 18.6 appears.

Enter your text into the Profile window and then choose OK to save it to the AIM servers.

FIGURE 18.6
Set the information you want displayed when your buddies request information on your account.

Setting Your iChat AV Buddy Icon

A unique feature of the AIM service is the capability to set custom thumbnails of all your contacts and yourself—these are known as *buddy icons*. Your buddy icon is automatically transmitted to your friends so that they can see whatever you've set your icon to be. Similarly, if they've set custom icons, they show up automatically on your system.

By default your personal AIM buddy icon is the image set in the Address Book application, or the icon used for your account image. To replace it with one of your choosing, drag a new image into the image well beside your name at the top of the Buddy List window, or choose Buddies, Change My Picture from the menu.

An editing window appears to enable you to position and scale the image, as shown in Figure 18.7. Drag the image so that the section you want to use as an icon is centered in the bright square in the middle of the window; then use the zoom slider underneath the image to zoom in and out. The center square shows the icon that will be set—albeit not necessarily the same size it will be in iChat AV. When you're satisfied with the image, click Set.

If you want to choose another image from a file, click the Choose button to open a standard file selection window. Users with a camera attached have a Take Video Snapshot button at the bottom of the window. Clicking this button displays a live video preview, gives you roughly 3 seconds to primp and preen, and then automatically takes a snapshot that you can use as a buddy icon. This provides an easy way to create a new icon to match your mood.

FIGURE 18.7
Position and
crop your
image.

Given that it is so easy to create and switch button icons, you'll soon end up with a library of icons. To switch to any icon you've used recently, click your thumbnail image in the Buddy List window. A palette of frequently used icons displays, enabling you to switch to icons in an instant.

Managing Your Buddy List

Virtually everything that goes on in iChat starts with the Buddy List. When you log in to AIM through iChat, the full Buddy List window appears onscreen to show which of your friends are online (not grayed out), whether they're available to chat, and what conferencing capabilities (Audio/Video) are available to them, as demonstrated in Figure 18.8.

FIGURE 18.8
You can easily
see who's avail-
able to chat and
their capabili-
ties using the
Buddy List; the
listings for peo-
ple who aren't
connected are
dimmed.

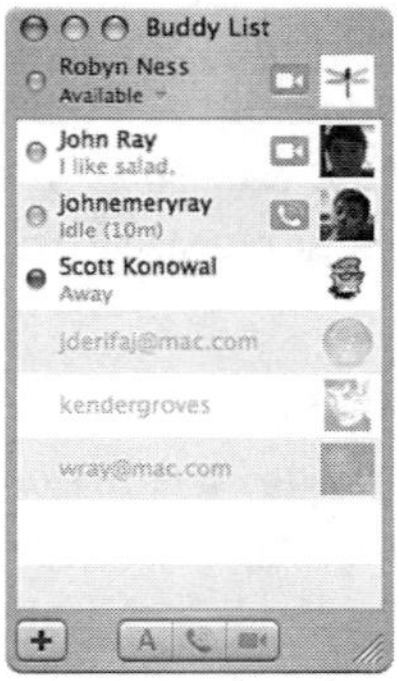

The video camera icon shows video availability, whereas the telephone represents an audio chat–ready contact. If you see multiple stacked video/audio icons, this indicates that your buddy can join a multi-party video or audio chat. You can customize what details are displayed in the Buddy List and use the iChat AV View menu to sort it by different criteria.

Bonjour and Jabber chatting, if active, open virtually identical windows displaying the active users on your local subnet and Jabber server, respectively.

Adding Buddies

Because your buddy list is stored on the AIM servers, you must be logged in to manage the list. To add a buddy, click the + button at the bottom of the iChat Buddy List window or choose Buddies, Add Buddy from the menu.

A window containing your Address Book entries appears, as shown in Figure 18.9. If the person you want to add to your Buddy List has an AIM or .Mac listing, highlight the person and click Select Buddy.

FIGURE 18.9
Add your AIM and .Mac buddies to your list.

If the person doesn't show an instant messaging name, you are prompted for the information. If the buddy-to-be isn't currently in your Address Book at all, click the New Person button to create a new entry. Enter the person's screen name, as well as a real name and email address in the window that appears. You can drag an image file (if available) into the image well to set a custom buddy icon. Click the Add button to save your new Buddy.

Address Book and iChat are integrated such that adding a new buddy to iChat automatically adds a new card in Address Book. However, because your buddy list is stored on the Instant Messenger server, you can't remove a buddy simply by deleting an Address Book card. Instead, you must select the buddy in the Buddy List and choose Buddies, Remove Buddy.

Also, keep in mind that deleting a buddy from the Buddy List does not remove the person's card from the Address Book.

Edit Buddy Info

To edit any information for a buddy that is already stored, select the buddy in the list and then choose Buddies, Get Info. The Info window, shown in Figure 18.10, provides quick access to your Address Book buddy information.

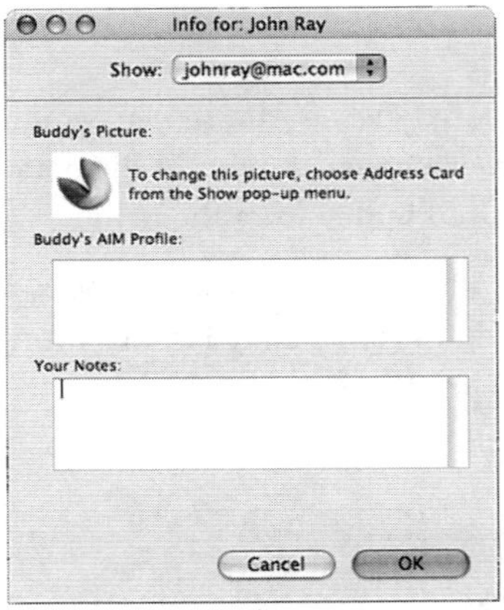

FIGURE 18.10
Edit your buddies and override their ugly and/or horrifying icons.

As with the initial setup, here you can set all the contact information for your buddy, as well as a custom buddy icon. If you *do* set a custom icon, you can choose to always use it in your buddy list. If this option is not set, your buddy icon can be overridden by any custom icon set on the remote system.

Set Buddy Actions

From the Info window, you can also access Buddy Actions by choosing Actions from the Show pop-up menu. A Buddy Action, displayed in Figure 18.11, is simply something that happens when one of your contacts becomes available or does something interesting.

In this example, I've set iChat to speak the text "Anne is here!" and bounce the Dock item repeatedly when this Buddy becomes available. Additionally, by checking the box Perform Actions Only Next Time Event Occurs, the action automatically is removed after the first time it is used. I have something very important to say to Anne today, thus the setting.

Seven possible events can be used to trigger a buddy action:

▶ Buddy Becomes Available—Your buddy has become available for IM'ing.

▶ Buddy Becomes Unavailable—Your buddy is no longer available for IM'ing.

▶ Message Received—Your buddy has received an IM that you sent.

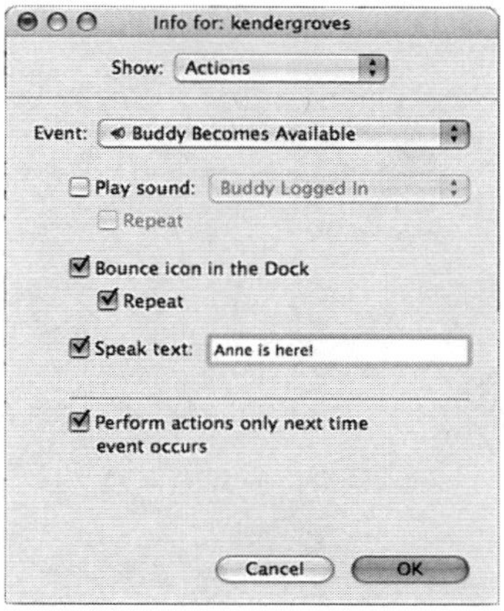

FIGURE 18.11
Buddy actions
automatically
react when your
contacts do
something.

▶ Text Invitation—Your buddy has sent you a text chat invitation.

▶ Audio Invitation—Your buddy has sent you an audio chat invitation.

▶ Video Invitation—Your buddy has sent you a video chat invitation.

▶ Buddy Accepted A/V Invitation—Your buddy has accepted an A/V chat invitation that *you* have sent.

As you set actions for events, a megaphone icon appears beside the event that contains an action. This lets you keep track of what events trigger actions without having to select and inspect each one.

There is no action for speaking the contents of the messages sent to you.

View a Buddy's Capabilities and Profile

Much as you have capabilities (to conduct audio chats, hold video conferences, and so on), so do your buddies. To get a summary of what IM capabilities a buddy on your list has, along with a copy of his profile, select him in your Buddy List and then press Command+I to open the Info window. Next, use the Show pop-up menu to choose his account name, as seen in Figure 18.12.

The profile is shown at the top of the window, followed by a text area where you can type your own notes that will be stored locally. Finally, the IM features supported are at the bottom of the window. If you have problems communicating with one of the methods discussed in this chapter, chances are it is not an available capability.

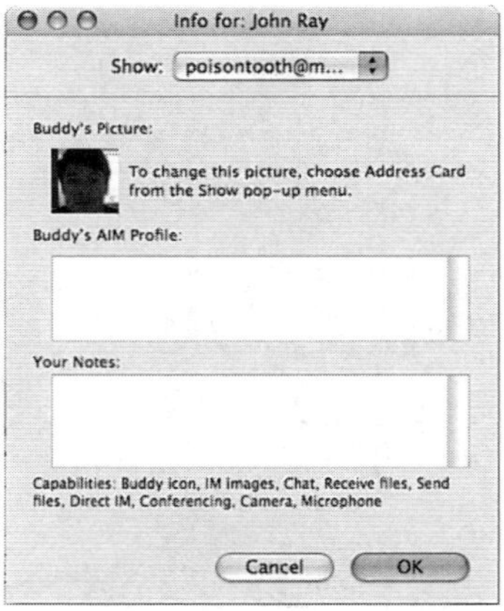

FIGURE 18.12
View the profile
and capabilities
of your buddies.

Managing Buddy Groups

To better manage your buddy list, you can arrange your buddies into groups. After creating the groups, you can choose which groups (or group) are displayed at once.

To access the groups feature of iChat AV, choose View, Use Groups from the menu. A collapsible heading for each group appears in the Buddy List, as shown in Figure 18.13. Clicking the heading toggles between hiding and showing the group members. A default group Buddies contains all your buddies.

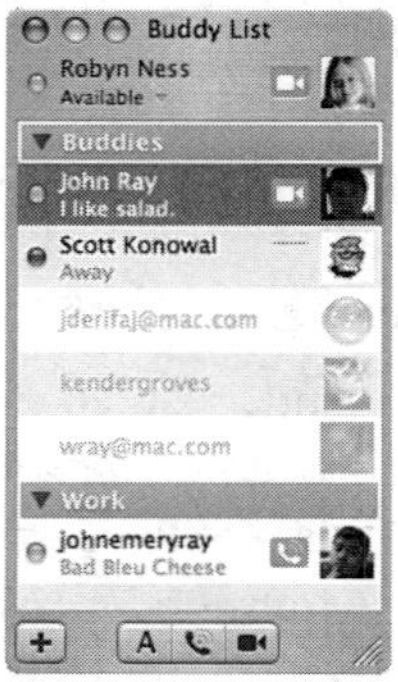

FIGURE 18.13
Arrange buddies
into groups.

To add a new group, click the + button at the bottom of the Buddy List and choose Add Group. When prompted, type a name for the group and click Add. The empty group is added to your buddy list.

To edit existing groups, click the + button again and choose Edit Groups to open a group management window. You can rename groups by double-clicking their names in the list or selecting them and clicking Rename. You can remove groups (and the buddies they contain) by selecting their names and clicking the – button. You can also add new groups within this view by using the + button.

After adding a group, add buddies to it by dragging their names in the Buddy List onto the group names. To remove a buddy from a group, drag the buddy back into the default Buddies group.

Blocking and Allowing Buddies

Your buddies are, presumably, actually your buddies—or at least people that you have some intention of talking to. If you're like me, however, you rarely want to talk to *everyone* all the time. iChat AV enables you to choose who can see you are online and who can start a chat session with you. This information is configured on an account-by-account basis, meaning that different accounts can allow or block different people.

To configure your block/allow list, open the Accounts pane of the iChat Preferences, choose the account you want to configure, and then click the Security button, as shown in Figure 18.14.

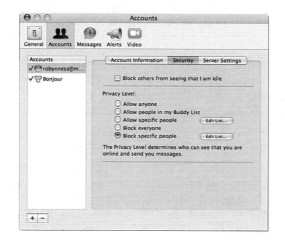

FIGURE 18.14
Set who can and can't chat with you.

By default, your IM account allows anyone to see you are online and initiate a chat with you. Using the radio buttons, you can choose to be visible only to those individuals you've added to your buddy list, or to a specific list of people.

An alternative approach is to configure who is *blocked* rather than allowed. The Block Everyone button prevents *anyone* from seeing you are online. The Block Specific People setting, on the other hand, allows everyone except individuals that you choose.

To edit either the Allow or Block lists, click the Edit List button. Use the + and – buttons in the window that appears to add and remove screen names from the list. Note, however, that you *must* use screen names in the allow/block lists; iChat does not warn you if you don't, but then these features do not work as expected.

Initiating IM and A/V Conferencing

In iChat AV, you can use three types of messaging to communicate: text, audio, and video. These three options are represented by the text ("A"), phone, and video camera icons at the bottom of your buddy list. To start a messaging session with one of your buddies, just select a name in the list and click the appropriate icon at the bottom of the Buddy List.

Alternatively, you can double-click your buddy's name to start a text chat, or click the telephone or video icon by a buddy picture to start an audio or video chat.

In the event you want to start a Text Chat *without* first adding the person to your buddy list, you can create a one-time chat with a "non-buddy" by choosing New Chat with Person (Shift+Command+N) from the File menu and typing the screen name of the person with whom you want to chat.

If your buddies' icons display multiple overlapping telephone and video camera icons, this indicates they can participate in a multi-party chat. If you are equipped to host a multi-party conference, select all the participants by Command-clicking their buddy list entries, and then clicking the camera or phone icon at the bottom of the Buddy List. If not all the participants are available when you start the session, don't worry—you can add audio and video conference members at any time during the session.

By the Way

The iChat AV menu extra can also be used to start a chat session by choosing a buddy name from the menu. If the buddy has multiple means of communicating (besides simple text), iChat displays a window with three buttons (Text, Audio, Video) and enables you to choose your preferred chat method.

For those who prefer to use the menus, the Buddies menu also enables you to initiate conferencing sessions—including two special chat types: one-way audio and one-way video. These are useful if you want to send audio or video to someone without a camera. They can type their responses to you and hear your audio stream or watch your video stream.

Now, let's take an in-depth look at how each of the communications methods works when chats are initiated.

Communicating Via Text Messaging

Starting a text messaging session opens an empty message window. Type your message in the field at the bottom of the window and press Return on your keyboard. If you're into sending *emoticons*, or smiley faces, there is a convenient pull-down smiley menu on the right side of the input field. Basic formatting controls (bold, underline, font, and so on) are found under the Format menu and can be used to style your text.

After your message has been sent, it appears in the upper portion of the window, along with whatever reply the other person sends. The text of a session can be saved by choosing File, Save a Copy As from the menu.

If you receive a message while not already engaged in a chat session with the sender, you are alerted, and a message window appears. If you click on the window, it displays an area for you to type a response (immediately accepting the invitation) or provides you the option of clicking Block to block the request and further messages from the buddy, Decline to turn down the chat with your buddy, or Accept to start chatting. If you enter a response and press Return, it is assumed that you have accepted the chat. If you decline, the sender receives a message that you have declined the invitation to chat. If you block a request, the sender is added to a list of blocked senders who can no longer see when you are logged in to iChat. (The list of blocked senders can be reviewed and edited under the Security settings of the Accounts pane of the iChat preferences.)

You can add the person you're currently chatting with to your Buddy List by choosing Buddies, Add Buddy from the menu, or show his or her Address Book entry by choosing Buddies, Show In Address Book.

By the Way

If, during the course of a conversation, the remote party closes the connection or gets bumped offline, the chat window stays open. If he or she comes back, a message to that effect appears in the already open window, and you can resume the conversation where you left off.

Customize the Chat Window Appearance

If you find the conversation bubbles overwhelming, you can use View, Show as Text to disable them (and Show as Balloons to turn them back on). You can also customize the font and font color for both your messages and your buddies'.

Further chat window View settings include the option to choose how buddies are identified in a chat (using their pictures, names, or both), the capability to set a customized picture as the chat background, and the option to clear the background picture.

Send and Receive Files

In addition to sending ordinary text messages, iChat enables you to send files. To send a file, drag its icon into the message area of a chat window and press Return on your keyboard. The recipient can then drag the file onto the desktop. If you send image files, they appear inside the chat window as part of the conversation. (For maximum compatibility with people using AIM programs other than iChat, it's recommended that you stick with JPEG and GIF image formats.)

By the Way

> You can force confirmation before a file is sent by choosing Confirm Before Sending Files in the Messages pane of the iChat AV preferences. This allows you to verify that you are sending the file you intended before it's too late!

When you find yourself on the receiving end of a file transfer, the file appears as a small icon with a link in your iChat message window. Clicking the link opens a status window that displays the copy progress. By default, all downloads are made to the Desktop folder. This can be changed in the General pane of the iChat preferences.

Send and Receive Links

A hyperlink can also be sent as a special iChat object. To send a hyperlink, drag the bookmark from your browser, use the Edit, Add Hyperlink option to enter in a clickable URL, or just type or paste it in, and the URL is recognized automatically.

If you receive a link in an instant message, it appears as underlined text, just like a web browser. Click the link to open the URL in your default browser.

Direct Messages

AIM messages are not (usually) a direct line of communication between people. Instead, all IM traffic is routed through instant messaging servers—in the case of AIM, it's AOL's servers. Although this conveniently avoids many connection problems with firewalls and inbound traffic, it also leads to privacy concerns about who could potentially be watching your chat. In addition, the extra time required to transmit through a central server can slow file transfers between individuals. To avoid this, users can activate a direct instant messaging session where all information is passed directly between the participants' computers.

To do this, choose the buddy to whom you want to send a direct IM, and from the menu select Buddies, Send Direct Message (Command-Option-Shift-M). If both you and the recipient are connected directly to the Internet, an IM session starts, exactly as it would through the AOL servers.

Multi-party Chat Sessions

As you've probably guessed, you can easily participate in chats with different people simultaneously, but each chat session would be in a separate window. You can also start a chat session with multiple people where all participants can see messages and type simultaneously.

To start a group chat, follow these steps:

1. Highlight the buddies you want to invite to chat, and then Control-click on any of the names and choose Invite To Chat, or just click the "A" button at the bottom of the Buddies List.

2. Type a message inviting the participants. When the invited buddies receive the chat request, they can choose to accept or decline. If they accept, they can send and receive messages as part of the group, as shown in Figure 18.15.

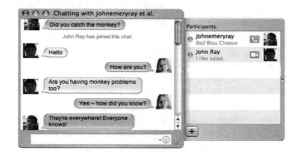

FIGURE 18.15
Start multiperson chats in iChat AV.

To add buddies to a Chat, use the + button at the bottom of the participants drawer to select their names.

All multi-party chats are given a Chat Name any AIM users can use to join the chat, even if they aren't on your Buddy List. To choose a Chat Name, select View, Chat Options and type a Chat Name in the provided field.

To join a chat when you know the Chat Name, choose File, Go to Chat and enter the Chat Name. Other chat applications should offer the same feature, but how it is accessed varies.

Create/Join a Persistent Chat Room

The Go to Chat feature can also be used to create a persistent chat room that other users can join. To start a persistent chat, choose File, Go to Chat (Command-G) from the menu. When prompted, type the name of an existing chat room (if you want to join a chat someone else has created), or make up your own name. The iChat AV chat window appears with *no* participants. Others can join your chat room by using the Go to Chat feature on their copy of iChat AV.

Some chat names (including those with punctuation) are unacceptable for creating a chat room. If iChat AV does not return a chat window immediately on using Go to Chat, the name you typed is invalid.

Save Chat/Messaging Transcripts

To save the contents of a chat to a text file, choose File, Save a Copy As from the menu. This creates a file that you can later open and review in iChat by choosing File, Open. If you prefer, you can automatically save transcripts of all your text chats by choosing Automatically Save Chat Transcripts in the Messages pane of the application preferences.

Requirements for Audio and Video Chats

iChat enables ordinary users to hold high-quality full-motion video/audio conferences with their friends and colleagues. Up to 10 people (including yourself) can participate in an audio chat, and up to 4 in a video chat. Unfortunately, with the new features come lofty new system requirements.

By the Way

iChat AV works with recognized Mac OS X video sources—FireWire camcorders, webcams, and analog A/V conversion devices, such as the Dazzle FireWire Bridge. Apple's own iSight camera (www.apple.com/isight/) is cost effective and produces high-quality images. If the $150 price tag is within range, I recommend the iSight purchase. If not, the iBot camera is available for the $30–60 range on eBay and works fine with iChat AV.

If you do not have a video camera, you can use iChat AV as an audioconferencing solution with any system-recognized microphone, and you can participate in one-way video conferences with someone who has a video camera.

On the computer side, iChat AV requires *at least* a 600MHz G3 for *single-party* video-conferencing. If you attempt to use video on a slower machine, it reports that video is not available on your computer.

The requirements for multi-party conferencing are even higher. If you plan to use the multi-person video/audio chat features, you need at least a dual-processor 1Ghz G4 to host a video chat and at least a single-processor 1GHz G4 or a dual-processor 800Mhz G4 to join one.

Finally, no matter what high-end CPU platform or video hardware you may own, you need a lot of network bandwidth to accommodate audio or video streams. The low-end requirements are 56Kbps for audio, and 128Kbps for video and 1000Kbps for hosting multi-party conferences.

Realistically, 56k modem users may be able to audioconference if they have a stable and noise-free connection, but the best experience comes from a dedicated digital connection. xDSL, cable, and LAN users should be able to carry high-quality audio/video streams easily, but even these connections may not be able to host multi-person chats.

Conversing Via Audio Chats

When an audio chat has been initiated, a window containing the names and icons of each of the participants appears. Beside each conference member is a volume meter; as the person speaks, the meter flashes, making it easy to determine who is talking at any given point in time. A multi-party audio conference is shown in progress in Figure 18.16.

An audio conference begins as soon as the first participant accepts the invitation. The conversation can carry on while iChat waits for other invitees to join.

FIGURE 18.16
The audio chat window displays the microphone input level for each participant along with Add Participant, Mute, and Volume controls.

At the bottom of the conference window is your own volume input meter, along with controls for adding participants, muting your microphone, and controlling the output volume of your speaker. If you are conversing with only a single person, iChat displays only your input level and volume controls.

The input level meter can be used to gauge whether your microphone is positioned correctly, or whether you need to adjust the input level within the Sound pane of the Mac OS X System Preferences. An iSight user in an average office environment should see a few bars' worth of "flicker" (background noise) on the left side of the bar. If background noise approaches 1/5 of the total bar length, you may need to reduce the gain or find a quieter place to chat.

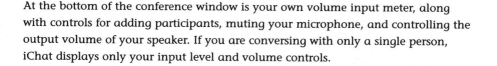

During a chat, you can adjust the volume by using the chat window's volume slider, or quickly mute the conversation by clicking the Mute button, which looks like a crossed-out microphone.

If the volume is too high, you may experience feedback as the microphone starts to pick up the speaker sounds. You can fix this by lowering the volume or positioning the microphone farther away from your speaker.

> To change the sound input source (if more than one is available) for your machine, use the Microphone pop-up menu in the Video pane of the iChat preferences.

Invite Additional Audio Chat Participants

To invite additional members to an audio chat, click the + button in the audio window and choose an audio-enabled member from the pop-up list. You can add only participants that meet the minimum requirements for an audio chat—meaning they must be running Mac OS X 10.4 and have at least a 1Ghz G4 (or dual-processor 800Mhz G4).

If you start an audio chat with a user that doesn't support multi-party conferencing, you cannot add more members.

Respond to an Audio Chat Request

If you are on the receiving end of an audio chat request, you are prompted with an incoming chat alert (similar to an incoming text message) and, after the alert window is clicked, given the option of accepting or declining the chat—or making a *text* reply. If you choose a text reply, you effectively open a new text chat with the remote party, and the audio chat is canceled.

> Even if your buddy doesn't have an audio input source, you can still have a one-sided audio chat. Use the Buddies, Invite to One-Way Audio Chat option to start a one-way chat.

Conducting Video Chats

A video chat works virtually identically to an audio chat but with the added bonus of being able to *see* as well as hear the remote participants. When a video chat is initiated, you see a preview of yourself until the chat is accepted. In the case of a single-party chat, after a connection is established your image shrinks to the lower-right corner of the window, and your buddy's smiling face fills the rest of the window.

You can resize your mini preview by moving your cursor over it and then dragging the resize handle that appears. You can also click and drag the mini preview to any of the four corners of the window.

Multi-party chats are a bit more interesting, as shown in Figure 18.17. When multiple individuals are invited to a chat, each person's image is displayed as a 3D panel surrounding the smaller image of you. The effect is similar to sitting at a table with your colleagues. You can see them and they can see you without having to search the screen for a window with their pictures.

FIGURE 18.17
Video chats—
be seen and
heard.

To take a picture of a video conference, choose Video, Take Snapshot (Option+Command+S).

Did you Know?

At the bottom of the video chat window is a microphone button for muting the audio portion of chat and a button with two opposing arrows for expanding the view to fill the whole screen (Control-Command-F). The + button is also present and active in multi-party–capable chats and can be clicked to display a menu allowing you to invite another person to the conference. Up to four (including yourself) individuals can participate in a video conference simultaneously.

When in full-screen mode, moving the mouse displays several button controls above your preview image: an "X" to close the chat, a microphone to mute, and double arrows to shrink back to a windowed view. Again, use the drag handle that appears in the upper-left corner of the preview to resize your own image onscreen or click and drag the entire mini preview window to move it to another corner.

To pause the video display at any time, use Video, Pause Video.

Respond to a Video Chat Request

When receiving a video chat request, clicking the alert window gives you a preview of your own video feed so that you can make sure that you've dressed yourself properly before clicking the Accept button to start the chat. Like the audio chat, you can also decline a chat request or send a text reply instead of video.

Applying Parental Controls

If you have children, you probably want to know who they are chatting with—or at least protect them from unwanted chat requests. To set parental controls for non-administrative user accounts, open the Accounts pane of the OS X System Preferences, select the user you want to restrict, and click the Parental Controls button, as demonstrated in Figure 18.18.

FIGURE 18.18
The iChat parental controls can protect your children from inappropriate conversations.

Click the Configure button to create a Buddy List for the account. Use the + button to open the Address Book window, and select an address book entry with an AIM account or create a new entry. This works identically to the process of setting up your own buddy list, discussed earlier in the chapter. To remove buddies, click the – button. When finished, click OK; the account is now restricted.

Setting Event Alerts

In the default iChat configuration, you have to pay attention to your screen to see who is logged in or what is going on. To change this, alerts can be set to notify you of events such as logins and logouts.

Under the Alerts pane of the application preferences, choose what iChat does when you or your buddies log in or out. Use the Event pop-up menu to choose an event to modify; then click the check boxes for the actions you want to apply, such as playing sounds, speaking text, and bouncing icons. This is similar to the individual Buddy Actions discussed earlier, but applies to *everyone*—not just a specific person.

Turn Repeated Ring On and Off

When a conference request first comes in, your computer will ring...and ring...and ring...and ring.... If you absolutely despise hearing this sound over and over, Apple provides a way to force the iChat from playing it repeatedly.

Within the Video pane of the iChat preferences, uncheck Play Repeated Ring Sound when Invited to a Conference.

Using the Connection Doctor

Depending on your and your buddies' connections, video and audio chats may be a bit choppy or sporadic. If something isn't working, it could very well be a lack of network bandwidth.

To get an idea of your connection's capacity, choose Video, Connection Doctor. The Connection Doctor is displayed in Figure 18.19. There are two display views—Statistics and Error Log. Use the Show menu at the top of the window to select them.

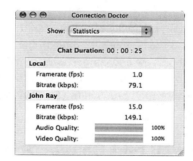

FIGURE 18.19
The Connection Doctor displays stats on your current A/V connection.

Watch the audio and video quality during the conversation. If they are not in the 90–100% range, you may have an unsatisfactory conferencing experience. The bitrate measurement tells you exactly how much data is being sent locally and remotely.

Adjusting Bandwidth

Some choppiness-related problems can be corrected by limiting the amount of data streamed to your chat partner. Usually, iChat AV determines the proper streaming rate automatically, but in some cases you may want to try setting the value yourself. To do this, use the Video pane in the iChat AV preferences, shown in Figure 18.20.

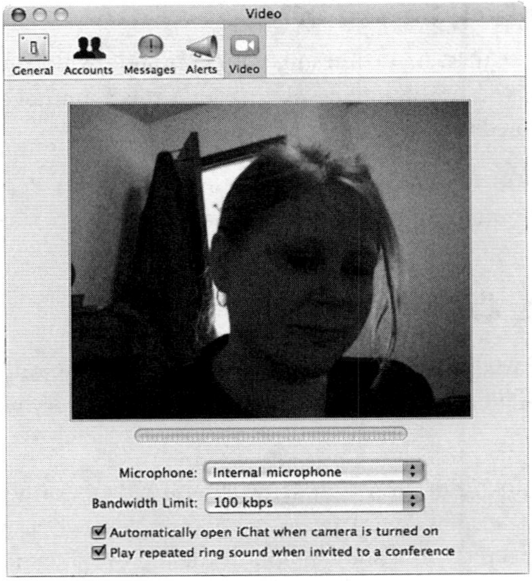

FIGURE 18.20
Adjust your
iChat AV prefer-
ences

The bandwidth limit is initially set to *none*, meaning that iChat attempts to stream data as quickly as possible to the remote site. You can limit the bandwidth to anywhere from 100Kbps to 2Mbps. Low-end connections should restrict the bandwidth to 100Kbps, whereas cable and xDSL users may be able to get away with 200kbps or possibly 500kbps. Only local or high bandwidth (T1/T3/ATM) connections should attempt the upper settings.

Diagnosing Firewall and Connection Errors

The Connection Doctor can also be used to view errors that occur in making the connection to remote audio and video chat partners. To view the error log, open the Connection Doctor and choose Error Log from the Show pop-up menu. iChat AV displays all the connections it attempted to make and what failed.

By the Way

Often, failure of a conference is due to a firewall conflict. iChat AV's audio and video features work well as long as one side of a connection is not behind a firewall or connection-sharing device, such as a router. To use video/audio conferencing behind a firewall, you must enable ports 5060 UDP (conference notifications) and 16384-16403 UDP (audio and video) to be passed through to the iChat AV computer. To read Apple's tech note on this topic, visit docs.info.apple.com/article.html?artnum=93208.

Summary

Apple's iChat AV can be used for instant messaging as well as for computer-to-computer audio and video chats. In this chapter, you learned how to set up iChat and add other people to your buddy list. You also learned how to initiate and join one-on-one instant messaging sessions, group chats, and chat rooms. You then learned about iChat's audio/video options, which require a microphone (or microphone-equipped computer) and a camera, respectively. Finally, we discussed the Connection Doctor, which can help you diagnose connection problems related to audio and video conferencing.

CHAPTER 19

Using iCal

Apple's iCal application is a personal calendaring system that you can use to manage your schedule and even email invitations to events. It also supports network calendar publishing so that you can share your calendar, or share the calendars of other iCal users.

Depending on the version of Mac OS X you have, iCal may already be installed on your computer inside the Applications folder. If not, you can download it from www.apple.com/ical.

---

iCal gets its name from both Apple's marketing department and the calendar standard it supports—iCalendar. The iCalendar format can be used to define a series of event objects within a calendar object, and a series of alarms within each event.

By basing iCal on a standard, Apple has opened the door to integration with other common calendaring solutions, and the exchange of information to and from computers running on different operating systems, such as Windows.

By the Way

The iCal Interface

On starting iCal, you see a three-paned window, shown in Figure 19.1, that will serve as your workspace while using the application.

The upper-left corner contains the Calendars list. Each calendar you've added or subscribed to is displayed here. By default, iCal comes with two calendars—home and work. You can feel free to delete these or use them. You can add new calendars by clicking the + button at the bottom-left side of the window, or by choosing File, New Calendar (Option-Command-N) from the menu. Delete calendars by highlighting them in the list and pressing the Delete key or by choosing Edit, Delete.

Calendars with a checked check box in front of them are "active" and are displayed in the main calendar view to the right of the calendar list.

FIGURE 19.1
The iCal work-space gives you complete con-trol over your schedule.

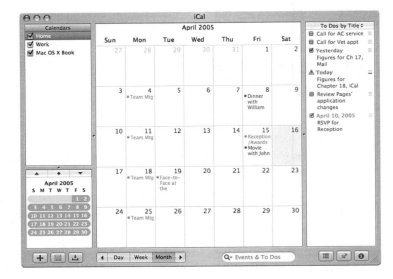

Directly beneath the calendar list is another pane, which can show either a mini-month view or any notifications made in response to invitations you've sent. When showing mini-months, you can move through the months by using the three icons (up arrow, diamond, and down arrow) to move back, to the current month, or to the next month, respectively. Clicking a date within one of the mini-months changes the main calendar view to that day.

By the Way

You can collapse the mini-month view by using the divider line between it and the calendar list, or by clicking the calendar icon at the bottom of the iCal window.

Along the bottom of the iCal window are several additional controls. The Day, Week, and Month buttons determine the view style of the main calendar—whether you're looking at a single Day, Week, or Month. The arrows to either side of these buttons move forward and back to the next appropriate calendar "unit" (Day, Week, or Month).

In the bottom center of the window is a single search field. Typing in this field dis-plays (as you type) a list of events that match the string of characters you've entered. Figure 19.2 shows a calendar search in action. The search works across *only* the calendars currently checked in your calendar list.

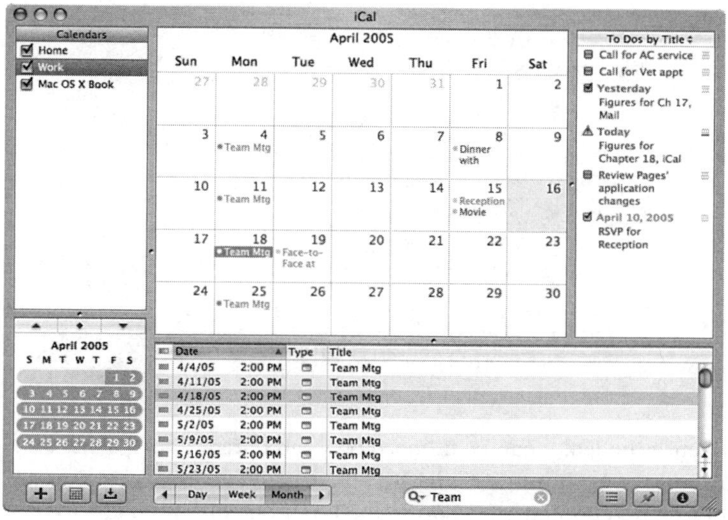

FIGURE 19.2
Search for an
event in your
calendars.

Double-click an event to which you want to jump and it is highlighted in the main calendar view pane.

Finally, to the right of the search field are three additional buttons. The first button hides or shows the search results. The second shows or hides a new pane to the right of the main calendar view containing to-do items. The third opens a window drawer containing detailed information about the currently selected event, calendar, or to-do item.

Adding and Editing Events

Adding an event is easiest within the Day or Week calendar views. Highlight the calendar that should hold the event, navigate in the main calendar view to the day where you want to create an event, and then click and drag from the start time to the end time. As you drag, the event end time is displayed near your cursor.

A New Event box is drawn that covers the selected time, and when you release the mouse button, the subject (title) is highlighted. Start typing immediately to enter a new subject (title), or double-click the event subject to edit it after it has been deselected. Figure 19.3 shows a Day view with a new event (Meeting with Anne) added.

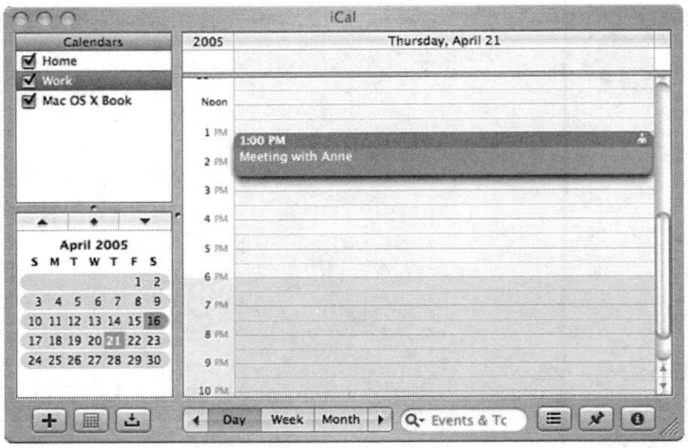

FIGURE 19.3
Add new events by clicking and dragging to cover the desired time span.

[iCal interface screenshot showing Calendars panel with Home, Work, Mac OS X Book, April 2005 calendar, and Thursday, April 21 day view with a 1:00 PM "Meeting with Anne" event]

After an event is added, it can be dragged between different time slots, or days. The event duration can be changed by putting the cursor over the bottom or top edge of the event block and dragging it to resize the box. You can also add new events by using File, New Event from the menu (Command-N). This creates a new 1-hour event on the selected day. Use the editing techniques discussed previously to position and change its duration.

Although events on the same calendar cannot be "drawn" over the same time slot, you can make two events at the same time with the same duration by creating them in separate time slots and then dragging them to the same slot.

If you prefer working within the Month view, you can add new events by double-clicking on the calendar cell (but not the date number) of a day. This creates a new event and opens the Information window, which provides access to the time/duration values for the event.

If you'd prefer to edit the event duration by dragging, you can quickly jump to the Day view by double-clicking the date (number) in the Month view.

To set these attributes, quickly jump to the Day view by double-clicking the day's number within the Month view.

To remove any event, highlight it in any of the three calendar views; then press your Delete key, or choose Edit, Delete.

Event Invitations

Events don't usually happen in a vacuum. If you're planning a party and no one else knows they're invited, you may have a problem. iCal supports the notion of event invitations and acceptance. After creating an event, you can invite other people listed in your address book to the event, and they can then accept or decline.

To send an invitation, switch to the Day or Week calendar view so that the event for which you want to send invitations is visible. Next, open the Information window. You should see a field called Attendees. Here, you can simply start typing email addresses or names. If they are recognized as Address Book entries, they are automatically completed. Press Return between multiple addresses. After an address is added and "recognized," it becomes an object in iCal. You can use the small pull-down menu attached to each attendee to choose between multiple email addresses stored for them, or to remove them or manually edit their email addresses, as shown in Figure 19.4.

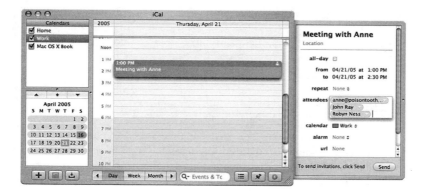

FIGURE 19.4
Enter your event's attendees.

Alternatively, you can invite people in your Address Book to the event by choosing Window, Address Panel (Option-Command-A), and dragging their individual vCards or a group vCard from the Addresses window onto the Info window. An icon of a person appears in the upper-right corner of the event in Day or Week view mode.

> You can create a calendar event to meet with someone in your Address book by opening the Addresses window and dragging the icon next to a name directly to your calendar. That person is automatically added as an attendee. (Note, however, that you'll still have to officially send the invitation.)

Did you Know?

At this point, you've officially told iCal that you want to invite the listed people, but you haven't yet sent invitations. To do this, you can click the Send button at the bottom of the Information window.

When you click the Send Invitations button, iCal works with Mail to send an invitation file to the people on the list. You'll also notice that the attendees are displayed with an arrow icon in front of their names. This indicates that they have been invited, but are not yet confirmed as attending the event. Confirmed attendees are displayed with a check mark, whereas declined attendees show an *X*.

Invitation recipients, assuming that they have iCal installer, can double-click the invitation icon in their email. The iCal application on the invitee's system displays a notification in the Notifications pane and provides details in the Info window, shown in Figure 19.5.

FIGURE 19.5
An invitation is
in progress.

<table>
<tr><td>**By the Way**</td><td>Earlier in the chapter you were told that iCal uses the iCalendar standard for storing information about events. That means that people using other iCalendar-based scheduling programs, such as Microsoft Outlook, will be able to read invitations generated by iCal.

However, sending invitations to people who don't have compatible calendaring software should be done the old-fashioned way—by sending a personally written email. (The iCal-generated messages are meant to be interpreted by computers and are not exactly friendly to human readers!)</td></tr>
</table>

Event Info

As you've seen, invitation management is one use of the Information window as it applies to events. You can also use the Information window to change event descriptions, durations, and schedules. Ten fields are available when an event is selected:

▶ Title—The name of the event being edited.

▶ Location—An arbitrary value, presumably where the event is taking place.

▶ All-Day—Whether it is an all-day event (not scheduled for a specific time).

▶ From/To—The date/time/duration of the event.

▶ Repeat—If an event occurs every several days, weeks, months, or years, use the Repeat field to set how often it appears on your calendar. You can also choose when the recurrences end, if ever, and when the event ends, if ever.

▶ Attendees—Covered previously.

▶ Calendar—The calendar on which the event is stored.

▶ Alarm—Choose to display a message, send an email, or play a sound. After choosing an action, a second field appears, enabling you to set the number of minutes, hours, or days before an event starts that the action will take place.

▶ URL—A URL that is pertinent to the given event.

▶ Notes—General notes and other information you might want to store about an event.

If you want to store time zone information with events, you can add a Time Zone field to the Event Information display by using the iCal application preferences.

By the Way

To Do Lists

A to-do item differs from an event in that it doesn't take place at a certain time but often must be *completed* by a given date. iCal can track your to-do items by using the To Do list. Click the pushpin icon in the lower-right corner of the iCal window to display the To Do list, shown in Figure 19.6.

You can sort the items in a To Do list by due date, priority, title, calendar, or manually by clicking the header above the list. You can also choose to show or hide completed items.

By the Way

To add a new item to the list, highlight the calendar that should contain the to-do item and then double-click within the To Do list pane, or choose File, New To Do (Command-K). A new item is added to the list. By default, new to-do items have no deadline, and you can flag them as "finished" simply by clicking the check boxes in front of them.

FIGURE 19.6
The To Do list contains a list of things to do.

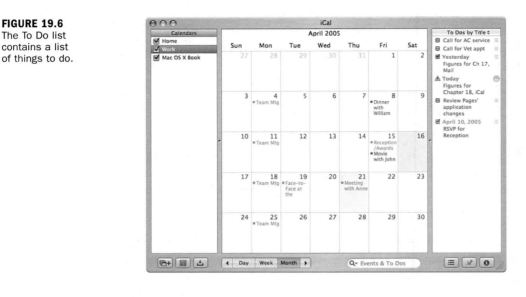

To Do Info

To add notes about a to-do entry and set a deadline, highlight the item in the To Do list and then click the Info button at the lower right to open the Information window.

The To Do Info window enables you to enter extended text information about the item, choose whether it has been completed, assign it a priority, pick a due date, pick the calendar of which it should be a part, and assign an appropriate URL for extended information.

Calendar Publishing and Subscribing

One of the most useful features of iCal is the capability to publish calendars to a .Mac account (or to other computers set up to be WebDAV servers) so that the others can subscribe to your calendar to view your schedule.

To publish an existing calendar to the Internet, highlight the calendar within your calendar list and then choose Calendar, Publish from the menu. The dialog shown in Figure 19.7 is displayed.

First, give your calendar a title.

Next, choose the information you want to be published:

▶ Publish Changes Automatically—Automatically update your published calendar when you make local changes in iCal.

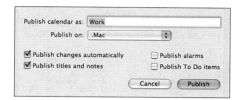

FIGURE 19.7
Publish your
calendar to a
.Mac account or
WebDAV share.

▶ Publish Subjects and Notes—Publish the subject and note fields for events.

▶ Publish Alarms—Publish alarm information (alarm type, time, and so on) along with your events.

▶ Publish To Do Items—Include any to-do items in the calendar as part of the publication.

Finally, choose whether you're using a .Mac account or a web server (WebDAV). If you're using .Mac, iCal automatically uses the .Mac account information contained in the Internet System Preferences. Otherwise, it prompts for the WebDAV URL, login, and password.

> You can change any of these attributes later by selecting the calendar and opening the Information window.

Did you Know?

Click the Publish button to send your calendar to the remote server. Published calendars are denoted by a "transmission" icon appearing after their names in the Calendar list.

After publishing, you are prompted with the option to Send Mail with your calendar information to those who might be interested in subscribing. You can also choose Visit Page to see a Web view of your Calendar. The Visit Page option is available only to .Mac subscribers and provides a fully interactive Web view of your calendar; non-Mac.com members can still visit the Web page to see the calendar.

You can update a published calendar with the latest changes by choosing Calendar, Refresh (Command-R) from the menu or by choosing Calendar, Refresh All (Shift+Command+R) to refresh *all* published calendars. To completely remove a published calendar, use Calendar, Unpublish.

Subscribing to a calendar is easier than publishing. In many cases, it's as simple as clicking a webcal:// URL in your web browser—this automatically creates a subscription in iCal. Apple has published a wide range of interesting online calendars in its iCal library at www.apple.com/ical/library/.

Calendars available in the iCal Library cover topics ranging from official holidays to sporting event rosters, movie releases, and music tour schedules. It's definitely worth a visit!

To manually enter a subscription, choose Calendar, Subscribe (Option-Command-S). The subscription window shown in Figure 19.8 is displayed.

FIGURE 19.8
Enter URL to subscribe to a calendar.

Subscribe to: [   ]

Cancel   Subscribe

Enter the URL of an appropriately prepared iCal source and click Subscribe. After a few seconds, the subscribed calendar appears in your calendar list (differentiated from local calendars by the "shortcut" arrow following its name). You can refresh a subscribed calendar by choosing Calendar, Refresh (Command-R).

iCal Preference Options

A few final preferences can be set from iCal's General and Advanced preferences, shown in Figures 19.9 and 19.10.

Under the General preferences, you can activate the following options:

▶ Use Days Per Week and Start Week On to choose whether iCal recognizes a work (5-day) or normal (7-day) week, and what day of the week the calendar should use as the start day.

▶ Use the Day Starts At, Day Ends At, and Show settings to set the start and end points in a calendar day, and of those hours, how many are visible onscreen simultaneously without scrolling.

▶ To add a display of the event time within the Month view, click the Show Time in Month View check box.

▶ To create a special calendar to display birthday information stored in your Address Book, check the box for Show Birthdays calendar. (The Birthdays calendar is read-only because it gets its data from your Address Book—to make changes, you have to work through Address Book.)

▶ If you have a .Mac account, you can also choose to synchronize your calendars with other computers.

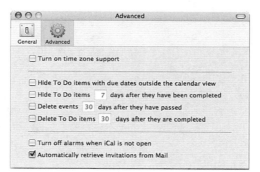

FIGURE 19.9
Set a few
iCal format
preferences.

FIGURE 19.10
Choose which
to-do items to
show.

The Advanced preferences control time-zone support, several aspects of to-do lists, and whether iCal alarms should sound even when iCal isn't open.

iCal Menus

A few minor additional features are available from the iCal File menus that have not yet been covered in the course of this discussion.

As usual, the File menu is used to create new calendars, events, and to-do items. It can also, however, export and import calendar files.

▶ Import—Import calendar data from Entourage, or import iCalendar or vCal format files.

▶ Export—Export the active calendar to an iCalendar format file.

▶ Print—Print a copy of the active calendar view.

Summary

iCal is a useful application for managing your schedule. With it, you can keep track of your own meetings, events, and to-do items—or even subscribe to the calendars others have set up. You can also use iCal to issue invitations to events in your calendar or share your full calendar so that family and friends will know what you're up to.

PART IV

Apple's iLife Applications

CHAPTER 20

Introducing iLife

The CEO of Apple, Steve Jobs, has spent a lot of time in the past few years talking about making the Mac the center of your digital life-style. iLife carries this vision forward by bringing together five easy-to-use digital media applications already available from Apple—iTunes, iPhoto, iMovie HD, iDVD, and GarageBand. These applications include features that enable you to conveniently cross over from one to another. For instance, you can build a slideshow of your digital photographs in iPhoto with accompanying music from your iTunes music library (maybe even something you've composed yourself in GarageBand) and then, with the click of a button, transfer that slideshow to iDVD for finishing touches and writing to disc.

Now let's take a brief look at the five applications that make up iLife.

iTunes

If you like music, iTunes (shown in Figure 20.1) was made for you. iTunes allows you to encode music from CDs in MP3 and other common digital formats for storage on your computer—a great option for easy access and organization. You can also use iTunes to design and burn your own custom mix CDs. If you want to expand your music collection, you can use iTunes to access Apple's iTunes Music Store, where you can purchase songs or albums for download in digital format.

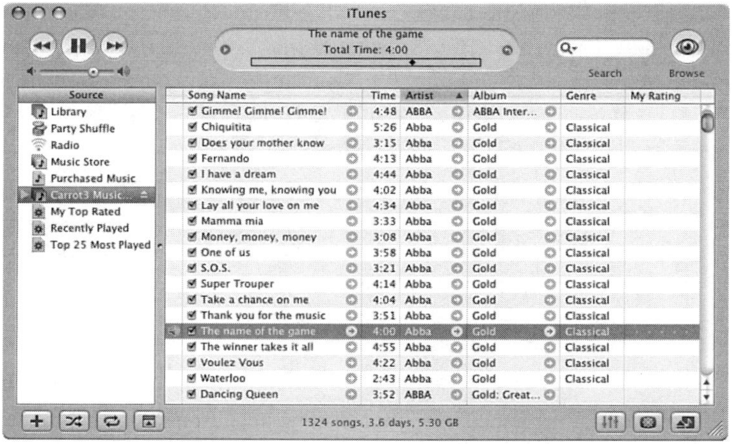

FIGURE 20.1
Here's a glimpse of iTunes.

MP3 is a compression system that reduces the size of a music file by a factor of 10 to 15, or more. How's this magic accomplished? By removing data that the human ear either cannot hear or doesn't hear as well. Audio quality can be almost indistinguishable from a CD, or, if you opt for more compression, audibly different.

> GarageBand was designed to integrate with iTunes. You can create your own music in GarageBand and then bring it into iTunes, where it can be used the same as any other track in your music library.

iTunes is also perfectly suited for handling streaming MP3s. If you've never listened to Internet radio before, you'll appreciate how quickly and easily iTunes enables you to find the type of music you want to hear and start listening.

iTunes also interacts with the Internet to look up information about your CDs, such as the artist and song title, based on album.

You'll learn how to use iTunes in Chapter 21, "Using iTunes."

By the Way

> Another element of iTunes is the iTunes Music Store, which allows you to purchase and download song files from participating recording companies.

iPhoto

Have a digital camera? If so, you may have struggled to keep track of image files with difficult-to-remember names such as 200214057. With Apple's iPhoto, there's an easy way to store, organize, edit, and share your photographs. iPhoto even connects directly to many digital cameras, so you can skip loading special software.

Perhaps iPhoto's greatest strength is that it allows you to visually search your entire photo collection easily. Tiny thumbnail images, demonstrated in Figure 20.2, enable you to scan hundreds of your pictures at a time for the one you want. (If you need to see each image in greater detail, you can also increase the size of this preview.) You can also use the built-in Calendar View to show photos by month, week, or day.

By the Way

> iPhoto can connect directly to your email program to make sending photo files easy—it even scales the file sizes down for faster sending and receiving.

Chapter 22, "Using iPhoto," covers iPhoto in detail.

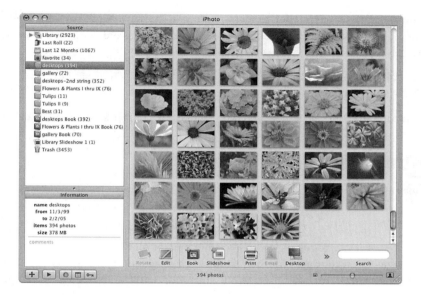

FIGURE 20.2
iPhoto makes it easy to manage a lot of images.

GarageBand

If your musical aspirations aren't satisfied by designing the perfect playlist in iTunes, it's time to give GarageBand a try (see Figure 20.3).

FIGURE 20.3
Compose music easily by using GarageBand's loops or its keyboard.

This application, the newest member of iLife, gives you the tools to create your own music, even if you don't read music or play an instrument. Simply mix and match elements from an extensive library of beats and instrumental riffs, neatly organized by instrument, style, or genre. Each element is added in its own track so you can edit or remove it easily as your composition evolves. You also can record your own elements and apply audio effects, such as fade and distortion, to get just the sound you want.

When you are satisfied with your composition, export it to iTunes to burn to CD, export it to your iPod, or use it in iPhoto, iMovie, or iDVD.

More details about using GarageBand are presented in Chapter 23, "Using GarageBand."

iMovie HD

At one time, editing a home video was a chore. You had to sit and copy each section separately from your camcorder to your VCR in the order it was to be viewed. Pros call this *linear* editing because everything is put in place in the exact sequence.

iMovie HD, an easy-to-use digital video editor, makes all that unnecessary. Editing a digital video on a computer for the first time is a revelation because you can copy the clips or segments in any order you want. Then, during the editing process, you put things in order. This process is called *nonlinear*, and it's much more flexible.

By the Way

iMovie is a ground-breaking application. Traditionally, nonlinear digital video editing was available only to professionals willing to spend thousands of dollars. iMovie brought these capabilities to hobbyists, and now iMovie HD offers the capability to capture and edit high-definition video for a more professional quality.

Although iMovie HD, shown in Figure 20.4, is astoundingly simple to learn, it includes advanced features that you can use to make the most of your video footage. You can combine separate video clips with transitions, add sound effects and voiceovers, create title text, and export your final work into formats others can view.

By the Way

A large part of what makes iMovie work so well is FireWire, the connection standard discussed in Chapter 11, "Working with Displays and Peripheral Devices." In fact, to work with digital video from your camcorder with iMovie, you must have a computer and a camera with FireWire ports. Digital video files can be very large, and getting them onto your computer would be impossibly slow without FireWire.

How can you tell whether your Mac came with FireWire ports? Check the connection panel and see whether you have any FireWire connectors. You can identify them by their peculiar shape: thin, oval at one end, squared off at the other.

Digital video cameras usually have a slightly different style Firewire connector (small, like a slightly misshapen rectangle) that may be labeled IEEE 1394 or iLink in the camera documentation.

If you don't have a FireWire connection, you can still use iMovie for making slideshows from still photos.

FIGURE 20.4
iMovie HD
makes video
editing a joy.

Chapters 24 through 28 cover most of the things you can do with iMovie HD, including adding effects and exporting.

iDVD

One of the fastest-growing consumer electronics products is the DVD player. A DVD puts the contents of an entire movie on a disc the same size as a CD. Using Apple's iDVD, you can create your own DVDs, complete with navigation menus and motion (moving) menus. (You can even transfer home movies from your camera to a DVD in one easy step.)

iDVD, shown in Figure 20.5, enables you to share your home movies and still images, and integrates with both iPhoto and iMovie.

To burn your iDVD projects to DVD, you need access to a Mac that has a SuperDrive, which can play CDs and DVDs and burn both.

You also need DVD-R, DVD-RW, DVD+R, or DVD+RW media. Although these discs may look like CDs, their capacity is much greater—4.7GB, which is large enough to hold at least an hour of average video and many image files.

The DVDs you write will play on most DVD players and the DVD drives on a personal computer. However, some of the oldest DVD players, made during the first year the format was introduced, cannot play them.

By the Way

FIGURE 20.5
iDVD lets you share your digital video and digital images, using professional-quality features.

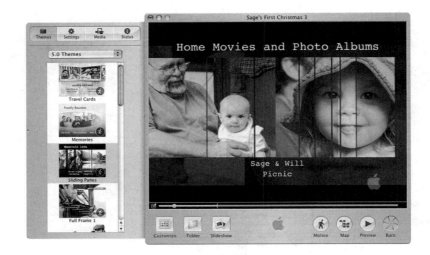

Like the other applications included in iLife, iDVD was designed to offer a wide range of features that are easy to use. We'll talk more about iDVD's features in Chapter 29, "Exploring the iDVD Interface," and Chapter 30, "Creating DVDs in iDVD."

System Requirements and Necessary Tools

Before you go any further, you need to make sure your system meets the requirements to run the iLife applications. First, your Mac must be running Mac OS X 10.2.6 or later. Your computer also must have 256MB of RAM and a display with a resolution of at least 1024×768. Your computer's processor needs at least a G3 to run iTunes, iPhoto, and iMovie. GarageBand requires at least a 600MHz G3 or, if you plan to use GarageBand Software Instruments, a G4. Because of the encoding required to produce a DVD, iDVD requires a 733MHz G4 processor or faster. Finally, if you will be installing all five iLife applications, you need 4.3GB of hard drive space; if you're planning to install only iTunes, iPhoto, and iMovie, you need 250MB of space.

By the Way

Because of the size of the GarageBand and iDVD applications, they come on an installation DVD rather than on a CD. This means your computer must have a drive that reads DVDs, such as a Combo Drive or SuperDrive, for you to install them.

In addition to these system requirements, you'll also need the right tools to meet the expectations you have of the applications that make up iLife:

▶ For making your own CDs (containing data, music, photographs, and so on), your computer must have a drive capable of writing CDs. Alternatively, you could use an external CD burner that is compatible with Mac OS X.

- ▶ To get full mileage from iPhoto, you need a compatible digital camera.
- ▶ If you want to use iMovie, you must use a digital video camera that uses either FireWire (also known as IEEE 1394 or i.Link) or USB2 technology and your computer must have a compatible connection port. (FireWire and USB2 allow large digital video files to be transferred between your camera and your computer. Without one of them, there is no feasible way to work with video on your computer.)
- ▶ To burn DVDs of iDVD projects, you must have access to a Mac equipped with Apple's SuperDrive, which can read and write both CDs and DVDs. (Note that although external DVD burners are sold, they do not work with iDVD.)

When you know what your computer needs to do its job, you're ready to move forward.

Installing the iLife Applications

Now that you've heard about the delights that await you when you use iTunes, iPhoto, iMovie, iDVD, and GarageBand, and you know about any additional requirements of those applications, how do you get them? Several options are available.

First, check your Applications folder to see whether they are already installed. If you find them, check their version numbers to make sure that you have the latest software. You can visit Apple's iLife website for information on the latest versions. (This book covers the versions of iTunes, GarageBand, iPhoto, iMovie, and iDVD included with iLife '05.)

Apple often makes minor updates to its applications that make them run better, so be sure to run Software Update to make sure your versions are up to date.

If you don't find these versions of the applications on your hard drive, you need to purchase the iLife software package.

iTunes, for both Mac and PC, is available for free via download from Apple's website.

By the
Way

To install, double-click the installer icon or disc icon that appears on your desktop and follow the prompts. You are asked to authenticate yourself first, which means that you enter the password for an account allowed to administer the computer—such as the computer owner's account. When you do that, just click OK for the license agreement and click the various Continue and Install buttons. The software will be set up on your computer in short order.

Summary

This chapter introduced you to iLife '05 and the applications it encompasses. iTunes can be used to turn your Macintosh into the centerpiece of your entertainment system. iTunes gives you access to audio media in a straightforward and entertaining manner, and its special features make organization a snap. The recent addition of the online Music Store provides a convenient source for high-quality versions of recent releases. iPhoto helps you manage and share your digital photographs. With features for editing and sharing your work, you can easily spend hours perfecting your images and preparing them for display. GarageBand helps you compose music, even if your only musical training is years of listening. By combining and refining snippets of percussion and instrumentation, you can create an original work and easily share it with others. (If you are more musically advanced, GarageBand also enables you to record and mix your own music.) iMovie HD, a digital video editing application, enables you to turn your home movies into finished products with titles, music, and transitions. It also lets you share your movies in several popular formats. Finally, iDVD lets you share your video or still photos in the popular DVD format, with features that rival those of professionally made DVDs. If you're a music enthusiast, digital photographer, or budding filmmaker, iLife '05 is for you.

CHAPTER 21

Using iTunes

Apple's iTunes enables you to organize and encode digital music files and also burn them to CD or share them with other iTunes users on your local network.

iTunes, versions 4 and higher, also connect to Apple's iTunes Music Store where you can purchase high-quality song tracks, or entire albums, online. We talk about how it works later in the chapter.

Setting Up iTunes

The first time you launch iTunes, it runs through a setup assistant to locate MP3s and configure Internet playback. At any time during the setup procedure, click Next to go to the next step, or click Previous to return to the preceding step. Clicking Cancel exits the setup utility and starts iTunes.

The first step of the setup process, displayed in Figure 21.1, enables you to set Internet access options.

iTunes is perfectly suited for handling streaming MP3s. If you've never listened to Internet radio before, you'll appreciate how quickly and easily iTunes enables you to find the type of music you want to hear and start listening. If you plan to use another streaming music player, tell iTunes not to modify your Internet settings.

iTunes also interacts with the Internet to look up information about your CDs, such as the artist and song title. The Yes, Automatically Connect to the Internet radio button, selected by default, enables this feature. To force iTunes to prompt you before connecting to the Internet, click No, Ask Me Before Connecting. Click Next when you've made your selections.

The setup step asks whether you want to go to the iTunes Music Store or go to your own iTunes Library on completing the setup. (If you choose not to explore the music store immediately, you can still reach it through the iTunes interface; you get a closer look at the music store later in this chapter.)

Click Done to begin using iTunes.

FIGURE 21.1
Choose how
iTunes works
with your
Internet
applications.

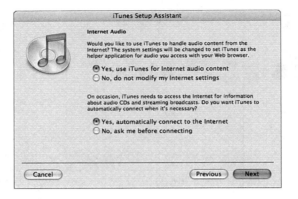

The iTunes Interface

Everything you need to do anything in iTunes is found in the main window, shown in Figure 21.2.

FIGURE 21.2
A single iTunes
window provides
access to
almost all appli-
cation functions.

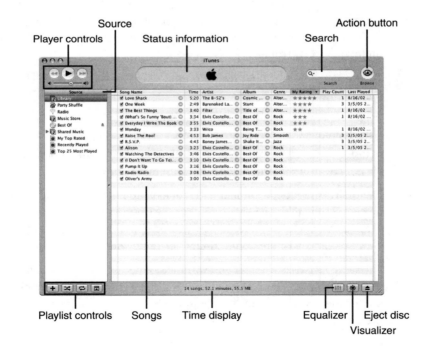

The main control areas are listed here:

▶ Player controls—The player controls play or pause, rewind, fast-forward, and adjust the output volume of the currently playing track. Clicking directly on the sound slider moves the volume adjustment immediately to that level.

▶ Status information—Displays information about the currently playing song. The top line displays the artist, the name of the song, and the name of the album. Clicking each of the status lines toggles between different types of information. Likewise, the Elapsed Time line can be toggled to display remaining time and total time.

The progress bar shows how far the playback of the current song has progressed. Dragging the progress bar handle moves the playback back or forward in the audio track.

Finally, a stereo frequency monitor can be displayed by clicking the arrow on the left side of the status display while a song is playing.

▶ Search—Typing a few letters into the iTunes Search field immediately displays all audio tracks in the current playlist or library that match the string in any way (artist, song, album).

▶ Action button—The action button performs a different function depending on what source is currently being viewed. As you work in different areas of the program, this button changes to an appropriate action for that area:

   ▶ Library—When viewing the main song library, clicking the action button toggles between two different browse modes. The first mode, shown previously in Figure 20.2, is similar to the Finder's List view. Each audio track is listed on its own line. The second mode uses a layout similar to the Column Finder view: The first column lists the artist, and the second column shows the albums for that artist. Finally, a lower pane shows a list of the song tracks for that artist and album.

   ▶ Party Shuffle—Party Shuffle is a feature that enables iTunes to choose the order of songs and display it so you can make adjustments. (Party Shuffle is discussed further in the section "Creating and Working with Playlists" later in this chapter.) Its action button is Refresh, which reloads the songs cued to play next if you change settings.

   ▶ Radio Tuner—The Radio Tuner's action button is Refresh, which reloads all available stations from the iTunes Internet radio station browser.

- ▶ Music Store—With Music Store selected, the action button toggles between two different browse modes as it does in the main song library.

- ▶ Playlist—A *playlist* is your own personal list of music that you've compiled from the main library. Playlists are the starting point for creating a CD. When you're viewing a playlist, the action button is Burn CD.

- ▶ CD—When a CD is inserted, iTunes prepares to import the tracks to MP3 files. The action button is Import when a CD is selected as the source.

- ▶ Visual Effects—No matter what source is selected, iTunes can always be set to Visualizer mode to display dazzling onscreen graphics. When the visual effects are active, the action button opens the Visualizer Options window for setting visual effect options.

▶ Source—The Source pane lists the available music sources. Attached digital music players, CDs, playlists, the central music library, iTunes Music Store, and Radio Tuner make up the available sources.

Did you Know?

Double-clicking a source icon opens a new window with only the contents of that source. This is a nice way to create a cleaner view of your audio files.

▶ Songs—A list of the songs in the currently selected source. When in the main Library view, you can click the action button to toggle between a simple list and a column-based browser. Double-clicking a song in the list starts playback of the selected list beginning at that song. To change the visible fields in the list, choose Edit, View Options from the menu. Among the available pieces of information for each song are Time, Artist, Album, Genre, Play Count, and the time it was Last Played.

▶ Playlist controls—Four playlist controls are available: Create Playlist, Shuffle Order, Loop, and Show/Hide Song Artwork. As their names suggest, these buttons can be used to create new playlists, control the order in which the audio tracks are played back, and show/hide song artwork.

By the Way

Most music you purchase from the iTunes Music Store comes with artwork, but you can add artwork to other song files. To add artwork, click the Show or Hide Song Artwork button and choose the song you want to be associated with the artwork. Then, drag any image file in .JPG, .PNG, .GIF, or .TIFF to the space at the lower left of the iTunes window.

▶ Time display—At the bottom of the iTunes window is information about the contents, playing time, and total file size of the currently selected music file. The default mode displays approximate time; clicking the text toggles to precise playing time.

▶ Equalizer—The Equalizer, shown in Figure 21.3, enables you to choose preset frequency levels by musical genre or to set them manually by dragging the sliders. The mode defaults to Flat, which means that all the controls are set in the middle of their range.

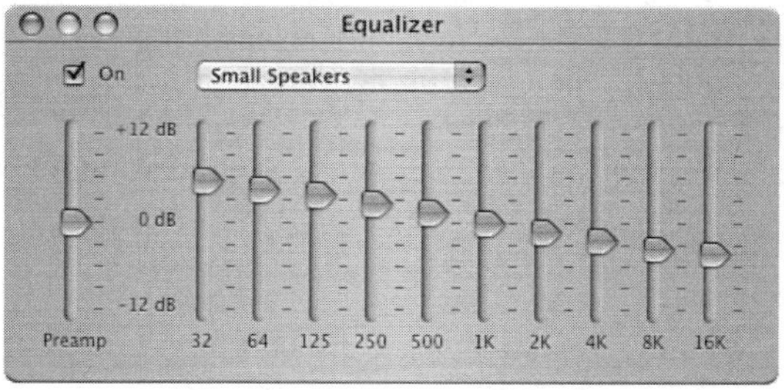

FIGURE 21.3
Choose how iTunes plays your music using iTunes' built-in equalizer.

▶ Visualizer—Turns the visualization effects ("music for the eyes") on and off.

▶ Eject Disc—Ejects the currently inserted CD.

Audio Control Keyboard Controls

The iTunes player controls work on whatever source you currently have selected. After a song plays, iTunes moves to the next song. You can also control the playing via keyboard or from the Controls menu:

▶ Play/Pause—Spacebar

▶ Next Song—Command-right-arrow key

▶ Previous Song—Command-left-arrow key

▶ Scroll Up or Down—Up- or Down-arrow keys

▶ Volume Up—Command-up-arrow key

▶ Volume Down—Command-down-arrow key

▶ Mute—OptionCommand-down-arrow key

Some of these functions are also available from the iTunes Dock icon. Click and hold the Dock icon to display a pop-up menu for moving between the tracks in the current audio source.

To randomize the play order for the selected source, click the Shuffle button (second from the left) in the lower left of the iTunes window. If you want to repeat the tracks, use the Loop button (third from the left) in the lower-left corner to toggle between Repeat Off, Repeat All, and Repeat One.

The iTunes window is a bit large to conveniently leave onscreen during playback. Luckily, two other window modes take up far less space. Quite illogically, you access these smaller modes by clicking the window's Maximize button.

After clicking Maximize, the window is reduced to the player controls and status window. Even this window is a bit large for some monitors, though. To collapse it even more, use the resize handle in the lower-right corner of the window to show only the player controls.

To restore iTunes to its original state, click the Maximize button again.

Visualizer

The iTunes Visualizer creates a graphical visualization of your music as it plays. While playing a song, click the Visualizer button (second from the right) in the lower-right corner of the iTunes window, or select Visualizer, Turn Visualizer On (Command-T) from the menu to activate the display. Figure 21.4 shows the Visualizer in action.

The Visualizer menu can control the size of the generated graphics as well as toggle between full-screen (Command-F) and window modes. To exit full-screen mode, press Esc or click the mouse button.

While the windowed Visualizer display is active, the Options action button in the upper-right corner of the window is active. Click this button to fine-tune your Visualizer settings.

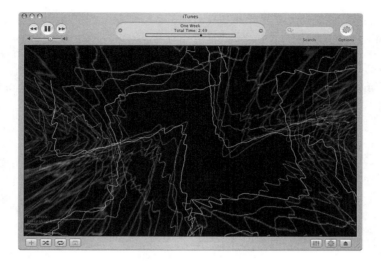

FIGURE 21.4
The Visualizer displays images to match your music.

Adding Song Files

Encoding, or *ripping*, CDs enables you to take the tracks from a CD and save them in the MP3 (MPEG Layer 3), AAC, AIFF, or WAV format.

Import Options

You can choose these options in the Import pane of the iTunes preferences, as shown in Figure 21.5.

Here are the basic distinctions between these formats:

▶ AAC files give you better quality than MP3s in a smaller file size, but may not be supported by all MP3 players.

▶ AIFF files are CD-quality, but much larger than both MP3 and AAC files.

▶ Files encoded with Apple Lossless encoding are about the same quality as AIFF files, but take up about half the size. They can be played in iTunes and on iPods that come with a Dock connector.

▶ MP3 files offer the option of compact file sizes and broad compatibility with MP3 players, but sound quality varies widely depending on the data rate.

▶ WAV files are large like AIFF files, but are more widely used with Windows computers.

The Settings pop-up menu enables you to choose a data rate in kilobits per second. The higher the data rate, the better the quality of the encoded music. For MP3s, anything lower than 128Kbps is different from (and inferior to) the quality of a regular audio CD. The iTunes Music Store sells 128Kbps AAC files, which are much better quality than 128Kbps MP3s. Remember also that the higher the data rate, the more disk space a music file occupies on your hard drive.

FIGURE 21.5
Pick an encoding type here.

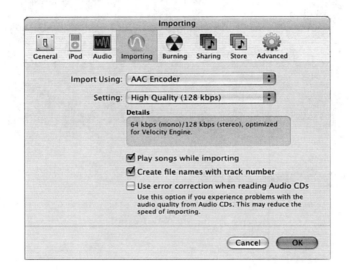

In the Import pane, you can also choose whether to play songs while importing them and whether to keep the track numbers with the filenames so that the album order can be maintained later.

The final option, Use Error Correction When Reading Audio CDs, should be used only if you are experiencing difficulties importing music from a given CD. Error correction attempts to fix any flaws in the tracks, but slows down the overall import.

Importing Song Files

iTunes makes it easy to import song files in common digital audio formats. In this section, we show you how to create MP3s from your CDs. (See the discussion on burning preferences in the section "The iTunes Preference Options" later in the chapter to learn about the options for burning in formats other than MP3.)

To import song files from a CD and encode them in digital format, find the CD you want to use and then follow these steps:

1. Insert the CD into your Macintosh's optical drive.

2. iTunes queries an Internet CD database to get the names of all the tracks on your disk. If you chose not to have this happen automatically during iTunes setup, select Advanced, Get CD Track Names from the menu and click the Stop button.

3. Click the CD name in the Source pane to display all the available tracks.

4. Select the tracks you want to encode by checking and unchecking the boxes in front of each song title. If no tracks are selected, the entire CD is imported.

5. Click the Import action button at the upper right of the iTunes window, as shown in Figure 21.6, to encode the selected tracks. As the tracks are importing, a small graphic appears to show whether it has been imported or is currently being imported.

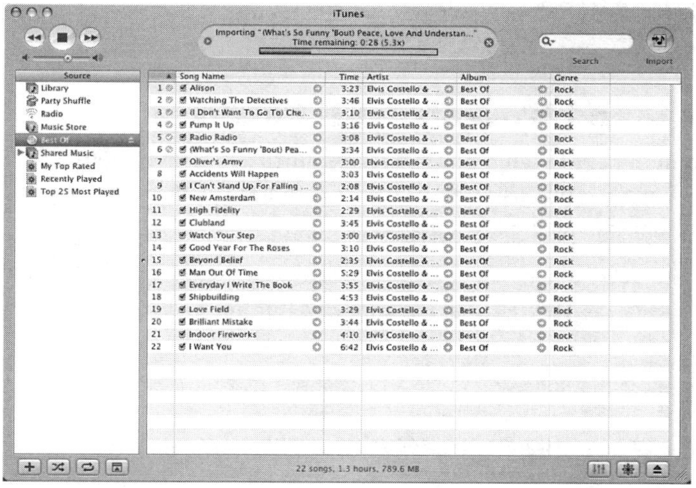

FIGURE 21.6
Importing a track from a CD.

By default, the encoded files are stored in Music/iTunes/iTunes Music found in your home directory. An entire CD can take from 5–74 minutes to process, depending on the speed of your CD-ROM drive. To pass the time, you can continue to use iTunes while the tracks are imported. When the import finishes, your computer chimes, and the music files are available under the Library source listing.

If you're working with an existing library of song files rather than a CD, you can easily add them to your library. Choose File, Add to Library from the menu to choose a folder that contains the files. Alternatively, you can simply drag a folder of files from the Finder into the Library song list.

The process of importing music files takes time. Each file is examined for ID3 tags (which identify information such as artist and title of a song) and is cataloged in the iTunes database.

The CDDB Internet database contains information on hundreds of thousands of CDs. In the unlikely event that your CD isn't located, it is listed as Untitled.

If iTunes couldn't find your song information, or you aren't connected to the Internet, you can edit each song file's stored artist/title information by hand by selecting the file and choosing File, Get Info (Command-I) from the menu. (If you need to enter the same information, such as album or artist, for several songs, select them all before choosing File, Get Info from the menu. Whatever you type will be applied to all selected songs.)

You can even submit your updated information back to the Internet CD database by choosing Advanced, Submit CD Track Names from the menu.

After you add songs to your music library, iTunes enables you to easily assign ratings to them. Locate the My Rating column in the song listings and click on the placeholder dots to add from one to five stars for each song. To sort by rating, simply click the My Rating header.

Creating and Working with Playlists

The key to many of the remaining iTunes features lies in creating a playlist. As mentioned earlier, a playlist is nothing more than a list of songs from your library. To create a new playlist, follow these steps:

1. Click the Create Playlist button in the lower-left corner of the iTunes window, or choose File, New Playlist (Command-N) from the menu.

You can import the songs on a CD and create a playlist simultaneously. After allowing the CDDB Internet database time to fill in the song information for the tracks on your CD, use the key-command Command-N to create a new playlist, select all the CD tracks, and drag them to the playlist. The songs are added to the playlist as they are imported.

2. The new playlist ("untitled playlist") is added to the list in the Source pane. Select the playlist and rename it. Now you're ready to add songs to the playlist.

3. Select Library in the Source pane.

4. Verify that the song you want is in the main library. If it isn't, you must first add the song to the library.

5. Select one or more songs in the Songs pane.

6. Drag your selection to the playlist in the Source pane.

The selected songs are added to your playlist. Click the playlist to display the songs. You can drag the tracks within the song pane to choose their order.

Using the Smart Playlist option, you can automatically create playlists based on criteria such as genre or your personal song ratings. Simply choose File, New Smart Playlist from the menu; set your criteria; and name your playlist. As an added bonus, Smart Playlists can also be set to update themselves with the Live Updating option as new material is added to your music library.

By the Way

You can use iTunes' Party Shuffle feature in conjunction with your playlists to randomize their order and still view which songs are coming up in the play cue. Choose Party Shuffle from the Source pane, and then select the playlist you want to use as the source. The top portion of the window lists songs from that source in the order iTunes has chosen, but you can drag songs around to change their order. Uncheck the box in front of a song to skip it.

Did you Know?

Sharing Music on Your Local Network

After you've added music and created playlists, you may want to share your music with others on your local network. You can share your entire library or selected playlists. You also can share but require a password to limit listeners to those you invite. The settings for these options are located under the Sharing pane of the iTunes preferences (shown in Figure 21.7), which you can access under the iTunes application menu.

FIGURE 21.7
The Sharing preferences enable you to let others listen to your music library.

The first of the Sharing options is a check box for your computer to look for music shared by other iTunes 4 users on your local network. If checked, any libraries or playlists located appear in blue in the left side of the iTunes window, as shown previously in Figure 21.2.

If you want to share your music, you can choose to share the entire library or specific playlists. You can also give your collection a catchy name or leave it as the default, as shown earlier in Figure 21.7.

By the Way

> The rules for sharing don't apply to music purchased in the iTunes Music Store, the use of which is discussed in the next section. To listen to music in a shared library or playlist that has been purchased from the Music Store, you need to double-click the song and authorize your computer to play it because there are limits on the number of computers that can access each purchased song.

If you want to share with only those you invite, check the Require Password box, type the word or phrase you want to require, and click OK at the bottom of the preference window to activate. Now, those who try to access your music see a pop-up window, as shown in Figure 21.8, that asks for the password.

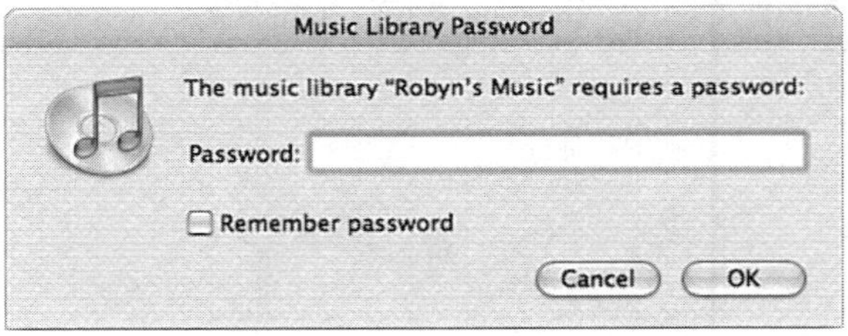

FIGURE 21.8
Prospective listeners must know the password to share your music.

Finally, you can see at the bottom of the Sharing preferences pane how many users are currently listening to your shared music.

The iTunes Music Store

One feature of iTunes that is getting a lot of attention is the iTunes Music Store, which allows you to browse available songs and albums, listen to short samples, and then purchase song files online. To access this feature, click the icon labeled Music Store located just above your playlists on the left side of the iTunes window. While in the music store, the area that typically displays your local music files is replaced by a list that you can navigate as you would a web page, as shown in Figure 21.9.

FIGURE 21.9
The "home page" of iTunes Music Store.

The songs purchased from the iTunes Music Store are in AAC format.

By the Way

In the music store, you can view lists of today's top songs and albums, look through new releases, browse by genre, or perform searches by song, artist, album, or composer name. When you find something that interests you, you can listen to a short clip of the song to see whether you want to purchase the full version. At the time of this writing, individual songs cost 99 cents, and full albums were around $10.

Earlier, you learned how to make a playlist in iTunes. If you make a playlist containing songs available from the iTunes Music Store, you can post it on the iTunes Music Store for others to see by creating an iMix. To create your iMix, simply design a playlist of eligible songs and click the arrow to the right of it in the Source list.

By the Way

As you click links to move around in the store, buttons at the top of the Music Store portion of the window, as shown in Figure 21.10, tell you where you are and enable you to move back and forward and to return to the home page.

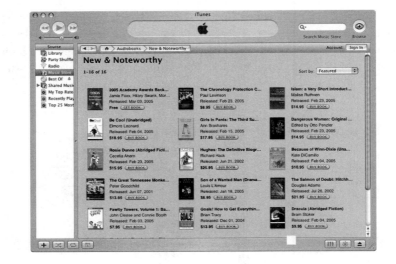

Power Search, Browse, and Requests

Although some people might enjoy browsing the iTunes Music Store in the web browser–like interface, others might find other options easier to use. In the left column are the options Power Search and Browse Music, as well as special categories for charts and audiobooks (refer to Figure 21.9), which provide more structured interfaces for searches.

Did you Know?

While the iTunes Music Store is "active" in iTunes, the search box at the top right can be used to search the store rather than your local files.

Power Search, as shown in Figure 21.11, provides fields for Song, Artist, Album, Genre, and Composer. This allows people who know precisely what they're looking for to locate it efficiently. If no results are found and you seem to have misspelled your search term, iTunes may offer an alternative spelling to help you.

The results for the power search can be sorted by song name, time (or length of track), artist, album, or relevance. (You can also sort by price, but at this time all prices for individual songs are the same!)

FIGURE 21.11
Enter any information you are sure of to see whether the Power Search can help you find it.

The Browse option, as shown in Figure 21.12, is like a more straightforward version of the main music store interface. When you choose a genre in the left column, artists for that genre appear in the middle column. Choosing an artist displays albums in the right column. Selecting an album displays the song tracks in the album in the bottom pane, where you can listen to a sample or make a purchase.

FIGURE 21.12
Browsing is a powerful way to search for specific songs, or to locate unfamiliar artists in a favorite genre.

If you don't know which album contains the song you're looking for, select All from the Album column to see a sortable list of all songs by your chosen artist that are available in the iTunes Music Store.

Making a Purchase

Now that you know how to find a song, let's see how to buy! The first step is to create an account, which you initiate by clicking the Sign In button at the upper right of the Music Store pane. This opens the window shown in Figure 21.13, where you can create an account from scratch or use your existing .Mac account or your AOL account (if you set one up).

FIGURE 21.13
Create an account for the iTunes Music Store, or use your .Mac or AOL account.

Sign In to download music from the iTunes Music Store
To create an Apple Account, click Create New Account.

(Create New Account)

If you have an Apple Account (from the Apple Store or .Mac, for example), enter your Apple ID and password. Otherwise, if you are an AOL member, enter your AOL screen name and password.

Apple ID:
[   ]   Example: steve@mac.com

Password:
[   ]   (Forgot Password?)

(Cancel) (Sign In)

To create an account, you need to fill out a form with your email address, a password you want to use, and your credit card information. When you are finished creating your account, you can sign in to make your purchase.

Apple has made a strong attempt to keep your iTunes Music Store account, which is tied to your credit card, safe from others who use your computer. When you finish using your account, you can click the Sign Out button. To reactivate your purchasing privileges, you have to sign in again with the email address with which you signed up and your password. If you or (someone else) should happen to mistype your password three times in a row, your account will have to be reset before login can continue.

To reset your account, you need to go to the iForgot Web site at https://iforgot.apple.com/ and enter your Apple ID. You have the option to have the password sent to the email address you provided when you created your account or to answer a security question to reset your password. Then you need to change your password to continue your login to the iTunes Music Store.

When you are logged in to the music store, you can locate a song you want to purchase and click the Buy Song button at the end of the row. In the Store pane (shown in Figure 21.14) of the iTunes preferences—which you can access under the iTunes menu—you can choose whether to buy songs using one-click download or to create a shopping cart so you can select a number of songs and purchase them all at once.

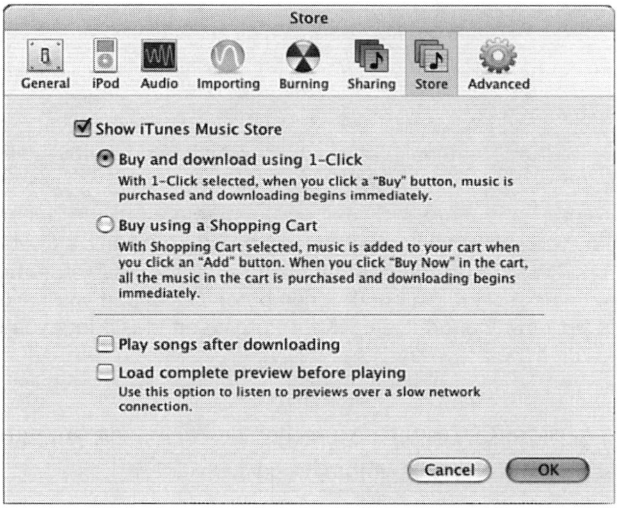

FIGURE 21.14
Choose your purchasing options.

When you click the Buy Song button, the file begins to download, and its status appears in the Status Information area at the top of the iTunes window. After you've downloaded your first song, another playlist appears in the Source pane. Called Purchased Music, this playlist is just like any other playlist: songs purchased from the music store appear in it, but you can delete them from the playlist, and they will still remain in your library.

Interacting with Purchased Music

Song files from the iTunes Music Store respond a bit differently than other song files in iTunes. Songs purchased by each iTunes Music Store account can be played on five computers, and the first time you try to play a purchased music file you have to authorize the current computer as one of them. (This is a measure taken to make sure that the files are not traded widely among users, which would deprive artists and record companies of revenue from the works they release.) The Authorize Computer window, shown in Figure 21.15, requires you to enter the password of the iTunes Music Store account set up on that computer.

FIGURE 21.15
You must for-
mally authorize
a computer for
it to be able to
play music
downloaded
from the iTunes
Music Store.

By the Way

Songs purchased from the music store cannot be shared to other users on your local network through the Sharing options discussed earlier.

Under the Advanced menu are two useful options related to the iTunes Music Store. First, because only five computers can be authorized to play your iTunes Music Store purchases at a time, Deauthorize Computer lets you remove the permission so you can assign it to another computer. Second, if you have purchased music but not yet downloaded it, Check for Purchased Music lets you see the files and download them.

When burning music to CD, as the next section describes, you can burn only seven CDs of a single playlist composed of purchased songs.

Burning CDs and Exporting to MP3 Players

After a playlist has been built, you can drag its name from the Source pane to any listed MP3 player source. The files are automatically copied to the connected player. If the player does not have enough available space, you must remove files from your playlist or select the external player and remove tracks from its memory. (We give special attention to using iTunes with Apple's iPod at the end of this chapter.)

Watch Out!

Not all Macs have a built-in CD burner. If yours doesn't, you can connect an external CD-burning drive. iTunes works with a number of makes and models from many popular brands. Even if you can't burn a CD, you can still rip tracks from an audio CD using your computer's CD drive.

If you have a Mac with a supported CD burner, you can use a playlist to burn an audio CD laid out exactly like the playlist. (You can burn only songs that have been added to a playlist and are saved in your iTunes music folders—songs on a connected iPod or in a shared playlist cannot be burned.)

When burning CDs, you have a choice between a couple types of CD media. The first type, CD-R, is a write-once CD. That means you can write your files to it just once, and that's it. If you make a mistake, you have to throw the failed CD away and use another. The CD-RW media can be erased and used over and over again, up to 1,000 times. In that way, it's like a regular drive except that CD drives run slower.

If you plan on using the files only temporarily and replacing them over and over again, the extra cost of the CD-RW is worth it. Otherwise, stick with the CD-R.

Regarding the price of blank CDs, well, the best thing to do is try a brand and see whether it works. If you get a lot of disk errors, try a different brand. The big names, such as Fuji, Imation, Maxtor, and Verbatum, should work with any CD burner. Try a few of the private store labels before buying a large bundle.

To make a CD, insert a blank CD into your computer's CD drive (if it came with a CD burner) or into a connected CD burner.

With the CD in place, double-check your playlist and then click Burn CD to make your custom disc. A 650MB CD can hold about 74 minutes of music. If your playlist is too large to fit on one CD, iTunes burns as many songs as will fit and then prompts you to insert another CD for the remaining songs.

You can print the list of songs in a playlist as an insert for a CD case. To do this, select the playlist and choose File, Print from the menu. In the Print window that appears, select the option for CD Jewel Case Insert, choose a design from the Theme pop-up window, and click the Print button. After your printer delivers the page, fold or trim the page to fit into a CD case.

Depending on the speed of your CD burner, making a CD can take up to half an hour. When you're finished, you can eject the CD (click the Eject button at the lower right of the iTunes window). Repeat the previous steps to make more playlists and more CDs. ***Begin Watch Out!*** It is important to keep your computer and its display from going to sleep in the middle of burning a CD. Before burning, open the Energy pane of the System Preferences and drag the Sleep option sliders for computer and display to Never.

Listening to Internet Radio

Depending on your connection speed, Internet radio could be your ticket to a whole new world of music. Unfortunately, most dial-in modems result in poor sound quality, but DSL and cable modem users can listen to much higher-quality streams. To see what's available and start listening requires only a few clicks:

1. To display a list of available streaming stations, click Radio in the Source pane. After a few seconds of querying a station server, a list of available music genres is displayed.

2. You can expand each genre to show the stations in that group by clicking its disclosure triangle. Stations are listed with a Stream (station) name, Bit Rate, and Comment (description). The bit rate determines the quality of the streamed audio—the higher the bit rate, the higher the quality...and the higher the bandwidth requirements.

3. Double-click a station to begin playing, or select the station and then click the Play button. iTunes buffers a few seconds of audio and then starts playing the streaming audio. If iTunes stutters while playing, look for a similar station that uses a lower bit rate.

Converse to what seems logical, you can drag stations from the Radio Tuner source and play them in a playlist. The playlist plays as it normally would, but starts playing streaming audio when it gets to the added Internet radio station.

You cannot burn a radio station to a CD or store it on an iPod or on other types of external MP3 devices.

The iTunes Preference Options

As you can see, building playlists in iTunes and making CD copies can be done in just a few minutes. If you want to look at the power of the program, however, there are some useful options to get you better-quality CDs and fine-tune the program.

You find them under Preferences in the iTunes application menu.

Here's a brief look at the preference panes:

▶ General—When you click the General icon (see Figure 20.16), you can set four clusters of preferences. In the first section, you can pick a text size from the two pop-up menus and whether to show Party Shuffle and Radio in the Source list.

The second grouping enables you to choose whether the musical genre (such as Country or Rock) should be displayed in your play list. You can also choose to group compilations when browsing and to show links to the Music Store, which enable you to quickly perform a power search using the current song's information (song, artist, and album).

The option On CD Insert lets you indicate with the pop-up menu what to do when you insert a music CD. The default is Show Songs, but you can also decide to both play and import the contents of a CD automatically.

The Internet option simply enables you to select the same choices you made when the original iTunes Setup Assistant appeared.

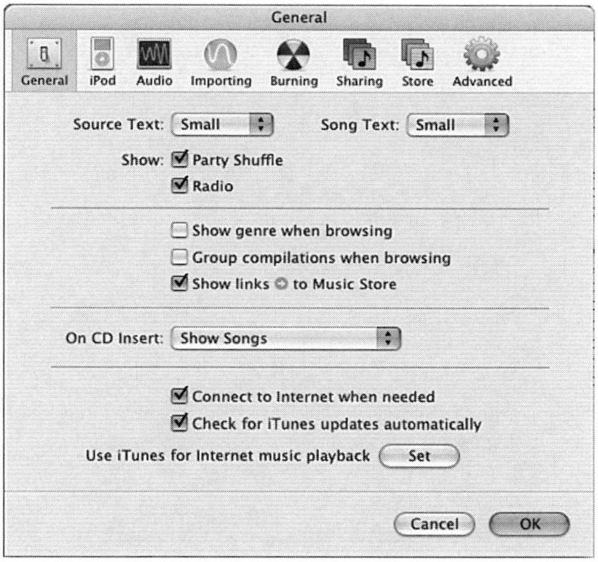

FIGURE 21.16
Choose various display options for iTunes here.

▶ iPod—The iPod preferences, shown in Figure 21.17, appear only if an iPod music player is connected to your computer. In this pane, you can choose whether to automatically synchronize your iPod music library with your iTunes music library, or with specific playlists in your iTunes library, or to manually manage your playlists and libraries. Under the General pane of the iPod preferences, you can specify whether attaching your iPod automatically launches iTunes. The next section spends more time discussing using an iPod with iTunes.

▶ Audio—The Audio preferences, shown in Figure 21.18, allow you to enable and set the number of seconds for Crossfade Playback, an effect that overlaps the end of one track with the beginning of the next to decrease dead air time. You can also choose to enable Sound Enhancer and choose an amount of enhancement from low to high. There is also an option to automatically adjust the volume level to be more even between different songs. The final option directs iTunes to automatically look for speakers connected with AirTunes, a wireless speaker option.

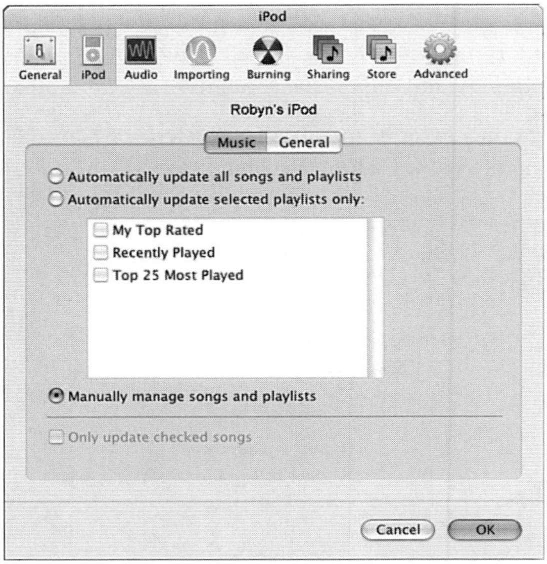

FIGURE 21.17
Choose whether
to sync your
iTunes library
and iPod
automatically or
manually.

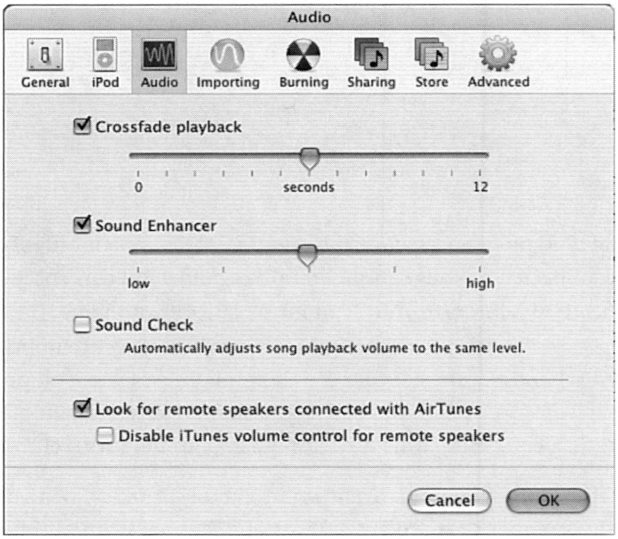

FIGURE 21.18
The Audio pref-
erences relate
to sound quali-
ty, volume, and
track overlap.

▶ Importing—You learned about the Importing preferences earlier in the section
  "Import Options." These settings pertain to format of music imported from CD
  and how iTunes behaves during import.

▶ Burning—The Burning preferences (shown in Figure 21.19) are specific to the kind of CD burner you are using and how you want the gap between musical tracks handled.

The disc format you choose under the Burning preferences really does matter. If your playlist includes AAC files, make sure to use Audio CD or Data CD format—the MP3 format does not work.

▶ Sharing—The Sharing options were discussed earlier, in the section "Sharing Music on Your Local Network." These settings enable you to look for music shared by others on your network and to choose what of your own music to share.

▶ Store—The Store settings, shown in Figure 21.20, enable you to choose whether to purchase one song at a time (one-Click) or many songs all at once (shopping cart). You can also choose whether to play songs you've purchased immediately after they download and whether to load entire song previews before listening.

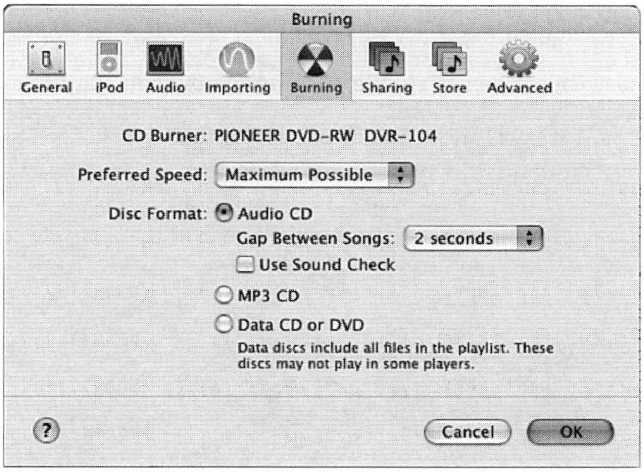

FIGURE 21.19
The settings for your CD burner are shown here.

▶ Advanced—The Advanced options, shown in Figure 21.21, include where on your system to store your music, whether to keep the folder organized, and whether to copy files to the folder when you add them to the library.

There is a setting for what degree—low, medium, or high—to which you want streaming media to be buffered. (That basically means, "How much of a file playing over the Internet do you want to have waiting in reserve before it begins to play on your local machine?" Because network connections aren't always consistently fast, setting buffering to low can result in stop-and-start audio that makes listening difficult.)

FIGURE 21.20
Customize your settings for the iTunes Music Store.

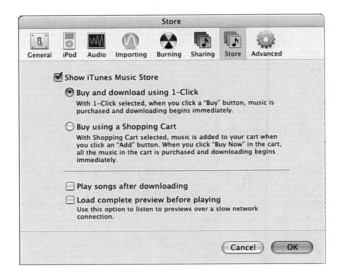

You can also choose how to shuffle your music—by individual song or by album.

Finally, you can select the option to allow the minimized iTunes window to float on top of all other windows on your desktop.

FIGURE 21.21
Change the location of your music library folder in the Advanced section of the iTunes preferences.

Using Your iPod with iTunes

Apple's tiny digital music player, the iPod can serve double duty. You can use it as an extra FireWire hard drive for your computer as mentioned in Chapter 11, "Working with Displays and Peripheral Devices," or you can stick with its core function, which is a handheld (or pocket-held) music device.

Making your iPod work with your Mac is an almost automatic process, so we take only a brief look.

To dock your iPod to your Mac, plug the FireWire cable that comes with your iPod (or any regular FireWire cable, for that matter) into your iPod and into your computer's FireWire port. When connected, your iPod appears in the Source list in iTunes. Depending on your iTunes preference settings, iTunes opens automatically, and synchronizes its music library with the one on your iPod.

If you connect your iPod to a computer other than the usual one, you will be asked whether you want to replace the iPod's music libray with the contents of the iTunes library for the current computer. Be careful not to accidentally synchronize!

If you prefer to transfer your music manually between your iPod and iTunes library, you can set that preference in the iTunes preferences, as shown in Figure 21.17. You can then drag songs between your iPod and your music library or playlists in the Source list.

Summary

The iTunes software can quickly convert your CDs into a library of digitized music or vice versa, and give you access to thousands of radio stations that play the kind of music you want to hear and—through the iTunes Music Store—to many new releases, 24 hours a day. It even syncs with your iPod to make your music portable. If you're a music enthusiast, Mac OS X is the operating system for you.

CHAPTER 22

Using iPhoto

Apple's iPhoto offers all the functions you need for working with digital photographs—importing, organizing, editing, and sharing.

The iPhoto Window

The iPhoto window, shown in Figure 22.1, contains several distinct areas.

The viewing area on the right changes to provide different functionality in Organizing view, Edit view, Book view, and Slideshow view. The tools displayed along the bottom of the photo viewing area change depending on the current view.

The Source list along the left side is available regardless of the view that is currently active. The Source list contains a number of elements. The Photo Library contains all the images imported by iPhoto. Last Roll is a special unit that contains the most recently imported pictures, and Last 12 Months contains all the images imported in the last year. Under these are albums, the special sets of pictures you put together, if you've created any. Selecting one of these items fills the viewing area with thumbnail images of its contents. Special items for any iPhoto books or slideshows you've created will also appear in the Source list, and selecting one will open the appropriate view so you can make changes.

Figure 22.1
The iPhoto win-
dow contains all
the settings you
need to import,
organize, and
edit your photos.

You can resize the contents of the viewing area by using the zoom slider at the bottom right. To jump between the smallest and the largest possible display sizes, click on the small and large image icons at either end of the resize slider.

If others on your local network are iPhoto users, you might see additional albums in the Source list: shared photos. In the iPhoto preferences, you can set iPhoto to look for shared photos and share your library or specific albums. Through this fea- ture, you can browse the images of others on your local network who've shared their photos, and they can browse yours. While you can see other users' photos, they first must be copied to your own photo library if you want to edit them.

There are also five buttons below the Source list:

▶ Add button—Enables you to create a special group of chosen photos that you can arrange in any way.

▶ Play button—Plays a full-screen slideshow, complete with music, of all the photos currently selected. (Slideshows are discussed further in the section, "Creating Slideshows.")

▶ Information button—Opens the Information pane to display details about the selected item in the Source list or selected photo or photos. See the section "Viewing Photo Information" below.

Additional details about a selected image can be accessed by choosing Photos, Get Info from the menu. This opens a window containing information about the image file, camera settings, and any keywords you've applied.

▶ Calendar button—Opens the Calendar pane, which enables you to view photos for a selected source by year or month. See the section "Viewing by Date" below.

▶ Keyword button—Opens the Keyword pane, in which you can search by iPhoto's default keywords. (You will first need to apply keywords—see the section "Using Keywords" below.)

As you use different views in iPhoto, some of the buttons below the Source list may be grayed out to show they aren't available.

Importing Image Files

The first time you connect a supported camera to your computer and set the camera to its playback or transfer mode, iPhoto opens automatically. If it doesn't, you can manually launch iPhoto either from the Dock or the Applications folder. When your camera is detected, the iPhoto window switches to Import view.

In addition to importing images in the commonly-used JPEG format, iPhoto can also import RAW images. RAW images are uncompressed, which means the camera is literally storing every bit of data it took in when capturing the image. Storing images as RAW files reduces the number of images that will fit on your camera's storage device. JPEG images are compressed by your camera to reduce the amount of image data saved, which lets you store more images as smaller image files.

While JPEG format is fine for creating standard size prints, RAW format allows for printing even larger images and offers more flexibility in image editing. If you want to save the highest-quality images possible to maximize your options, check your camera's documentation to see if RAW image format is available.

Because some digital cameras can capture short video clips as well as still photos, iPhoto can import these video clips in MPEG format for you to store with the still clips on the same roll. iPhoto labels video clips with a video camera icon and the length of the clip. Double-click a video clip to play it in the QuickTime Player. (See Chapter 7, "Using QuickTime and DVD Player.")

You can then add the clips to iMovie or iDVD projects using the Media Browsers in those applications. (See Chapters 24 through 30 for more information about iMovie HD and iDVD.)

The Import view, shown in Figure 22.2, displays import status, space to name the roll and describe the contents, an option to delete images from the camera after they're stored in iPhoto, and the Import button.

Figure 22.2
The Import view enables you to follow the progress of your files as they're transferred from the camera to your computer.

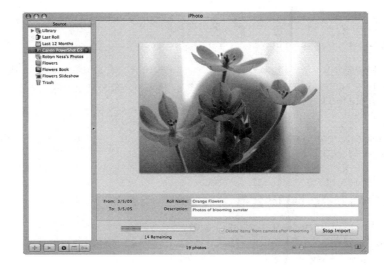

To import the photos on your camera, fill in information about the roll and click the Import button in the lower-right corner of the window. If the box for Erase Camera Contents After Transfer is checked, iPhoto asks you to approve deletion of the original photo files from the camera.

By the Way

If you don't opt to delete images from your camera after importing to iPhoto, the next time you import iPhoto asks if you want to import duplicates of the images you've already imported.

Each image appears in the Import view as it is imported, along with the number of photos remaining to be transferred. When the import is complete, the new images appear in the photo viewing area in Organize view, along with any other images in your iPhoto Library.

To import images already stored on your hard drive or other media, select them and drag them onto the Photo Library icon at the upper left, or choose File, Add to Library from the menu. Preview images appear as each photo is imported, as if the images were another "roll" of film.

If you change your mind about importing, click the Stop Import button at the lower right. iPhoto asks if you want to keep any photos transferred so far.

> After your photos have been imported and deleted from your camera's memory, don't forget to shut off your camera to save the charge on the batteries!

Organizing and Searching Images

The iPhoto window in Organize view, shown in Figure 22.1 above, enables you to view thumbnail images of many photos at once so you can easily locate the one you want. In Organize view, you can also choose ways to share your images, which we'll talk about in the section "Sharing Your Photos" later in this chapter.

> By default, new *rolls* (groups of pictures imported at one time) are added to the bottom of the viewing area in the Organize view, but you can change that so that the most recent roll is at the top inside the Appearance pane of the iPhoto preferences.

By the Way

Selecting and Deleting Images

In Organize view, you can select an image in the viewing area by single-clicking it. You can select a group of consecutive pictures by clicking just outside the edge of the first photo and dragging to create a box connecting all the photos that you want to select, or select a group of nonconsecutive pictures by holding down the Command key as you click the desired images.

> You can select a series of photos by selecting the first one and then holding down the Shift key on your keyboard while clicking the last photo. You can also hold down the Control key to selectively deselect any photos in the group by clicking them.

By the Way

If you want to delete a photo or several photos that are visible in the viewing area, select the photos you don't want to keep, and then press the Delete key on your keyboard or choose Photos, Move to Trash from the menu. In the original version of iPhoto, when you deleted a photo it was truly gone forever. In more recent versions, deleted photos are stored in a special Trash folder, much like the one for your entire system. If you are sure that you don't want any of the items in the Trash, choose File, Empty Trash from the menu.

> You can view the contents of the Trash by selecting its icon on the left side of the iPhoto window. If you decide to save a photo that you sent to the Trash, you can drag it back to your Photo Library or choose Photos, Restore to Photo Library from the menu. Alternately, you can Control-Click on a photo to open a contextual menu that includes the Restore to Photo Library option.

You can also drag selected photos to your desktop, which makes additional copies of them, or into a new album, which is discussed later in this chapter.

Viewing Photo Information

To view information about an item in the Source list or for a selected image, click the Information button below the Source list.

The Information pane opens to display details. For example, in Figure 22.3, the Photo Library is selected, so the information section displays the name of the selection, the range of dates for the images it contains, the number of images it contains, and the total file size of its contents. If a specific image were selected, the given information would be the image title, date and time taken, any rating you've given, format of the image, size of image in pixels, and file size. The Information pane also includes a field to add comments about the selected item.

Figure 22.3
The Information pane displays information about a selected photo or group of photos.

By the
~~Way~~

You can edit some of the information in the Information pane, including the title, date, time, and rating for an individual image. If you want to set the date and time for a group of photos to the same thing, choose Photos, Batch Change from the menu.

If you want to view specific information for all the photos shown in Organize view, you can display the images in your viewing area with their titles, keywords, film rolls, and ratings by selecting those options from the View menu.

Selecting Titles displays the title of each image beneath its thumbnail in the viewing area.

The View, Keywords option shows any keywords you've attached to an image file to the right of its thumbnail image. We look further at applying keywords in a moment.

Displaying by Film Rolls divides the photos in the viewing area into sections labeled with roll number and date of import. Click the arrow next to a roll to hide the images it contains, and click again to show them.

If you've rated your photos, choosing View, My Ratings displays the number of stars you've assigned. Assigning ratings is discussed further in "Smart Albums," later in this chapter.

> You can tell iPhoto to order the images in your Photo Library by film roll, date, or title by selecting the appropriate option in the Sort Photos submenu of the View menu.

By the Way

Using Keywords and Searches

A good way to organize your photo collection is with keywords. When applied, keywords appear next to the image thumbnails in the viewing area when you choose View, Keywords from the menu, as discussed above.

To apply iPhoto's default keywords, choose Photos, Get Info from the menu and open the Keywords pane of the Photo Info window, shown in Figure 22.4. Then, select an image thumbnail in the viewing area and check the keyword or keywords you want to apply. (You can also apply the same keyword or set of keywords to a group of images by selecting them as described in the section, "Selecting and Deleting Images.")

> Included in the keyword list is a check mark symbol, which acts somewhat differently than the other keywords. Whereas other keywords are visible only when you've chosen to display them in the View menu, the check mark is always visible in the lower-right corner of the thumbnails to which it has been applied. Also, the check box cannot be renamed or deleted as the other keywords can.

By the Way

Figure 22.4
The Keywords pane of the Photo Info window allows you to apply keywords.

You can create new keywords, or edit or remove the default keywords, in the Keywords pane of the iPhoto Preferences. (Note, however, if you edit a default keyword, that change is passed along to any photos assigned the previous keyword.)

If you've added several keywords of your own, you may have to expand the Keywords pane to reveal them. To do this, click and drag the border dividing the Keywords pane from the Source list.

To remove a keyword, open the Keywords pane of the Photo Info window, select the image, or uncheck the keyword or keywords you want to remove.

To search by keyword, click the Keyword button below the Source list to reveal the Keywords pane, shown in Figure 22.5. Click the individual keyword buttons to set your search criteria—iPhoto displays in the viewing area images with any of the selected keywords. Click a selected keyword again to deselect it, or click reset to remove all selected keywords.

If you want to search by text in addition to keywords, use the Search field on the right side of the toolbar. This search enables you to locate photos by words contained in their film roll, title, filename, keywords or comments. As you type, iPhoto limits the photos shown in the viewing areas to only those that match the search. To clear the search and view all images for the selected source, click the X in the Search field.

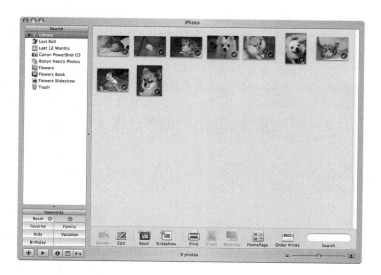

Figure 22.5
The Keywords pane allows you search by keywords.

View Photos by Date

In addition to searching your photos by keyword and other text, iPhoto allows you to search by date using the Calendar pane, shown in Figure 22.6.

Figure 22.6
The year view of the Calendar pane lets you view photos by month or year taken.

To view photos by month or year, click the Calendar button below the Source list and choose your photo library or an album in the Source list. Use the up and down arrows at the top of the Calendar pane to find the year of interest. Click the year label at the top of the pane to select all photos taken in that time, or click a month to view only that month's worth.

If you find inconsistencies in how your photos are dated, you can change the date and time information in the Information pane.

If you want to see only photos taken on a specific day, double-click a month to show the month view of the Calendar pane and then choose the day of interest. To switch months, use the up and down arrows. Double-click the month label at the top of the calendar to return to year view.

To display photos from multiple months, switch to year view and hold down the Command key as you click each month.

To display photos from multiple days, switch to month view and hold down the Command key as your click each day. To select an entire week, click the dot to the left of the week in month view.

To show all the photos in your library, click the "x" button at the top right of the Calendar pane.

Creating an Album

You can't arrange the individual images in your Photo Library just any old way. To choose the sequence of a set of images, you must create an album and add the photos you want to work with. (Keep in mind that every photo imported into iPhoto will appear in your Photo Library; adding photos to albums doesn't move them out of the Photo Library.)

You can choose whether to arrange the photos in an album by film roll, date, or title by using the View, Arrange Photos option in the menu, just as you can for your Photo Library. However, for albums there's another option that lets you arrange your images manually, which gives you the power to arrange them in any order you see fit.

Albums are a useful way to organize your photographs into collections, especially if you have many photos. Albums are also a basic unit in iPhoto that can be used when creating books, slideshows, and web pages, which we'll discuss in the sections "Creating an iPhoto Book," "Creating Slideshows," and "Sharing Your Photos."

The option to make a new album is available from any view in iPhoto. To create a new album, perform the following steps:

   1. Click the "+" button below the Source list, or choose File, New Album from the menu.

2. In the window that appears, type a name for your album. (If you change your mind later, you can double-click the name of the album in the Source list to change it.)

3. When you've named your album, click OK.

The album you created appears at the end of the list of albums in Source list. If you want to change the order of your albums, select the one you want to move and drag it to a new position. A black bar indicates where the album will be inserted, as shown in Figure 22.7. If you want to remove an album, select it and press the Delete key on your keyboard. Unless the album is empty, you see an alert asking you to confirm deletion.

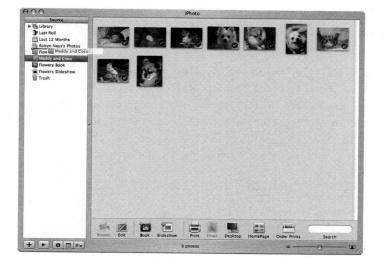

Figure 22.7
Reorder your albums by dragging them around in the list.

> If you want to organize your albums even further, you can create folders in the Source list and move albums (or even books and slideshows) into them. For example, you can create folders for each year or for special topic to neatly hold all related items in the Source list. To create a folder, choose File, New Folder from the menu, name your folder, and then drag items into it. You can then expand the folder to see what's inside or collapse it to save space.

By the Way

To add images to your album, make sure that you're in Organize view and select the images you want from the viewing area. You can select them one at a time or in groups. Drag your selection to your album name until a black border appears around it. As you drag, a faded version of one of the selected images appears behind your cursor, along with a red seal showing how many items you're dragging.

> The images within albums are something like aliases on your desktop: You can delete a photo from an album without affecting the original file. However, when you delete an image from the Photo Library, it also disappears from any albums to which it has been added.

After you've created an album and added images, you can open the album and drag the contents into any order you want. You can also remove images from the album by selecting them and pressing the Delete key on your keyboard. Because the photos in your albums are always a part of the Photo Library, only the album copy is removed. (If you want to delete a photo altogether, you'll need to delete it from the Photo Library as you learned earlier.)

Smart Albums

In addition to the albums you compile by hand, you can have iPhoto automatically generate albums based on criteria you set. These albums are called Smart Albums.

To create a Smart Album, choose File, New Smart Album from the menu. The Smart Album window, shown in Figure 22.8, appears in which you add conditions for including images or whole existing albums in the smart album. You can have iPhoto search any text associated with a photo, comments, date, filename, keyword, rating, roll, title, or combinations of those things. You also can set conditions to exclude photos or whole albums based on those criteria.

Figure 22.8
Set the criteria for including photos in your smart album.

Smart Album name:	Special Photos
Match the following condition:	
Keyword is ⊘	⊖ ⊕
	Cancel OK

> Ratings are a very useful tool for creating smart albums to show off only your best work. To add ratings to a selected photo or group of photos, choose Photos, My Ratings, and then select a number of stars to represent your rating. With ratings in place, you can set criteria to display only your five-star images.

If you want to have more conditions, click the "+" button to the right of the first condition to see another condition group. If you want to remove a condition, click the "–" button. When you are done, click OK and your new smart album appears in the Source list. If you need to change the smart album criteria, select it in the Source list and choose File, Edit Smart Album.

Editing Photos

iPhoto's Edit view enables you to improve your existing photos by cropping them, adjusting their coloration, and performing simple retouching.

To edit a photo, select it in Organize view and click the Edit button, or double-click a thumbnail image. A screen similar to that shown in Figure 22.9 appears, with a large view of the photos and a number of editing tools in the toolbar. While in Edit view, you can use the Previous and Next buttons at the bottom right to move through a group of images without going back into Organize view, or use the photo browser at the top of the viewing area to scroll through all the photos in the selected source. To switch back to Organize view from Edit view, click the Done button.

Figure 22.9
In Edit view, you can crop your images or change their color properties.

> When editing a photo that's been added to an album, bear in mind that any changes appear in both the Photo Library and the album.

By the Way

Cropping a Photo

A major function available in Edit view is *cropping* or trimming away the unimportant edges around a subject. iPhoto enables you to constrain the size of your cropped images to fit the common photos sizes, including 4×6, 5×7, and 8×10, as well as ratios such as square, 4×3, and a size to fit the resolution of your computer display.

Depending on the resolution of the images produced by your digital camera, you might not be able to crop to a small section of a photo without the resulting image becoming grainy or fuzzy. This is a problem especially if you plan to make printed versions of your photos because the images might look okay onscreen, but look terrible on paper. When ordering prints or books, watch out for the low-resolution warning symbol, which looks like a yellow traffic sign. This symbol appears during creation of a book or while ordering prints if iPhoto determines that an image's resolution is not sufficient for the requested size of the finished image.

To crop an image, open it in Edit view and follow these steps:

1. Set a Constrain option if you want to maintain a specific width-to-height ratio.

2. In the viewing area, a selection box appears centered over the photograph, as shown in Figure 22.10. To reposition the selection box, move your mouse pointer to the center of the selected area until it changes to a hand and then drag the box where you want it. To resize the selection box, position your cursor along an edge so it changes to an arrow, and drag the edge of the selection box. If you want to clear the selection box and redraw it where you want it, click on the photo but outside the selection box, so that your cursor changes to lines that look like a plus sign. Then place your mouse pointer at one corner of the object or scene you want to keep, and click and drag to form a selection box around it.

Figure 22.10
Drag your cursor to create a box containing the part of the photo you want to keep.

3. Click the Crop button to apply your change and see the result in the viewing area.

If you don't like the look of the cropped image as well as you liked the original, you can undo your most recent edit by choosing Edit, Undo from the menu.

> After you make changes to images in iPhoto, you can always revert to the image as it was first imported by choosing Photos, Revert to Original from the menu. This enables you to make changes freely without fear of losing your original. However, if you achieve an effect you like, you might want to duplicate the photo in that state before trying additional edits. To do so, select the desired photo and choose Photos, Duplicate from the menu. That way, choosing Revert to Original after further editing returns you to that state rather than the original form of the image.

Changing Image Coloration

In addition to cropping, you can edit your photos by changing their color. iPhoto's Enhance, Red-Eye, Retouch, B&W, and Sepia tools offer preset color adjustment functions.

The Enhance tool changes the coloration of the selected image. Specifically, it adjusts the colors in the photo for maximum contrast. To use it, simply click the Enhance button. If you don't like the results, you can always choose Edit, Undo from the menu.

The Red-Eye tool is useful for reducing red tint from the eyes of people and pets. To correct red eye, click the Red-Eye button and then click in the center of the red spot your wish to remove. A black-ish area is applied, following the edges of the area you selected. Click the Red-Eye button again to deactivate the tool.

Use the Black & White option to convert an entire image to black-and-white, and the Sepia option to tint an entire photo rosy brown like an old-time photograph.

The Retouch option allows you to blend specks and imperfections in your photos into the areas surrounding them. When using Retouch, your mouse cursor appears as a set of crosshairs and a green dot appears on the Retouch tool icon. You use these crosshairs to target image flaws. It may help to use the size slider to magnify the image so that you can see the area you want to retouch, as shown in Figure 22.11. When you have Retouch cursor positioned near a discolored spot, click your mouse button and watch the color in the region around your cursor even out. When done, click again on the Retouch tool icon to return to normal editing mode.

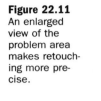

Figure 22.11
An enlarged view of the problem area makes retouching more precise.

Using the Adjust Palette

While iPhoto's preset color tools are helpful, the Adjust tool gives you more options. Clicking the Adjust button opens the Adjust palette, shown in Figure 22.12, in which you can fine-tune an array of image settings. (The Adjust button may not be visible if your window isn't wide enough to show all the options. In that case, an arrow icon will appear to show there are more options. Click the arrow to open a menu of additional tools.)

Figure 22.12
The Adjustment palette includes sliders for a range of color settings, as Straighten option for leveling crooked photos, and a histogram to represent color distribution in the current photo.

You can edit your images with the Brightness and Contrast sliders. Brightness makes a photo either lighter or darker overall—it can fix minor problems from under- to overexposure. Contrast increases the difference between light and dark elements by making lighter areas lighter and darker areas darker. Contrast also increases the saturation of colors.

> Although the settings in the Adjust palette are good for small corrections, keep in mind that they can't save a photograph shot in really poor conditions. Applying them too heavily only makes a photo look over-processed.

Watch Out!

You can also change the Saturation, Temperature, and Tint sliders. The Saturation setting ranges from grayscale (or black and white) to exaggerated versions of the original colors. Temperature settings refer to the coolness (blue tones) or warmness (orange tones) underlying an image. Tint settings change the balance between red and green tones. Temperature and Tint settings can be used to correct for discoloration due to lighting conditions at the time a photo was shot.

> When making changes with the Adjust palette, you can hold down the Control key on the keyboard to see the original version of the photo. Release the Control key to return to the adjusted version. If you feel your adjustment are off-track and want to start over, click the Reset Sliders button at the bottom of the Adjust palette to start fresh.

By the Way

The Sharpness setting changes the amount of softness in edges in the subject matter of a photo. (Visualize the hard edges of an office building versus the soft edges of a furry pet.) Increasing sharpness can compensate for slightly out-of-focus images, while decreasing sharpness can lend a softer appearance to a subject.

The Straighten slider allows you to rotate an image by an arbitrary number of degrees. This comes in handy for photos in which buildings seem to be leaning. As you drag the Straighten slider, a grid appears over your image and the image rotates. (As the image rotates, iPhoto appears to zoom in on it as its edges are cut off to maintain 90-degree angles at the corners.)

The Exposure slider enables you to mimic different camera exposures for a given image. (Exposure has to do with the amount of light that the camera takes in while capturing an image. Over-exposure results in a washed out, pale image; under-exposure creates a dark image.) This setting is most effective on images in RAW format, which are uncompressed and contain the most image information for iPhoto to work with.

Histogram and Levels

At the bottom of the Adjust palette is a histogram depicting how the colors in the image are distributed between black and white. If the histogram doesn't touch the left side, there is no true black in the image; if it doesn't touch the right side, there is no true white in the images.

The separate color graphs in the histogram represent the levels of red, blue, and green in an image. Red, blue, and green are the primary colors of light, which are combined to produce all other colors. You can see how the colors change as you move any of the Adjust sliders, except Straighten, which doesn't effect color.

Using the Levels slider below the histogram, you can alter the appearance of an image to have darker darks or lighter lights. If an image is pale from over-exposure, you can increase the darkness by dragging the slider on the left side to the point at which the histogram starts. If an image is too dark from under-exposure, you can increase the brightness by dragging the slider on the right side to the point at which the histogram ends.

By the Way

> Changing the levels essentially increases contrast between light and dark areas. Be aware, however, that you are sacrificing image detail for greater contrast.

Using Other Photo-Editing Software with iPhoto

If you choose, you can edit your photos in a separate image-editing application, such as Adobe Photoshop Elements.

To open an iPhoto image file in another image editing program, click and drag an image thumbnail from the Organize view onto the icon for the photo-editing program.

Did you Know?

> If you plan to edit with an outside program frequently, you can go into the General pane of the iPhoto Preferences and set images to open automatically in the outside program when double-clicked.

If you do choose to edit your photos in a program other than iPhoto, keep in mind that changes saved to an original image from an outside program replace the original file in iPhoto's folders, so you cannot revert to the original image as you normally would. If there is a chance that you'll ever want the original, it is best to make a duplicate before you begin editing by choosing Photos, Duplicate from the menu. If you choose to further edit an image that has already been altered from within iPhoto, the image already is a copy, so you can revert to the original version.

To check whether a file is an original or a copy before you begin editing, look at the Photos menu to see whether Revert to Original is an available option or is grayed out. If it is grayed out, the photo you're working with is the original.

Creating an iPhoto Book

Book view, shown in Figure 22.13, is a specialized option used to arrange an album's photos into a book format, including any supporting text. You can then order copies of your book.

Figure 22.13
Book view enables you to arrange the photos in an album for publication as a book.

To create a book from an album, select it in the Source list and click the Book button in the toolbar of the Organize view, or choose File, New Slideshow from the menu.

A window appears in which you can choose a book type and a theme for your book, as shown in Figure 22.14. The Book Type options include a large hardcover and small, medium, and large softcover versions. The Theme options, including Story Book, Picture Book, and Folio, differ in their picture layouts and built-in text areas, and how the photos are arranged on the page.

Your options for theme change according to the book type you set.

Figure 22.14
Choose your
book type and
theme.

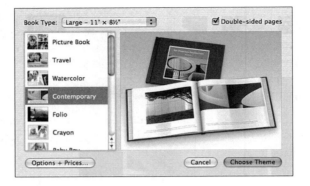

After you make your selections, click the Choose Theme button. iPhoto asks if you would like to arrange your photos manually or have iPhoto automatically place the photos. If you choose to have iPhoto do it automatically, the photos in the selected album are placed in your template in the order in which they appear; otherwise, a blank book is created in which you can add images. In the Source list, a new item also appears to store the settings for your book.

If you change your mind about the theme you chose, you can switch it easily by clicking the Themes button in the toolbar to reopen the window shown in Figure 22.14.

It's best to choose the look you want for your book carefully before you start customizing it. If you change from one theme to another, you lose any text (except photo titles and comments) or special page formatting you've made.

Working with Images in Books

Designing books in iPhoto is a simple matter of dragging and dropping images onto the pages created from the theme you chose.

While designing books, it is helpful to know that you can view the main viewing area as a single page or as two facing pages, called a *page spread*, as shown in Figure 22.13 above. Also, in Book view, the photo browser at the top of the viewing area can show either the pageview of all the pages in your book, also shown in Figure 22.13 above, or any unplaced photos that have yet to be added. To switch between these modes, click the buttons on the left side of the photo browser.

To rearrange images already added to a book, simply drag them between pages. To move images between pages that aren't facing each other, switch the photo browser to pageview as described above and drag images from the pages in the main viewing area to a new page in the photo browser.

To remove a photo from a page, select it in the main viewing area and press the Delete key on your keyboard. In case you want to add the removed image to another page, it becomes an unplaced image.

To add image to the book, set the photo browser to display unplaced images. Then, select an image and drag it to a page in the main viewing area. Page templates will adjust themselves as you add photos, but the maximum number of images allowed is determined by the theme you chose.

To quickly add all the unplaced photos for your book, click the Autoflow button in the toolbar. All unplaced photos will be added to pages in the order in which they occur.

Did you Know?

Working with Pages

For designing your book, iPhoto enables you to change page styles and to add, remove, and rearrange pages.

Some designs offer several different page styles to display a given number of images. To change the design of an existing page in your book, select it in the main viewing area and click the Page Design button in the toolbar. A menu opens to list all the page styles for your chosen theme that use the current number of photos.

To change the page style to one that shows a different number of photos, choose the number of photos to appear on the page from the Page Type pop-up menu and then select a page design. If you decrease the number of photos on a page, extra photos from your original page are stored as unplaced photos. If you increase the number, any unplaced photos are added to your book in the order in which they appear.

To insert a new page, select the page after which the new page should appear and click the Add Page button in the toolbar. To remove a page, select it and choose Edit, Remove Page from the menu.

If you are viewing page spreads in the main viewing area, iPhoto will add two facing pages when you click the Add Page button. However, it will only delete the selected page or pages when you choose to remove a page.

By the Way

To rearrange pages, set the photo browser to page view. Then, select and drag pages to new positions. If you are viewing page spreads instead of single pages in the main viewing area, facing pages move as one unit.

Working with Text

Page styles in some themes include text elements for you to customize.

To enter your own text, click once on the text in the main viewing area. A blue box appears to show which text area is editable, as shown in Figure 22.15. Select the placeholder text, delete it, and type your own.

Figure 22.15
Click placeholder text to edit it.

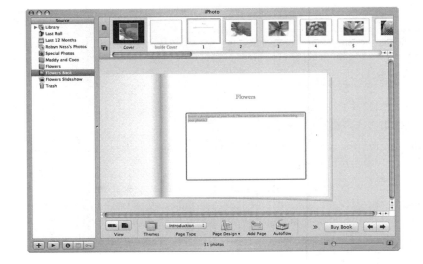

You can spell-check text in the currently selected text area by choosing Edit, Spelling and then the Spelling sub-option from the menu. Note, however, you can only check spelling in the currently-selected text area.

Click the Settings button to change font consistently for all different headings and text elements in your book.

Completing Your Book

After adding photos, arranging them on pages, and customizing text, your book is nearly complete. However, before you order a printed copy, you should preview your book one last time to make sure everything appears as you want it.

While you can click through the pages of the book individually within iPhoto, it can be difficult to see text clearly. To create a version of your book that can be resized, or even printed, choose File, Print from the menu. After iPhoto has a chance to assemble your book, the Print window will appear where you can preview the book file. In the preview, you can zoom in on pages to proofread text that is difficult to see within iPhoto in order to make corrections before it's too late.

When you are satisfied with the design of your book, click the Buy Book button to choose a quantity and provide your billing and shipping information.

If you have not changed all the placeholder text, a warning will appear to tell you that text will not be printed in your book. Click OK to continue or Cancel to replace the text with your own.

By the Way

Creating Slideshows

If you want to create an onscreen presentation of photos in your iPhoto Library, you have two choices.

The first is a very basic slideshow that simply plays photos in the selected source with your choice of background music. The second is a carefully crafted slideshow in which you set a transition for each slide individually.

For a basic slideshow, choose your photo library or an album from the Source list and click the Play button below the Source list. The window shown in Figure 22.16 appears, in which you can set the transition between images, the duration each image stays onscreen, whether the slides are shuffled and whether they repeat, whether the images are scaled to fit onscreen, whether a motion effect (known as the Ken Burns Effect) should be applied, as well as whether to display titles, ratings, and slideshow controls. In the Music pane of the window, you can select music to accompany the show. When you've made your settings, click Play to start the slideshow.

The Ken Burns Effect is a technique of panning across a still photo to change what is shown onscreen or to zoom in or out for emphasis. It is the namesake of an award-winning documentary filmmaker. Details are given below. (The technique is also available in iMovie, as discussed in Chapter 27, "Working with Still Photos and Sound in iMovie.")

By the Way

If you move your mouse while in a slideshow, controls appear to enable you to move forward or backward through the show. You can also easily apply ratings to the photos by using the slideshow controls. Simply click the placeholder for the number of stars representing your rating.

Did you Know?

Figure 22.16
Set a basic
transition and
slide duration
for your entire
set of slides.

Slideshow

Settings   Music

Transition: Dissolve

Speed:

Play each slide for   3   seconds
☐ Shuffle slide order
☑ Repeat slideshow
☐ Scale photos to fill screen
☑ Automatic Ken Burns Effect
☐ Show titles
☐ Show my ratings
☐ Show slideshow controls

(Save Settings)   (Cancel) (Play)

While a simple slideshow works well for viewing your photos and choosing favorites, there are times you want more precise control for a more polished presentation. To be able to apply individual transitions and customize the Ken Burns Effect, click the Slideshow button at the bottom of the main window when in Organize view, or choose File, New Slideshow from the menu. The Slideshow view, shown in Figure 22.17, opens. Also, a slideshow item with the same name as the album from which it was created appears in the Source list—this item stores the settings you choose for the slideshow.

Figure 22.17
Set transitions
and effects for
each individual
slide.

The toolbar in Slideshow view enables you to play your slideshow full-screen or to preview it within the viewing area.

From the toolbar, you can also apply effects (such as sepia), transitions (such as dissolve), and the Ken Burns Effect to individual images or groups of images. To apply effects or transitions, select an image and choose an option from the pop-up menu. Click the Adjust button to open a window in which you can fine-tune transitions.

The Ken Burns Effect allows you to choose a start point and an end point for panning across an image or zooming in or out. To apply it, select an image and check the box for Ken Burns Effect. Then use the zoom slider at the lower right to zoom in or out on the image. Click the Start/End slider to end and change the zoom, the position onscreen, or both of the image. To test settings, click the Preview button.

The Settings and Music buttons give access to settings similar to those for a basic slideshow. For example, use the Settings option to set default transitions for slides without individual settings.

Sharing Your Photos

iPhoto offers a variety of ways for you to enjoy your photos, both in print and digitally. They are located in the Share menu and, by default, most are shown in the toolbar along the bottom of the iPhoto window when it is in the Organize view.

> You can choose which sharing options appear in the toolbar by choosing from the menu Share, Show in Toolbar and the sharing option you wish to add.

Did you Know?

Sharing Printed Photos

For those who want to share their photos the traditional way—on some sort of paper—iPhoto offers three button choices at the bottom of the window: Book, Print, and Order Prints.

iPhoto books, as discussed above, enable you to order a bound book of an album as you designed it in Book view. Clicking the Book button creates a new book from the currently selected item.

Clicking the Print button enables you make print settings for the selected item, including page size, margin width, and number of copies. iPhoto also includes a range of templates for printing multiple photos on a single page, as shown in Figure 22.18, or for printing greeting cards.

Figure 22.18
Use the Style
pop-up to
choose a page
template—N-Up
style gives the
option to
choose the
number of
images per
page.

Clicking the Order Prints connects you to a website where you can choose what to order and supply your billing information.

Sharing Photos Digitally

To share your photos digitally with others, you can use the Email option, which enables you to easily email a photo stored in iPhoto. Clicking the Email button brings up the Mail Photo window in which you can choose the size of the image and whether to include the image title and comments. Click the Compose button to open a mail window containing the selected photograph and then add the email address of the recipient.

The Desktop option enables you to choose a single photo from your collection for use as a desktop background on your computer display. To set a desktop, simply select the image you want and click Desktop. Your desktop background is immediately replaced with the selected image. (To change your background back to a non-iPhoto background, open the Desktop & Screen Saver pane of System Preferences and choose a different image.)

If you are a .Mac member, as discussed in Chapter 16, "Exploring .Mac Membership," you can also use the HomePage and .Mac slides options for sharing. Clicking the HomePage button enables you to select up to 48 images from your Photo Library or a specific album to insert into a basic Web page layout that will be stored in your .Mac account. You can view a sample page in my .Mac account at homepage.mac.com/robynness/PhotoAlbum30.html.

The .Mac Slides option lets you upload a set of images to your .Mac server space, or iDisk, that can be used as a screensaver by anyone running version 10.1.5 or later of Mac OS X. You can offer only one slideshow at a time, but this is a fun way to share pictures with friends and family. When you update the slides, their screensavers will also be updated the next time they are connected to the Internet. To create .Mac slide, select an album you wish to share and choose Share, .Mac Slides from the menu.

After you upload a .Mac slideshow, how can you share it with your family and friends? Tell them to go to the Desktop & Screen Saver pane of System Preferences and choose .Mac from the list in the Screen Saver settings. Then they need to click the Options button and, in the Subscription window that opens, type your .Mac membership name and click OK. (They may also need to uncheck any previous .Mac screensaver to which they are subscribed in order to view yours. By default, a .Mac slideshow of recent products is the selected option.) It will take a few moments for the images to be downloaded from the Internet to their computers.

If you want to test drive a .Mac slideshow, you're welcome to subscribe to mine, which features my own photographs of flowers and leaves. Simply enter *robynness* as the .Mac membership name in the Subscriptions window.

By the Way

If your Mac has a CD burner or you have access to a DVD burner, you have two additional options for sharing your images digitally: Burn Disk and Send to iDVD.

The Burn option allows you to burn an album, or your entire library, to a CD or DVD. Simply choose Share, Burn Disc from the menu and insert a blank disc when prompted. Then click the Burn button again to write to the disc.

Send to iDVD magically exports selected photos into iDVD as an iDVD slideshow so you can customize it and write it to DVD. We'll talk more about iDVD in Chapter 29, "Exploring the iDVD Interface," and Chapter 30, "Creating DVDs in iDVD."

The iPhoto Preference Options

The iPhoto preferences, shown in Figure 22.19, enables you to customize several functions of the program.

General

The first grouping of preference options in the General pane controls what appears in the Source list. Here, you can choose whether to have special albums for the last 12 months and the last roll imported. You can also choose whether to show the photo count next to items in the Source list.

Double-click Photo refers to the action that occurs when you double-click on a thumbnail image in Organize view. The default setting is to open in iPhoto's Edit view, but those who want to edit with an external program might want to select the radio button for Opens in Other, and then select an application on their hard drives. You can also choose the option to open in Edit window, which is a separate window that presents the standard editing tools in a slightly different way.

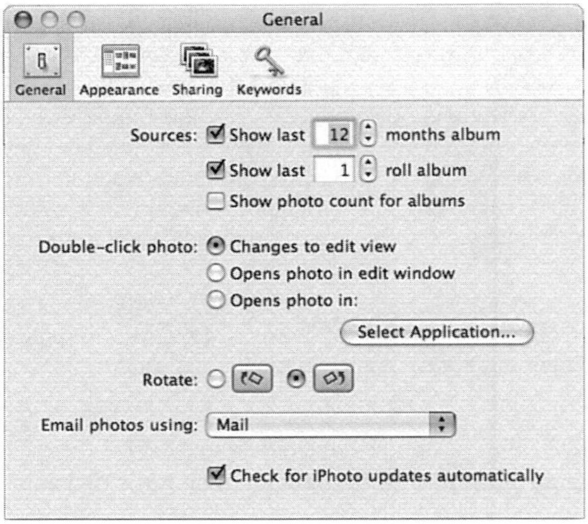

Figure 22.19
Customize the
appearance of
the iPhoto view-
ing area, the
action associat-
ed with double-
clicking a photo,
the direction of
image rotation,
and your default
email program.

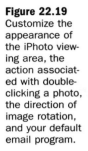

The Rotate options let you choose whether to rotate images clockwise or counter-
clockwise by default. (Remember, you can reverse the default direction by holding
down the Option key.)

The Email Photos Using preference enables you to choose which installed email program is used when you select Email from the Organize view. By default, it is set to
Mail, which was installed with Mac OS X. If you've installed another email program, you have the option to select it.

The option Check for iPhoto Updates Automatically has iPhoto notify you upon start
up if an update is available for download.

Appearance

The options in the Appearance pane let you customize the appearance of the iPhoto
viewing area. You can choose whether a drop shadow, a outline, or both appears
around thumbnails and full images. You can also choose a background shade for
the viewing area; your options are white, back, and shades of gray.

The check box for Organize View alters how thumbnails are positioned. It doesn't
make much difference if all the images in your library have the same dimensions.
However, if some are horizontal and others vertical, choosing Align Photos to Grid

By the Way

When working in separate Edit windows, you can have more than one photograph
open at a time.

will keep the same number of pictures per row rather than squeeze in however many will fit. The option Place Most Recent Photos at the Top does exactly what it says; if unchecked, the most recent photos are added to the end (or bottom) in the rows making up your Photo Library.

You can also choose the size of the text in the Source pane.

Sharing

The Sharing preferences refer to options for sharing your photos with others on your local network, as discussed earlier in the section "The iPhoto Window." Choose whether to look for shared photos and whether to share yours. You can also choose to share only selected albums or to require a password to view any of your photos.

Keywords

The Keywords preferences enable you to add new keywords or rename or remove existing keywords. These options were discussed in the section "Using Keywords and Searches."

Summary

This chapter covered the different views of iPhoto: Import, Organize, Edit, Book, and Slideshow. You learned how to make albums, edit and crop your photos, lay out your own photo book, and configure a slideshow. You also looked at the various ways in which iPhoto helps you share your images both in print and onscreen.

CHAPTER 23

Using GarageBand

Whether you're an experienced musician or someone who can barely hum, GarageBand enables you to create original musical compositions. All you have to do is mix and match stock *loops*, or repeatable segments of beats and notes. Best of all, as you add new loops, GarageBand matches tempo, beat, and key to make you sound like a pro.

> The loops that come with GarageBand are royalty-free. That means your compositions really are yours to distribute freely...unless, of course, you re-create a song that's already been written.

By the Way

You can also record music from your own instruments or use the onscreen keyboard to pick out a melody. Then edit the result until it sounds as ideal as you hear it in your head.

When you're finished with a song, you can export to it iTunes, where you can make your own CD—literally—or use it with your iPhoto, iMovie, and iDVD projects for an added personal touch.

> If you want to share your compositions with a wider audience, you can upload your files to MacJams, a website for GarageBand users. Go to www.macjams.com/ for more information.

By the Way

The GarageBand Interface

The GarageBand application consists of a main window for combining beats and notes, a keyboard for recording your own melodies, and several more specialized windows for editing and adding effects to the notes in your song.

We begin by exploring the main window, and then discuss the other elements as they become relevant.

By the Way

When you open GarageBand, the first thing you see is a window with the options to Create a New Project or Open an Existing Project. If you choose to start a new project, the New Project window appears so you can name your tune, choose a place to save it, and set the basic tempo, time signature, and key. You can bring this window up at any time by choosing File, New from the menu.

Did you Know?

Use the Tempo slider to set how fast or slow your composition will play in beats per minute (bpm).

Time signature refers to how many notes are grouped together in a *measure*, which is the unit by which the notes in a song are divided into smaller sections. Time signatures look like fractions—two numbers separated by a line. The top number indicates the number of beats per measure, and the second number shows which type of note in the measure gets a single beat. The time signature you choose can help you achieve different rhythms to match different genres—for instance, most rock music has a 4/4 time signature, whereas waltzes are played in 3/4 time.

By the Way

Key identifies the set of pitches on which a composition is based. Changing the key shifts the whole piece up or down.

The main window, shown in its default state in Figure 23.1, is made up of several regions and controls.

FIGURE 23.1
The main window in default mode.

> If you don't see the Mixer, click the arrow in the Track header to slide it open.

Did you Know?

▶ Timeline—Where you build your composition by adding measures of music. The Timeline contains some important controls and gauges, as shown in Figure 23.2.

▶ Onscreen Keyboard—Allows you to record notes. (If the keyboard is not visible, you can open it by choosing Window, Keyboard from the menu.) The keyboard is discussed in the section "Recording Original Music."

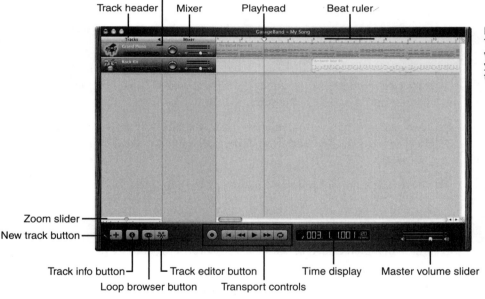

FIGURE 23.2
The Timeline is where you build your composition.

▶ Tracks—Holds the different layers of instrumentation added to a song.

▶ Beat Ruler—Marks the "time" in the Timeline in beats and measures counted out at the top of the Timeline.

▶ Playhead—Represents the current point in the composition.

> There are two kinds of tracks: software instrument tracks and real instrument tracks. The difference is whether they contain actual audio recordings or audio generated by your computer.

By the Way

▶ Track headers—Labels the *tracks*, or individual layers of instrumentation added to a song. Each Track header contains several buttons:

   ▶ Record—Enables or disables recording for the track.

   ▶ Mute—Silences the current track.

   ▶ Solo—Plays only the current track. (Click the button again to unsolo the track.)

   ▶ Lock—Prevents a track from being edited. (This also renders a track to the hard drive to free up processing power.)

   ▶ Show Track Volume or Pan Curve—Displays the track volume or track pan curve in a row below the selected track. (Track Pan refers to the stereophony of a track, or how the left and right speaker each play a track.)

▶ Mixer—Controls the volume and track pan setting for each track. Use the track pan position control to make sounds appear to come from one speaker more than the other. Use the volume slider to balance the tracks.

▶ Zoom slider—Changes the amount of the Timeline that is visible at a time. Use it to see a close-up of the Timeline, or zoom out to see a longer stretch of your work.

▶ New Track button—Adds a new blank track to your project.

▶ Track Info button—Reveals additional information about a selected track.

▶ Loop Browser button—Opens the Loop Browser, a pane in which you can sort and search prerecorded music. (The Loop Browser is discussed further in the next section.)

▶ Track Editor button—Opens a pane where you can edit the notes in a track. This option is examined in depth in the section "Using the Track Editor."

▶ Transport controls—Control the standard functions for Record, Return to the Start, Play, Rewind, and Fast Forward. The last control is the Cycle button, which sets the section in your composition for which you will record music, either from real or electronic instruments. (This is described further in the section "Recording Original Music.")

▶ Time Display—Indicates the position of the playhead, either in musical time or in regular time.

▶ Master Volume slider—Sets the overall loudness of your song. Above it are level meters that show how loud the song is at a particular time.

Working with Prerecorded Loops

Loops are the basic building blocks for songs in GarageBand. They are prerecorded measures of music that you can mix and match. To help you find a loop in the right style or genre, or performed by the right instrument for your composition, GarageBand includes a pane called the Loop Browser, as shown in Figure 23.3.

FIGURE 23.3
The Loop Browser, in Button view, helps you narrow down the selection of loops included with GarageBand.

To open the Loop Browser, click the button that looks like an eye at the lower left of GarageBand's main window. Then start clicking buttons to select an instrument, genre, or style. As you click, the options displayed in the far right of the Loop Browser change to show only those loops that meet your selection criteria. For each loop, the browser shows its name, tempo, the key it's using, and the number of beats it contains.

If you know a term that is in the name of the loop you are seeking, you can enter that word in the search text field at the bottom of the Loop Browser.

Also, you can change the Scale pop-up menu to narrow your selection. The options are Any, Minor, Major, Neither, or Good for Both. Major and Minor refer to two basic types of keys in the seven-note scale structure commonly used in Western music. The distinguising characteristic is the distance between each of the seven notes in a scale. Major keys are generally considered brighter and bolder than minor keys, which can sound heavy or gloomy.

Did you Know?

There are two views of the Loop Browser: Button view and Column view. To switch between them, click the view buttons at the lower left of the Loop Browser.

Click one of the loop options to audition it before adding it to your project. If you like what you hear, click on the loop and drag it into the Timeline. A new track is added containing one segment, or region, of the loop, as shown in Figure 23.4.

FIGURE 23.4
One region of a loop now appears in the Timeline.

If you want the loop to repeat for several regions, which is something loops are designed to do, position your mouse cursor over the right edge of the loop until the cursor changes to a looping arrow, and then drag for as many measures as you want the loop to repeat. An example of a repeating loop appears in Figure 23.5.

FIGURE 23.5
A loop doing what loops do best—repeating to make continuous background music.

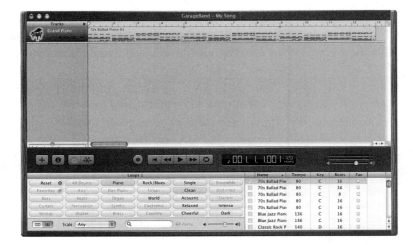

If you find a loop you really like to use in your projects, you can check the box at the end of its row to add it to a special category of Favorite loops.

If you try to drag a loop without the looping cursor visible, you either move the loop in its track or stretch it. Not that either of those things is against the rules, but if you are trying to make repeating loops it can be frustrating to merely move a loop region back and forth.

You can extend GarageBand's loop assortment by purchasing one (or more) of Apple's Jam Packs. More details can be found at www.apple.com/ilife/garageband/jampacks/.

If you decide you don't like the loop you've added, select it and press the Delete key on your keyboard. Note, however, that the track is still there in case you want to try a different loop in that place. If you want to remove the entire track, you must select it and choose Delete Track from the Track menu.

Recording Original Music

Although the basic prerecorded loops that come with GarageBand can be put together to make complex music, there might be times when you want to record your own melody from real instruments or software instruments.

You can use the onscreen music keyboard, shown in Figure 23.1, to play a song, or you can purchase a microphone to record your own instruments.

The onscreen music keyboard that appears in Figure 23.1 displays fewer keys than a real piano. If you want to expand the range of notes available, click the resize arrow at the lower right and drag to show more keys. (If you want to shift the section of keys visible rather than resize, click the arrows at either end of the keyboard.)

To record from the onscreen keyboard, select Track, New Track from the menu. In the New Track window that appears (see Figure 23.6), choose Software Instrument and the specific sound you want to apply. (The instrument icon at the bottom of the New Track window doesn't affect the sound; it changes only the track's icon label.) Click OK to close the window.

Then click the Record button (the round button below the list of tracks), and pick out notes on the keyboard. Any other tracks you've added to your song play in the background, unless you've muted them.

As you record, you can hear a metronome keeping time, but that sound isn't recorded.

FIGURE 23.6
Choose an instrument sound and a style.

As you record, a region appears in the Timeline with marks to indicate the notes you've played. When you've recorded enough, click the Play button, which highlights when you record as your composition plays, to stop recording. You can treat the recorded region as you would a prerecorded loop from the loop browser.

Working with Real Instruments

If you want to record a real instrument, you need to connect a microphone. Then you have two choices for adding a new track into which to record.

By the Way

If you plan to record from a real instrument, be sure you have enough space on your hard drive. Each minute of high-quality audio requires approximately 10MB of disk space.

Choose Track, New Basic Track from the menu if you want to record the original sound of the instrument, or choose Track, New Track and then open the pane for Real Instruments (shown in Figure 23.7) to choose some effects settings and the channel for your input source, which is the microphone you'll be using to record your sound.

You can also choose whether the track is recorded in Mono (the default setting) or Stereo (an option if two channels are available from your input source). Turning on Monitor enables you to hear what's picked up by the microphone without having to record first. This is good for practicing with the background music, but it should be turned off for actual recording because of potential feedback problems.

FIGURE 23.7
Set your input channel and whether it is mono or stereo.

> You can click the Track Info button to open the Track Info window for the selected track, so the settings you make when creating a new track aren't irreversible. The next section discusses the Track Info window.

Did you Know?

To record, move the playhead to the point at which you want to start recording and click the Record button. Play the instrument and click the Play button when you are ready to stop recording.

> If you want GarageBand to count out a measure before your recorded playing begins, choose Count In from the Control menu.

Did you Know?

Your real instrument track appears in the Timeline in purple with a waveform instead of discrete line segments to represent the recorded sound.

> You can add existing music files you've created previously in GarageBand, even full songs, to your new songs by dragging each file from iTunes into the GarageBand window. A track is created and the imported file appears purple with a waveform, just like instruments you record, to indicate that the notes are a sound recording and not a digital representation.

By the Way

Customizing Tracks

After you've added a track or two to your project, you might want to make changes to how they sound.

You can make overall changes to tracks containing software and real instrument regions in the Track Info window. This window lets you apply different instrument sounds to the selected track, as well as apply or remove effects that give the track a particular mood associated with its style or genre.

Software Instrument Tracks

To open the Track Info window, select the track, or region in the track, you want to work with and click the button labeled with a capital *I* that appears under the Tracks column. If you select a software instrument track, you see options similar to those in Figure 23.8. (If the lower portion of the Track Info window is hidden, click the Details disclosure triangle to reveal it.)

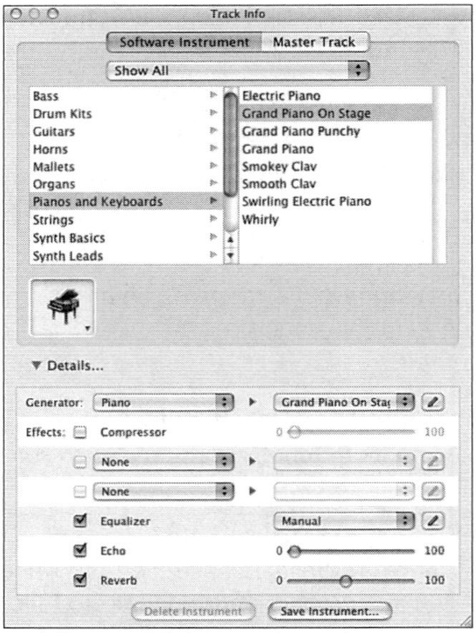

FIGURE 23.8
Modify your original track by applying a new generator or changing the effects.

You can choose a different instrument to produce the sound and style, which replaces the original preset options, but you keep the notes that were there. Under Details, you can change the instrument settings using the Generator pop-up menu rather than the columns at the top of the Track Info window. You can also choose between preset qualities for your chosen instrument/generator using the pop-up menu to the right of the Generator pop-up menu.

Also under Details, you can try out different effects that alter the amount of bass, distortion, vibration, and many other characteristics that contribute to musical style.

If you change from the preset options for a track, and then change it again, you are prompted to save your first set of changes. That's because what you created is not stored as a default, so you wouldn't be able to return to it if you later decided it was the perfect sound. If you don't think you want to save a change, feel free not to save.

As you make changes in the Track Info window, they are applied to the affected track and you can leave the window open as you play your song to try out the new settings. (The Save Instrument button at the bottom of the Track Info window is for those times when you construct a sound you want to keep for other projects. It's not necessary to click this button to apply your changes.)

Combining notes and effects in real time can be hard work for your computer's processor. As you preview your song, you might see a message that there are too many tracks, effects, or notes in your project for it to be played. To maximize processor performance, you need to open the System Preferences panel (choose System Preferences from the Apple menu), and then go to the Energy Saver pane. Click the button for Show Details and choose Highest from the pop-up menu for processor performance.

Also, you can monitor the effort your computer is giving to play your composition by watching the playhead arrow change colors from yellow to orange to red as its workload increases.

Real Instrument Tracks

If you choose a real instrument track, your options in the Track Info window change slightly (see Figure 23.9).

The top half of the window should look familiar, but the Details section allows you to apply only effects, not modifications to the sound style as with software instruments.

To reduce ambient noise from recorded real instruments, try applying the Gate effect.

The changes you make are available for you to listen to, just as with software instrument tracks.

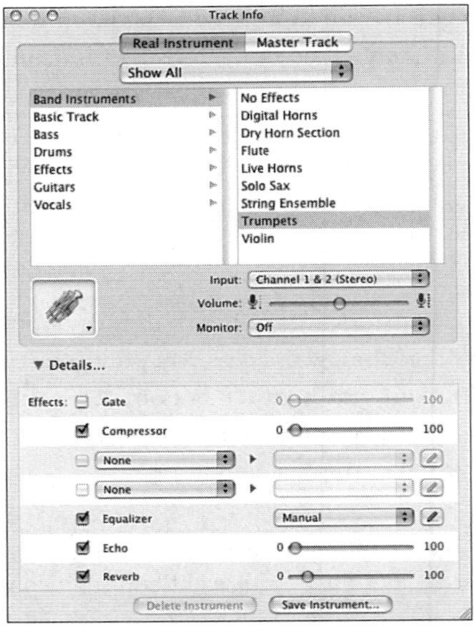

FIGURE 23.9
Under Details are options for changing the sound of real instrument tracks.

Master Track

The Track Info window also gives you options to change the fundamental structure of a project beyond the sound of the individual tracks that it contains. While working with either software instrument or real instrument tracks, you can click the pop-up menu at the top of the Track Info window to switch to Master Track, as shown in Figure 23.10.

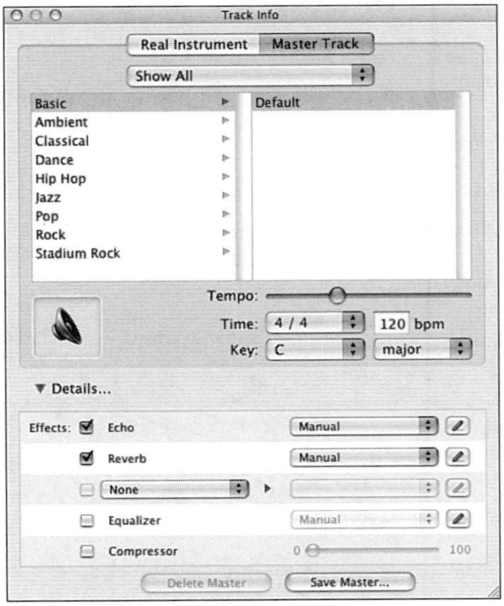

FIGURE 23.10
Change the key, the time signature, or the tempo of a song, or apply and adjust an overall style.

The Master Track settings apply to an entire song. You can use them to change a project's key as well as its time signature and tempo. You can also add effects to all the tracks in your project. Changes made to the time signature change the measure markings on the Timeline, and changes to the tempo, key, or effects are audible when you play your composition.

Adjusting Volume

In addition to adjusting the generating instrument and effects for individual tracks and the key, time signature, tempo, and effects for an entire song, you can adjust volume by track or for the whole. To change a track's overall volume, you need to open the Mixer to the left of the Tracks column, as shown in Figure 23.11. (If the Mixer is hidden, click the right-pointing arrow in the Tracks header.)

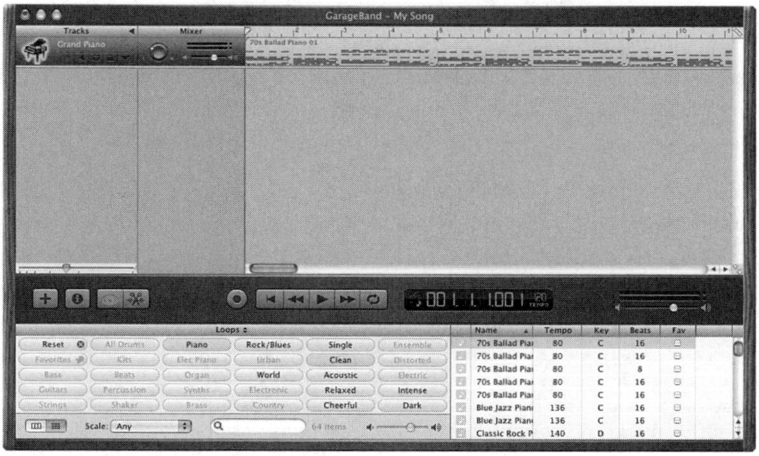

FIGURE 23.11
Change a track's volume or change the balance between speakers.

Drag the slider to adjust the volume. You can also change the amount of sound coming from the left or right speaker by adjusting the track pan control. The monitor bars above the volume slider show each track's relative volume as you preview it.

To adjust the volume of your entire composition, use the volume slider below and to the right of the Timeline. It also has level meters above it to show the volume level for each speaker at a given instance in your project.

If you want to fine-tune a track's volume to make it fade in or out at specific points, click the down arrow in the Tracks column to reveal the track's volume curve, as shown in Figure 23.12.

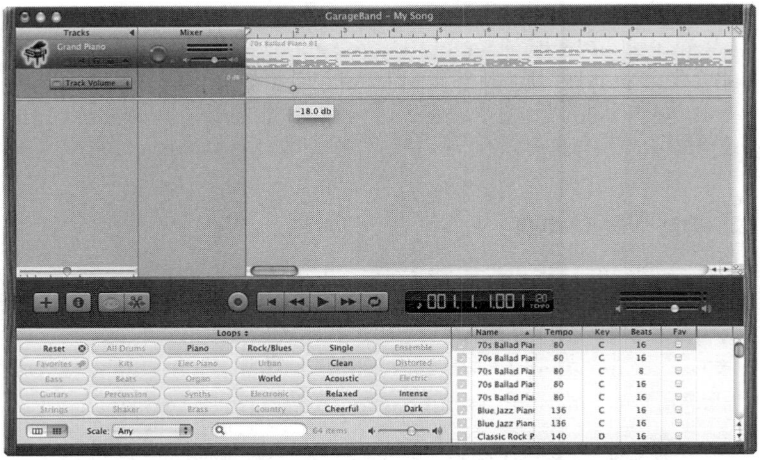

FIGURE 23.12
Adjust the volume level for specific portions of a track by changing the volume curve.

To change the volume curve, click and drag the line representing volume. This adds a control point, which breaks the volume curve into segments. To remove a control point, click to select it, and press the Delete key on your keyboard.

In addition to changing the volume curve for a track, you can also change the Track Pan curve to control the volume of the left and right speakers. To do this, click the down arrow in the Tracks column and choose Track Pan from the pop-up menu in the row that appears under the selected track. (If you changed the Track Pan settings for the track, you will see two separate lines to represent volume to each speaker; otherwise, the lines overlap because the volume for each speaker is equal.)

By the Way

In addition to adjusting volume curves for individual tracks, you can also adjust the volume curve for the master track that controls the entire project. Choose Track, Show Master Track from the menu to reveal the master track at the bottom of the Timeline. Adjust its volume curve as discussed earlier.

Using the Track Editor

So far in this section, you've learned ways to modify the sound and volume of a track or an entire song without changing the individual notes. But there are times when you want to edit a track to add notes, move the notes around, or transpose a track.

By the Way

With transposing, the relationship between notes stays the same but their key or pitch changes. For example, you can change a group of notes so they are played a fifth higher or lower than before.

To change notes themselves, you need to open the Track Editor by clicking the button that looks like a pair of scissors with sound waves springing from its sides. The Track Editor for a software instrument track appears in Figure 23.13.

FIGURE 23.13
The Track Editor for software instruments shows notes and enables to you move them around or add more.

In the Timeline portion of the Track Editor, notes appear as blocks in a grid. The grid represents time horizontally and pitch vertically. To change a note, click the block representing it and drag it up or down to change its tone. Drag it left or right to change when it occurs in your song. To alter a note so it takes up more or less time, click an edge and drag it left or right. As you click on each block, the note it represents sounds.

When working with loops, only the first region is editable—the rest are duplicates of it, so any changes carry over.

If you record music from a software instrument, you might find that notes aren't exactly on the beat, and this can sound sloppy. If you click the Fix Timing button, notes are aligned with the closest beat on the grid. You can change the grid to represent different fractions of a beat by using the slider at the bottom of the Region column.

If you want to transpose the track, drag the slider labeled Transpose. Keep in mind that dragging by increments of 12 will give you the same notes in a different octave than the original, but you can also change the key by choosing numbers that aren't multiples of 12.

Exporting a Song to iTunes

When you are satisfied with your song, you can export it to iTunes, where it will be added to your iTunes Library and treated just like any other music file. From there, you can add the song to your iPhoto, iMovie, or iDVD projects, transfer it to CD or iPod, or simply listen through iTunes.

To export your song, choose File, Export to iTunes from the menu. A status window appears, as shown in Figure 23.14, to show you how encoding is progressing. The playhead also progresses to show where in the song encoding is.

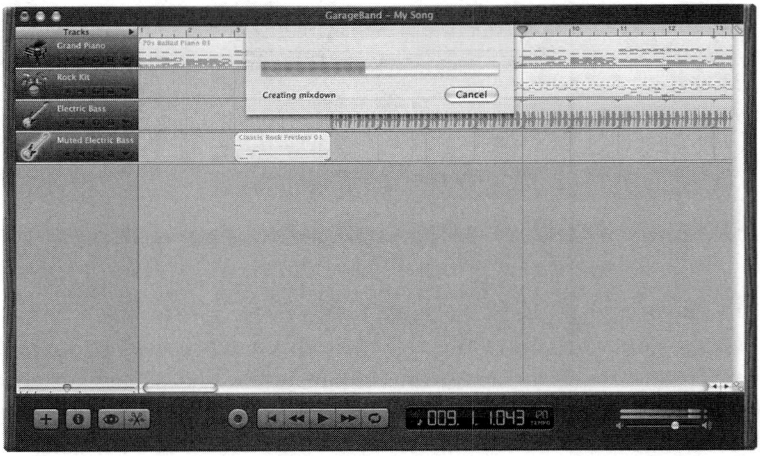

FIGURE 23.14
Processing can take a few minutes, especially for very complex songs with many tracks or notes.

By the Way

> By default, your song is exported in AIF format, which results in a higher quality file for the size than an MP3. However, some music players aren't compatible with AIF. If you find you need to switch the format, you can convert between file types with iTunes, as discussed in Chapter 21, "Using iTunes."

When GarageBand is finished exporting, iTunes opens and you find your song in the iTunes Library listing, as shown in Figure 23.15. The information about your song is the title you saved it under, as well as the artist name and album that you can set in the GarageBand preferences.

Did you Know?

> If you export a song with a name, artist, or album, but then change your mind, you can click once on each of these details in the iTunes window to make them editable.

Now it's time to discuss the preference settings.

FIGURE 23.15
A newly export-
ed song in
iTunes.

Preferences

The GarageBand Preferences are split into categories: General, Audio/MIDI, Export, and Advanced.

In the General settings, you can decide whether to have the built-in metronome play during recording or during both recording and playback. You can also choose whether to see a message if GarageBand is about to replace unsaved changes when you apply a new setting. When you check the Keyword Browsing setting, it filters the returned results in the Loop Browser to show only those with a similar key to your project. Finally, if you have customized the arrangement of Loop Browser categories, you can reset it back to the default.

Among the Audio/MIDI settings are pop-up menus that control which input and output devices GarageBand uses. Also, if you have any recognized MIDI devices, they are listed near the bottom of the window. The Optimize For preference gives you the choice between maximizing the number of tracks that can be added (a large buffer that allows GarageBand to "plan" allocation of its resources) and mini-mizing the time you need to wait while recording live instruments (a smaller buffer that cuts GarageBand's reaction time). The Keyboard Sensitivity slider controls how input from an external MIDI keyboard is interpreted. The central concept for this setting is *velocity*, a measure of how hard you press each key of a MIDI-compatible instrument. Increasing the sensitivity means that playing softer will results in higher velocity levels, while decreasing it means that higher velocity levels are created only when you play harder.

With the Export settings, you set your composer and album names and specify which playlist to add to hold your original compositions. You can also choose whether loops you install or create are available to other users of the same computer.

Under Advanced preferences are choices for how many tracks to allow each for real and software instruments. (Remember, processing and playing audio is quite intensive in GarageBand because every part is editable. You might want to limit your tracks to improve sound quality in playback and exporting.) You can also choose the number of different "voices" that are combined to form a single track. Finally, you can choose whether to convert software instrument loops added to the Timeline to real instrument loops. (Real instruments are purely audio files and require less processing power than software instruments; however, you can make fewer modifications to software instrument tracks.)

Summary

GarageBand is a music composition and editing tool that enables you to mix and match prerecorded loops or record your own music, either from real instruments or software instruments. You can edit loops, individually change their volume, and add special sound effects to get the mood you want. When you're finished with your song, GarageBand can encode your work and export it to iTunes, where you can use it as you would any other music file.

CHAPTER 24

Exploring the iMovie HD Interface

iMovie HD lets you take video that you've recorded with a video camera and make your own movies. It gives you the power to be your own movie director. In Hollywood, the process of deciding which parts of the footage end up in the final product is called *editing*. Movie editors craft the various scenes to fit together—in essence, they're making the same kinds of decisions that you'll make for your iMovie.

> The "HD" in iMovie HD stands for *high definition*, a high-resolution video format that produces higher-quality pictures than standard video. To make use of iMovie's HD compatibility, however, you need to start with HDV, footage captured by an HD-compatible camera.
>
> iMovie also lets you capture standard video (bit HDV) directly from iSight cameras, which were introduced in Chapter 18, "Using iChat AV." We discuss further details in Chapter 25, "Working with Video and Clips in iMovie HD."

By the Way

Basic Stages of Making an iMovie

There are six general stages in making iMovies: shooting, importing, editing, adding video effects, adding sound effects, and sharing.

> If that sounds like a lot of stages, you'll be happy to know that iMovie HD also allows you to make a "Magic Movie," where all you do is connect your camera and let iMovie add basic titles, credits, and transitions that you can customize with ease.

By the Way

Shooting

Shooting video is simply the process of using your digital camcorder to record scenes or events for your iMovie. Most people find themselves using the built-in microphone on their camcorder to record sound with their video, but you don't necessarily need to do this.

With the right equipment, you can record sound separately and then import it into your iMovie. For example, you might shoot some footage of an event and want to record yourself separately, making narrative commentary about the footage.

There are really no limits to what you can do when shooting video; you're limited only by how many blank tapes you have and how well charged your batteries are. Keep in mind, though, that you can work with only a limited amount of the footage you have shot because iMovie temporarily stores your production on your computer's hard drive. That means that the available free space on your hard drive has a direct relationship to the amount of video you can edit at one time. For example, you can shoot as much video as you want, but you might not be able to edit all 10 tapes worth of footage at one time.

Importing

The way that you get video into the computer so that you can use it in iMovie is called *importing* video. Apple makes it so simple to import video that you don't really need to think of it as a separate stage in the process of making an iMovie. You simply shoot your video, connect your camcorder to your Mac with a FireWire cable, and click a button. iMovie captures the video for you and automatically processes the incoming video into separate clips.

By the Way

> Some video cameras that aren't FireWire-ready can still be used with iMovie. If you are using an MPEG-4 video camera, you may be able to transfer video to your computer using USB or USB2. When you connect this type of camera to your Mac, it appears as a hard disk on your desktop, with the video you've recorded as a file. You can copy these video files to your hard drive by selecting and dragging as you would any other file. After the video is saved on your drive, you can import it into iMovie.

You learn how to import video in Chapter 25.

Editing

Some people find that editing video is their favorite part of working with iMovie. This is where you get to make the creative decisions that cause the final product to take form. The most common adjustments that iMovie enables you to make when editing video are the *start* and *end* of an individual video clip. For example, let's say that you bring a new video clip into iMovie. It's a scene of a friend standing in front of a building, talking about an event, and the total length of the clip is about 2 minutes long.

But when you look at the clip in iMovie, you notice that at the beginning of the clip there's a little boy sticking his tongue out at the camera while walking by in the background. One option is to leave this type of accidental action in a clip, but ultimately you'll probably find yourself wanting to remove or add things to your iMovie—thus you'll want to learn how to edit.

If you want to edit the boy out of the scene in this example, iMovie gives you the ability to pick a new start for the clip. For example, you could start the clip 2 seconds later.

You'll learn the details of editing scenes in Chapter 25.

Adding Video and Sound Effects

iMovie gives you a number of tools and special effects that you can use to enhance your iMovie. In traditional video or film production, the same stage is referred to as *post-production*: when a movie or television show is tweaked and developed, special effects are added, and final decisions are made about how the production will turn out.

iMovie is simple to use, but powerful, and one of the places it shines is in the category of video and sound effects. iMovie comes with many built-in effects, including visual effects like Brightness/Contrast and Adjust Colors and a sound effects library.

We explore video effects in Chapter 26, "Adding Titles, Transitions, and Effects in iMovie," and sound effects in Chapter 27, "Working with Still Photos and Sound in iMovie."

Sharing

iMovie offers several options for sharing your movies: from exporting them back to videotape through your camera to exporting for use with iDVD. We cover the options in depth in Chapter 28, "Exporting iMovies."

The iMovie Interface

iMovie is a simple yet powerful video editor that enables you to develop your video project with three main tool areas (see Figure 24.1): the Monitor, tool pane, and Timeline/Clip Viewer. The Monitor is where you preview a video clip or your entire movie. The tool pane changes to reveal options related to Clips, Photos, Audio, Titles, Transitions, Effects, or iDVD. The Clips pane, which is the default option for the tool pane, enables you to look at all the clips you have to work with at a glance. The Timeline/Clip Viewer is a special area at the bottom of the screen where you can put together your clips and make decisions about when you want them to start and end.

iMovie Monitor

The iMovie Monitor is the center of activity. After you've created a new project, the action happens in the Monitor window, which is used both to capture and preview video in iMovie. The Monitor is a powerful tool that enables you to switch between looking at video that's coming from your camcorder and the clips that you already have on your Mac by toggling the import/edit control, labeled with camera and scissors icons, below the Monitor.

FIGURE 24.1
The overall iMovie workspace: The Monitor, Clips Pane, and Timeline Viewer.

Monitor　　　　　　　　　　　　　　　　　Clips pane

Timeline viewer

The controls for the Monitor window are much like what you use on a DVD player and VCR, enabling you to quickly move through your video or jump to a specific location.

Clips Pane

The value of the Clips Pane, visible to the right of the Monitor window in Figure 24.1, quickly becomes apparent when you connect your camcorder to the Mac for the first time and start capturing clips. The Clips Pane is like a pantry for video—when you capture video, you load up the shelf with clips, and you can take a quick glance to see what you have to work with.

As you'll see in later chapters, this area gives you several additional tools to enhance your video productions, including photos, audio, titles, transitions, and effects.

Timeline/Clip Viewer

The Timeline Viewer, visible along the bottom of the iMovie interface in Figure 24.1, consists of three tracks: one for video and two additional tracks for audio. The Timeline Viewer lets you see the elements of your movie (clips, transitions, sound effects) as they progress over time. It also enables you to make adjustments to your video clips, such as changing the start and end times of each clip, and to work with multiple audio clips, such as by adding different sounds.

The Clip Viewer (see Figure 24.2) offers another way of looking at video clips that you've added to your movie. You switch between the Timeline Viewer and Clip Viewer by using the buttons below the Monitor that show the icon of a film frame (for Clip Viewer) or clock face (for Timeline Viewer).

In the Clip Viewer, video clips are treated more like icons. You can easily click and drag an individual clip to position it differently and thus have a different order for your video production. We'll take a closer look at the Clip Viewer in Chapter 24.

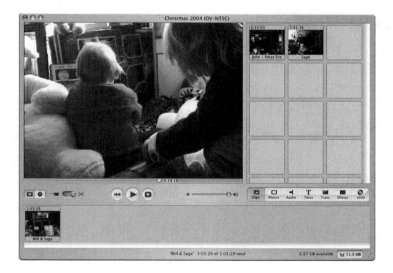

FIGURE 24.2
The Clip Viewer offers an alternative way to work with clips.

Other Important Controls for the Timeline

A row of controls appear at the very bottom of the iMovie window when the Timeline Viewer is visible (refer to Figure 24.1).

The first control is the Zoom slider, which enables you to zoom in on the Timeline to see more detail. As you add more and more scenes to the Timeline, the proportion of the whole that each one takes up shrinks—and so do the rectangles representing those clips. Use the Zoom slider to focus on one part of the Timeline by selecting a clip and dragging the Zoom controller to the right.

Next is the Clip volume control, labeled with the icon of a speaker. This slider controls the overall volume of the selected video clip or sound effect.

By the Way

> If the Zoom slider control button moves sluggishly when you try to drag it, you could instead click on the spot along the slider path where you want to set it. The button will jump precisely to that spot with ease.

Trash and Free Space

The bottom control row also includes a couple of helpful things to manage your iMovie project: the free space indicator and a miniature trash can so that you can easily get rid of video clips that you don't need any more.

iMovie Preferences

Before you begin any projects, let's take a brief look at the options in the iMovie Preferences panel, which can be opened from the iMovie application menu. The Preferences window, shown in Figure 24.3, contains a relatively small number of options and is categorized into General, Import, and Payback.

FIGURE 24.3
There are only a few iMovie preferences for you to configure.

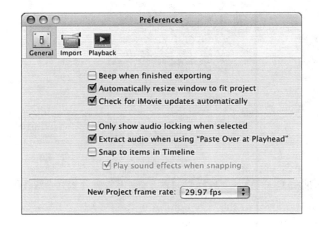

General Preferences

The General preference options are

▶ Beep When Finished Exporting—Alerts you when the export of your movie is done. (Exporting iMovies is covered in Chapter 28.)

▶ Automatically Resize Window to Fit Project—Allows iMovie to resize the iMovie window to fit the size of your video.

▶ Check for iMovie Updates Automatically—Allows iMovie to alert you if Apple issues an upgrade to iMovie.

The second grouping is related to how iMovie handles audio. (Working with audio is covered in detail in Chapter 27.)

▶ Only Show Locked Audio When Selected—Hides the indicators for locked audio unless you have selected a clip that is affected by locked audio. Checking this option removes some of the clutter from a complex movie project with added sound effects.

▶ Extract Audio when Using "Paste Over at Playhead"—Checking this box means that if you paste one clip on top of another, the original audio track appears as a separate audio track, rather than with the new audio track layered over it.

▶ Snap to Items in Timeline—iMovie enables you to add sound effects in two audio tracks. Check Snap to Items in Timeline to align an audio element to the start of a clip. When that option is checked, you can also check the option Play Sound Effect When Snapping for additional help with aligning video and audio elements precisely.

The last section of the General preferences is for manually setting the frame rate. The *frame rate* of digital video is the number of images displayed in a second as they flash by, like frames in a traditional movie. If you are importing video from your camera, iMovie HD automatically detects frame rate. However, if you create a movie out of still photos, you need to specify a frame rate.

The frames per second measurement for your project depends on a variety of factors, including the country you live in. In North America or Japan, televisions use a system called National Television Standards Committee (NTSC). If you use the NTSC digital video system, the measurement is most often 29.97 frames per second (fps). If you live in Europe, you probably use the PAL system for working with video, which uses a frame rate of 25.

Did you Know?

Import Preferences

The Import Preferences contain three options. The first is a pair of radio buttons where you can choose whether clips imported from the camera are placed in the Clip pane or placed directly in the Timeline Viewer. If you are making an iMovie and want to be sure to keep all the scenes in order, choose to have the clips go directly into the Timeline; otherwise, storing them in the Clip pane while you decide what clips to add makes good sense.

Start New Clip at Each Scene Break enables you to choose whether iMovie imports your video as clips, based on when you stopped and restarted filming. If you want to import your video as a continuous clip, be aware that iMovie limits a single clip to less than 2GB. You learn how to import clips in Chapter 24.

Apple recommends that you keep the option to Filter Audio from Camera checked. If you hear clicks or popping in imported clips, double-check that Filter Audio is enabled.

Playback Preferences

The options for Playback Preferences are split into two sections.

The Quality settings enable you to choose how iMovie plays your movie and video clips when previewing. You can choose between standard-quality images, which plays more smoothly on computers with slower processors; high-quality images, which produces a better image but requires more effort from your computer; or highest-quality, which produces the best image and requires even more effort from your computer. By default, iMovie sets the quality to high if your computer's processor can handle it. It's best to leave those settings unless you are experiencing video playback problems, such as stuttering and skipping.

The Play DV Video Through to DV Camera setting enables you to watch recording on the camera and your Mac simultaneously while you import your clips.

Starting a New Project

Now that you've seen the iMovie interface, it's time to look at how to start a new project.

By the Way

> When iMovie creates a project, it puts all your video material in one location on the hard drive—by default, the Movies folder in your home directory. When you import video, all the clips end up in the project; and even though there are separate files, everything stays together.

Before you can begin working on making iMovies, you must know how to create a new project. iMovie makes this easy by bringing up a special screen (shown in Figure 24.4) if you don't already have a project started. (If you have already created a project, or even several projects, iMovie tries to open the one last opened on your computer.)

FIGURE 24.4
A startup screen appears if you haven't already started a project.

To create a new project, follow these steps:

1. Start iMovie. If you get the window shown in Figure 24.4, click the Create a New Project button.

   If you don't get this window when you start iMovie, you can choose File, New Project from the menu bar to get the same thing.

2. When you create a new project, iMovie brings up the Create Project window, where you can give a name to your project and choose where you want to save the project. (If you don't want to save the project in your Movies folder, choose another location.)

3. Although iMovie automatically detects the appropriate video format when you connect a standard definition (DV) camera, a high-definition (HD) camera, or iSight camera, you may need to set a format for your project if you want to override that setting. Click the disclosure triangle labeled Video Format to choose between DV, DV Widescreen, HDV 1080i, HDV 720p, M-PEG4, or iSight.

> Consult the manual for your camera if you have questions about which setting your video footage will use.

By the Way

4. When you're satisfied with your settings, click Create.

Chapter 24 shows you how to import video from your digital video camera.

Summary

In this chapter, you were introduced to the basics of the iMovie interface. You took a closer look at the Clips pane (where video clips are stored), the Monitor (which lets you see the clips), and the Timeline/Clip Viewer (which gives you another way to interact with clips), as well as iMovie's preference settings. You also learned a little bit about iMovie's capabilities and how to start a new project.

CHAPTER 25

Working with Video and Clips in iMovie HD

This chapter focuses on working with video, from importing video clips to moving them around within iMovie. You'll learn the way that a video camera can be connected to your Mac and the process of importing video through that connection. You'll also learn some basics of video editing and working with film clips.

Connecting Video Cameras

Today, virtually every video camera that you can purchase includes a FireWire connection, which you may remember from Chapter 11, "Working with Displays and Peripheral Devices." (FireWire is also known as iLink or IEEE 1394 in some product documentation, but they all work the same.)

> As you learned in the previous chapter, you can also connect MPEG-4 devices to your Mac to import video using USB (not recommended for large amounts of video) or USB2. However, you cannot take advantage of some iMovie HD features, such as Magic iMovies and automatic scene separation.

When you want to connect your digital video camera to your Mac, you must use a FireWire cable. Some cameras come with such a cable, but you can also purchase it separately.

The cable that you need to use has two different kinds of connectors: a smaller end that's known as a 4-pin connector and a larger one on the other side that's known as a 6-pin connector. The smaller, 4-pin connector is the kind most often found on digital video cameras, and the larger 6-pin connector is most often found on computers.

After you connect the FireWire cable to your computer, you can connect the other, smaller end to the video camera. The location of the FireWire port on a video camera varies, but it's usually behind some kind of protective cover. Review your camera's documentation if you need help locating it. Figure 25.1 shows the smaller 4-pin end of a FireWire cable and the corresponding port on a digital video camera.

FIGURE 25.1
Getting ready to
plug the smaller
end of the
FireWire cable
into a video
camera.

Connecting Your Video Camera

This section takes you through the process of setting up iMovie and connecting a video camera so that you can import video.

1. Connect your video camera and computer using a FireWire cable as described previously.

2. Turn on the camera, and set it to playback mode. (Consult your camera manual for the appropriate settings. Insert a tape on which you've recorded video into the camera if you haven't already.

3. Open iMovie and choose Create New Project from the startup window, or if previous iMovie opened when you started iMovie, choose File, New Project to create a new project.

4. iMovie automatically switches to Camera mode when you plug in most cameras and turn them to playback mode. But if that doesn't occur, click the Camera/Edit Mode switch in iMovie to switch to Camera (DV) mode.

After you've connected your camera, iMovie displays a message in the monitor window confirming that your camera is connected, as shown in Figure 25.2.

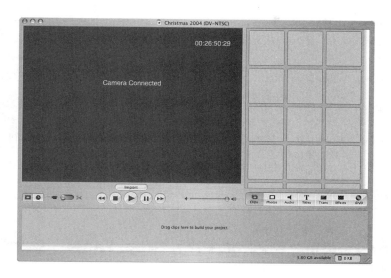

FIGURE 25.2
iMovie confirms
when a video
camera is
turned on and
plugged in.

It's easy to record video to a tape and then forget to rewind it—so you might put the tape in your video camera and press Play to preview it, but not see anything or see a blank blue screen! The material is still there, earlier on your videotape; you just have to rewind to get to it.

By the Way

Importing Video from an iSight Camera

In addition to capturing video from a video camera that records to a tape or other storage media, iMovie can be used with Apple's iSight camera, discussed in Chapter 18, "Using iChat AV," to record video directly. iMovie converts the footage to the DV format as it is stored so you can work with it just like other video.

To use your iSight to record directly to iMovie, first attach your iSight and open the privacy shutter. Then launch iMovie and switch to Camera mode, and click the small arrow immediately to the left of the Camera mode icon to select iSight from the pop-up menu. Click the button labeled Record with iSight to begin recording, and click again to stop recording. The clips recorded appear in the Clips pane just like those imported from a video camera.

Working with Video

If you're new to working with digital video on your Mac, all you really need to keep in mind is that you're using your camera and your computer as if they were a TV and a VCR.

In essence, iMovie becomes your computer VCR, but instead of recording a program from the television, iMovie records video from your video recorder.

This section focuses on importing selected clips of video, but you can also have iMovie import the contents of an entire video tape. If you have your iMovie Import preferences set to start a new clip at each scene break, it automatically creates separate clips for each scene you recorded.

Also, if you just want to create a movie from your footage quickly, you can opt to make a Magic iMovie, which is essentially a movie where iMovie automatically inserts credits and basic transitions between your scenes. When a Magic Movie is created, you need only type a title screen and your movie is ready to share. We talk about how to create a Magic iMovie near the end of this chapter.

Understanding Cueing: Play, Stop, Fast-forward, Rewind

When working with video on your Mac, you use standard controls to capture and access your video, such as Play, Stop, Fast Forward, and Rewind.

When you want to import video, you need to find a spot in your video where you want to start a clip, and that's where cueing comes into play. Depending on where you left off in the tape when you used your video camera to record your video, you might need to play, rewind, and so on to position and review your footage.

Did you Know?

Digital video takes up a lot of storage space. Although you can choose to let iMovie import all of the scenes, being select as you import may be necessary to keep from running out of available space.

You can do this positioning with the camera itself, by looking at its miniature screen. But one of the most enjoyable things about working with digital video through FireWire is that you can control your camera with buttons in the iMovie screen. So when you connect your camera, you don't necessarily have to use the buttons on the camera itself. When connected through FireWire, iMovie can actually control the camera, so you can use the Play/Fast-forward/Rewind buttons (see Figure 25.3) right in iMovie to go through your tape.

Use iMovie to Find a Spot on Your Videotape

Assuming that you successfully connected your video camera to your computer (as explainer earlier in this chapter), follow these steps:

1. Click the Rewind button to rewind the tape.

FIGURE 25.3
The play controls in iMovie.

Rewind | Play | Fastforward
Stop Pause

2. Click the Play button to begin playing your video.

You might need to adjust the sound on your computer as you preview your video.

Watch Out!

3. While the video is playing, try clicking the Fast-forward button to fast-forward through the video while you're watching it. Click again to stop the tape.

4. If your video is still playing, click the Stop button, and then click either the Fast-forward or Rewind button. This method of moving through a tape is faster, but you can't see the video moving by.

5. Using the play controls, find a spot in your videotape where you want to start importing a clip.

There's no official term for fast-forwarding or rewinding from a complete stop. But if you're new to video, you could think of it as *step starting*, where the tape isn't moving and you have to take a step in a particular direction (backward or forward) to get things going. Step starting is the fastest way to get to a certain point on your tape. In contrast, watching footage going by when you're fast-forwarding or rewinding could be thought of as *play previewing*. In other words, you press the Play button and then press Fast-forward or Rewind. The disadvantage is that things go slower, but you can see exactly what's going on.

It can sometimes be helpful to start importing a clip just a little before where you want to create a video clip so that you can make a fine adjustment to the starting point of your video clip in iMovie.

Importing Video

When you import video from a FireWire-compatible camera, one nice thing that iMovie can do is separate your clips for you automatically. If you set your iMovie preferences to automatically start a new clip at scene breaks, iMovie breaks the clips automatically wherever you stopped filming and then started shooting a new scene.

Did you Know?

If you already have video clips saved, you can import them into your current iMovie project by choosing File, Import from the menu. In the window that appears, you then need to locate the video file, select it, and click Open.

After you've completed the two previous tasks (connecting your video camera and finding a spot in your tape to start recording), follow these steps:

1. Open iMovie and start a new project.

2. Make sure your camera is connected and in playback mode.

3. Click the Import button to start importing footage (refer to Figure 25.3).

4. When you've imported the section you want to work with, click the Stop button.

5. Now click the Camera/Edit Mode switch and drag it to switch to Edit mode so that you can begin to work with your clips. (You can also click the Clips pane to automatically switch to Edit mode.)

By the Way

When importing video, keep in mind that you must keep an eye on the amount of space available on your hard drive. Remember that if you're planning to export your iMovies for use in an iDVD project (see Chapter 28, "Exporting iMovies"), you need as much space as your project is taking up in iMovie—in other words, when you plan to export for iDVD, you need twice as much space.

Moving Around in a Clip

One of the most enjoyable parts about playing with footage in iMovie is the way that you can easily move around in a clip in the same way that you might use the remote control on your VCR or DVD player to find a spot in a movie. In iMovie, as you're editing your creation, you'll often want to move through various parts of individual clips or the overall movie as it takes shape. Rather than play through the entire movie, you can quickly get to the spot that you want with a control called the *playhead*, which is located at the bottom of the Monitor window (see Figure 24.4).

FIGURE 25.4
A close-up view of the playhead, along with the time stamp for that spot in your video clip.

Go to a Specific Spot in a Clip

After you've acquainted yourself with the clips to get an idea of what you have to work with, you'll want to target specific moments in the clips for use in your project.

If you don't already have the clip from the previous task open, open it so that you can have something to work with.

To go to a specific spot in a clip:

1. Click on the playhead, and hold down the mouse button.

2. Drag the playhead horizontally to the left or right to find the spot that you want. Notice how the position of the playhead is expressed as the number of minutes, seconds, and frames next to the playhead as you drag it.

Rename a Clip in the Clips Pane

After you are familiar with the content of your clips, you may want to rename them with more informative labels than Clip 01, Clip 02, Clip 03, and so on.

To rename a clip, follow these steps:

1. Select a clip in the Clips pane by clicking it; the selected clip turns blue.

2. Move the mouse over the text in the clip and click. The area behind the text turns white, and you can type a new name in for the clip (see Figure 25.5).

FIGURE 25.5
Renaming a clip: 1) select a clip; 2) click on its name; 3) type a name.

Another way to see the clip name is to double-click a clip in the Clips pane, which brings up the Clip Info window.

Making Basic Edits

To give you a better taste of how the iMovie interface gives you the power of video editing, we take a look at how to make a basic edit using a combination of the Clips pane, the Monitor, and the Timeline Viewer.

Preparing a Clip

This section goes through the process of making an adjustment to a clip, but first you need to drag the clip into the Timeline Viewer. To prepare the clip, click on it in the Clips pane and drag it down to the uppermost track of Timeline Viewer, which is where you put video clips.

After you drag the clip, the Video Monitor looks the same, but the clip now appears on the Timeline Viewer rather than the Clips pane, as illustrated in Figure 25.6.

Split a Video Clip at the Playhead

Now that you have a clip ready to go, you can make an adjustment to it. In this scenario, the adjustment you want to make is to delete some extra footage at the end of the clip.

To delete extra footage:

1. Drag the playhead in the Monitor to somewhere close to the end of the clip—to a point just before the clip switches to something you don't want in your movie.

2. Choose Edit, Split Video Clip at Playhead to mark the spot so that iMovie knows where one clip ends and the next begins. In essence, you've just created two separate clips from one original clip (see Figure 25.7).

FIGURE 25.6
The clip as it appears in the Timeline Viewer.

FIGURE 25.7
The newly split clip.

3. In the Timeline Viewer, click the unwanted clip and choose Edit, Clear from the menu. The extra footage is removed, and the desired footage remains.

You don't have to move clips to the Timeline to split them. You can choose a clip in the Clips pane and preview it in the Monitor window; then place the playhead and split the clip as described in step 3.

If you don't want to delete the video you split, you can select it and drag it back to the Clips pane for use later.

Edit with Direct Trimming

Besides splitting a clip at the playhead, which results in two clips, you can also edit with direct trimming right in iMovie's Timeline. Direct trimming doesn't produce "leftovers" the way splitting a clip does, because the trimmed footage is hidden but still part of the original clip until you empty the trash.

To trim a clip, first drag it to the Timeline and select it. Then place your mouse cursor over the right or left edge of the clip so the cursor changes to a double-sided arrow. Next, click and drag the cursor toward the center of the clip, as shown in Figure 25.8, as you watch the video in the Monitor. (For additional information about where you are in the clip, the time code for the amount you've trimmed appears next to the playhead above the Timeline as you drag.) When you get to the part of the clip you want to use in your movie, let up on the mouse and the trimmed clip slides into place.

FIGURE 25.8
Click on a clip and drag toward the center to trim a clip.

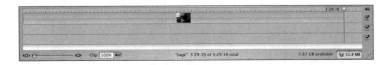

You can tell which ends of a clip have been trimmed because they appear with straight edges in the Timeline, rather than rounded corners.

In addition to trimming a single clip, you can also click and drag a selected clip's edge to overwrite an adjacent clip by holding down the Control key. This means you can reposition a clip and edit the adjacent clip in one motion.

If you discover you've trimmed too much, place your cursor on the side you've trimmed and drag away from the center of the clip to restore what you want to keep. Remember, however, that you can't restore trimmed video after you've emptied the trash.

Delete a Clip from the Clips Pane

One of the more common tasks in basic video editing is deleting unwanted video footage. Doing so is easy in iMovie:

1. Click on a clip in the Clips Pane to select it.

2. Either drag the clip into iMovie's Trash until the Trash well darkens or select Edit, Clear from the menu.

You'll probably want to get into the habit of emptying the Trash after you've deleted a clip, or at regular intervals, so that you can keep the maximum amount of hard drive space available to work on your movie.

3. Choose File, Empty Trash to empty the Trash.

Empty the Trash only when you are positive you won't need a discarded clip later—you can't undo emptying the Trash.

Watch Out!

4. Click Empty Trash and Save Project in the confirmation window that comes up. Then see how much space you have freed up by checking the free space indicator at bottom-right of the iMovie window.

If you click on iMovie's Trash icon, a window appears to show you what movie clips and elements you have discarded. If you want to rescue something from the Trash, you can select it and drag it back to the Clips Pane. If you aren't positive you want to delete everything in the Trash, you can select individual items to delete, leaving the other items until you're sure you won't need them.

By the Way

Restore Clip Media

No one is perfect, and sooner or later you'll decide that you want to start over again when adjusting clips. One way to back up is to go through a repeated series of undo steps by pressing Ctrl-Z on your keyboard or choosing Edit, Undo.

Another way is to use the Restore Clip option, which enables you to start over again by bringing clips back to their original state.

If you edit clips, you can restore clips to the condition in which were only up until the last time you emptied the trash, so be careful to clean up only after you're happy with your edits.

Watch Out!

1. Click one of the clips in the Timeline that you made by splitting the original clip.

2. Choose Advanced, Revert Clip to Original from the menu.

3. Click OK in the dialog box that appears to restore the original clip.

If you split a clip at the playhead but keep both resulting clips, restoring one of them doesn't merge pieces of the original clip back together. If you restore one of the pieces, the restored clip will contain the footage from the other clip.

Preview an iMovie Project

When you want to view your iMovie to see how it is progressing, click the Play button without any clip selected. iMovie plays all the clips in succession in the Monitor.

Previewing an entire movie is as simple as previewing a single clip; just remember not to have any one clip selected when you click the Play button. (If you do have a clip selected, iMovie plays only that clip instead of your entire movie.) To preview, follow these steps:

1. Open an iMovie project with clips that have been dragged into either the Timeline Viewer or the Clip Viewer.

2. Click somewhere other than on a clip to make sure that you don't have any clip selected—they should all be a white color.

3. Make sure the playhead below the Monitor is at the far left and that the time code reads 0:00:00. If it isn't, drag the playhead to that position to preview your project from the beginning.

4. Click the Play button below the iMovie Monitor, and iMovie plays through all the clips, giving you a preview of your entire iMovie.

In Clip Viewer, iMovie draws a small red marker that moves slowly to the right in the Clip Viewer area as you watch your movie. The position of the red marker corresponds to where the playhead is positioned in the Monitor window as well. Both the playhead and the red marker are essentially tools for keeping track of where you are in your movie project.

Also, small vertical lines in the scrubber bar below the Monitor correspond to where one clip ends and another begins. This feature is sort of like a timeline you have even when you're in the Clip Viewer.

Check the Size of an iMovie Project

Just about the time you start getting hooked on iMovie, you might realize that your Mac doesn't have an endless amount of hard drive space, and you need to think a bit more about how much space your projects are taking up.

Did you Know?

Chances are that you'll have enough space on your hard drive to work on a few projects at the same time, unless you're working on full-length movies from day one. When you're finished and have exported your iMovies to tape or iDVD, you can burn the raw files in your iDVD project folder to CD or DVD or move them to an external hard drive.

It's good to keep an eye on things so that you can decide when you have to delete or archive your collection of accumulated media files.

1. Double-click the icon on your hard drive to launch a Finder window.

2. Locate the folder with your iMovies—when you created a new iMovie project, you named it something.

3. Select the folder and choose Get Info from the Action pop-up menu. An Info window appears, as shown in Figure 25.9.

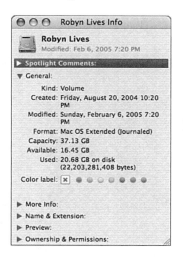

FIGURE 25.9
Showing information about the size of your movie project.

Did you Know?

If you saved your movie in the default folder, it is in the Movies folder within your home folder.

The Info window gives you a variety of information, including the size of your folder.

Working with iMovie's Clip Viewer

As you learned in Chapter 24, "Exploring the iMovie Interface," the Clip Viewer is an alternative to the Timeline Viewer and might be preferable for some as a way to work with clips. In some ways, the Clip Viewer is the "lite" version of iMovie.

Although the Timeline view provides an excellent way to work with clips and is easy to use, the Clip Viewer is even easier. If you want to have a simplified introduction to working with iMovie, you might want to work in the Clip Viewer. Also, children might find it easier to play with iMovie in the Clip Viewer because there are fewer skills to master—just clicking, dragging, and dropping.

Adding and Rearranging Clips

In the Clip Viewer, you can do just about everything you can in the Timeline Viewer, including adding transitions, effects, and titles. One of the only major differences is that you can't work with audio in the Clip Viewer. (When you try to drag a sound effect into the Clip Viewer, it switches you back to the Timeline.)

Figure 25.10 shows the Timeline with three successive video clips arranged from left to right. The leftmost part of the Timeline Viewer represents the beginning of the movie, and the rightmost part of the Timeline Viewer represents the end of the movie.

FIGURE 25.10
Three clips in the Timeline Viewer.

Now take a look at the Clip Viewer in Figure 25.11, which you access by clicking on the film frame symbol at the left corner of the screen.

The video clips represented in Figure 25.11 are the same video clips that you saw in Figure 25.10.

FIGURE 25.11
The same three clips in the Clip Viewer.

Add Clips

Adding clips is simple in the Clip Viewer. You can basically handle things the same way that you will learn to do in the Timeline Viewer: by dragging clips into the Clip Viewer from the Clips pane.

1. Open an iMovie project that has several clips in it.

2. To access the Clip Viewer if it's not already open, click the film frame icon in the lower-left corner of the screen.

3. Choose a clip for your iMovie by single-clicking one of the clips in the Clips pane, holding down the mouse button, and dragging it down toward the Clip Viewer area. When you have the mouse arrow over the Clip Viewer area, you can let go of the mouse button and drop the clip there.

4. To add another clip, repeat steps 2 and 3 to drag the next clip down and drop it to the right of the first clip.

When you've finished dragging clips into the Clip Viewer, they are lined up in a row. If one of the clips is a blue color, that simply means it's selected. If you want to deselect it, you can click somewhere other than on the clips in the Clip Viewer.

Rearrange Clips

The Clip Viewer comes in particularly handy for rearranging clips if you want to reposition one clip after another or easily try different combinations of scenes. For comparison, you might want to try clicking on a clip in the Timeline Viewer to move it around, as shown in Figure 25.12.

Now switch back to the Clip Viewer and you're ready to reposition:

1. Open an iMovie project with at least three clips in it, and click on the film frame icon at the lower left to see the Clip Viewer.

2. Click the first clip, and holding down the mouse button, drag the clip to the right, until a space opens up between the second and third clips (see Figure 25.13).

3. Let go of the mouse button to drop the clip in place.

Enhancing Clips in Clip Viewer

Adding transitions, effects, and titles in the Clip Viewer works the same as adding them in the Timeline. You learn how in Chapter 26, "Adding Titles, Transitions, and Effects in iMovie HD."

Creating a Magic iMovie

If you want to create a basic movie quickly, you'll love the Magic iMovie feature, which allows you to make a few choices and then sit back and let iMovie HD do the rest.

To create a Magic iMovie, connect your camera and set it to playback mode as explained earlier in this chapter. Next, start iMovie and click Make a Magic iMovie button in the startup window or choose File, Make a Magic iMovie from the menu. You'll need to give your project a name and choose a location in which to save it, as you would for any other new project. (If you are using a camera other than a standard DV camera, you also need to choose a video format.) When you're finished, click the Create button.

The window shown in Figure 25.14 appears, where you can make some simple choices for your Magic iMovie. (For the first option, you can revise the name you just gave your project.)

FIGURE 25.14
Making a Magic
iMovie requires
a few simple
decisions.

If you would like, you can choose which transition to apply between scenes.

As iMovie imports your video, it recognizes where you stopped and started the camera and automatically makes divisions between clips. Transitions help link these separate scenes together in a less abrupt way than just stopping one and beginning another. After your Magic iMovie is created, you can choose to edit the transition if you change your mind. (Adding transitions to non-Magic iMovies is covered in Chapter 26.)

If you would like a musical soundtrack to play in the background of your Magic iMovie, make sure the second check box is checked and click the Choose Music button, which opens the Choose Music window shown in Figure 25.15.

To select songs from your iTunes library, simply drag the songs from the listing on the left side of the window to the space on the right. If you don't add enough music to play as long as the video in your movie, the song repeats until the video ends. If you have more music time than video time, the music ends when the video does. (If you change your mind and want to delete a song you've added, select it and press the Delete button on your keyboard.)

If you want to use music from a CD instead of music from your library, click the Eject the CD-ROM button to the right of the music source popup and insert your CD in the CD drive. Then click the music source popup, choose your CD, and drag songs to the list on the right side of the window.

By the Way

FIGURE 25.15
Choose songs
from your iTunes
library or a CD,
and then adjust
the volume.

Use the volume slider near the lower right to set a volume level for your musical sound-track. If you want to hear only the soundtrack, slide the control all the way to the right.

When you're finished selecting music and setting volume, click OK to finalize your music choices.

The last Magic iMovie option is the Send to iDVD check box. If you don't want to make any adjustments to your Magic iMovie before sharing it, you can check the box for this option. This opens your Magic iMovie in iDVD so you can prepare a DVD and burn it to disk for sharing. Otherwise, uncheck the box to have your Magic iMovie open in iMovie so you can make changes before writing it to DVD. (Using iDVD is covered in Chapter 29, "Exploring the iDVD Interface," and Chapter 30, "Creating DVDs with iDVD.")

When you are satisfied with your Magic iMovie settings, click Create and let iMovie do its thing. One last thing: If you have a lot of video, be patient as the clips are imported—importing video is quite resource intensive!

Summary

In this chapter, you learned how to import video, using the FireWire interface to capture it. You also learned about some introductory, basic video editing tasks, such as adding clips to the Timeline Viewer, making adjustments, and deciding to do it all over again to make it perfect. You also learned how to work with clips in the Clip Viewer. Finally, you learned how simple it is to create a basic iMovie with the Magic iMovie feature.

CHAPTER 26

Adding Titles, Transitions, and Effects in iMovie

This chapter looks at some enhancements you can make to your movies and clips. Titles are covered first, enabling you to add text portions to your movies (or even write a text-only movie). Then you learn about transitions, which enable you to enhance your iMovies with between-clip features, such as fade in, fade out, cross dissolve, and others. Finally, you can explore visual effects, which can be applied to the clips themselves to change color or add special effects, such as lighting effects, sparkles, or fog.

Titles

When you're ready to try adding a title to your iMovie, you'll be working in a new area of iMovie: the Titles pane. Until now, you probably spent most of your time simply capturing video and working with clips in the Clips pane, the Monitor, and the Timeline or Clip Viewer. But now you start switching back and forth between various panes of tools. Click the Titles button above the Timeline or Clip Viewer on the right side to reveal to the Titles pane.

When the Titles pane comes up, you see a number of options, including ways to adjust the font, color, and size of the letters in your title, as well as a list from which you can select different titles (see Figure 26.1).

But if you're new to digital video, don't worry about all the options. You can add a title to your iMovie simply by choosing one (such as Bounce In To Center) from the list, clicking on it, and dragging it into the Timeline. (If you want to keep the title you gave your project and use the name set up for the current account, you don't even have to enter text—iMovie uses those pieces of information as the default text.)

Sooner or later, you'll want to take advantage of all the things you can do to spruce up and modify titles to give your productions a customized touch. To get your feet wet, let's take a look at a couple of the basic titles included with iMovie HD. Later, we dive into adjusting and customizing titles.

FIGURE 26.1
The Titles pane.

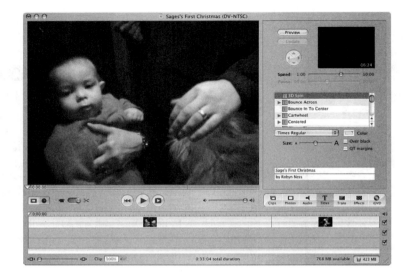

Sample Titles—Centered Title and Centered Multiple

Near the top of iMovie's title list is the item Centered. If you click it, you see a couple of options: Centered Multiple and Centered Title. Centered Title makes your title fade in and then out, centered in the middle of your screen. You can get a sense of how it will look in your movie by clicking on it. A preview plays, as shown in Figure 26.2.

By the Way

To help you organize the long list of titles, some are categorized under a heading marked with an arrow, or a "disclosure triangle." You can reveal or hide the titles under a heading by clicking the arrow. In many cases, disclosure triangles indicate which titles have a "Multiple" option, but sometimes they also indicate the availability of variations on one theme.

At first glance, Centered Multiple might sound like an abstract algebraic principle, but after you start playing with it, its value becomes apparent. Centered Multiple is an example of a title to which you can add multiple screens of text. (When you use any of the titles ending in the word *Multiple*, iMovie makes it easy to create an entire opening credit sequence by enabling you to add text to some titles.)

To enter your own text for a title, delete the placeholder text in the fields near the bottom of the Titles pane and type your own (see Figure 26.3).

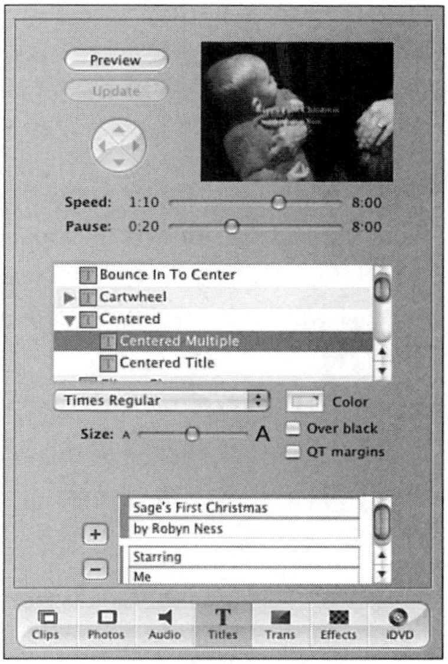

FIGURE 26.2
A sample title.

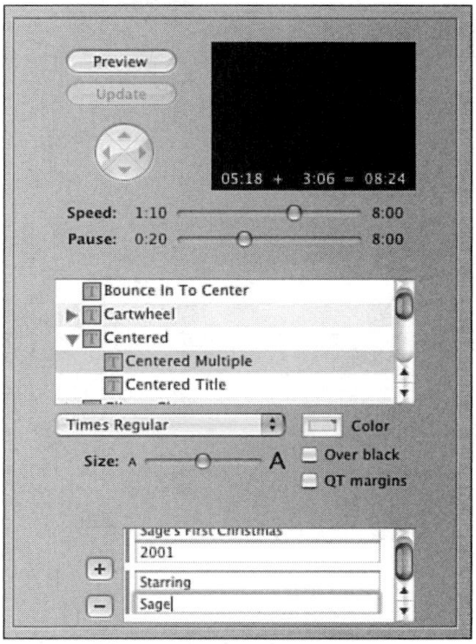

FIGURE 26.3
The text input area in the Titles pane.

With a multiple-line title, such as Centered Multiple, you can click the + button to add more title fields. If you've added a few, drag the blue scrollbar to the right of the text to reveal them.

Now that you've gotten a taste of two basic titles, take a moment to consider all the titles you have available by looking through the list in iMovie. Remember, if you click one it previews in the small window at the top of the Titles pane.

Using Titles Over Black

A simple way to have titles is to use the default, which appears in white text against a black background. This focuses your attention on the title itself. To accomplish this, you simply click on the Over Black option in the Titles pane (refer to Figure 26.3).

Overlay (over Video) Titles

Another method you might want to try is to uncheck the Over Black option so that your title appears over a video clip, as shown in Figure 26.4. The only requirement is that you have a video clip in the project!

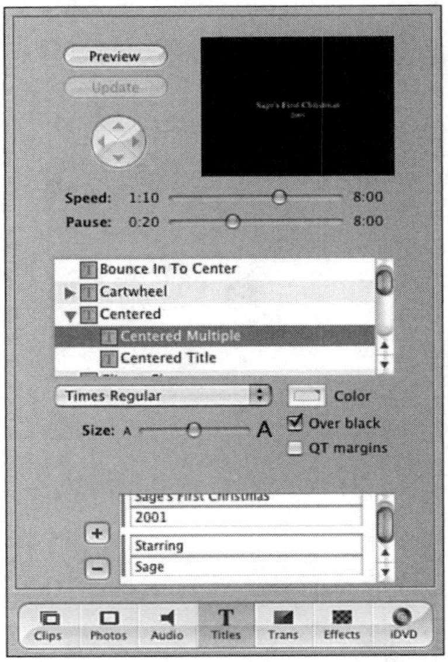

FIGURE 26.4
Clicking on a title with Over Black unchecked to see a mini-preview with the title displayed over a video clip.

Adding Titles

The ultimate goal of making titles is to introduce or otherwise enhance your movie. You could have a title at the beginning, a rolling credit at the end, and any number of titles in between to introduce different scenes (reminiscent of silent movies?) or sections (such as in a training video).

Earlier in this chapter, we talked about the two different ways that titles can work: either displayed against a black screen (Over Black), or as an overlay displaying directly over video. Either approach can be fun and work in different situations, but you might want to start out with a standard Over Black title (by clicking the Over Black check box).

Adding a title to a movie is as easy as adding a clip to a movie; it's a similar, almost identical process. In fact[-el]it is identical.

1. Open an iMovie project and drag a clip into the Timeline or Clip Viewer.

2. Open the Titles pane and click on a title of choice. If you'd like, enter your own title text in the text field or fields near the bottom of the pane.

3. Click on the title you select once again and drag it down into the Timeline or Clip Viewer until your video clip moves aside to make room for the title (see Figure 26.5). Drop the title into the open space.

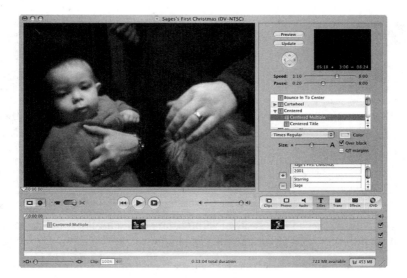

FIGURE 26.5
Dragging a title from the Titles pane down to the Timeline Viewer in front of the video clip.

Notice in Figure 26.6 how the small red bar travels from left to right underneath your title to indicate that the title is being processed.

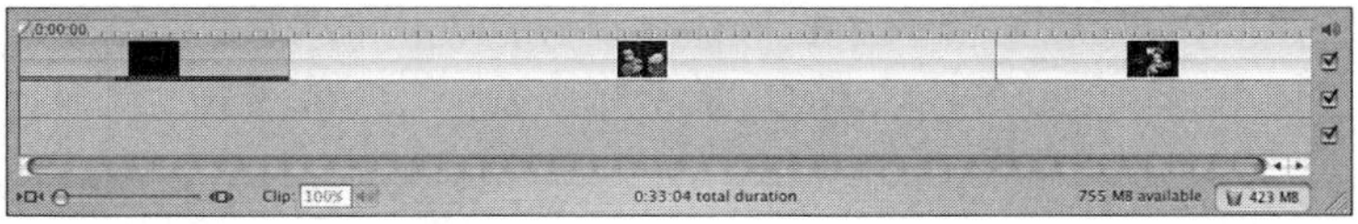

FIGURE 26.6
A little red bar going to the right underneath the title in the Timeline indicates that your Mac is processing your title.

With your title in place, try clicking on the playhead and dragging it through your title to get a quick glance at how the title animates.

After you've added a title to your movie, you can select it in the Timeline or Clip Viewer (it changes to blue) and make adjustments to it. Then you need to click Update for iMovie to process your new settings.

You can actually layer different titles in iMovie. For instance, you can add one long-duration title that is set over black and have other titles that aren't set over black cross over the top of it.

iMovie can quickly display a miniature preview in the Titles pane when you make changes. But digital video takes a lot of processing power. So for it to catch up with changes when you add a title to your movie, it has to be processed before you can get the final preview of how it'll look onscreen.

Adjusting Titles

As soon as you start trying out the different titles, you'll want to know how you can adjust them, and Apple has done an excellent job again of making things easy and intuitive, yet flexible. Essentially, you can do no tweaking at all or as much as you want.

The following steps describe how to make adjustments to a title.

1. Select a title from the list in the Titles pane. This example uses Drifting.

2. Click the Text Size slider, marked with a small and a large capital A, and drag it to the left or right to change the size of your title text.

3. To choose a different color for the text, click once on the Color button. A pop-up menu of colors appears (see Figure 26.7).

4. Click on a color that you want to use for your text, and then click somewhere outside the pop-up menu to deselect it.

5. Click and drag the blue Speed slider (just below the preview area) to the left or to the right to see how it affects the behavior of the title text.

6. To see the preview of a title with the changes you've made, click on the Preview button and it appears in the Monitor.

FIGURE 26.7
Use the color
picker to
choose a color
for your text.

Transitions

Transitions could be thought of as the bread and butter of video editing. Or, perhaps, as the peanut butter that makes scenes stick together.

When you deal with clips, if you choose wisely, one clip can cut to another without anything between the clips. To get a better understanding of the concept of a *cut*, try watching a few minutes of television or a movie and looking for the spots where the camera switches from one view to another—this usually happens most rapidly in music videos. Some people prefer cutting from one scene to another without any blending.

But there are times when you want to find a way for one clip to lead smoothly to another, and a transition is a perfect way to accomplish this.

Figure 26.8 shows the Transitions pane in iMovie, which you can access easily by clicking the Trans button. The Transitions pane enables you to choose transitions to use in your iMovie, as well as make some simple adjustments to the way each transition appears.

You can see mini-previews of the iMovie transitions in the preview area of the Transitions pane. Because transitions are based on the clip or clips to which they are applied, you need at least two clips in your movie to see an example of every transition. (Some transitions can be applied to a single clip, but most are designed for use between two clips.)

FIGURE 26.8
The Transitions
pane.

By the Way

The icon in front of each transition in the Transitions pane tells you where it can be added. For example, Fade In shows an icon with a darker blue triangle on the left side, which means it has to be added on to the left of (or before) a clip. The icon for Fade Out has a darker blue triangle on the right side, so it has to be added to the right of (or after) a clip. Most of the transitions show darker blue triangles on both the left and right sides, which means the transition has to be placed between two clips.

To view the mini-previews, select a clip that follows another clip in your movie project and click through the list of transitions.

Sample Transition—Cross Dissolve

To get a better understanding of transitions, it's helpful to take a look at the Cross Dissolve transition. Simply put, a cross dissolve blends one scene into another.

Imagine a movie containing two clips. If you watched the movie as is, when one video clip ended, it would simply cut from one video clip to another. But a cross dissolve could help the scenes blend. Essentially, over the course of a Cross Dissolve transition you see less of the first clip and more of the second. Figure 26.9 represents the blending of two video clips.

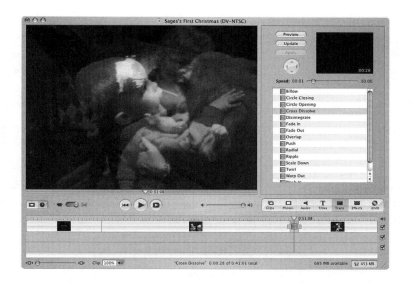

FIGURE 26.9
Cross Dissolve: At the beginning, you see the first clip. Toward the middle, you still see the original clip, but you also see a fair amount of the second clip "merged in" with the original clip. At this stage, both clips are semi-transparent. At the end, you see the second clip.

Transitions, such as cross dissolves, overlap with the video clips in a project. Longer transitions overlap with more of the video, obscuring more of the original imagery. As a general rule, the length of a clip overlapped by a transition is half of the duration of the transition (because most transitions are shared between two clips).

Working with Transitions

Transitions are easy to work with. Just as with other enhancements that you can add to an iMovie, a transition takes a few moments to process, and if you add many transitions to your iMovie, you might have to wait a few minutes. But when the processing is done, you have a nice way to spice up your iMovie. It's worth experimenting to find and develop your own style.

Transitions can be fun to work with, but be careful not to upstage your video clips with too many distracting transitions.

In general, there are three ways of working with transitions: adding, updating, and removing.

Add a Fade In

Adding a transition is as simple as clicking to select it, dragging it into the Timeline or Clip Viewer, waiting for a moment while it processes, and then watching it to see how you like it.

Keep in mind that to try a transition, you must have at least one video clip in your project. Some transitions are better suited to be before or after a clip (rather than in between), such as the Fade In transition, which is a good way to start off your iMovie.

1. Open an iMovie project and add a video clip.

2. Click the Trans button in the main iMovie window to access the Transitions pane.

3. Click the Fade In transition. After a transition is selected, a mini-preview of it plays in the window at the upper right.

4. Select the Fade In transition and drag it to a point in the Timeline or Clip Viewer to the left of the clip you want to fade in. The clip moves aside (see Figure 26.10) to make room for the transition, indicating that you can release the mouse button to drop the transition in place.

FIGURE 26.10
Release the mouse button to insert a transition in the space next to a clip.

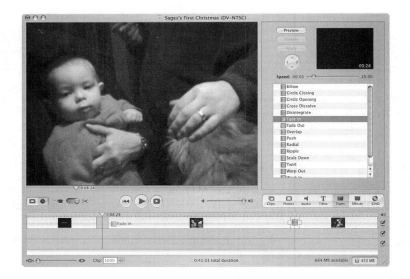

By the Way

To which side of a clip you drag a transition depends on the transition being added. If you try to place a transition on the wrong side of a clip, an error message tells you whether the transition you have chosen must be placed before or after a clip.

Transitions that require two clips to work—such as Cross Dissolve, Overlap, and Push—give you an error if they aren't sandwiched between two clips. (Somewhat confusingly, this error message is the same one that appears when you place a transition on the wrong side of a single clip—the one that tells you to place the transition on the opposite side of where you've placed it. If you follow that advice with only one clip in the Timeline, another error tells you to place the transition on the opposite side.)

A red processing indicator (see Figure 26.11) shows progress as the transition is processed. Wait until it is done before previewing your movie.

When the processing is finished, drag the playhead through the transition to see how your iMovie now starts black, and the video clip slowly fades in.

Add a Push

Although a Fade In can be added when only a single clip has been added to your project, most transitions are designed to go between two clips. One example is the Push transition, in which the second clip "pushes" the first one off the screen as it appears.

To add a push:

1. Open an iMovie project and add at least two video clips.

2. Click the Trans button in the main iMovie window to access the Transitions pane.

3. Click the Push transition.

4. The Push transition is a special kind of transition because you can choose the direction from which it starts. To do this, click one of the direction arrow buttons to the left of the mini-preview area, as shown in Figure 26.12. (This control is not active unless it applies to the selected transition.)

5. When you are satisfied with your direction setting, select the Push transition from the list and drag it to a point in the Timeline or Clip Viewer between two clips. The clips move aside to make room for the transition, indicating that you can release the mouse button to drop the transition in place.

If you want to add the same transition several places in your movie, select the clips that will be affected and then choose a transition from the Transitions pane. Click the Apply button to add transitions to all the selected clips. (Remember that the rules for placing transitions before, after, or between clips still must be followed.)

By the Way

FIGURE 26.12
Choose a starting direction for the Push transition.

Change and Replace a Transition

At some point, you might want to change a transition that's already been added, and doing so is easy:

1. Open your iMovie project in which you have a transition that you want to replace. In Figure 26.13, you see our trusty sample project. In this scenario, we've decided that we want the fade out to be longer; that is, the fade should start earlier in the clip.

2. Click on the transition to select it; it will be highlighted in blue.

3. Click on the blue Speed slider in the Transition pane to adjust the Speed setting.

Did you Know?

The higher the Speed setting, the more seconds of space the transition takes up. So, if you want a longer transition, you want a higher Speed setting—toward 10:00. For a shorter transition, you want a lower setting—toward 00:01.

3. Click the Update button in the Transition pane. When the processing is done, drag the playhead back and forth on the Timeline to see the effect of the adjusted transition, or position the playhead to the left of the transition and click the Play button below the Monitor window.

FIGURE 26.13
Selecting the
transition.

Compare the relative lengths of the transition and video clip in Figures 26.13 and
26.14. Notice how the transition in Figure 26.17, which has been adjusted to 10:00,
is longer and therefore takes up more space in the Timeline than the original transition shown in Figure 26.13. The transition starts earlier in the video clip.

FIGURE 26.14
Viewing the
results of the
adjusted transi-
tion, which has
to process first.

Replacing a transition works in a similar way, except that you choose a different transition than the one originally in place and add it by clicking the Update button. If the new transition can be applied where the old one was, the old one is removed to make room for your new choice.

Remove a Transition

Removing a transition is simple:

1. Open the iMovie project in which you have a transition that you want to remove.

2. Click on the transition to select it; when selected it is highlighted in blue.

3. Choose Edit, Clear from the menu, and the transition is removed.

> To select all the transitions at once, select one transition and then choose Edit, Select Similar Clips from the menu. You can then delete all the clips at once.

Effects

Effects represent another way that you can enhance your iMovies by adding something to them. You take plain video and make it stand out or spice it up to create your own movie-making style.

For example, if you want to give a historic feel to a portion of your iMovie, you could use an effect to make the movie either black-and-white or a sepia tone to give it the feel of an early moving picture.

Sometimes the video you use might give you ideas. For example, there might be a scene in a movie that's supposed to represent a person's dreams, and you could use the Fog effect to give that scene a surreal feeling. Maybe you could even combine it with another effect to change the colors around, and when the person in your iMovie wakes up, everything returns to normal, and you don't see the effects anymore.

In essence, to add an effect, you simply choose a clip in the Timeline or Clip Viewer and then choose and apply an effect—you can make adjustments anytime you want.

Did you Know?

> If you want to add an effect to only a portion of your iMovie, use the Split Video Clip at Playhead command (for a refresher, see the section "Preparing a Clip" in Chapter 25, "Working with Video and Clips in iMovie HD") to separate a portion of your video and then apply the effect to it.

Effects are similar to transitions and titles in that the magic happens in the relevant pane in iMovie (see Figure 26.15); the Effects pane gives you a convenient place to try out different things.

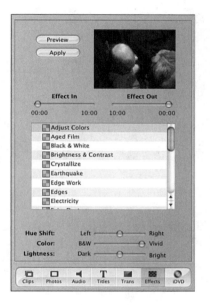

If you like to keep things as simple as possible, you can simply choose an effect; but iMovie also enables you to customize each effect if you choose to. You might find that you start by simply adding effects with their default settings and then end up coming back to the Effects pane to try different options when you get ideas for how some adjustment could work better for a particular clip.

When you select a clip in your project, you can click through the list of Effects to see a mini-preview at the top of the Effects pane.

By the Way

Sample Effect—Brightness/Contrast

When you use an effect in iMovie, you choose a clip, such as the one in Figure 26.16, and decide you want to do something to it. In this case, it's a video clip in which the picture came out a bit dark.

But with a bit of tweaking, using the Brightness/Contrast controls, you can improve the clip so that you can see the subject better (see Figure 26.17).

FIGURE 26.16
A dark clip
before the
Brightness/
Contrast effect
is applied.

FIGURE 26.17
The clip after
the Brightness/
Contrast effect
is applied.

Watch Out!

Because effects are simple to add, it can be easy to overdo effects, making things so "affected" that they look worse than when you began. So, if you want to preserve the quality of the video, you have to keep things somewhat balanced by not going overboard and using the most extreme settings in each effect.

Working with Effects

When you try out effects, you can experiment without waiting for iMovie to process, or render, an effect, which can take several minutes. Then when you've made a decision, you can apply the effect and allow iMovie to render it, and you can continue to add other effects to that clip if you want.

If you want to experiment with effects, try creating a copy of your original clip to use for comparison. The copy can also come in handy if you need to restore an original, but have already emptied iMovie's trash.

In general, the options when working with effects are Preview, Apply, and Restore Clip.

Previewing

The Preview button enables you to see an effect on the main Monitor area in iMovie. It becomes active when you select an effect in the Effects pane.

When you first click on an effect in the Effects pane in iMovie, a mini-preview appears. It is helpful to get a general sense of what the effect does, but ultimately it's nicer to see how the effect looks at normal size, in the main iMovie Monitor area.

Applying

Applying an effect is simply the process of going beyond the preview stage and actually having iMovie change your video clip by employing the effect on the clip you have currently selected. At this point, iMovie processes (or *renders*) the effect, which may take several minutes. The status of the processing appears as a red bar at the bottom of the affected clip in the Timeline or Clip Viewer (see Figure 26.18).

FIGURE 26.18
If you're happy with the preview, you can click Apply to render the effect.

If you apply an effect to a clip that already has a transition, you see a message saying that the effect will invalidate an existing transition and requesting your permission to re-render it. If you don't click OK, the effect is not applied.

Restoring Clips

After you apply an effect, if you want to go back to how the clip originally was, choose Advanced, Revert Clip to Original from the menu.

You can restore a clip back to only the state in which it was immediately after you last emptied iMovie's trash.

Enhance a Clip with Brightness/Contrast

This example takes a video clip that came out dark and uses the Brightness/Contrast effect to tweak the video so that you can see the people in the video better.

1. Open an iMovie project, and if you haven't already done so, add a clip.

2. Select the clip and open the Effects pane.

3. Select the Brightness/Contrast effect as shown in Figure 26.16.

4. Start increasing the contrast by clicking the blue slider button, holding down the mouse button, and dragging a small bit to the right to bring out the brighter colors and distinguish the darker colors from them.

5. Click the Brightness slider button and slowly drag it to the right, keeping an eye on the video clip.

   At any time, you can click the Preview button in the Effects pane to see how things look in iMovie's Monitor area, or watch the mini-preview window as you adjust the settings.

6. When you like how the previews look, click Apply, and iMovie begins to process the video.

When iMovie is done processing your clip, you can play the movie to see how the effect looks.

By the Way

> Sometimes, after you apply an effect and iMovie begins to render it, you change your mind. What do you do to stop iMovie from rendering the rest of the clip? If you press the Command key and the period on your keyboard at the same time while iMovie is rendering any element, that process is cancelled, and the clip remains as it was before you started.

Enhance a Clip with Rain

Some effects, such as Brightness & Contrast, affect a clip's coloration. Others, such as Rain, Fog, and Glass Distortion, are more like special effects layered on top of a clip.

To apply the Rain effect:

1. Open an iMovie project, and if you haven't already done so, add a clip.

2. Select the clip and open the Effects pane.

3. Select the Rain effect as shown in Figure 26.19.

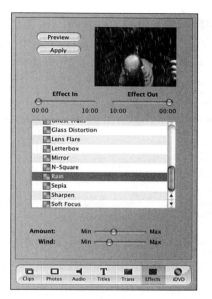

FIGURE 26.19
Customize the
appearance of
the Rain effect.

4. Adjust the settings near the bottom of the window for Amount and Wind.

5. When you like how the previews look, click Apply, and iMovie begins to process the video.

Some effects can be used together, such as Fog and Black & White, but others interfere with each other, such as Sepia and Black & White. Experiment to see which ones can be layered.

Did you Know?

Making Changes to Effects

After you've tried effects by simply applying them to successive clips, you'll probably discover that you want to make things more interesting or customized.

You can drag and drop transitions, but the drag-and-drop feature doesn't work with effects.

By the Way

Because you've already applied an effect to a clip, you need to reapply the changed effect. To do this, select the clip for which you want to change the effect, choose the new effect you want, change its settings, and then click Apply. A sheet window appears in some cases to let you know that the new effect invalidates the previous one. You must choose OK for your new effect to be processed.

Change and Update an Effect

The following example picks up where the last one left off. This example uses the Effect In and Effect Out features in the Effects pane to slowly increase the impression that the effect has on the clip over the space of a few seconds. It brings in the effect to give the clip a unique feel and then fades it out.

1. Select a clip in your project that has an effect applied to it.

2. Click the blue slider in the Effect In area of the Effects pane, and drag it a bit to the right to choose the length of time that it takes for the effect to develop to full strength.

3. Now click the Effect Out slider and drag it to the left to choose how long it takes for the video to return to normal.

4. Click the Apply button to reapply the effect with these new settings.

When you click the Apply button, iMovie starts to process the video. In a short while, you can preview to see the final version. Of course, if the effect doesn't measure up to your expectations, you can repeat steps 1–4, trying out different adjustments until you're happy with the effect.

Summary

In this chapter, you found out how you can bring your iMovies one step closer to their Hollywood (or living room) debut by learning about titles, transitions, and effects. You learned how easy it is to make and adjust titles in iMovie. You also learned how iMovie enables you to add professional-looking transitions to a project, which can help digital video to look and feel more like a real movie. Finally, you saw how, in certain situations, an effect such as Brightness/Contrast can actually help you see your video better if it was shot in a setting where there wasn't much light.

CHAPTER 27

Working with Still Photos and Sound in iMovie

If you've added view clips to your project from your camera or from other sources, they've almost certainly had sound accompanying them. What if you decide that you don't like the sound that goes along with your movie clip? Do you have to reshoot the video just for a new audio track? No, not at all. iMovie HD enables you to use dozens of canned sound effects, record audio from your computer's microphone (if available), use music from your iTunes library, or even take the sound from other video clips and use them with different video sequences.

Photos and iMovie HD

iMovie HD is known for the ease with which it allows you to import and manipulate digital video with special effects and transitions. IMovie HD also integrates completely with iPhoto, providing instant access to your photograph library.

Photographs can be worked with much like video clips. You can apply the same effects and transitions, as well as use a special effect designed specifically for digital photographs—an effect dubbed the "Ken Burns Effect." This effect, which is discussed later in this chapter, can add motion and depth to otherwise still images. Figure 27.1 shows a still image within the Timeline—it appears identical to a video clip.

iMovie HD supports a number of native image formats through QuickTime's media framework. TIFFs, JPEGS, and even PDF files can be dragged into an iMovie project as a source of still images.

FIGURE 27.1
Still images work virtually identically to video clips within iMovie.

Adding Photos to iMovie

There are two ways to add photos to iMovie HD, either from files on your desktop, or via iPhoto integration. Because iPhoto is the preferred method, we'll start there.

The best and cleanest way to handle importing images into iMovie HD is to first import them into iPhoto. iMovie automatically connects to your Photo Library and provides access to all your digital images the same way it does with digital music and iTunes. The basics of working with iPhoto are explained in Chapter 22, "Using iPhoto."

By the Way

> You should start iPhoto at least once before using iMovie; otherwise, the iPhoto/iMovie integration will not be complete, and iMovie may behave strangely when you attempt to access photo features.

iPhoto Integration

To add a photograph that you've previously stored within your Photo Library, click the Photos button in the icon bar in the lower-right portion of the iMovie window. The Photo pane appears, as shown in Figure 27.2.

At the top of the pane are the controls for the Ken Burns effect, followed by the library of available iPhoto images. The pop-up menu at the top of the image catalog can be used to limit the images being displayed to any of the iPhoto albums.

FIGURE 27.2
The Photo pane provides direct access to iPhoto images.

> If you're asking yourself who Ken Burns is and why there is an effect in his honor, you'll find out in just a moment.

By the Way

To add a photo to your project, choose the album or category that contains the image you want to use and then scroll through the image catalog to find the exact picture you want to add. (If you want only a still shot of the image, uncheck the box for Ken Burns Effect.) Drag the image to the Timeline or Clip Viewer at the bottom of the iMovie window.

When you add a still image, iMovie behaves exactly as if you were adding a video clip with a specific duration. (You can change the duration of a still image by dragging the slider in the Photos pane that is labeled with a rabbit (for quicker) and a turtle (for longer-lasting). Figure 27.3 shows a collection of three images that have been added to the Clip Viewer in iMovie.

Adding Photos Directly

You can easily add photos directly to iMovie by dragging the image files from your desktop into the Clips pane, the Clip Viewer, or the Timeline Viewer. In all these cases, iMovie adds the image, just as if it were a video clip.

FIGURE 27.3
Just think of
still images as
video clips with-
out much video.

The Ken Burns Effect

The Ken Burns effect is a method of bringing life to still images that was pioneered by the filmmaker Ken Burns, who has created many award-winning documentaries, and whose work has been nominated for an Academy Award.

For a complete background on Ken Burns and his work, visit
http://www.pbs.org/kenburns/.

The effect is really simple. Instead of just putting a photograph onscreen while someone narrates, a virtual "camera" pans over the image, zooming in or out as it goes. A photograph of a bouquet of flowers, for example, could start zoomed in on one particular flower and then zoom out, centering the bouquet on the screen as it goes. When the effect is used properly, the end result can make the viewer forget that he is not watching live video.

To use the Ken Burns effect in iMovie, first make sure that you are in the Photos pane. Then select the image to which you want to apply the effect. At the top of the Photos pane are the controls that you use to determine the path that the virtual camera is to take, how far in or out the virtual camera is zoomed, and how long the resulting video clip will be.

For example, I've chosen a picture of a flower to which I want to apply the effect. I've decided that I want to start out zoomed in on one of the petals and then zoom out to show the entire flower. To do this, I drag the slider to the Start position and then click and drag the image within the image well at the top of the Photo pane. This enables me to center where the camera starts when the effect is applied. Next, I adjust the zoom level, either using the slider control or by directly typing in the Zoom field. Figure 27.4 shows the start settings of my Ken Burns effect.

To complete the effect, I need to repeat the same process for the End point of the effect. This time, I move the slider to the Finish position, click and drag the image so that it appears as I want it in the image well, and then adjust the zoom so that I can see the entire flower, as shown in Figure 27.5.

FIGURE 27.4
Choose the start point and zoom for the image.

To preview the Ken Burns effect before you actually apply it to an image, click the Preview button. To reverse the path that the virtual camera takes (effectively switching the Start and End settings), click the Reverse button. If you want the total time the transition takes to last longer (or shorter) than 5 seconds, adjust the duration slider, or type directly into the Duration time field. Finally, to add the image with the Ken Burns effect to the Timeline or Clip View, click the Apply button. The effect may take several minutes to apply (watch the progress bar that appears over the image in the Clip Viewer or Timeline).

The settings you choose when adding the Ken Burns effect to a photograph are used as the default for subsequent images you add. Because iMovie attempts to apply the Ken Burns effect to everything, make sure that what it's doing is really what you want.

By the Way

FIGURE 27.5
Set the end
point and zoom
level to com-
plete the effect.

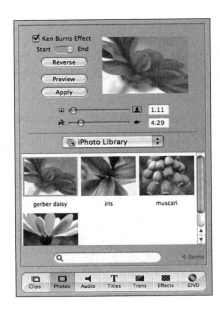

Still Images from Video

One final source for still images is a video clip itself. iMovie makes it easy to create a
still image from any frame in a video file. To do this, switch to the Timeline Viewer
and drag the playhead until the image that you want to use as a still appears within
the main viewer. Next, choose Edit, Create Still Frame from the menu. iMovie adds a
still image with a 5-second duration to the available iMovie clips.

By the Way

> Surprisingly, when you create a still image from a video clip, iMovie does not
> attempt to apply the Ken Burns effect!

Still Images and Duration

A point of confusion when working with still images is the duration, and how duration can be changed. A still image that does not have the Ken Burns effect applied
is, by default, treated as a 5-second video clip. To change the length of time that it is
displayed onscreen, simply double-click it within the Timeline or Clip Viewer. The
Clip Info window, as shown in Figure 27.6, appears, where you can manually enter
how long the clip should last.

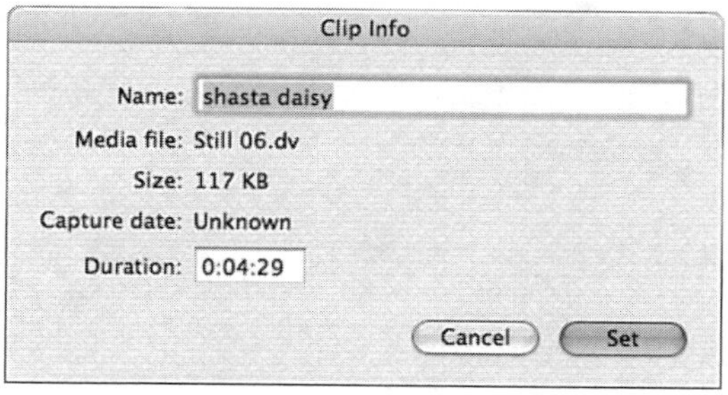

FIGURE 27.6
Change how
long a still
image is
displayed.

The same, however, cannot be said for an image that has had the Ken Burns effect applied. Double-clicking a Ken Burns image shows a noneditable duration.

The reason for this difference is an image that has had the Ken Burns effect applied to it is effectively a piece of video. It has different frames that iMovie calculated based on the settings you gave it. A "real" still image is just a single frame that iMovie understands should display for a set time.

To change the duration of a Ken Burns effect image, select the image within the Timeline or Clip Viewer; then click the Photos button to switch to the Photos pane. The selected image is shown in the Ken Burns preview, and the settings used to create the image are loaded. Adjust the duration using the duration slider; then click the Apply button to re-render the effect with the new duration.

Still Images, Effects, and Transitions

iMovie makes it simple to apply effects and transitions to images that you've added to your project. In fact, there is virtually no difference between working with still or Ken Burns effect image clips and video clips. There are two specific situations, however, when things don't work as you'd expect:

- ▶ Clip Duration—Sometimes the length of a still image clip isn't long enough for the speed you've set for a given transition (a wipe, fade, and so on) to be applied. In this case, iMovie tells you to adjust the speed of the transition, as shown in Figure 27.7. Alternatively you could adjust the duration of your still image (as discussed previously).

- ▶ Convert Still Clip to Regular Clips—Sometimes, when you apply an effect that changes over time—such as "Ghost Trails," which makes each frame shift slightly to create a "blurring" appearance—iMovie will apply and render the effect, but nothing seems to change in your movie. Nothing appears to happen because nothing is moving in the frame.

FIGURE 27.7
Some shorter
clips require
faster transi-
tions speeds.

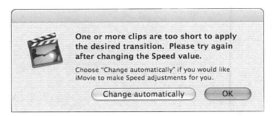

One or more clips are too short to apply the desired transition. Please try again after changing the Speed value.

Choose "Change automatically" if you would like iMovie to make Speed adjustments for you.

Change automatically   OK

Sound in iMovie HD

In an iMovie project, sound often plays almost as important a part as video. Sound and music can set the stage for a romance, suspense, comedy, or thrills. It can help create pacing for the movie and smooth through otherwise troublesome video transitions. If you've been using iMovie HD to import and edit movies from your camera, you already have audio in your projects. Movie clips themselves can contain embedded sounds, and these are usually transferred and saved along with the movie files. Although this is convenient if you only want to use the sounds you've recorded with your camera, it doesn't give you the flexibility to mix sounds or add additional sounds to your movie.

Audio Tracks

To accommodate additional sound effects, iMovie includes two sound tracks that can hold any sound, music, or audio that you want. Figure 27.8 shows the three available iMovie tracks: Video/Audio, Audio Track 1, and Audio Track 2.

There is no difference in functionality between the audio 1 and 2 tracks. You can use one track to hold sound effects, the other for background music, or mix and match them as you choose. In addition, each track can overlap audio clips, allowing you almost limitless layers of audio. You could, for example, have a base piece of background music in Audio Track 1; then perhaps an environment sound track layered on top of it, and, finally, sound effects layered on top of that in Audio Track 2.

By the Way

You've probably figured this out, but you must be in the Timeline Viewer rather than the Clip Viewer to see the available audio tracks.

You can move sounds added to either of the audio tracks to the other track by clicking and dragging between the tracks in the Timeline. No matter what type of sound you're adding, it is referred to within iMovie as an *audio clip*.

FIGURE 27.8
Audio can be part of a video track, or can be added to either of the two audio tracks.

Audio Playback

However you've decided to layer your audio, iMovie automatically composites it correctly when you play back your movie project. If you've included audio clips in all the tracks, they'll automatically all play back when you play the movie.

Sometimes this can get to be a bit of a pain as you try to fine-tune your special effect sounds and don't want to hear the dialog from your video tracks, or the background music you've added. To enable you to focus on a single set of audio, Apple has provided the ability to control audio playback by using the three check boxes to the right of the video and audio tracks, shown previously in Figure 27.8.

You can also control the movie's overall volume by using the volume control slider to the right of the main playback controls.

Working with Audio

There are a number of different ways to add audio to a project, so we start with one of the most common (and useful). Then we discuss how to work with audio clips that have been added to a Timeline, and, finally, examine other means of importing audio.

Accessing the iTunes Music Library

Adding audio to an iMovie project takes place through the Audio pane, accessed by clicking the Audio button in the icon bar above the Timeline Viewer on the right side of the iMovie window. Figure 27.9 shows the iMovie window with the Audio pane active.

FIGURE 27.9
Access Audio import features in the Audio pane.

Your iTunes library is the default source for audio that is added to the project. You can use the pull-down menu at the top of the iTunes listing to choose between your iTunes playlists, or type a few characters into the search field at the bottom of the song list to filter the songs that are shown.

Did you Know?

> When using the search field to find your iTunes music, you'll notice that an "X" appears at the end of the field after you've typed in a few characters. Clicking the "X" clears out the search results and returns you to the full list.

If you want to preview a song, you can choose it from the list and then click the Play button underneath the list to listen to the song.

Watch Out!

> You must remember that using copyrighted material is against the law. Be sure that any songs you're using on a movie are public domain or properly licensed. If you're making the movie just for yourself, you can use music you own, but if the final product will be widely distributed, you cannot include copyrighted material.

Adding iTunes Audio to the Project

After you've located the song file that you want to add to the iMovie project, position the playhead where you want the sound to be inserted, click within the audio track that should receive the sound file, and then click the Place at Playhead button in the Audio pane. iMovie takes a few seconds (or minutes, depending on the length of the file), and then the corresponding audio clip appears in the selected audio track as a colored bar labeled with the name of the audio file, as shown previously in Figure 27.8.

There is no obvious means of telling which audio track is currently selected. The last track you clicked is the one used for inserting audio.

If you happen to end up with audio inserted in the wrong track, simply click and drag the audio from one track to another.

Another, perhaps more elegant, way to add audio clips to the project is to drag a name from the list in the Audio pane to the audio track where it should be inserted. As you drag the item into the Timeline, the playhead moves to show you where the audio will be inserted when you stop dragging.

You can even extend this technique to the Finder by dragging audio files directly from your desktop into the Timeline.

Manipulating Audio Within the iMovie

After a piece of audio has been added to an audio track, it can easily be manipulated to match up with your video tracks, or the volume can be changed to better mix with the video or other audio files.

Repositioning Audio

Sometimes you place a sound in a movie, and it "just doesn't fit," or doesn't sync up with the video. To move an audio clip, click and drag it horizontally within the Timeline. The audio segment moves to any position you want within the project. While you are dragging, the playhead automatically tracks the start position of the audio, enabling you to position it perfectly within the project, as shown in Figure 27.10

If you decide that you want to remove an audio clip from the project, simply click on it, then press Delete or choose Edit, Clear from the menu.

Using Timeline Snapping

To help you precisely align sound effects with the start and end of a video clip, iMovie includes a feature called *Timeline snapping*. When activated, Timeline snapping produces a snapping sound as you align the beginning or end of an audio or video clip with the beginning or end of another clip. It also displays a yellow bar to mark those alignment points, as shown in Figure 27.11.

To use Timeline snapping, hold down the Shift key as you drag a selected video or audio clip. When you hear the snap or see the yellow bar indicating perfect alignment, you can stop dragging.

FIGURE 27.10
Drag the audio
clip to reposi-
tion it.

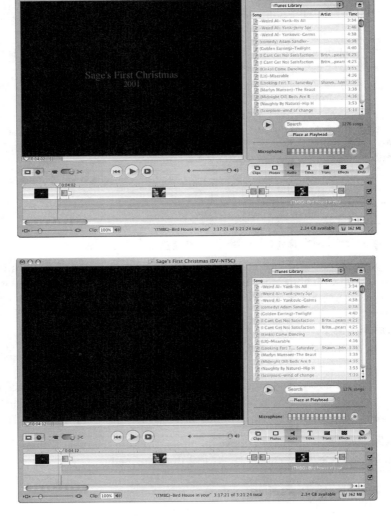

FIGURE 27.11
Timeline snap-
ping give you
visual (and
audio) cues to
help you align
video and audio
clips.

You can enable Timeline snapping in the iMovie preferences so it is on by default. That way, you don't even need to hold down the Shift key. (If you enable it, holding down the Shift key temporarily turns it off.) You can also choose to silence the snapping sound and leave only the visual cue that clips are all lined up.

Showing Audio Track Waveforms

In addition to Timeline snapping, you can use audio track waveforms to line up audio clips and video. *Waveforms* are representations of the volume of sounds in an audio track. Loud sounds have longer "waves" and silence appears as a blank space. An example appears in Figure 27.12.

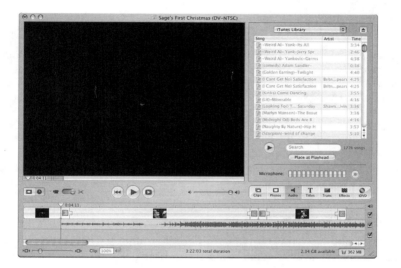

FIGURE 27.12
Audio track waveforms help you see the sound in an audio clip.

To display waveforms, choose View, Show Audio Waveforms from the menu. Audio tracks and video tracks with sound will have their waveforms overlaid on them so you can position sound based on high points and silences.

Locking Audio to a Video Clip

Often the act of moving audio around is an attempt to synchronize it with a piece of video. iMovie's capability to position on a frame-by-frame basis makes this simple, but what if you decide later that you want to reposition the video clip? If you drag the video, all your hard work synchronizing the audio will be lost.

To "lock" a piece of audio to the video track, select the audio that you've positioned where you want it; then choose Advanced, Lock Audio Clip at Playhead from the menu. The audio track is then "attached" to the video that occurs at the same place as the audio. Moving the video track within the Timeline moves the audio as well, keeping your synchronization intact. You can tell a lock is in place by graphical "pushpins" that appear on the audio and video tracks, as shown in Figure 27.13.

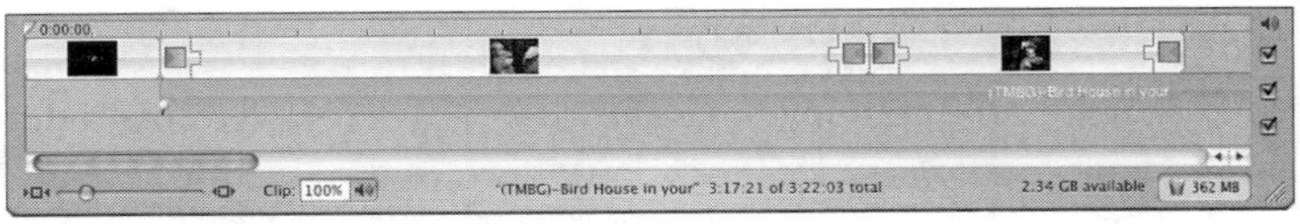

FIGURE 27.13
Pushpins
denote an audio
track that is
locked to a
video track.

To unlock an audio clip, select it within the audio track; then choose Advanced, Unlock Audio Clip from the menu.

Watch Out!

> Locking audio to a video clip works one way. It does not lock the video to audio. If you drag the video clip, the audio moves with it, but not vice versa. Dragging the audio only repositions the lock to the video, potentially losing any synchronizing work you've done.

By default, all locked audio clips are displayed with the pushpins all the time. To change the display so that the pushpins are shown only when the audio clip is selected, be sure to check the Only Show Audio Locking When Selected option within the iMovie preferences.

Using Crop Markers

Like video, audio clips can be cropped to affect how much or how little of a clip is played. Simply position your cursor over the start or end point of an audio clip until the cursor changes to show a vertical bar with an arrow pointing toward the center of the clip. Then drag toward the center until the clip ends where you want it to stop. The cropped edge loses its rounded corners, as shown in Figure 27.14.

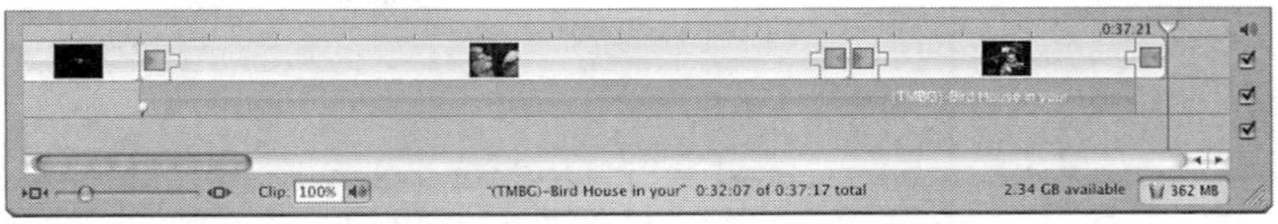

FIGURE 27.14
A trimmed clip
has a straight
edge to show
where it has
been shortened.

If you change your mind before you empty iMovie's trash, you can position your cursor over the trimmed end until a double-sided arrow appears, and drag the clip back to its full length.

Adjusting Volume

To change a clip's overall volume level, highlight the clip within any of the tracks (remember, even the video track's audio can be adjusted here); then click and drag the volume adjustment at the bottom of the iTunes window, or type a new volume level (100% being the "default" volume) into the field beside the volume slider. Multiple clips can even be selected at once (Shift-click) and adjusted simultaneously with this control.

But suppose that you want soft background music in one portion of your movie, but want it to slowly build to a blaring orchestra in another? In iMovie, adjusting the volume curve is as simple as clicking and dragging.

To alter the volume level within a specific part of an audio or video clip, choose View, Show Clip Volume Level from the menu. Within a few seconds, all the audio clips (and the video clips that contain audio) display lines through them. These lines represent the volume level of the clips.

To change the volume curve, click and drag the volume line within the clip. As you drag, an adjustment *handle* (a big yellow dot) appears. Dragging this dot up or down raises or lowers the volume at that point. To carry the volume change through to a different part of the clip, click wherever you want another volume adjustment handle to be added, and the level changes are carried through to that point.

Each handle that is added also carries with it a transition point that determines how the audio clip transitions to the new volume level (will it happen abruptly? smoothly?). The transition point is displayed as a small magenta square to the right of the adjustment handle. The point can be dragged so that it is right above or below an adjustment handle, making for an immediate transition in volume, as shown in Figure 27.15.

FIGURE 27.15
Moving the transition point directly above or below the adjustment handle causes an immediate volume transition.

To smooth things out a bit, the transition point can be dragged all the way along the volume line up to another adjustment point. The transition then occurs all the way between these two points. For example, Figure 27.16 shows the same volume adjustment being made as in Figure 27.15, but the transition takes place over a much larger span of the audio clip.

> If you are having difficulties setting a smooth volume transition, it may help to zoom in on the Timeline Viewer using the zoom slider at the bottom left of the iMovie window.

By the Way

Volume adjustment can be used to ramp down an audio clip while ramping up another (similar to video transitions that blend the end of one clip with the beginning of another; this is called a cross-fade), or to create any number of other effects within your project.

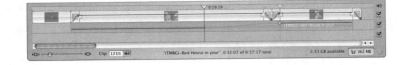

FIGURE 27.16
The transition point can be used to spread the volume transition out over a long span of the audio clip.

Splitting Audio

If you want to play part of a sound or song at one time, and another part at another time, you have two choices: You can import the audio clip twice, or you can simply "split" the existing clip into different pieces and use each part wherever you want. To split an audio clip, position the playhead where you want the clip to break; then choose Edit, Split Selected Audio Clip at Playhead from the menu.

Lines appear at the location of the split within the selected audio clip to show the clip split into two pieces, as shown in Figure 27.17.

FIGURE 27.17
Using the split feature creates two audio clips separated at the location of the playhead.

After you split a clip, click outside the pieces of the split clip to deselect the two pieces, and then click on the one you want to reposition; otherwise, both pieces are selected and you can't move them separately.

Other iMovie Audio Sources

Now that you've learned how to work with audio clips in iMovie, let's take a quick look at the other sources of audio available for adding audio clips to your project. At the top of the Audio pane is a pop-up menu with additional choices for importing audio clips. As you've already seen, the iTunes Library and playlists are available.

iMovie Sound Effects

A great source for canned sound effects is the included iMovie sound effects library, accessed by choosing iMovie Sound Effects from the top of the Audio pane. The iMovie sound effects, shown in Figure 27.18, encompass a wide range of environmental and special effect sounds. The "Skywalker Sound Effects" (named for filmmaker George Lucas's Skywalker Ranch) are extremely high-quality effects that can be used to create an impressive sound track.

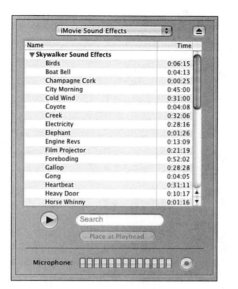

FIGURE 27.18
Choose from
dozens of built-
in sound
effects.

You can add sound effects using the same methods described earlier for songs from
your iTunes library.

Audio CDs

To add a sound track from an audio CD, put the CD in your computer's CD-ROM
drive and then wait a few seconds. iMovie automatically switches to Audio CD
mode, queries the Internet CD database to get a list of track names, and then displays the contents of the CD in the Audio pane.

Choose the song you want to add to one of your iMovie audio tracks; then either use
the Place at Playhead button or drag the song to the Timeline to add it to the project.

Recording a Voice Track

If you want to narrate a portion of the video, position the playhead where you want
to start recording from your computer's microphone; then click in the audio track
that should receive the audio. Finally click the red Record button to the right of the
Microphone label at the bottom of the Audio pane. A graph of the level of sound
input is shown beside the label as it records. To stop recording live audio, click the
Record button again.

The new audio clips are added to your project with the sequential labels "Voice
01," "Voice 02," and so on.

Extracting Audio from Video Clips

As we've already mentioned, the video track often also contains audio that accompanies a video clip. When adjusting volume, you can adjust the volume of a video clip just as you would an audio clip in an audio track.

Having video so closely tied to audio, however, has a disadvantage: You cannot manipulate the audio and video independently of one another. Thankfully, iMovie allows you to "decouple" the audio and video from one another. To do this, select a video clip with audio; then choose Advanced, Extract Audio from the menu. After a few seconds, the audio from the video clip appears in the audio track below the video clip.

After audio is extracted from a video file, it can be manipulated like any other audio clip.

By the Way

> There is another reason you may want to extract audio from your video. Some iMovie users find that video gets out of sync with its audio track on projects longer than 20 minutes, especially when their clips were recorded as 12-bit instead of 16-bit audio. (Check your video camera documentation to see if you can avoid the problem altogether by setting your camera for 16-bit audio.) One fix for this problem if you've already got the footage imported is to extract the audio before sharing your project.

In some cases, audio extraction happens automatically. If, for example, you cut and paste a video clip using the Paste Over at Playhead option of the Advanced menu, iMovie automatically extracts the audio of the original clip and moves it to an audio track so that it is not replaced by the paste-over. The video clip that is pasted over is lost, but the audio remains.

You can disable this feature by deselecting Extract Audio when using "Paste Over at Playhead" from the iMovie preferences.

Summary

In this chapter you learned how to use photographs and audio in iMovie. You learned how still images can be added to iMovie projects and how they can be made "dynamic" through the use of the Ken Burns effect. In iMovie, a still image behaves almost exactly like a standard video clip and can have all the same transitions and effects applied. Although simple to use, iMovie's audio features enables novice editors to create layered audio tracks with ease. You learned how to work with a variety of audio sources available for adding sound to your video project.

CHAPTER 28

Exporting iMovies

In this chapter, you take a look at what you can do with your movies after you complete them: You can prepare them for email, web, and disc delivery. When your iMovie is edited and ready to share, you can deliver it in two basic ways: by tape (using a video camera) or by file (which can be delivered by email, the Web, or disc such as CD or DVD).

Choosing a Way to Share Your iMovie

When you're ready to export your iMovie, simply choose File, Share from iMovie's menu bar. Then, choose one of six options in the sheet that appears (see Figure 28.1): Email, HomePage, Videocamera, iDVD, QuickTime, or Bluetooth.

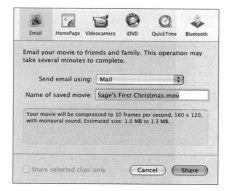

FIGURE 28.1
Choosing File, Share opens a window in which you can choose how you want to share your movie.

▶ Email—If you want to email a short movie, the Email option saves your movie as a QuickTime movie at an emailable size and, when complete, opens a new email message containing the movie attachment.

> If you want to send only select clips, and not an entire movie, select them before choosing Share from the File menu. The check box for Share Selected Clips Only is available for you to mark.

By the Way

▶ HomePage—People with .Mac memberships can use the HomePage option to export a movie directly to their .Mac HomePage. The file is compressed for the Web and stored as a streaming QuickTime, which means the full movie won't have to download before playback begins.

▶ Videocamera—When you choose Videocamera, you need to connect a video camera to your computer, as you did when you imported a video clip, and send the finished iMovie back out to Mini-DV or Digital-8 tape. From there, you can watch the finished product by connecting the camera to the television, recording from the camera to a VHS tape in your VCR, or sending the tape off to have several copies duplicated.

▶ iDVD—When you choose to share to iDVD, the option is basically a preset that generates a high-quality video file that iDVD then converts for use on a DVD disc. It takes up the largest amount of hard-drive space of any of the export options.

In addition to exporting to iDVD from the export dialog box, iMovie's iDVD pane lets you add "chapters" to your movie, which are then displayed in your iDVD project. We talk about how later in this chapter, in the section "Exporting iMovies to iDVD."

▶ QuickTime—QuickTime is a video format developed by Apple that compresses audio or video files so they are as small as possible while still retaining a reasonable quality. When you export to QuickTime, you have a wide range of options, based on the intended use of your movies. The one you choose results in a particular kind of file or amount of compression. For example, when you export an iMovie that you want to email to someone, it creates a relatively small file because it must travel over the Internet, and you don't want the person on the other end to have to wait too long to download the attachment. When you want to burn a CD with iMovie, the CD can hold a much larger file than an email could handle, so the movie quality is much better; however, it's still not as good as the original iMovie. The section "Sharing via QuickTime" takes a closer look at some of the QuickTime options.

Did you Know?

You can export a movie for email either under the Email section or the QuickTime section. If you want to send it right away, exporting from the Email section creates a new message and attaches your movie; if you want to prepare a movie but may not send it right now, exporting for email from the QuickTime section lets you save the movie wherever you want.

▶ Bluetooth—Bluetooth is a technology that enables various devices to exchange information without connection cables if they are in range of each other. If you have a Bluetooth-enabled device, such as another computer or a handheld device, you can export your movie in this way.

Emailing iMovies

When you want to email an iMovie, you use your email program to attach the iMovie file to a new message. If you've never emailed an attachment before, keep in mind that uploading the attachment can take a few minutes, depending on whether you're using a 56K modem or a higher-speed DSL or cable modem connection.

Also keep in mind that it will probably help you to choose a special name for the email version of your iMovie, such as `my movie-email`.

Export to Email

To send an iMovie via email:

1. Choose File, Share, and then choose the Email option from the row of icons along the top of the sheet that appears.

2. Choose the email program you use and give your movie a name, if different than the name of your iMovie project.

3. Click Share. iMovie shows the status of your movie as it compresses, as shown in Figure 28.2.

FIGURE 28.2
iMovie provides an estimate of time remaining for file compression.

4. iMovie creates a new message, using the program that you chose to send email.

5. Compose a message and click the appropriate button to send your message.

By the Way

Some email providers have file size limitations, and others put quotas on the mailboxes of their account holders. If you want to share a long movie, you should consider writing it to CD or DVD and sending it by mail—or look into sharing over the Web.

Sharing Movies over .Mac

If you have a .Mac account and have your .Mac membership information set up in the .Mac pane of the System Preferences, you can share your movies online easily.

Simply choose File, Share from the menu and click the HomePage option. After a few minutes of compression, iMovie uploads your movie to your .Mac account and opens your default web browser, where you can customize the page containing the movie, as shown in Figure 28.3.

FIGURE 28.3
In the web interface for your .Mac account, you can choose a location in your .Mac account and a page theme for displaying your movie.

For more details about setting up a .Mac membership, refer to Chapter 16, "Exploring .Mac Membership."

Making Videotapes from iMovie

To view an iMovie on television from a tape, the first step is to export the movie to your video camera. Then you can either connect your video camera to your television or make a VHS tape from your digital tape (Mini-DV or Digital-8).

> When you're going back out to tape, some of the main considerations are how much time you have left on the tape and how long your iMovie is. You'll generally want to put your iMovie at the beginning of the videotape so it's easy to get to.

By the Way

Export to Camera

When you've finished your iMovie and are ready to take it to the next level, exporting to a video camera enables you to display it on the television. With a few simple steps, you can make the video ready to share in a one-time event, where you play the video only from the camera. Or, after you have exported the video from iMovie to your video camera, you can then go on to make a tape from there.

1. Load a blank tape into your video camera and turn it on. (Be sure you aren't about to record over something you want. Remember to label those tapes!)

2. Connect your digital video camera to your computer with a FireWire cable.

3. In iMovie, choose File, Share Movie, and choose Videocamera (see Figure 28.4).

4. If you haven't set up your camera, choose how many seconds of black to show before and after your movie on the tape.

5. Click Share. iMovie waits until your camera is set to VTR mode before transferring the movie.

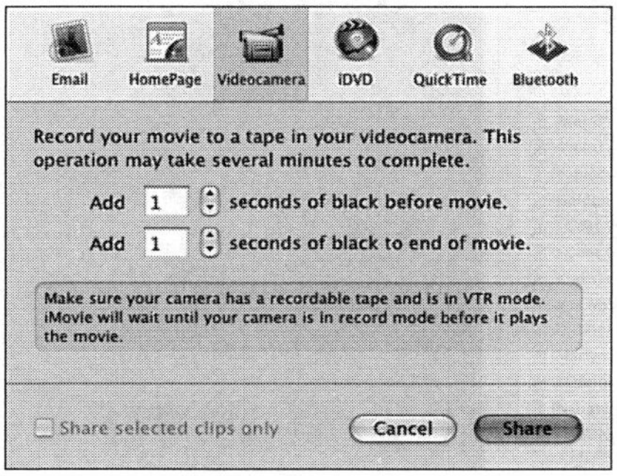

FIGURE 28.4
When exporting to video camera, you add several seconds of black to the beginning and end of your movie.

If you want to make VHS copies of the digital tape that you just made, you can connect your video camera to your VCR using standard RCA cabling, where you connect a series of cables to the Video Out and Audio Out jacks of your camera. The video connector is usually indicated by a yellow color. Two cables carry the audio, where each cable carries half a stereo signal (the left audio channel is the white connector; the right audio channel is the red connector). (See Figure 28.5.) Then connect the cables to the Video In and Audio In jacks of your VCR (see Figure 28.6).

FIGURE 28.5
The Video/
Audio Out con-
nectors on a
typical video
camera.

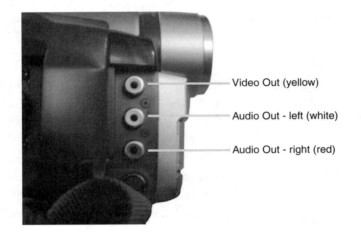

Video Out (yellow)

Audio Out - left (white)

Audio Out - right (red)

FIGURE 28.6
The Video/
Audio In connec-
tors on the back
of a typical VCR.

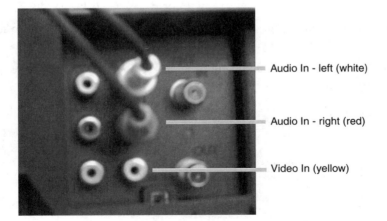

Audio In - left (white)

Audio In - right (red)

Video In (yellow)

Exporting iMovies to iDVD

Distributing your iMovies on DVD is the ultimate in digital video. You start by recording your footage digitally, editing it in iMovie, and retaining the digital quality by going directly to DVD. iMovie makes creating DVDs simple by linking up with iDVD.

Export to iDVD

There is an option for iDVD in the Share sheet, as shown in Figure 28.7. If you want to export your movie to iDVD as a whole, or export only selected clips, simply click the Share button.

Alternatively, you could open the iDVD pane on the right side of the iMovie interface and click the Create iDVD Project button. It takes a moment for your movie to open in iDVD, where you can customize the menus and add movies.

FIGURE 28.7
Exporting an iMovie for iDVD.

Add Chapters to Your Movie

Besides maintaining video quality, DVDs offer another benefit to your iMovies: chapters. Adding chapters enables you to segment your video project so that people viewing the completed DVD can skip straight to the part they want to see, just like on a commercial DVD.

Follow these steps to add chapters to an existing iMovie:

1. Open a finished iMovie project and be sure you are in Timeline view.

2. Click the iDVD button in the main iMovie window to display the iDVD pane.

3. In the Timeline Viewer, move the playhead to the point in your movie at which you want to start a new chapter.

4. In the iDVD pane, click the Add Chapter button.

5. A row for the newly created chapter appears in the iDVD pane, where you can type in a Chapter Title, as shown in Figure 28.8.

6. A small yellow diamond appears in the Timeline Viewer to mark the location of chapters, as shown in Figure 28.9.

7. You can repeat steps 4 through 6 until you've added up to 99 chapters to your iMovie.

8. When you are finished adding chapters, click the Create iDVD Project button to open your iMovie in iDVD, as shown in Figure 28.10, where you can choose themes to customize the menu that displays your chapters.

By default, iDVD saves your project in the Documents folder of your user account with the file extension .dvdproj. (We talk about customizing your presentation in iDVD in Chapters 29, "Exploring the iDVD Interface," and 30, "Creating DVDs in iDVD.")

FIGURE 28.8
Type a descriptive title for your chapter.

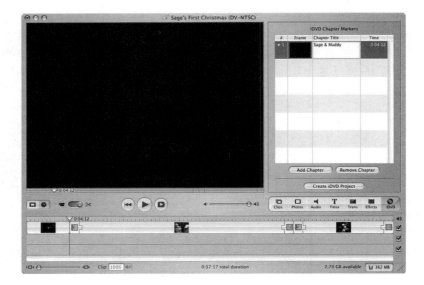

FIGURE 28.9
Chapter markers appear as yellow diamonds at the top of the Timeline.

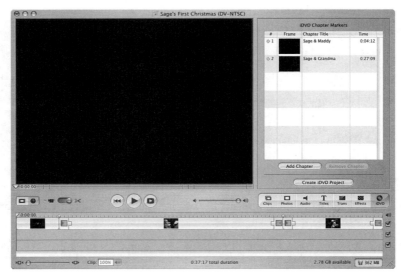

FIGURE 28.10
This is an iMovie with chapters after export to iDVD.

Sharing via QuickTime

Sharing options for Email and HomePage also save your project in QuickTime format, but the QuickTime sharing option gives you several additional preset options, including preparing your movie to share on the Web using web servers other than the .Mac server. You can also choose to export your full-sized movie or a compressed version to fit on a CD-ROM.

> While exporting your movie as a full-size QuickTime movie does preserve picture quality, there is a difference between that and exporting your movie for iDVD. In the previous section, you learned to add chapter markers to your movie for use with iDVD—those markers are not maintained in the QuickTime format.

Watch Out!

The difference between all these QuickTime options is the level of compression, which is directly related to the quality of the picture.

> If none of the QuickTime options are right for your needs, you can choose Expert Settings, which opens a window where you can choose other file formats, such as AVI (a common format for Microsoft Windows users) and AIFF (sound file only).

By the Way

Putting iMovies on the Web

Putting iMovies on the Web is a bit more involved than putting them on tape or sending them via email, but taking the time to figure out how to do it can make for an ideal way of sharing your iMovies with people who are far away.

There are two ways that iMovie can save your movie for delivery on the Web: as a web movie or as a streaming web movie. A web movie is uploaded to a standard web server, and a streaming web movie is uploaded to a streaming web server.

Here are some terms and concepts that are helpful to consider; entire books and series of books have been written about each item, but just taking a look at each can be helpful later when you start to put more things of your own up on the Internet.

- ▶ Server—A *server* is the name for the computer used as the central storage location for web pages. When you create a web page on your computer, you have to upload the files to a server. Then, when people view your web page, they are connecting to the server computer.

- ▶ Standard server (for web movies)—This is the most common type of server. When you put your movie on the server and a person requests the file through their web browser, it doesn't play until enough of the file is downloaded. A standard server is basically any server that doesn't have QuickTime streaming capability. If you're not sure what kind of server you have and you don't know that it's specifically capable of streaming QuickTime, chances are it's a standard server.

- ▶ Streaming server (for streaming web movies)—True streaming video is when you can watch a video without downloading the entire file. Streaming video enables you to watch video in *real-time*, meaning that you establish a connection with a streaming server and watch the video as if it were a miniature television show. True streaming video basically means that you have a smoother, higher-quality experience. Streaming video is usually more expensive and more complicated to set up, but many companies and individuals find that the effort and expense are worth it. In addition to QuickTime, other forms of streaming video that you might recognize include RealMedia and Windows Media. All forms of streaming video require some kind of player application, such as QuickTime, to be present on a person's computer.

By the Way

Keep in mind that even true streaming video is still dependent on how fast your connection is—video can be streamed on typical 56K modems, for example, and the streaming version is smoother than a non-streaming version, but the quality is not as good as you would have on a higher-speed connection such as cable or DSL.

Export a Web Movie for Use on a Standard Web Server

You'll probably want to use the Web Movie option to save your iMovies, unless you specifically know you'll be using the file on a QuickTime streaming server. The next section looks at the streaming server, as well as investigates an easy-to-use method of streaming video provided by PlayStream.

1. Choose File, Share; then choose QuickTime.

2. Choose the Web option in the Compress Movie For pop-up menu (see Figure 28.11).

3. Click Share and save your iMovie to a location on your hard drive from which you can then upload it to a web server.

4. Using an FTP application or a web page creation program such as Dreamweaver, upload your file to your website.

FIGURE 28.11
Exporting an iMovie as a web movie, for a standard web server.

5. Using a web page creation tool, make a link to your iMovie in a web page. Here's some sample HTML link code:

```
<a href=http://www.floraphotographs.com/flower.mov>View a flower montage
video.</a>
```

Figure 28.12 shows an iMovie playing in the QuickTime browser plugin. (Refer to Chapter 7, "Using QuickTime and DVD Player," for more information about viewing QuickTime movies in your web browser.)

Even though this isn't a streaming server, QuickTime has the capability to play as much of the movie as you've downloaded. If you have a fast connection, it can be almost as if it were a streaming clip. (Note, however, that the viewer might have to adjust the QuickTime preferences to play movies automatically to get this effect.)

FIGURE 28.12
The iMovie
plays when you
click on the link.

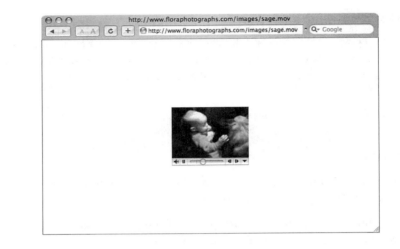

When you are sharing your iMovies with people on a website, you might want to include instructions for people visiting your web page to describe how they can actually download the file to their hard drive instead of watching it on the web page. Instruct Mac users to hold down the Ctrl key on their keyboard, click the movie link, and choose the Save Link As or Download Link to Disk option. Instruct Windows users to right-click the link and choose the Save Target As option to save the file to disk.

By the
Way

You might also want to instruct people that, to view your iMovie, they might need to download and install the latest version of QuickTime, which is a free download available from www.apple.com/quicktime/download.

Export an iMovie for a Streaming Server

Exporting your iMovie as a streaming web movie for use on a streaming server is similar to exporting your iMovie as a web movie for use on a standard server.

1. Choose File, Share; then choose QuickTime.

2. Choose the Web Streaming option in the Compress Movies For pop-up menu.

3. Click the Share button and save your file on your hard drive in a location you can find later to upload to the streaming server. You might want to name the file so that you can easily distinguish it later as a streaming file, something like my movie-streaming.mov.

4. Use your FTP program or web page creation and upload tool to upload the iMovie to the streaming server.

As mentioned earlier, setting up a QuickTime file for a streaming server can be more complex and might require some experimentation and research. At the minimum, you must set up a web account with a host company capable of QuickTime streaming.

You also might want to investigate a company such as PlayStream, whose mission is to make the process of streaming video as easy as possible. PlayStream has special accounts that exist only to host streaming video. So if you already have a web page, you can put your video on a PlayStream account and link to it from your current web page. PlayStream offers a free 15-day trial, and its accounts enable you to host the common formats of streaming video, including QuickTime video, Real Media, and Windows Media, so you can reach the maximum audience. Preparing your video for the different formats can require downloading or purchasing additional software, but it might be worth it because most people usually have the ability to view video encoded for either the Real Player or Windows Media Player.

For some people, it might actually be easier to try a service such as PlayStream and use full streaming video instead of getting web creation software. PlayStream enables you to simply use your browser to upload files, and you don't even need your own web page—when you upload files, you're given a link that you can email to people to get them directly to your video.

Upload a Streaming Web iMovie for PlayStream

If you want to try the PlayStream option, you can sign up for a free 15-day trial at www.playstream.com. It's a way of getting right into putting your iMovie on the Web without spending any money.

1. Go to www.playstream.com and log in; then click the Content link.

2. Click the Upload Files link to locate the streaming web movie file you saved earlier to your hard drive.

3. Click the Upload File button to upload the file to your space on PlayStream. A window pops up that gives you a progress indicator of the upload.

4. After the file is uploaded, select the text in the Stream Link field and copy the link into memory by choosing Edit, Copy from the menu at the top of the screen.

5. Paste the link text somewhere you can get it later, such as in an email to yourself or in a text document.

6. To allow access to the movie, insert the Stream Link text in an email, use it as a link on a web page, or just paste it right into your web browser.

Burning iMovies to CD

If you have a CD burner and want to share your iMovies via CD, you can simply save as a CD-ROM movie, which generates a QuickTime movie file small enough to burn to CD. Anyone on a Mac can see the movie without installing special software. Many Windows PCs have QuickTime software installed, but if it's not on your recipient's computer, the free download is available from www.apple.com/quicktime/download.

Export an iMovie for CD-ROM

To export an iMovie for CD-ROM, follow these steps:

1. Choose File, Share; then choose QuickTime.

2. Choose the CD-ROM option in the Compress Movie For pop-up menu.

3. Click Share and save your file in a location on your hard drive where you can find it later.

After you've exported your movie, you can burn it to disc as you would any other data CD, as described in the section "Burn Disc" in Chapter 2, "Using the Finder."

By the Way

> You can also use third-party CD-burning software (such as Roxio's Toast) to burn your CD to disc. The process can vary, but typically you drag your CD-ROM movie file into the program and choose the option to burn a data CD (as opposed to an audio/music CD). When using third-party software, be sure to read your documentation to find out if there are special settings to make a CD that is readable by both Macs and a PCs. (The discs you burn directly from the Mac OS X Finder will work on a PC, but third-party software gives you more control over CD format, which can sometimes have unintended consequences.)

Sharing with Bluetooth Devices

If you have a Bluetooth-enabled computer, you can export your movie to share with other Bluetooth devices in your vicinity. To do this, choose Share from the File menu and click the Bluetooth option. Then click the Share button. This saves a version of your file inside a Bluetooth folder, inside the project folder for your iMovie. The file can be shared with other Bluetooth devices via Bluetooth File Exchange.

Summary

In this chapter, you learned how to take your iMovies and share them in several different ways, including by email, videotape, and CD. You also learned how to add chapter markers for use with iDVD. Some methods, such as streaming web video, might require more effort than others, but learning how to put an iMovie on the Web can open up new audiences for your creative works. You literally gain the ability to go worldwide with your iMovies!

CHAPTER 29

Exploring the iDVD Interface

DVD video is a form of *digital* video, and much like the way digital video is stored on a computer hard drive, digital video is stored as data files on the DVD disc. It used to be that putting together a DVD project was complex, requiring the DVD author to perform many steps and have a significant amount of knowledge about the underlying technology. iDVD simplifies the process of DVD authoring—it's as easy as dragging and dropping files into the iDVD window, and iDVD handles encoding the files.

> Remember, you must have access to a DVD writer to burn your iDVD project to a disc. In addition to Apple's own SuperDrive, iDVD 5 also supports some external DVD writers. See www.apple.com/ilife/idvd for more information.

This chapter begins with a look at DVD basics by investigating the way that DVD video works. It then takes a look at iDVD, Apple's revolutionary, easy-to-use DVD-authoring software.

> Apple issued an important update for some SuperDrive-equipped computers. This update prevents permanent drive damage when some models of SuperDrive manufactured by Pioneer are used with newer high-speed media. To see whether you need to install this update, follow these steps:
>
> 1. Open the Apple System Profiler application, which can be found in the Utilities folder in the Applications folder.
> 2. Open the Devices and Volumes tab.
> 3. Expand the CD-RW/DVD-R item by clicking the disclosure triangle.
> 4. Examine the information given. If Pioneer is the vendor, you may need the update. To find out for sure, look at the Product Identification code. For drives with the Product Identification DVR-104, no update is required if the Device Revision number is A227 or higher. For drives with the Product Identification DVR-103, no update is required if the Device Revision number is 1.90 or higher.
>
> If your drive comes from Pioneer and doesn't have the upgrade in place, go to the Apple Web site (www.apple.com), search for "SuperDrive update," and then download and install it before attempting to write a DVD.

The iDVD Interface

The iDVD interface, shown in Figure 29.1, has two distinct parts: the viewing area and the Customize drawer. The viewing area is where you can see how your project looks at a given time, but it also acts as work space for arranging item menus and for creating slideshows of still images.

FIGURE 29.1
The iDVD inter-
face.

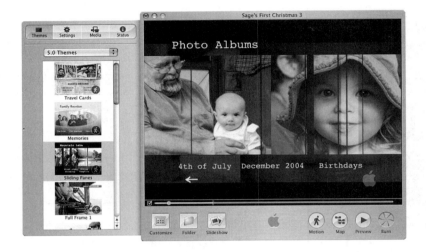

Below the viewing area are seven buttons: Customize, Folder, Slideshow, Motion, Map, Preview, and Burn. Let's examine what they do.

Customize Button

When you click the Customize button, the Customize tray opens along the left side of the iDVD window, as you saw earlier in Figure 29.1. The Customize tray consists of several different panes with controls for different tasks. Let's take a brief look at what you can do in each pane.

Themes Pane

The defining characteristic of a DVD is that it enables you to watch digital video inter-actively on your television. It's possible to make a DVD disc that goes directly to the video when you put it into a DVD player, but most DVDs have some kind of menu.

By the Way

A DVD *menu* is simply a screen that gives you several choices, with selectable buttons of some kind that lead directly to video or to other menus.

Apple has put together a number of customizable templates, called *themes*, which enable you to make professional-looking menus for your DVD projects. You can choose a theme from the list in the Themes pane of the Customize window, shown earlier in Figure 29.1.

> By default, the Apple logo is shown in the lower-right corner of all the themes. To remove it, open the iDVD preferences and uncheck the box for Show Apple Logo Watermark.

By the Way

Some available themes have video clips as backgrounds, and some also include sound. These themes enable you to include what's known as a *motion menu* on your DVD. You can even set your own motion backgrounds in some themes by dragging a movie or series of still photos into a customization area known as a *drop zone*.

Applying and customizing themes is discussed in the next chapter.

Settings Pane

After you've chosen a theme, you may want to go beyond the default colors chosen for text. To customize a theme, open the Settings pane to select colors and text (see Figure 29.2).

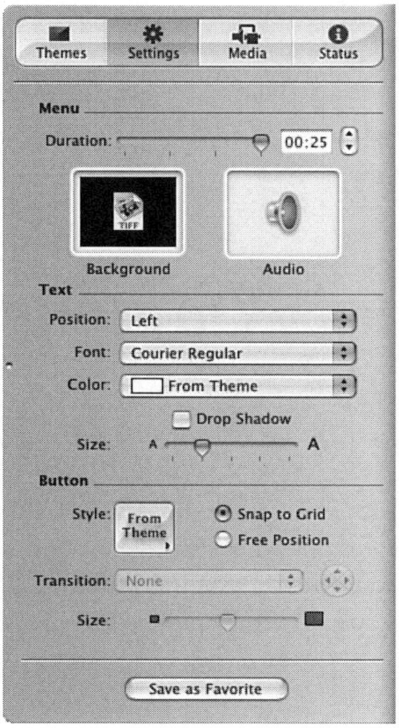

FIGURE 29.2
iDVD enables you to choose your own color and font for text.

Also in the Settings pane is the option to choose different styles of button shapes for your DVD screens. You can also change, or remove entirely, any background music for the menus.

When you choose to customize your DVD, and if you like what you've done, you can save the settings for later use in a Favorites list. A customized theme can be saved so that you can access it later for other projects.

The Media Pane

You can insert a variety of DVD content, including audio files, still photos, and movies. The Audio settings in the Media pane, shown in Figure 29.3, integrate with your iTunes library to enable you to add background music to your chosen DVD theme.

FIGURE 29.3
Select songs from your iTunes library.

In addition to integrating with your iTunes library, iDVD connects directly to your iPhoto library. From the Photos option of the Media pane, shown in Figure 29.4, you can drag and drop photos to create slideshows, which we'll look at shortly, or to customize themes that contain special drop zones where you can put in one of your own images or video clips.

FIGURE 29.4
Drag and drop photos from your iPhoto library.

Make sure that you've upgraded to the latest version of iPhoto and launched iPhoto at least once (so that it can perform file system changes) before trying to integrate with iDVD.

By the Way

The Movies option lists all the movies stored in the current user's Movies folder, which is the default location for iMovie HD to store your projects. (You can add folders in the Movies section of the iDVD preferences.)

Status Pane

The Status pane (see Figure 29.5) shows you the size of your project in running time or disc space—click the text to the right of the status bar to toggle between the two. The additional status bars show the number of minutes of motion menu, the number of tracks, and the number of menus that have been added to your current project. (These numbers do matter; your DVD project is limited to 1GB (15 minutes) of motion menu, 99 video tracks or slideshows, and 99 menus of any kind.)

When you make your own DVDs, iDVD has to *encode* the video into a special format so that a DVD player can play it properly. iDVD gives you an update on how the encoding is coming along in the lower portion of the Status pane.

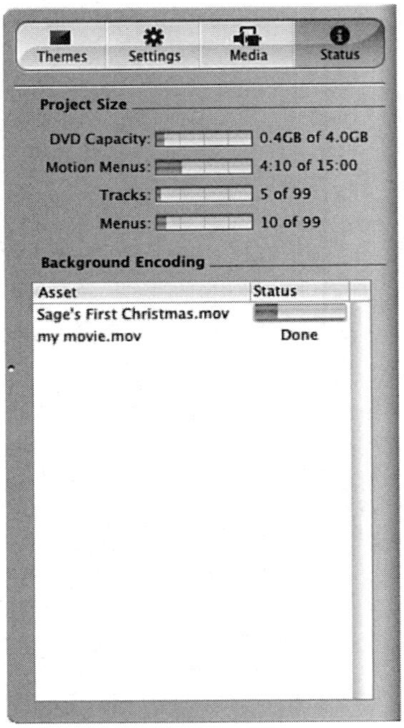

FIGURE 29.5
Keep track of
the size of your
DVD project.

**Did you
Know?**

You can't burn a project to DVD until iDVD is finished encoding the video.
However, if you turn on Enable Background Encoding in iDVD's preferences, iDVD
encodes video as it is added to your project. With background encoding enabled,
you can continue to work, and you won't have to wait as long for encoding to finish when you are ready to write a DVD.

Folder Button

Although you can add individual items (such as movie clips) directly to your DVD
menus, you can also create folders in the menu to add a secondary menu in which
to add even more movie clips and slideshows. You may want to use folders to organize your content neatly into subcategories. Also, there is a limit of 12 items per
menu—if you need to add more than 12 movie clips or slideshows you have to create a secondary menu, or submenu, for the overflow.

To create a folder, simply click the Folder button at the bottom of the iDVD window
and a new menu item is added to link to your new folder. Double-clicking the menu
item for a folder in the viewing area opens this submenu so that you can work with
it as you would the top-level menu.

You'll know you are in a submenu rather than the main menu if a button marked by an arrow appears in the menu. (Refer to Figure 29.1 for an example.)

Did you Know?

Slideshow Button

The Slideshow button enables you to add a series of still photos to a DVD and to choose background music. DVD slideshows are a nice way to share digital pictures, so that people who watch your DVD can see the pictures on their televisions. Just as when you're working with video clips in iDVD, creating a slideshow is as easy as dragging and dropping digital pictures into the iDVD window (see Figure 29.6).

FIGURE 29.6
Slideshow editing window with individual images.

When you drag digital pictures into the editing window, you can easily rearrange them and preview the show. There's also an option for iDVD to display navigation on the screen so that when a person views your DVD, there's a visual reminder to press the arrow keys on the remote to move through the slides. See Figure 29.7 for an example.

You may recall from Chapter 22, "Using iPhoto," that you can easily export a slideshow created in iPhoto to iDVD.

By the Way

Click the Return button at the lower right to stop working with slideshow contents and return to the DVD menu.

FIGURE 29.7
Slideshow preview showing arrows that indicate there are additional slides to view.

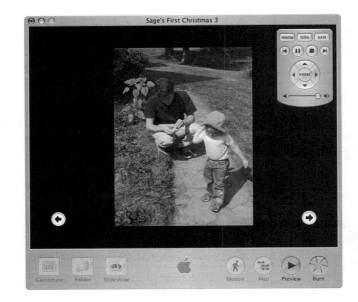

Motion Button

You might discover that sometimes when you're working on a DVD project, you want to turn off the motion in a motion menu. (Recall that you can add motion menus with iDVD, and this movement can be distracting while you are trying to design your DVD.) You can turn off motion in menus temporarily by clicking the Motion button.

Map Button

If you want a general overview of your project's structure, click the Map button. A DVD "map" appears in the viewing area, as shown in Figure 29.8. Double-click an item to go directly to a screen in your project so you can edit it. Click the Return button, or the Map button again, to exit the map.

By the Way

> The box at the top left of the Map view is for content you want to play automatically when the DVD is loaded. Here, you can put a video clip, a single still image, or a series of images.

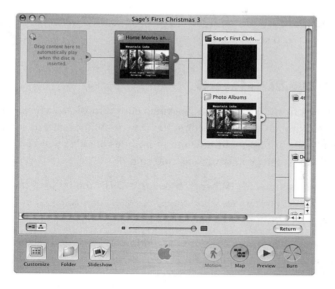

FIGURE 29.8
The DVD map
gives you an
easy way to see
what you've
added to a DVD
project.

Preview and Burn Buttons

As you work on your DVD project, you can test it by clicking the Preview button. This plays the current version of your project as it would appear on a finished DVD, including menus and video clips. A DVD controller appears onscreen during the preview so you navigate as you would in the finished DVD (refer to Figure 29.7).

When you are satisfied with your project, you're ready to burn a DVD disc. You simply click the Burn button to activate it (see Figure 29.9) and then click it again.

FIGURE 29.9
Clicking the
Burn button.

When you click the Burn button a second time, your DVD writer opens so that you can insert your DVD disc.

iDVD Capabilities

When you're just starting out with a few video clips and DVD screens, you might not need to think much about exceeding iDVD's capabilities. But at some point, you'll probably be curious about how many minutes of video you can fit on a DVD, how many menu screens you can have, and so on.

- ▶ Items on a menu = 12—When you create a DVD, the buttons on the menu screen can lead to movies, slideshows, or other menus. iDVD enables you to have up to 12 buttons on each screen.

- ▶ Images in a slideshow = 99—You can add up to 99 digital pictures to each slideshow that you have on your DVD.

- ▶ Tracks on a DVD = 99—You can add a total of 99 movies and or slideshows to a DVD project, assuming that the total amount of video used in the movie portion of your DVD does not exceed 90 minutes.

- ▶ Menus in a DVD = 99—You can add a total of 99 menus to a DVD Project. Because motion menus use short video clips, you're limited to using 1GB worth, or 15 minutes, on a DVD project.

- ▶ GB of data on a DVD = 4—The total size of your project can't exceed 4GB, including movies, photos, audio, and menus. (The number of minutes of video that will fit on a DVD depends on the quality of the video you want to output.)

The iDVD Preference Options

Before you move on to Chapter 30—where you'll learn how to design DVDs, customize menus, and add DVD-ROM content—it's a good idea to take a brief look at the iDVD preferences, which are divided into General, Slideshow, and Movies options.

General Preferences

The General Preference settings, shown in Figure 29.10, affect entire projects. Under the Project Settings header are check boxes for the following three options:

FIGURE 29.10
A typical config-
uration for the
General prefer-
ences—if you
live in North
America!

▶ Show Drop Zones—As you learned earlier in this chapter, drop zones are areas in iDVD themes where you can insert photos or movie clips of your own. If the Show Drop Zones option is checked, these regions are labeled "Drop Zone" so that you can recognize them more easily during the design process.

▶ Show Apple Logo Watermark—If this option is checked, an Apple logo appears on the menu screens in your project.

▶ Delete Rendered Files on Closing a Project—Each DVD project you create con-sists of the raw files and the files that have been encoded for DVD. To save space on your hard drive, you can select this box to remove the encoded files each time you close a project. (Because the encoded files can be constructed from the raw files, iDVD creates them again if you open the project.)

> Deleting rendered files may also be useful if you burn a DVD that simply doesn't work. Deleting the encoding and starting over fixes problems related to corrupt files.

By the Way

In Encoder Settings, you can choose between encoding your project for best quality or best performance. Best quality gives the best quality for your specific project, so movies more than 60 minutes long will be made to fit, and movies less than 60 minutes long will be encoded at a higher than usual quality because the space is available. Best performance uses a standard encoding quality that isn't determined in response to the size of your project. (Best performance can't be used with DVDs that are more than 60 minutes long.) If you choose best performance, you can also choose whether to enable background encoding, which allows iDVD to encode your project's content to DVD format while you work. If you choose best performance with background encoding, you don't have to wait as long for your DVD project to finish encoding before you burn your DVD.

The Video Standard options are NTSC or PAL. As discussed in Chapter 24, "Exploring the iMovie HD Interface," video standards differ by region. These standards specify the picture dimensions as well as a frame rate. If your intended audience lives in North American or Japan, be sure to use NTSC; if your viewers will be from Great Britain, choose PAL.

The final option in the General preferences is to reset warnings. Click the Reset button to begin showing warning messages that you had opted not to see again. For example, iDVD allows only 12 items per menu and warns you if you try to add a 13th item. If you check Do Not Ask Me Again on the warning message, iDVD no longer explains why it can't add another item to the menu.

Slideshow Preferences

The Slideshow preferences affect how iDVD copes with images you add to slideshows. The first check box is Always Add Original Slideshow Photos to DVD-ROM, which includes the raw image files on the DVD along with the DVD-version of the slideshow. This gives your audience access to the original images for printing, editing, or otherwise working with on a computer.

Checking the second option, Always Scale Slides to TV Safe Area, scales each image in a slideshow to leave room around the edges of the screen. This ensures that extreme edges of your images are not cut off when played on some older television screens. When slides are scaled to fit the TV safe area, a black border appears around each image. You learn how to create slideshows in Chapter 30.

Movies Preferences

Movies preferences, shown in Figure 29.11, enable you to choose whether iDVD recognizes available chapter markers when a movie is imported. (Recall from Chapter 28, "Exporting iMovies," that chapter markers can be added in iMovie to allow you to skip to a specific place in a movie clip or movie.) The options are to automatically create chapter markers, never create them, or to ask each time a project is opened.

You can also choose where on your system iDVD searches for video clips to list in the Movies pane discussed earlier in this chapter. (By default, iMovie tries to save files in an account holder's Movies folder, so that's the default place the iDVD will look. If you prefer to save your projects to the desktop, you can tell iDVD to also look on the desktop.)

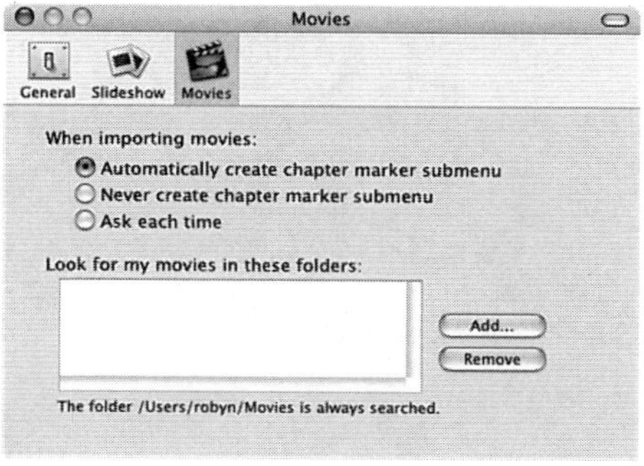

FIGURE 29.11
Choose how to
cope with chap-
ter markers and
where to find
movie files.

Summary

In this chapter, you learned about the basic DVD features, as well as some background about DVDs in general. You became acquainted with the iDVD interface and the various options it provides for making a variety of DVD projects that can include a combination of movies and digital pictures. You also saw the controls you'll use to customize your DVD menus, as well as to preview your project and burn it to DVD.

CHAPTER 30

Creating DVDs in iDVD

This chapter delves into constructing a DVD—from adding content to customizing the look of the menus to burning your project to DVD. For those who want a basic DVD fast, the One-Step feature is also explained. It also offers some tips and tricks for getting started with a project. Let's start there—at the beginning!

Preparing the DVD Project

Before you start a new project in iDVD, you may want to adjust a few settings and make sure your computer is up to the task. There are no particular rules about what you have to do first, but it's a good idea to save your project frequently—the keyboard shortcut for saving is Command-S. As you work on your project, you can get in the habit of choosing File, Save at regular intervals so that you don't lose your work if lightning happens to strike or your Mac freezes up for some reason.

Before you even open iDVD, it's a good idea to check the amount of space available on your hard drive. Video clips and DVD files take up a lot of space, and you should make sure that you have room to complete your project. To view the amount of space available, select your hard drive in the Finder or in a Finder window, and choose File, Get Info from the window to see the amount of space available. Keep in mind that your computer needs 4.7GB for the encoded files that will be written to the DVD, in addition to the space taken up by any files you add to your DVD.

The final video will take up to 4.7GB and will need double that as iDVD builds the image.

To prepare for this project, you need to put a few things in order to set the stage for importing video into the DVD project:

1. Launch iDVD and create a new project. You are prompted to name and save your project automatically. (By default, iDVD projects are saved in a user's Documents folder, but you can choose a different location.)

2. Choose iDVD, Preferences to bring up the Preferences window (see Figure 30.1).

The name you give your project is the name that will be applied automatically to the DVD disc when you burn your completed project. However, you can change the original project name by choosing Project, Project Info from the menu. Then, in the window that opens, simply type a new Disc Name and click OK.

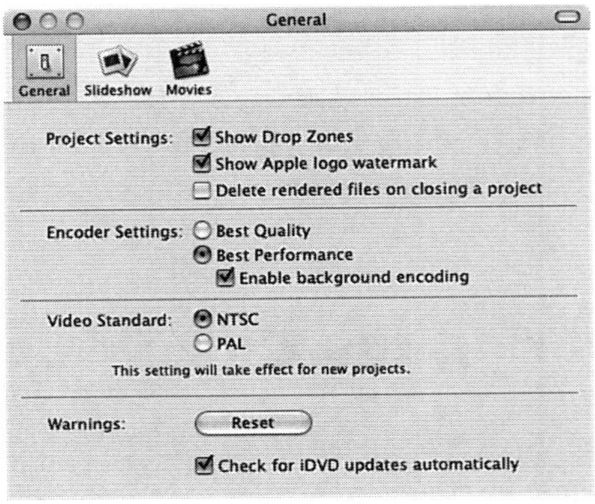

FIGURE 30.1
The iDVD preferences.

3. In the Preferences window, click to uncheck the Show Apple Logo Watermark option. This removes the Apple logo from the lower-right corner of the DVD production. Of course, you can leave it in if you want. When you're finished, close the Preference window.

4. In the main iDVD window, click the Customize button in the lower-left corner, click the Themes icon if necessary, and click to select a theme (see Figure 30.2). (Using the pop-up menu in the Themes pane, you can choose subsets of themes or all available themes. You can also view any themes you've customized and saved as Favorites.)

5. To customize the title in your theme, double-click the text so that it's selected (as shown in Figure 30.3), and you can start typing.

FIGURE 30.2
You can use the iDVD Themes pane to select a background for your iDVD project. This example uses the Sliding Panes theme.

FIGURE 30.3
The placeholder text can be replaced with your own text.

Importing Files

You learned in Chapter 28, "Exporting iMovies," that you can create an iDVD project directly from iMovie if you want. That opens your iMovie directly into iDVD, including any chapter markers you've added to make it easier for viewers to skip to specific scenes.

If you want to add clips rather than your entire iMovie, there are three methods for importing video:

▶ Select File, Import, Video.

▶ Open the Media pane in the Customize drawer and select Movies from the pop-up menu to see movie files saved in your Movies folder.

▶ Drag the file directly into the DVD from a Finder window.

By the Way

> Remember that video clips imported with iMovie have been encoded automatically in the appropriate format for them to be compatible with iDVD. iDVD supports only QuickTime movies with linear video tracks. Other formats, such as QuickTime VR, MPEG-1 and MPEG-2, Flash, streaming or encrypted movies, or QuickTime spanned movies, are not supported by iDVD.
>
> If you try to import a file that is not compatible with iDVD, a message saying `Unsupported File Type` appears.

Using the Media Pane

The integration between iDVD, iTunes, iPhoto, and iMovie is apparent in the Media pane, which links directly to the folders on your hard drive that contain your iTunes library, your iPhoto library, and the default location for storing iMovie projects. The Media pane gives you direct access to these elements so that you can incorporate them into your DVD projects.

For these sections to function, however, you need to make sure that you are using compatible versions of each of these applications. See Chapter 20, "Introducing iLife," for more information.

To use the Audio and http://www.betarecordings.com/beta-site/CrazyPhotos/47_Christmas_NYE_LA_05/13.jpgPhotos sections, you also need to have opened iTunes and iPhoto at least once after they've been updated to compatible versions so that your media libraries can be cataloged in a format that iDVD understands.

By the Way

> Although iPhoto and iTunes make it more difficult to move the location of your media, iMovie lets you store your movie files anywhere you want. To solve the problem of the Movies browser not knowing where to locate your movie files, you can add paths to them in the Movies section of the iDVD preferences.

Importing Video Clips

To import a video clip stored on your computer or a connected storage device, open the folder containing your video clips and drag one directly from the Finder into the iDVD window.

When you choose a theme for your DVD in iDVD, the DVD buttons consist of either small images or text buttons that represent the video clips you've imported. If your theme uses text buttons, the name of the clip you've added appears as the label of the button (see Figure 30.4). To change the label, click a text button once to select it and then again to select the text label. (If you click twice too close together, you Preview the selected clip.)

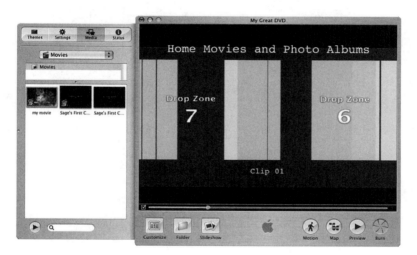

FIGURE 30.4
You can drag QuickTime movies directly into the iDVD window, and the filename becomes the DVD button name.

If you have more clips to add, continue dragging the clips into the project and renaming them as needed.

At this point, you can click the Preview button in the main iDVD window to preview the project, as shown in Figure 30.5. Previewing is a good way to find out whether you chose the clips you intended to use.

As you add files to your project, it's wise to keep an eye on the size of your files. (DVDs hold a lot of information, but video takes up a lot of space!) You can monitor the size of your project in the Status pane, as shown in Figure 30.6.

FIGURE 30.5
Preview your
project to watch
the video clips
you've added.

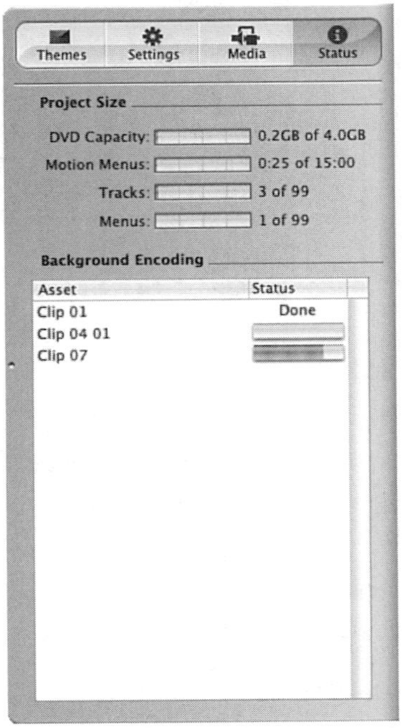

FIGURE 30.6
Encoder status:
iDVD can
encode your
video clips while
you work on
your project.

Remember, you may need to click the Customize button to get to the Status tab.

As you learned in Chapter 29, "Exploring the iDVD Interface," you can't burn a project to DVD until iDVD has finished encoding the video. If you turn on Enable Background Encoding in iDVD's preferences, you don't have to wait as long for encoding to finish when you're ready to write a DVD.

Did you Know?

Customizing DVD Menus

DVD menus consist of a background and a series of buttons that lead to other parts of the DVD—such as video clips, which you just learned to add. This section takes a closer look at iDVD themes and how to customize them.

As you learned earlier from importing video, every element you import appears on the menu as either a button or text label. How they appear by default depends on the theme you've selected.

By the Way

Types of Themes

iDVD makes it easy to choose a background theme for your DVD project and to customize it for your project. Most of the themes for the latest version of iDVD include *Drop Zones*, which are areas where you can add your own slideshows, movies, or still images.

There are two basic categories of themes:

▶ *Static background* themes display a regular, nonvideo image. An example is Full Frame 2, which displays a still photo of your choosing.

▶ *Motion* themes display short video repeats. An example of a Drop Zone theme is Sliding Panes, which you saw earlier in this chapter as well as in the previous chapter, where a series of images and black bars move across the screen.

When a motion menu is selected, a "scrubber bar" appears at the bottom of the iDVD window, as shown earlier in Figure 30.4. Drag the scrubber along the scrubber bar to quickly scan the menu's motion. If the motion menu begins with an introductory video, it appears as a gray region at the left of the scrubber bar. To turn off the intro, uncheck the box in front of the scrubber bar.

By the Way

Different types of themes suit different purposes, but switching between them isn't difficult. You can always click on a different theme when you're working on your project—iDVD enables you to play and experiment as much as you want. The elements in your DVD and the titles you've given them carry over between themes.

Some of the themes, such as Wedding White, include music. Setting background audio is discussed later in this chapter.

Choose a Theme

After you've started a new project, follow these steps:

1. Click the Customize button in the lower-left corner of the main iDVD window to display the Themes pane. If the Themes pane is not visible, click the Themes button.

2. Select a theme in the Themes pane, and it automatically appears in the main iDVD window.

If you choose a theme that has background sound or motion (indicated by a small circular walking man symbol), or displays previews of the project clips as video buttons, you might want to temporarily disable the sound or motion if it becomes distracting or seems to slow your computer's reaction time.

You can do so by clicking the Motion button at the bottom of the main iDVD window, which displays an icon of a walking person.

The theme you select is applied only to the menu that appear in the main iDVD window. To apply a new theme to menus across your entire project, or to all the menus inside a given part of your project, choose Advanced, Apply Theme to Project or Advanced, Apply Theme to Folder from the menu.

Using the same theme across all the menus of DVD lends a professional look, but iDVD also includes theme variations that coordinate with each other, such as Travel 1 and Travel 2.

Working with Drop Zones

Some themes include Drop Zones, or areas that you can customize by adding movies or still images. To add a movie or image to themes containing a Drop Zone, select the media file and drag it on top of the Drop Zone, as shown in Figure 30.7.

If you are using a Drop Zone theme and you want to add a movie as content to your project, drag it to an area of the screen that is not a Drop Zone. It becomes a text button. If you want, you can change it to a picture button in the Settings pane of the Customize window. We talk more about customizing buttons shortly.

FIGURE 30.7
The borders of
the Drop Zone
change when
you drag a file
on top of it.

When your file is added, it fits inside the Drop Zone, as shown in Figure 30.8.

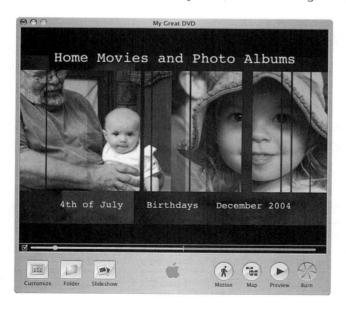

FIGURE 30.8
The Drop Zone
now displays
the file you
added.

The aspect ratio of the image you insert is preserved, with the image scaled to fit against either the top and bottom or left and right edges of the region. If the best part of the image doesn't fall in the center of the space, you can drag the image to choose which portion of the image is visible in the Drop Zone.

When you drag a movie to a Drop Zone in a DVD menu, the movie you added plays over and over again when the menu is onscreen. You can set the duration of the movie by using the Duration slider in the Settings pane of the Customize drawer. You can choose how long you want the movie to play in each loop, up to a maximum of 15 minutes total per DVD.

To remove a file from the Drop Zone, drag the image or movie out of the Drop Zone.

Customizing Text in Titles and Labels

The Text area of the Settings pane enables you to customize the title and label text that appears on your DVD screens. To make changes to the title, select the title or click on the background of the DVD menu. To make changes to the label text of the menu items, select one of them—changes made are applied to all menu items to keep them consistent.

The following list corresponds to the options in the Text section of the Settings Tab, shown in Figure 30.9.

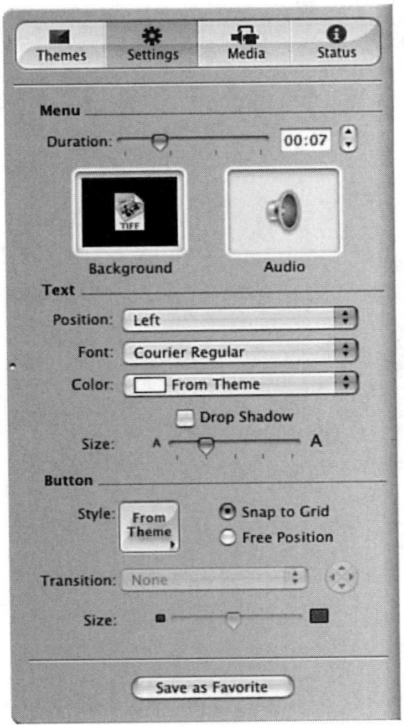

FIGURE 30.9
Options for changing the text in iDVD.

You can customize your title and labels with the following settings:

▶ Position—When used to customize titles, enables you to choose a preset position, such as Left, Center, Right, or Custom, which allows you to drag the title to precisely the place you want it. When used to customize the labels of menu items, enables you to choose a preset position, such as Top, Center, Bottom, Left, or Right, or to hide the text.

▶ Font—Enables you to choose a different style of text.

▶ Color—Enables you to choose a color for your title text.

▶ Drop Shadow—Enables you to shadow behind the title text.

▶ Size—Enables you to make the text bigger or smaller.

DVD Buttons—Video and Text

In iDVD, you can have two different kinds of buttons, depending on the theme that you choose. In some themes, there are text buttons, which contain only text labels (refer to Figure 30.8).

In other themes there are video buttons, which include text labels and a preview of the video clip or slideshow to which they lead (see Figure 30.10).

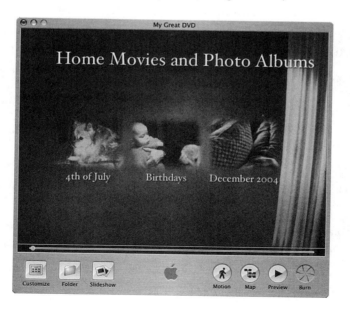

FIGURE 30.10
Video buttons showing previews of the clips to which they lead.

Earlier in this chapter, an example demonstrated that text buttons are created automatically when you import video clips into a theme. That occurred because most of the recent iDVD themes use text buttons by default. If you choose a theme that uses video buttons by default, such as Wedding Bronze Two, video buttons are created for each video clip you import.

Though themes default to one kind of button or the other, you can change text buttons to video buttons, or vice versa, in the Button section of the Settings pane (see Figure 30.9 above). To make a change, click the Style menu to see the options and select the one your want to apply. If you select a video button style, the Size slider enables you to resize the buttons.

By the Way

> To reposition your buttons anywhere you want them, select Free Position instead of the Snap to Grid option.
>
> One note of caution: If you choose to use Free Position for your buttons, be careful not to position them in ways that your viewers will find difficult to use! You may even want to turn on the TV Safe Area feature under the Advanced menu. This puts a border around the region of your menu that is most likely to be visible across different models of televisions. (In case you are wondering, the preset button positions used with Snap to Grid already fall safely inside the TV Safe Area.)

If you change your mind about the changes you've made, choose the first option, From Theme, to revert to the default style for your chosen theme.

Adjust a Video Button

iDVD gives you a number of ways to make simple adjustments to a video button right in the main iDVD window. The automatic setting is for the button to start playing the movie from the beginning, but you can change where the video displayed on the button starts or have just a single frame of the movie appear, instead of a video clip.

1. Click a video button to get the adjustment controls, as shown in Figure 30.11.

2. Click the slider and drag it to the desired position within the video button to change where the video clip starts.

3. If you don't want the video button to be in motion, uncheck the Movie option and use the slider to choose the frame you want to use as a still image.

4. When you're finished adjusting, click on the video button again and you see the customized video button.

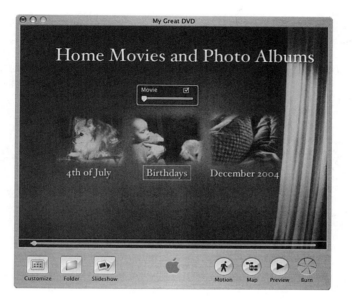

FIGURE 30.11
Clicking a video button gives you the button controls.

When working with video buttons, remember that they are in motion as you're working on them only if you have motion in iDVD turned on. If the Motion button at the bottom of the main iDVD window is green, motion is activated. Similarly, unless you specifically uncheck the Movie option as described earlier, your video buttons move.

By the Way

Adding Submenus

In Chapter 29, you learned that iDVD enables you to add up to 12 menu items per screen. To add more than 12 items to your DVD, you need to add additional screens, or submenus, to your DVD project. Each submenu can contain an additional 12 items until you hit the limit of 99 movies or slideshows, or no more than 15 minutes' worth of motion menus.

iDVD represents submenus with the metaphor of folders. Think of DVD folders just as you do the folders on your hard drive. You can put multiple items in a folder, and to get to the contents, you click on the folder. Similarly, in iDVD, the folder provides viewers a way to go to another set of options.

When you add a DVD folder, you add it to the main menu. You can then add more folders to the main menu or within other folders.

As you learned in Chapter 28, "Exporting iMovies," chapter markers can be set in iMovie for export to iDVD. When you import a movie with chapter markers, iDVD creates a button with the title of the movie, so the viewer can play the entire movie, and a Scene Selection button that links to a scene submenu, so the viewer can select which scenes to watch and in what order. If you want, however, you can set your iDVD preferences so that scene submenus are never created or so that iDVD asks what you want on each imported movie.

Add a DVD Folder

You can add a folder to a theme that includes text buttons or video buttons.

Follow these steps to get a sense of how things work:

1. Import a video clip as you learned earlier in this chapter.

2. Click the Folder button at the bottom of the main iDVD window to add a folder. If you are using a theme that supports video buttons, iDVD adds a button that displays an icon that looks like a folder (see Figure 30.12). (If your theme supports text buttons, your folder is added as a button labeled My Folder.)

FIGURE 30.12
When added, a new folder appears with a generic icon like the one at the lower right.

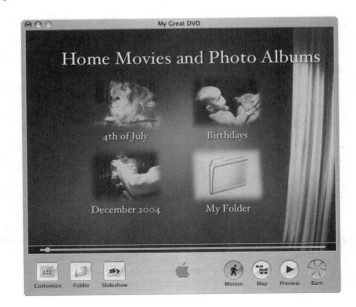

3. Double-click the new folder button in your menu to get to the new folder screen you have just added (see Figure 30.13).

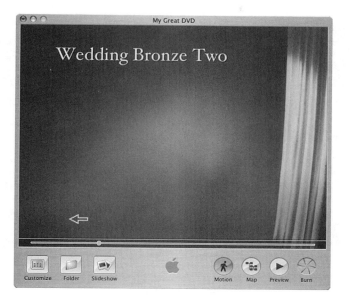

FIGURE 30.13
Double-clicking on the newly added button takes you to the new folder screen.

4. Drag additional files into the new submenu. If you want, customize the buttons, using the techniques you learned earlier. Then click on the small arrow in the lower-left corner of your submenu, as shown earlier in Figure 30.13, to get back to the main menu.

5. Single-click on the folder button in the menu to activate the button controls.

6. Use the slider in the button controls to choose which button from your submenu you want to feature. (The changes that you made to the video buttons on your submenu are carried over to this preview.)

When you're finished, you will have a video button on your main menu that leads to a submenu.

As your DVD project grows, it can be helpful to view its structure. Click the Map button to show an "organization" chart of your project, including any video clips, slideshows, and submenus you've added. In the map, double-click a video clip to preview it, or a slideshow or submenu to open it for further customization.

Customizing Menus

Although Drop Zones give you a lot of opportunity to make a theme your own, customizing a menu by adding your own overall background or theme music is something you also might want to do.

You can drag elements into two wells in the Background section of the Settings area in iDVD (see Figure 30.14).

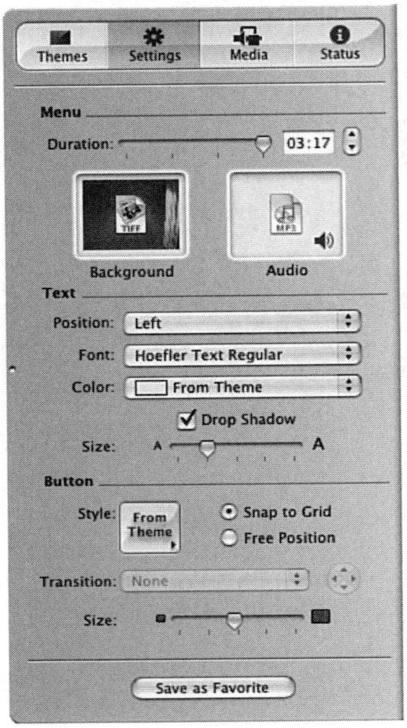

FIGURE 30.14
The Image/
Movie and
Audio wells in
the Background
section of
iDVD's Settings
pane.

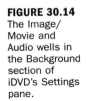

To add a new background image to a DVD project, you must have an image prepared that you want to drag in. It could be a digital picture you have taken or an image that you've prepared in a graphics program. Although iDVD can resize your background image, Apple suggests you make sure that your image is sized to 640×480 to fit the screen exactly.

To import a new background image,

1. Open a Finder window containing the file that you want to be the new background and position it next to iDVD.

2. Click and drag the file into the Image/Movie well in the Background section.

The new background file becomes the new image you see in your DVD menu.

If you like the changes that you've made in customizing your DVD project, you can save this customized theme in the Favorites list of iDVD. Click the Save as Favorites button at the bottom of the Settings tab and give your creation a name in the dialog box that appears. When you want to choose your special theme, you can access it in the same Themes list where you normally choose a built-in theme by clicking the pop-up menu and selecting Favorites. The main value of this Favorites option is that it saves you from having to manually adjust things on every screen in a custom DVD project.

By the Way

Add a Sound to a DVD Menu

If you want to add a sound to your DVD menu, you can drag it into the Audio well in the Background area of the Settings pane.

1. Open your iDVD project. In the main iDVD window, click the Customize button to see the tray window.

2. Click the Settings tab in the drawer.

3. Drag a sound file into the Audio well in the Background section of the Settings tab (refer to Figure 30.14).

The icon in the Audio well changes to reflect the type of file that you're dragging in.

You can check the name of the sound file and its duration by moving your mouse over the Audio well.

By the Way

If you decide that you no longer want the sound that you've added to a project, drag the sound file icon from the audio well to anywhere outside the iDVD window. (When no audio file is set as the menu's background, the audio well appears as it did in Figure 30.9.)

If you want to temporarily silence a menu to keep it from playing over and over again as you work, you can click the speaker icon in the lower right of the audio well to mute it.

By the Way

DVD Slideshows

This section examines how to work with DVD slideshows in iDVD. DVD slideshows are a way to enhance a DVD production; they enable you to add digital pictures to a DVD project.

Using iDVD to create a slideshow is as simple as using other parts of the program; it's a matter of dragging your files directly into the iDVD window. After adding your pictures to the slideshow in your DVD project, you can make a number of adjustments if you want.

You may recall from Chapter 22, "Using iPhoto," that you can export a slideshow created in iPhoto directly to iDVD—including the slide duration and background music. However, slideshows created in iPhoto and exported to iDVD cannot be edited in iDVD. Also, slideshows exported from iPhoto are added to the top level of the DVD project. If you want to add a slideshow to a submenu or want to keep your customization options open, you need to create the slideshow in iDVD. (But don't worry—that's not difficult!)

Create a Slideshow

Before you can create a slideshow, you must open a new iDVD project or reopen an ongoing DVD project to which you want to add a slideshow.

1. Open your DVD project.

2. Click the Slideshow button at the bottom of the main iDVD window to create a slideshow.

By the Way

To customize the name of your slideshow, click the My Slideshow label. (A later section describes how to customize the thumbnail image of the button.)

3. To get into the slideshow editing window, double-click on the My Slideshow button that appears on your main DVD screen. From there, you can add slides and make adjustments to your slideshow (see Figure 30.15).

Add and Arrange Slides

Adding slides to an iDVD slideshow is as easy as dragging and dropping the files into the iDVD window. You can drag files in from the desktop, or you can drag images from your iPhoto library by using the Photo section of the Media pane. (Remember, to open the Media pane, you need to click the Customize button at the bottom of the iDVD main window.) You can also use the File, Import, Image option.

1. Open your iDVD project and click on the Slideshow button in the main iDVD window to reveal the Slideshow editing window shown previously in Figure 30.15.

FIGURE 30.15
The Slideshow
editing window.

2. If you are importing photos from your iPhoto library, open the Media pane and choose Photos from the pop-up menu. If you are importing photos from somewhere else on your hard drive, position a Finder window with the picture files you want to import to the left of the iDVD window.

> Before you try to import photos from iPhoto to iDVD, make sure you have opened iPhoto at least once to let it update the format in which photos are stored. Otherwise, your iPhoto library may be incompatible with iDVD.

Watch Out!

3. Click on one of the desired image files and, while holding down the mouse button, drag the file into the slideshow editing window. Figure 30.16 shows a slideshow with several photos in it.

You can drag multiple files at once into the slideshow editing window. To accomplish this, place the mouse pointer near one of the image thumbnails, click and hold down the mouse button, and drag upward and over all the images you want to add. Then click directly on one of the selected thumbnails, and drag them all over at once.

You can reposition and adjust the slides added to a slideshow according to your taste, once again by dragging and dropping.

To move a slide, select it and drag it to the position where you want it. As you drag, the other slides move aside to show you where the selected slide will land if you release the mouse button.

FIGURE 30.16
Images added
to a slideshow
are numbered.

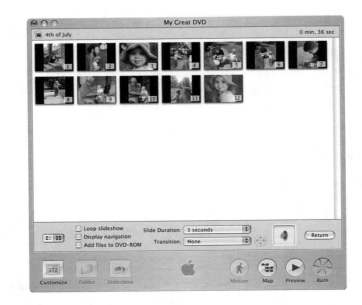

Slideshow Options

The slideshow editing window has a variety of options that you can use to adjust both the order of slides and how the slides behave.

Loop Slideshow

If you want your slideshow to play over and over again automatically, check the Loop Slideshow option.

Display Navigation

The Display Navigation option causes arrows to be displayed on your slideshow screens, as shown in Figure 30.17, that are a reminder that there are previous or remaining slides.

Adding Picture Files to DVD-ROM

When you add a slideshow to your DVD project, the images are encoded as part of the DVD. If someone wanted to work with one of the images as a file to print or send in an email, she wouldn't be able to do this. However, the Add to DVD-ROM option enables you to add the individual slides to your DVD as graphics files—a nice option for enabling people to watch the slideshow, as well as put the DVD in their computers to have the picture files available.

FIGURE 30.17
Display arrows in an iDVD preview. They represent how a person can use the arrow keys on a DVD remote to go through slides.

When you burn your final DVD with this option checked, the slides in your slideshow are also added to your DVD as individual image files. These files are accessible to any computer with a DVD-ROM drive. Adding other kinds of DVD-ROM content is covered in more detail in the section, "DVD-ROM Content—Including Computer Files on a DVD."

Setting Slide Duration

The Slide Duration option enables you to set the time that a slide displays on a screen.

The Manual setting basically means that the user presses the right or left arrow on the DVD remote control to advance to the next slide or go back to a previous slide. But if you want a slideshow to run on its own, you can adjust the duration. To adjust a slide's duration, click the Slide Duration pop-up menu and choose a duration.

> In the Slide Duration popup menu, the Fit to Audio option is available only after you've added background music to your slideshow, as is discussed shortly. Also, after you've added an Audio file, the default setting becomes Fit to Audio, and the Manual option is no longer available.

Transition

The Transition settings determine the way iDVD transitions between slides in the slideshow.

You can choose None, or you can choose from a range of transitions including Dissolve, where one photo fades out as another fades in; Cube, where the images appear as if they're the sides of a rotating cube; and Mosaic Flip, where square pieces of each slide flip to reveal new pieces of the next slide.

To the right of the Transition pop-up is a direction selector that becomes active if you've chosen a transition that can be activated starting from the left, right, top, or bottom. Click the corresponding arrow in the direction selector to choose one.

Audio

The Audio option enables you to add a sound file to a slideshow. It works the same as adding audio to a menu, as discussed earlier in the chapter. You simply drag a file into the well. To delete, drag the audio file from the Audio well out of the iDVD window.

> It has been reported that background music in iDVD slideshows stutters in some DVD players. The problem seems to lie with how these DVD players cope with chapter breaks, which are used to allow navigation between photos in a slideshow. You may want to forego background music if you want to be certain to avoid annoying and distracting audio problems.

DVD-ROM Content—Including Computer Files on a DVD

DVD is a flexible medium for creating and sharing interactive presentations, but the possibilities aren't limited to images and video intended for onscreen viewing. You can also include files on a DVD that people can access on their computers. This feature, mentioned in the section on iDVD slideshows, is known as DVD-ROM.

Adding DVD-ROM content isn't anything that you have to do; it's just great to have the flexibility to add computer files to your DVD. However, there are two things to consider when deciding whether to add DVD-ROM content:

▶ Does the person have a DVD-ROM drive? Most newer computers have DVD-ROM drives, but not all of them. If the person you want to share files with doesn't have a DVD-ROM drive, you would be better off creating a CD.

By the Way

> The purpose of the DVD-ROM feature in iDVD is to add extra material to video DVDs. It isn't recommended as a way to back up your data files. Instead, use the Burn Disc option available in the Finder's File menu to burn a data DVD.

▶ Is the person on Mac or Windows? If you're burning files to a DVD and you want a person on Windows to be able to use them, be sure to include the appropriate file extensions on your files.

Microsoft Windows relies on the file extension to recognize which application is needed to open a file. For example, JPEG files need a .jpg at the end for a Windows machine to launch a program capable of displaying JPEGs. Many Mac programs automatically put on a file extension, but you need to be sure to use them if sending your DVD to Windows users.

You can easily add computer files to your DVD using iDVD:

1. Launch iDVD and open your project.

2. Choose Advanced, Edit DVD-ROM Contents from the File menu.

3. This opens the DVD-ROM Contents window, as shown in Figure 30.18.

Name	Size
▶ 📁 Slideshows	46 MB

New Folder   Add Files...

FIGURE 30.18
Add DVD-ROM files—and view what's been added—in the DVD-ROM Contents window.

4. Drag files and folders into the DVD-ROM Contents area.

As you drag large media files in as DVD-ROM content, remember to keep an eye on the size of your project. (This information appears at the top of the Status pane.)

Watch Out!

To add files from your hard drive and connected drives, you can also click the Add Files button at the bottom of the window. This brings up a window in which you can navigate to the file, as shown in Figure 30.19.

iDVD doesn't move the files you add as DVD-ROM content, or make duplicates of them. Instead, it creates a reference to the file on your system. If you delete a file or move a file after you've added it to the DVD-ROM list, its name appears in red to tell you something's wrong. If you try to burn the disc anyway, the Missing Files window appears to tell you which files cannot be found.

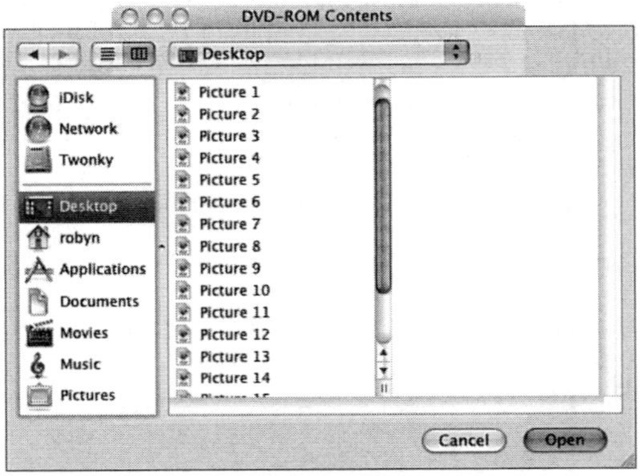

FIGURE 30.19
Select files from your hard drive or connected drives to add to your DVD.

As you add files, you might want to organize them with folders. To add a folder, click the New Folder button at the bottom of the DVD-ROM Contents window and give the fresh folder a name.

To delete a file from the DVD-ROM Contents list, select it and press the Delete key on your keyboard.

Archiving DVD Projects and Creating Disc Images

When you're finished creating your DVD project, you have three options: You can write it to DVD from the computer you've been using, save a disc image of your project and write it later, or archive your project so you can move it to another computer.

By the Way

If you create a disc image of your project, you can use Apple's SuperDrive to burn a DVD, or you can use an external DVD burner.

To archive your project, choose File, Archive Project from the menu. A window similar to a Save window appears, as shown in Figure 30.20, where you can name your project and choose where to save it.

FIGURE 30.20
Archive your
project so you
can open it
in iDVD on
another Mac.

> Sometimes, because of problems with file permissions, archived projects don't
> open as expected when shared with a user who didn't create the file. If you expe-
> rience trouble, select the archived project and open an Info window by choosing
> File, Get Info from the menu. Then, open the Ownership & Permissions section
> and be sure you can both read and write to the item.

By the Way

You can also choose whether to save themes and encoded files with your project.
You may choose not to include either of these things if you want to minimize the
size of the archived project. If you don't include encoded files, the copy of iDVD to
which you transport your archived files can re-encode your files. If you don't include
themes, the computer to which you are transferring the files supplies them if it has
the ones you chose available. (If your theme is not available, however, it is not
applied unless you have archived it with your project.)

If you archive a project, you can open it in iDVD and make changes. If you are finished with your project and want to save only a completed version of the resulting
DVD, you can create a disc image. A disk image is just like a real DVD, except it
exists as a file on your computer instead of as a file burned to a DVD disc.

> Creating a disc image is a good way to test your project before writing it to DVD.
> That way, you can make sure there are no errors without wasting a blank DVD.
> Also, if you create a disc image, you can always write it to DVD later—just select
> the disc image in the Finder and choose File, Burn Disc from the menu.

Did you Know?

To create a disc image, choose File, Save As Disc Image from the menu. A Save window appears, in which you can name the file and choose a location in which to
save it. Click the Save button to continue. A progress window, as shown in Figure
30.21, indicates how your disc image is progressing.

When iDVD is finished, a file with the extension .dmg appears in the location you
chose. To interact with the disc image as you would a DVD, double-click it to open
the DVD Player application. (Refer to Chapter 7, "Using QuickTime and DVD
Player," for more information about playing DVDs on your Mac.)

FIGURE 30.21
Creating a disc
image requires
the same file
processing as
writing a DVD.

Burning Your DVD

Burning a DVD is really as simple as clicking a button and waiting for your master-
piece to be created. There are, however, several steps you should take to be sure that
the DVD really is ready to go: Previewing the contents, preparing your computer,
and, finally, burning the DVD. These steps are covered in detail now.

Previewing Your Project

Before you burn your finished DVD to disc, you should preview it to make sure that
everything is exactly as you want it. Although it's tempting to skip this step when
your project is so close to being completed, you will have to burn the project all over
again, and end up waiting twice as long to view it, if you made any mistakes. To
preview your project, follow these steps:

1. Click the Preview button.

2. In the remote control that appears on your screen, click the arrow buttons to
   select a menu button (refer to Figure 30.17). When you press Enter, the content
   linked to the selected button plays.

3. Repeat step 2 until you've tried all the elements in your project, even those in
   submenus, to make sure that you finished all the portions of your project.

4. When you have tested everything, click the Preview button or click the Exit
   button on the remote control to return to edit mode.

By the Way

While previewing your project, make sure that you have motion activated so that you can see any motion effects in the menus or menu buttons. You'll know motion is activated if the Motion button is green.

Preparing Your Computer

After you've tested your DVD project and are certain everything is as you want it in the final version, you're almost ready to burn your project to a DVD disc. Before you do so, however, you need to do a couple of things to make the process go smoothly.

First, you should quit out of any other applications you have running, such as iMovie or Mail. Burning DVDs is a resource-intensive process, and it's best to let your computer focus all its processing power on iDVD.

Next, make sure that your Mac doesn't go to sleep in the middle of burning. (This doesn't seem to affect all Macs, but it's better to be safe than to waste a DVD-R.) To do this, go to the Apple menu at the upper left and open the System Preferences. Choose Energy Saver from the Hardware section, and set the slider that controls the length of inactivity before the computer sleeps to Never (see Figure 30.22).

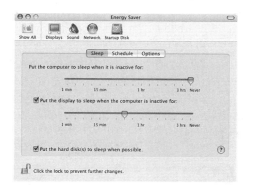

FIGURE 30.22
Open the Energy Saver pane of the System Preferences to ensure that your computer doesn't sleep during disc burning.

Burning Your DVD

After you've tested your project and prepared your computer, burning the actual disc is simple. Just check the Status pane of the Customize drawer to see that all encoding is completed, and be sure that you don't want to add anything else to your project.

By the Way

> There are many options in DVD media. Recordable DVDs (DVD-R) enable you to write data a single time to a disc, whereas DVD-RW discs can be reused. There is also a slightly different format of each, DVD+R and DVD+RW. Both DVD-R and DVD-RW will work in any Mac with a SuperDrive. However, the DVD+R and DVD+RW formats can be used only by newer Macs, such as G5s and Mac Minis. Visit www.apple.com/ilife/idvd/featureoverview.html for specifics about compatibility.

1. Click the Burn button. When clicked, the gray button retracts to reveal a pulsing button in its place.

2. You are prompted to insert a blank DVD in your disc drive.

By the Way

> If you have forgotten to add content to a slideshow or have deleted a file used in your project, iDVD warns you so you can correct the problem.

With a disc in place, iDVD begins processing the menus and any other files in your project. A status window, similar to the one shown in Figure 30.21, appears to show its progress.

Watch Out!

> If your DVD project is large or uses very high-quality video, it might take hours for your DVD to be written. Be careful not to press the Eject key while burning is in progress. This may interrupt burning and result in an unusable disc.

It takes a while for your computer to create the disc. Exactly how much time depends on your computer's processor and how much content is on the disc. Generally, it takes two to three times the length of the video on the disc for that video to be encoded and written.

Testing Your DVD

After your DVD is written, there's one step yet remaining—make sure that the disc works! To find out whether the disc has been created correctly, the best option is to try it in the computer that wrote it. If the DVD works in your computer, chances are good that it will play in most newer DVD players and DVD-drive equipped computers.

1. To test your DVD, insert it into your computer's drive.

2. The DVD Player application should open automatically with your DVD main menu visible.

3. Using the remote control that appears on your screen, click the arrows to select a button and click Enter to watch that segment of your DVD.

Creating OneStep DVDs

So far, this chapter has focused on carefully crafting a DVD project by adding content and customizing menus before burning it to DVD. However, sometimes you need a simple, straight-forward DVD to share video quickly. iDVD's OneStep DVD feature meets this need by enabling you to burn DVDs directly from your digital video camera. (However, you cannot edit your video in any way or add menus.)

To create a OneStep DVD, connect your digital video camera, turn it on, and set it to VCR mode. Insert a blank DVD in your drive. Then, launch iDVD and choose OneStep DVD from the welcome window that appears, or choose File, OneStep DVD from the menu if another project is already open. iDVD automatically rewinds the tape in your camera and imports the video it contains.

As the video is imported, iDVD displays a thumbnail image to show its progress, as shown in Figure 30.23. Two time indicators are also displayed—one showing the amount of video imported and the other showing the amount of video that could be imported, given the space on your hard drive.

FIGURE 30.23
While importing video for a OneStep DVD, iDVD shows its progress.

To choose where iDVD begins recording rather than letting it rewind to the beginning of a tape, cue up the portion of the tape you want and then click the Play button on your camera to start importing immediately.

To stop importing video, click the Stop button at the bottom of the OneStep DVD window. iDVD displays a window to ask whether you want to Cancel the project or Continue to burn the video imported to DVD. If you don't interrupt the importing process, iDVD continues until the tape ends, there is no remaining footage on the tape, or there is no room remaining on the hard drive.

After importing, iDVD encodes the video and the sound for DVD. Once again, a thumbnail is displayed to show the progress. When encoding is complete, iDVD writes the DVD and ejects it when finished.

You can cancel your OneStep DVD up until it finishes encoding and your DVD media will be left blank.

Summary

In this chapter, you learned how to create a DVD, including adding content, designing menus, and burning disks. You saw how DVD menus are put together, using a combination of backgrounds and buttons (and don't forget the movie clips, slideshows, and computer files!). You also learned how to archive a project, create a disc image, and use the One-Step DVD feature.

PART V

System Administration and Maintenance

CHAPTER 31

Sharing Your Computer with Other Users

As you know from previous chapters, Mac OS X is a true multiuser operating system because everyone who works on the computer can have a separate, private area in which to store personal files. Although you don't have to use the multiuser capabilities of your Mac, they affect the system's structure in terms of both their benefits and problems, and may require special attention.

Understanding User Accounts

In a multiuser system, everyone who works on the computer can have a separate account in which to store personal files. In practice, that means when one user saves a document to the desktop, it does not appear on the desktop that the other users see when they log in to their accounts. Also, each person can set system preferences that show up only when he or she is logged in. Users can customize the Dock and the desktop appearance and expect them to remain that way.

> **By the Way**
>
> An interesting feature of multiuser operating systems is related to a feature called remote access. Because the operating system assigns a separate desktop to each account, multiple users can use different files on a single computer at the same time. Although this requires connecting to the machine from another computer and enabling remote login, the OS is designed to cope with different simultaneous processes so that users can work as though they were alone on the system.

The home folders for user accounts are located in the Users folder of the Mac OS X hard drive, as shown in Figure 31.1. A house icon is used in the Finder window toolbar to represent the current user's home folder. Inside the home folder are several different folders, which were discussed briefly in Chapter 2, "Using the Finder," during the discussion about file structure.

FIGURE 31.1
Every user has
a home folder in
which to store
files.

Although individual users can see the contents of most other files on the hard drive, they cannot see most of each other's files. Users in a multiuser system can set permissions on their files that restrict access to keep their work private. They can specify whether a file can be read or altered by everyone, by a limited number of other people, or only from within the account in which the files were created.

For example, Figure 31.2 shows what the home folder of the user jray looks like to another user. Most of the folders have an icon with a red circle containing a minus sign. That means these folders are not accessible to normal users who do not own them. (However, a special class of users with administrative access can access almost anything on the system. We discuss administrative users later in this chapter and again in Chapter 33, "Securing Your Computer.")

FIGURE 31.2
By default,
other users are
restricted from
accessing all
but the Public
and Sites
folders.

You can change the permissions on a file or folder that you own under the Ownership & Permissions section of the Info window (Commmand-I). Permissions are discussed further later in this chapter.

Adding and Editing User Accounts

When you first installed Mac OS X, an account was created that used the name you supplied. The system uses the short name you gave as your account name, but you can use either your full or short name to log in to the system. Because the account created first can access sensitive system settings and install new software, it's referred to as an *administrator account*.

When logged in with an administrator account, you're granted the privilege of adding other users, and you can choose to give them administrative privileges as well. Remember, however, that creating additional administrator accounts means that other people can add new accounts and modify the system, so you should do so judiciously. Be sure that you trust your users not to delete important files or disrupt the system in other ways before you give them administrator privileges.

New user accounts are added from the Accounts Preferences pane, shown in Figure 31.3.

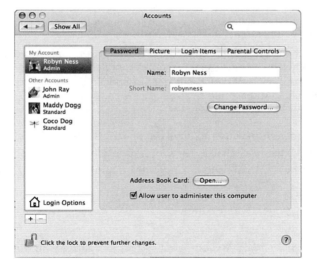

FIGURE 31.3
The left side of the Accounts Preferences pane lists current users and enables you to edit them or add new ones.

To create a new user account, follow these steps:

1. Click the "+" button at the lower left of the Accounts pane. If the "+" button appears faded, or "grayed out," you need to click the lock icon at the lower left and type your password to authorize making changes in this set of preferences.

2. Type the name of the person using the account, as well as a short name to be displayed for logging in.

> Note that although you can change many things about a user account later, you can't alter the short name used to log in without performing some complicated maneuvers. (That's because the system uses this short name as an identifier in a lot of hidden system files.) Choose wisely the first time.

3. Type a password once, and then type it again to verify it. The Password Hint box is for a short description or question to remind the user of the password if it is forgotten.

Watch Out!

> If you are serious about password-protecting your computer, you should pick your password carefully. A family member's name or birthdate may be relatively easy for people close to you to guess, and words that are in the dictionary are relatively easy for a determined hacker to crack.
>
> If you want help choosing a password, click the key icon next to the new password field that is visible either when creating a new account or changing an existing password. The Password Assistant window opens with a randomly-generated password for your consideration. If you don't like the suggestion, you can change the type of password that is generated, such as "Memorable" or "Numbers Only," and the length of the password.
>
> You can also change the type to manual, and try your own password ideas. The graph for quality indicates how easily the password could be cracked, based on length, complexity, and whether it is a word existing in the dictionary. Tips may also appear to help you choose stronger passwords.

4. If you want your new user to have administrative powers, as discussed previously, check the box labeled Allow User to Administer This Computer. (We talk about further limitations that can be set on non-administrators in just a moment.)

5. Click the Create Account button.

As soon as you click Create Account, your system recognizes your new user, who has a folder in the Users folder.

By the Way

> When you create an additional account, you may see a window asking whether you want to turn off automatic login. Automatic login means that when you turn your computer on, your account is automatically available—but when you have more than one user account, you may want to enable login so you can choose an account. The "Logging In" section a little later in this chapter talks more about logging in to multiuser systems.

If you want to change the picture associated with your own account, click the Picture button near the top of the Accounts pane. Choose an icon to represent the new user, as shown in Figure 31.4. (This picture shows up next to the user's name in the login screen, as discussed in a moment, as well as in the user's Address Book and in iChat.)

FIGURE 31.4
Choose an icon to represent a user.

> **By the Way**
>
> You can edit an existing user account, including changing the name, password, and password hint. Simply select the user account to be edited from the list at the left, and then change the Name or click the Reset Password button. Remember, however, that you can't easily change the short name after an account has been created.
>
> To alter the name or password for the currently active administrator account, you must enter your current password to provide authorization. If you have forgotten your password and need to reset it, you need to use your installation discs, as discussed in Chapter 35, "Recovering from Crashes and Other Problems."

Parental Controls

If you want to further control the access of users who aren't allowed to administer the computer, you can click the Parental Controls button to choose their level of access to various applications and system functions. After you activate any of these controls, the label under the affected Account switches from Standard to Managed so you can easily recognize where changes have been made.

By the
Way

> If you don't see any options under Parental Controls, you may have selected a user account with administrator privileges, for which you can't set limits.

As shown in Figure 31.5, the applications that can be controlled are Mail, iChat, Safari, and Dictionary. To activate them, check the box in front of each, click the Configure, and respond to the options or instructions presented. Let's take a closer look at what is controlled by each of these applications and their configuration options.

FIGURE 31.5
Check a box and configure the settings for each application.

If applying parental controls to the Mail application, you can restrict who can exchange email with the current managed user by adding the email addresses of trusted people, as shown in Figure 31.6. Messages that come from other addresses are not received, but you can choose to have notifications delivered to another address so approval can be given. (See Chapter 17, "Using Mail," for more about this application.)

The settings for iChat are similar to those for Mail: List the name and AOL Instant Messenger (AOL) identifier of trusted people, and only those buddies are then recognized by iChat. (See Chapter 18, "Using iChat AV," for more about this application.)

You can also control which websites can be visited with the Safari web browser. To set parental controls for Safari, you will need to check the box for Safari in your account, and then log in from the account the controls are being applied to and open Safari. To set acceptable websites in Safari, just add them to Bookmarks—but you must first type an administrator name and password. (When parental controls are set for Safari, you see a lock symbol on top of Safari's usual Bookmarks icon in the Bookmarks bar.) If a user tries to visit a site that has not been added to the Bookmarks, the message shown in Figure 31.7 is displayed. (See Chapter 14, "Using Safari," for more about this application.)

FIGURE 31.6
Set trusted email addresses as well as an address to receive notification of email sent from unapproved addresses.

FIGURE 31.7
Safari doesn't display sites that aren't bookmarked.

Setting parental controls for the Dictionary application blocks the display of a set of words, including profanity, that may be inappropriate for children or other sensitive users. (Because there is nothing to configure—parental controls are either on or off—the Configure button is replaced with an Info button.)

The Finder & System parental controls are a bit different from those for the applications we've already discussed. You need to choose what kind of limits to place on the managed account.

The options are

▶ Some Limits—With the Some Limits options (shown in Figure 31.8, you can set whether users can access System Preferences, change passwords, modify the Dock, burn CDs or DVDs, administer printers, or allow use of programs that aren't approved if they are needed by an approved application. You can also control which applications are available to the managed user.

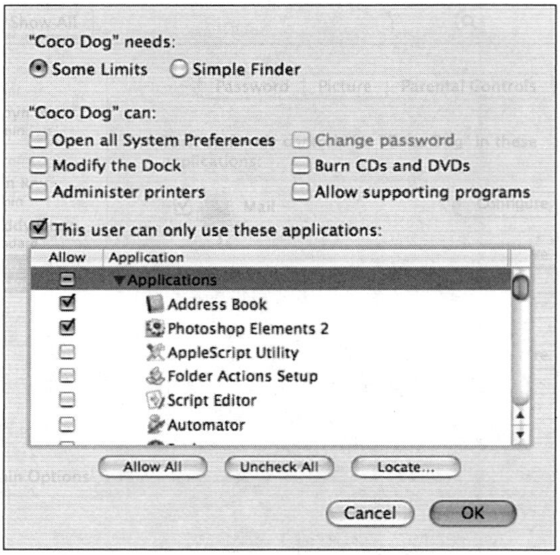

FIGURE 31.8
Restrict access to specific system functions or applications.

▶ Simple Finder—If you want to pare down the options for a given user to make things less confusing, you can enable a setting called Simple Finder, which simplifies system navigation by allowing the user to open only applications that appear in the My Applications folder.

Deleting User Accounts

Now that you know how to add a user, you should also know how to remove a user. This again requires you to open the Accounts Preferences pane. To delete a user account, select the account to be deleted and click the "-" button at the lower left. In this way, you can delete any user account except the last administrator account. (At least one account must exist, and it has to be an administrator account.) The sheet window shown in Figure 31.9 appears to confirm your choice. You have the option to Delete Immediately, which doesn't save anything in the user account, or to click OK, which stores the deleted user's files as a disk image (.dmg file) in the Deleted Users folders. (If you choose OK and find later that you don't want the contents of the deleted account, you can open that folder and delete the .dmg file.)

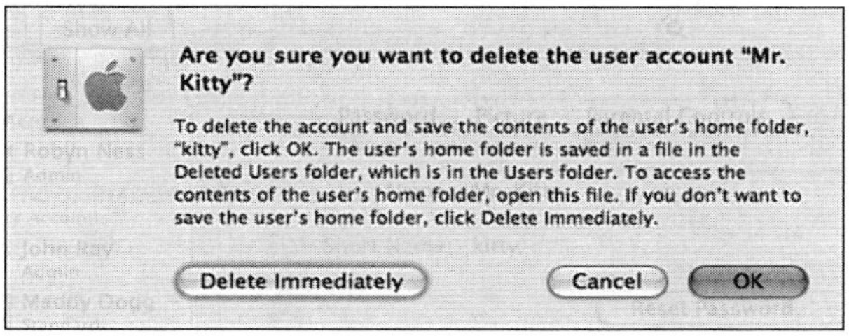

Are you sure you want to delete the user account "Mr. Kitty"?

To delete the account and save the contents of the user's home folder, "kitty", click OK. The user's home folder is saved in a file in the Deleted Users folder, which is in the Users folder. To access the contents of the user's home folder, open this file. If you don't want to save the user's home folder, click Delete Immediately.

Delete Immediately   Cancel   OK

FIGURE 31.9
When a user account is deleted, that user can no longer log in.

When the first account is deleted, the Deleted Users folder is created. You may choose to retain or delete the .dmg file of the deleted user's account. If you want to remove the entire Deleted Users folder, you can drag it to the trash, but you need to enter an administrative user's password to authorize the action.

By the Way

Logging In

Now that you know how to create additional accounts, you may be wondering how your users will access them. One aspect of maintaining a multiuser system is keeping track of who can use the computer, to which files they have access, and where their work is stored. These objectives are met by requiring people to sign in before using the machine. This process of identifying yourself to the system, which involves presenting a username and password, is known as a *login*.

If you're logged in on a Mac that's used by other people with their own accounts, it's a good habit to log off when finished. This allows the computer to return to a state that enables others to log in. If someone forgets to log off, that person's account and files could be accessed by anyone because the system does not know that the owning user is no longer at the controls. (This isn't necessarily a serious problem for home users, but it's neater to have everyone's files in their own account.)

By default, Mac OS X sets the system to log in automatically to the account of the first-created user every time the computer starts up. In this mode, your computer doesn't require you to enter your username and password. If you don't see a need to force a login each time your computer turns on, you can keep this setting.

However, if other people have access to your computer, you might want to create separate accounts for them and require them to log in. Many people dislike the idea of requiring a login to use their computers, but it is a good idea to disable automatic login if your computer has more than one user. Why? Without required logins, your documents and system settings can be modified by whoever uses the machine. Besides, giving each user his own desktop can cut down on clutter, prevent accidental deletion of files, and enable everyone to customize settings.

To change your system so that it requires each user to log in, open the System Preferences and click the Accounts button in the System section. Click the Login Options item at the lower left to view the login preferences, as shown in Figure 31.10. From those options, uncheck the box in front of Automatically Log In As [Username]. We look at the options for customizing the login window in the next section.

FIGURE 31.10
Login options include setting your system to automatically log in when your computer starts.

Customizing the Login Window

The screen in which users supply their names and passwords is referred to as the *login window*. Figure 31.11 shows an example.

Although the login window looks simple, several of its characteristics can be altered in the Login Options window of the Accounts Preferences pane, which appeared in Figure 31.10. You can indicate what you want the login window to look like: either a list of usernames with an associated picture, as shown in Figure 31.11, or two blank fields for username and password. When a login picture format is used, clicking on a user reveals a space to type the user's password.

FIGURE 31.11
Mac OS X gives
the option to
choose an icon
to represent
each user.

You can configure several additional options related to logging in or what is active at the login window. Choose whether to include the Shut Down and Restart buttons login window and whether to show password hints on the login window. You can enable at the login window the Input menu to change the keyboard layout to support different languages or national standards, or to enable the VoiceOver feature, a spoken English interface to assist the visually impaired. (Refer to Chapter 5, "Setting System Preferences and Universal Access Options," for more about VoiceOver.)

Fast User Switching

The bottom check box under Login Options (refer to Figure 31.10) enables or disables *fast user switching*, a feature useful for families of shared computers. In earlier versions of Mac OS X, if you added multiple user accounts to your computer, you had to close your applications and then choose Log Out from the Apple menu before another user could access the system from the same computer. In Mac OS 10.3 and 10.4, fast user switching preserves your current desktop but lets another user log in and use her account. Users whose accounts are logged in but not onscreen can then return to where they left off.

With fast user switching enabled, a menu item appears near the upper-right corner of the menu bar—the switching menu. Displaying the menu reveals a list of local user accounts along with a Login Window option. Choosing a user's name prompts for that user's login information and then switches to that user's desktop. Choosing the Login Window selection leaves your applications running but displays the login window—allowing other users to log in without disrupting your workspace.

If you want to be able to switch to another user account without entering that user's password, the other user *must* have a blank password.

User accounts that are "active" (have running applications) are denoted with orange check marks in front of their names in the switching menu and the login screen, as shown in Figure 31.12. Switching to an active account is almost instantaneous.

FIGURE 31.12
Active sessions are denoted by orange check boxes in the switching menu and login screen.

Users should log out (Shift-Command-Q) completely when finished using the computer. Shutting down or restarting your computer while there are active sessions could result in lost data for users who are still logged in. Also, if you try to shut down while other accounts are active, you need to enter an administrator name and password to authorize it.

File Permissions

In addition to letting you decide who can log in to your computer, Mac OS X enables you to control who can interact with your files. If you create a file while you're logged in to your account, you own that file. Without your password, other users can be prevented from accessing your folders and files in any way; they can neither read nor alter your files and folders that are not stored in your Sites or Public folders. For example, the folders in the home folder created for each user have some of these restrictions set by default.

Changing privileges in a file or folder is done though the Info panel of the Finder, as discussed in Chapter 4, "Working with Folders, Files, and Applications." These are the steps to use this panel:

1. Highlight the icon of the file or folder whose access you want to change. Users who are administrators can change the permissions on almost any file, but those who are normal users can change the permissions only on files they themselves own.

2. To open the Info panel, choose Get Info from the Action pop-up menu at the top of a Finder window or from the File menu. Alternatively, you can use the key command Command-I.

3. Open the Ownership & Permissions section of the panel and click the disclosure triangle in front of Details to show levels of access, as shown in Figure 31.13. If the lock button shows a closed lock, click it to unlock the settings.

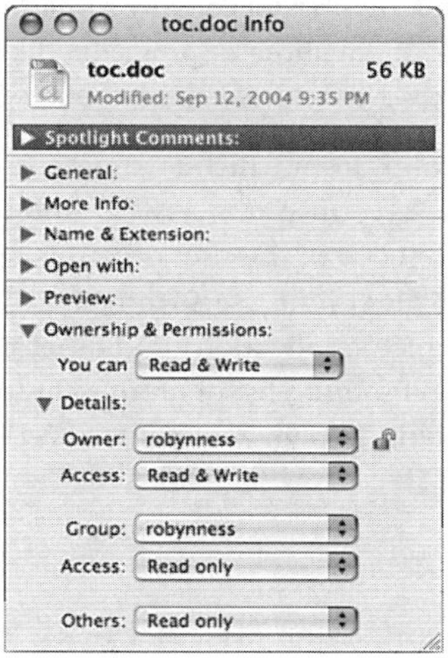

FIGURE 31.13
Protect or share your files by changing permissions in the Info window.

4. Access can now be set so that different users have different privileges. The main options for levels of access are Read & Write, Read Only, and No Access. For folders, there is also the Write Only option, which enables a drop-box feature so that users can copy files into the folder, but only the owner can view its contents.

> You may have noticed that you can set permissions such that even you can't read or write to files you own. Why is that option available? If you've ever accidentally deleted an important file, you'll understand why. Sometimes it's best to impose a few rules on yourself to avoid bigger problems. Remember, though, that file owners can always change the permissions, even after they've turned off read or write access for themselves.

By the Way

5. When you've set the permissions you need, close the pane.

> When changing access options for a folder, you also have the Apply to Enclosed Items button to apply the access rights you've selected to all files and folders within the original folder.

By the Way

Understanding Groups

You might have noticed that the Ownership & Permissions section of the Info panel enables you to specify permissions for the owner of the file, the group to which that user belongs, and others. But what is a group? Let's look at that concept briefly now.

In Unix systems, on which Mac OS X is based, users can be classified into many different groups so that they can access, or be excluded from accessing, certain information. In other words, some files are needed by more than one person but shouldn't be accessed by everyone. To facilitate appropriate file sharing, groups are defined to identify who can have access to which system features.

There are many possible groups from which to choose in the Owner and Group pop-up menus of the Ownership & Permissions section. Among the groups recognized by the system are the names for each of the user accounts on your computer, which are used to assign ownership of files to the users who created them. There is also an option labeled System, to which applications and other things available for system-wide use are assigned. The remaining list of groups contains specialized groups that you don't need unless you plan to treat Mac OS X as a Unix system.

Summary

Multiuser systems are new territory for most Mac users, but the basics aren't difficult to understand. This chapter introduced you to this concept as it relates to Mac OS X and explained different types of users, user groups, and file privileges and how to work with them. You also explored some of the settings you need to create, delete, and edit user accounts and to change read/write file permissions.

CHAPTER 32

Sharing Files and Running Network Services

The Macintosh has always made it simple to share files with other Macs on the same network and over the Internet. Mac OS X's strong Unix roots bring even more sharing capabilities to the Mac, including the capability to connect to Windows systems. In this chapter, you learn how to activate various sharing features.

Sharing Services

A *service* is something that your computer provides to other computers on a network, such as running a web server or sharing files. In Mac OS X, you can enable or disable all the standard information-sharing services from the Services settings of the Sharing pane in System Preferences, as shown in Figure 32.1.

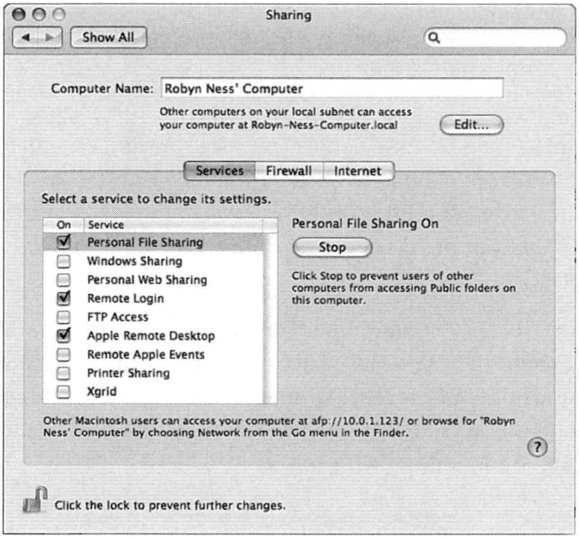

FIGURE 32.1
The Services options of Sharing Preferences enable you to choose which sharing services you want running on your computer.

Watch
Out!

Be aware that turning on or off any service in the Services Preferences of the Sharing pane activates that service for all user accounts on a computer. If sharing is on for one user, it's on for everyone. If it's off, it's off for everyone!

You can enable or disable the following services:

▶ Personal File Sharing—Share your files with other Mac users across a local network. We discuss activating AppleTalk, if needed, in just a moment.

▶ Windows Sharing—Share your files with Windows users on your local network.

▶ Personal Web Sharing—Use Mac OS X's built-in web server to serve web pages from your own computer.

▶ Remote Login—Allow users to interact with your computer remotely with Secure Shell (SSH) command-line access.

▶ FTP Access—Allow access to your machine via FTP (File Transfer Protocol).

▶ Apple Remote Desktop—Enable individuals using Apple's full version of Remote Desktop to access your computer.

By the
Way

Essentially, Apple Remote Desktop enables someone to look over your shoulder (or even take the controls if needed) as you work, without being in the same room. To make this work, the remote viewer does need to purchase and install a copy of Apple's Remote Desktop, but this is a great option for people in learning labs or help-desk situations!

▶ Remote Apple Events—Enable software running on other machines to send events to applications on your computer with the AppleScript scripting language. Coverage of this option is outside the scope of this book, but the basics of AppleScript are discussed in Chapter 36, "Introducing Automator and AppleScript."

▶ Printer Sharing—Grant other computers access to the printers connected to your computer. With this service enabled, your printers appear in the Printer Setup Utility's printer list for other users on your local network. General information about connecting to printers is covered in Chapter 12, "Printing, Faxing, and Working with Fonts."

Did you
Know?

In addition to sharing printers with other Mac users, you can share printers with Windows users by enabling both Printer Sharing and Windows Sharing in the Services pane of the Sharing Preferences.

▶ Xgrid—Share your Mac's unused processing capacity with others on the network. With specially-written software and proper configuration, Xgrid makes it possible to share a computer's resources when they are not needed for the tasks it is running locally. (Because it requires Xgrid-compatible software, we don't cover this option further.)

The Firewall section of the Sharing control pane contains a list of all the options in the Services section, with the exception of Xgrid. A *firewall* sits between the outside network and network services on your computer to protect your computer from network-based attacks. The Firewall options enable you to activate Mac OS X's built-in firewall software to prevent access to your computer through those services you don't want to run. Chapter 33, "Securing Your Computer," discusses this further.

Now, let's take at look at starting and using these services.

Activating Personal File Sharing and AppleTalk

Personal File Sharing is Apple's method of sharing files with other Mac users over a network, via either TCP/IP or AppleTalk. AppleTalk is an older protocol for browsing and accessing remote workstations that share files or services, such as printers. With the introduction of Mac OS X, Apple has been transitioning to use of the TCP/IP-based Service Locator Protocol (SLP) and a local network-based services feature called Rendezvous, mentioned in Chapter 18, "Using iChat AV." However, you might still need to enable AppleTalk to access older devices or Macs running pre-OS X operating systems.

Follow these steps to share your files with another Mac user:

1. Determine whether you need to use AppleTalk to access computers and printers on your network. If all the other computers are Mac OS X machines and your printer is USB-based, you probably don't need AppleTalk support—skip ahead to step 8. If you're not sure, go to step 2.

2. Open the Network preferences, found in the Internet & Network section of System Preferences.

3. Use the Show pop-up menu to choose the device you're using to access your network (such as AirPort or Ethernet).

4. Click the AppleTalk button to reveal the options shown in Figure 32.2.

5. Check the Make AppleTalk Active check box. (To make the change, you might first have to click the small lock button at the bottom of the window and type an administrator's username and password.)

By the Way

If you don't recall the difference between administrators and non-administrators, you may want to review Chapter 31, "Sharing Your Computer with Other Users." For now, all you need to know is that the first-created user account is an administrator account. Other accounts may or may not be administrators, depending how they were set up.

6. If necessary, choose an AppleTalk Zone to use. You might want to speak to your network administrator if you aren't sure what to choose.

7. Click Apply Now.

8. Open the Sharing Preferences pane, as shown previously in Figure 32.1, and check the box for Personal File Sharing, or highlight it and click the Start button.

9. Close the System Preferences window.

Your Mac OS X computer should now be able to share files with other Macs on your network. We talk about how to actually connect to other users' files later in this chapter in the section "Connecting to Shared Folders."

Activating Windows Sharing (Samba)

Windows computers use a different protocol than the Mac for file and print sharing. To share files with Windows computers, your Mac must employ the same protocol through a piece of software called Samba.

To turn on Windows Sharing (Samba), open the Sharing System Preferences to the Services section and then either click the check box in front of the Windows Sharing option, or highlight the option and click the Start button. The Sharing pane updates, as demonstrated in Figure 32.3.

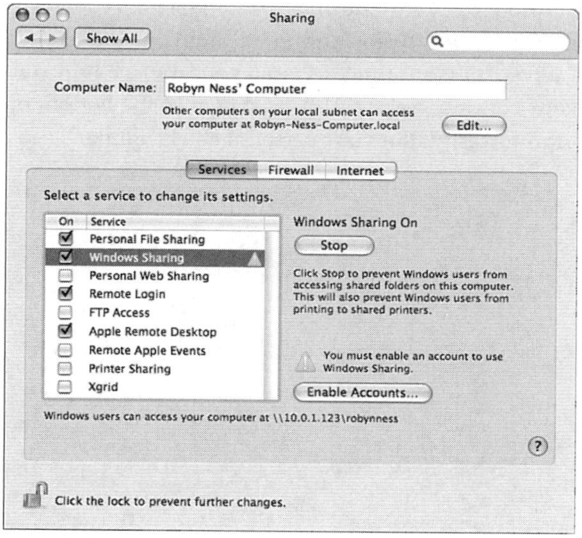

FIGURE 32.3
Activate Samba for file sharing with Windows computers by using the Sharing preference pane.

As shown in Figure 32.3, you are prompted to enable an account to use Windows Sharing. Click the Enable Accounts button to select which accounts to authorize. When you choose an account from the list, you are asked for the password.

Like AppleShare file sharing in Mac OS X, the default Samba configuration is set up to share each user's home directory. The user's home directory can be accessed through the path that appears in the Sharing preferences pane in the Services section when Windows Sharing is highlighted, as in Figure 32.3. (We talk about accessing files from a computer running Windows in the section "Connecting from a Windows Machine.")

Activating Web Sharing

Mac OS X makes it easy to run a simple web server using a popular and powerful open source server called Apache. (Apache is actually the server that powers most Internet websites. It's built to run complex sites, including e-commerce and other interactive applications, and it's running on your desktop as a part of Mac OS X.)

Mac OS X can share a personal website for each user on the computer. In addition, it can run a master website for the whole computer, entirely independent of the personal websites.

To turn on Web sharing, open the Sharing System Preferences(shown in Figures 32.4) and check the box for Personal Web Sharing, or highlight it and click the Start button. The Apache server starts running, making your website immediately available. Make a note of your personal website URL as shown at the bottom of the window and then start Safari to verify that your personal site is online.

FIGURE 32.4
Turn on Web Sharing and note the address of your website.

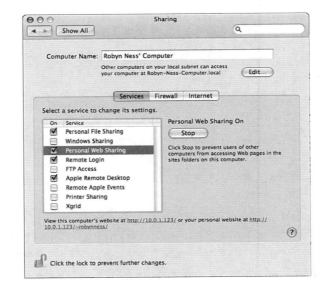

With Safari running, enter your personal website URL, which should be in the following format:

```
http://<server ip or hostname>/~<username>
```

The tilde (~) is extremely critical. It tells the server that it should load the Web pages from the Sites folder located inside the user's home directory. Note that after you activate Web sharing for one user, it's active for all users, so make sure that all users are ready to have their websites shared with the rest of the world.

Assuming that you entered your URL correctly, you should see the default Mac OS X home page, as demonstrated in Figure 32.5.

FIGURE 32.5
Apple includes a default personal home page.

To edit your website, just look inside your Sites folder. The default page is generated from the file index.html and the Images folder.

> Under Mac OS X's user interface, it isn't possible to change your home page's filename. When you start creating files, make sure that the first page you want to be loaded is named index.html; otherwise, your site might not behave as you want.

Watch Out!

To edit an HTML document, you can open it in a text editor, such as the TextEdit application discussed in Chapter 6, "Using Calculator, Graphing Calculator, Preview, and TextEdit."

> If you are interested in making your own simple web pages, I highly recommend *Teach Yourself HTML and XHTML in 24 Hours*. If you would to learn more about the Apache web server, check out *Apache Server Unleashed*.

By the Way

You may have noticed that two website addresses are shown at the bottom of the screen when Web Sharing is activated: There's one for your own account and one without the ~<username> portion. The one that doesn't specify an account is the website for the computer rather than a specific user. If you haven't already done so, enter that address in a browser now. If no one with access to your system has created a new page for your computer, you should see something similar to the page shown in Figure 32.6.

FIGURE 32.6
The default
page for your
system looks
different than
your default
personal page
(shown in Figure
32.5).

This is the system website, and it can be used for anything you want, but you must do a bit of digging to reach the directory that holds it.

The system-level site is in the Documents folder, located in a folder labeled Webserver inside the hard drive's Library folder. (Note that there are several folders labeled Library at various levels in OS X—this one is at the same level as the Applications and System folders.) Any administrator can make changes to this directory, so make sure that the other admin users on the system understand its purpose and that they don't assume that it's related to their personal websites.

Viewing Website Statistics

For every visit made to a website located on your computer, the Apache web server makes an entry in its log files. These log files can tell you who looked at your files, what they looked at, and the IP addresses of their computers. Keeping track of this kind of information helps you understand who the audience for your website is and what types of information they're seeking. (If your site has more than one page, seeing what pages people visit can show you what people like—or what they can find— and what may need more work!)

The logs for your server are located in the /var/log/httpd directory and are named access_log and error_log by default. You can open these files in a text editor, view them from the command line, or use the Console application to monitor them by following these steps:

1. Open the Console application located inside the Utilities folder of the Applications folder.

2. From the File menu, select Open Quickly, select /var/log, select httpd, and, finally, select access_log.

3. A window such as the one displayed in Figure 32.7 opens with the contents of the Apache access_log file.

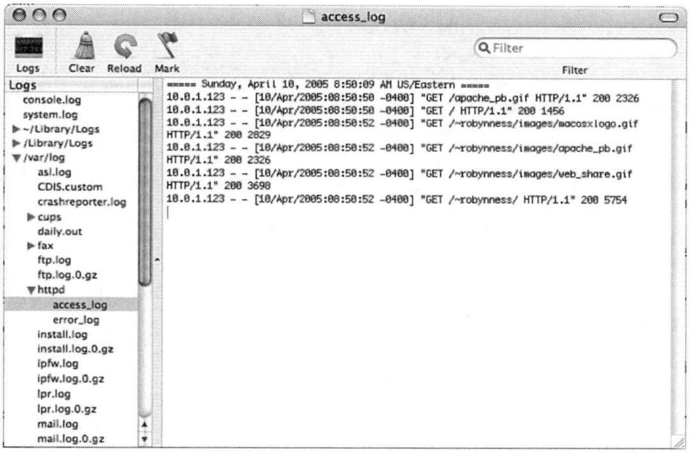

FIGURE 32.7
The Console application can be used to monitor your logs.

As you and other users access the websites on your computer, you can view information about each of the hits within the log window. Each row displayed is a record of what computer has visited your site, what was viewed, and when it was viewed. Take, for example, the following log entry:

```
10.0.1.116 - - [30/Jan/2005:19:13:38 -0400] "Get /~robyn http/1.1" 301 336
```

Essentially, this means that the computer with the IP address 10.0.1.116 visited on the 30th of January, 2005, at 7:13 p.m. to view the default page for the user "robyn." The extra numbers at the end of the entry are a code reporting how the web server responded to the request and the size of the file (in bytes) served to the viewer's computer for the given item.

> Hits represent each of the page elements that are served to create a web page. The list of hits in Figure 32.7 is from viewing the page shown in Figure 32.6, and the system-level default web page once each. (There are so many rows of information because the web pages and each image they contain count as separate hits.)

By the Way

Although accurate, this information can be difficult to interpret—especially if many visitors have viewed your website. You can install a number of applications (both free and commercial) to help translate the raw web logs into something a bit more meaningful. To help you get started, take a look at the following products and websites:

▶ Analog—www.summary.net/soft/analog.html

  Analog is a robust, fast, free program for analyzing web statistics. Reports include basic bar graphs and pie charts.

▶ Webalizer—www.mrunix.net/webalizer/

  Webalizer is a web server log file analyzer that runs on OS X (and many other Unix and Unix-based systems). It handles large log files as well as partial files, and generates easy-to-read graphs. Best of all, it is entirely free.

▶ Summary—www.summary.net/summary.html

  Summary produces web statistic summaries of just about anything that can be determined from web page requests, including search terms that lead to a page and various types of errors that occurred on a site. It is available for a free 30-day trial.

▶ Traffic Report—www.seacloak.com/

  Traffic is another web statistics analyzer that presents a wide variety of reports. It is available in a lite and full version, with pricing to reflect the levels of functionality. A 30-day free trial is available.

▶ Sawmill—www.sawmill.net/

  Sawmill produces attractive, easy-to-read web statistics reports with graphs and color-coding. It is available for a free 30-day trial.

Activating Remote Login and FTP

Two additional methods of file sharing available in Mac OS X are FTP and SSH. FTP (File Transfer Protocol) simply provides cross-platform file-transfer services. The second type of sharing, SSH (secure shell), enables a remote user secure access to the command prompt of a Mac OS X computer from almost any computer anywhere in the world—and the ability to transfer files with better security than available through FTP.

Both of these protocols can be turned on in the Services section of the Sharing preferences. SSH is turned on through the Remote Login check box, as shown previously in Figure 32.4. Activate FTP by clicking the Allow FTP Access check box. Alternatively, you can highlight the option you want to activate and click the Start button.

Now that you know how to turn these services on, let's see what they can do for you!

Remote Login (SSH)

SSH, or as Apple calls it in Sharing preferences, Remote Login, is a new concept for most Mac users. If you've seen a Windows or a Linux computer before, you've probably occasionally seen someone open a command prompt and start typing text commands instead of working with an icon-filled desktop. Although SSH isn't the command line itself, it provides a secure means of accessing the command line from a remote location. In an SSH connection, the entire session is encrypted. As such, administrators can use SSH to log in to their systems and edit user accounts, change passwords, and so on, without the fear of giving away potentially sensitive information (such as passwords) to those who are watching network traffic for information to exploit.

For the most part, all you need to know about SSH is that from the Terminal application located inside the Utilities folder in the Applications folder you can access your account on a remote system by typing

```
ssh <username>@<ip address or hostname>
```

(The specific information for your computer is shown at the bottom of the Sharing window after SSH is enabled.)

After you enter this command, the remote machine prompts you for the account password and then gives you full control over your account and the resources to which you have access. It's as if you launched the Terminal application directly on the affected computer. (If you're wondering what exactly you can do with SSH, don't worry! We talk more about using the command line from the Terminal application in Chapter 37, "Using Basic Unix Commands.") If you're not interested in the command line, don't worry—there's absolutely no reason why you have to use SSH. If you prefer a GUI solution to remote system administration, check out Apple's Remote Desktop application, mentioned in a note in the section "Sharing Services" earlier in this chapter. It enables you to do things such as use your work computer from home and vice versa.

> If you're planning to serve FTP and SSH only occasionally, shut off the services in the Sharing window until you're ready to use them. This closes some potential points of attack on your computer. You can still use the Mac OS X clients and command line to access other SSH/FTP servers, but remote users can't connect to your machine.

Watch Out!

FTP

With FTP enabled via the Sharing preferences on your computer, a remote user can type into a web browser a URL of the form:

```
ftp://<client number>.<ip address or hostname>
```

This tells the web browser to contact the Mac OS X computer running the FTP server. From there, the user is prompted to enter any valid username and password for the computer being accessed (as shown in Figure 32.8).

FIGURE 32.8
Authentication requires a valid username and password.

FTP File System Authentication

Enter your user name and password to access the server at the URL "ftp://10.0.1.123/."

Your name and password will not be sent securely.

Name

Password

☐ Remember this password in my keychain

Cancel   OK

After a user has connected via FTP, a special icon appears on the desktop to represent the remote system that is now linked to, or *mounted on*, your desktop. When double-clicked, a Finder window containing the files on the remote system appears.

Although the built-in FTP option provides some basic FTP functions, most users prefer to use heartier third-party software. Here are some of the most popular options:

▶ Fetch—www.fetchsoftworks.com/

Fetch is a full-featured FTP client that enables you to resume file transfer if interrupted. (The cursor appears as the silhouette of a running dog to show when transfers are in progress.) A 15-day trial is available.

▶ Interarchy—www.interarchy.com/

Interarchy enables you not only to transfer files but also to diagnose connection problems.

▶ Transmit—www.panic.com/transmit/download.html

Transmit enables you to transfer files and create a list of frequently accessed servers—all in a user-friendly interface. You can download a free trial version that doesn't expire, but you have to purchase Transmit to unlock all the features.

If you need to share files over the Internet, FTP is one of the best ways to do so. It's a fast, effective, and efficient protocol. Unfortunately, it's also not easy to work with behind firewalls, and it transmits its passwords and data unencrypted so they can be monitored easily by unauthorized parties. If you set up a non-administrator account, perhaps called Transfers, for the sole purpose of moving non-confidential files around, these security issues shouldn't be much of a problem. Firewalls, on the other hand, are something you might need to discuss with your network administrator before you activate FTP.

You learn how to use FTP from the Finder in the next section.

Connecting to Shared Folders

Your Mac OS X computer can connect to a number of types of network resources from the Finder, specifically:

▶ Macintosh systems—Other Mac computers that are sharing files via AppleTalk or AppleShare IP.

▶ Windows/Linux computers—If Windows or Linux computers are using SMB or CIFS file sharing (the standard for most Windows networks), your Mac can access the files easily.

▶ WebDAV shares—WebDAV is a cross-platform file-sharing solution that uses the standard web protocols. The .Mac iDisk storage uses WebDAV.

▶ FTP servers—File Transfer Protocol servers are a popular means of distributing software on the Internet.

▶ Linux/BSD NFS servers—NFS is the Unix standard for file sharing. Your Mac (being Unix-based) can obviously talk to them as well.

To connect in these various ways, choose Go, Connect to Server (Command-K) from the Finder menu. This opens a new dialog box, shown in Figure 32.9, that enables you to connect to remote computers.

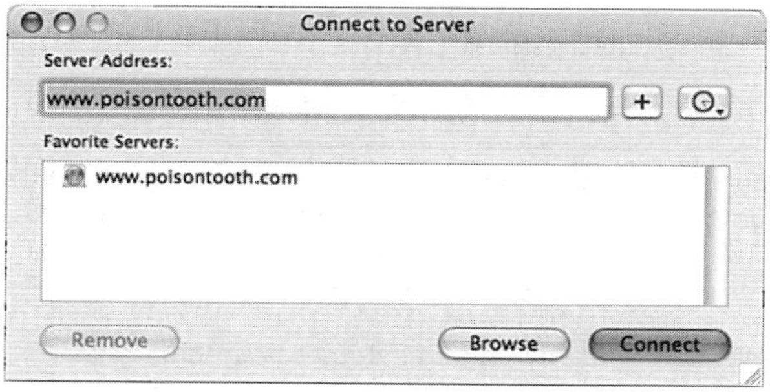

FIGURE 32.9
The Finder has the power to connect you to remote volumes directly.

To make the connection to Macintosh and Windows servers, enter the address of the server you want to access and then click Connect. After a few seconds, you're prompted for a username and a password, as shown in Figure 32.10.

Click Connect. You may then see a window similar to Figure 32.11, where you can choose different accounts on the remote computer. After you choose one and click OK, the volume is mounted on your desktop. Double-click the icon to access the remote computer.

By the Way

If you're connecting to another Mac OS X computer, you can use either an account holder's full name or short name to connect. You must enter a valid password for that account.

Connecting to WebDAV and NFS shared volumes is similar.

Your network administrator should be able to give you the exact information you need, but for the most part, the URLs follow a format like this:

FTP shares: ftp://*<server name>/<shared volume>*

For example, I have an FTP server named Xanadu on my network (poisontooth.com) containing a folder called `waternet` at the root level of the server. To access it, I would type `ftp://xanadu.poisontooth.com/waternet` and then click Connect.

WebDAV is even simpler. WebDAV shares are actually just web resources, so they use the same URLs that you would type into your web browser. For example, to access the iDisk storage of your Mac.com account, you would type `http://idisk.mac.com/<your Mac.com username>`.

NFS follows the same pattern. If the remote server is configured to allow connections, an NFS connection URL looks like this: nfs://*<server name>/<shared volume>*.

Connecting from a Windows Machine

Earlier in this chapter, you learned how to enable Windows Sharing. Now, we'll talk about how someone on a Windows computer can connect to your computer.

> The following steps are for Windows XP. Those running different versions of Windows may have to consult other documentation because some features may be labeled, or even accessed, differently.

By the Way

There are essentially two options for connecting. For a Windows computer on your own network, you can browse to a shared Mac account in the following way:

1. Open the Control Panel from the Windows Start menu.

2. Choose Network and Internet Connections from the items under the header Pick a Category.

3. Choose My Network Places from the list along the left with the header See Also.

4. Under the header Network Tasks, choose View Workgroup Computers.

5. Under the header Other Places, choose Microsoft Windows Network.

6. Double-click the Workgroup icon to see a screen similar to Figure 32.12, in which the shared Mac appears as an option.

7. Double-click the desired Mac OS X Client to initiate contact. You then have to enter the username and password of the Mac account holder to access the account.

FIGURE 32.12
Choose a Mac that's part of the current PC's Windows Workgroup.

Keep in mind that the person logging from Windows must be identified as the same user the Mac account recognizes, meaning that it is necessary to use the username and password of the account on Mac OS X when you log in to Windows. Be sure to enter your username in all lowercase characters and the password just as you entered it in Mac OS X.

After logging in, the Windows user double-clicks the account icon to view the folders in the Mac user's account, as shown in Figure 32.13.

For Windows XP users outside your local network, the connection process requires them to map a path to your shared account, using the address displayed in the Sharing window when you enabled it for Windows Sharing (similar to the address shown at the bottom of Figure 32.3.)

Here are the steps to map a networked drive:

1. Open the Control Panel from the Windows Start menu.

2. Choose Network and Internet Connections from the items under the header Pick a Category.

3. Choose My Network Places from the list along the left with the header See Also.

4. Choose Add a Network Place from the list along the left with the header Network Tasks.

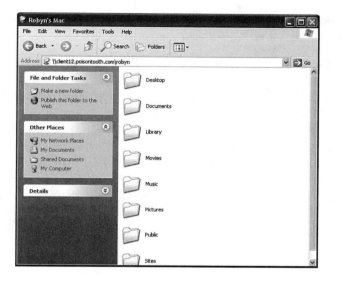

FIGURE 32.13
The familiar files of an OS X user's home folder in an unexpected interface!

5. A wizard appears to guide you. Click Next and select the Choose Another Network Location option.

6. Click Next to see the screen shown in Figure 32.14. There, type the path given in the Sharing pane of your Mac. (Be sure to type it exactly as shown, including the backslash characters.) Then click Next. You may have to wait a moment as the Windows computer locates the requested account.

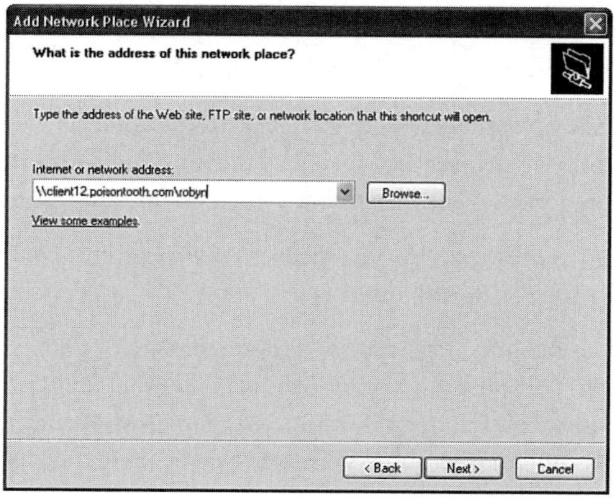

FIGURE 32.14
Enter the path to the shared Mac OS X account carefully.

7. If all goes well, you see the screen shown in Figure 32.15, where you can give a name to the network place your computer has just identified. Click Next.

8. The final screen of the wizard requires you to click Finish to wrap things up.

To connect to a mapped network drive, open the Control Panel and choose Network and Internet Connections. Under the See Also heading on the left side of the window, choose My Network Places. You then see the place you just added under the Internet header in the middle of the screen. You can double-click it to view the folders in the Mac user's account, as shown previously in Figure 32.13.

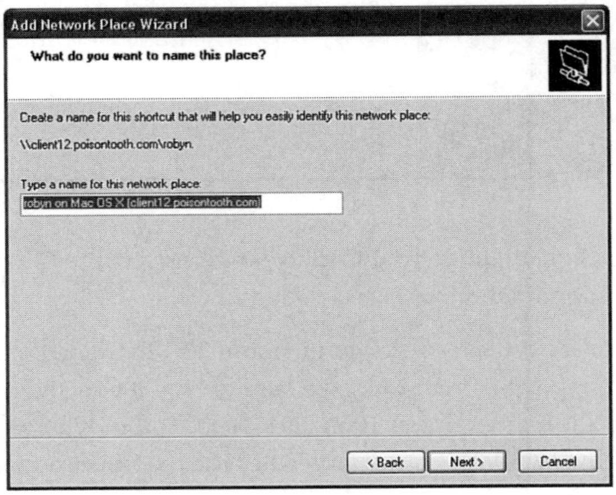

FIGURE 32.15
Give a short but descriptive name to the shared account.

Sharing Your Internet Connection

If you have multiple computers that need access to the Internet, but only one Internet connection, you can set up Mac OS X to share the connection it has with other computers on your network. Here are some possible configurations:

▶ If your primary connection is via AirPort, any machines connected to it via ethernet can connect to the Internet.

▶ If your primary connection is an ethernet connection, your machine can become an AirPort base station and share its connection with others using AirPort wireless technology (assuming that the sharing computers all have AirPort cards). It can also share with other computers that use ethernet.

▶ If your connection is a modem, your machine can share connections through both AirPort and ethernet.

Watch Out!

Even though this sounds like a truly wonderful feature, it should be used with caution. Some network arrangements can be disrupted when their member computers start sharing Internet connections. Check with your network administrator, or any nearby network administrators of wireless networks, before you try this.

To share your Internet connection, open the Internet section of the Sharing System Preferences, shown in Figure 32.16, set the Share Your Connection From pop-up menu to the type of connection used, and check the box for the type of connection that will be connecting. After you have these settings in place, click the Start button.

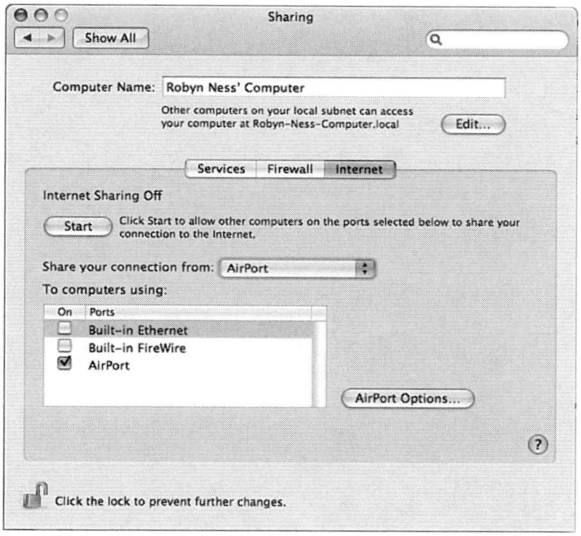

FIGURE 32.16
Share your network connection with a friend.

Summary

The Macintosh has always made it simple to share file information between computers. Mac OS X keeps the process simple but imposes some limitations for which users might not be prepared. At the same time, it opens up compatibility with Windows and Linux computers by adding SMB/CIFS and WebDAV support. In addition to the standard file sharing services, Mac OS X can be configured to act as an FTP or SSH server, making it possible to access information and control your computer from anywhere on the Internet.

CHAPTER 33

Securing Your Computer

Mac OS X is a powerful Unix-based operating system, and with that power comes the responsibility to minimize security risks. If your computer is used by other people, it's wise to secure it against users who may not realize the consequences of their actions, or those who may intend to wreak havoc. If you're connecting your computer to the Internet, it's necessary to take preventive measures to guard against unwanted connections over the network.

For information about Apple's security recommendations and recent software updates related to security, visit the Apple Product Security web page at www.apple.com/support/security/.

Local Security

Mac OS X is a true multiuser operating system. In Mac OS X, you have complete control over who can do what, but you must realize that exercising that control is essential if you intend to have a shared computer that doesn't self-destruct after one or two adventurous users decide to play around.

Problems due to local users might not seem likely, but an unmanaged public computer can easily be turned into a powerful tool of attack—sometimes unintentionally. (As you learned in Chapter 32, "Sharing Files and Running Network Services," and will explore further in just a moment, even turning on network services can expose your computer to risk from malicious strangers.)

Much of local system security is common sense coupled with a reasonable amount of watchfulness. Because implementing a local security policy is easier than maintaining network security, that's where we start.

Your first decision is what type of computer you're setting up.

If the machine is destined to be in a public library and serve as both a Unix and a Macintosh workstation, your security considerations are far more complicated than if it sits at your desk and has only you as a user.

Let's take a look at a series of steps you can take to minimize the risks to your system. Some obviously don't apply to your particular circumstances, but they're worth noting regardless.

Create Only "Standard" Users

Many people aren't clear on what happens when you create a user in Mac OS X. As you learned in Chapter 31, "Sharing Your Computer with Other Users," two types of user accounts can be created in the Accounts pane of the System Preferences: admin users and standard users. The only difference when setting up accounts is checking the box that reads Allow User to Administer This Computer. A user who has this check box set can

- ▶ Add or delete users and their files

- ▶ Remove software installed in the system-wide Applications folder

- ▶ Change or completely remove network settings

- ▶ Activate or disable the web service, FTP service, or SSH (secure shell)

Though at least one user account—the one created when you first started OS X—should to be an admin user, it is better to grant admin privileges sparingly unless you are confident your other users can manage the responsibility and understand the implications of what they do.

Removing Administrative Access from an Existing User

Although it's unlikely that users who are given administrative privileges will completely destroy the system, they can make life difficult for others even if they don't mean to. However, users with more curiosity than judgment are not ready for the responsibility of administrative powers.

Deleting files in the System or Library folders or tampering with default folders or files in user directories should be done only for a good reason.

To remove administrative access from an existing user, follow these steps:

1. Open the System Preferences.

2. Click the Accounts item under the System section.

3. Select the name of the user to edit in the list along the left.

4. Uncheck the Allow User to Administer This Computer box, as shown in
   Figure 33.1.

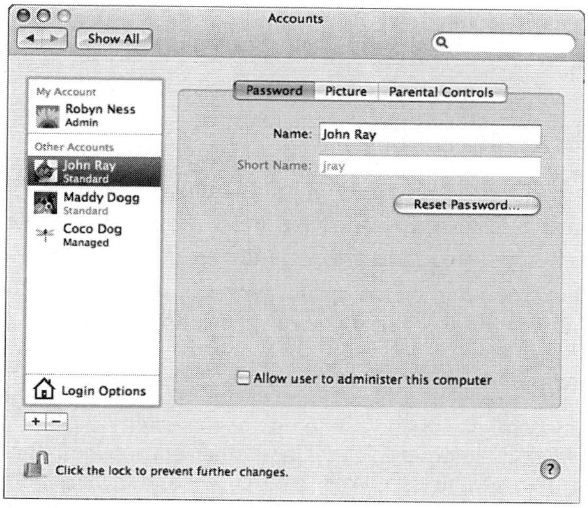

FIGURE 33.1
Create as few
administrative
users as
possible.

If you try to change the administrative access for the first-created user account,
there must be another account that remains an administrative account—otherwise
no one would be able to install software or add new users. Also, before the
change is made, you are asked to enter a password to authorize it.

By the Way

If your computer has only a few accounts for people you know, this local security
precaution is probably the only one you need. However, if you want your system to
be a bit more impenetrable, keep reading.

Disable Usernames

It's obvious that Apple wanted to create a system that would be friendly and accessible for any level of user. In doing so, it also set a few defaults that make it easy for a
public system to be "cracked" by a persistent attacker with direct access to the
machine. One precaution that's easy to take is not to display login names on the
Login Preferences panel. To shut off this feature, follow these steps:

1. Open System Preferences.

2. Click the Accounts button in the System section.

3. Choose the Login Options button at the bottom of the list of users.

4. Click the Display Login Window as Name and Password radio button to select it.

5. Close the window to save the settings.

Now, let's take a look at ways to secure your system online.

Network Security

There are two steps to network security: figuring out what your machine is doing and disabling those things that you'd rather it not do. Neither of these tasks is as easy as it sounds because you must check a number of places before you can be sure that your machine is secure. The end result, however, is a Mac OS X computer that you can leave online without worrying about the consequences.

> This chapter focuses on security issues related to Mac OS X, but the software you install on your system may open your computer to security exploits. For example, web browsers, such as Internet Explorer, and other applications that receive data over a network may be vulnerable. Your best defense is to visit the security sections of software manufacturers' web sites regularly. The Microsoft Security web site is online at www.microsoft.com/security/.

Disabling Network Services

As discussed in Chapter 32, your Mac OS X computer has several built-in methods of sharing information over the web—through network shares, FTP, and more. Each of these features relies on a special Mac OS X background application called a *service*. As its name implies, a service provides additional functionality to the system. With network services, this functionality can be accessed remotely over a network connection. Therein lies the potential for someone to access and modify your computer over the network.

Each network service that runs on your computer requires a *port* that can be used to accept incoming connections. Think of network ports as power receptacles with multiple outlets. Connections to your computer are "plugged" in to the outlet and then communications can begin. Mac OS X has the capability to accept many incoming connections via many different ports. You can enable many of the commonly used ports under the Services section of the Sharing Preferences, as detailed in Chapter 32.

The biggest risk of having several network services active is that there could be a bug or backdoor associated with one of them. The Mac OS X architecture uses complex applications to provide its network services. Improperly setting up one of these services, or failing to keep your system updated, could open your account to being accessed by an unauthorized user who can tamper with your files. Even worse, it is possible for an intruder to take over your machine and use it to launch attacks on even more computers!

If you need to run services that use some of the less common ports, as with some types of file sharing or instant messaging, you can activate them under the Firewall section of the Sharing preferences. Click the button labeled New and choose a port name or, if none apply, choose Other. If you choose Other, you need to set the port number or range; talk to your system administrator if you feel there are custom settings you should configure.

By the Way

When your computer is connected to the Internet via a direct connection to a cable modem or DSL line, it can be a target for attack from outside. The more network services that are running, the greater the chance that a potential intruder can discover and compromise your system.

Disabling Network Sharing Services

Your first concern should be the network services that Apple included with your system. Although it's tempting to go through your system and activate every feature, doing so isn't always a good idea. If you turn on everything in the Sharing preferences, your system would have the following services and ports active:

▶ FTP Access (port 20 or 21)—FTP is a quick and easy way to send and retrieve files from a computer. FTP Sharing starts an FTP server on your computer. Unfortunately, it provides no password encryption and is often targeted by attackers. If you don't have to use FTP, don't enable it.

▶ Remote Login—SSH (port 22)—The secure shell enables remote users to connect to your computer and control it from the command line. It's a useful tool for servers, but it presents a security risk to home users.

▶ Personal Web Sharing (port 80)—Your personal web server is a server called Apache. Apache is a stable program and should be considered the least of your concerns, unless you've manually customized its configuration files.

▶ Windows File Sharing (port 139)—Enables Windows users to access the shared folders on your computers. If you enable this feature, you are prompted to enable each user account in which you want to use it. (Windows File Sharing requires a less secure method of storing passwords than would be used otherwise, so only enable accounts that need it.)

▶ svrloc (port 427)—The Service Locator Protocol enables remote computers to detect what services are available on your computer over the Internet.

▶ afpovertcp (port 548)—The Apple File Protocol is used to share your disks and folders over a network. If you have Personal File Sharing turned on, be aware that potentially anyone on the Internet can connect to your computer.

▶ Printer Sharing (port 631)—Enables other users on the network to use printers connected to your computer. If you trust the users on your network to print responsibly, enabling this feature poses little risk.

▶ ppc (port 3031)—Program-to-program communication enables remote applications to connect to your computer and send it commands. It's unlikely that you would need this feature in day-to-day use. PPC is controlled by the Remote Apple Events setting in the Sharing Preferences panel.

To disable any of these built-in network services, follow these steps:

1. Open System Preferences under the Apple menu or by clicking its icon in the Dock.

2. Click the Sharing item under the Internet & Network section.

3. In the Services preferences, uncheck the boxes for the listed services to toggle them on and off, as shown in Figure 33.2.

FIGURE 33.2
The Sharing Preferences pane controls the built-in network services.

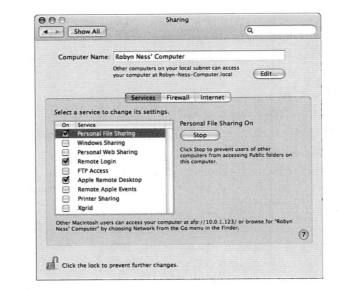

Firewalls

The ultimate solution to network security is the use of a *firewall*, a piece of hardware or software that sits between your computer and the Internet. As network traffic comes into the computer, the firewall looks at each piece of information, determines whether it's acceptable, and, if necessary, keeps the data from getting to your machine.

> You might be asking yourself, "If a firewall can be a piece of software that runs on my computer, how can it both look at network traffic and keep it from reaching my machine?" After all, to look at the information and determine whether it's trouble, the data obviously must have reached my computer!
>
> That's true, but firewall software operates at a low level, intercepting network traffic before your computer has a chance to process it and make it available to components such as your web server or FTP server.

By the Way

Software Firewalls

Using a software firewall is the quickest way to get unwanted traffic blocked from your machine.

Mac OS X includes a built-in personal firewall, accessible from the Firewall section of the System Preferences Sharing settings shown in Figure 33.3.

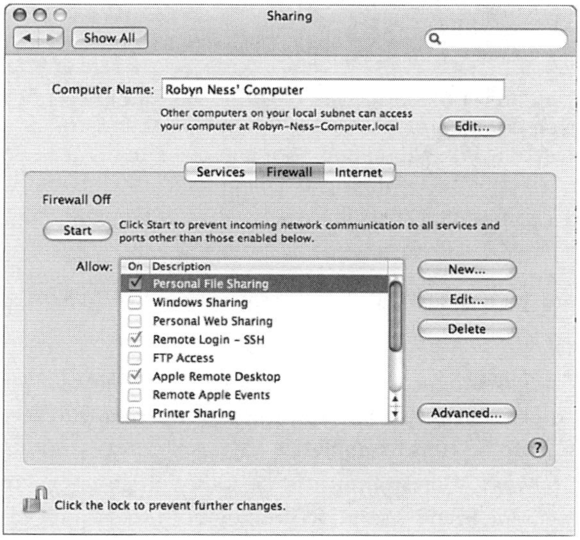

FIGURE 33.3
The Mac OS X personal firewall can be enabled to secure the services/port you don't want to operate.

To activate the firewall, click the Start button. Checked boxes appear next to those services/ports that you've turned on under the Services setting of the Sharing preferences.

Because disabling a port disables its service and unenabled ports require no securing, you must go to the Services pane to change the status of the services in the Firewall pane.

In addition to starting or stopping your personal firewall, you can add and delete additional ports to be opened between your computer and the outside world. This may be necessary for some people who want to play games online, use some specific file sharing or Internet chat software, or interact in other ways via a network. Consult your system administrator or ISP if you have questions.

> If you need even more flexibility, several other firewall builder packages make it easy to point and click your way through setting up a firewall on your computer. You may want to consult another source, such as *Maximum Mac OS X Security*, by John and William Ray (Sams Publishing, 2003), for deeper coverage of security issues.

Hardware Firewalls

A growing number of network hardware appliances can virtually eliminate the threat of attack by making your computer unreachable from the Internet. Although slightly more expensive than a software-only solution, they provide a worry-free answer to the problem of network security!

By the
Way

> As you shop for a hardware firewall, you might notice that many of the devices you see are advertised as routers. A *router* is simply a generic term for a network device that moves network information from one place to another. For your personal system, it routes information from your computer to the Internet and vice versa. During the process of routing data, the device also performs its firewall activity.

Here are a few Mac-friendly firewall solutions you might be interested in checking out:

▶ Apple AirPort (www.apple.com/airportextreme/)—The Apple wireless network server can make an effective firewall when configured with the option to Share a Single IP Address Using DHCP (Dynamic Host Configuration Protocol) and NAT (Network Address Translation). Although more expensive than other options, it's a Mac-friendly solution and a great way to gain security and go wireless at the same time.

▶ LinkSys cable/DSL routers (www.linksys.com)—Largely responsible for creating the first mass-produced personal firewall, LinkSys has a variety of different options available for home users. LinkSys offers both traditional wired and wireless products.

▶ NetGear routers (www.netgear.com)—Much like the LinkSys routers, the NetGear offerings are available in wired and wireless configurations and feature easy web configuration and an attractive price point.

The biggest drawback to using a personal hardware firewall is that if you run a web server (or other processes that enable people to connect to your machine over the Internet), you must specially configure the firewall to let requests pass through to your computer. This isn't usually difficult, but it requires more than simply plugging it in and having it work.

Summary

Mac OS X security presents several challenges for Mac users. Its underlying Unix subsystem makes it an attractive target for network crackers as well as any unscrupulous person who might have access to the system. In this chapter, you learned several ways to help protect your system from both local and network attacks by limiting access to critical features and shutting off network services that you might not need. The topic of security is broad, so consider this chapter only a start to maintaining a secure computer—not an end-all guide.

CHAPTER 34

Maintaining Your System

In this chapter, you learn some maintenance tips that will help keep your computer running smoothly and keep your files safe. Because Apple frequently releases critical security updates and patches that should be installed quickly, we talk first about automating system software updates. Then we discuss the importance of backing up your files so that you won't lose all your hard work and important data in the event of system disruption. Finally, we check out a built-in tool for monitoring the effort expended by your system.

Automating Software Updates

Mac OS X enables you to receive software updates from Apple over the Internet, so you don't have to go looking for the updates to the operating system or Apple-created software. You can enable this feature in the Software Update Preferences pane of the System Preferences.

Running Software Updates Manually

Although automating software updates can take most of the burden off you, sometimes you want to force your system to search for recent updates rather than wait for your scheduled time. For example, when Apple releases a new version of a fun application such as iChat—see Chapter 18, "Using iChat AV"—you may be eager to get your hands on it.

Here's how you can check for updates anytime:

1. Launch the System Preferences application from the Dock or the Applications folder. (Or choose Software Update from the Apple menu and skip to step 4.)

2. Click the Software Update pane, which opens the screen shown in Figure 34.1.

3. If you want to check for updates right now, click the Check Now button. Your computer uses the Internet connection you've configured to contact Apple's support website to check for possible updates. (If you aren't connected to the Internet, Software Update lets you know it can't retrieve updates and provides a button to open the Network Diagnostics assistant, which can help you connect.)

4. If updates are available for your computer, you see a screen listing what's available, as shown in Figure 34.2. From there you can click the check boxes for the items you want and accept the download process.

FIGURE 34.1
Apple enables
you to download
the latest
updates for your
computer auto-
matically over
the network.

FIGURE 34.2
The Software
Update window
displays a list of
updates for your
system.

5. Click the Install Item button, and type the username and password of an administrative user to authorize the updates.

6. When the downloads are complete, the software installers launch, and your computer is updated with the new software. Then usually there is an "optimizing" process, which allows the update to function with full efficiency. (For some updates, you may be prompted to click the Restart button to finish the process.)

By the Way

Depending on the software package, you might see a license agreement at some point in time during the installation. Just click OK to proceed.

Setting Up Regular Software Updates

If you want to have your computer check for Apple software updates automatically, check the Check for Updates box and then click the pop-up menu to set the interval. You can choose Daily, Weekly, or Monthly. (Weekly is best, considering the unpredictable nature of software updates.)

After you've set the schedule, quit System Preferences. After you've set up your automated update schedule, Software Update checks Apple's website at the specified intervals as soon as you log in to your computer and have a connection to the Internet. The window shown in Figure 34.2 appears where you can see what updates are available.

Of course, if your computer isn't on when the scheduled update is set to take place, it just doesn't happen. The check is skipped until the next scheduled run.

By the Way

Sometimes the list of updates includes features you don't need or want, such as iPod updates when you don't own an iPod. Although not checking the box for those items prevents them from being installed, they may continue to show up in your Software Updates window unless you choose Update, Ignore Update from the menu. If you ever change your mind, you can choose Software Update, Reset Ignored Updates from the menu to make the updates visible again and allow the system to perform any you decide are needed.

Did you Know?

Installed Files

Many users, for good reason, want to keep track of what software has been installed on their system. Opening the Software Update preference pane and clicking the Installed Updates button displays a log of installed updates. This listing is shown in Figure 34.3.

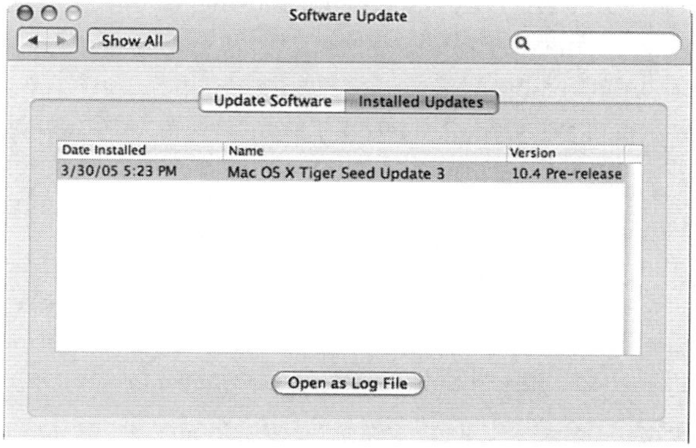

FIGURE 34.3
The Installed Updates pane displays a list of installed update packages.

Backing Up Your Data

Although keeping a secure and updated operating system is important, it is not as important as maintaining an archive of your important data.

When a program or computer crashes, it's possible that one or more files on your computer's drive can be affected (especially if you're working on a file when the computer locks up). Even though Mac OS X offers strong resistance to system failure, the world is unpredictable, and the potential for events ranging from simple human error to theft make backups an important consideration.

Backup Strategies

You can follow different types of backup techniques, depending on the kind of documents you're creating and how many of them there are. Here's a brief look at the sort of things you can do without having to buy extra software:

▶ Select backups—You already have copies of your programs on a CD, or can obtain them if you really need them. A complete packet of CDs came with your computer, containing all the software Apple installed on your computer. In addition, most new software you buy will also come on an installation disk of some sort. So the fastest backup method is just to concentrate on the documents you make with those programs.

Watch
Out!

> If you purchase software that must be downloaded, it's wise to create backup copies in case of system failure. Or, if you can download the software freely but need a code to unlock it, you may simply want to store your codes in a safe place so that you can recover use of applications for which you've paid.

▶ Full backups—Even though you already have a separate copy of the software, it can be time-consuming to restore all your software and redo special program settings. If you back up everything, however, it's easier to restore a program with your settings intact without fuss or bother. In addition, having a complete backup of your computer's drive is extra protection in case something happens to both the computer and software disks. The downside, however, is that making a full backup can be time consuming and requires a large amount of storage space.

▶ Incremental backups—This technique requires special software (such as Retrospect, which is described later), but it is designed to make a backup strictly of the files that have changed since your last backup. A thorough backup plan might include a full backup at regular intervals, say once a week, and then a daily incremental backup. This method also takes a lot less time, and you don't need as much disk space to store it all.

Data Storage Options

Another part of your backup plan is deciding where and how to store the data you will be copying from your hard drive. The best method is to use a separate storage drive (such as an external hard drive) or a device (such as CD burner) with media (disks) that you can remove. That way you can store the backups in a separate location for the ultimate in safekeeping. That's the method the big companies use.

Here are some storage options you should consider:

> It's just not a good idea to back up your files to the same drive as the one on which they were made (such as your Mac's hard drive). If something should happen to that drive, or the entire computer, your backup would be gone.

Watch Out!

▶ Data CDs—Many Macs come equipped with a drive that can burn CDs. You can use this drive to copy your files to a CD/R or CD/RW disc (the latter is the one that's rewritable). This is a convenient and inexpensive way to copy your valuable data on a medium that will last for years. If you don't have a built-in CD burner on your Mac, no problem. There are plenty of low-cost external drives that can work from your computer's FireWire or USB ports (but of course the first runs much faster).

> Does your Mac have Apple's SuperDrive? If so, you can also burn data DVDs in the same way you make a CD. The advantage is that you can store much more data on the DVD—4.7GB compared to 650MB or 700MB for a CD. Though DVDs are more expensive than CDs, this might be a good option if you have a well-populated hard drive.

By the Way

▶ External backup drive—Iomega Jaz, Peerless, or Zip drives are convenient, and the drives and disks aren't too expensive. Several varieties of tape drives also work with backup software as fairly stable backup media.

▶ Networked disks—If your computer is on a network, a drive on another Mac (or actually even a Windows-based PC set up to handle Mac files) can be used for your regular backups. Before you set up a networked drive for this purpose, you should set up a strategy with those who run the network. Some companies plan on having all files backed up to one drive or drives, and then they do their own special backup routine on those files.

▶ Internet backups—If you have a good Internet connection and you don't want to back up a large number of files, you can use backup via the Internet. An easy way to get storage space is to sign up with Apple's .Mac program, as discussed in Chapter 16, "Exploring .Mac Membership." As part of the package, you get 100MB of iDisk storage space at Apple's web servers, and you can buy extra space if you need it. Visit www.mac.com to sign up. However, unless you have really fast Internet access, the process of copying files to your iDisk is slow.

By the Way

> After you've set up a .Mac account, you can access your iDisk. Click the iDisk icon on the Finder's toolbar to connect to your disk. If you aren't connected to the Internet, the service is dialed up first.

Here are some additional considerations related to storing backups of your data:

▶ Careful labeling—Make sure that your backup disks are carefully labeled according to date and content. Often something such as "Backup for February 28, 2005" is sufficient. (If you have more than one disk for a date, remember to label the different volumes.)

By the Way

> CDs and DVD media are write-once media, which means that when you burn one of these discs that's it, unless, of course, you opt for CD/RW media, where you can rewrite data up to 1,000 times.

▶ Reuse of media—If you need to keep an older version of a file, you need to keep the backup in a safe place. However, if you are using reusable media and you no longer need a file from a particular time range, there's no problem in putting that storage media back into service for newer backups.

▶ Making multiple backups—If your files contain important data on them (financial or otherwise), make a second backup and store it in a secure location (such as a bank vault). In the unlikely event something happens to your home or office, you'll be protected.

There's one more important element in a backup plan—setting a consistent schedule. It's a good idea to set aside a time to do your backup at regular intervals—perhaps at the end of your work day before leaving your office (or before shutting down your computer for the day if you're at home). Remember, it does no good to intend to backup your files if you never actually do it, so try to work out a system and a schedule that you can maintain over time.

Copying Your Hard Drive

In addition to the methods previously mentioned for storing your data, your Mac comes equipped with a piece of software that turns files into *disk images* that are read by computers as if they were CDs. This software, called Disk Utility, is located in the Utilities folder within the Applications folder of your hard drive. Disk Utility is mainly used to fix file permission discrepancies and hard drive errors, but it also includes a slick tool that is useful for creating an exact duplicate of your hard drive. Disk Utility even has built-in CD-burning capabilities to make turning a disk image into a real CD a matter of a few clicks.

In Chapter 2, "Using the Finder," you learned how to burn a CD from the Finder.

By the Way

Creating Disk Images with Disk Utility

There are two ways to generate an image in Disk Utility: by copying an existing item, or by creating an empty image file, mounting it, and then copying files to it.

To create an empty image file:

   1. Open Disk Utility, as shown in Figure 34.4, and don't select any drives.

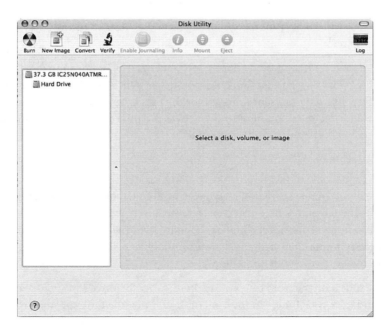

FIGURE 34.4
Disk Utility lists in its sidebar all drives connected to your computer, including your internal hard drive.

2. Click the New Image icon in the toolbar. The dialog box shown in Figure 34.5 appears.

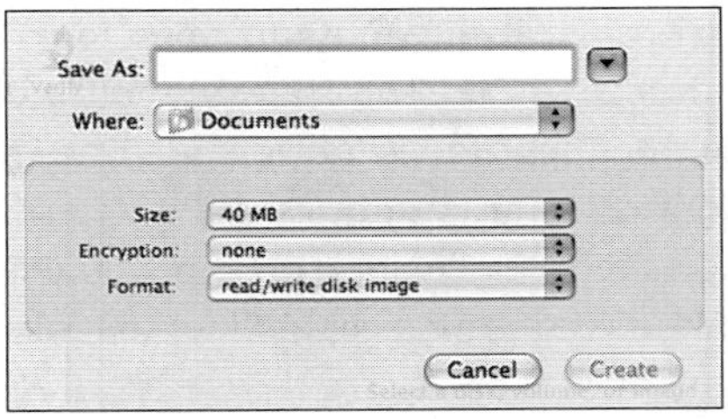

FIGURE 34.5
Make a new
image and then
copy files to it.

Save As:	
Where:	Documents
Size:	40 MB
Encryption:	none
Format:	read/write disk image

Cancel   Create

3. Fill in the Save As field to give a name to the image file.

4. Choose a size for the image from the Size pop-up menu. There are a variety of preset sizes for common media, such as Zip disks, CDs, DVDs, and a Custom setting for arbitrary sizes.

By the Way

For each image you create, you must have enough free space on your hard drive. For example, to create a CD image, you need approximately 650MB free. Currently shipping Apple computers come with at least 10GB drives, so this really shouldn't be an issue.

5. If you want to encrypt the disk image, choose AES-128 in the Encryption pop-up menu.

6. Choose a format in the Format pop-up menu. The options are Read/Write Disk Image, which takes up a set amount of space, or Sparse Disk Image, which fills only the space needed for the files it holds. (Sparse disk images are used for the distribution of software over the Internet—why require customers to download more than they need to?)

7. Click Create.

After the blank image is created, it appears in the sidebar in the Disk Utility window as well as the location where you choose to save it. A "mounted" version of the image also appears in that location as a white disk drive. To add files to the image, drag them onto the mounted drive. (You can double-click the drive just as you would a folder to review its contents.)

To create a disk image from an existing drive, select the drive in the sidebar of Disk Utility and click New Image in the toolbar. In the window that appears, similar to the one shown in Figure 34.4, give your disk image a name, choose a location to save it, and pick an image format and whether to encrypt. Finally, click the Save button.

A Progress window appears to show how much of the image has been created. Depending on the size of the drive being duplicated, it may take a while.

After you have a disk image of your data, you can move it over the Internet or network to a safe storage place or burn an actual CD of it.

To burn a CD from Disk Utility, follow these steps:

To burn a CD from within Disk Utility with an external burner, you must have your CD writer connected and powered on. Check Apple's website for supported writers.

By the Way

---

1. Open Disk Utility.

2. Locate the disk image you want to burn in the sidebar of the Disk Utility window.

3. Place a blank CD-R or CD-RW in your CD writer.

4. Select the image in the sidebar, and click the Burn button in the toolbar.

5. Click OK in the confirmation window to begin burning.

Using Backup Software

If you have many files, or if your files need to be backed up from more than one Mac OS computer on a network, you'll do better with some backup software.

Such software can

▶ Perform scheduled backups—You can set the software to perform the backups at a regular time (daily, every other day, weekly, whatever). At the appointed time, you only need to have the backup media in place and the computers turned on for the process to go.

Although automatic backups are great, a backup can stop dead in its tracks if the media runs out of space, the media isn't ready, or the computer is shut down by mistake. If you have many files, make sure that your disks have enough space, or be prepared to check the backup process every so often in case of trouble.

Watch Out!

▶ Perform networked backups—With the right software, backups can be done from all computers on a network to one or more backup drives.

▶ Back up the entire drive or selected files or folders—When you set up your backup, you can instruct the software to limit the backup to the items you want. By default, they do the entire drive and then incremental backups for each disk, unless you pick a full backup.

Choosing Backup Software

When you've decided on the backup software route, you need to know what to choose. Fortunately, several good Mac OS software packages give you great automatic backups. They vary in features, and you should pick one based on what you need.

Here's a brief description of backup programs:

▶ Backup—For home users who just want to make sure that their critical data is backed up to CD, DVD, or iDisk, Apple's aptly named Backup may be the right answer. Shown in Figure 34.6, Backup is a simple piece of software capable of selecting common file types (such as Word documents), system information (such as Safari preferences), or arbitrary files and folders and backing them up to your Mac's CD- or DVD-burning drive or .Mac iDisk. It does not currently offer incremental backups, nor a way of performing unattended backups.

FIGURE 34.6
Apple's Backup is a simple tool for backing up data files.

Back Up	Items	Size	Last Backed Up
☑	Address Book contacts	484K	--
☐	Stickies notes	--	--
☑	iCal calendars	4K	--
☑	Safari settings	1.89M	--
☐	Internet Explorer settings	--	--
☑	Keychain (for passwords)	56K	--
☐	AppleWorks files in Home folder	--	--
☑	Excel files in Home folder	--	--
☐	FileMaker files in Home folder	--	--
☐	iTunes playlist	--	--
☐	PowerPoint files in Home folder	--	--
☑	Word files in Home folder	--	--
☑	Files on Desktop	--	--

Back up to iDisk
0   62 MB   125 MB
iDisk backups scheduled Fridays at 12:30PM   5 Items, 2.43 MB used
Backup Now

By the Way

Backup is a .Mac membership exclusive application. This means that to download and use the tool, you need to pay the $100 entrance fee (www.mac.com). See Chapter 16, "Exploring .Mac Membership," for more information about the benefits of .Mac.

▶ Data Backup from ProSoft Engineering (www.prosoftengineering.com/products/data_backup.php) is a complete personal backup system that picks up where Apple's tool leaves off. It offers advanced features such as scheduling, compression, mirroring, synchronization, incremental backups, and an "evolutive" mode that preserves different versions of files as they change across backups. For personal workstations, Data Backup X is difficult to beat.

▶ Retrospect—From Dantz (www.dantz.com), this is a heavy-duty backup program that does just about everything you can imagine in backup planning with little fuss or bother. You can use it to create a complete backup plan simply by answering some basic questions. Backups are compressed (to save space) and saved in a special format for efficient retrieval. Unlike other backup programs, Retrospect can work with tape drives, which can store many megabytes of files on little cartridges. Retrospect can also work with Internet-based backup services. For large networks, there's the Retrospect Network Backup Kit and even a Windows version with similar features.

▶ Retrospect Desktop—This program distills the most important features of Retrospect and puts them in a smaller, less-expensive package.

Activity Monitor

After looking at software updates and backing up data, we round out this system management discussion with a look at system resources. With the multitasking capabilities of Mac OS X, you may find it interesting to check what your system resources are being used for.

Activity Monitor, found in the Applications/Utilities folder, can illustrate system activity with simple graphs for CPU, System Memory, Disk Activity, Disk Usage, and Network activity. Figure 34.7 shows Activity Monitor at work.

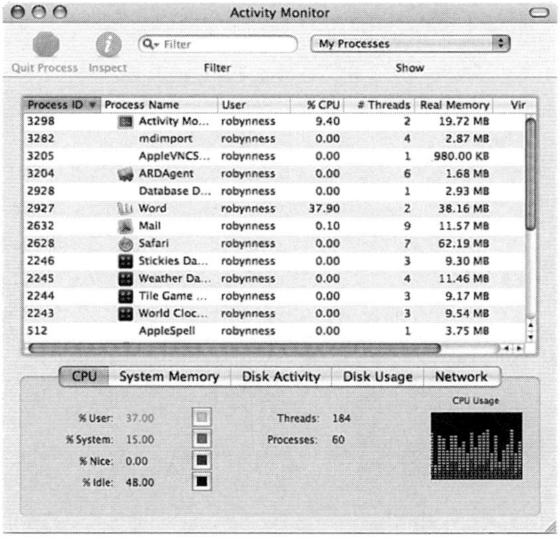

FIGURE 34.7
The Activity Monitor shows how active your computer is on a number of different measures.

At the top of the window is a live list of active processes. From the Show pop-up menu, you can choose whether to view only your own processes, all processes, or other subgroups of processes. The data displayed about each process includes the percentage of CPU time, the amount of memory it consumes, and the user running it. If your system seems sluggish, you can choose a process in the list and click the Quit Processes button in the toolbar to exit a program. Note, however, that you should quit something only if you know what it's doing—otherwise, underlying system functions that are important may be disrupted.

Summary

Mac OS X gives you a great deal of flexibility, but it also requires more responsibility to run. To successfully keep your computer running smoothly and safely, you must stay current with system patches and create backups. If system performance problems arise, it may be beneficial to understand the effort your computer is expending to do the tasks you ask of it. The chapter began with a look at Apple's automated software updates. Next, it looked at several options for backing up your data, including burning data CDs and creating disk images to transfer over the Internet or network to a safe storage place. To finish up, you learned about the Activity Monitor Utility, which enables you to observe your computer's processor function.

CHAPTER 35

Recovering from Crashes and Other Problems

In this chapter, you learn ways to react to application and system crashes and ways to be proactive about virus protection. You also learn to use your OS X installation CD to reset your password and, in times of widespread system failure, to reinstall your operating system.

Application Crashes

Sometimes, out of the blue, the application you're trying to use freezes up or disappears altogether. These events are commonly referred to as "crashes."

<table>
<tr>
<td>

If you experience a lot of crashes in a specific application, you may want to see whether you can download a software update from the developer's website—frequently, software companies release a free patch to correct an instability problem. Also, sometimes preference files associated with an application are corrupted, which can cause an application to operate erratically. If a preference file is causing a problem, you can correct it by removing the file and resetting your preferences. Typically, preference files are stored in the system-wide Library folder in another folder called Preferences.

</td>
<td>

Did you Know?

</td>
</tr>
</table>

Application Unexpectedly Quits

One of the more common kinds of crashes involves an application quitting. Suddenly, without warning, the document window disappears from the screen, and you see a message similar to the one shown in Figure 35.1.

<table>
<tr>
<td>

Unfortunately, when a program quits while you're working on a document, all the work you've done since the last time it was saved is gone—unless the application has a recovery feature that autosaves, such as Microsoft Word. For that reason, get in the habit of saving your documents often so that you don't lose much if something goes wrong.

</td>
<td>

By the Way

</td>
</tr>
</table>

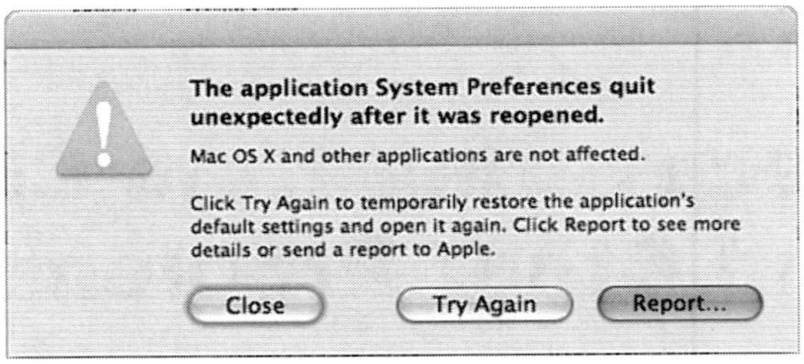

FIGURE 35.1
This unfriendly
message might
sometimes
appear when
you're working
on a document.

> The application System Preferences quit
> unexpectedly after it was reopened.
>
> Mac OS X and other applications are not affected.
>
> Click Try Again to temporarily restore the application's
> default settings and open it again. Click Report to see more
> details or send a report to Apple.
>
> Close   Try Again   Report...

Mac OS X is designed to be stable despite localized problems with applications, so if one application unexpectedly quits, you can continue to work in others without needing to restart.

Force Quit

Not all crashes cause an application to quit. Sometimes the application just stops running. The mouse might freeze, or it might move around but not do anything.

By the Way

> Sometimes an application appears to be unresponsive because it is in the middle of a resource-intensive task. The keyboard shortcut Command-[period] can be used to interrupt active processes in some applications to return your system to your control. If an application isn't responding because it's busy, you may want to try this command (or let the application finish its task) instead of force-quitting it—just be sure that the application you wish to interrupt is the one you have selected.

If this happens, follow these steps to force-quit the application so you can restart it:

Watch Out!

> If you must force-quit an application, you lose unsaved changes because the application is not functioning well enough to save. Yet another reason to save often!

1. Force-quit the program. Hold down the Cmd-Option-Esc keys, or click on the Finder icon in the Dock; then choose Force Quit from the Apple menu. You see a Force Quit Applications window as shown in Figure 35.2.

2. Normally, the application you were just running is selected. If not, select the application.

3. Click Force Quit. Over the next few seconds, Mac OS X should make the program quit. If it fails to occur, try again. Sometimes it takes two tries for the system to get the message.

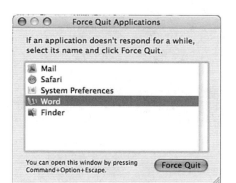

FIGURE 35.2
Choose the application to force-quit from this window.

4. If the program really doesn't quit, go to the Apple menu and choose Restart. At this point, there might be systemwide instability, and it doesn't hurt to start from scratch.

By the Way

At times, you may not be able to restart your computer by choosing Restart. (For example, if you can't move your cursor or you can't access the Restart option from the menu.) If that occurs, hold down the power button on your computer for several seconds to shut down your computer.

An occasional Mac OS X system error is called a *kernel panic*. When this type of error occurs, instructions in several languages to restart your computer appear onscreen. These instructions tell you to hold down the power button for several seconds. If holding down the power button does not restart your computer, use the instructions in the section "System Crashes" to force a system restart.

Restarting Classic

Earlier you were told that other applications in OS X aren't affected if one crashes. Here's where you learn the exception: If the application happens to be running in the Classic environment (see the section on running Classic applications in Chapter 4, "Working with Folders, Files, and Applications"), Classic itself becomes unstable and should be restarted. To restart Classic, follow these steps:

1. Quit all your open Classic programs.

2. Launch the System Preferences application from the Dock, the Apple menu, or the Applications folder.

3. Click the Classic icon to open the Classic Preferences pane (see Figure 35.3).

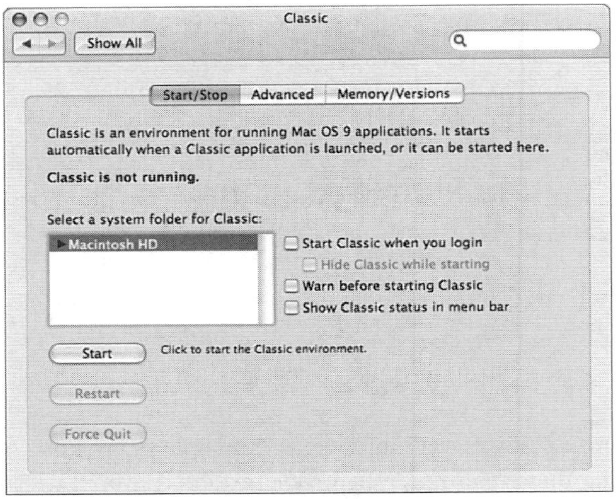

FIGURE 35.3
You can restart
or configure
Classic from
this preferences
pane.

4. Click the Restart button. If it fails to work, click Force Quit (see the "Forcing a Restart" section) and OK the choice; then try Restart again.

By the Way

> If you don't plan on using a Classic application after using the Force Quit function, you don't have to restart that environment. Whenever you do launch a Classic application, Classic is restarted as part of the package.

System Crashes

At times, your computer may freeze up altogether—refusing to let you interact with any applications or shut it down. This is known as a *system crash*.

An occasional system crash is normal behavior for any computer. However, if you encounter crashes several times a day, something is definitely wrong. You might be seeing a conflict with some new software or hardware you've installed, or be experiencing the initial symptoms of a dying hard drive.

Fortunately, there are ways to check for the cause of such problems. Consider the following:

▶ Recent software installations—What did you do just before your computer began to crash? If you just installed some new software, maybe one of those files is causing a conflict. You'll want to check the program's documentation (or Read Me, if there is one) to see whether the publisher is aware of any problems.

▶ Recent hardware upgrades—If you just installed a RAM upgrade on your computer and it is now crashing, maybe the RAM module you installed is defective. It's always possible and not easy to test for. You might want to consider removing the RAM upgrade, strictly as a test. Then work with your Mac to see whether the crashes go away. If they do, contact the dealer for a replacement module. If you've installed an extra drive, scanner, or other device, disconnect it (and turn off its software) and see whether the problem disappears.

▶ Hardware defects—As with any electronic product, there's always the slight chance one or more of the components in your computer might fail. In the vast majority of cases, however, a software conflict (or defective RAM) causes constant crashes. If you've tested everything and your Mac still won't work reliably, don't hesitate to contact Apple Computer or your dealer and arrange for service.

> Hard drive failure can be difficult to predict. The best course of action is to have a regular backup plan in place so you won't lose your important files. See Chapter 34, "Maintaining Your System," for more information about backing up your data.

By the Way

Forcing a Restart

If your computer refuses to shut down or restart in the normal fashion, you have to force the process by using the reset function. Resetting is done in different ways on different models of Macs. On flat-panel iMacs and other newer models, you must press and hold down the power button for five seconds. After the computer shuts down, turn your computer on as you normally would.

On some Macs, you may have to search for a tiny button labeled with a triangle-shaped icon and then press it. (On some older models you may need to use the point of a pencil or a straightened paperclip to press the button.) As soon as you press and release the reset button, your Mac should restart normally.

> Consider this action only if the previous process doesn't work because it's much more drastic. If attempting to reset your Mac fails, your only remaining option is to unplug it, wait 30 seconds, plug in your Mac again, and turn it on. At this point, you should be able to start normally, except that you might find the startup process pauses for some extra seconds at the Checking Disks prompt on the Mac OS X startup screen. A forced shutdown can cause minor disk directory damage, which is fixed during the startup process. This should not be any cause for concern.

By the Way

Resetting PRAM

PRAM (pronounced P-RAM) is a battery-powered portion of your computer's memory where default settings for basic functions (including video display and what's connected to certain types of ports) and some system preferences (including the startup disk) are stored. If, on starting your computer, the picture doesn't display properly or other basic functions (such as the time) don't reflect the preferences you've set, you may need to reset the PRAM.

By the Way

> If you frequently have to reset your PRAM or your clock resets itself each time you shut down, it may be time to replace your computer's internal battery.

To reset, or "zap," the PRAM, restart your computer while holding down the keys Command-Option-P-R. Wait for your computer to chime twice before releasing the keys. (The screen also flashes when the PRAM has been reset.)

Watch Out!

> Although resetting the PRAM is sometimes necessary, remember that doing so resets many of your Mac's essential preferences and may result in loss of some settings. The bottom line is that you may not want to do this without reason.

Protection Against Viruses and Other Malicious Code

Malicious code is any program written to disrupt, rather than assist. Perhaps the most familiar kind of malicious code is the computer virus. Without getting overly technical, a computer virus is a chunk of code that attaches itself to a document or program and is passed passively from computer to computer. Viruses are often transferred via infected email attachments and Internet downloads. After an infected file is opened, the virus is set in motion. Some viruses are written to destroy files and cause damage to the hard drives of infected computers.

Another type of malicious code are worms, which differ from viruses in that they can transmit themselves across networks rather than waiting to hitch a ride on another program. Worms have been used to instruct infected computers to contact a specific website at a given time to overwhelm the site and take it offline.

Few viruses or worms affect Mac OS X. Unfortunately, this doesn't mean that they can't, or won't, be created. For that reason, it's a good idea to install anti-virus software and to update it frequently.

Other types of malicious code include spyware and adware. (Spyware monitors users' activities without their knowledge, whereas adware delivers advertising without users' permission.) Although a majority of spyware and adware is focused on PC users, a savvy Mac user will be on the alert for suspicious activity to head off any problems.

By the *Way*

As with any software product, a specific set of features might be more appealing to you, but any of the programs I'm describing will do the job.

▶ Norton AntiVirus—This program, published by Symantec, at www.symantec.com, is designed to check for viruses every time you insert a disk into a drive, mount a networked disk on your computer's desktop, or download a file from the Internet; the latter is courtesy of its Safe Zone feature. So-called suspicious activities are also monitored. You can perform scheduled scans, where the program launches automatically at a predetermined hour and scans your drives. One intriguing feature is called Live Update, where the program logs on to the publisher's site every month and checks for updates to protect against newly discovered viruses.

Such features as Live Update, which retrieve minor program updates and new virus definitions, don't mean that you'll never have to pay for a new version of the software. You may have to purchase a yearly subscription or regular software upgrades to maintain effective virus protection.

By the *Way*

▶ Virex—This is published by McAfee, at www.mcafee.com (see Figure 35.4). Many of the features offered by Norton AntiVirus are also available with Virex. The program scans files from a networked drive or the ones you download, and it performs scheduled scans. A special technology called *heuristics* is designed to check for virus-like activity to help protect you against unknown viruses. Updates to the program are usually offered on a monthly basis and are available via its Auto Update feature.

Virex is part of the package available to those who subscribe to .Mac. If you're in the market for virus software, check out Chapter 16, "Exploring .Mac Membership," to see whether Virex and the other perks are worth the price!

Did you *Know?*

▶ VirusBarrier—A third contender, VirusBarrier, comes from Intego (www.intego.com), a software publisher whose product line also includes Internet protection and security software. Similar to the virus protection applications, there's an automatic update feature so that your virus protection remains current.

FIGURE 35.4
Virex offers
drag-and-drop
detection and
regular updates.

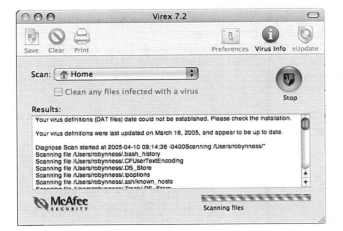

Buying and installing virus software isn't necessarily a guarantee that you'll be protected.

New viruses are discovered all the time. The publishers of virus software share information, so everyone can be protected in case a new virus strain crops up. You should check a publisher's website at least once a month for virus definition updates. The information on how to keep updated is usually included with the publisher's documentation. Using a program's capability to do automatic scheduled updates is a real plus.

Restoring the Administrator Password

If the Mac OS X administrator password is forgotten or misplaced, Apple provides a facility for restoring a password. Boot your computer from the Mac OS X install CD (hold down the C key while turning on your computer with the CD in the CD-ROM drive). When the Installer application starts, choose Reset Password from the Installer application menu.

Detected Mac OS X volumes are listed along the top of the window. To reset a password, follow these steps:

1. Click the main boot drive to load the password database for that volume.

2. Next, use the pop-up menu to choose the user account that you want to reset.

3. Fill in the new password in both of the password fields.

4. Finally, click Save to store the new password.

After rebooting your system, you can immediately log in with the new password.

Fixing Hard Drive Problems

Your computer comes with a tool that can check for and repair minor hard drive problems. The program is called Disk Utility, and you'll find a copy in the Utilities folder inside the Applications folder. (Chapter 34, "Maintaining Your System," looked at Disk Utility as a tool for making a disk image of your hard drive.)

If you begin to see system errors related to denied permissions or failures to access needed components, you can run the First Aid component of Disk Utility to verify or repair file permissions. Open Disk Utility and then click the First Aid button. Finally, select the drive or drives whose permissions you want to verify or repair (see Figure 35.5). The process may take several minutes, but you can watch as Disk Utility lists all the files on your computer for which the current permissions don't match what they should be.

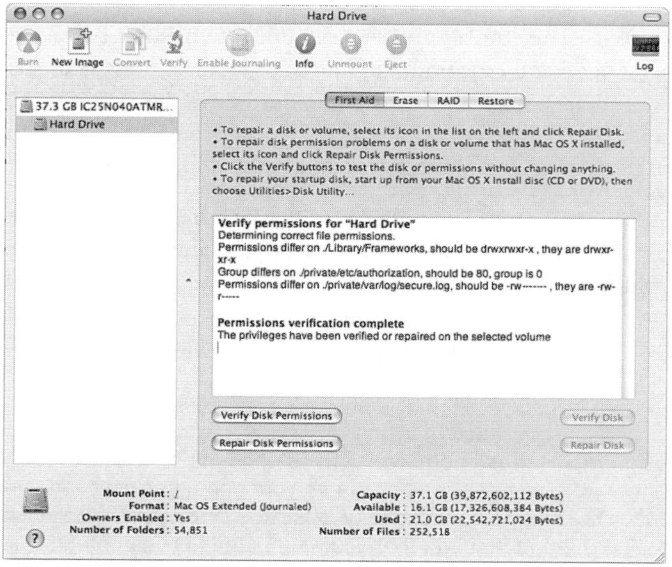

FIGURE 35.5
The First Aid component of Mac OS X's Disk Utility can check your drive for basic directory problems and fix them.

After you install software, you may want to use Disk Utility to repair file permissions— sometimes software installers make changes to file ownership or permissions that result in slower system performance or even failures by other applications.

In addition to identifying and fixing permissions problems, Disk Utility can verify and repair drives. This feature can be used for preventive maintenance. If you repair your hard drive periodically, you may avoid the "sudden" appearance of a larger hard drive failure. (Hard drives, as storage devices that are continuously in use, can develop localized problems before a user becomes aware of them.)

Note, however, that you cannot repair directory problems on a startup drive (the drive from which the operating system is running) from the Disk Utility application on your hard drive. If you need to repair your main drive, you need to boot from your system installation CD and run a version of Disk Utility from that disk. To do this, insert the CD and restart your computer while holding down the C key. When your system is booted, choose Open Disk Utility from the Installer application menu and run the repair.

The nice thing about Disk Utility is that it's free, but it's not a 100% solution. Several popular commercial programs offer to go beyond Disk First Aid in checking your drive and repairing catalog damage.

Here's a brief description of several hard drive diagnostic programs and what they do:

▶ DiskWarrior—This single-purpose program is from Alsoft (www.alsoft.com), a publisher of several Mac utility products. Its stock in trade is the capability to rebuild, rather than repair, a corrupted hard drive directory file. The original catalog is checked to locate the files on your drive and then that information is used to make a new directory to replace the damaged one.

▶ Norton Utilities—From Symantec (http://www.symantec.com/sabu/sysworks/basic/), this is the oldest available hard drive maintenance and repair package. Additional components of the package can optimize your drive to speed up file retrieval and to recover your drive in the event a crash makes it inaccessible. The program can also help you recover the files you delete by mistake.

Watch
Out!

> Though Norton Utilitieshas been around for a while, older versions of Norton Utilities cannot work with the file system on your computer, which is known as HFS+ (or Mac OS Extended). At the very least, they might even make catalog damage worse, and the end result is that your computer's drive contents will become unavailable. In addition, you cannot scan disks running Mac OS X unless you use version 6.0 or later of this program.

▶ TechTool Pro—In addition to hard drive repairs, TechTool Pro (www.micromat.com) can optimize the drive and even run a wide range of diagnostic checks on all your computer's hardware and attached devices. One great feature is the capability to perform an extended test of your computer's RAM. This might be helpful if you suddenly face a lot of crashes after doing a RAM upgrade. To add to its bag of tricks, TechTool Pro can also do virus checks. To check a Mac OS X drive, you need to restart from your TechTool Pro CD.

► Drive 10—As the name implies, this is a special-purpose utility from the publisher of TechTool Pro (www.micromat.com), designed to diagnose hard drives running Mac OS X. Although it can run a pretty hefty suite of tests, you need to restart your Mac from the supplied CD to fix problems. Running a scan first is a real time-saver; you have to restart only if a problem is reported.

If you choose any of the disk repair packages, be sure to use them as directed in the instructions.

Watch Out!

Optimizing Your Hard Drive

In the course of normal use of your Mac, the computer is constantly writing various files, deleting others, and fitting them into unallocated spaces on the hard drive. Over time, the hard drive becomes fragmented, where different parts of a single file are split into sections and spread out wherever they fit.

The demands that large files, such as digital video, place on the hard drive can cause this fragmentation to have a significant impact in the length of time needed to read or save a file. *Defragmenting* basically takes the various parts of each file from different sections of the hard drive and reassembles them into one contiguous block. That allows the computer to read the file without having to jump around the hard drive.

There is some debate about whether optimizing drives running OS X is really beneficial for typical users. Although there may be some a small benefit immediately after optimizing a fragmented drive, crowding all the files together during optimization means that any subsequent changes to the files will result in new fragmentation that negates prior optimization. On the other hand, if you work with large files in iMovie or iDVD, disk optimization may benefit you enough to make it worth your while.

By the Way

To defragment and optimize your hard drive, you must purchase a drive tool such as those mentioned previously.

Reinstalling System Software

Why do you want to reinstall system software? Perhaps your Mac is unstable, no matter what you do, and all your efforts to clean things up have failed.

There is a drastic method to fix everything, but it's not something you would do normally, and that's to run your Mac Restore CD (or CDs, because some models come with several). When you do that, however, you might lose all your custom program settings, and (if you opt for the Erase Disk option), all the files you created on your Mac. What's more, if you have updated your Mac Operating System, all that will be lost as well. So I mention it here as an option, but only as a last resort.

By the
Way

> Reinstalling Mac OS X does not necessarily replace your system accounts, information, or configuration. There are, however, a few drawbacks: Most notably, the system updates are replaced by the original version of the operating system. After running the Mac OS X Installer to recover a damaged system, you must force an update on your computer by going to the Software Update setting of the System Preferences and clicking the Check Now button, or by choosing Software Update from the Apple menu.

Here are the steps you need to follow to reinstall OS X with your System Installer CD:

1. Get out your system installation CD, press the CD button, and insert the CD in your CD drive.

2. Restart your Mac. If need be, force a restart as described previously.

3. As soon as you hear the computer's startup sound, hold down the C key. This enables your computer to start from your system CD.

4. The installer launches automatically.

5. After your system installation is finished, go ahead and restart and check that everything is working properly.

Summary

System crashes and application quits can be inconvenient, but you learned in this chapter that you are not helpless against them. You learned to force-quit unresponsive applications and to restart unresponsive computers. You discovered the secret of resetting your password with your system install CD. You also learned how to set up a preventive regime to defend against computer viruses. You learned about some disk repair options. Finally, you learned how to reinstall your operating system in case your computer begins to experience widespread failures.

PART VI

Advanced Topics

CHAPTER 36

Introducing Automator and AppleScript

For years, one of Apple's most compelling technologies within the Mac OS (even before Mac OS X!) has been the AppleScript scripting language. Unfortunately, AppleScript *is* a programming language; it requires at least elementary programming skills. Starting with Mac OS X 10.4, everything changes. Tiger introduces Apple's new scripting environment designed for average users—Automator.

Automator

Automator enables you to make repetitive tasks automatic. It is built around the idea that applications carry out actions to create a *workflow*. Workflow is the path that work takes as it is completed.

For example, the workflow for sending an email message with an attachment might be:

1. Collect the content for the email (text, files, and so on).

2. Compress the files.

3. Start the email application.

4. Create a new message.

5. Enter the text content.

6. Add the compressed files as an attachment.

7. Send the message.

In this example, two applications are used: The Finder and Mail. Each of these applications carries out actions within the workflow. The Finder collects, organizes, and compresses files. Mail composes and sends the message.

In Automator you can create workflows that automatically integrate applications and their associated actions—enabling one application to send information to another seamlessly. All that is required to build a workflow similar to the one described here (or much more complex!) is the ability to drag and drop.

Workflows are linear, meaning that you don't need to worry about branching. Although this does limit what you can do somewhat, you'll find that Automator is still a *very* flexible tool.

In the event that things do go wrong in Automator, the workflow can be debugged and corrected with just a few points and clicks.

Actions and Data Flow

Automator works with very simple data types such as folders, files, email messages, URLs, text, and so on. Actions have clearly labeled data type requirements for input and output that must match up with other actions' requirements. For example, the Compress Files action takes files and folders as input, and produces a file as output. It can't be connected to an action that uses URLs, but *can* be connected to an action that creates a new email message that accepts files and folders and adds them as attachments to the message.

All available actions are sorted based on how well they will work with the action you've currently added or selected in your workflow. Not to over-simplify things, but using Automator is a bit like connecting the dots.

The Automator Interface

The Automator interface, shown in Figure 36.1, is very similar to Apple's "i" applications. Along the left side of the application window are two columns: the Library, which lists Automator-compatible applications, and Actions—the tasks that applications can carry out. Below the columns is a collapsible information area that provides documentation for the currently selected object. If you aren't sure what something does, selecting it displays more detailed information in this area.

The majority of your workflow composition takes place in the large pane on the right side of the window. Actions are added to this area to create an interconnected chain of applications—that is, the workflow.

Execute finished workflows by using the Play and Stop buttons at the top of the window.

Action Search

Library   Actions   Workflow Controls

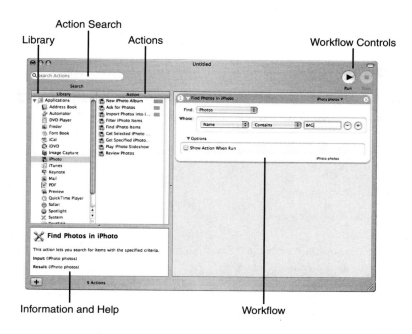

Information and Help   Workflow

FIGURE 36.1
Use the Automatic interface to carry out tasks.

Creating a Workflow

To create a new workflow, start dragging actions into the workflow pane. As they are added to the flow, actions appear as numbered blocks within the pane, as shown in Figure 36.2.

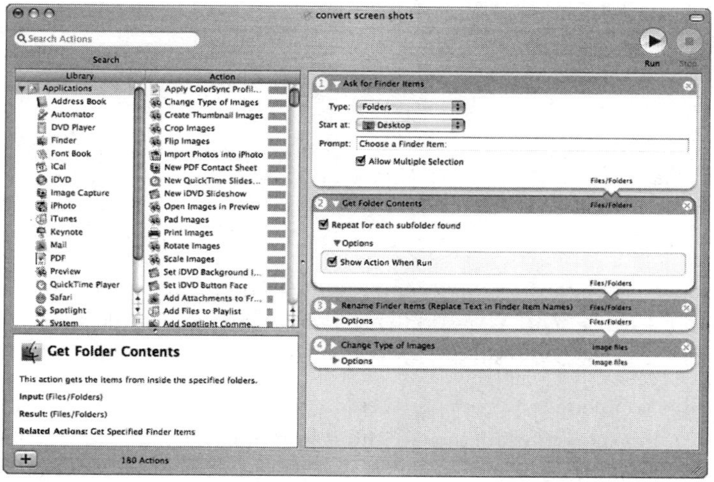

FIGURE 36.2
Drag actions into the pane on the right to create your workflow.

You can select the Applications folder in the Library column to display all available actions at once. The icon next to each action indicates to which application it will be applied.

To get you started, let's create a simple workflow that downloads the text from a URL (or URLs) that you specify, and then creates an iPod note based on the page content.

This workflow consists of three actions:

1. Get Specified URLs

2. Get Text from Webpage

3. New iPod Note

Find these actions in the Library list, and then drag them, one by one, into the workflow area, as shown in Figure 36.3.

FIGURE 36.3
Create a simple workflow by dragging the actions into the workflow.

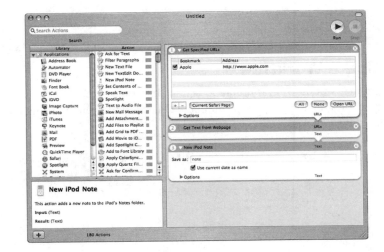

After all the actions are added, you need to configure a few properties of the actions.

The first action, Get Specified URLs, requires that you provide it with one or more URLs. Use the + and – buttons, respectively, to add and remove URLs. The sole purpose is to feed the URLs you specify into the next action, Get Text from Webpage.

Get Text from Webpage requires no additional settings. This action downloads all the text from the URLs that are passed into it from the previous action. After it is finished, it passes information into the third and final action, New iPod Note.

The New iPod Note action creates a new note that you can read by using the scroll wheel on your iPod. By default, the new note is named "note." To save the note based on the current date, click the Use Current Date as Name check box.

This workflow is now ready to run. If you have an iPod connected to your system, click the Run button and in a few seconds a text version of the URL you specified is uploaded to your iPod as a note labeled with the current date.

To configure this workflow to be executed every day automatically, see the section "Managing Workflows."

Workflow Actions

As soon as actions are added to a workflow, they can be removed, rearranged, and minimized with only a few clicks. Use these shortcuts to help maintain a clean and manageable workflow:

▶ Deleting Actions—To delete an action, select it in the list by clicking, and then press the Delete key—or simply click the X button in the upper-right corner.

▶ Reordering Actions—To change the order of a group of actions, drag them around within the list. The surrounding actions automatically renumber as you drag. On some systems, it can be difficult to get an action to properly "drop" where you want. In these cases, click the action number and then choose which other action you would like it to follow.

▶ Renaming Actions—By default, actions in the workflow inherit their names from the library. If you would like to rename an action to something specific for your workflow, choose Rename from the pop-up menu displayed by clicking the action's number.

▶ Disabling/Enabling Actions—If you no longer want to execute a given step in a workflow, you can disable it rather than delete it. This keeps the action in the flow, but passes the information through it unchanged. Keep in mind that if the action performed a data conversion, the workflow may no longer function. Choose Disable (and Enable) by clicking the action number.

▶ Collapsing/Expanding Actions—Actions can take up quite a bit of space in the workflow area. After an action is configured, it can be collapsed, saving a significant amount of screen space. To collapse/expand an action, click the disclosure triangle by the action name.

▶ Import Actions—If a third party, Apple, or you decide to provide additional actions for an application, you can import them into Automator by Choosing File, Import Actions. See developer.apple.com for more information on developing Automator actions.

> If you want to have as much space as possible in the workflow, you can choose to have the actions automatically collapse within the Automator application preferences.

User Control During an Action

The most useful options for an action are always displayed directly in the action block of the workflow, such as the Use Current Date as Name option used earlier. Many Automator actions, however, have a Show Action When Run check box. When enabled, the action displays an onscreen dialog to allow user interaction.

To access any additional settings, click the Options disclosure arrow at the bottom of the action block (if available). This expands the block, as shown in Figure 36.4.

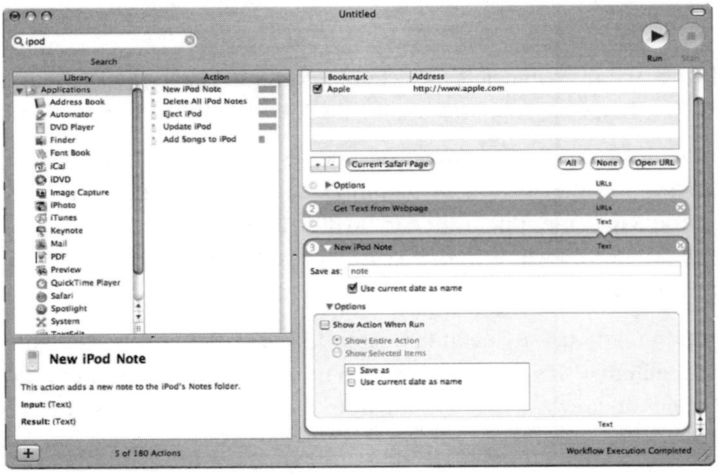

FIGURE 36.4
This is the same New iPod Note action you've seen already with additional options displayed.

In this example, you can choose how the iPod note is saved. For example, to show a Save As dialog for the note, click the Show Action When Run check box, then choose Show Selected Items, and check the Save As box.

Watch Out!

> Strangely, Automator allows you to configure additional options that conflict with the main settings. For example, if you were to use the Use Current Date as Name setting for the New iPod Note action, but also activate Show Action When Run and Save As, you would see a Save As dialog when the workflow is run, but you wouldn't be able to enter any text.

Running and Debugging Workflows

Workflows can be executed by clicking the Run button in the toolbar or by choosing Run (Command+R) from the Workflow menu. As a workflow executes, a green check mark appears in the lower left corner of each successfully completed action. If an action fails, a red X is displayed instead. Use the Stop button or choose Workflow, Stop (Command+.) to cancel execution in the middle of a workflow.

Workflows don't always work as planned—either because an error occurred somewhere during the execution of an action, or there was a logical error during the creation of the workflow. In many cases errors are caused by either inappropriate or a lack of data being handed off to an action. When this occurs you'll notice that the input and output data types are highlighted in red. You *must* pass compatible data between actions, but Automator does allow you to add incompatible actions.

When errors aren't immediately visible in red, there are two places to track down the problems: through Automator Logs and the View Results Action.

View Logs

Workflow logs record the output of actions as they are executed and display any results—including any errors that may occur. For example, if you used an action to fetch a URL but the web server wasn't accessible or the URL was wrong, this would be immediately visible in the Automator log, as shown in Figure 36.5.

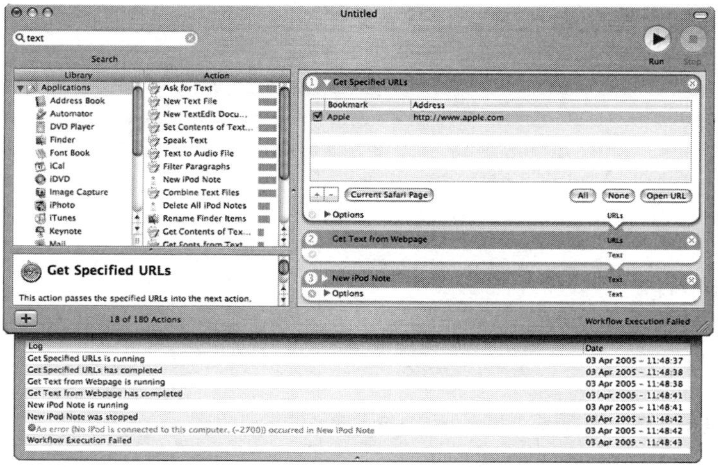

FIGURE 36.5
Use the Automator log to determine where things may have gone wrong.

View Results Action

The second error type, a logical workflow error, might not result in an actual visible error; rather, incorrect information is passed between actions. If you developed a workflow with an action that processes a group of files, but provided a folder as input, the action would essentially receive *no* input and probably produce no results. Here, the logical error would be forgetting to insert a Finder Get Folder Contents action before the action expecting the group of files. In these cases, the View Results action can be used as an important debugging tool.

View Results is found under the Automator application's actions and accepts *any* type of Automator input, stops the workflow, and then shows the information that was received from the preceding action. You can use the View Results action to ensure that the data you *think* is entering an action really is. For example, Figure 36.6 shows the results of the View Results action applied to an action that filters the contents of a folder based on the string green and then imports image files into iPhoto. Notice that View Results indicates that the results are not image files, yet the subsequent action operates on image files—indicating that I've obviously done something wrong.

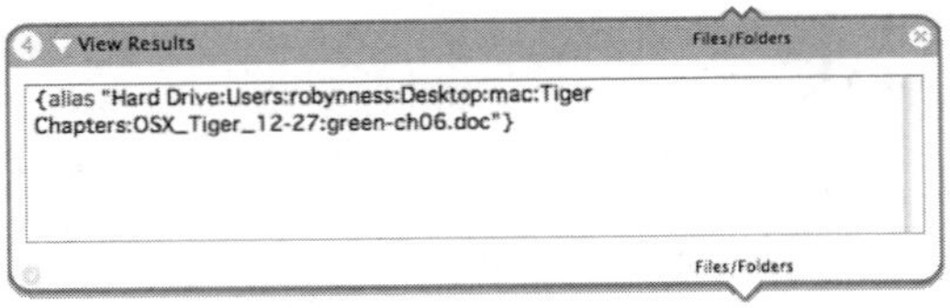

FIGURE 36.6
The View Results action can help you debug logical errors in the workflow.

> **By the Way**
>
> View Results can tell you whether there are no results returned from an Action, such as Filter Finder Items, to be passed along to the next Action. When this occurs, "()" appears in its message area.

Managing Workflows

After you've developed a workflow, you need to do something with it. Automator gives you quite a bit of flexibility in packaging your final workflows.

Save Workflows as Documents and Applications

You can save workflows as documents or applications by choosing File, Save As from the menu. Double-clicking a document workflow loads it within Automator—just as you'd expect. You can also create double-clickable applications that can be invoked directly from the Finder with a double click, or if files are dragged and dropped onto their icon. Workflows saved as applications can be imported into the Automator Library—which you'll learn about directly.

As soon as it is saved as a document or application, a workflow can be shared with other users who are running Automator, assuming they have the appropriate applications and actions installed for the workflow to function.

Add Workflows to the Automator Library

The Automator Library seems to be a combination of two rather different functions. First and foremost, the Library provides instant access to the applications that you can automate—you use it to select individual applications to view their actions, or the entire Applications folder to show all actions.

The second role for the Library is to contain collections of workflows. The My Workflows collection contains any workflows placed in `~/Library/Workflows`. Expand the collection by clicking the disclosure triangle in front of the name. Workflows stored in the collection are displayed and can be loaded if you double-click their names.

You can import into My Workflows by placing workflow documents in `~/Library/Workflows`, or by dragging a workflow from the Finder or Automator into the collection.

To create a new collection, use the + button at the bottom of the Automator window; this creates a new empty workflow collection that you can use just like My Workflows.

Apple provides several example workflows in the "Example Workflows" collection.

Saving Workflows as Plugins

Earlier in the discussion of Automator, you learned that you could create an Automator action that would repeat on a timed schedule. This is made possible by the capability for workflows to be saved as plug-ins for other applications and tools.

Six plug-in options are provided:

▶ Finder—When saved as a Finder plug-in, an Automator workflow immediately becomes available within an Automator submenu when a contextual menu (Control+Click) is invoked in the Finder. This enables you to create workflows that operate directly on the files selected in the Finder, as shown in Figure 36.7.

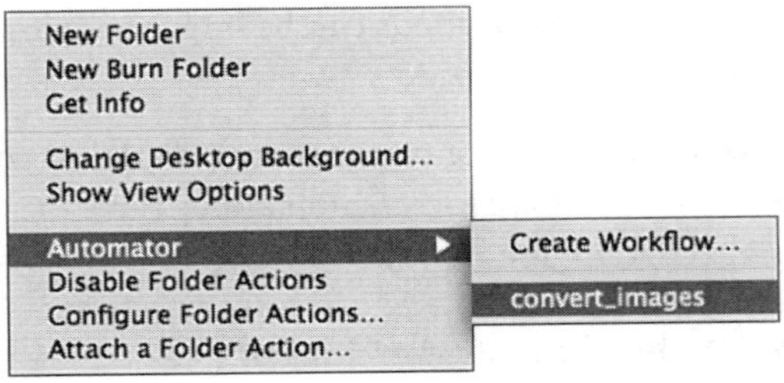

FIGURE 36.7
The Finder plug-
in enables you
to create your
own Finder con-
textual menus.

New Folder
New Burn Folder
Get Info

Change Desktop Background...
Show View Options

Automator ▶   Create Workflow...
Disable Folder Actions   convert_images
Configure Folder Actions...
Attach a Folder Action...

▶ Folder Actions—Folder actions are scripts that are activated based on an action that affects a folder. A workflow could be developed to scale and email all images dropped into a folder, for example. You learn more about configuring Folder Actions during the discussion about AppleScript later in this chapter.

▶ iCal Alarm—When a workflow is added as an iCal alarm, it can be set as the alarm action for any event. Repeating events can trigger a workflow at any interval you specify. Learn more about the iCal application in Chapter 19, "Using iCal."

▶ Image Capture—The Image Capture application, located in the Applications folder, can be used to import photos from a digital camera rather than from iPhoto. Image Capture can run a workflow after an image imports, which could be used to resize, crop, or otherwise package the images downloaded from your digital devices.

▶ Print Workflow—A Print workflow is accessed directly from the PDF menu of the Print window, providing the printing document as the input to the work-flow. Learn more about printing settings in Chapter 12, "Printing, Faxing, and Working with Fonts."

▶ Script Menu—The script menu is a menu extra that can be enabled by the AppleScript utility, discussed later in this chapter. After it is active, workflows appear in this menu and can be accessed from any application at any time.

The capability to interface and integrate with so many parts of the operating system makes Automator an intriguing tool that may very well change how we work with and control our computers.

AppleScript

Although Automator is a great tool for stringing together pre-built actions to create an automated workflow, it is not the first nor only means of automating actions on your Macintosh. AppleScript, originally introduced in the early 90's, provides much greater control over your entire system.

AppleScript is intended to provide a means for Macintosh users to develop complex scripts with the capability to evaluate conditions and branch, if needed. The syntax is surprisingly simple and can be understood even if you've never seen a programming language before. For example, take the following code:

```
tell application "Finder"
    activate
    close window "Applications"
end tell
```

It doesn't look like a programming language, but it is. This small example instructs Mac OS X to activate the Finder application and then close an open window with the title Applications.

Using a language that can almost be read aloud and understood, normal users can write scripts that combine the capabilities of multiple applications.

Using the Script Editor

The easiest way to get started with AppleScript is with the Script Editor. Besides being a context-sensitive programming editor, it also acts as a script recorder. You can open the Script Editor, click Record, and generate an AppleScript by using the editor to monitor your actions while interacting with a recordable application—unfortunately, very few are.

The Script Editor serves as your primary entry and testing point for any AppleScript development—either recorded or entered by hand.

Script Editor Controls

Launch the Script Editor from the AppleScript folder in the Applications folder to begin scripting. Figure 36.8 shows the initial editor window.

The Script Editor recording and editing tools include the following:

▶ Record/Stop/Run—Similar to a tape deck, these buttons are used to control recording and playback of an AppleScript. Click the Record button (Command-D) to start monitoring your system for Apple events within scriptable applications. These events are then stored in a script. The Stop button (Command-.) is used to stop recording, whereas the Run button (Command-R) executes the actions.

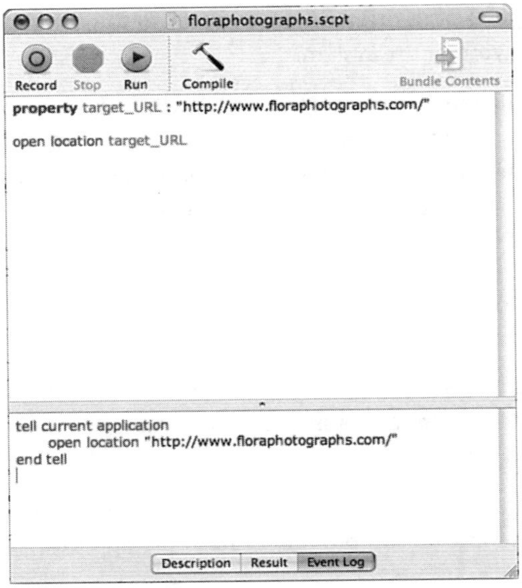

FIGURE 36.8
The Script
Editor is used
when editing or
recording
AppleScripts.

▶ Compile—Reviews the syntax of the current script for errors and automatically reformats the script if needed.

▶ Content—The content area is used to compose and edit script content. It functions like any Mac OS X text editor, but has the benefit of auto-formatting code when syntax is checked or the script is run.

▶ Description/Result/Event Log—This area is used to display information from or about the script, depending on the active button at the bottom of the window.

To start using the editor, click the Record button, switch to the Finder, and then open and drag a few windows around. As you work in the Finder, an AppleScript builds in the editor window. Click Stop to finish the code block and prepare it for execution. Figure 36.9 displays a script that has just finished generating.

You can immediately replay the recorded actions by clicking the Run button.

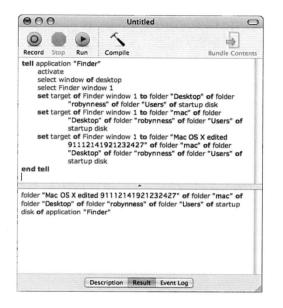

FIGURE 36.9
Click Record to
monitor your
actions and
build an
AppleScript;
then click Stop
to finish the
script.

Exploring the Scripting Dictionary

Obviously, the biggest draw to AppleScript is the capability to create scripts from
scratch. Recording is a good way to get a quick start but can't be used to generate
anything truly useful. The basic AppleScript syntax is covered later in the section
"Understanding AppleScript Syntax." Even this, however, is useless without knowledge of what commands an application can accept. Thankfully, each scriptable
application contains a dictionary that shows the scripting features it supports.

To access a scripting dictionary for any application, or scripting addition, choose
File, Open Dictionary from the menu. A list of the available scriptable applications
is displayed, as demonstrated by Figure 36.10. You can select multiple applications
by holding down the Apple key.

Be aware that some applications might not be shown. The Browse button at the bottom of the window opens a standard File Open dialog for choosing an arbitrary file.
After you pick an application from the default or browse view, a dictionary browser
window appears, as shown in Figure 36.11.

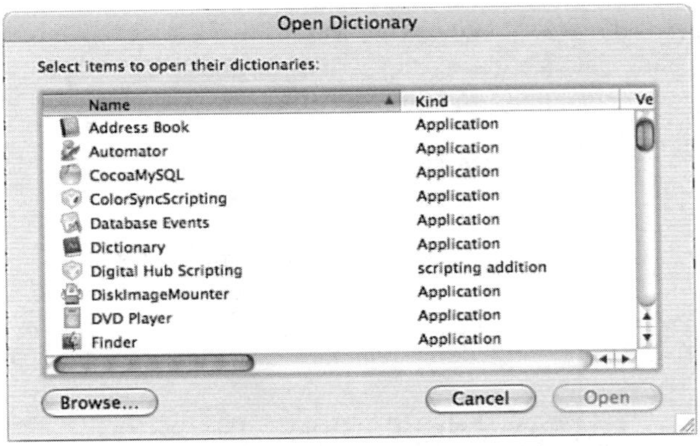

FIGURE 36.10
Choose from the available scriptable applications.

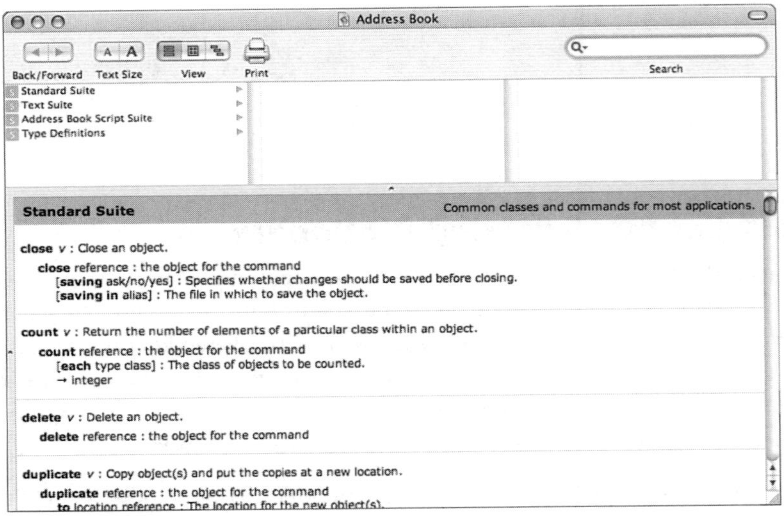

FIGURE 36.11
The dictionary documents the available AppleScript functions.

The browser toolbar works like many of Apple's other applications, the arrows moving back and forth through dictionary entries, and the search field providing an instant lookup of any key term you might need.

Below the toolbar are several columns. In the default view mode, the first column allows you to select suites of dictionary entries. A suite is simply a categorization for certain types of AppleScript functionality. The DVD Player, for example, has a DVD suite that contains all the necessary information for working with DVDs. Some applications may include other suites as well, such as a Standard suite, which provides everything you need to open and close documents, print, and so on. These additional suites are shared throughout the system and enable you to use a common syntax when doing everything from creating a new web browser window to creating a new text document.

When a suite is selected, all the available entries within that suite appear to the right, and a complete summary of all suite keywords is displayed in the pane below the columns, as shown in Figure 36.12.

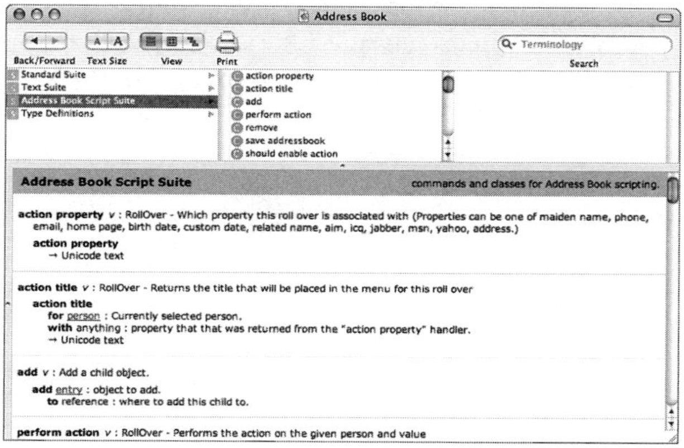

FIGURE 36.12
When a suite is selected, all entries are displayed in the lower pane.

To show a given entry within a suite, select it in the second pane and only its description appears. Each item within a suite is labeled as either a noun (*n.*) or a verb (*v.*). Nouns are *classes*, and you can either get information about them or act on them in some way. A class is an abstraction of a component of an application with which you work, such as a file. When you work with a class, you work with an instance of a class, which is called an *object*. Objects can have properties that can be set or modified to effect changes to the object. In some cases you may notice additional entries in the far right column after selecting an object. These are properties of the noun.

For example, the Address Book suite contains a Person object. For a given person, there are many different properties that can be assigned, as shown in Figure 36.13.

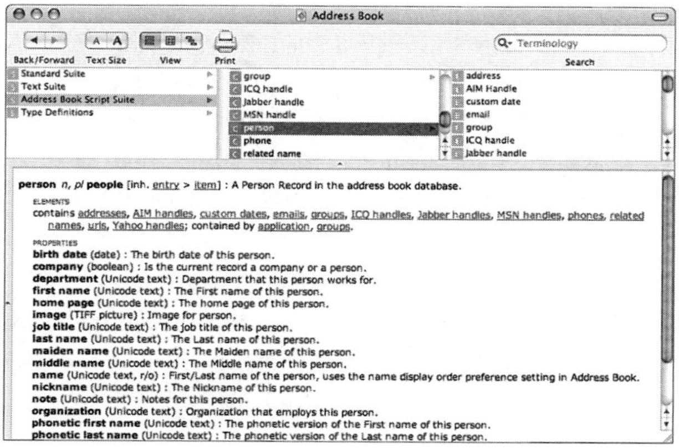

FIGURE 36.13
The Person object contains many attributes that describe a person.

Each property has a certain data type, such as an integer, image, text string, and so on. In this example, the Title attribute of a person is a text string, whereas the Image attribute is a TIFF.

By digging even further through the dictionary you can find that there is a specific object of the Address Book application called My Card, which is an instance of the Person class representing the current user, as shown in Figure 36.14.

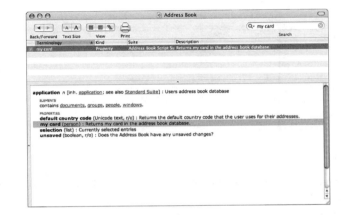

The only way to find everything you can do with AppleScript is to dig and experiment. The dictionary browser provides two other browsing modes to help.

Alternative Browsing Modes

By default, the dictionary browser shows suites. In some cases, however, you might be more interested in seeing a hierarchical view of what is contained within a given set of objects, or viewing an inheritance tree for the application from top to bottom. Both of these views are described here.

The Containment view, selected via the middle button in view controls of the toolbar, bases its display off of how objects are contained within one another. For example, the Address Book application starts with an Application container. Within that container are documents, groups, people, and windows—each of which, in turn, can contain additional elements. Groups, for example, can contain people and more groups.

The last viewing mode, Inheritance, uses the object hierarchy of the system to browse a dictionary. AppleScript is an object-oriented environment, and this means that classes can inherit information and features from parent classes, and sub-classes can, in turn, inherit information from them. Earlier, it was mentioned that the

Address Book application object contains a property called My Card, which is a Person object describing the currently active user. Although this property is specific to the Address Book application, other properties, such as the application name and version, are automatically inherited from a parent application object. A view of this inheritance is shown in Figure 36.15.

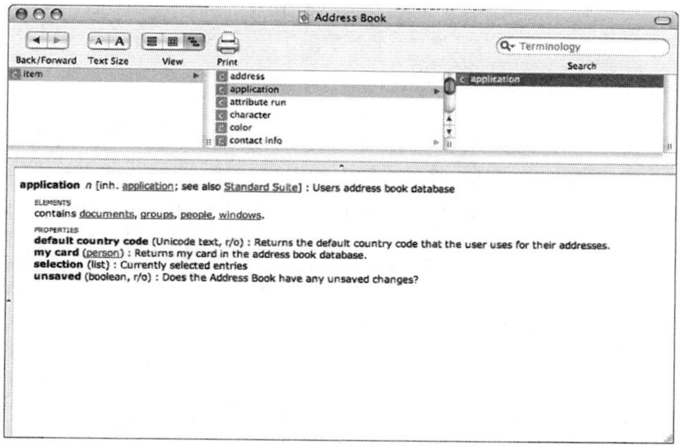

FIGURE 36.15
Objects inherit properties from parent classes.

Object-oriented programming is a bit beyond the scope of this book. If you find these views at all confusing, stick to the Suites view, which provides a much cleaner organization for most users.

Entering a Sample Script

Let's see how the Person class can be used to return an attribute about someone in the Address book. Go back to the main Script Editor window and enter the following (without line numbers):

```
1: tell application "Address Book"
2:   get the job title of my card
3:   set myTitle to the result
4:   display dialog myTitle
5: end tell
```

> If you switch between lower and upper case characters as you enter script in AppleScript, the Script Editor cleans up your code by changing everything to the correct case.
>
> **By the Way**

When finished, click the Run button and a dialog box appears with your Address Book title as the contents.

> If information required by the AppleScript is missing, such as the job title in this example, an error window opens in the Address Book application.

Line 1 indicates that instructions are to be sent to the Address Book application. Line 2 gets the job title for the Person object contained in the special property my card (me). Line 3 sets a variable called myTitle to the results of the previous get command. Line 4 displays a dialog box containing the contents of myTitle. Finally, line 5 stops talking to Address Book.

This example introduces the structure you will see in most AppleScript programs. The tell, set, and get statements form the basis of scripts. The objects and the parameters that can be modified, however, have to be looked up in the application's dictionary.

> The Script Editor features a Script Assistant that automatically completes recognized pieces of code as you type. Before you can use the assistant, you must first enable it within the Editing pane of the Script Editor preferences, and then quit and restart the editor.
>
> If the assistant recognizes what you're typing, it places an ellipsis (...) after your cursor. When this is displayed, pressing F5 shows the potential code completions. Use the up and down arrows to choose the one you want, and then press Enter to insert the code into your script.

Viewing Results

As seen in the preceding example script, when an AppleScript function returns a result, it is stored in a special temporary variable called result. This can be used to access a value without the need for additional variables. For example, lines 3 and 4 of the preceding script could be condensed to

```
display dialog the result
```

To display the contents of the result container within the Script Editor, choose View, Show Result (Command-2) from the menu, or click the Result button at the bottom of the Script Editor window. Tiger displays the current value of result below the script.

Tracing Events

To trace the execution of a script as it runs, use the Event Log. This log keeps track of the events (commands) sent to an application and displays the results that are returned immediately. Click the Event Log button or press Command-3 to show the Event Log in the lower pane of the Script Editor window. Figure 36.16 shows the Event Log after replaying a simple script to get the location of a Finder window.

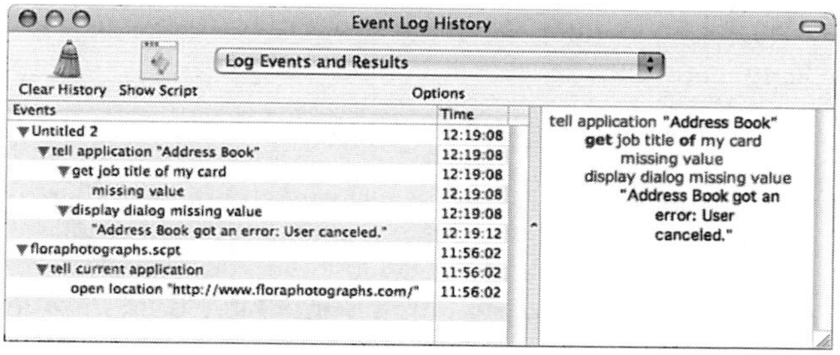

FIGURE 36.16
The Event Log can be used to monitor script execution.

Saving Scripts

After creating a script that functions the way you want, you can save it in several different ways. Select File, Save As, and then choose from the following options, depending on what you want to do with the script:

There are five possible file formats for scripts:

- ▶ Script—Saves the script as a compiled binary file.

- ▶ Application—Saves the script for double-click execution under Mac OS X.

- ▶ Script Bundle—A noncompiled binary form of the script packaged with a text file containing the description.

- ▶ Application Bundle—Saves the script for double-click execution under Mac OS X, along with a text file containing the description and an icon file saved with an .icns extension.

- ▶ Text—Saves the contents of the script in a plain-text file.

In addition to the file format, you can also choose the line ending format if saving to a text file, and whether the file should be Run Only (not allow editing), display a Startup Screen, and be set as Stay Open (to not close after it finishes executing).

Changing Scripting Preferences

The Script Editor automatically highlights and formats AppleScript as you type. To change the default font styles and formatting, choose Preferences from the application menu.

The five categories of Script Editor preferences are as follows:

- ▶ General—The default scripting language to be used. AppleScript is the only language available unless you install third-party software.

▶ Editing—Control line wrap settings, control tab indentation, and enable/disable the Script Assistant.

▶ Formatting—Choose font size, color, syntax highlighting, and so on.

▶ History—Enable or disable a running history of AppleScript-generated results and events.

▶ Plugins—Display any third-party plug-ins that have been installed.

Understanding AppleScript Syntax

AppleScript uses a programming model based on an English-like structure.

By the Way

> Many of the building blocks discussed here can be entered into the Script Editor automatically if you Control-click within your script and then choose from the many prewritten code fragments displayed in the pop-up menu that appears. You still have to fill in the details, but you don't have to remember the exact syntax.

Send Instructions to an Application: `tell`

The basic building block of an AppleScript is the `tell` statement. `tell` is used to address an object and give it instructions to perform. A `tell` line is written in one of two common forms: a block or a single statement. The block format enables the programmer to send multiple commands to an application without stating its name each time.

For example, the following two statements are identical, but the simple and block forms of `tell` are used in their structures:

```
tell application "Finder" to empty trash
```

and

```
tell application "Finder"
    empty trash
end tell
```

Both of these short scripts cause the Finder to empty the Trash. Although the second form might seem more verbose, it is likely to be the most commonly encountered form. Most scripts interact with objects to perform complex compound operations rather than simple commands. In addition, the second version of the AppleScript is easier to read, and makes it easier to view the functional components. Maintaining readable code is a good idea no matter what programming platform you're using.

In addition to breaking up code with `tell` blocks, long lines are typically split with a code-continuation character. To break a single long code line across multiple lines, press Option-Return to insert a code-continuation character.

Did you Know?

Manipulating Variables: `set`/`get`

In AppleScript, variables are automatically created when they are created with the `set` command. A variable name can be any combination of alphanumerics as long as the first character is a letter. No special prefixes are required to denote a variable within the code.

Although type conversions happen automatically in many cases, a variable type can be explicitly given directly in the `set` statement:

```
set <variable/property> to <value> [as <object type>]
```

For example, both of the following lines set variables (`thevalue` and `thevalue2`) to 5, but the second line forces the variable to be a string:

```
set thevalue to 5
set thevalue2 to 5 as string
```

In programming, a *string* is a type of variable that acts as a grouping of characters, such as a word or phrase. In this example, a number that is forced to act as a string cannot be used for mathematical operations. Variables containing numbers are often treated as strings when they represent phone numbers, numbers in addresses, or other numbers that act as labels or categories. It makes no sense to add, subtract, multiply, or divide them.

By the Way

In addition to setting variables, the `set` command can act on an object's properties to effect changes on the system. Earlier you saw how an AppleScript could get the "title" of the active person object in Address Book. Similarly, `set` can alter the file type. For example:

```
1: tell application "Address Book"
2:   display dialog "Enter a new job title for yourself:" default answer ""
3:   set myNewTitle to the text returned of the result
4:   set the job title of my card to myNewTitle
5: end tell
```

In line 3 of this code fragment, `set` is used to alter the job title for the active user's card. Previously, you had only read information—now you can change it!

As you've already seen, to retrieve values from variables, or properties from objects, you would use the get command. get, by itself, retrieves the value of an object or variable and stores it in the result variable:

```
get the <property/variable> [of <object>]
```

Traditional programmers might feel uncomfortable with retrieving results into a temporary variable (result); in that case, they can use an implicit get to immediately store the results in another variable or object property:

```
set <variable/property> [of <object>] to the <property/variable> [of <object>]
```

Here the get is implied. This form of get and set is preferred for creating concise and readable code.

Working with Lists

You've seen that variables can take on simple values, such as numbers or strings, but they can also contain more complex values in the form of lists. Lists are equivalent to arrays in more traditional programming languages. A list is represented by a comma-separated group of values, enclosed in curly brackets { }. For example, the following line sets a variable, thePosition, to a list containing two values:

```
set thePosition to {50, 75}
```

Lists are often used to set coordinate pairs for manipulating onscreen objects, but can contain any object. In fact, lists even can contain lists of lists. For example:

```
set theListOfPositions to {{50, 75}, {65, 45}, {25, 90}}
```

Here, a variable called theListOfPositions is set to a list of lists. Item 1 of the list is {50,75}, item 2 is {65,45}, and so on.

When dealing with list values, you can reference individual items within a list by referring to them as just that: items. For example, assume that you've run the following command:

```
set thePosition to {50, 75}
```

To retrieve the value of the first item in the list, use

```
get item 1 of thePosition
```

When dealing with lists within lists, just embed item statements within one another. Assume, for example, that this list has been entered:

```
set theListOfPositions to {{50, 75}, {65, 45}, {25, 90}}
```

To retrieve the value of the second item of the second list within a list, you could write

```
get item 2 of item 2 of theListOfPositions
```

List Abstraction

In many cases, the names of lists and the elements they contain have been abstract-ed within the application dictionaries. For example, the Address Book application defines people as the plural form of the person object. In other words, people is a list of person elements. Because you know this, you can access any person in the address book by referencing his or her item number in the people list.

For example, to reference the name of the first person in the people list, I could use

```
get the name of item 1 of people
```

However, because the system already knows that a person object is an element of the people list, this can also be rewritten as simply

```
get the name of person 1
```

You can apply this same syntax wherever the dictionary includes the an abstraction for a list and its elements.

Again, the power of these commands is based in the dictionaries of AppleScript applications. Exploring the scripting dictionaries is the best way to uncover the capabilities of the AppleScript platform.

Using Flow Control: If

A common programming construct is the if-then-else statement. This is used to check the value of an item and then react appropriately. The syntax for a basic if statement is

```
If <condition> then
    <action>
end if
```

For example, the following code asks the user to input a value, checks to see whether it equals 5, and outputs an appropriate message if it does:

```
1: display dialog "Enter a number:" default answer ""
2: set theValue to (text returned of the result) as integer
3: if theValue = 5 then
4:    display dialog "Five is my magic number."
5: end if
```

Line 1 displays a dialog prompt for a user to enter a value. Line 2 sets a variable `theValue` to the text returned from the dialog and forces it to be evaluated as an integer. Line 3 checks `theValue`; if it is equal to the number 5, line 4 is executed. Line 4 displays an onscreen message, and line 5 ends the `if` statement.

The `if` statement can be expanded to include an `else` clause that is executed if the original condition is not met.

```
1: display dialog "Enter a number:" default answer ""
2: set theValue to (text returned of the result) as integer
3: if theValue = 5 then
4:    display dialog "Five is my magic number."
5: else
6:    display dialog "That is NOT my magic number."
7: end if
```

In this modified version of the code, line 6 contains an alternative message that is displayed if the condition in line 3 is not met.

Finally, the `else` itself can be expanded to check alternative conditions using `else if`. This enables multiple possibilities to be evaluated within a single statement:

```
1: display dialog "Enter a number:" default answer ""
2: set theValue to (text returned of the result) as integer
3: if theValue = 5 then
4:    display dialog "Five is my magic number."
5: else if theValue = 3 then
6:    display dialog "Three is a decent number too."
7: else
8:    display dialog "I don't like that number."
9: end if
```

The latest version of the code includes an `else if` in line 5. If the initial comparison in line 3 fails, line 5 is evaluated. Finally, if line 5 fails, the `else` in line 8 is executed.

Creating Iteration with `repeat`

Another common programming construct is the loop. AppleScript uses a single-loop type to handle a variety of looping needs. The `repeat` statement has several different forms that cover `while`, `until`, and other types of traditional loops.

There are six different forms of the `repeat` statement:

▶ Repeat indefinitely—Repeat a group of statements indefinitely, or until the `exit` command is called.

```
repeat
  <statements>
end repeat
```

▶ Repeat #—Using the second loop format, the user can choose the number of times a loop repeats.

```
repeat <integer> times
  <statements>
end repeat
```

▶ Repeat while—Loop indefinitely while the given condition evaluates to true.

```
repeat while <condition>
  <statements>
end repeat
```

▶ Repeat until—Loop indefinitely until the given condition evaluates to true. This is the inverse of the repeat while loop.

```
repeat until <condition>
  <statements>
end repeat
```

▶ Repeat with—Called a for/next loop in more traditional languages, this form of the repeat loop counts up or down from a starting number to an ending number. Each iteration updates a variable with the latest loop value.

```
repeat with <variable> from <starting integer> to
<ending integer> [by <increment>]
  <statements>
end repeat
```

▶ Repeat with list—Like the standard repeat with style loop, the repeat with list loop runs over a range of values, storing each value in a named variable during the iterations of the loop. The difference is that the value range is specified with a list, rather than an upper and lower integer value. This enables the loop to operate over anything from numbers to strings to lists of lists.

```
repeat with <variable> in <list>
  <statements>
end repeat
```

For example, consider a short script that cycles through each of the individuals in your address book and displays the name of each. To do this, you need use the second to last loop type, and you also need to know how many people are in the address book and how to reference each one.

A bit of poking around in the dictionary quickly reveals that you can return the number of elements in any list by using the Standard suite verb count with the syntax count of <list name>. You also learned earlier (in "List Abstraction") that

Address Book abstracts the list of all `person` objects as `people`, and that you can reference an individual element of the `people` list as simply `person <#>`, so the script can be written as

```
1: tell application "Address Book"
2:     repeat with i from 1 to count of people
3:         get the name of person i
4:         display dialog the result
5:     end repeat
6: end tell
```

Creating Subroutines

An important building block that you need for creating large AppleScripts is the *subroutine*. Subroutines help modularize code by breaking it into smaller, more manageable segments that can return specific results to a controlling piece of code. There are two types of subroutines in AppleScript: those with labeled parameters and those that use positional parameters. A *parameter* is a piece of information passed to a subroutine when it is called.

Positional parameters will be the most familiar to anyone who has used another programming language. This type of subroutine, which is the easiest to define and use, depends on being called with a certain number of parameters in a certain order.

Labeled parameters, on the other hand, rely on a set of named parameters and their values, which can be sent to the subroutine in any order. This can be used to create an English-like syntax, but adds a level of complexity when the code is read.

Because positional parameters can be used for almost any type of development and fit in with the structure of other languages discussed in this book, they are the focus here.

The syntax of a positional parameter subroutine is shown here:

```
on <subroutine name> ([<variable 1>,<variable 2>,<variable n>,...])
  <statements>
  [return <result value>]
end <subroutine name>
```

Each positional parameter-based subroutine requires a name, a list of variables that will be supplied when called, and an optional value that will be returned to the main application. For example, the following beAnnoying routine takes a string and a number as parameters, and then displays a dialog box with the message. The display is repeated until it matches the number given.

```
1: on beAnnoying(theMessage, howAnnoying)
2:   repeat howAnnoying times
3:     display dialog theMessage
4:   end repeat
5: end beAnnoying
```

Line 1 declares the subroutine beAnnoying and its two parameters: theMessage and howAnnoying. Line 2 starts a loop that repeats for the number of times set in the howAnnoying variable. Line 3 displays a dialog box with the contents theMessage. Line 4 ends the loop, and line 5 ends the subroutine.

As expected, running this piece of code does absolutely nothing. It is a subroutine, and, as such, requires that another piece of code call it. To call this particular routine, you could use a line such as

```
beAnnoying("Am I annoying yet?",3)
```

This causes the subroutine to activate and display the message Am I annoying yet? three times.

A more useful subroutine is one that performs a calculation and returns a result. The following example accepts, as input, an integer containing a person's age in years. It returns a result containing the given age in days.

```
1: on yearsToDays(theYears)
2:   return theYears * 365
3: end yearsToDays
```

Because this subroutine returns a value, it can be called from within a set statement to store the result directly into a variable:

```
set dayAge to yearsToDays(90)
```

When working in subroutines, you must explicitly define variables that are used only in the subroutine, as opposed to those that can be accessed from anywhere in the AppleScript application. A variable that is visible to all portions of a script is called a *global variable* and is defined in the global declaration. Similarly, the local keyword can be used to limit the scope of a variable to only the code contained within a subroutine. For example, try executing the following AppleScript:

```
1: set theValue to 10
2: reset()
3: display dialog theValue
4:
5: on reset()
6:   local theValue
7:   set theValue to 0
8: end reset
```

In line 1, a variable called `theValue` is set to 10. In line 2, the reset subroutine is called, which appears to set the contents of `theValue` to zero. Yet, when the result is displayed in line 3, the original value remains. The reason for this strange behavior is the inclusion of line 6. Line 6 defines `theValue` as a local variable to the reset subroutine. This means that any changes to that variable do not extend outside the subroutine.

To gain the behavior you expect (the contents of `theValue` are set to zero everywhere), swap the `local` keyword with `global`:

```
1: set theValue to 10
2: reset()
3: display dialog theValue
4:
5: on reset()
6:    global theValue
7:    set theValue to 0
8: end reset
```

This tiny modification tells the reset subroutine that it should use the global representation of the variable `theValue`. When `theValue` is set to zero in line 7, it replaces the initial value set in line 1.

Additional AppleScript Tools and Resources

To finish this chapter, it's a good idea to look at some additional tools on your system and other resources for AppleScript information. Apple has a strange habit of hiding AppleScript from its users. Although this has improved from Jaguar to Panther and Panther to Tiger, things that you'd expect to be plainly visible are tucked away.

Script Menu

The Script Menu is a menu extra to your menu bar that can be used to quickly launch AppleScripts. Apple has included dozens of scripts you can use with your applications immediately. To turn this feature on, you must run the AppleScript utility within the AppleScript folder and click the Show Script Menu check box.

Any compiled scripts placed in the Scripts folders inside either the system-level or user-level Library folder become accessible from the menu. To create submenus for categorizing scripts, just create multiple folders within the `Scripts` folders. As with everything in Mac OS X, items stored in `/Library/Scripts` are accessible by all users, whereas those in your personal `~/Library/Scripts` folders can be used by only you. If you prefer to see only your own scripts, you can choose to not show Library scripts from within the AppleScript utility.

To remove the Script menu, Command-drag it from the menu bar, or turn it off within the AppleScript utility.

Folder Actions

Folder actions are scripts executed when folders are opened, modified, or moved. Actions are configured either via the Script menu's Folder Actions submenu or when a Folder is selected in the Finder and invoked in the contextual menu (Control-click).

First, Folder Actions must be enabled. Choose Enable Folder Actions from a folder's contextual menu or from the Script menu.

Next, you can attach a Folder action to a selected folder, using either the Attach Folder Action or Configure Folder Actions options from the same menu.

Add Folder action prompts you for a folder action script to attach to the highlighted folder, whereas Configure Folder Actions opens the Folder Actions Setup application, shown in Figure 36.17, that provides access to *all* Folder actions configured for your account.

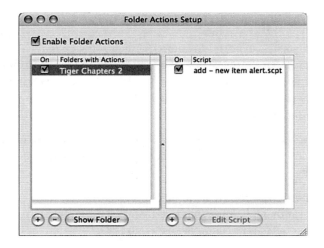

FIGURE 36.17
Configure Folder Actions provides a "control center" for adding and removing folder actions.

Within the Folder Actions Setup window, use the Enable Folder Actions check box to globally enable or disable actions. To add a new action, click the "+" button below the left column and choose a folder to which you want to attach an action. When added to the folder list, highlight it and use the + button in the right column to choose a folder action script that you want to attach to the folder. The – buttons can be used to remove folders and attached scripts, whereas the Show Folder and Edit Script buttons open the highlighted folder and open the selected script in Script Editor.

To get started with folder action scripts, Apple has included basic scripts in /Library/Scripts/Folder Action Scripts, including

- ▶ `close - close sub-folders.scpt`—Closes any open subfolders when the folder with the attached script is closed.

- ▶ `add - new item alert.scpt`—Displays an alert when new items are added to the folder with the attached script.

- ▶ `open - show comments in dialog.scpt`—Shows any comments stored when the folder with the attached script is opened.

Also included are several scripts for operating on images, providing simple graphic conversions and alterations if you just place files in a folder.

Properly formed Action scripts should be placed in either `/Library/Scripts/ Folder Action Scripts` or `~/Library/Scripts/Folder Action Scripts`. Apple has provided an excellent tutorial on how to set up a folder action script at www.apple.com/applescript/folder_actions/.

Scripting Additions

Enterprising developers who open the power of their software to the AppleScript model constantly expand AppleScript. The most common type of scripting addition is a new application. Applications that you install under Mac OS X may or may not be scriptable—be sure to check the documentation or try opening the software's dictionary while using the Script Editor.

In addition, some developers may deliver extensions to AppleScript in the form of a scripting extension. These extensions are not applications themselves but libraries of additional functions that can be used in any AppleScript.

Downloaded AppleScript extensions should be stored in `~/Library/ScriptingAdditions` or the system-level directory `/Library/ScriptingAdditions` for access by all users.

Other Sources of AppleScript Information

AppleScript is a capable language that offers many advanced features impossible to cover in the amount of space this title allows. What is provided here should be an ample start to creating scripts of your own and editing scripts included with Mac OS X. If you're interested in more information on advanced AppleScript syntax, I strongly suggest that you check out the following resources:

▶ AppleScript Language Guide—developer.apple.com/documentation/
AppleScript/Conceptual/AppleScriptLangGuide/

▶ AppleScript in Mac OS X—developer.apple.com/documentation/AppleScript/
Conceptual/AppleScriptX/Concepts/ScriptingOnOSX.html

▶ The AppleScript Sourcebook—www.AppleScriptSourcebook.com/

▶ *AppleScript in a Nutshell,* Bruce W. Perry, ISBN: 1565928415, O'Reilly

Summary

Automator is an amazing tool that provides a point-and-click solution for automating repetitive tasks in many popular Mac OS X applications. For tasks too complex for Automator, AppleScript provides a powerful solution for automating tasks on your Mac. Its Script Editor offers even novice users the ability to record their interactions directly to an AppleScript. Give it a try—you may be surprised by how easy the syntax can be.

CHAPTER 37

Using Basic Unix Commands

Unix-based operating systems are powerful and stable, but traditionally, people had to access Unix systems from the command line, by typing text commands in a text-only window. For this reason, many average computer users have been intimidated by their complexity. As you found out way back in Chapter 1, "Introducing Mac OS X," Apple has harnessed that power and stability while maintaining the ease of a traditional Macintosh by designing Mac OS X with a Unix subsystem.

> By creating Mac OS X, Apple has become the largest producer of Unix-based operating systems on the planet!

By the Way

If you've been using Mac OS X for a while now, you might be wondering what all this command-line talk is about—after all, you certainly haven't needed to type a command on your system, nor have any of your applications required you to access a command prompt. That's precisely what Apple intended when creating Mac OS X.

Beneath the gorgeous veneer of Mac OS X's graphical interface lies the powerful BSD (Berkley Software Distribution) version of the Unix platform. This layer sits behind many of the tasks you perform on your machine and coordinates the actions that make using your Macintosh possible. Although you don't have to directly interact with this underlying system to complete your day-to-day tasks, you can—if you choose to do so.

Terminal: Your Window to the Underworld

The Terminal application (/Applications/Utilities/Terminal) provides your point of access to the BSD subsystem of Mac OS X. Opening Terminal creates a new window with a beckoning command prompt, just waiting for some input, as shown in Figure 37.1.

You can customize the appearance of the Terminal application in a number of ways, such as changing the font, resizing the window, and setting a title. You do so with the Terminal Inspector, which you launch by choosing Terminal, Window Settings in the menu.

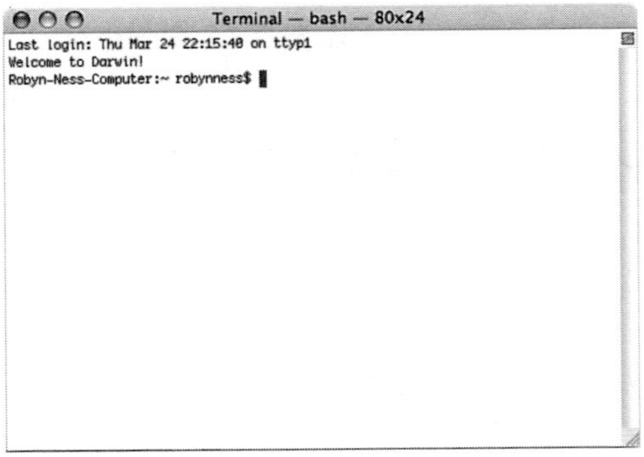

FIGURE 37.1
Terminal opens
a window into
the Unix layer of
Mac OS X.

One of the most important changes you can make is setting an unlimited scrollback buffer. As you use the Terminal program and begin to explore Unix, you will want to "scroll back" to check on the output of commands that you've entered using the scrollbars. By default, the Terminal remembers 10,000 lines. This might seem like a lot, but those who use Terminal to do serious operations will quickly see that it isn't. To change to an unlimited scrollback buffer, follow these steps:

1. Open the Terminal application Window Settings, found in the application menu.

2. Click the Buffer option in the pop-up menu at the top of the window.

3. Select the Unlimited Scrollback radio button, shown in Figure 37.2.

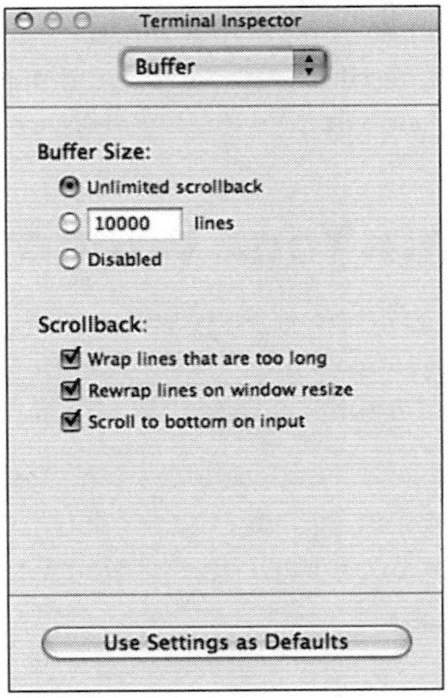

FIGURE 37.2
An unlimited
scrollback
buffer helps you
keep track of
the things
you've done.

4. Close the settings by closing the window or click Use Settings as Defaults.

5. Open a new Terminal window by choosing File, New Shell from the menu (Command-N).

6. The new window is ready for use with an unlimited scrollback buffer.

Now that you've found the command prompt, let's see what you can do with it. Whenever possible, I'll try to relate the command-line tools to their graphical Mac OS X alternatives.

Basic Commands for Working with Files

As you work with the Mac OS X Finder, you get to know a sequence of mouse commands for working with the files and folders on your system. These same actions can be carried out from the command line very easily.

Basic Commands

Let's start with some of the basic commands for listing, moving, and copying files. Obviously, you can't do much with your files unless you can see them, so we start with the ls (or list) function.

ls

Typing ls at the command prompt displays all the available files in the current directory (folder). Because the Terminal opens to your home directory and you haven't learned how to change directories, you probably see a list of the files inside your home that's similar to the list following list:

```
[client18:~john] john% ls
Desktop      Library    Music      Public
Documents    Movies     Pictures   Sites
```

As you know, your Mac OS X files also have permissions on them. To view the listing with permissions showing, use ls -l, and you see a list similar to the following:

```
[client18:~john] john% ls -l
total 94296
drwx------    9 john    john         306 Jul 25 01:11 Desktop
drwx------   49 john    john        1666 Jul 10 23:55 Documents
drwx------   41 john    john        1394 May 30 18:58 Library
drwx------    6 john    john         204 Mar 30 02:40 Movies
drwx------    3 john    john         102 Mar 30 02:40 Music
drwx------    6 john    john         204 Jul 10 23:55 Pictures
drwxr-xr-x    6 john    john         204 Mar 30 02:40 Public
drwxr-xr-x   16 john    john         544 Jul 10 23:55 Sites
```

For the most part, the listing is straightforward. The second column is a count of the number of files in a directory. The third and fourth columns are the owner and group, respectively. The fifth column contains the file size, whereas the sixth and seventh columns are the modification date and filename.

The first column, however, is filled with strange letters, such as drwx (repeated several times). The first character of this sequence of letters indicates what kind of file it is. In the listing example, the first characters are all the letter *d*—for directories. The rest of the nine letters represent read, write, and execute permissions for the user, group, and everyone, respectively.

By the Way

The Mac OS X GUI doesn't provide a control over the execute permission of a file. This attribute, as its name suggests, controls whether the file can be executed or, in Mac terms, *run*. If execute is set for a directory, you can move through, or *traverse*, it.

For example, assume that you see a column with drwxr-xr--. Following the pattern described, the first letter, d, indicates that this is a directory, and the next three letters, rwx, show that the owner has read, write, and execute permissions. The middle three positions, r-x, show read and execute permission for everyone within the file's group, and the last two, r--, tell us that everyone else has read permission for the file.

Special "abbreviations" are used to represent two special files (you can see these when you use **ls -al**):

▶ .—A single period represents the current directory.

▶ ..—Two periods represent the parent directory of the current directory.

You can use this directory notation with the other commands covered in this section.

cp

The next command we look at is the cp, or copy command. Copy, as its name suggests, is used to copy files or directories of files. The syntax for cp is simply

```
cp <source file path> <destination file path>
```

For example, to copy the file test.txt to testcopy.txt, you would type

cp test.txt testcopy.txt

This does nothing more than create an exact duplicate of the file test.txt named testcopy.txt in the same directory. To copy a file to another directory, just include the file's full pathname.

In the case of copying a directory, you must perform a *recursive* copy, which copies the contents of the folder and the contents of any folders within the source. Do this by supplying the -R option to cp. For example, if I want to copy the directory /Users/jray/testfiles and all of its contents to the folder /Users/robyn/ otherfiles, I use the following command:

```
cp -R /Users/jray/testfiles /Users/robyn/otherfiles
```

Simple enough, isn't it? You might recognize this as the equivalent of Option-dragging a file within the Finder, or using the Copy contextual menu command.

Did you Know?

If you play with cp, you might notice that it cannot copy Macintosh-specific files (applications, files with custom icons, and so on). To get around this, you can use the ditto command, which copies one directory to another, complete with all the information that makes a Macintosh file special.

mv

"Moving" right along, the mv command can move a file or directory from one place to another or rename it. It uses the same syntax as cp:

```
mv <source file path> <destination file path>
```

This is the same as clicking and dragging an icon from one place to another within the Finder.

For example:

```
mv myfile.txt myoldfile.txt
```

This moves the file myfile.txt to myoldfile.txt, effectively renaming the file. Like copy (cp), you could move the file to another directory by using its full pathname.

For example:

```
mv myfile.txt /Users/robyn/robynsfilenow.txt
```

Here the file myfile.txt is moved to /Users/robyn and stored with the new name: robynsfilenow.txt.

rm

Now that you can list, move, and copy files, you should probably also learn how to delete them. The rm (remove) command erases a file from your system. It's extremely important that you pay attention to what you're doing with rm because no Undo command or Trash exists from which to remove a deleted file.

When using rm, I recommend using the -i option along with it. This forces the system to ask you before removing a file. The basic syntax for rm is

```
rm -i <filename>
```

If you want to remove an entire directory, you must also add the -r option to the mix to force rm to go through the directory and remove all the files within it. For example, suppose that you want to remove a directory called myjunkfiles, including all the files inside it. To do that, type the following:

rm -ri myjunkfiles

The rm command steps through each file in the directory and prompts you to confirm that the file should be deleted.

Watch
Out!

> For your own good, you should learn to recognize the command that can remove *everything* on your system without asking twice—rm -rf. Essentially, this command tells your system to delete all folders and all the files in them. Never, ever use it—even if someone tells you to.

Wildcards

When working with files, you can use a few special symbols in place of characters in the filename. Specifically, the following sequences are available:

▶ *—Matches any number of characters in a filename

▶ ?—Matches a single unknown character

▶ [0—9]—Matches a range of characters

For example, if I want to list only the files in a directory that contain the letters *memo* anywhere in their names, I would type

ls *memo*

If, on the other hand, I want to be a bit more specific, such as listing all files that start with *memo* and end with exactly two characters that I don't know, I could use

ls memo??

Finally, to be even more exact, I could match a range of characters using the format [<start>—<end>]. Assume that I have a group of files, all named memo, followed by two extra characters—some of which are numbers. To list all the memo files followed by the numbers, I could enter

ls memo[0-9][0-9]

Wildcards make it easy to work with groups of files and directories without having to list each name separately.

Editing Files with `pico`

Creating and editing files is another important part of mastering the Mac OS X command line. This is a definite necessity for performing remote administration of the system, enabling you to make changes to your system's configuration from almost any terminal connected to the Internet.

A number of text editors are available that you can use from the Mac OS X command line:

▶ emacs—The emacs editor is a powerful editor that can be used for programming and basic editing tasks.

▶ vi—vi is the editor of choice for die-hard Unix fans. It's fast and omnipresent—it's available on just about any Unix machine that exists. (By the way, vi is pronounced *V-I*, not *Vee*.)

▶ pico—The pico editor is a modern editor for beginners. Like vi, it's fast, but it's much simpler to use and is the focus of our attention here.

To use pico, start it from the command line with the name of the file you want to edit or from a new file that you want to create:

```
pico <filename>
```

Figure 37.3 shows the pico editor running.

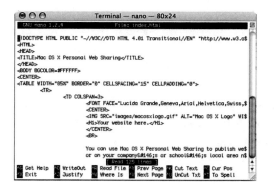

FIGURE 37.3
Pico is an easy-to-use command-line editor. (As you can see, it can even be used to make changes to the HTML for a Web page.)

To operate pico, use the arrow keys on your keyboard to move the cursor around the screen. Typing enters new text, whereas pressing Delete removes existing characters. You can also use a number of control characters during editing:

▶ Control-G—Opens a help screen with basic usage instructions

▶ Control-O—Writes (saves) the file

▶ Control-R—Reads a new file into the editor

▶ Control-Y—Jumps to the previous page

▶ Control-V—Jumps to the next page

▶ Control-W—Searches the file for a given sequence of characters

▶ Control-X—Exits pico

By the Way

You can certainly use pico to read files as well as edit them, but if you just want to quickly scroll through a file, use `more <filename>` to move through the file a page at a time.

File Permissions

The final file operations that we look at are how to modify permissions. You've already discovered how you can tell what the permissions of a file are (using ls)—now it's time to see how you can change them.

chown

By default, you own every file that you create. That's fine, but you might want to change a file's owner so that you can give it to someone else. The chown command (change ownership) performs this task with ease. Although you can also do this in the Finder, you can use the command-line chown command with filename wildcards to handle multiple files simultaneously.

To use chown, all you need is the name of the file you want to change and the username of the person to whom you want to assign ownership:

```
chown <username> <filename>
```

To change the ownership of a file called test.txt to the user jray, you would type

```
chown jray test.txt
```

You might need to prefix the line with the sudo command, which you learn about a bit later in this chapter.

chmod

The chmod command (change mode) modifies file permissions—the read, write, and execute attributes that you saw earlier when learning about the ls function.

The chmod command takes as its parameters a filename and the permissions that you want to assign to it. The permissions are given through use of a symbolic representation based on the letters u, g, o, and r, w, and x. The u, g, and o are user, group, and other, respectively. The letters r, w, and x represent the read, write, and execute permissions.

Combining these letters with + and -, you can add or subtract any permission from any type of access level:

```
chmod <permission> <filename>
```

For example, to remove write permission for the owner of a file named nowrite.txt, you would enter

```
chmod u-w nowrite.txt
```

Likewise, to add read permission for other users (the rest of the world), use this syntax:

```
chmod o+r nowrite.txt
```

As you can see, the Unix commands give you a much greater level of control than using the equivalent Get Info feature in the Finder.

Managing files in Unix is the same as managing files in Mac OS X's Finder, but instead of mouse actions, typed commands are used to tell your computer what to do. Before moving on, try editing a few files and using the basic mv and cp commands to move them around. When you feel comfortable with the process, move on to the next section, "Process Management." There you learn how the Unix side of your computer views running applications.

Process Management

As you use your Mac OS X computer, you create dozens of processes and support processes that you probably never realized existed. In Chapter 34, "Maintaining Your System," you learn about some of the GUI tools that enable you to manage these processes in a point-and-click manner. In this section, however, you see the commands that can provide the raw data of what is happening on your system.

Viewing Processes

To view the active processes on your computer, you can use one of two commands. The first command, ps, creates a process listing of whatever's running in the foreground (or, if it's modified, everything that's running). The second command, top, shows a list of the applications using up the most resources on your computer.

ps

To use the ps command, all you need to do is type **ps** at the command prompt. This generates a list of the processes that you control on the computer. For example:

```
[localhost:~] jray% ps
  PID  TT  STAT      TIME COMMAND
  707 std  Ss     0:00.25 -tcsh (tcsh)
```

Here, the process is my command-line shell (tcsh), which isn't very interesting. To list *everything* that's running on a Mac OS X computer, add the argument -ax to the command, like this:

```
[localhost:~] jray% ps -ax
  PID  TT  STAT      TIME COMMAND
    1  ??  SLs    0:00.05 /sbin/init
    2  ??  SL     0:02.75 /sbin/mach_init
   41  ??  Ss     0:01.94 kextd
   68  ??  Ss     0:22.85 /System/Library/Frameworks/ApplicationServices.framew
   70  ??  Ss    40:38.78 /System/Library/CoreServices/WindowServer
   72  ??  Ss     0:07.96 update
   75  ??  Ss     0:00.01 dynamic_pager -H 40000000 -L 160000000 -S 80000000 -F
  103  ??  Ss     0:00.61 /sbin/autodiskmount -va
  127  ??  Ss     0:03.28 configd
  185  ??  Ss     0:00.38 syslogd
  218  ??  Ss     0:00.02 /usr/libexec/CrashReporter
  240  ??  Ss     0:01.37 netinfod -s local
  247  ??  Ss     0:04.32 lookupd
  257  ??  S<s    0:05.72 ntpd -f /var/run/ntp.drift -p /var/run/ntpd.pid
  270  ??  Ss     0:01.38 /System/Library/CoreServices/coreservicesd
  277  ??  Ss     0:00.00 inetd
  288  ??  S      0:00.00 nfsiod -n 4
  289  ??  S      0:00.00 nfsiod -n 4
  290  ??  S      0:00.00 nfsiod -n 4
  291  ??  S      0:00.00 nfsiod -n 4
  298  ??  S      0:00.27 DirectoryService
...and so on.
```

By the Way

If the list generated by ps –ax is overwhelming, type **ps -ax ¦ more** to view the list in sections that fit your Terminal window. Press Enter to progress line by line through the list. Type **q** to go back to the command prompt.

For each process, you'll notice a `PID` number in the listing. This is the process ID, and it uniquely identifies the program running on your computer. There's also a `TIME` field, which contains how much cumulative processor time the software has used on your machine.

> You might also notice the TT and STAT columns in the listing. These display a process's controlling terminal and status. Unfortunately, these topics are beyond the scope of this book and are best addressed by an advanced book, such as *Mac OS X Unleashed* from Sams Publishing.

By the Way

Keep track of the `PID` values—you'll need them in a few minutes.

top

If you want a more interactive means of monitoring what's running on your system, try using the `top` command. The utility, shown in Figure 37.4, shows a listing of the most active and processor-intensive applications running on your machine. It can provide a good means of uncovering unusual activity on your computer and answering why your system is sluggish at a given point.

When you run `top`, the most active processes are shown at the top of the listing. Usually the Mac OS X components (such as the Finder) rank very highly in the list. Watching the `CPU` (percentage of CPU being used), `TIME` (total amount of CPU time the application has consumed), and `RSIZE` (amount of memory the application is using) columns gives you the most useful information about what your computer is doing. If you see an unusual piece of software that you didn't install (perhaps your coworker's copy of Seti@Home) in the listing, you can write down its `PID` and then force it to quit.

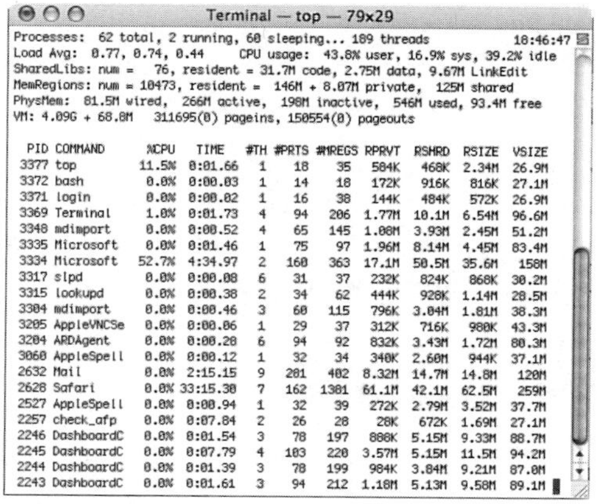

FIGURE 37.4
Use *top* to get an interactive view of the processes on your computer.

> To quit top, you need to type the key command **q** (as in "quit"). That returns Terminal to a command line where you can continue entering commands.

From the command line, you can use Unix to force any application to quit. Although powerful, this can also pose a danger to the system: Users can easily force important parts of the operating system to quit!

Killing Processes

As violent as it sounds, the action of forcing a running Unix process to quit is called *killing* it. Appropriately enough, this action uses a command called kill.

The kill command's actions don't need to be as drastic as forcing an application to quit. In reality, the kill command simply sends a signal to a process that can be interpreted in a number of ways. Sometimes, the kill command simply causes the software to reload its configuration, whereas in other instances the kill command does indeed force the software to exit.

The two most common signals you'll encounter are HUP (to force a reload) and KILL (to truly kill a process). Along with a signal, the kill command also requires a process ID (the numbers supplied in the PID column of the ps or top commands). Armed with this information, you can kill a process by using this syntax:

kill -<signal> <process id>

For example, to force a process with the ID of 1992 to quit, I would type

kill -KILL 1992

> Killing a process with the KILL signal does not save any data that the application is processing. Use this as a last resort for gaining control of a piece of software.
>
> Also be aware that indiscriminately killing processes on your system could make Mac OS X unstable or even crash the operating system.

The kill command can be used remotely to control what's running on your machine and shut down processes that shouldn't be active. In the next section, you learn how to gain complete control over the command line.

Server Administration

Although everything that you've learned so far in this chapter is valid, it isn't necessarily completely functional. For example, you can't change the owner of a file you don't own. In most cases, that's fine, but for complete control over the machine, you should be able to do whatever you want.

The command that makes this possible is sudo. When sudo is placed in front of any other command, it enables you to execute the command as the root user. Root has complete control over everything on your system, so be careful when using the command; you could end up removing all the files from your computer.

For example, to kill a process that you didn't create, you could use the following:

```
sudo kill <signal> <process ID>
```

sudo starts, asks you for your user password, and then executes the given command with root's permissions.

The commands themselves stay the same but gain a whole new level of capability. Using this technique, you can easily remove, copy, or rename files belonging to other users.

> Don't let the power go to your head! Other people who use or store files on your system should have a right to privacy, unless you explicitly tell them otherwise. Reading files you don't own is unethical and, depending on the circumstances, may be illegal.

By the Way

Getting Help with Manpages

Almost every function and utility that exists on your system includes a built-in help file called a *manpage* (manual page). The man command returns all the information you need to understand the arguments a given utility takes, how it works, and the results you should expect. Consider the more command, for example. Although this has been mentioned only briefly, you can quickly learn more information about it by typing

```
man more
```

For example:

```
[localhost:/etc] john% man more
man: Formatting manual page...
MORE(1)                                              MORE(1)
NAME
       more, page--file perusal filter for crt viewing
SYNOPSIS
       more  [  -cdflsu  ] [ -n ] [ +linenumber ] [ +/pattern ] [
       name ...  ]
       page more options
```

```
DESCRIPTION
       More is a filter which allows examination of a  continuous
       text  one screenful at a time on a soft-copy terminal.  It
       normally pauses after each screenful, printing the current
       file name at the bottom of the screen or --More-- if input
       is from a pipe.  If the user then types a carriage return,
       one  more  line  is  displayed.  If the user hits a space,
       another screenful is displayed.  Other  possibilities  are
       enumerated later.
...and so on...
```

This is only a tiny portion of the total manpage for the more command. There are more than five pages of information for this function alone!

> If you don't know exactly what command you're looking for, use apropos *<key-word>* to search through the manpage information for a given word or phrase.

Other Useful Commands

Thousands of other commands and utilities on Mac OS X could potentially be covered in a Unix chapter. Instead of trying to do the impossible and document them all in 15 to 20 pages, we finish the chapter by listing a few interesting functions that you can explore (remember to use man!) if you choose to do so.

- ▶ curl—Retrieves information from a given URL. Useful for downloading files from the command line.

- ▶ ncftp—A simple, yet surprisingly user-friendly FTP client.

- ▶ cat—Displays a file's contents.

- ▶ file—Shows a file's type (what it contains).

- ▶ locate—Quickly finds a file based on the text in its name.

- ▶ find—Locates files based on their size, modification dates, and so on. This is the Unix equivalent of the Finder's Find feature.

- ▶ grep—Searches through a text file for a given string.

- ▶ shutdown—Shuts down a Mac OS X computer.

- ▶ reboot—Reboots a Mac OS X computer.

- ▶ date—Displays the current date and time.

- ▶ uptime—Shows the amount of time your computer has been online and what the current system load is.

- passwd—Changes your Mac OS X password.

- df—Shows the amount of free and used space on all available partitions.

- du—Displays disk usage information on a directory-by-directory basis.

- tar—Archives and de-archives files in the Unix tar format.

- gzip/gunzip—Compresses and decompresses files.

Again, I want to stress that this should serve as a starting place for exploring the Unix subsystem. You will find commands that aren't listed in this chapter. However, with the documentation provided here, you're prepared for how they work and understand how to get more information about them.

> **By the Way**
>
> If this chapter has whetted your appetite for using the command line, I highly recommend *Mac OS X Tiger Unleashed*, which covers many of the topics discussed in this book, but with greater technical detail and much more attention to the Unix side of Mac OS X.

Summary

In this chapter, you learned some of the basics of the Unix command line. You should now be capable of performing many of the standard Finder functions from a command prompt. Although many gaps exist in what was covered, Unix is a broad topic and one that takes years to master. It can be hoped that you're on your way to becoming a future Unix guru!

CHAPTER 38

Exploring the Utilities Folder

Tucked inside the Applications folder is a folder called Utilities, which stores a treasure trove of helpful applications. Some of those "utilities" are employed by your system to carry out common tasks, whereas others are tools that you can use for specific purposes. In this chapter, we talk about each of these applications and, where appropriate, refer back to previous chapters where they were mentioned.

> You may find extra items in the Utilities folder in addition those described here. For example, if Mac OS X's Software Update finds a hardware update for iPod, iSight, or even your computer's built-in disc drive, that update is installed in the Utilities folder until the device it affects is run. You can delete these items, which are typically clearly labeled, after they have been installed.

Unlike the categorization structure used by the System Preferences, the items in the Utilities folder aren't in any particular order. However, for organizational purposes, we've grouped the applications in the Utilities folder into four categories: System Tools; Network Tools; Imaging, Audio, and MIDI Tools; and System Helpers.

System Tools

You Mac is a complex machine that runs many processes and has many components, some of which you may not even know about! System Tools are useful for taking an in-depth look at your Mac, which you may want to do in case of system difficulties or merely as an interesting window into the workings of your Mac.

Activity Monitor

As discussed in Chapter 34, "Maintaining Your System," Activity Monitor reveals what processes are running on your system and how much CPU time they consume. This can be helpful for finding out which applications are monopolizing system resources if your computer seems bogged down.

Console

Console is a specialized window for reading system logs, which record events related to applications or even network activity. Refer to Chapter 32, "Sharing Files and Running Network Services."

Disk Utility

Disk Utility is OS X's built-in hard drive repair tool—with the extra function of creating disk images of drives and allowing you to burn them to CD or DVD. Chapter 35, "Recovering from Crashes and Other Problems," discusses the repair aspects, and the disk copy element is covered in Chapter 34, "Maintaining Your System."

Disk Utility can also be run from your system installation disk. Use the version from the disk if you need to repair your main hard drive because drive repair can't be run from itself!

Migration Assistant

Migration Assistant is an application designed to help you transfer the contents of another Mac to the current one easily. To use this application, you need to connect the two computers via FireWire, which can handle the transfer of large quantities of data quickly. When the computers are connected, the Migration Assistant takes you through options step by step to make sure that all the information you need is transferred.

System Profiler

System Profiler is useful if you ever need to call for technical support and are asked for your computer's exact system configuration. The System Profiler's sole purpose is to collect data on your computer, peripherals, and software, and prepare a report of the results.

You can also open the System Profiler from the Apple menu. To access the System Profiler, choose About This Mac from the Apple menu, and then click the More Info button in the window that appears.

The information in the System Profiler is divided into three categories: Hardware, Software, and Network. (These can be expanded to show details if you click their disclosure triangles.)

Hardware

The Hardware section, shown in Figure 38.1, displays general information such as the machine model, the amount of built-in memory, and your computer's serial number.

The additional items under Hardware give summaries of the devices connected to your computer (including internal disks and storage devices, video and sound cards, and modems). Here are some of the items displayed in the Hardware section:

▶ ATA—Advanced Technology Attachment (ATA) refers to a standard for internal CD-ROM and disk storage; view details about your hard drive, such as model, capacity, and serial number.

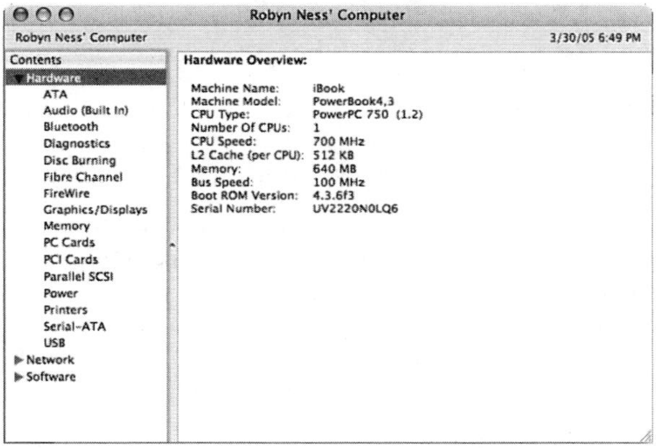

FIGURE 38.1
The main Hardware screen presents an overview of your system configuration.

▶ Disc Burning—Details about your computer's disc drive, such as whether it can burn CDs or read DVDs.

▶ FireWire—An Apple-developed bus technology that supports speeds of 400Mbps, which is often used with high-speed storage and digital video cameras. (FireWire is also known as IEEE 1394 and, in Sony devices, as iLink.) If you have any FireWire devices connected, you can see details about them here.

▶ Graphics/Displays—Details about your graphics card and display.

▶ Memory—Details about the location, type, and amount of memory installed in your computer.

▶ Printers—Details on any printers that you've added with the Printer Setup Utility. (See Chapter 12, "Printing, Faxing, and Working with Fonts," for more about connecting to a printer.)

▶ USB—Universal Serial Bus is used for connecting external peripherals, such as scanners, printers, cameras, keyboards, and mice—as well as lower speed storage devices. View details about any USB devices connected to your computer, as shown in Figure 38.2.

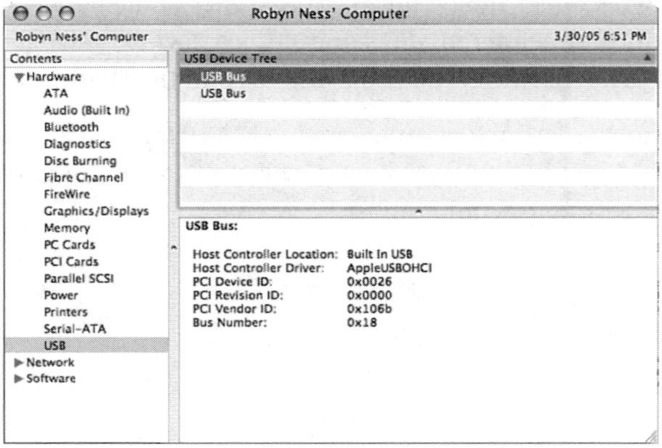

FIGURE 38.2
Identify your keyboard, mouse, and any other USB peripheral.

By the Way

Use of USB and FireWire peripheral devices is discussed briefly in Chapter 11, "Working with Displays and Peripheral Devices."

Network

The Network category lists details about the hardware available to your computer for connecting to networks. (Configuration of these devices for network access is discussed in Chapter 13, "Connecting to the Internet.")

Software

The Software section displays general information about the version of the operating system, the computer name, and the user currently logged in. There are also two subsections—Applications and Extensions.

▶ Applications—The Applications section displays all the installed applications on your drive in alphabetical order, regardless of where they are installed. You can use the list to see what versions are installed and where an item is located.

▶ Extensions—Extensions help the operating system interact with hardware, such as network cards and peripheral devices. In this section, you can learn information such as the version, location, and developer about each extension.

▶ Fonts—The Fonts section contains a list of all fonts installed on your system. Refer to Chapter 12 for more about using fonts and managing them with the Font Book application.

▶ Frameworks—Frameworks are libraries of helper files used by applications to carry out their function. They are typically stored in your System/Library folder. In this section, you can see what frameworks the applications on your system have installed.

▶ Logs—Earlier in this chapter, you learned about the Console utility, which is used to view system logs. The Logs section of the System Profile also gives access to this information, which may include failed attempts by your system to access files or hardware that can give you clues about the source of problems with your system. The two types of logs available are console and system logs. The `console.log` item records errors having to do with the applications run on your computer. The `system.log` item reports events related to the operating system and networking, which are largely outside a user's control.

It's not unusual for errors and failure to be recorded in the `console.log` file and for you to have no idea that they occurred. If you haven't noticed anything strange with your system, don't worry about entries about elements not found or exceptions raised.

Watch
Out!

▶ Preference Panes—An alphabetical list of the sections in the System Preferences. See Chapter 5, "Setting System Preferences and Universal Access Options," for coverage and cross-references related to System Preference settings.

▶ Startup Items—An alphabetical list of services and functions your system activates on startup.

Terminal

Terminal is an application that provides a window, or shell prompt, into which you can type commands directly to the system. Chapter 37, "Using Basic Unix Commands," discusses some basic uses of Terminal.

Network Tools

Networking relates to how your computer interacts with other computers. The items in this section include setup assistants for various network-able devices, as well as utilities for storing and looking up network information. These applications are more advanced than those in the previous sections, and their use is described only briefly here. However, if you are interested in learning more, you may want to pick up a copy of *Mac OS X Tiger Unleashed*, which discusses them thoroughly.

AirPort Admin Utility and AirPort Setup Assistant

In Chapter 13 you learned that one option for networking was a wireless connection called AirPort. Although at that time we talked about connecting to an existing AirPort network, the AirPort Admin Utility and the AirPort Setup Assistant are used to set up the wireless base station that conveys a wireless signal to computers.

Bluetooth Utilities

Bluetooth refers to a wireless technology standard that allows compatible devices to interact with each other with little setup by the users—quite simply, Bluetooth devices send out signals that can be received by other Bluetooth devices. Bluetooth File Exchange enables you to browse files on other Bluetooth computers, both Mac and Windows-based.

Directory Access

Directory Access is used to access directory servers, such as Window's Active Directory Server. It is used to configure where Mac OS X gets its account information. For example, in a computer lab, a server would contain a listing of all the accounts, and each computer would be set up to use Directory Access to get account settings from the server when an account holder logged in.

NetInfo Manager

The NetInfo Manager is a window into a database of information on your system about your computer's setup and files, its users, and its network.

For example, you can select the Users folder (or directory) from the list and then choose your account. Among other things, you'll see your username, password hint, and the path to the user picture you chose as your login icon—which you can also access from the Accounts pane of the System Preferences.

In the other categories are more advanced settings related to the Unix underpinnings of OS X, many of which you don't have the option to change from the graphical interface.

Watch Out!

> For an average user, it's not wise to make system changes with NetInfo Manager. The information it accesses is vital to the operation of your computer, and mistakes made may be difficult to fix. (Even experienced system administrators are advised to make duplicates of the original information before changing settings here.)

Network Utility

Network Utility, shown in Figure 38.3, contains a collection of functions commonly used by people who manage or work with networks. Most of these functions display information or are used to test network connections.

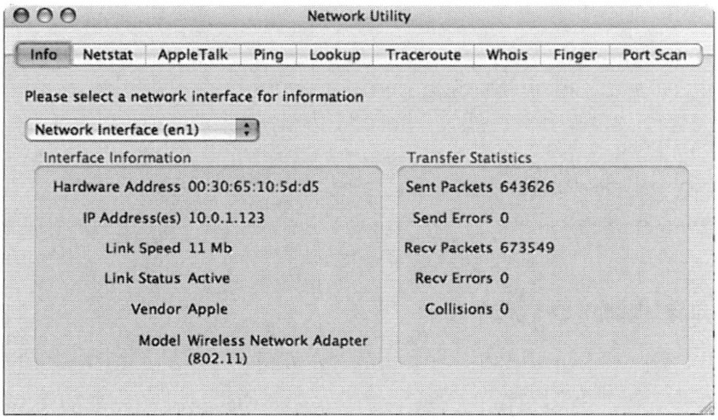

FIGURE 38.3
Network Utility
collects several
network admin-
istration tools
into a single
resource.

Following is a brief description of the options available:

- ▶ Info—Lets you see information about the installed network cards, including whether they are connected and to which IP address. It also lists any errors in transmission that have occurred.

- ▶ Netstat—Shows all the connections to and from your computer. It is of most use to server operators who need to see who is connected to the computer at a particular instant.

- ▶ AppleTalk—Shows AppleTalk zone details as well as statistics and errors.

- ▶ Ping—A function that enables you to test whether a remote machine is responding and how fast the connection is. (Essentially, this is a low-level con- tact between machines that is used to see whether a machine is online.)

- ▶ Lookup—Translates between IP addresses and hostnames.

- ▶ Traceroute—Shows the path required to connect to a given IP address or host- name.

- ▶ Whois—Enables you to look up who owns and administers a domain name. Note that when using the default whois server options, you may be directed to another host for more detailed information.

- ▶ Finger—Lets you look up information on a specific user on systems that have this service enabled. Finger was traditionally a feature of Unix-based systems that, when supplied with a username, returned information about a user, such as a real name and whether the user was currently logged in. (Large institutions, such as universities, may offer this service.)

▶ Portscan—Used to test which services (such as FTP and file sharing) are running on a computer, but should not be used on any but your own computers.

Portscan is nothing to play with. Scanning other people's networks can be interpreted as suspicious behavior—it's one of the ways malicious hackers find vulnerable systems to hack into—and if portscans are being performed by your computer, your ISP may receive letters of complaint.

ODBC Administrator

ODBC stands for Open Database Connectivity. The ODBC Administrator is an application that can be used with the appropriate database drivers to provide database access to ODBC-aware applications, such as FileMaker.

Imaging, Audio, and MIDI Tools

The applications discussed here are related to MIDI composition, Mac OS X's built-in screen reader, and imaging. For imaging, Mac OS X includes applications to measure onscreen color and to calibrate your display as well as to create screen captures. It also includes a digital music composition tool.

Audio MIDI Setup

The Audio MIDI Setup utility enables you to view and customize settings for audio and MIDI devices.

MIDI, an acronym for Musical Instrument Digital Interface, is a protocol for creating music with electronic devices. If you connect MIDI hardware to your Mac and launch the Audio MIDI Setup, you can check for device drivers or customize your MIDI setup in the MIDI Devices section.

In the Audio Devices section, you can view which peripheral devices and built-in hardware are available and, with selected devices, change their configuration.

ColorSync Utility

ColorSync Utility helps you calibrate your display. You learn about monitor calibration in Chapter 11, "Working with Displays and Peripheral Devices."

DigitalColor Meter

The next application, DigitalColor Meter, measures and reports the color of an onscreen pixel, or the average color of a group of pixels. It comes in handy when trying to find an exact match for any color appearing on your display.

When launched, DigitalColor Meter opens the window shown in Figure 38.4.

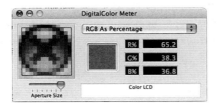

The section at the left of the window displays an enlarged view of whatever is currently under the mouse cursor. Immediately to the right of the enlarged view is a color well that contains the sampled color. Adjusting the aperture slider controls the number of pixels sampled from 1×1 to 16×16. (For apertures greater than 1×1, the displayed color is the average of several pixels surrounding the mouse cursor.)

To the right of the color well is a numeric representation of the currently selected color. The pop-up menu at the top of the window determines the color space.

To match an onscreen color with a web color, select RGB As Hex in the DigitalColor Meter's pop-up menu. The three sets of letter/number combinations describe the color.

By the Way

Grab

Mac OS X enables you to make a screen capture, or an exact snapshot of your screen at the current moment, by pressing Shift-Command-3 for full-screen captures or Shift-Command-4 for partial screens. The Grab application can do things that are not possible with the built-in screenshot function. Grab can capture screen information in four different ways:

Screen captures created with Shift-Command-3, or partial screen captures created with Shift-Command-4, are in PNG format. They appear on the desktop as `Picture number`. Although this method works for quick screen captures, Grab offers a few more features.

By the Way

▶ Selection (Shift-Command-A)—Captures a portion of the screen, which the user determines by drawing a rectangle.

▶ Window (Shift-Command-W)—Captures a selected window, determined by which window is clicked after the Grab capture is initiated.

▶ Screen (Command-Z)—Captures the entire screen.

▶ Time Screen (Shift-Command-Z)—Captures the screen with a 10-second delay. That gives you time to position your windows, pull down (or pop up) menus, and so on. You can take screenshots with menus in the down position in Mac OS X!

No matter what method you use, Grab displays a window with short instructions on how to proceed. This window is *not* included in the final screenshot, despite appearing onscreen as the shot is taken.

For example, to capture a timed screenshot:

1. Choose Capture, Timed Screen from Grab's menu. Grab displays the window shown in Figure 38.5.

FIGURE 38.5
Timed screen-
shots give you a
chance to get
things in order.

2. Click the Start Timer Button.

3. As the clock counts down, change your screen into the arrangement you want. At the end of 10 seconds, Grab captures the screen and opens the image in a new window.

4. Choose File, Save from the menu to save the image in Tiff format.

Grab saves images in TIFF format. If another image format would be more appro-priate, you can open the image in the Preview application, discussed in Chapter 6, "Using Calculator, Graphing Calculator, Preview, and TextEdit," and select File, Export from the menu. You can then choose from a number of common image formats.

When taking a screenshot, you can choose to superimpose a cursor of your choice over the screen; by default, no cursor is shown at all. Choose Preferences under the Grab application menu to change the cursor that will be used. Figure 38.6 shows the preferences.

FIGURE 38.6
Grab can include a cursor of your choice in a screen capture.

In the Pointer Type section, click the button for the cursor you want to use.

The preferences can also toggle the camera shutter noise that is played when an image is captured. Select or deselect the Enable Sound check box as you see fit.

VoiceOver Utility

Designed to benefit the visually impaired, VoiceOver Utility enable you to access your Mac through speech, sound cues, and keyboard commands. Refer to Chapter 5, "Setting System Preferences and Universal Access Options," for details about setting up VoiceOver Utility.

System Helpers

At the start of this chapter, you learned that the Utilities folder is home to several applications that help your computer perform necessary tasks. Let's take a quick look at them.

Installer

The Installer utility is used by many applications when they are installed. It essentially provides the wizardlike interface that appears with many of Apple's applications.

Java

Java is programming language specifically written to create programs that can be run on any operating system, or even from web pages, easily. Inside the Utilities folder is a Java folder containing several applications for installing and running with Java-based applications, or applets.

Keychain Access

Keychain Access is the utility that maintains all your application passwords. It was discussed in Chapter 8, "Working with Address Book, Keychain Access, iSync, and Ink."

Printer Setup Utility

As covered in Chapter 12, "Printing, Faxing, and Working with Fonts," the Printer Setup Utility enables you to configure available printers and choose your default.

StuffIt Expander

To reduce their size, files are often compressed, especially those distributed via email or a web site. StuffIt Expander uncompresses these files so that you can read them. StuffIt Expander is covered in Chapter 9, "Installing Additional Software," in connection with installing downloaded software.

Summary

This chapter has examined the contents of the Utilities folder located inside the Applications folder. Several utilities can be used to monitor system functions, including the System Profiler. Others relate to networking options, such as the Airport Setup Assistant. A few are useful, targeted applications, such as Grab. There are also several applications used by your system for specific purposes, such as Installer and Keychain Access. For the most part, these applications are tucked away in the Utilities folder because the average user doesn't need to use them from day to day or can access them in some other way, but isn't it nice to know that all this stuff is there for a reason?

Index

How can we make this index more useful? Email us at indexes@samspublishing.com

How can we make this index more useful? Email us at indexes@samspublishing.com

718

Source pane

How can we make this index more useful? Email us at indexes@samspublishing.com

Your Guide to Computer Technology

www.informit.com

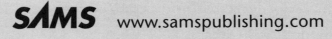